ADVANCED ANSI COBOL

DISK/TAPE

PROGRAMMING EFFICIENCIES

ANAHEIM PUBLISHING COMPANY
Specialist in Data Processing Textbooks

INTRODUCTION TO DATA PROCESSING

Our Computerized Society, Logsdon & Logsdon
The Computers In Our Society, Logsdon & Logsdon
The Computers In Our Society Workbook, Logsdon & Logsdon
Introduction To Flowcharting and Computer Programming Logic, Shelly & Cashman

BASIC

Programming In BASIC, Logsdon
Programming In BASIC With Applications, Logsdon

STRUCTURED COBOL

Introduction To Computer Programming Structured COBOL, Shelly & Cashman
Advanced Structured COBOL Program Design and File Processing, Shelly & Cashman

COBOL

Introduction To Computer Programming ANSI COBOL, Shelly & Cashman
ANSI COBOL Workbook, Testing & Debugging Techniques & Exercises, Shelly & Cashman
Advanced ANSI COBOL Disk/Tape Programming Efficiencies, Shelly & Cashman

RPG II

Computer Programming RPG II, Shelly & Cashman

RPG

Introduction To Computer Programming RPG, Shelly & Cashman

SYSTEMS ANALYSIS AND DESIGN

Business Systems Analysis and Design, Shelly & Cashman

ASSEMBLER LANGUAGE

Introduction To Computer Programming IBM System/360 Assembler Language, Shelly & Cashman
IBM System/360 Assembler Language Workbook, Shelly & Cashman
IBM System/360 Assembler Language Disk/Tape Advanced Concepts, Shelly & Cashman

FORTRAN

Introduction To Computer Programming Basic FORTRAN IV-A Practical Approach, Keys

PL/I

Introduction To Computer Programming System/360 PL/I, Shelly & Cashman

JOB CONTROL - OPERATING SYSTEMS

DOS Utilities Sort/Merge Multiprogramming, Shelly & Cashman
OS Job Control Language, Shelly & Cashman
DOS Job Control for Assembler Language Programmers, Shelly & Cashman
DOS Job Control for COBOL Programmers, Shelly & Cashman

FLOWCHARTING

Introduction To Flowcharting and Computer Programming Logic, Shelly & Cashman

ADVANCED ANSI COBOL

DISK/TAPE

PROGRAMMING EFFICIENCIES

By:

Gary B. Shelly
Educational Consultant
Fullerton, California

&

Thomas J. Cashman, CDP, B.A., M.A.
Long Beach City College
Long Beach, California

ANSI COBOL
Program Conversion
David Beers

ANAHEIM PUBLISHING CO.

1120 E. Ash, Fullerton, Ca. 92631

(714) 879-7922

Fifth Printing

July 1977

Sixth Printing

October 1977

Seventh Printing

April 1978

Library of Congress Catalog Card Number 74-21838

ISBN 0-88236-105-8

Printed in the United States

PREFACE

The System/360, and System/370, as well as most other medium to large scale computers, utilize many peripheral devices in addition to a card reader-punch and a printer. Included among these peripherals are direct-access devices and magnetic tape devices. It is essential that a business programmer have a knowledge of these devices, their uses, and the COBOL instructions and techniques to utilize these devices.

This book is designed to present both an introduction to magnetic tape and direct-access devices and the programming methods used for these devices. The methods presented in this text are, for the most part, applicable to all computers and all ANSI COBOL compilers, although all applications shown in this book have been written to be executed on a System/360 operating under the Disk Operating System. A prior knowledge of basic COBOL programming, such as presented in the text INTRODUCTION TO COMPUTER PROGRAMMING ANSI COBOL, is assumed.

Every effort has been made to present the concepts of direct-access and magnetic tape processing in a simplified manner through the use of realistic programming problems, numerous examples and illustrations, and completely documented and fully programmed examples. The approach is to first introduce the student to a typical application, explain the COBOL statements required to process the data, and conclude the chapter with an illustration of the input, output, and complete program to solve the problem. Each of the problems illustrated has been fully tested and run under the ANSI COBOL compiler of the Disk Operating System.

The seven programs presented in the text explain the following concepts and operations: Magnetic tape sequential processing, sequential file updating, DASD sequential processing, DASD indexed sequential processing (including sequential retrieval, random retrieval and updating, loading and adding records), COBOL subroutines, segmentation for use with overlays, an introduction to virtual storage, and the use of the Report Writer feature of ANSI COBOL.

In addition, each chapter includes techniques to be used with the ANSI COBOL language which reflect industry-accepted methods and techniques and produce efficient COBOL programs. Included are such topics as definitions of data items, data usage in mixed modes (including conditional statements, arithmetic statements, and move statements), data conversion, the binary data format, decimal point alignment and sign control, and the efficient usage of subscripting. It is intended that the inclusion of these techniques will aid the student in being aware of the best uses of the various capabilities of the COBOL language.

A comprehensive set of appendices is included for student reference covering such topics as Disk/Tape Concepts, COBOL Format Summary, COBOL Reference Summary, computer storage requirements of various COBOL statements, and the job control statements for the disk operating system necessary to process magnetic tape and direct-access files. The appendices are intended to serve as reference material, but it is suggested that the student be introduced to the material covered so that it can be used in a meaningful manner. In addition, a programming assignment is presented at the end of each chapter, and a case study is presented at the end of the text. These problems should be coded by each student and run on the computer which is available at the school.

When the student has completed the study of the material contained in the text, he should have a firm foundation in the use of magnetic and direct-access devices when programmed using COBOL. He should be able to make decisions concerning file usage and file organization for magnetic tape and direct-access devices. In addition, he should have an understanding of the methods used by COBOL and the most efficient manner in which to code a COBOL program.

This text, used in conjunction with the previous volume INTRODUCTION TO COMPUTER PROGRAMMING ANSI COBOL, should provide schools giving vocational data processing training with a comprehensive set of instructional materials for an in depth course of instruction in COBOL. In addition, ideas and techniques presented in this text will provide instructional and reference material for the experienced COBOL programmer.

The authors would like to thank the many data processing instructors from across the country who have made constructive criticisms after having used the COBOL Disk/Tape textbook for the COBOL D compiler. In addition, we would like to thank Ms. Jackie Rough, who typed most of the manuscript, and Ms. Kay Kreidel, who did most of the drawings, and both of whom survived the many idiosyncrasies of the authors.

Gary B. Shelly

Thomas J. Cashman, CDP

TABLE OF CONTENTS

Prepare Job Control Cards For Testing

Prepare Test Data

Test Program Using Valid Test Data

Test the Program Using All the Test Data

Verify Test Results With Analyst

Prepare Final Documentation

Case Study

MAGNETIC TAPE SEQUENTIAL FILE UPDATING

CHAPTER 1

MAGNETIC TAPE SEQUENTIAL FILE UPDATING

1

INTRODUCTION

Although COBOL programs written to process routine business reports involving addition, subtraction, multiplication and division with related major, intermediate and minor totals, and problems utilizing table lookup and table search techniques illustrate important programming concepts, much of the programming effort of the business application programmer using COBOL is devoted to the more complex task of **FILE MAINTENANCE** involving the use of both magnetic tape and magnetic disk as a form of input and output.

File maintenance refers to the task of maintaining accurate, up-to-date business records for a company. In any business organization it is necessary to maintain permanent **MASTER** records relating to the operation of the business. These master records are designed to reflect the current status of the business. For example, in all businesses it is necessary to have a master file of all employees, a master payroll file with year-to-date earnings for tax purposes, a master file reflecting the amount of money due the company from customers, etc. In many installations these master files are maintained on magnetic tape.

MASTER FILE UPDATING

Once a master file has been created, it is periodically necessary to update this file with current information so that the file always contains the most recent data. Typically, file updating procedures take three forms: additions, deletions, and changes.

An **ADDITION** takes place when a new record is added to an already established master file. For example, in a customer sales system, if a new customer is acquired, it would be necessary to add a record to the master file reflecting the acquisition of the new customer.

A **DELETION** becomes necessary when data currently stored on the master file is to be removed. For example, if a customer is lost, that is, the customer no longer purchases from the company, it would be necessary to delete the corresponding master record from the file.

A **CHANGE** must be made to the master file whenever the data on the master file no longer contains accurate, up-to-date information. For example, in a customer sales system, when a new sale is made, the sales amount must be added to the sales amount in the master record to reflect the sale to the customer.

SEQUENTIAL FILE UPDATE

When there are numerous records in the master file which frequently require updating, that is, when there are numerous and frequent additions, deletions, and changes to the master file, magnetic tape is a very efficient type of storage. When master records are stored on magnetic tape, these records must be arranged sequentially on the basis of some control field. For example, in a customer sales system the records would probably be arranged on the tape in ascending sequence on the basis of the customer number. When file updating takes place the master file is processed against a **TRANSACTION** file containing additions, deletions, and changes. This transaction file must also be arranged in ascending sequence.

SEQUENTIAL UPDATING thus involves the reading of a sequential master file, the reading of a sorted sequential transaction file and the creation of a new, updated master file. Normally, an exception report which lists transaction errors such as invalid transaction codes is also created.

Figure 1-1 illustrates, through the use of a system flowchart, the basic concept of a file updating procedure in which a master file stored on magnetic tape is updated by sorted transaction records stored on punched cards.

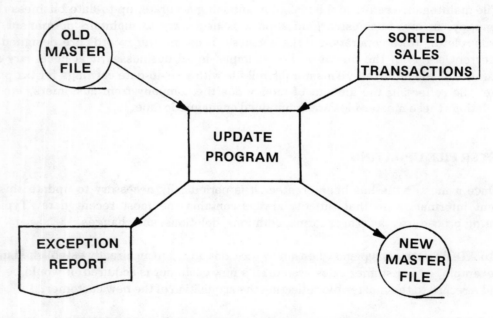

Figure 1-1 System Flowchart of Sequential Update

From the flowchart it can be seen that after the updating process has been completed the output consists of a new updated master tape reflecting all additions, deletions, and changes to the original master file and, in addition, a printed exception report listing any transaction records in error, such as one containing an invalid code.

It should be noted that on the next file updating cycle the newly created master file becomes input to the system and any new transaction records for the next period are then processed against this file. The "old master" file can then be discarded, although most installations normally retain the "old master" files for at least three generations back in case difficulties are encountered, such as the current master file being accidentally damaged or destroyed.

SAMPLE PROBLEM

The program presented in this chapter illustrates a technique to sequentially update a master file stored on magnetic tape with sorted transaction records stored on punched cards. The master file contains the year-to-date sales amounts for customers. This master file is to be updated with the new sales figures for the month. In addition, the update program will add customers or delete customers from the master file as needed. An error listing will also be produced which contains a list of any transaction records with errors such as invalid transaction codes.

The format of the master file is illustrated in Figure 1-2.

MASTER FILE - INPUT

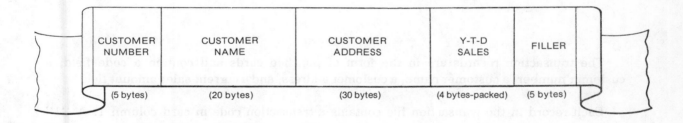

Figure 1-2 Master File - Input

The customer master file contains the customer number, the customer name, the customer address and the year-to-date sales field. Note that the year-to-date sales is to be stored on the tape in a packed decimal format. Storing data in a packed decimal format can reduce the amount of space required to store numeric fields on the tape. For example, a seven digit numeric field can be stored in only 4 bytes on tape, thus saving 3 bytes of tape storage for each record. In addition, if the field is stored in a packed format, programming efficiencies result as the compiler does not have to pack the field prior to performing calculations.

The format of the transaction records is illustrated below.

TRANSACTION FILE - INPUT

CODE	CUST NUM	CUSTOMER NAME	CUSTOMER ADDRESS	CURRENT SALES AMOUNT	
0 0	0 0 0 0	0 0 0 0 0 0 0 0 0 0 0 0 0 0 0 0 0 0 0 0	0 0 0 0 0 0 0 0 0 0 0 0 0 0 0 0 0 0 0 0 0 0 0 0 0 0 0 0 0 0	0 0 0 0 0 0	0 0 0 0 0 0 0 0 0 0 0 0 0 0 0 0 0
1	2 3 4 5 6	7 8 9 10 11 12 13 14 15 16 17 18 19 20 21 22 23 24 25 26	27 28 29 30 31 32 33 34 35 36 37 38 39 40 41 42 43 44 45 46 47 48 49 50 51 52 53 54 55 56	57 58 59 60 61 62 63	64 65 66 67 68 69 70 71 72 73 74 75 76 77 78 79 80
1 1	1 1 1 1	1 1 1 1 1 1 1 1 1 1 1 1 1 1 1 1 1 1 1 1	1 1 1 1 1 1 1 1 1 1 1 1 1 1 1 1 1 1 1 1 1 1 1 1 1 1 1 1 1 1	1 1 1 1 1 1	1 1 1 1 1 1 1 1 1 1 1 1 1 1 1 1 1
2 2	2 2 2 2	2 2 2 2 2 2 2 2 2 2 2 2 2 2 2 2 2 2 2 2	2 2 2 2 2 2 2 2 2 2 2 2 2 2 2 2 2 2 2 2 2 2 2 2 2 2 2 2 2 2	2 2 2 2 2 2	2 2 2 2 2 2 2 2 2 2 2 2 2 2 2 2 2
3 3	3 3 3 3	3 3 3 3 3 3 3 3 3 3 3 3 3 3 3 3 3 3 3 3	3 3 3 3 3 3 3 3 3 3 3 3 3 3 3 3 3 3 3 3 3 3 3 3 3 3 3 3 3 3	3 3 3 3 3 3	3 3 3 3 3 3 3 3 3 3 3 3 3 3 3 3 3

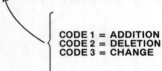

CODE 1 = ADDITION
CODE 2 = DELETION
CODE 3 = CHANGE

Figure 1-3 Transaction File - Input

The transaction records are in the form of punched cards and contain a code field, a customer number, a customer name, a customer address, and a current sales amount field.

Each record in the transaction file contains a transaction code in card column 1. A "1" punch indicates that the transaction record is an addition; a "2" indicates a deletion, and a "3" indicates a change.

MAGNETIC TAPE OUTPUT

The output will consist of an updated magnetic tape master file consisting of the new master records reflecting all additions, deletions, and changes to the original file. The format of this magnetic tape file will be identical to the master file used as input, as illustrated in Figure 1-2.

PRINTED EXCEPTION REPORT - OUTPUT

In addition to the master output tape file an exception report is to be prepared listing all transaction records in error. This report will list (1) all transaction records which do not have a valid code, that is, cards in which there is not a "1", "2", or "3" in the Code field; (2) transaction records for deletions or changes which do not have a corresponding master record in the master file; (3) duplicate master records. This condition occurs when a transaction record indicates an add, but there is already a record with that specified customer number in the master file.

The printer spacing chart is illustrated in Figure 1-4.

XX/XX/XX		EXCEPTION REPORT		PAGE XXX
CODE	CUST NO.	AMOUNT	ERROR	
X	XXXXX	XXXXXXX	DUPLICATE MASTER RECORD	
X	XXXXX	XXXXXXX	INVALID TYPE CODE	
X	XXXXX	XXXXXXX	NO MASTER RECORD	

Figure 1-4 Printer Spacing Chart

SEQUENTIAL UPDATE LOGIC

The flowchart logic for a file updating procedure is illustrated on the following pages. The basic logic requires the following basic steps: (1) a transaction record is read; (2) a master record is read; (3) the customer number of the master record and the transaction are compared to determine if the master record is equal to, less than, or greater than the transaction record; (4) the required processing is performed based upon the comparison.

The logic of this file updating procedure should be analyzed carefully and thoroughly understood prior to reviewing the coding for the problem explained on subsequent pages of this chapter. The following master and transaction records are used in the analysis of the logic of the sequential update beginning on page 8.

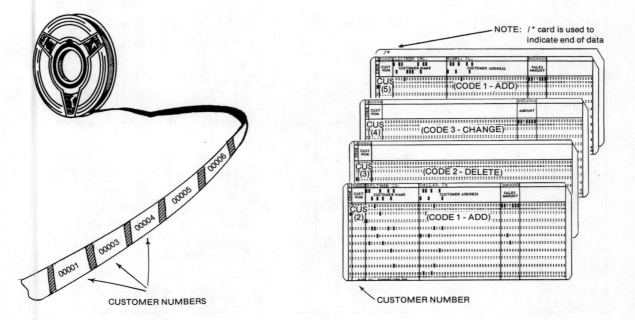

Figure 1-5 Sample Data For Sequential Update Processing

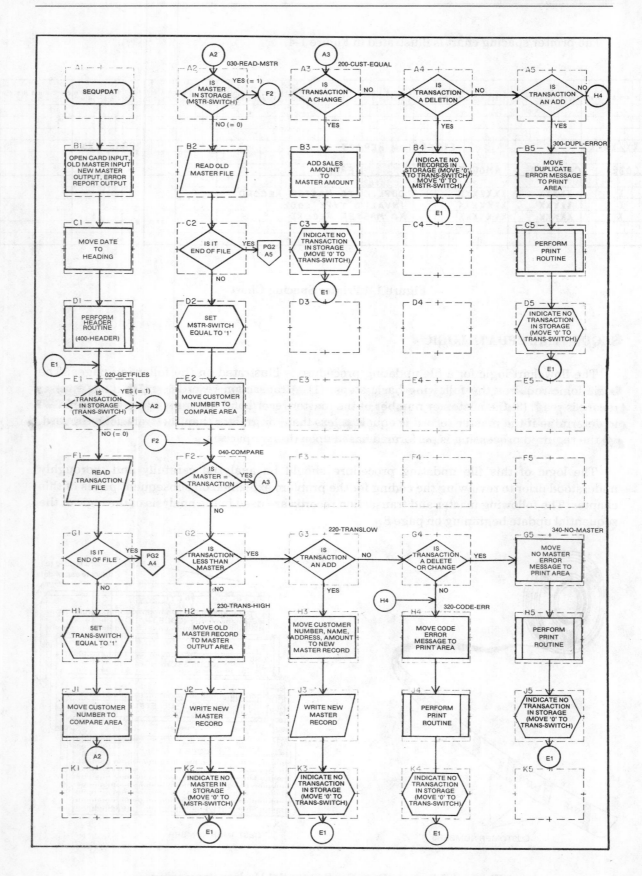

Figure 1-6 Sequential Update Program Flowchart - Part 1 of 2

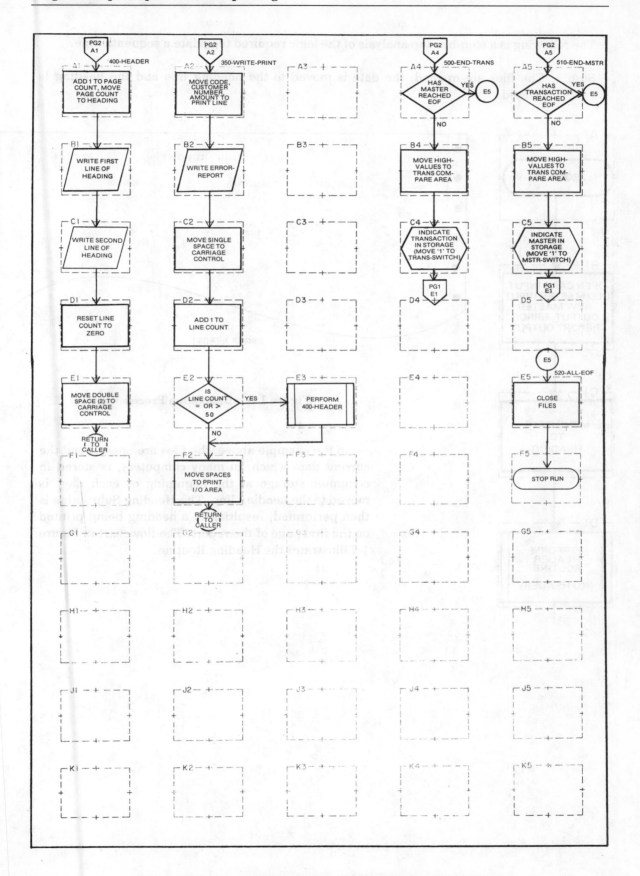

Figure 1-7 Sequential Update Program Flowchart - Part 2 of 2

The following is a step-by-step analysis of the logic required to update a sequential file.

Step 1: The files are opened, the date is moved to the heading line and the heading is printed.

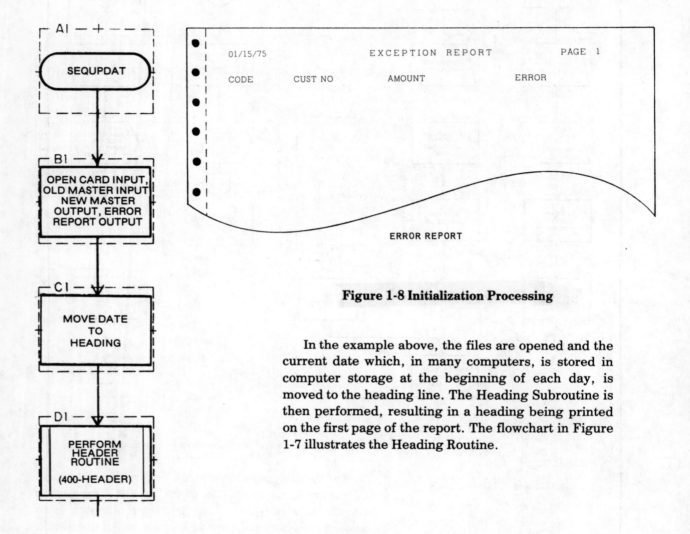

ERROR REPORT

Figure 1-8 Initialization Processing

In the example above, the files are opened and the current date which, in many computers, is stored in computer storage at the beginning of each day, is moved to the heading line. The Heading Subroutine is then performed, resulting in a heading being printed on the first page of the report. The flowchart in Figure 1-7 illustrates the Heading Routine.

Step 2: A transaction record is read from the card reader.

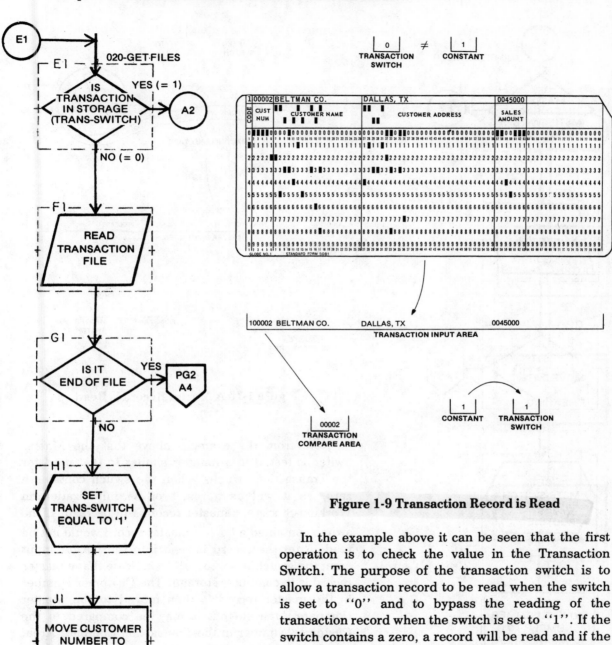

Figure 1-9 Transaction Record is Read

In the example above it can be seen that the first operation is to check the value in the Transaction Switch. The purpose of the transaction switch is to allow a transaction record to be read when the switch is set to "0" and to bypass the reading of the transaction record when the switch is set to "1". If the switch contains a zero, a record will be read and if the switch contains a "1", a transaction record will not be read. The Transaction Switch was initialized with a value of zero in Working-Storage, so a record will be read.

After Checking for End-of-File, the value in the switch is set to "1" because a transaction record is now in computer storage to be processed. The Customer Number in the input record is then moved to the Transaction Compare Area in computer storage so that it may be compared to the Customer Number which will be read from the master file. Control is then passed to block A2.

Step 3: A master record is read from the master file which is stored on tape.

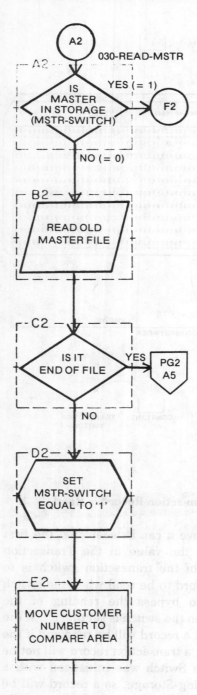

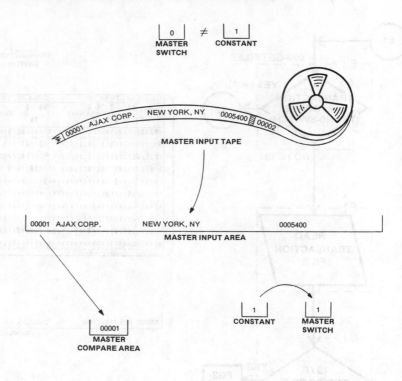

Figure 1-10 A Master Record is Read

Note from the example above that the Master Switch is tested in a manner similar to that used for the Transaction switch. When the switch contains a zero, as it will as a result of its initialization in Working-Storage, a master record will be read. If the switch contained a "1", a master record would not be read. After the record is read into the master input area, the switch is set to "1" to indicate that a master record is in computer storage. The Customer Number in the master record is then moved to the Master Compare Area so that it may be compared to the Customer Number in the Transaction Compare Area.

It should be noted from the examples in Figure 1-9 and Figure 1-10 that two input areas are used in the program - one for the transaction record, and one for the master record. This is done because the two records must be in computer storage at the same time in order for them to be processed.

Step 4: The Customer Numbers in the Transaction Compare Area and the Master Compare Area are compared and the appropriate action is taken.

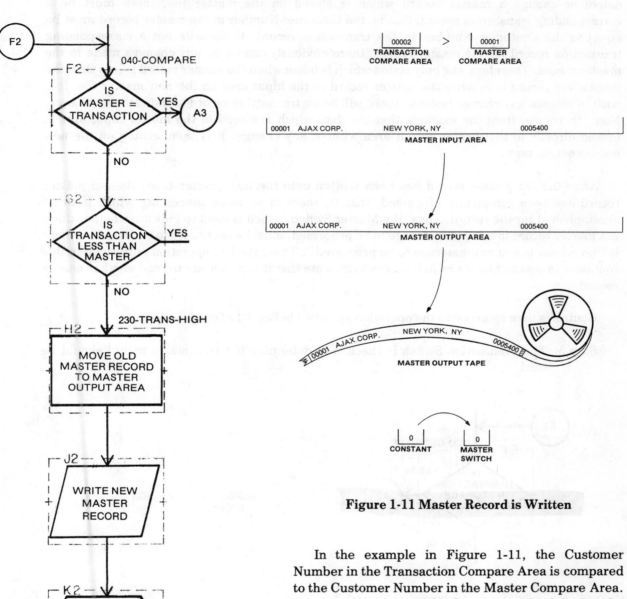

Figure 1-11 Master Record is Written

In the example in Figure 1-11, the Customer Number in the Transaction Compare Area is compared to the Customer Number in the Master Compare Area. As can be seen, the Customer Number in the Transaction Compare Area, which contains 00002, is greater than the Customer Number in the Master Compare Area, which contains 00001. Thus, both "no" paths of the decision symbols are taken because the number in the Master Compare Area is not equal to the number in the Transaction Compare Area (Box F2 in the flowchart) and the number in the Transaction Compare Area is not less than the number in the Master Compare Area (Box G2).

As was noted previously, the three operations which may be performed when updating a sequential master file are adding a record, deleting a record, and changing a record. In order to delete or change a master record which is stored on the master file, there must be a corresponding transaction record, that is, the Customer Number in the master record must be equal to the Customer Number in the transaction record. If there is not a corresponding transaction record for the master record, there obviously cannot be any changes made to the master record. Therefore, the only action which is taken when the master record is less than the transaction record is to write the master record in the input area on the new master file. It is written without any change because there will be no transaction record to indicate any change. Note, therefore, from the example that the data which is stored in the master input area is moved directly to the master output area without any change. It is then written on the new master output tape.

After the old master record has been written onto the new master tape, the old master record has been completely processed, that is, there is no more processing which is to be accomplished for the record. Thus, the Master Switch, which is used to indicate whether there is a master record in computer storage to be processed, must be set to zero to indicate that there is "no master in computer storage to be processed". Thus, the last operation performed in this routine is to set the Master Switch to zero to indicate that it is necessary to read another master record.

Control is then returned to the operation specified in Box E1 of the flowchart.

Step 5: The Transaction Switch is checked to determine if a transaction record should be read.

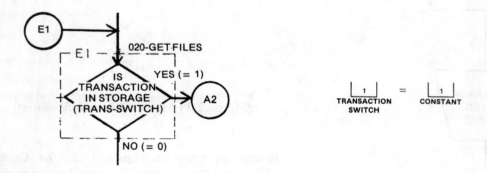

Figure 1-12 Test For Transaction Read

The transaction record which was read in Step 2 has not yet been processed. This is indicated by a "1" in the Transaction Switch; therefore another transaction should not be read. As there is a "1" in the transaction switch control is transferred to the read master routine (Box A2).

Step 6: Another master record is read.

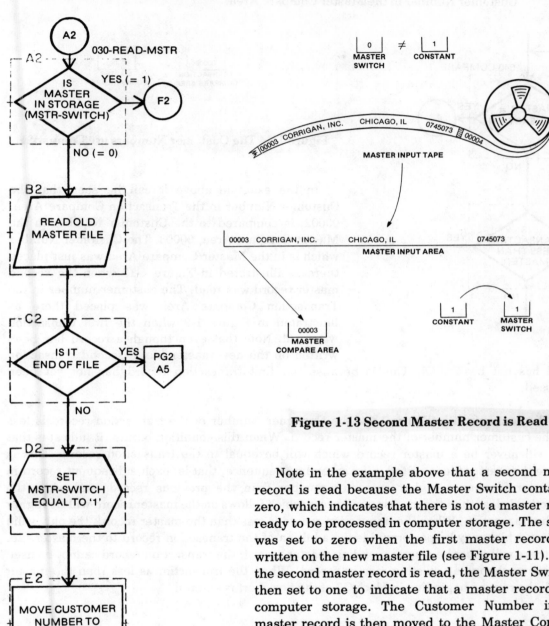

Figure 1-13 Second Master Record is Read

Note in the example above that a second master record is read because the Master Switch contains a zero, which indicates that there is not a master record ready to be processed in computer storage. The switch was set to zero when the first master record was written on the new master file (see Figure 1-11). After the second master record is read, the Master Switch is then set to one to indicate that a master record is in computer storage. The Customer Number in the master record is then moved to the Master Compare Area to be used in comparisons with the transaction record.

Step 7: The Customer Number in the Transaction Compare Area is compared with the Customer Number in the Master Compare Area.

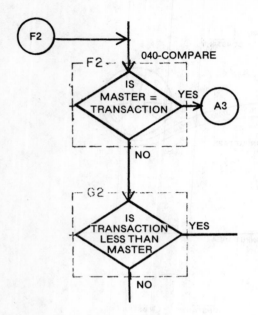

Figure 1-14 The Customer Numbers are Compared

In the example above it can be seen that the Customer Number in the Transaction Compare Area, 00002, is compared to the Customer Number in the Master Compare Area, 00003. The Customer Number which is in the Master Compare Area was just placed there as illustrated in Figure 1-13 when the second master record was read. The customer number in the Transaction Compare Area was placed there as illustrated in Figure 1-9 when the first transaction was read. Note that even though a record has been written on the new master file, a second transaction record has not been read. This is because the first transaction record has not yet been processed.

In the comparison in Figure 1-14, the Customer Number of the transaction record is less than the customer number of the master record. When this condition occurs, it indicates that there will never be a master record which will be equal to the transaction record. This is because the master file is sorted in an ascending sequence, that is, each subsequent record in the master file has a higher customer number than the previous record, and when the transaction is less than the master, any record which follows on the master record will be higher than the transaction. When the transaction record is less than the master record, the only valid operation which may be performed is the addition of the transaction record to the master file. Since there will never be a corresponding master record, the transaction record cannot be used to delete or change an existing master record. When the transaction is less than the master record, the routine beginning in block G3 of the flowchart is entered.

Step 8: The Transaction Code in the transaction record is checked to verify that the transaction record contains a "1" to indicate that the record is to be added to the master file. If it does contain the value "1", the transaction record is added to the new master file.

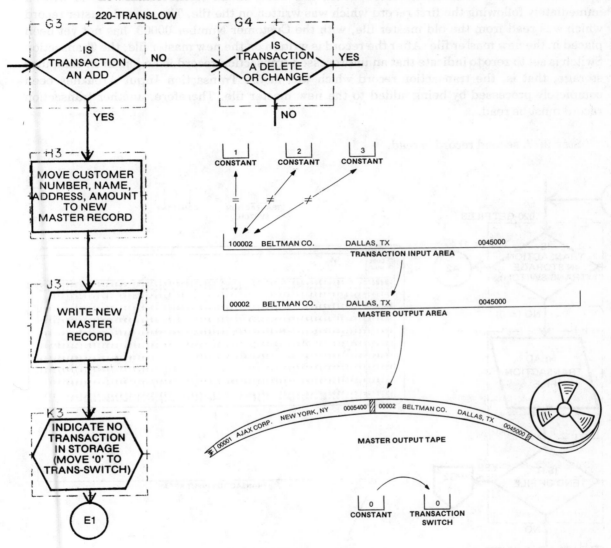

Figure 1-15 Transaction Record is Added to Master Output File

As was noted previously, the Transaction Code in the transaction record is used to indicate the function of the transaction record. The three types of operations which may be performed by transaction records are to add a record (code = 1), delete a record (code = 2), or change a master record (code = 3). Again, in order for a transaction record to delete or change a master record, the Customer Number in the transaction record must be equal to the Customer Number in the master record. Since the transaction Customer Number is less than the master record, the only function which may be performed is to add the transaction record to the master file. Thus, the comparisons illustrated in Figure 1-15 ensure that the Transaction Code is equal to "1", which indicates that the transaction is to be added to the master file. Any other Transaction Code will be treated as an error and a message will be printed on the error report. As can be seen from the example, the Transaction Code is valid because it is equal to "1".

Since the transaction record is to be added to the new master file, the Customer Number, the Customer Name, the Customer Address and the Amount are moved from the Transaction Input Area to the Master Output Area. The record is then written on the master output tape. Note also that the transaction record which has been added to the master file is written immediately following the first record which was written on the file. The second master record which was read from the old master file, with the Customer Number 00003, has not yet been placed in the new master file. After the record is written on the new master file, the Transaction Switch is set to zero to indicate that an unprocessed transaction record is no longer in computer storage, that is, the transaction record which was in the Transaction Input Area has been completely processed by being added to the new master file. Therefore, another transaction record must be read.

Step 9: A second record is read.

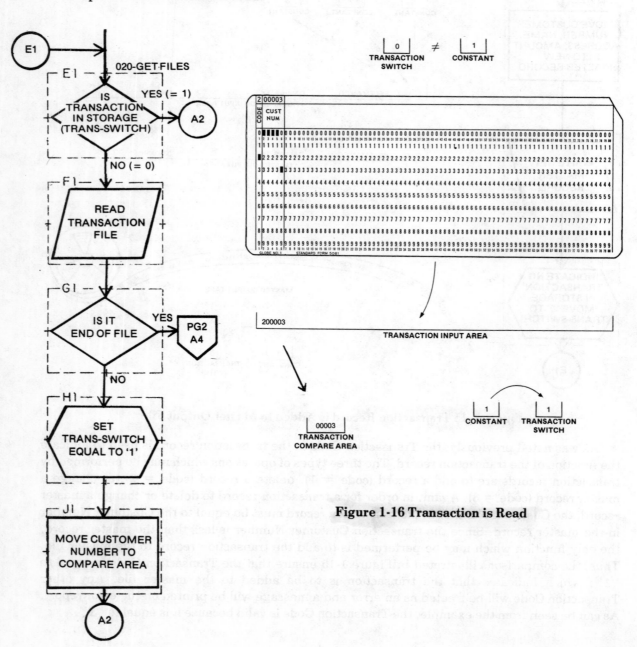

Figure 1-16 Transaction is Read

Note in Figure 1-16 that the second transaction record is read and placed in the Transaction Input Area. The Transaction Switch is then set to one to indicate that a transaction record is in computer storage and the Customer Number from the transaction record is moved to the Transaction Compare Area. Note also that the only data contained in the transaction record is the transaction code, 2, and the customer number, 00003. As noted previously, the code 2 indicates that the transaction record is to cause a master record to be deleted. Thus, since no data is to be changed in the master or added to the master file, the only data required is the transaction code to indicate a delete and the customer number of the master record to be deleted. The operation in Box A2 of the flowchart is performed next.

Step 10: The reading of a master record is bypassed.

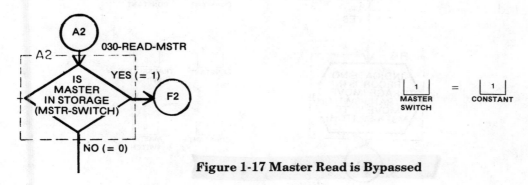

Figure 1-17 Master Read is Bypassed

Note in the example above that after the transaction record is read, the master switch is tested to determine if a master record is in computer storage. In Figure 1-13, a master record was read and it has not yet been processed. Therefore, the master switch which was set to ''1'' in that example has not been reset to zero to indicate that a master need be read. Therefore, the reading of a master record is bypassed since the one in computer storage has not yet been processed.

Step 11: The Customer Number in the Transaction Compare Area is compared with the Customer Number in the Master Compare Area.

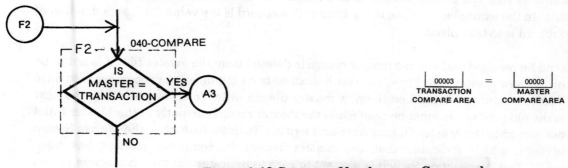

Figure 1-18 Customer Numbers are Compared

Note in the example in Figure 1-18 that when the Customer Numbers in the Transaction Compare Area and the Master Compare Area are compared, they are found to be equal. When the Customer Number in the transaction record is equal to the Customer Number in the master record, the two valid operations are to change the master record by adding the amount in the transaction record to the amount in the old master record or to delete the master record from the new master file. Thus, the next step in block A3 is to determine the type of operation to be performed on the master record.

Step 12: The Transaction Code is checked.

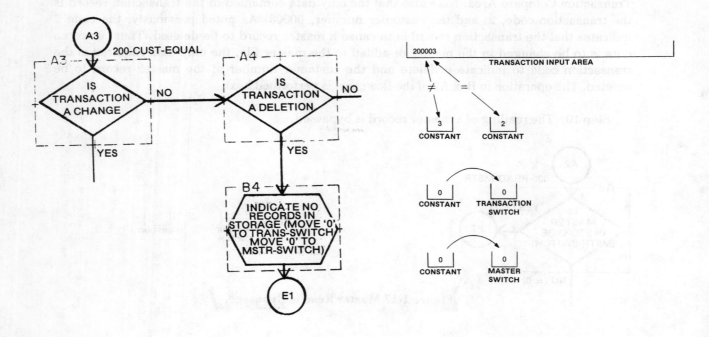

Figure 1-19 The Delete Transaction is Processed

In the example above, the transaction code must be checked to determine what processing is to take place. When the customer numbers are equal, the most likely code is "3", which indicates a change in the master record. Therefore, this code is checked first. In the example, the code is not equal to a "3". The next most likely code, and the only other valid one, is a "2", which indicates that the master record is to be deleted. Thus, the next code checked is the delete code. In the example, the code in the transaction record is the value "2", so a deletion of a master record is to take place.

It should be recalled that when a master record is deleted from the master file, it is not to be written on the new master file. Thus, the result desired from the deletion processing is to have the old master record not written on the new master file. In order to accomplish this, the next record on the old master file must be read while the master record currently in the Master Input Area is not moved to the Master Output Area and written. In order to do this, the Master Switch is set to zero, which indicates that the master record in computer storage has been "processed". The Transaction Switch is also set to zero to indicate that the transaction record has been processed. Note again that the master record which was read in Figure 1-13 is not written on the new master. Thus, the record is effectively deleted from the new master file.

After the switches have been set to zero, control is returned to block E1 where the next transaction record is read.

Step 13: The next transaction record is read.

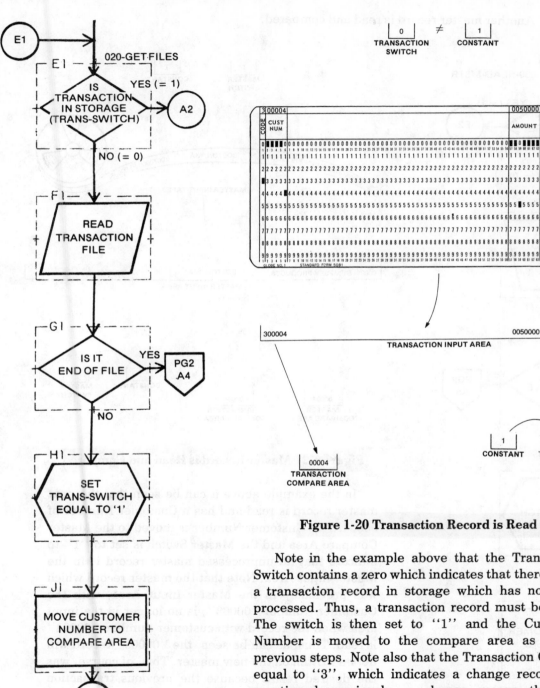

Figure 1-20 Transaction Record is Read

Note in the example above that the Transaction Switch contains a zero which indicates that there is not a transaction record in storage which has not been processed. Thus, a transaction record must be read. The switch is then set to "1" and the Customer Number is moved to the compare area as in the previous steps. Note also that the Transaction Code is equal to "3", which indicates a change record. As mentioned previously, a change means that the amount field is the corresponding master record is to be incremented by the Amount field in the transaction record. Since the Amount field is the only field which is to be acted upon in this transaction, the Name field and the Address field do not contain any values.

After the transaction record is read, a check is made to determine if a master record must be read.

Step 14: Another master record is read and compared.

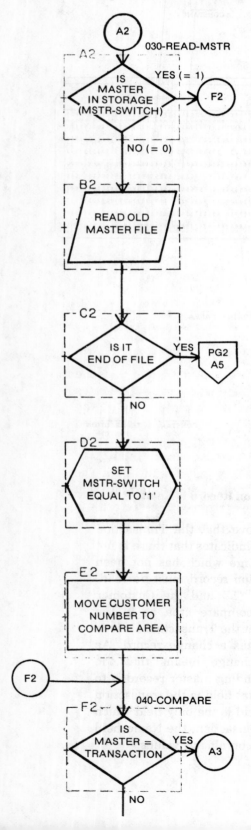

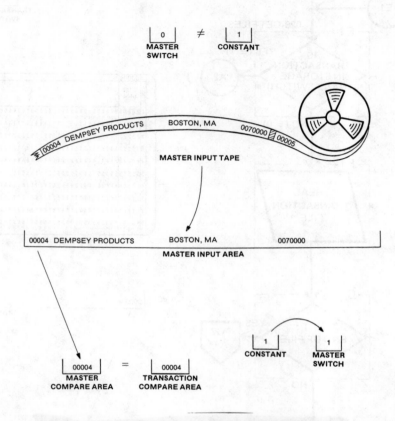

Figure 1-21 Master Record is Read and Compared

In the example above it can be seen that the next master record is read and has a Customer Number of 00004. This Customer Number is moved to the Master Compare Area and the Master Switch is set to "1" to indicate that an unprocessed master record is in the Master Input Area. Note that the master record which was previously in the Master Input Area, with the Customer Number "00003", is no longer in the input area when the record with customer number "00004" is read. Thus, as can be seen, the "00003" record will not be written on the new master. This, of course, was the desired result because the previous transaction requested that the master record be deleted.

When the Customer Number in the master record is compared to the Customer Number in the transaction record, they are found to be equal, that is, they are both 00004. Thus, the routine in block A3 is entered.

Step 15: After the Customer Numbers are compared and found to be equal, a check is made of the code field in the transaction record.

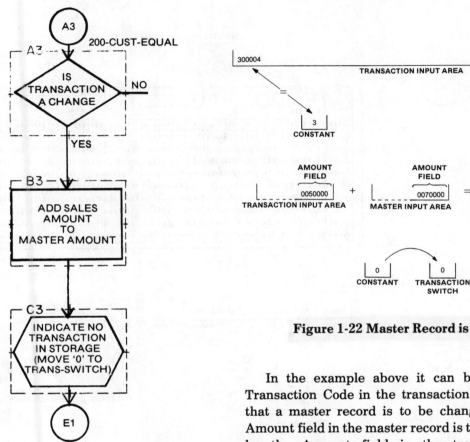

Figure 1-22 Master Record is Changed

In the example above it can be seen that the Transaction Code in the transaction record indicates that a master record is to be changed, that is, the Amount field in the master record is to be incremented by the Amount field in the transaction record. Therefore, the Amount in the Transaction Input Area is added to the Amount in the Master Input Area. The Transaction Switch is then set to zero to indicate that there is no unprocessed transaction record in computer storage. This is because the Amount in the transaction record has been added to the master record and there is no more to be done with the transaction record. Note that the Master Switch is not set to zero. This is because the master record is not moved to the new master output area and written on the new master file. Since the old master record has not been written on the new master, it is still considered an unprocessed record even though the Amount field has been updated. The reason that the old master record is not written after the Amount is updated is that the possibility exists that there may be more than one transaction record to update a master record, that is, the Amount in the master record may be incremented by more than one transaction record. Thus, the master record should not be written on the new master file until all of the transaction records which reference that record are processed. This happens only when the Customer Number in the master record is less than the Customer Number in the transaction record. When this occurs, all of the transaction records will have been processed for the master record.

Step 16: The next transaction record is read.

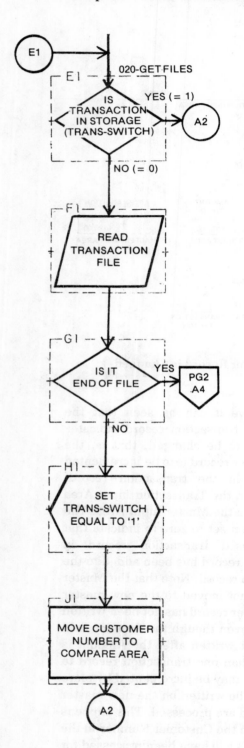

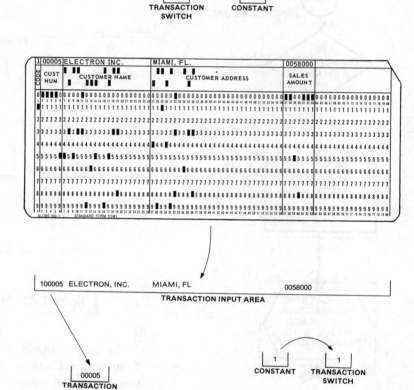

Figure 1-23 Transaction Record is Read

As in the previous examples, when the Transaction Switch is equal to zero, it indicates that there is not a transaction record in computer storage. Thus, a transaction record is read into the Transaction Input Area. In addition, the Transaction Switch is set to "1" to indicate that an unprocessed transaction record is in storage and the Customer Number in the transaction record is moved to the Transaction Compare Area. Control is then passed to block A2, which determines if a master record must be read.

Step 17: The master file is not read because a master record is in computer storage. The Customer Numbers are compared to determine the action to be taken.

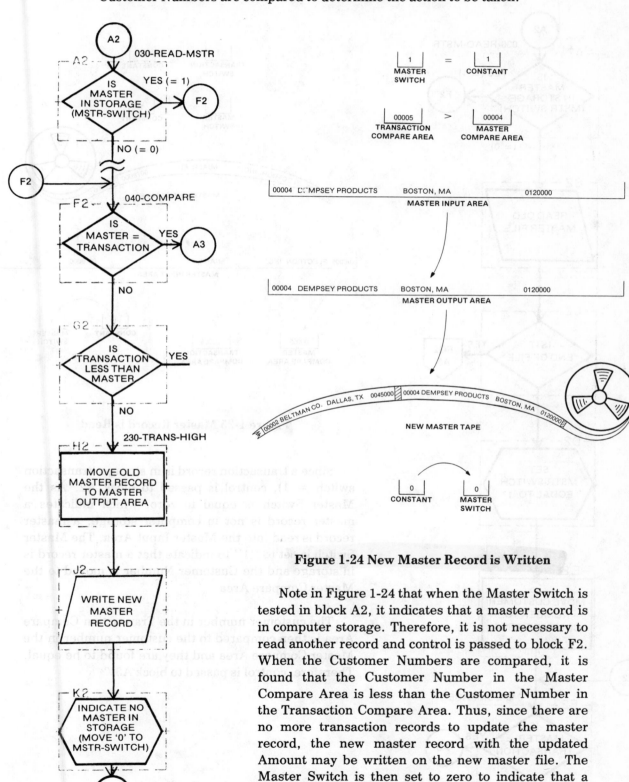

Figure 1-24 New Master Record is Written

Note in Figure 1-24 that when the Master Switch is tested in block A2, it indicates that a master record is in computer storage. Therefore, it is not necessary to read another record and control is passed to block F2. When the Customer Numbers are compared, it is found that the Customer Number in the Master Compare Area is less than the Customer Number in the Transaction Compare Area. Thus, since there are no more transaction records to update the master record, the new master record with the updated Amount may be written on the new master file. The Master Switch is then set to zero to indicate that a master record must be read.

Step 18: The next master record is read.

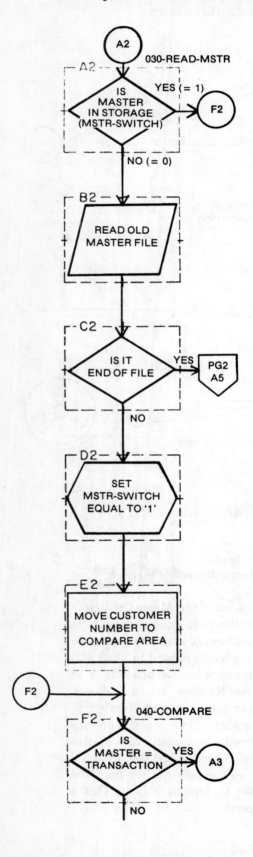

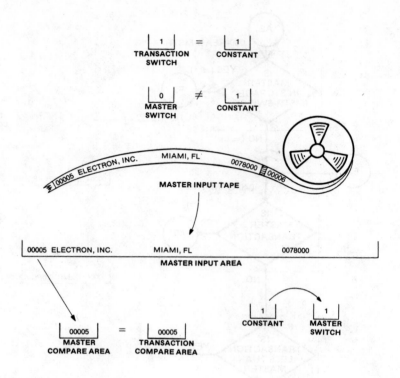

Figure 1-25 Master Record is Read

Since a transaction record is in storage (transaction switch = 1), control is passed to block A2. As the Master Switch is equal to zero, which indicates a master record is not in computer storage, a master record is read into the Master Input Area. The Master Switch is set to ''1'' to indicate that a master record is in storage and the Customer Number is moved to the Master Compare Area.

The customer number in the Transaction Compare Area is then compared to the customer number in the Master Compare Area and they are found to be equal. Therefore, control is passed to block A3.

Step 19: The Customer Numbers in the Transaction Compare Area and the Master Compare Area are found to be equal. The "equal" routine is then entered and the appropriate action taken.

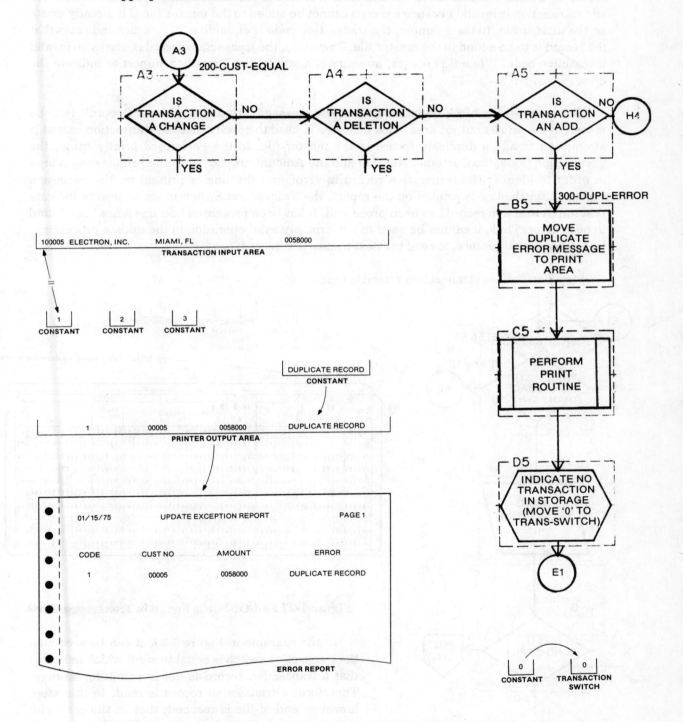

Figure 1-26 Invalid Transaction Record is Processed

In the example in Figure 1-26, it can be seen that the routine in block A3 is entered when the customer numbers are equal. As was noted previously, the valid operations when the customer numbers are equal are to delete the master record from the master file and to update the master record by adding the amount in the transaction record to the amount in the master record. An add transaction is invalid because a record cannot be added to the master file if it already exists on the master file. In the example, the transaction code is equal to a ''1'', which indicates that the record is to be added to the master file. Therefore, the transaction record contains an invalid transaction code. When this occurs, an entry is made on the Exception Report to indicate the error.

The statement in block B5 indicates that the message ''Duplicate Master Record'' is to be moved to the printer output area. This message is used to specify that the transaction record is attempting to add a duplicate record to the master file. In the Performed print routine, the Transaction Code, the Customer Number and the Amount are moved to the printer output area in order to identify the transaction record in error and the line is printed on the exception report. After the line is printed on the report, the Transaction Switch is set to zero to indicate that the transaction record has been processed. It has been processed because it has been found to be in error. Thus, it cannot be used to perform any valid operation in the update processing. It is necessary, therefore, to read the next transaction record.

Step 20: The next transaction record is read.

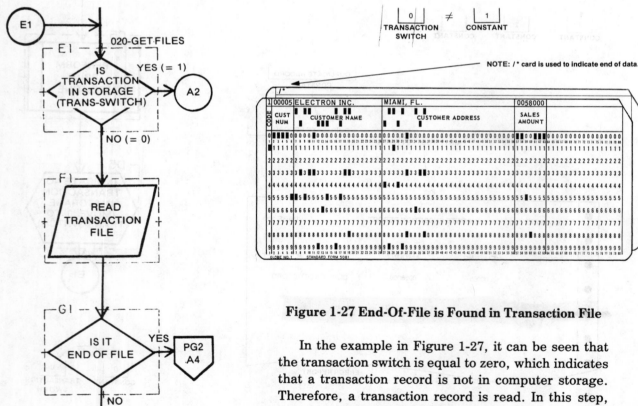

Figure 1-27 End-Of-File is Found in Transaction File

In the example in Figure 1-27, it can be seen that the transaction switch is equal to zero, which indicates that a transaction record is not in computer storage. Therefore, a transaction record is read. In this step, however, end-of-file is reached, that is, the card with the /* is read. Therefore, the end-of-file routine is entered. Note the use of the ''off-page connector'' to indicate that the routine to be entered is illustrated on another page of the flowchart. This symbol is always used when control is to be transferred to a routine which is illustrated on a page of the flowchart other than the one where the transfer of control takes place.

Step 21: The end-of-file routine for the transaction file is entered.

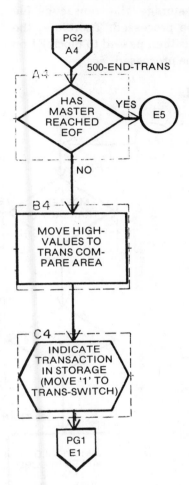

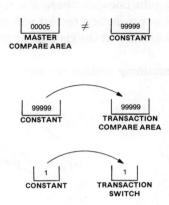

Figure 1-28 Transaction End-of-File is Processed

When two files are being processed within the same program, such as the transaction file and the master file in this example, the program cannot be ended when only one file has reached the end. Both files must reach end-of-file before the program can be ended. Thus, when end-of-file is reached for the transaction file, the first operation to be performed is to test if the master file has reached end-of-file. If it has, then the program can be terminated. If it has not reached end-of-file, then the remainder of the master file must be processed before the program can be terminated. In this example, in order to test if the master file has reached end-of-file, the value in the Master Compare Area is compared to the value "99999". It should be noted that in a COBOL program, the figurative constant HIGH-VALUES is moved to the compare area. HIGH-VALUES will always be the highest value in the collating sequence of the computer. This is a value which is moved to the Master Compare Area when the master file has reached end-of-file. Thus, if the value is not equal to "99999", in the example above, it indicates that the master file has not yet been completely processed. If the master has not reached end-of-file, the value 99999 is moved to the Transaction Compare Area. This value accomplishes two objectives: first, it indicates that the transaction file has reached end-of-file, so that when the master file reaches end-of-file, the master end-of-file routine will be able to determine that the transaction file has been completely processed and the program will be terminated; second, it ensures that when the Customer Number in the Master Compare Area is compared to the value in the Transaction Compare Area, the master will always be low. This is required because there are no more transaction records to be processed against master records. Therefore, the remaining master records will always be treated as if they are less than the transaction records and cause the writing of the remaining master records on the new master tape.

The Transaction Switch is then set to "1" to indicate that there is a transaction record in computer storage. Even though there is not actually a record in storage, the transaction file must not be read again because there are no more records to be processed. Therefore, the switch is set so that a transaction record will not be read. Control is then passed to block E1 on Page 1 of the flowchart so that the remaining master records may be processed.

Step 22: The remaining master records are read and processed.

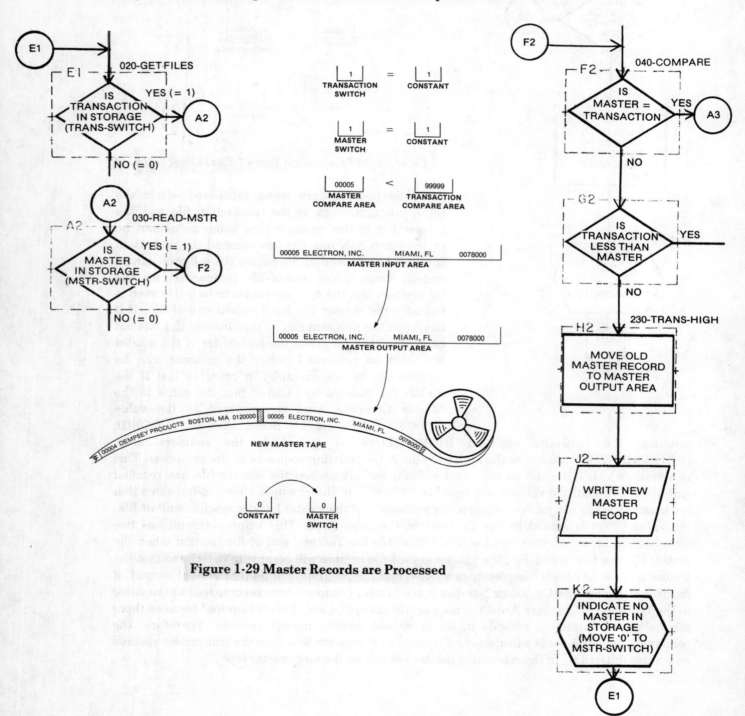

Figure 1-29 Master Records are Processed

Since the transaction switch indicates a record in storage (block E1), control is transferred to the master reading routine (A2). The first test when the routine in block A2 is entered is to determine if there is a master record in computer storage. In Figure 1-29, there is a master in storage, so a master record is not read. When the Customer Number in the Master Compare Area is compared with the value in the Transaction Compare Area, it is found that the master is less than the transaction. This will always be true when the transaction file has reached end-of-file because the value "99999" (or HIGH-VALUES) is contained in the Transaction Compare Area. Thus, the records which remain on the old master will merely be rewritten on the new master because there are no transaction records to update the records on the old master file.

Step 23: The master file is processed until the end of the master input file is found. The master end-of-file routine is then entered.

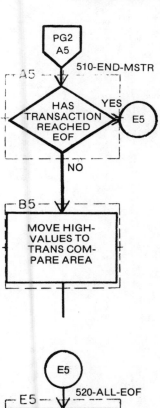

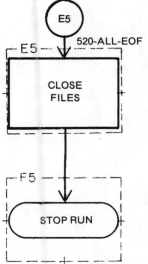

Figure 1-30 Master End-Of-File Routine is Entered

Note in Figure 1-30 that the first test performed is to check if the transaction file has reached end-of-file. In this example, it has because the Transaction Compare Area contains the value "99999". As was noted previously, this value is moved to the Transaction Compare Area when the end of the transaction file is found. Thus, since both files have been completely processed, the program is terminated.

It can be seen from the flowchart in Figure 1-30 that if the transaction file had not reached end-of-file, the value 99999 is moved to the Master Compare Area and the Master Switch is set to "1" in the same manner as used for the transaction file. Thus, if the master file reached end-of-file before the transaction file, the remainder of the transaction records must be processed.

It should be noted that since the Customer Number of the transaction records will always be less than the Customer Numbers in the Master Compare Area after the master has reached end-of-file, the only valid transaction code for a transaction record after the master has been completely read is an "add" (transaction code = 1). Any other code will cause an error message to be written on the Exception Report (see Figure 1-6). This is because there are no master records to be changed or deleted since there are no more master records.

The process of sequentially updating master files is quite common in business applications and should be thoroughly understood for the basic file update logic presented in this chapter can be applied to many types of business programming problems such as payroll, inventory control, etc.

DEFINING MAGNETIC TAPE MASTER FILES

The tape files which are used for the input and output master files must be defined in the Input-Output Section of the Environment Division and in the Data Division of the COBOL program. The definitions of both the input and output files and their respective data records are illustrated below.

```
002030  INPUT-OUTPUT SECTION.
002040  FILE-CONTROL.
002050
002060      SELECT TRANSIN
002070          ASSIGN TO SYS007-UR-2540R-S.
002080      SELECT MSTRIN
002090          ASSIGN TO SYS024-UT-2400-S-MSTRIN.
002100      SELECT MSTROUT
002110          ASSIGN TO SYS027-UT-2400-S-MSTROUT.
002120      SELECT PRTFLE
002130          ASSIGN TO SYS013-UR-1403-S.


003020  FD  MSTRIN
003030      BLOCK CONTAINS 56 RECORDS
003040      RECORD CONTAINS 64 CHARACTERS
003050      LABEL RECORDS ARE STANDARD
003060      DATA RECORD IS MSTRIN-IO.
003070  01  MSTRIN-IO.
003080      03  CUST-NUMB-MSTRIN      PICTURE X(5).
003090      03  CUST-NAME-MSTRIN      PICTURE X(20).
003100      03  CUST-ADDR-MSTRIN      PICTURE X(30).
003110      03  SALES-AMT-MSTRIN      PICTURE S9(5)V99
003120                               USAGE IS COMPUTATIONAL-3.
003130      03  FILLER               PICTURE X(5).


004020  FD  MSTROUT
004030      BLOCK CONTAINS 56 RECORDS
004040      RECORD CONTAINS 64 CHARACTERS
004050      LABEL RECORDS ARE STANDARD
004060      DATA RECORD IS MSTROUT-IO.
004070  01  MSTROUT-IO.
004080      03  CUST-NUMB-MSTROUT     PICTURE X(5).
004090      03  CUST-NAME-MSTROUT     PICTURE X(20).
004100      03  CUST-ADDR-MSTROUT     PICTURE X(30).
004110      03  SALES-AMT-MSTROUT     PICTURE S9(5)V99
004120                               USAGE IS COMPUTATIONAL-3.
004130      03  FILLER               PICTURE X(5).
```

Figure 1-31 Definitions of the Master Files

INPUT-OUTPUT SECTION

Note in the Select statements for the magnetic tape files the "name" entry, that is, the entry following the organization "S" entry, is different for both files. This name entry may be used when disk or tape files are being defined in order to specify a name which will be used to identify the file when the job control statements of the various operating systems reference the file. In the case of the input master file, the "name" is **MSTRIN**, which is the same name used for the filename entry. There is no requirement that this name entry be the same as a filename. It may be any name desired by the programmer. The name for the output file is **MSTROUT**, which is the same as the filename. Again, there is no requirement that this name be identical.

DATA DIVISION

From the example in Figure 1-31 it can be seen that the file definitions for both the input and the output master files are virtually identical. This is because the output file which is created out of one run of the program will be the old master file which is input to the program for the next run of the program. Thus, the files, which contain fixed-length blocked records, must have the same blocking factor, the same record length, and the same labelling on the tape volumes.

The data records defined in the Data Division are structured in the same way for both the tape input file and the tape output file so that the data which is written on the output file will be readable as an input file on the next updating cycle. It should be noted that when packed-decimal (Computational-3) data is to be written on a file, such as the **SALES-AMT-MSTROUT** field, then in order for the compiler to treat this data as signed numeric data when reading the file as input it must also be defined as Computational-3 in the input record.

HOUSEKEEPING ROUTINES

The first steps in a sequential update program, as with most other programs, is to perform certain housekeeping routines. The files must be opened, the date retrieved, and the headings printed on the first page of the report. The coding to perform these activities in the sample program is illustrated in Figure 1-32.

EXAMPLE

```
007030  010-START.
007040         OPEN INPUT TRANSIN, MSTRIN,
007050              OUTPUT MSTROUT, PRTFLE.
007060         MOVE CURRENT-DATE TO DATE-H1.
007070         PERFORM 400-HEADER THRU 400-EXIT.
```

Figure 1-32 Housekeeping Routines

Note that the files being opened are the transaction file (**TRANSIN**), the old master file (**MSTRIN**), the new master file (**MSTROUT**), and the exception report printer file (**PRTFLE**). The **OPEN** verb must be issued before processing of the files can begin. In addition to preparing a tape file for processing, the **OPEN** routine checks the labels on the tape volume to ensure that the proper tape is being used. The tape label information is supplied to the **OPEN** routine by the Job Control statements which would be used for the execution of the program.

After the files are opened, the current date, through the use of the identifier **CURRENT-DATE**, is moved to the heading line to be printed in the heading. The identifier **CURRENT-DATE** is a special name which is available with the IBM ANSI COBOL compiler to represent the date. The current date is stored at the beginning of each day by the operator in a permanent area of storage. The date is stored in the normal format of **MM/DD/YY**. On other compilers, this same name or a similar name is usually available so that the current date which is stored in main storage will be available to COBOL programs. Note that this is an alternate method to using an Assembler Language subroutine to extract the date and is probably superior because main storage will be saved as the assembler subroutine need not be included in the program. The main disadvantage is that if the program is compiled at some future date on a compiler which does not support this special identifier, the program will have to be changed.

READING THE INPUT FILES

The basic logic in a sequential update is to read a transaction record, read a master record, then compare the transaction record with the master record, that is, compare the controlling field in these records (in the sample program this field is the customer number), and process the records dependent upon a high, low, or equal condition. If an unequal condition occurs, normally either the transaction record or the master record will be processed but not both. Thus, after an unequal condition, it is necessary to read only the type of record which was just processed because the record not processed is still in main storage ready to be processed. To accomplish this, switches are established which indicate whether or not a transaction or master record should be read.

At the **020-GETFILES** routine illustrated in Figure 1-33, the first test is to determine if a transaction is already in main storage. This is done by checking the value in the switch **TRANS-SWITCH**. If the switch is equal to '0', it indicates a transaction record is not in main storage and that a transaction record must be read. The first time, of course, a record will not be in main storage so a **READ** command is issued to read the transaction file. The **TRANS-SWITCH** is then set to '1' to indicate a transaction record is in main storage.

EXAMPLE

```
008090 020-GETFILES.
008100     IF TRANS-SWITCH NOT = 0
008110 !       GO TO 030-READ-MSTR.
008120     READ TRANSIN AT END GO TO 500-END-TRANS.
008130     MOVE '1' TO TRANS-SWITCH.
008140     MOVE CUST-NUMB-TRANS TO CUST-NUMB-TRANS-C.
008150 030-READ-MSTR.
008160     IF MSTR-SWITCH NOT = 0
008170 !       GO TO 040-COMPARE.
008180     READ MSTRIN AT END GO TO 510-END-MASTER.
008190     MOVE '1' TO MSTR-SWITCH.
008200     MOVE CUST-NUMB-MSTRIN TO CUST-NUMB-MSTRIN-C.
```

Figure 1-33 Routine to Read Transaction File and Master File

A similar test is performed for the master file records. The first time, an unprocessed master record will not be in main storage, so a master record is read and the switch **MSTR-SWITCH** is set to '1' to indicate the record is in storage.

In order to read a tape input file, the **READ** verb is used in the same manner as reading a card file. The filename **MSTRIN** is entered immediately after the **READ** verb and the end-of-file processing is determined by the **AT END** portion of the **READ** statement. When reading magnetic tape, the end-of-file is indicated by the tape mark following the last data record.

Note in the routine shown above that the customer number of the transaction record and the master record are moved to separate areas which are used for compare purposes. This is done because these compare areas will be used after the files have reached end-of-file and the I/O areas in the File Section of the Data Division are not available after the file has reached end-of-file. Therefore, to use common compare areas before and after the file has been completely read, the customer numbers are moved to a compare area.

COMPARING MASTER AND TRANSACTION

The next step is to determine whether the customer number in the transaction record is equal to, less than, or greater than the customer number in the master record.

This routine is illustrated in Figure 1-34.

EXAMPLE

```
ØØ9Ø1Ø  Ø4Ø-COMPARE.
ØØ9Ø2Ø     IF CUST-NUMB-TRANS-C IS = CUST-NUMB-MSTRIN-C
ØØ9Ø3Ø        GO TO 2ØØ-CUST-EQUAL.
ØØ9Ø4Ø     IF CUST-NUMB-TRANS-C IS < CUST-NUMB-MSTRIN-C
ØØ9Ø5Ø        GO TO 22Ø-TRANSLOW.
ØØ9Ø6Ø     GO TO 23Ø-TRANS-HIGH.
```

Figure 1-34 Routine To Compare Customer Numbers

TRANSACTION HIGH

When the customer number in the transaction record is higher than the customer number in the master record, it indicates that there is no updating to be performed on the master record. This is because all the remaining records on the transaction file are sorted in an ascending sequence and therefore, there will never be an equal condition between the current master record and a transaction record. Thus, the master record is written onto the new master file without being changed. See Figure 1-35.

EXAMPLE

```
Ø11Ø3Ø  23Ø-TRANS-HIGH.
Ø11Ø4Ø     MOVE MSTRIN-IO TO MSTROUT-IO.
Ø11Ø5Ø     WRITE MSTROUT-IO.
Ø11Ø6Ø     MOVE 'Ø' TO MSTR-SWITCH.
Ø11Ø7Ø     GO TO Ø2Ø-GETFILES.
```

Figure 1-35 Transaction High Routine

The **WRITE** verb is used to write the tape output record. The first entry following the **WRITE** verb is the name of the I/O area as defined in the File Section of the Data Division.

Although not shown in the routine in Figure 1-35, it should be noted that the "**FROM**" entry could be used in the Write sentence for tape if the record is to be written from a work area defined in the Working-Storage Section of the Data Division.

After the record is written on the new file, the switch which indicates that an unprocessed master record is in storage is set to '0'. This indicates that there is not a master record in storage, which is the desired indication because the record has been processed by being written on the new master file. See the flowchart in Figure 1-6.

At the **020-GETFILES** routine, a test is first made to determine if a transaction record is in computer storage. Since the switch was set to '1' when the transaction record was read, and the switch was never reset to '0', a branch around the **READ** for the transaction record will take place. Next, when a check is made for an unprocessed master record, the switch is equal to '0' because it was set to '0' in the **230-TRANS-HIGH** routine. Therefore, a master record will be read.

TRANSACTION LOW

When the transaction record is low, it indicates that the transaction is not to be used to delete or change a master record because there is not a master record which will match the transaction record. This is because all the remaining master records on the old master file will be higher in sequence than the transaction record. Therefore, the only valid function the transaction can perform is an add function, that is, inserting a new master record between two existing master records. The routine used when the transaction record is low is illustrated in Figure 1-36.

EXAMPLE

```
010020  220-TRANSLOW.
010030      IF CODE-TRANS IS = '1'
010040          NEXT SENTENCE
010050      ELSE
010060          IF CODE-TRANS IS = '2' OR CODE-TRANS IS = '3'
010070              GO TO 340-NO-MASTER
010080          ELSE
010090              GO TO 320-CODE-ERR.
010100      MOVE CUST-NUMB-TRANS TO CUST-NUMB-MSTROUT.
010110      MOVE CUST-NAME-TRANS TO CUST-NAME-MSTROUT.
010120      MOVE CUST-ADDR-TRANS TO CUST-ADDR-MSTROUT.
010130      MOVE SALES-AMT-TRANS TO SALES-AMT-MSTROUT.
010140      WRITE MSTROUT-ID.
010150      MOVE '0' TO TRANS-SWITCH.
010160      GO TO 020-GETFILES.
```

Figure 1-36 Transaction Low Routine

When the transaction is low, the transaction code must contain the value "1" or it is in error. Thus, the first statement in the routine is used to ensure that the transaction is a valid add transaction. The first **IF** Statement will check for the value "1". If the code is a "1", then the next sentence, which begins processing the transaction, will be executed. It should be noted that in the majority of cases, the value will be "1", since most transactions will be properly prepared. Therefore, the check for a "1" takes place first so that a minimum of execution time will be used in checking the code. If the invalid codes were checked first, in the majority of cases the errors would not be found and the check for the "1" would have to take place anyway. It is normally good programming procedure that when more than one condition is to be checked in a sequence such as found in the routine, above, the most likely condition to be found is checked for first. This procedure will save execution time, especially in a case where thousands and thousands of records may be processed by the routine.

If the code does not indicate an add (code = "1") then a check is made to determine if the code indicates a delete (code = "2") or a change (code = "3"). If so, the routine **340-NO-MASTER** is entered to print the appropriate "no master" message on the Exception Report. If the transaction code is invalid, that is, it does not indicate an add, delete, or change, a branch is taken to the routine **320-CODE-ERR** to issue the "invalid code" message on the Exception Report.

If the transaction code indicates the record is an add transaction, the fields are moved from the transaction fields to the master output area. When the moves are complete, the added master record is written on the new master file. A '0' is then moved to the switch which indicates an unprocessed transaction record is in computer storage. This is because the transaction has been processed by adding it to the master file. A return is then made to the **020-GETFILES** routine.

At the **020-GETFILES** routine, a transaction record is read because **TRANS-SWITCH** is equal to '0'.

A master record is not read, however, because **MSTR-SWITCH** was set to '1' when the master record was read and was not altered in the **220-TRANSLOW** routine.

TRANSACTION EQUAL TO MASTER

When the customer number on the transaction file is equal to the customer number on the master file, it indicates that either a change to the master record or a deletion of the master record is to take place. An addition of a master record cannot occur because a master record is already on the master file. The routine which is entered when the transaction and the master record are equal is illustrated in Figure 1-37.

EXAMPLE

```
009030 200-CUST-EQUAL.
009040     IF CODE-TRANS IS = '3'
009050         ADD SALES-AMT-TRANS TO SALES-AMT-MSTRIN
009060         MOVE '0' TO TRANS-SWITCH
009070         GO TO 020-GETFILES.
009080     IF CODE-TRANS IS = '2'
009090         MOVE '0' TO MSTR-SWITCH
009100         MOVE '0' TO TRANS-SWITCH
009110         GO TO 020-GETFILES.
009120     IF CODE-TRANS IS = '1'
009130         GO TO 300-DUPL-ERROR
009140     ELSE
009150         GO TO 320-CODE-ERR.
```

Figure 1-37 Transaction Equal Routine

When the transaction customer number is equal to the master customer number, the most likely action to be taken is to change the master record. Therefore, the first check in the routine is to determine if the transaction record is a change record (code = '3'). If so, the amount field in the transaction record is added to the sales field in the old master record. A '0' is then moved to **TRANS-SWITCH** to indicate that there is not an unprocessed transaction record in storage. This will cause the **020-GETFILES** routine to read a new transaction record. The indicator for the master record, however, is not set to zero. This is so that more than one transaction record can update a master record. If the next transaction record is high, the updated master record will be written by the **230-TRANS-HIGH** routine and the next master record will be read. The transaction record will never be lower because the transactions are sorted in ascending sequence.

The next most likely transaction code when the customer numbers are equal is the value '2', which indicates a delete function. When a delete transaction is found, a '0' is moved to both **TRANS-SWITCH** and **MSTR-SWITCH**. This indicates that neither a transaction record nor a master record is unprocessed in storage. Thus, when the **020-GETFILES** routine is entered, both a transaction record and a master record will be read. This deletes the old master record from the new master file because the old master record is never written to the new master file before another old master record is read. Thus, the deleted record is never written on the new master file. The transaction record has been processed, so a new transaction record must also be read.

If the code field contains neither a '3' nor a '2', then it is in error because a change and delete are the only two valid transactions. If the code is equal to a '1', then it appears that the transaction record is attempting to add a record already on the master and the **300-DUPL-ERROR** routine is entered to print the appropriate message on the listing. If the code is not equal to '1', then the **320-CODE-ERR** routine is entered to print the error message on the Exception Listing.

END-OF-FILE

When two files are being read, one file will reach the end of its data before the other file. The transaction file will reach end-of-file first if the last transaction record is less than or equal to the last record on the master file. The master file will reach end-of-file if its last record is less than the last record on the transaction file. Thus, the end-of-file routines must check the status of the other file before determining that the job is complete.

The end-of-file routines for both the Transaction Records and the Master Records are illustrated below.

EXAMPLE

```
015020   500-END-TRANS.
015030       IF CUST-NUMB-MSTRIN-C IS = HIGH-VALUES
015040           GO TO 520-ALL-EOF.
015050       MOVE HIGH-VALUES TO CUST-NUMB-TRANS-C.
015060       MOVE '1' TO TRANS-SWITCH.
015070       GO TO 020-GETFILES.
015080
015090   510-END-MASTER.
015100       IF CUST-NUMB-TRANS-C IS = HIGH-VALUES
015110           GO TO 520-ALL-EOF.
015120       MOVE HIGH-VALUES TO CUST-NUMB-MSTRIN-C.
015130       MOVE '1' TO MSTR-SWITCH.
015140       GO TO 020-GETFILES.
015150
015160   520-ALL-EOF.
015170       CLOSE  MSTRIN, MSTROUT,
015180              TRANSIN, PRTFLE.
015190       STOP RUN.
```

Figure 1-38 End of File Routines

The **500-END-TRANS** routine is entered when the transaction file reaches end-of-file. It first checks if the master file has reached end-of-file. If so, the update processing has been completed and the job can be completed. If not, it moves **HIGH-VALUES** to the transaction record compare area. The figurative constant **HIGH-VALUES** represents the highest value in the collating sequence of the computer being used. Thus, when a customer number from a master record is compared to the transaction compare area, the master file will always be low (i.e. the transaction record is high). Therefore, the transaction high routine (**230-TRANS-HIGH**) will always be entered and the old master record will be written on the new master file with no changes. This is the desired result because there are no more transaction records to update or change the master file. A '1' is also moved to **TRANS-SWITCH** so that no more transaction records will be read. The transaction end-of-file routine then branches to the **020-GETFILES** routine to read the remainder of the old master records.

The **510-END-MASTER** routine is entered when the old master reaches end-of-file. It checks if the transaction file has reached end-of-file. It does this by comparing the value in the transaction compare area to **HIGH-VALUES**. If the transaction compare area contains **HIGH-VALUES**, then the **500-END-TRANS** routine has been entered previously and therefore the transaction file has reached end-of-file. If this has happened, the **510-END-MASTER** routine goes to the **520-ALL-EOF** routine to complete the program. If not, this routine moves **HIGH-VALUES** to the master compare area. Placing this value in the compare area of the master record will make the customer number in any transaction records read lower than the master records. Thus, after end-of-file is reached on the master file, the transaction low routine (**220-TRANSLOW**) will always be entered when a transaction record is read. This is the desired routine because there cannot be a match between a transaction record and a master record since there are no more master records. Therefore, the transaction record must either be an addition to the master file or it is in error. A '1' is moved to **MSTR-SWITCH** to indicate that a master record is in storage so that the master file will not be read again. The master end-of-file routine then branches to the **020-GETFILES** routine to read the remainder of the transaction records.

When both files are completed, the **520-ALL-EOF** routine is entered to close the files and stop the run. The format notation for the **CLOSE** statement is illustrated below.

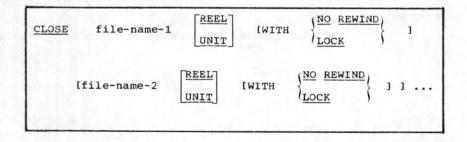

Figure 1-39 Format Notation: CLOSE Statement

Note that the close statement in the sample program does not make use of any of the options illustrated in Figure 1-39. Therefore, the tape volumes on which the files **MSTRIN** and **MSTROUT** are recorded, will be rewound to the load point. This rewind to the load point is the default value if none of the options are specified.

It should be noted also that when the tape volume is rewound to the load point as a result of the Close Statement, the tape is positioned for processing if it is subsequently opened again. Therefore, unless the **LOCK** option is used, a tape file which is closed can be opened again and processed. For example, an output tape may be created in a program, be closed and rewound, and then be opened as an input file so that the information stored by an earlier portion of the program can be used as input to a subsequent portion of the same program. If the **LOCK** option is used, the tape file cannot be subsequently reopened.

MASTER FILE CREATION

In the previous explanation of the sequential update logic, it was assumed that the master file had been created and stored on magnetic tape. In actual practice, the master file must be created before it is updated.

In order to create the master file, data which will comprise the master file is normally recorded on punched cards and a program is written to transfer the information contained on the punched cards to magnetic tape. In many applications, the program used to create the master file is the same program used to update the file. This is accomplished by having a "first-time" routine, that is, a master creation routine, in the update program.

The "first-time" routine, which is executed only when the master file is initially created, reads the card file and writes the new master file on magnetic tape, thus performing a function similar to the addition routine in the update program. The addition routine writes a record on the new master file when one did not exist previously. Thus, with minor modification to the update program, the addition routine can be used to create the master file.

In order to incorporate a "first-time" routine into an update program, there must be some type of external indicator available for the program to test indicating whether or not it is the "first-time". Again, it should be noted that when it is the "first-time", the program will be used to create the master file. The method of setting an external indicator to be tested by the program will vary dependent upon the compiler and the computer being utilized. On some computers there is a "hardware switch", that is, a switch on the console of the computer, which can be set in an "on" or "off" status and which can be tested by the program. On other computers there are switches which are actually bits or bytes within storage which are set by various types of job control statements. The Disk Operating System utilized on the System/360 and System/370 has switches, called the User Program Status Indicators (UPSI), which are set by statements in the job stream processed by the operating system. The User Program Status Indicators are contained in a byte of storage called the **UPSI BYTE**. Each bit of this byte can act as a switch because its value can be either '0' or '1'. The bits are controlled (turned "off" and "on") by means of a job control card. For example, at the beginning of a job all the bits in the **UPSI** byte are set to zero, as illustrated in Figure 1-40.

EXAMPLE

Figure 1-40 Example of UPSI Byte

A job control card may then be used to turn "on" bit '0' prior to executing the program, as shown below.

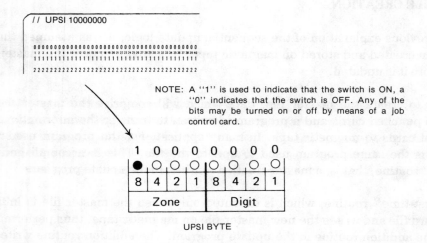

NOTE: A "1" is used to indicate that the switch is ON, a "0" indicates that the switch is OFF. Any of the bits may be turned on or off by means of a job control card.

Figure 1-41 Example of "Turning On" UPSI Switch

Although the methods of setting and resetting the indicators may vary as noted, in general the technique used in the sample program compiled under DOS will illustrate the method used in all COBOL programs.

The first requirement is normally that the external switch, whether it be a hardware switch or a bit or byte in main storage, must be defined in the Special-Names portion of the Environment Division. The Special-Names paragraph of the Environment Division is used to give identifiers to certain functions which must be performed or which must be identified. The name which is associated with the identifier is usually unique to the compiler being used, since the computer has its own unique method of setting external switches. For example, on the NCR Century 200 computer, the Special-Names used are **SWITCH-1**, **SWITCH-2**, etc. because there are hardware switches which are used on the computer console. When using the ANSI compiler under DOS, the names used are **UPSI-0**, **UPSI-1**,..., **UPSI-7**. These names reference the eight bits of the **UPSI** byte which can be used as switches and are set by means of a job control statement. **UPSI-0** references bit 0, **USPI-1** references bit 1, etc.

In the sample program, bit 0 of the **UPSI** byte is to be used to indicate whether or not the master file has been created. If the bit is equal to 1, it indicates that there is no master file and that it must be created by the program using the first-time routine. If the bit is equal to 0, it indicates that there is a master file and that the normal update processing should be done. Thus, when the master file is to be created, an **UPSI** job control card must be used to set bit 0 equal to 1. At the conclusion of the job, the DOS job control routines will reset the bit to zero.

Bit zero of the **UPSI** byte must be given an identifier. The coding in the sample program to accomplish this is illustrated below.

```
002030 ENVIRONMENT DIVISION.
002040 SOURCE-COMPUTER.      IBM-360-F30.
002050 OBJECT-COMPUTER.      IBM-360-F30.
002060 SPECIAL-NAMES.
002070     C01 IS TO-TOP-OF-PAGE
002080     UPSI-0 ON STATUS IS UPSI-0-ON
002090         OFF STATUS IS UPSI-0-OFF.
```

Figure 1-42 Use of Special-Names Paragraph to Define External Indicators

It will be noted that the **ON** status and the **OFF** status are specified so that both can be tested within the program. The general format of the statement illustrated in Figure 1-42 is shown below.

```
SPECIAL-NAMES.
     function-2 ON STATUS IS condition-name-1
                OFF STATUS IS condition-name-2
```

Figure 1-43 General Format for Testing External Switches

Note from the general format above that function-2 must be a special word which indicates the function to be tested. In the example in Figure 1-42, this function is specified as **UPSI-0**, which is a special IBM name. On other computers and other compilers, this name may vary, but the function of the name, that is, to specify an externally set switch, will be the same. The condition-name-1 entry is a programmer chosen word which is used in the program in much the same way a level-88 condition-name is used.

FIRST-TIME ROUTINE

The first-time routine must test the external switch to determine if there is an old file. In order to test the switch, the condition-name specified in the Special-Names portion of the program must be tested. The routine used in the sample program is illustrated below.

```
007020  010-START.
007030      OPEN INPUT  TRANSIN,
007040             OUTPUT MSTROUT, PRTFLE.
007050      MOVE CURRENT-DATE TO DATE-H1.
007060      PERFORM 400-HEADER THRU 400-EXIT.
007070      IF UPSI-0-ON
007080          GO TO 510-END-MASTER.
007090      OPEN INPUT  MSTRIN.
007100  020-GETFILES.
```

Figure 1-44 Example of First-Time Routine

Note from the example in Figure 1-44 that the transaction file (**TRANSIN**), the new master file (**MSTROUT**) and the Exception Report file(**PRTFLE**) are opened, but the master input file (**MSTRIN**) is not opened as the first statement in the program. This is because it must first be determined if a master file has already been created. This is determined by checking the external switch. After the heading is printed on the Exception Report, the condition-name **UPSI-0-ON** is checked. If the switch is ''on'' it indicates that there is no master input file, and that it must be created. Since the Addition routine is to be used to create the master file, some indication must be set in the program so that the Add routine will always be entered. This can be accomplished by the end-of-file routine for the master file (**510-END-MASTER**). Thus, as shown in Figure 1-44, when the external switch is ''on'', the **510-END-MASTER** routine should be entered.

The **510-END-MASTER** routine, as shown in Figure 1-38 moves a '1' to **MSTR-SWITCH** to indicate a master record is in storage and also moves **HIGH-VALUES** to the master file compare area. Although there is no master record, this routine will accomplish what is necessary for the first-time creation routine because it ensures that the old master file will not be read (this is necessary because there is no old master file) and that the **220-TRANSLOW** routine (i.e. the Add Routine) will always be entered because the transaction customer number will always be less than the old master customer number. Thus, when the **020-GETFILES** routine is entered, only the transaction file will be read and only the **220-TRANSLOW** routine will be entered. This is the desired result to create the master file the first time. It should also be noted that the type code in the transaction record must be equal to '1' (Add) or the transaction record is invalid.

If the external switch is not "on" it indicates that there is an old master file. Therefore, as illustrated in Figure 1-44, the input file **MSTRIN** will be opened and processing will take place as previously explained.

It should be noted that since the input master file **MSTRIN** may not be opened at the beginning of the program if it is not available, so too it may not be present to be closed at the conclusion of the program. Therefore, as illustrated below, the end-of-file routine for the program must check the status of the external switch.

EXAMPLE

```
016130  520-ALL-EOF.
016140      IF UPSI-0-OFF
016150          CLOSE MSTRIN.
016160      CLOSE MSTROUT,
016170          TRANSIN,
016180          PRTFLE.
016190      STOP RUN.
```

Figure 1-45 End-Of-File Routine

Note from the example that if the external switch is off, then it indicates that there is an input master file and the file is closed. If the switch is "on", there is not a master file and the Close Statement should not be issued for the master input file. The master output file, the transaction input file, and the printer file must be closed everytime regardless of whether there is a master input file because they are always used in the program.

SAMPLE PROGRAM

The following pages contain the documentation for the sample file updating problem, including the format of the input, the format of the output, and the program listing.

INPUT

The input to the sample program is a sorted transaction file and the old master file. The transaction file is on cards and the master file is on tape. The record layouts for the two files are illustrated on page 46.

Transactions Records

FIELD	FIELD NAME	PICTURE	POSITION	NO OF DIGITS	LENGTH
Transaction Code	CODE-TRANS	X	1	1	1
Customer Number	CUST-NUMB-TRANS	X(5)	2-6	5	5
Customer Name	CUST-NAME-TRANS	X(20)	7-26	20	20
Customer Address	CUST-ADDR-TRANS	X(30)	27-56	30	30
Sales Amount	SALES-AMT-TRANS	S9(5)V99	57-63	7	7

Note: In the Transaction Code field, a ''1'' indicates an addition or load, a ''2''
       indicates a deletion, and a ''3'' indicates a change.

Master Records

FIELD	FIELD NAME	PICTURE	POSITION	NO OF DIGITS	LENGTH
Customer Number	CUST-NUMB-MSTRIN	X(5)	1-5	5	5
Customer Name	CUST-NAME-MSTRIN	X(20)	6-25	20	20
Customer Address	CUST-ADDR-MSTRIN	X(30)	26-55	30	30
Sales Amount	SALES-AMT-MSTRIN	S9(5)V99 Comp-3	56-59	7	4
Filler		X(5)	60-64	5	5

OUTPUT

The output consists of the updated master file with the same record layout as shown above
and an error listing.

The format of the error listing is shown below.

PROGRAM

The following is the listing of the program which sequentially updates the customer sales master file. Note in the Procedure Division the use of the Note statement. When used as the first word in a paragraph, the Note statement causes the paragraph to be considered a comment. Thus, as shown in the sample program, a note paragraph can be used to explain what processing will be done in the following paragraph. This type of documentation within the program listing is very necessary so that future debugging and maintenance of the program can be made as easy as possible. Note also the fact that each paragraph name is preceeded by a number and that these numbers are sequentially ascending as the Procedure Division coding continues. This technique is used for readability of the source listing. Note that when a paragraph name is referenced in a sentence the reader can go directly to the paragraph because he knows the location, within the Procedure Division, of the paragraph. Although not a required technique, this method does provide for better documentation of the source listing for future debugging and maintenance.

Note also at pg/line 003100, the amount field in the transaction record is defined as Picture S9(5)V99, and then is redefined as Picture X(7). The reason that this is done is so that the amount field can be printed on the Exception Report. As was noted previously, when an update of a master record takes place, the amount field is added to the amount contained in the master record. In order for this addition to take place properly, the field must be defined as a numeric field with two digits to the right of the decimal point - S9(5)V99. When this field is moved to the output area for the Exception Report, however, a numeric move would require that editing of the numeric field take place. It should be noted, however, that the possibility exists that this amount field could contain blanks. This could happen, for example, with a delete transaction. If a field which is defined as numeric is edited, and it contains blanks, a program check interruption would occur on the System/360 or the System/370. Therefore, in order to make it possible to move the amount field to the Exception Report regardless of what is contained in the field, the field is redefined as an alphanumeric field - Picture X(7). Thus, whatever is contained in the Amount field will be moved properly to the output area for the exception report and a program check interruption will not occur.

```
     1                          IBM DOS AMERICAN NATIONAL STANDARD COBOL          CBF CL3-4          09/12/74

     00001    001010 IDENTIFICATION DIVISION.                                     SEQUPDAT
     00002    001020 PROGRAM-ID.      SEQUPDAT.                                   SEQUPDAT
     00003    001030 AUTHOR.          SHELLY.                                     SEQUPDAT
     00004    001040 INSTALLATION.    LONG BEACH.                                 SEQUPDAT
     00005    001050 DATE-WRITTEN.    07/10/74.                                   SEQUPDAT
     00006    001060 DATE-COMPILED.   09/12/74.                                   SEQUPDAT
     00007    001070 SECURITY.        UNCLASSIFIED.                               SEQUPDAT
     00008    001080 REMARKS.         A SEQUENTIAL MASTER FILE ON MAGNETIC TAPE IS TO  SEQUPDAT
     00009    001090                  BE UPDATED BY SORTED TRANSACTIONS CONTAINED IN   SEQUPDAT
     00010    001100                  A CARD FILE AND A NEW MASTER IS TO BE CREATED.   SEQUPDAT
     00011    001110                                                             SEQUPDAT
     00012    001120                                                             SEQUPDAT
     00013    001130 ENVIRONMENT DIVISION.                                        SEQUPDAT
     00014    001140                                                             SEQUPDAT
     00015    001150 CONFIGURATION SECTION.                                       SEQUPDAT
     00016    001160 SOURCE-COMPUTER.  IBM-360-F30.                               SEQUPDAT
     00017    001170 OBJECT-COMPUTER.  IBM-360-F30.                               SEQUPDAT
     00018    001180                                                             SEQUPDAT
     00019    001190 SPECIAL-NAMES.                                               SEQUPDAT
     00020    001200     C01 IS TO-TOP-OF-PAGE                                    SEQUPDAT
     00021    002010     UPSI-0 ON STATUS IS UPSI-0-ON                            SEQUPDAT
     00022    002020             OFF STATUS IS UPSI-0-OFF.                        SEQUPDAT
     00023    002030                                                             SEQUPDAT
     00024    002040 INPUT-OUTPUT SECTION.                                        SEQUPDAT
     00025    002050                                                             SEQUPDAT
     00026    002060 FILE-CONTROL.                                                SEQUPDAT
     00027    002070     SELECT  TRANSIN                                          SEQUPDAT
     00028    002080         ASSIGN TO SYS007-UR-2540R-S.                         SEQUPDAT
     00029    002090     SELECT  MSTRIN                                           SEQUPDAT
     00030    002100         ASSIGN TO SYS024-UT-2400-S-MSTRIN.                   SEQUPDAT
     00031    002110     SELECT  MSTROUT                                          SEQUPDAT
     00032    002120         ASSIGN TO SYS027-UT-2400-S-MSTROUT.                  SEQUPDAT
     00033    002130     SELECT  PRTFLE                                           SEQUPDAT
     00034    002140         ASSIGN TO SYS013-UR-1403-S.                          SEQUPDAT
     00035    002150                                                             SEQUPDAT
     00036    002160                                                             SEQUPDAT
     00037    002170 DATA DIVISION.                                               SEQUPDAT
     00038    002180                                                             SEQUPDAT
     00039    002190 FILE SECTION.                                                SEQUPDAT
     00040    002200                                                             SEQUPDAT
     00041    003010 FD  TRANSIN                                                  SEQUPDAT
     00042    003020     RECORD CONTAINS 80 CHARACTERS                            SEQUPDAT
     00043    003030     LABEL RECORDS ARE OMITTED                                SEQUPDAT
     00044    003040     DATA RECORD IS TRANS-IO.                                 SEQUPDAT
     00045    003050 01  TRANS-IO.                                                SEQUPDAT
     00046    003060     03  CODE-TRANS          PICTURE X.                       SEQUPDAT
     00047    003070     03  CUST-NUMB-TRANS     PICTURE X(5).                    SEQUPDAT
     00048    003080     03  CUST-NAME-TRANS     PICTURE X(20).                   SEQUPDAT
     00049    003090     03  CUST-ADDR-TRANS     PICTURE X(30).                   SEQUPDAT
     00050    003100     03  SALES-AMT-TRANS     PICTURE S9(5)V99.                SEQUPDAT
     00051    003110     03  SALES-AMT-TRANS-X   REDEFINES  SALES-AMT-TRANS       SEQUPDAT
     00052    003120                             PICTURE X(7).                    SEQUPDAT
     00053    003130     03  FILLER              PICTURE X(17).                   SEQUPDAT
     00054    003140                                                             SEQUPDAT
     00055    003150 FD  MSTRIN                                                   SEQUPDAT
     00056    003160     BLOCK CONTAINS 56 RECORDS                                SEQUPDAT
     00057    003170     RECORD CONTAINS 64 CHARACTERS                            SEQUPDAT
     00058    003180     LABEL RECORDS ARE STANDARD                               SEQUPDAT
     00059    003190     DATA RECORD IS MSTRIN-IO.                                SEQUPDAT
     00060    003200 01  MSTRIN-IO.                                               SEQUPDAT
     00061    004010     03  CUST-NUMB-MSTRIN    PICTURE X(5).                    SEQUPDAT
     00062    004020     03  CUST-NAME-MSTRIN    PICTURE X(20).                   SEQUPDAT
     00063    004030     03  CUST-ADDR-MSTRIN    PICTURE X(30).                   SEQUPDAT
     00064    004040     03  SALES-AMT-MSTRIN    PICTURE S9(5)V99                 SEQUPDAT
     00065    004050                             USAGE IS COMPUTATIONAL-3.        SEQUPDAT
     00066    004060     03  FILLER              PICTURE X(5).                    SEQUPDAT
     00067    004070                                                             SEQUPDAT
     00068    004080 FD  MSTROUT                                                  SEQUPDAT
     00069    004090     BLOCK CONTAINS 56 RECORDS                                SEQUPDAT
     00070    004100     RECORD CONTAINS 64 CHARACTERS                            SEQUPDAT
     00071    004110     LABEL RECORDS ARE STANDARD                               SEQUPDAT
     00072    004120     DATA RECORD IS MSTROUT-IO.                               SEQUPDAT
     00073    004130 01  MSTROUT-IO.                                              SEQUPDAT
     00074    004140     03  CUST-NUMB-MSTROUT   PICTURE X(5).                    SEQUPDAT
     00075    004150     03  CUST-NAME-MSTROUT   PICTURE X(20).                   SEQUPDAT
     00076    004160     03  CUST-ADDR-MSTROUT   PICTURE X(30).                   SEQUPDAT
     00077    004170     03  SALES-AMT-MSTROUT   PICTURE S9(5)V99                 SEQUPDAT
     00078    004180                             USAGE IS COMPUTATIONAL-3.        SEQUPDAT
     00079    004190     03  FILLER              PICTURE X(5).                    SEQUPDAT
     00080    004200                                                             SEQUPDAT
     00081    005010 FD  PRTFLE                                                   SEQUPDAT
     00082    005020     RECORD CONTAINS 81 CHARACTERS                            SEQUPDAT
     00083    005030     LABEL RECORDS ARE OMITTED                                SEQUPDAT
     00084    005040     DATA RECORD IS PRINT-IO.                                 SEQUPDAT
     00085    005050 01  PRINT-IO.                                                SEQUPDAT
     00086    005060     03  FILLER              PICTURE X(5).                    SEQUPDAT
     00087    005070     03  CODE-PRINT          PICTURE X.                       SEQUPDAT
```

```
     2

00088  005080     03  FILLER               PICTURE X(6).                        SEQUPDAT
00089  005090     03  CUST-NUMB-PRINT      PICTURE X(5).                        SEQUPDAT
00090  005100     03  FILLER               PICTURE X(4).                        SEQUPDAT
00091  005110     03  SALES-AMT-PRINT      PICTURE X(7).                        SEQUPDAT
00092  005120     03  FILLER               PICTURE X(7).                        SEQUPDAT
00093  005130     03  ERROR-PRINT          PICTURE X(46).                       SEQUPDAT
00094  005140                                                                   SEQUPDAT
00095  005150                                                                   SEQUPDAT
00096  005160  WORKING-STORAGE SECTION.                                         SEQUPDAT
00097  005170  77  MSTR-SWITCH             PICTURE X        VALUE '0'.          SEQUPDAT
00098  005180  77  TRANS-SWITCH            PICTURE X        VALUE '0'.          SEQUPDAT
00099  005190  77  PG-CNT                  PICTURE S999     VALUE ZERO          SEQUPDAT
00100  005200                              USAGE COMPUTATIONAL-3.               SEQUPDAT
00101  006010  77  VARIABLE                PICTURE 9.                           SEQUPDAT
00102  006020  77  LINE-COUNT              PICTURE S999                         SEQUPDAT
00103  006030                              USAGE COMPUTATIONAL-3.               SEQUPDAT
00104  006040  77  CUST-NUMB-TRANS-C       PICTURE X(5)     VALUE LOW-VALUES.   SEQUPDAT
00105  006050  77  CUST-NUMB-MSTRIN-C      PICTURE X(5)     VALUE LOW-VALUES.   SEQUPDAT
00106  006060  01  HEADER1.                                                     SEQUPDAT
00107  006070     03  FILLER               PICTURE XXX      VALUE SPACES.       SEQUPDAT
00108  006080     03  DATE-H1              PICTURE X(8).                        SEQUPDAT
00109  006090     03  FILLER               PICTURE X(17)    VALUE SPACES.       SEQUPDAT
00110  006100     03  FILLER               PICTURE X(44)    VALUE               SEQUPDAT
00111  006110           'EXCEPTION REPORT'.                                     SEQUPDAT
00112  006120     03  FILLER               PICTURE X(5)     VALUE 'PAGE '.      SEQUPDAT
00113  006130     03  PG-H1                PICTURE ZZ9.                         SEQUPDAT
00114  006140     03  FILLER               PICTURE X        VALUE ' '.          SEQUPDAT
00115  006150  01  HEADER2.                                                     SEQUPDAT
00116  006160     03  FILLER               PICTURE X.                           SEQUPDAT
00117  006170     03  FILLER               PICTURE X(46)    VALUE               SEQUPDAT
00118  006180      '  CODE    CUST NO.    AMOUNT                ERROR'.          SEQUPDAT
00119  006190     03  FILLER               PICTURE X(34)    VALUE SPACES.       SEQUPDAT
00120  006200                                                                   SEQUPDAT
00121  007010                                                                   SEQUPDAT
00122  007020                                                                   SEQUPDAT
00123  007030  PROCEDURE DIVISION.                                              SEQUPDAT
00124  007040  -                                                                SEQUPDAT
00125  007050                                                                   SEQUPDAT
00126  007060  NOTE-001.                                                        SEQUPDAT
00127  007070     NOTE ***************************************************************SEQUPDAT
00128  007080     *    THIS PROGRAM IS USED TO UPDATE A CUSTOMER SALES         *SEQUPDAT
00129  007090     *    SEQUENTIAL MASTER FILE BY SORTED TRANSACTIONS           *SEQUPDAT
00130  007100     *    STORED ON A PUNCHED CARD FILE.  A FIRST-TIME            *SEQUPDAT
00131  007110     *    ROUTINE IS INCORPORATED INTO THE PROGRAM TO            *SEQUPDAT
00132  007120     *    CREATE THE MASTER FILE IF NO OLD MASTER FILE           *SEQUPDAT
00133  007130     *    EXISTS.                                                 *SEQUPDAT
00134  007140     *                                                           *SEQUPDAT
00135  007150     *    THE BASIC LOGIC USED IS TO COMPARE THE CUSTOMER        *SEQUPDAT
00136  007160     *    NUMBER ON THE OLD MASTER WITH THE CUSTOMER NUMBER      *SEQUPDAT
00137  007170     *    ON THE TRANSACTION RECORD.  IF  THE MASTER IS LOW,     *SEQUPDAT
00138  007180     *    NO UPDATE IS TO TAKE PLACE AND THE OLD MASTER          *SEQUPDAT
00139  007190     *    RECORD IS WRITTEN TO THE NEW MASTER FILE. IF THE       *SEQUPDAT
00140  007200     *    MASTER RECORD IS HIGH, THE TRANSACTION RECORD MUST     *SEQUPDAT
00141  008010     *    BE AN "ADD" TYPE (CODE = 1 ) OR IT IS IN ERROR. IF     *SEQUPDAT
00142  008020     *    THE CUSTOMER NUMBERS ARE EQUAL, THE TRANSACTION        *SEQUPDAT
00143  008030     *    RECORD MUST BE A DELETE (CODE = 2) OR AN UPDATE        *SEQUPDAT
00144  008040     *    (CODE = 3) OR IT IS IN ERROR. IF IT IS A DELETE        *SEQUPDAT
00145  008050     *    TRANSACTION, THE OLD MASTER RECORD IS NOT WRITTEN      *SEQUPDAT
00146  008060     *    ON THE NEW MASTER FILE. IF IT IS AN UPDATE             *SEQUPDAT
00147  008070     *    TRANSACTION, THE SALES AMOUNT FIELD IS UPDATED.        *SEQUPDAT
00148  008080     *                                                           *SEQUPDAT
00149  008090     *    AN ERROR EXCEPTION REPORT IS GENERATED FOR ANY         *SEQUPDAT
00150  008100     *    ERRORS IN THE TRANSACTION DATA.                        *SEQUPDAT
00151  008110     ***************************************************************.SEQUPDAT
00152  008120                                                                   SEQUPDAT
00153  008130                                                                   SEQUPDAT
00154  008140  NOTE-010.                                                        SEQUPDAT
00155  008150     NOTE ***************************************************************SEQUPDAT
00156  008160     *    THIS ROUTINE IS ENTERED TO OPEN THE FILES AND          *SEQUPDAT
00157  008170     *    DETERMINE IF THE FIRST-TIME ROUTINE MUST BE            *SEQUPDAT
00158  008180     *    PERFORMED. THIS IS DONE BY TESTING THE UPSI BYTE       *SEQUPDAT
00159  008190     *    IN THE COMMUNICATIONS REGION.  IF BIT 0 OF THE         *SEQUPDAT
00160  008200     *    BYTE IS EQUAL TO 0, IT INDICATES THERE IS A MASTER.    *SEQUPDAT
00161  009010     *    IF BIT 0 OF THE BYTE IS EQUAL TO 1, IT INDICATES       *SEQUPDAT
00162  009020     *    THERE IS NOT A MASTER FILE.  IN ADDITION, THE          *SEQUPDAT
00163  009030     *    DATE IS RETRIEVED TO BE PRINTED ON THE EXCEPTION       *SEQUPDAT
00164  009040     *    REPORT.                                                *SEQUPDAT
00165  009050     ***************************************************************.SEQUPDAT
00166  009060                                                                   SEQUPDAT
00167  009070  010-START.                                                       SEQUPDAT
00168  009080     OPEN INPUT  TRANSIN,                                          SEQUPDAT
00169  009090          OUTPUT MSTROUT, PRTFLE.                                  SEQUPDAT
00170  009100     MOVE CURRENT-DATE TO DATE-H1.                                 SEQUPDAT
00171  009110     PERFORM 400-HEADER THRU 400-EXIT.                             SEQUPDAT
00172  009120     IF UPSI-0-ON                                                  SEQUPDAT
00173  009130         GO TO 510-END-MASTER.                                     SEQUPDAT
00174  009140     OPEN INPUT MSTRIN.                                            SEQUPDAT
```

```
     3

00175   009150                                                                     SEQUPDAT
00176   009160                                                                     SEQUPDAT
00177   009170 NOTE-020.                                                           SEQUPDAT
00178   009180       NOTE ***********************************************SEQUPDAT
00179   009190     *    THIS ROUTINE IS ENTERED TO READ EITHER THE        *SEQUPDAT
00180   009200     *    TRANSACTION FILE OR MASTER FILE OR BOTH AND THEN GO *SEQUPDAT
00181   010010     *    TO THE PROPER PROCESSING ROUTINE.                 *SEQUPDAT
00182   010020     ***********************************************SEQUPDAT
00183   010030                                                                     SEQUPDAT
00184   010040 020-GETFILES.                                                       SEQUPDAT
00185   010050       IF TRANS-SWITCH NOT = 0                                       SEQUPDAT
00186   010060           GO TO 030-READ-MSTR.                                      SEQUPDAT
00187   010070       READ TRANSIN AT END GO TO 500-END-TRANS.                      SEQUPDAT
00188   010080       MOVE '1' TO TRANS-SWITCH.                                     SEQUPDAT
00189   010090       MOVE CUST-NUMB-TRANS TO CUST-NUMB-TRANS-C.                    SEQUPDAT
00190   010100 030-READ-MSTR.                                                      SEQUPDAT
00191   010110       IF MSTR-SWITCH NOT = 0                                        SEQUPDAT
00192   010120           GO TO 040-COMPARE.                                        SEQUPDAT
00193   010130       READ MSTRIN AT END GO TO 510-END-MASTER.                      SEQUPDAT
00194   010140       MOVE '1' TO MSTR-SWITCH.                                      SEQUPDAT
00195   010150       MOVE CUST-NUMB-MSTRIN TO CUST-NUMB-MSTRIN-C.                  SEQUPDAT
00196   010160 040-COMPARE.                                                        SEQUPDAT
00197   010170       IF CUST-NUMB-TRANS-C IS = CUST-NUMB-MSTRIN-C                  SEQUPDAT
00198   010180           GO TO 200-CUST-EQUAL.                                     SEQUPDAT
00199   010190       IF CUST-NUMB-TRANS-C IS < CUST-NUMB-MSTRIN-C                  SEQUPDAT
00200   010200           GO TO 220-TRANSLOW.                                       SEQUPDAT
00201   011010       GO TO 230-TRANS-HIGH.                                         SEQUPDAT
00202   011020                                                                     SEQUPDAT
00203   011030                                                                     SEQUPDAT
00204   011040 NOTE-200.                                                           SEQUPDAT
00205   011050       NOTE ***********************************************SEQUPDAT
00206   011060     *    THIS ROUTINE IS ENTERED WHEN THE CUSTOMER NUMBERS ON *SEQUPDAT
00207   011070     *    THE TRANSACTION FILE AND THE MASTER FILE ARE EQUAL. *SEQUPDAT
00208   011080     *    EITHER AN UPDATE OR A DELETION CAN TAKE PLACE. ANY *SEQUPDAT
00209   011090     *    OTHER TYPE OF TRANSACTION IS INVALID.              *SEQUPDAT
00210   011100     ***********************************************SEQUPDAT
00211   011110                                                                     SEQUPDAT
00212   011120 200-CUST-EQUAL.                                                     SEQUPDAT
00213   011130       IF CODE-TRANS IS = '3'                                        SEQUPDAT
00214   011140           ADD SALES-AMT-TRANS TO SALES-AMT-MSTRIN                   SEQUPDAT
00215   011150           MOVE '0' TO TRANS-SWITCH                                  SEQUPDAT
00216   011160           GO TO 020-GETFILES.                                       SEQUPDAT
00217   011170       IF CODE-TRANS IS = '2'                                        SEQUPDAT
00218   011180           MOVE '0' TO MSTR-SWITCH                                   SEQUPDAT
00219   011190           MOVE '0' TO TRANS-SWITCH                                  SEQUPDAT
00220   011200           GO TO 020-GETFILES.                                       SEQUPDAT
00221   012010       IF CODE-TRANS IS = '1'                                        SEQUPDAT
00222   012020           GO TO 300-DUPL-ERROR                                      SEQUPDAT
00223   012030       ELSE                                                          SEQUPDAT
00224   012040           GO TO 320-CODE-ERR.                                       SEQUPDAT
00225   012050                                                                     SEQUPDAT
00226   012060                                                                     SEQUPDAT
00227   012070 NOTE-220.                                                           SEQUPDAT
00228   012080       NOTE ***********************************************SEQUPDAT
00229   012090     *    THIS ROUTINE IS ENTERED WHEN THE CUSTOMER NUMBER, *SEQUPDAT
00230   012100     *    IN THE TRANSACTION RECORD IS LESS THAN THE CUSTOMER *SEQUPDAT
00231   012110     *    NUMBER IN THE MASTER RECORD. THE ONLY VALID        *SEQUPDAT
00232   012120     *    TRANSACTION IS AN ADDITION (OR, IF THE FIRST-TIME, *SEQUPDAT
00233   012130     *    A LOAD).                                            *SEQUPDAT
00234   012140     ***********************************************SEQUPDAT
00235   012150                                                                     SEQUPDAT
00236   012160 220-TRANSLOW.                                                       SEQUPDAT
00237   012170       IF CODE-TRANS IS = '1'                                        SEQUPDAT
00238   012180           NEXT SENTENCE                                             SEQUPDAT
00239   012190       ELSE                                                          SEQUPDAT
00240   012200           IF CODE-TRANS IS = '2' OR CODE-TRANS IS = '3'             SEQUPDAT
00241   013010               GO TO 340-NO-MASTER                                   SEQUPDAT
00242   013020           ELSE                                                      SEQUPDAT
00243   013030               GO TO 320-CODE-ERR.                                   SEQUPDAT
00244   013040       MOVE CUST-NUMB-TRANS TO CUST-NUMB-MSTROUT.                    SEQUPDAT
00245   013050       MOVE CUST-NAME-TRANS TO CUST-NAME-MSTROUT.                    SEQUPDAT
00246   013060       MOVE CUST-ADDR-TRANS TO CUST-ADDR-MSTROUT.                    SEQUPDAT
00247   013070       MOVE SALES-AMT-TRANS TO SALES-AMT-MSTROUT.                    SEQUPDAT
00248   013080       WRITE MSTROUT-IO.                                             SEQUPDAT
00249   013090       MOVE '0' TO TRANS-SWITCH.                                     SEQUPDAT
00250   013100       GO TO 020-GETFILES.                                           SEQUPDAT
00251   013110                                                                     SEQUPDAT
00252   013120                                                                     SEQUPDAT
00253   013130 NOTE-230.                                                           SEQUPDAT
00254   013140       NOTE ***********************************************SEQUPDAT
00255   013150     *    THIS ROUTINE IS ENTERED WHEN THE CUSTOMER NUMBER IN *SEQUPDAT
00256   013160     *    THE MASTER RECORD IS LESS THAN THE CUSTOMER       *SEQUPDAT
00257   013170     *    NUMBER IN THE TRANSACTION RECORD. WHEN THIS OCCURS, *SEQUPDAT
00258   013180     *    THE OLD MASTER RECORD IS MERELY WRITTEN ON THE    *SEQUPDAT
00259   013190     *    NEW MASTER FILE.                                   *SEQUPDAT
00260   013200     ***********************************************SEQUPDAT
00261   014010                                                                     SEQUPDAT
```

```
      4
00262  014020 230-TRANS-HIGH.                                          SEQUPDAT
00263  014030     MOVE MSTRIN-IO TO MSTROUT-IO.                        SEQUPDAT
00264  014040     WRITE MSTROUT-IO.                                    SEQUPDAT
00265  014050     MOVE '0' TO MSTR-SWITCH.                             SEQUPDAT
00266  014060     GO TO 020-GETFILES.                                  SEQUPDAT
00267  014070                                                          SEQUPDAT
00268  014080                                                          SEQUPDAT
00269  014090 NOTE-300.                                                SEQUPDAT
00270  014100     NOTE *****************************************************SEQUPDAT
00271  014110     *   THIS ROUTINE IS ENTERED WHEN AN ADD IS ATTEMPTED ON *SEQUPDAT
00272  014120     *   A CUSTOMER NUMBER ALREADY ON THE MASTER FILE.       *SEQUPDAT
00273  014130     ****************************************************.SEQUPDAT
00274  014140                                                          SEQUPDAT
00275  014150 300-DUPL-ERROR.                                          SEQUPDAT
00276  014160     MOVE 'DUPLICATE MASTER RECORD' TO ERROR-PRINT.       SEQUPDAT
00277  014170     PERFORM 350-WRITE-PRINT THRU 350-EXIT.               SEQUPDAT
00278  014180     MOVE '0' TO TRANS-SWITCH.                            SEQUPDAT
00279  014190     GO TO 020-GETFILES.                                  SEQUPDAT
00280  014200                                                          SEQUPDAT
00281  015010                                                          SEQUPDAT
00282  015020 NOTE-320.                                                SEQUPDAT
00283  015030     NOTE *****************************************************SEQUPDAT
00284  015040     *   THIS ROUTINE IS ENTERED WHEN AN INVALID CODE IS    *SEQUPDAT
00285  015050     *   FOUND IN A TRANSACTION RECORD.                     *SEQUPDAT
00286  015060     ****************************************************.SEQUPDAT
00287  015070                                                          SEQUPDAT
00288  015080 320-CODE-ERR.                                            SEQUPDAT
00289  015090     MOVE 'INVALID TYPE CODE' TO ERROR-PRINT.             SEQUPDAT
00290  015100     PERFORM 350-WRITE-PRINT THRU 350-EXIT.               SEQUPDAT
00291  015110     MOVE '0' TO TRANS-SWITCH.                            SEQUPDAT
00292  015120     GO TO 020-GETFILES.                                  SEQUPDAT
00293  015130                                                          SEQUPDAT
00294  015140                                                          SEQUPDAT
00295  015150 NOTE-340.                                                SEQUPDAT
00296  015160     NOTE *****************************************************SEQUPDAT
00297  015170     *   THIS ROUTINE IS ENTERED WHEN A CODE OF '2' OR '3' IS*SEQUPDAT
00298  015180     *   FOUND IN A TRANSACTION RECORD AND THERE IS NO       *SEQUPDAT
00299  015190     *   CORRESPONDING MASTER RECORD.                       *SEQUPDAT
00300  015200     ****************************************************.SEQUPDAT
00301  016010                                                          SEQUPDAT
00302  016020 340-NO-MASTER.                                           SEQUPDAT
00303  016030     MOVE 'NO MASTER RECORD' TO ERROR-PRINT.              SEQUPDAT
00304  016040     PERFORM 350-WRITE-PRINT THRU 350-EXIT.               SEQUPDAT
00305  016050     MOVE '0' TO TRANS-SWITCH.                            SEQUPDAT
00306  016060     GO TO 020-GETFILES.                                  SEQUPDAT
00307  016070                                                          SEQUPDAT
00308  016080                                                          SEQUPDAT
00309  016090 NOTE-350.                                                SEQUPDAT
00310  016100     NOTE *****************************************************SEQUPDAT
00311  016110     *   THIS ROUTINE IS ENTERED FOR ALL ERROR ROUTINES. IT *SEQUPDAT
00312  016120     *   MOVES THE CUSTOMER NUMBER, NAME AND ADDRESS AND THE *SEQUPDAT
00313  016130     *   SALES AMOUNT TO THE PRINT AREA AND WRITES THE       *SEQUPDAT
00314  016140     *   REPORT.                                            *SEQUPDAT
00315  016150     ****************************************************.SEQUPDAT
00316  016160                                                          SEQUPDAT
00317  016170 350-WRITE-PRINT.                                         SEQUPDAT
00318  016180     MOVE CODE-TRANS TO CODE-PRINT.                       SEQUPDAT
00319  016190     MOVE CUST-NUMB-TRANS TO CUST-NUMB-PRINT.             SEQUPDAT
00320  016200     MOVE SALES-AMT-TRANS-X TO SALES-AMT-PRINT.           SEQUPDAT
00321  017010     WRITE PRINT-IO AFTER ADVANCING VARIABLE LINES.       SEQUPDAT
00322  017020     MOVE 1 TO VARIABLE.                                  SEQUPDAT
00323  017030     ADD 1 TO LINE-COUNT.                                 SEQUPDAT
00324  017040     IF LINE-COUNT > 50                                   SEQUPDAT
00325  017050         PERFORM 400-HEADER THRU 400-EXIT.                SEQUPDAT
00326  017060     MOVE SPACES TO PRINT-IO.                             SEQUPDAT
00327  017070 350-EXIT.   EXIT.                                        SEQUPDAT
00328  017080                                                          SEQUPDAT
00329  017090                                                          SEQUPDAT
00330  017100 NOTE-400.                                                SEQUPDAT
00331  017110     NOTE *****************************************************SEQUPDAT
00332  017120     *   THIS ROUTINE IS ENTERED TO PRINT THE HEADINGS FOR  *SEQUPDAT
00333  017130     *   THE ERROR EXCEPTION REPORT.                        *SEQUPDAT
00334  017140     ****************************************************.SEQUPDAT
00335  017150                                                          SEQUPDAT
00336  017160 400-HEADER.                                              SEQUPDAT
00337  017170     ADD 1 TO PG-CNT.                                     SEQUPDAT
00338  017180     MOVE PG-CNT TO PG-H1.                                SEQUPDAT
00339  017190     WRITE PRINT-IO FROM HEADER1 AFTER ADVANCING TO-TOP-OF-PAGE.SEQUPDAT
00340  017200     MOVE SPACES TO PRINT-IO.                             SEQUPDAT
00341  018010     WRITE PRINT-IO FROM HEADER2 AFTER ADVANCING 2 LINES. SEQUPDAT
00342  018020     MOVE SPACES TO PRINT-IO.                             SEQUPDAT
00343  018030     MOVE 0 TO LINE-COUNT.                                SEQUPDAT
00344  018040     MOVE 2 TO VARIABLE.                                  SEQUPDAT
00345  018050 400-EXIT.   EXIT.                                        SEQUPDAT
00346  018060                                                          SEQUPDAT
00347  018070                                                          SEQUPDAT
00348  018080 NOTE-500.                                                SEQUPDAT
```

```
     5

00349   018090    NOTE *****************************************************SEQUPDAT
00350   018100    *      THIS ROUTINE IS ENTERED WHEN THE TRANSACTION FILE   *SEQUPDAT
00351   018110    *      HAS BEEN COMPLETELY READ. IT SETS THE SWITCH SO THAT *SEQUPDAT
00352   018120    *      NO MORE READ COMMANDS WILL BE ISSUED FOR THE         *SEQUPDAT
00353   018130    *      TRANSACTION FILE AND MOVES HIGH-VALUES TO THE        *SEQUPDAT
00354   018140    *      CUSTOMER COMPARE AREA TO INSURE THAT THE MASTER      *SEQUPDAT
00355   018150    *      RECORD WILL ALWAYS BE LOW.                           *SEQUPDAT
00356   018160    *****************************************************.SEQUPDAT
00357   018170                                                              SEQUPDAT
00358   018180 500-END-TRANS.                                               SEQUPDAT
00359   018190    IF CUST-NUMB-MSTRIN-C IS = HIGH-VALUES                    SEQUPDAT
00360   018200       GO TO 520-ALL-EOF.                                     SEQUPDAT
00361   019010    MOVE HIGH-VALUES TO CUST-NUMB-TRANS-C.                    SEQUPDAT
00362   019020    MOVE '1' TO TRANS-SWITCH.                                 SEQUPDAT
00363   019030    GO TO 020-GETFILES.                                       SEQUPDAT
00364   019040                                                              SEQUPDAT
00365   019050                                                              SEQUPDAT
00366   019060 NOTE-510.                                                    SEQUPDAT
00367   019070    NOTE *****************************************************SEQUPDAT
00368   019080    *      THIS ROUTINE IS ENTERED WHEN THE OLD MASTER HAS REACHED *SEQUPDAT
00369   019090    *      END-OF-FILE OR WHEN THE FIRST-TIME ROUTINE IS TO BE *SEQUPDAT
00370   019100    *      PERFORMED. IT MOVES HIGH-VALUES TO THE CUSTOMER     *SEQUPDAT
00371   019110    *      COMPARE AREA SO THAT RECORDS FROM THE TRANSACTION FILE *SEQUPDAT
00372   019120    *      WILL ALWAYS BE LOW IT ALSO SETS THE SWITCH SO THAT  *SEQUPDAT
00373   019130    *      NO READ COMMANDS WILL BE ISSUED TO THE MASTER FILE. *SEQUPDAT
00374   019140    *****************************************************.SEQUPDAT
00375   019150                                                              SEQUPDAT
00376   019160 510-END-MASTER.                                              SEQUPDAT
00377   019170    IF CUST-NUMB-TRANS-C IS = HIGH-VALUES                     SEQUPDAT
00378   019180       GO TO 520-ALL-EOF.                                     SEQUPDAT
00379   019190    MOVE HIGH-VALUES TO CUST-NUMB-MSTRIN-C.                   SEQUPDAT
00380   019200    MOVE '1' TO MSTR-SWITCH.                                  SEQUPDAT
00381   020010    GO TO 020-GETFILES.                                       SEQUPDAT
00382   020020                                                              SEQUPDAT
00383   020030                                                              SEQUPDAT
00384   020040 NOTE-520.                                                    SEQUPDAT
00385   020050    NOTE *****************************************************SEQUPDAT
00386   020060    *      THIS ROUTINE IS ENTERED WHEN BOTH THE TRANSACTION   *SEQUPDAT
00387   020070    *      FILE AND THE OLD MASTER FILE HAVE REACHED EOF. IT   *SEQUPDAT
00388   020080    *      CLOSES THE FILES AND STOPS THE RUN.                 *SEQUPDAT
00389   020090    *****************************************************.SEQUPDAT
00390   020100                                                              SEQUPDAT
00391   020110 520-ALL-EOF.                                                 SEQUPDAT
00392   020120    IF UPSI-0-OFF                                             SEQUPDAT
00393   020130       CLOSE MSTRIN.                                          SEQUPDAT
00394   020140    CLOSE MSTROUT,                                            SEQUPDAT
00395   020150          TRANSIN,                                            SEQUPDAT
00396   020160          PRTFLE.                                             SEQUPDAT
00397   020170    STOP RUN.                                                 SEQUPDAT
```

CHAPTER 1

PROGRAMMING ASSIGNMENT

INSTRUCTIONS

A salesman master file is to be created and updated. The format of the master file is illustrated below. This master file is to be stored on magnetic tape.

FIELD	PICTURE	POSITION	NO OF DIGITS	LENGTH
Department Number	XX	1-2	2	2
Salesman Number	XXX	3-5	3	3
Salesman Name	X(20)	6-25	20	20
Year-To-Date Sales	S9(5)V99 Comp-3	26-29	7	4
Months Employed	S9(3) Comp-3	30-31	3	2

The salesman master file is created or updated from sales transaction cards. The format of the cards is illustrated below.

In the transaction cards, the "type" field (card column 56) may contain the following values:

    1 = add or load   3 = change
    2 = delete

A single program should be written that will initially load the master file and will also update the file after it has been loaded. Processing should take place as follows:

1. An External Switch should be used to determine if the "first-time" routine in the program should be used. Any settings which the programmer deems sufficient can be used.

2. If a master exists, an addition (type = 1), a deletion (type = 2), or a change (type = 3) must be processed. An addition takes place when a new salesman is to be added to the master file. A deletion takes place when a salesman's number is to be removed from the master file. A change occurs when the Year-To-Date Sales Field is to be updated by the Current Sales Field in the Transaction record.

3. The Months Employed Field in the master record must be updated by 1 each time the master file is updated, regardless of whether the Current Sales in the master record is updated.

4. An exception report is to be created which identifies each transaction record with an error and the type of error must also be specified. The programmer is to design the format of this exception report.

5. Cards are to be sorted by salesman number within department.

6. Suggested test data is contained in Appendix G.

7 Sample job control statements are contained in Appendix F.

8. It is suggested that the tape file first be loaded and then dumped using a utility program. After it has been assured that the tape load is correct, it is suggested that the update program be executed and the output from this execution be dumped using the utility program once again. Note: In many schools it will be impossible to reserve a reel of tape for each student; therefore, the final run will consist of a load run followed immediately by the file update run.

9. It is the responsibility of the programmrer to assure that the program is correct by analyzing the test data and related outputs.

SEQUENTIAL ACCESS METHOD - DIRECT - ACCESS DEVICES

CHAPTER 2

SEQUENTIAL ACCESS METHOD –
DIRECT - ACCESS DEVICES
2

INTRODUCTION

For many applications, a Direct Access Storage Device (DASD) is an effective storage media. Direct access storage devices may process files organized sequentially as with magnetic tape but also offer the advantage of "random" retrieval of individual records from a file. The 3330 Direct Access Storage Device is illustrated below.

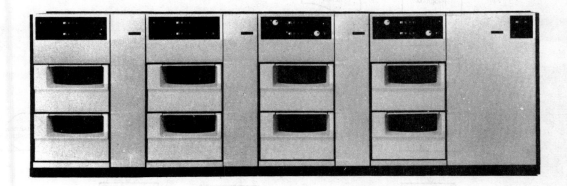

Figure 2-1 IBM 3330 Direct Access Storage Device

COBOL programs written to process data stored on direct access devices are similar in structure to COBOL programs written to process data stored on cards and tape. The file is defined in both the Environment Division and the Data Division and Input/Output commands such as **READ, WRITE, OPEN,** and **CLOSE** are used to actually process the files. There are three primary methods of file organization when using direct access devices. These methods include the **SEQUENTIAL FILE ACCESS METHOD**, the **DIRECT ACCESS METHOD**, and the **INDEXED SEQUENTIAL ACCESS METHOD**. Some compilers on the System/370 allow a fourth method, the **VIRTUAL STORAGE ACCESS METHOD**. This chapter will explain the Sequential File Access Method.

SAMPLE PROGRAM

The sample program presented in this chapter is the first of a series of four programs presented to illustrate a "typical" inventory system. Although most inventory systems in use are much more complex than the one presented here, the concepts presented are intended to illustrate basic programming methods and techniques useful in a wide variety of applications.

INVENTORY SYSTEM

The system flowchart is illustrated below.

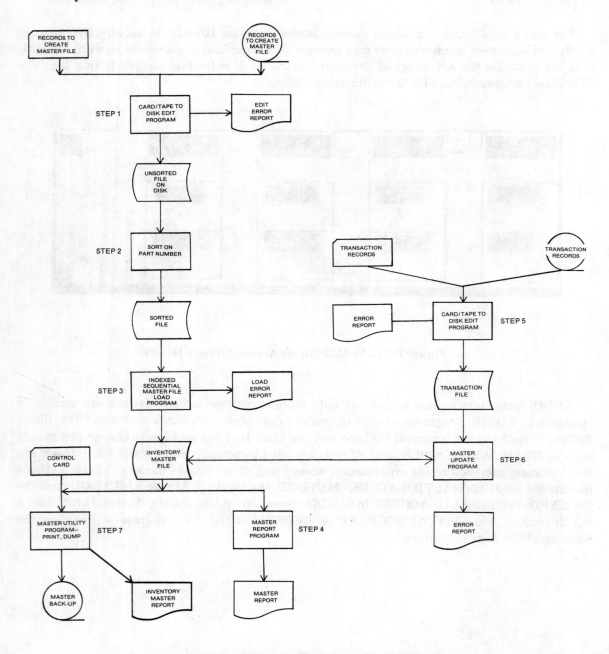

Figure 2-2 Inventory System Flowchart

The inventory system can be segmented into steps, as explained below.

STEP 1: Unsorted records from cards and tape are read and edited and a sequential file is created. The records created in step 1 are used to load the indexed sequential inventory master file. An error report is created which indicates edit errors, such as non-numeric fields. The program to create this sequential file is explained in this chapter.

STEP 2: The file created in step 1 is sorted on part number through the use of a Utility Disk Sort. This sort is supplied as a part of most operating systems and is executed through the use of control cards. An illustration of the job control and sort control cards used in this inventory system is contained in the appendices.

STEP 3: An Indexed Sequential inventory master file is loaded from the sorted file from step 2. An error report is generated for any errors occuring during loading, such as invalid type codes. The program to load the inventory master file is presented in Chapter 3.

STEP 4: After the inventory master file is created, it is normally desirable to print its contents. The program to sequentially retrieve the data in the master file is illustrated in Chapter 4.

STEP 5: The edit program from step 1 is also used to create a transaction file which will be used to update the inventory master file. The input records from cards and/or tape are read and edited and a transaction file is produced. Any update record in error is recorded on the error report.

STEP 6: The inventory master file is randomly updated from the transactions on the update transaction file created in step 5. Any transactions in error such as duplicate add records, are reported on the error listing. The update program is presented in Chapter 5.

STEP 7: The final step of the system is a "utility" program which performs two functions: "Dumping" the master file onto a tape for use as a back-up file and creating the Inventory Master Report from the master file. A control card is read to determine which of the functions is to be performed. This program is presented in Chapter 6.

The detailed processing, record layouts, report formats and program requirements are described in the chapters presenting the programs.

In addition to illustrating the use of direct access storage devices, the programs presented in the subsequent chapters illustrate a variety of programming techniques and considerations which are commonly required and used in business applications. Some of the concepts presented in this chapter include:

1. COBOL Programming Considerations
2. Permissible Comparisons, using alphabetic, alphanumeric and numeric fields
3. Numeric Tests
4. Effective use of the Perform Statement

COBOL PROGRAMMING CONSIDERATIONS

When designing and writing a COBOL program, the programmer should have four major goals in mind: 1) Completing the program in as little time as possible with as much accuracy and completeness as possible; 2) Having the program consume as little main storage as possible; 3) Having the program execute as fast as possible; 4) Design the program so the future debugging and maintenance performed by a programmer other than the original programmer will be as easy a task as possible.

It can be seen from these four goals that some conflicts may occur. For example, when programming to save main storage, that is, taking the time to consider all possible ways to write a routine, the time to complete the programming assignment may be increased. It is, therefore, one of the important tasks of a good programmer to balance each goal so that the best product is produced with as little cost as possible.

In general, these goals may be accomplished in a program by writing the program in as SIMPLE a manner as possible. It is a general rule of thumb that the best COBOL programs are those programs written in a simple, straight-forward manner. By writing in a simple manner, the programmer normally can code the program in a faster time than if involved routines are used and, more importantly, he can debug the program in less time and with more assuredness that the program is correct. In addition, the task of modification and maintenance of the program at some future date is normally made easier by programming in a straight-forward manner.

The key, therefore, to accomplishing the goals is not in the use of involved programming techniques but rather in the understanding of how COBOL works and what methods can be used by the programmer to make the COBOL program as efficient as possible while still keeping it relatively simple. It is toward this end that the characteristics of COBOL are presented in this and following chapters.

PERMISSIBLE COMPARISONS

In order to make the COBOL program as efficient as possible, the rules under which COBOL operates must be understood. One set of very important rules which must be followed are the rules for comparisons between fields defined as alphabetic, alphanumeric, and numeric. The following paragraphs review specific uses and areas of possible errors in the use of comparison instructions.

1 - Alphabetic Comparisons: A field defined as alphabetic (**PICTURE A**) can be compared to another alphabetic field or to an alphanumeric field (**PICTURE X**). In addition, an alphabetic field can be compared to the figurative constants **SPACE** and **ALL** 'character' when character is alphabetic. Note than an alphabetic field cannot be compared to any type of numeric field (**PICTURE 9**).

2 - Alphanumeric Comparisons: A field defined as alphanumeric (**PICTURE X**) is the most versatile of the field definitions. It can be compared with an alphabetic field, another alphanumeric field, or a numeric field (**PICTURE 9**) which is defined as a Display field. A comparison used for an alphanumeric field is defined as a **LOGICAL** compare. A logical compare is a bit by bit comparison of a value contained in one field with the value contained in another field. The equal or unequal condition is determined by which field contains the highest value in the collating sequence of the computer. The following example illustrates a logical comparison using two fields defined as alphanumeric and stored in the EBCDIC format. Note that the binary representation of the fields is shown.

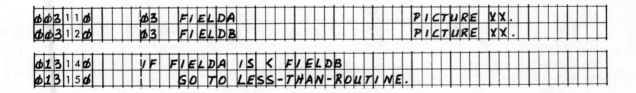

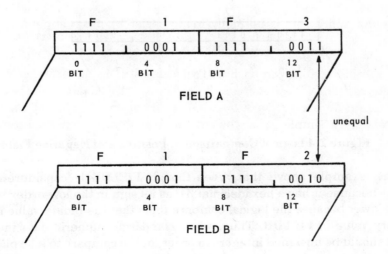

Figure 2-3 Logical Comparison of Alphanumeric Fields

In the example in Figure 2-3, the comparison of **FIELDA** and **FIELDB** begins with the first bit (bit 0) of the fields and continues to the right until an unequal condition is found. When an unequal situation is found, it is determined which field contains the lesser value. In the example, **FIELDB** contains a lower value because bit 15 in the field is equal to 0 while bit 15 of **FIELDA** is equal to 1. Therefore, in a logical comparison, **FIELDB** is considered less than **FIELDA**. Thus, the **LESS-THAN-ROUTINE** will not be entered as a result of this comparison.

When an alphanumeric field is compared to another alphanumeric field or to an alphabetic field, the comparison will be a logical compare and the correct indication will always be given as to the high, low, or equal status of the two fields. However, when comparing two alphanumeric fields containing numeric data, care must be taken because the sign of the numeric value, that is, whether it is positive or negative, is NOT considered. The compare is always a logical compare.

Thus, in the example shown below, the positive number will be considered less than the negative number.

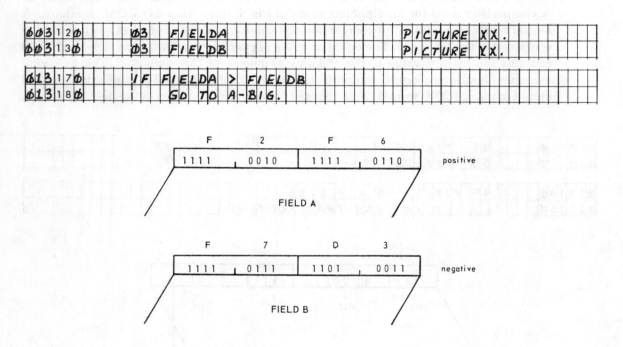

Figure 2-4 Logical Comparison of Positive and Negative Fields

Note in the example above that, even though **FIELDB** is considered negative (using EBCDIC code) because it has a hexadecimal 'D' as its sign in the low-order byte, **FIELDA** will be considered lower because the logical compare finds that the binary value in **FIELDA** is less than the binary value in **FIELDB**. Thus, when comparing numeric data in an alphanumeric field, the data should be unsigned integers in order for the compare to take place properly.

It should also be noted that an alphanumeric field can be compared to any of the figurative constants (**SPACES, ZEROS,** or **ALL** 'characters').

3 - Numeric Comparisons: A field defined as a numeric field (**PICTURE 9**) can be compared to another numeric field or to an alphanumeric field. If the numeric field is compared to an alphanumeric field, the same rules as described previously for alphanumeric fields holds true. If a numeric field is compared to another numeric field, a "numeric" comparison takes place. A numeric comparison considers the sign of the field when performing the comparison. Thus, in the example shown in Figure 2-4, the negative number would be considered less than the positive number because of the negative sign if both fields were defined as numeric.

On many computers, when a numeric comparison is performed, the fields must be in packed-decimal format. Thus, if the field is a **DISPLAY** field, it is packed to a Computational-3 format and then the comparison takes place. For example, two numeric fields read from a punched card will be stored in the zoned-decimal format (Display). If these fields are compared, they will be packed prior to the compare. The two numeric fields must contain valid signs (hexadecimal 'C', 'D', or 'F').

Any other values in the sign position of the low-order digit will cause a program check interruption and the program will terminate. It is necessary, therefore, to ensure that the data contained in a field defined as numeric is a properly signed value before performing the comparison. The **IF NUMERIC** class test can be used to ensure a validly signed field (see Page 65).

It should also be noted that a numeric field can only be compared to the figurative constants **ZERO** or **ALL** 'character' where the characters must be numeric.

As a result of the types of comparisons performed on the three fields as discussed above, certain rules should be followed by the programmer to ensure the most efficient program in terms of main storage usage and reliability of the program. These rules include the following:

1 - Whenever possible, define a field as alphanumeric, not numeric or alphabetic. The main reason for this rule is the versatility of alphanumeric fields as opposed to alphabetic and numeric fields and the fact that a logical comparison on an alphanumeric field takes less main storage than a comparison on a numeric field. For example, if a single digit is to be used for a switch, and is to have the value '0' or '1', it can be defined as either alphanumeric or numeric. If it is defined as numeric, each comparison to it will be a numeric compare. Thus, if the field is a Display field, it will need to be packed before each comparison is made. This operation consumes more storage and time than is necessary. If the field is defined as alphanumeric, a simple logical comparison is made on the field and time and storage are both saved.

This same rule holds for most Display numeric fields (a numeric field stored in the zoned decimal format). If, for example, a field which will always contain numeric data is to be compared to a constant in the program, it is more efficient to define both fields as alphanumeric and compare them than it is to define them both as numeric. Again, the data in a Display field must be packed before a numeric comparison can take place while this is unnecessary for an alphanumeric field. Care must be taken, however, that errors will not occur if a sign is to be considered. If a field can be positive or negative, it is normally best to perform a numeric comparison so that the sign will be considered.

2 - If a numeric comparison is to be performed on a numeric field, **ALWAYS** perform a test on the data in the field prior to the comparison to ensure that the data is a properly signed numeric value. If the data contained in the field is not numeric, incorrect results will occur and the job may be abnormally terminated.

3 - Whenever performing a numeric comparison, on many computers it is best , if possible, to have the two fields being compared be in the packed-decimal format. The least main storage and time will be consumed in a numeric comparison if both fields are Computational-3. The following conversions are made on the System/360 and System/370 if data is in a "mixed-format", that is, the two fields to be compared are not the same format.

A - Compare - Display to Computational-3: The Display field is converted to a Computational-3 format.

B - Compare - Display to Computational (Binary): Both the Display field and the Computational field are converted to Computational-3 or the Display field is converted to Computational format.

C - Compare - Computational-3 to Computational: The Computational data must be converted to Computational-3 or the Computational-3 data is converted to Computational.

D - Compare - Computational to Computational-3: The Computational data must be converted to Computational-3 or the Computational-3 data is converted to Computational data.

E - Compare - Computational to Display: Both the Computational and the Display fields must be converted to Computational-3 or the Display field is converted to Computational format.

F - Compare - Computational-3 to Display: The Display data must be converted to Computational-3.

G - Compare - Display to Display: Both the Display fields must be converted to Computational-3.

Thus, it can be seen that using mixed modes can be costly in both computer storage and in execution time. Again, it is best if both fields can be in Computational-3 format. If, for example, a value in a Display field is to be compared to a value in a Computational-3 field more than once, it would be better to move the Display field to a Computational-3 work area in Working-Storage and then perform the comparisons than to perform the comparison in the Display field each time it was necessary for the comparison. Moving a Display field to a Computational-3 Work area will cause the field to be packed.

4 - Whenever possible, the lengths of the two fields being compared should be equal. This is true for alphabetic, alphanumeric and numeric comparisons. With the exception of data fields defined as Computational-3, "filler" characters may have to be inserted before a comparison takes place when the fields are of unequal length. For example, if two alphanumeric fields are to be compared, the shorter of the two fields must be moved to a work area and filled with low-order blanks before the comparison takes place. Thus, to avoid unnecessary moves and therefore a wasting of core storage, fields should be of equal length.

5 - Whenever a field is defined as Computational-3, define it with an odd number of digits, not an even number of digits. In the example in Figure 2-5, the contents of a Computational-3 field are illustrated for the four digit number 3426.

EXAMPLE

```
005020  77  FIELD-EVEN                        PICTURE S9999
005030      !                                 USAGE COMPUTATIONAL-3.

005060  77  FIELD-ODD                         PICTURE S9(5)
005070      !                                 USAGE COMPUTATIONAL-3.
```

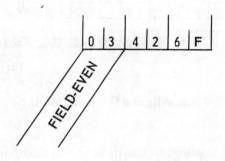

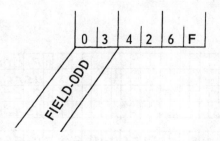

Figure 2-5 Example of Even and Odd Definitions of Computational-3 Field

Note that even though **FIELD-EVEN** is defined for four digits and **FIELD-ODD** is defined for five digits, the same core allocation is allowed for both because a Computational-3 field must contain an odd number of digits. When an even number of digits are defined for a Computational-3 field, COBOL must use additional instructions in the Procedure Division to properly set up the field to be operated upon. Thus, by always defining a Computational-3 field as an odd number of digits, even though it may contain an even number of digits, considerable main storage may be saved because fewer instructions are generated in the Procedure Division with no additional storage allocated in the Data Division.

6 - When performing numeric comparisons, the "fraction" portion of a number, that is, the number of digits to the right of a decimal point, should, if at all possible, always be the same. This is because when the decimal points are not "aligned", the COBOL compiler must generate instructions to align the fields.

The following example illustrates two methods of defining two fields which will be used in numeric comparisons.

METHOD 1

```
004020  77  FIELD-2                              PICTURE S999V99
004030                                           USAGE COMP-3.
004040  77  FIELD-1                              PICTURE S999V9
004050                                           USAGE COMP-3.

013070      IF FIELD-2 IS = FIELD-1 GO TO EQUAL-ROUTINE.
```

Figure 2-6 Non-Aligned Decimal Points

Note in method 1 that there is 1 position to the right of the decimal point for **FIELD-1** and two positions to the right of the decimal point for **FIELD-2**. When a comparison is performed on these two fields, the coding generated in the Procedure Division will first have to set the fields so that the decimals are aligned, which requires additional machine language instructions.

METHOD 2

```
004100  77  FIELD-2                              PICTURE S999V99
004110                                           USAGE COMP-3.
004120  77  FIELD-1                              PICTURE S999V99
004130                                           USAGE COMP-3.

004150      IF FIELD-2 IS = FIELD-1 GO TO EQUAL-ROUTINE.
```

Figure 2-7 Aligned Decimal Points

When the fields are defined as in method 2, no decimal alignment needs to be performed because they are already aligned. In addition, **FIELD-1**, in method 2, contains an odd number of digits which makes the coding even more efficient in the Procedure Division.

Consideration should be given to decimal alignment in the use of literals in the Procedure Division as well as the fields in the Data Division. For example, if it was desired to compare the value "5" to the value in **FIELD-2**, either of the two instructions shown in Figure 2-8 could be used.

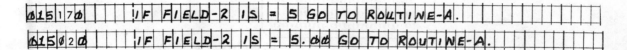

Figure 2-8 Illustration of Decimal Alignment With a Literal

When **FIELD-2** is compared to "5", the literal is not decimally aligned with **FIELD-2**. Therefore, the necessary instructions must be generated in the Procedure Division to align the literal. If **FIELD-2** is compared to the literal "5.00", no decimal alignment instructions need be generated. The literal "5.00" requires one more byte of core storage than the literal "5", but main storage can be saved in the Procedure Division because no alignment instructions are generated.

IF NUMERIC TEST

Previously it was noted that before a numeric comparison is performed on data in a numeric field, it is necessary to ensure that valid, signed numeric data is contained in the field. The class test **IF NUMERIC** provides a convenient means to test the data in the numeric field. It should be noted, however, that when the **IF NUMERIC** test is performed on a field defined as a signed numeric field, the low-order digit is assumed to contain the sign of the number. Thus, when a card is read with an "over-punch" in the low-order digit to indicate a sign, it would be stored as illustrated in Figure 2-9.

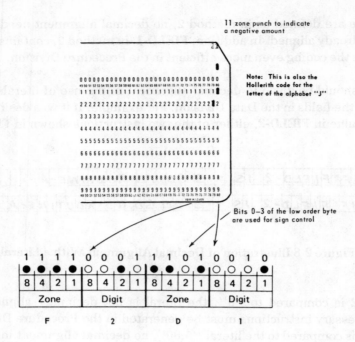

Figure 2-9 Representation of -21 in Core Storage

Note in the example above that the negative sign represented by the "11" punch in the card is stored in computer storage as a hexadecimal D (in the EBCDIC coding format) in the low-order sign position. A positive sign (hexadecimal C) would be stored if the card were over-punched with a "12" punch. When using the **IF NUMERIC** test with a signed numeric field, these signs are considered valid in the low-order byte. Note also that an 11-1 punch in a card is the letter of the alphabet J and that the 12-1 punch is the letter of the alphabet A; however, the field containing these characters in the low-order position would be considered numeric when using the **IF NUMERIC** test with a signed numeric field.

There are applications, however, when the **IF NUMERIC** test is used to flag any byte in the field which does not contain an absolute value, that is, a value with a sign of hexadecimal 'F'. Thus, a low-order byte with the hexadecimal sign 'D' or 'C' would be considered invalid because it would represent a letter of the alphabet, not a valid numeric character. When non-signed numeric values are read from a punched card, they are stored in computer storage as shown in Figure 2-10.

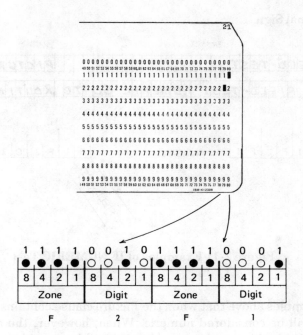

Figure 2-10 Representation of Absolute Value 21 in Core Storage

As can be seen in the example above, the sign is a hexadecimal 'F', which is treated as an absolute value, that is, it is treated as a positive value. If an absolute value must be contained in a field, as opposed to a signed or over-punched value, the field to be tested must be defined without an operational sign, that is, the ''S'' in the Picture clause must not be present. When the ''S'' is not present, the **IF NUMERIC** test will allow only a hexadecimal 'F' in the sign position; a 'C' or a 'D' will be considered the zone portion of a letter of the alphabet and not numeric. When the ''S'' is present in the Picture clause, fields with the signs 'C' and 'D' as well and the 'F' are considered value numeric fields. This is illustrated in Figure 2-11.

Example 1 - No Operational Sign

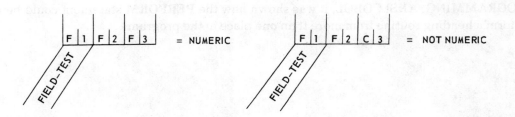

Example 2 - Operational Sign

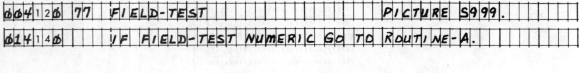

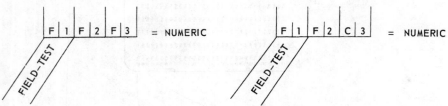

Figure 2-11 Examples of IF NUMERIC Test

Note from the examples above that when the Picture clause contains an operational sign (S), then a signed field will be considered numeric. When, however, the S is not included in the Picture, then only a field with the absolute sign 'F' will be considered numeric. It should be noted that the programmer can check for an absolute sign and also keep the efficiencies of a numeric field with the operational sign by simply redefining the field. Thus, in the example above, the **FIELD-TEST** field defined in Example 1 could be redefined with a sign (S) in the picture and this would allow the field with the operational sign to be used in arithmetic operations if the data in the field was to be changed.

The **IF NUMERIC** test can also be used with fields defined as alphanumeric (Picture X). When used with alphanumeric fields, only data with an absolute sign is considered numeric. Any data in an alphanumeric field with a low-order sign, such as a hexadecimal 'C' or 'D', will be considered non-numeric. Therefore, a field may be defined either as an alphanumeric field or as a numeric field without an operational sign in order to allow only data with an absolute sign to be considered numeric.

PERFORM STATEMENT

The **PERFORM** statement specifies a transfer of control from one portion of a program to another in order to execute some procedure. It directs that control is to be returned to the statement immediately following the point from which the transfer was made. The **PERFORM** statement is normally used to execute a subroutine, that is, a set of instructions which must be executed more than one time within a program. In the text INTRODUCTION TO COMPUTER PROGRAMMING, ANSI COBOL, it was shown how the **PERFORM** statement could be used to perform a heading routine from more than one place in the program.

The **PERFORM** statement has the following basic format:

PERFORM procedure-name-1 [THRU procedure-name-2]

Figure 2-12 Format Notation - PERFORM Statement

When the Perform Statement is used without the **THRU** option, the single paragraph stated in the Procedure-Name-1 entry is executed and then control is returned to the statement following the Perform statement. If the Thru option is used, the paragraph named in Procedure-Name-1 is entered and executed and the linkage back to the statement following the Perform statement does not occur until the paragraph named in Procedure-Name-2 has been executed. Thus, in the following example paragraphs P-1, P-2, and P-3 would be executed by the Perform statement.

EXAMPLE

```
015040         PERFORM P-1 THRU P-3.

018060  P-1.
018070         ADD 6 TO AMOUNT.
018080         MOVE AMOUNT TO AMT-PRT.
018090  P-2.
018100         ADD AMOUNT TO TOTAL-AMT.
018110  P-3.
018120         MOVE TOTAL-AMT TO TOTAL-PRT.
018130  P-4.
```

Figure 2-13 Example of the Use of the THRU Option in a PERFORM Statement

Note in the example in Figure 2-13 that none of the paragraphs executed as a result of the Perform statement contain coding that will cause a branch within the performed paragraphs, that is, no conditional statements or **GO TO** statements are contained in P-1, P-2, or P-3. It is permissible, however, to have conditional statements and **GO TO** statements within performed paragraphs. The only requirement is that there be a common exit point so that control will always return to the statement following the Perform statement. This common exit point can be established by using the **EXIT** statement. The following example illustrates performed paragraphs with conditional statements and **GO TO** statements using an **EXIT** paragraph as the common exit point.

EXAMPLE

```
Ø12Ø4Ø        PERFORM P-1 THRU P-4.
Ø16Ø6Ø  P-1.
Ø16Ø7Ø        MOVE Ø TO COUNTER.
Ø16Ø8Ø  P-2.
Ø16Ø9Ø        IF COUNTER = TYPE-IN
Ø16100            GO TO P-3.
Ø16110        IF COUNTER IS > TYPE-IN
Ø16120            MOVE 'INVALID TYPE' TO ERROR-PRT
Ø16130            GO TO P-4.
Ø16140        ADD 1 TO COUNTER.
Ø16150        GO TO P-2.
Ø16160  P-3.
Ø16170        MOVE TYPE-IN TO TYPE-PRT.
Ø16180  P-4. EXIT.
```

Figure 2-14 Example of Performed Paragraphs with Conditional Statements

In the example above, a counter is set to 0 and then is incremented by 1 in the routine. The value in the counter is compared to the field **TYPE-IN** to determine if the value in **TYPE-IN** is a given numeric value. If an equal condition occurs, that is, the value in **TYPE-IN** is equal to the number in the counter, the value in **TYPE-IN** is moved to a report area. If it is not, an error message is moved to a report area. When the processing in the paragraphs is complete, a return is made to the statement following the Perform statement by exiting at paragraph P-4. Thus, regardless of what occurs in the performed paragraphs, a common exit point is used to return to the statement following the Perform statement which called the subroutine.

It should also be noted that a paragraph or series of paragraphs which are being performed can themselves issue a Perform statement. The range of the Perform statement issued within a paragraph being performed must be entirely within the performed paragraphs or entirely outside the performed paragraphs.

In the sample program presented in this chapter, various fields are checked for valid numeric values. If the field does not contain numeric data, an entry is made on the error report indicating the invalid data. The following excerpt from the sample program shows the technique used to check the data and to write on the report in the case of an error.

EXAMPLE

```
Ø15Ø2Ø        IF PART-NUMB-WK IS NOT NUMERIC
Ø15Ø3Ø           MOVE 'PART NUMBER-NOT NUMERIC' TO ERROR-PRT
Ø15Ø4Ø           PERFORM 25Ø-WRITE-ERR THRU 25Ø-EXIT.

Ø18Ø6Ø  25Ø-WRITE-ERR.
Ø18Ø7Ø        IF LINE-COUNT > 5Ø
Ø18Ø8Ø           PERFORM 3ØØ-HEADER THRU 3ØØ-EXIT.
Ø18Ø9Ø        WRITE PRINT-IOA AFTER ADVANCING VARIABLE LINES.
Ø1811Ø        ADD 1 TO LINE-COUNT.
Ø1811Ø        MOVE SPACES TO PRINT-IO.
Ø1812Ø        MOVE '1' TO BAD-SWITCH.
Ø1813Ø        MOVE SINGLE-SPACING TO VARIABLE.
Ø1814Ø  25Ø-EXIT. EXIT.

Ø19Ø2Ø  3ØØ-HEADER.
Ø19Ø3Ø        ADD 1 TO PG-CNT.
Ø19Ø4Ø        MOVE PG-CNT TO PG-H1.
Ø19Ø5Ø        MOVE HEADER1 TO PRINT-IO.
Ø19Ø6Ø        WRITE PRINT-IOA AFTER ADVANCING TO-TOP-OF-PAGE.
Ø19Ø7Ø        MOVE DOUBLE-SPACING TO VARIABLE.
Ø19Ø8Ø        MOVE ZERO TO LINE-COUNT.
Ø19Ø9Ø  3ØØ-EXIT. EXIT.
```

Figure 2-15 Routine to Check Numeric Data and Write Error Report

In the routine shown in Figure 2-15, the part number (**PART-NUMB-WK**) is checked for an absolute numeric value. If it does not contain numeric data, an error message is moved to the report area and the **250-WRITE-ERR** routine is performed. This routine first checks if 50 lines have been printed on the report. If so, the **300-HEADER** routine is performed.

Note at this point that a subroutine being performed, **250-WRITE-ERR**, is the calling routine for another subroutine, **300-HEADER**. The **300-HEADER** routine is completely outside the limits set by the Perform statement at pg/line 015040. Therefore, the Perform will take place properly. As noted previously, a subroutine which is performed by a subroutine which is itself being performed must be either completely within the calling subroutine or outside the calling subroutine. After the heading subroutine returns control to the **250-WRITE-ERR** subroutine, the line is printed on the printer and control returns to the statement following the Perform statement at pg/line 015040.

It should be noted that each of the paragraphs being performed in the previous example are performed through the use of the Perform statement using the **THRU** option and that the Procedure-Name stated in the **THRU** option is always an **EXIT** paragraph. This is done for two primary reasons: 1) The use of the **THRU** option allows paragraph names to be inserted in a performed paragraph with no changes to any part of the Perform statement. Thus, if a change was necessary to a performed paragraph, and a paragraph name had to be added, the Perform statement would still be executed in the desired manner; 2) The use of the **THRU** option and the **EXIT** statement provides for better program documentation and understanding because the reader knows what paragraph(s) are to be performed and where the exit point from the performed paragraph is. Because of this, there is no doubt as to the function of the performed paragraph and where it starts and ends.

When a paragraph is being performed, it is possible to use a **GO TO** statement in the performed paragraph to branch out of the performed routine and NOT return to the statement immediately following the Perform statement. Except for very rare instances, this technique should NOT be used. By not returning to the statement following the Perform statement, the basic function of the perform is defeated and it makes a program much more difficult to follow because of the interrupted flow of the logic of the program. If a decision needs to be made following the execution of a performed paragraph, it is much better to set a switch and test the switch upon return from the performed paragraph than to make the decision in the performed paragraph to branch to another area of the program. Thus, if a subroutine were to be used to read an input file, an indication will be given at end-of-file. Instead of using a **GO TO** statement after the **AT END** clause in a Read statement, it would be much better to set a switch indicating end-of-file and let the routine following the Perform of the read paragraph determine if end-of-file has been reached. This is illustrated in the following example.

EXAMPLE

```
013050        PERFORM 200-READ-MSTR THRU 200-EXIT.
013060        IF EOF-SWITCH IS = '1'
013070            GO TO 500-MSTR-EOF.

014090  200-READ-MSTR.
014100        READ MASTER-IN AT END MOVE '1' TO EOF-SWITCH.
014110  200-EXIT.  EXIT.
```

Figure 2-16 Example of Performed Read Statement

Note in the example in Figure 2-16, that **EOF-SWITCH** will contain a ''1'' when end-of-file is reached on the master file **MASTER-IN**. The **IF** statement at pg/line 013060 will test the value in the switch and if it indicates that end-of-file has been reached, it will go to the end-of-file routine. From a debugging and program maintenance standpoint, this technique is easy to follow because the only function of the performed paragraph is to read the master file and the reader knows that control will always return to the statement following the perform statement.

As has been shown, the Perform Statement is quite versatile and can be a valuable command to use. It must be noted, however, that the Perform Statement itself consumes a number of bytes in the Procedure Division, the exact number of bytes depends upon the COBOL compiler. Thus, indiscriminate use of the Perform statement can lead to higher main storage usage for a program and excessive execution time. Some of the suggested uses of the Perform statement are described below.

1 - The Perform Statement should normally be used whenever a series of instructions are to be used more than once in a program. The storage required for the instructions to be performed should exceed the storage requirements for the Perform Statement itself. This determination assumes a knowledge of how many bytes will be used in the subroutine. Although determining an exact number of bytes in a subroutine is difficult and is probably more time-consuming than is practical, guidelines are presented in the appendices which can give some approximate storage requirements for different types of commands available in the COBOL language. Again, it must be noted that these requirements can vary greatly between machines and compilers. It is, however, necessary for the programmer to have some feel for the storage requirements so that his program can be as efficient as possible in the use of main storage.

2 - The Perform statement can be used when it is desirable to isolate one function in a program even though it is more costly, in terms of computer storage, to do so. For example, it is normally best that only one I/O command be written for each file defined in the program. In many programs, a **WRITE** command may have to be issued to the printer in many places in a program, that is, the Heading routine has to issue several Writes and the other routines in the program may issue writes. A single Write command could be written and performed at the various points in the program where a write to the printer is required.

Most Read and Write commands, if they are to be issued from more than one place in a program, should be performed because this ensures the reader who is debugging or performing maintenance on the program that he knows exactly what happens on every I/O command. In addition, such requirements as counting records on a file, transforming blanks to zeros, etc., can be performed at one central point and all processing routines can be assured that these functions have been performed.

3 - If the program is being written in a "modular" manner, the Perform Statement should be used for all processing and I/O subroutines. "Modularization" refers to the technique of having a "main-line" routine which is relatively short and simple and makes all the major logic decisions. The main-line routine controls the order in which all processing is to be done. The "processing subroutines" are called using a Perform Statement in the main-line routine. The processing routines accomplish all the processing done by the program such as taking totals, formatting reports, updating masters, etc. The main-line routine determines which of these processing subroutines should be executed. The Input/Output subroutines perform the same function as described previously in Number 2. The I/O subroutines are called by the processing subroutines again by using the Perform Statement.

By using the Perform statement properly, the program can be a more efficient program from a storage use and execution time standpoint, and can also be made much easier to debug and perform maintenance upon. Again, however, it should be emphasized that the Perform statement is costly in terms of core storage and must not be used indiscriminately throughout a program.

SAMPLE PROGRAM

The sample program presented in this chapter reads both tape and card input files and creates a sequential disk output file which, after being sorted, is input to create the indexed sequential master file. The program is also used to create a transaction file which is used to update the inventory master file. See Step 1 and Step 5 of the systems flowchart (Figure 2-2).

As each card or tape record is read, an "editing" process is performed to ensure that the input records contain valid data. Each numeric field in the input is checked to ensure that it contains either all blanks (in which case, zeros are moved to the output field) or all numeric data. If the field contains invalid data, an error message is issued and the record is not included on the output file.

INPUT

The record format of the punched card and magnetic tape input files and the sequential disk output file is identical. The card format is illustrated in Figure 2-17.

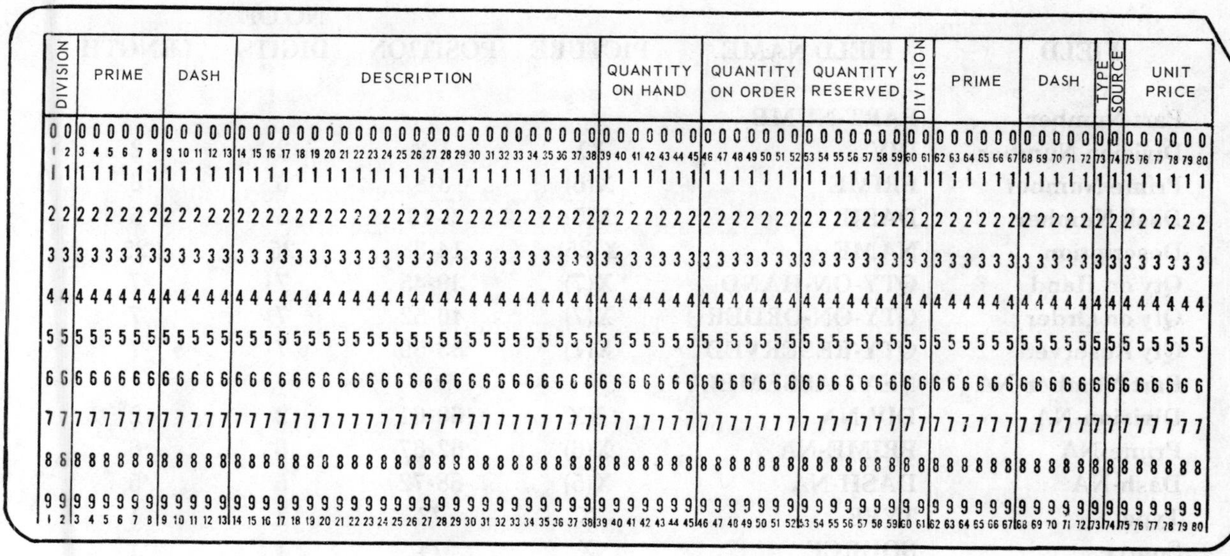

Figure 2-17 Card Format

The record length of the records is, as shown, 80 bytes. The tape input file contains 4 records per block. Thus, the block size is 320 bytes. The disk output file is to contain 44 records per block. Thus, the block size will be 3520 bytes.

The chart in Figure 2-18 summarizes the format of the record layout and includes the field name, the picture used for the field, the position of each field within the record, the number of digits in the field, and the length of each field in bytes. It should be noted that the names given in the field name column are not the complete names of the fields in the program. They are only the base names. Each field within a file is given a suffix to uniquely identify it from the corresponding field in another file. Thus, the description field name for the card input file is **NAME-CD**, the field name for the tape input file is **NAME-TP** and the field name for the work area is **NAME-WK**. This technique for naming fields in records should always be followed because it makes it easier for a programmer unfamiliar with the program to find fields in the program listing and to know which fields are logically a part of the same record or area.

FIELD	FIELD NAME	PICTURE	POSITION	NO OF DIGITS	LENGTH
Part Number	PART-NUMB				
Division Number	DIV	XX	1-2	2	2
Prime Number	PRIME	X(6)	3-8	6	6
Dash Number	DASH	X(5)	9-13	5	5
Description	NAME	X(25)	14-38	25	25
Qty on Hand	QTY-ON-HAND	X(7)	39-45	7	7
Qty on Order	QTY-ON-ORDER	X(7)	46-52	7	7
Qty Reserved	QTY-RESERVED	X(7)	53-59	7	7
Part Number-NA	NEXT-ASSEMBLY				
Division-NA	DIV-NA	XX	60-61	2	2
Prime-NA	PRIME-NA	X(6)	62-67	6	6
Dash-NA	DASH-NA	X(5)	68-72	5	5
Type	TYPE	X	73	1	1
Source	SOURCE	X	74	1	1
Unit Price	UNIT-PRICE	X(6)	75-80	6	6

Figure 2-18 Record Formats

The fields are defined as follows:

1. Part Number: The part number consists of a division number, a prime number, and a dash number. The part number identifies each part in an inventory.

   A. Division Number (DIV): The division number portion of the part number identifies the division of the plant in which the part is manufactured.

   B. Prime Number (PRIME): The prime number portion of the part number is the number given to each part which is in the inventory. It uniquely identifies the type of part.

   C. Dash Number (DASH): The dash number portion of the number can be used for various functions in a manufacturing environment. It may be a work order number, a purchase order number, a cycle control number, an assembly number, etc. For example, all dash 00001 parts may go into the first finished product, all dash 00002 parts may go into the second finished product, etc.

2. Description (NAME): The description field contains a description of the part.

3. Quantity on Hand (QTY-ON-HAND): The quantity on hand field specifies how many parts are in stock, that is, how many parts have been manufactured or purchased and are currently held in a storage area.

4. Quantity on Order (**QTY-ON-ORDER**): The quantity on order field specifies how many parts are on order. The parts on order may be either parts which are currently being manufactured in the plant or parts which have been ordered from an outside "vendor".

5. Quantity Reserved (**QTY-RESERVED**): This field contains the number of parts which have been reserved for use in other assemblies, the number of parts needed to keep a fixed number of parts on hand, etc. For example, the part may be a screw. If 10 screws are needed for assemblying a handle and 5 handles are being built, then 50 screws would be put on reserve so that they would be available for use. If there are more parts on hand and on order than are reserved, then there are "spares" of the part, that is, there are more parts than are needed. If there are more parts on reserve than on hand and on order, a "shortage" exists, that is, there are not enough parts to fill the needs. In this case, more parts must be put on order.

6. Part Number - Next Assembly: This field contains the part number of the next assembly part. The next assembly is the part into which the part described in the record will go. Thus, if the part in the record is a screw, and it goes into a handle, the part number of the handle is the next assembly number.

   A. Division Number - Next Assembly (**DIV-NA**): The division number of the part number for next assembly.

   B. Prime Number - Next Assembly (**PRIME-NA**): The prime number of the part for next assembly.

   C. Dash Number - Next Assembly (**DASH-NA**): The dash number of the part for next assembly.

7. Type (**TYPE**): The type field specifies the function of the record. The codes for the type field are:

   1 = Add Record
   2 = Delete Record
   3 = Change Quantity on Hand
   4 = Change Quantity on Order
   5 = Change Quantity Reserved
   6 = Change Next Assembly Part Number
   7 = Change Source
   8 = New Load
   9 = Change Unit Price

When the program is used in step 1 of the inventory system, that is, to create the sequential file which is used to load the inventory master, the type field should be equal to "8", which indicates a "new load" (i.e. a master record). When used in step 5, that is, when the program is used to create the transaction file which is used to update the inventory master file, any of the codes except "8" are valid.

8. Source (**SOURCE**): The source field indicates whether the part is a manufactured part (source = 1) or a purchased part (source = 2).

9. Unit Price (**UNIT PRICE**): The unit price indicates the price for one item.

OUTPUT

All numeric fields in the input records must contain numeric data or be blank. The type field must contain a value of 1-9. An error report is generated for each record which is in error.

The format of the report is illustrated below.

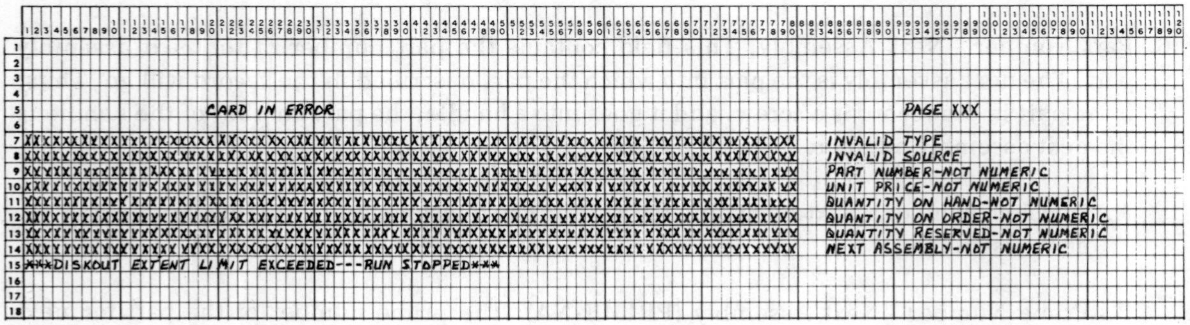

Figure 2-19 Error Report Format

As was mentioned, a sequential disk output file is also created in the program presented in this chapter. The required entries for creating a sequential disk file are illustrated in the following section.

SEQUENTIAL DISK PROCESSING

When processing a disk file in a sequential manner, the file must be defined in the File-Control paragraph in the Input-Output Section of the Environment Division and in the File Section of the Data Division. The following entry in the Environment Division would be made to define the sequential disk output file to be used in the sample program.

Figure 2-20 Select Statement for Disk Output File

The filename **DISKOUT** immediately follows the **SELECT** statement in the same manner used for cards, the printer, and tape. The **ASSIGN** statement assigns the output file to the device assigned to "SYS006" at the time the program is executed. The letters "UT" specify that the file is a sequential file on a device that is not considered a unit-record device. The entry 2314 states that the file will be contained on a 2314 disk drive. The file is sequential as defined by the "S" and the file will be referenced by the name **DISKOUT** in job control statements.

The file must be defined by a "FD" statement in the File Section of the Data Division. The following entry in the File Section is used to define the sequential disk output file used in the sample program.

```
003110  FD  DISKOUT
003120      BLOCK CONTAINS 44 RECORDS
003130      RECORD CONTAINS 80 CHARACTERS
003140      LABEL RECORDS ARE STANDARD
003150      DATA RECORD IS DISK-IO.
003160  01  DISK-IO                    PICTURE X(80).
```

Figure 2-21 File Section Entries for Disk Output File

The filename **DISKOUT** will be used for the disk output file and must immediately follow the "FD" entry. The physical record, or block, will contain 44 records and each record will contain 80 characters. This means that the block size will be 3520 characters (44 X 80). A blocking structure is determined for each file dependent upon the main storage available and the medium on which the file is to be stored. In this case, the maximum amount of main storage which can be allocated to the input/output area required to store the block is 3520 bytes. In most cases, it is advantageous to block as large as possible so that gaps which are required on both tape and disk between physical records can be kept to a minimum. It is always necessary to analyze the trade-off between disk storage (maximum usage) and main storage requirements (smaller blocks need less main storage I/O area) to find the optimum combination.

The **LABEL RECORDS ARE STANDARD** clause specifies that standard labels will be used for the disk file. All disk files must have standard labels and this entry is required for disk files. The data record will be **DISK-IO**, which is defined immediately following the **FD** entry. It should be noted that although, as discussed above, enough main storage must be available to store the entire block of records to be written on the disk, the 01 level entry only describes a single logical record. It does not matter what the size of a block is which is going to be stored on the disk; the data record only describes the single logical record. The block is made up of two or more of these logical records.

WRITE STATEMENT

In order to write a record or block of records onto a sequential disk file the **WRITE** verb is used. The following example illustrates the Write verb to write a record onto a sequential disk output file.

```
013030        WRITE DISK-IO FROM WORK-AREA
013040             INVALID KEY
013050             MOVE BAD-WRITE-ERROR TO PRINT-IO
013060             PERFORM 250-WRITE-ERR THRU 250-EXIT.
```

Figure 2-22 WRITE Verb to Write on a Sequential Disk Output File

The operand immediately following the **WRITE** verb is the name of the I/O area as defined by the level 01 entry in the File Section of the Data Division. The optional "**FROM**" word can be used if it is desired to write a record which is stored in a work area in Working-Storage. If the "**FROM**" option is not used, the record will be written directly from the I/O area defined the the File Section.

The **INVALID KEY** clause may also be required on some ANSI COBOL compilers, such as the DOS compiler for the System/360 and System/370. The imperative statements specified by the Invalid Key clause when writing a sequential disk output file will be executed when the Write statement is attempting to write a record outside the limits of the file. Thus, if certain limits have been defined for the file, and there is not room in the file for the record to be written, the Invalid Routine will be entered. In the example above, an error message will be written on the Exception Report. In addition, in the **250-WRITE-ERR** routine, an indicator will be set which will cause the program to be terminated.

PROGRAM

The following is the listing of the entire program to read a card and tape input file and create a sequential disk output file.

Note in the program that the following "editing" operations are performed to validate the input files.

1. **TYPE FIELD** - This field must contain the values 1-9.

2. **SOURCE FIELD** - This field must contain a space or the codes 1 or 2.

3. **PART NUMBER FIELD** - This field must contain an absolute numeric value - a negative part number is not valid.

4. **UNIT PRICE FIELD** - This file must contain an absolute numeric value or spaces. If it contains spaces, the spaces are replaced with zeros.

5. **QUANTITY ON HAND FIELD** - This field must contain numeric data or spaces. If it contains spaces, zeros are moved to the field.

6. **QUANTITY ON ORDER FIELD** - This field must contain numeric data or spaces. If it contains spaces, zeros are moved to the field.

7. **QUANTITY RESERVED FIELD** - If this field contains blanks, the blanks are replaced with zeros. Otherwise, the field must contain numeric data.

8. **PART NUMBER-NEXT ASSEMBLY** - This field may contain blanks or an absolute numeric value. If it contains blanks, zeros are moved to the field.

The routine to do the editing of the input data (**200-CHECK-NUMB**) is performed because the same routine is used to check both card input and tape input. When an error is detected in an input record (for example, a field is checked and does not contain numeric data) a "1" is moved to a programmed switch, **BAD-SWITCH** to prevent the invalid record from being recorded on the disk.

```
     1                              IBM DOS AMERICAN NATIONAL STANDARD COBOL              CBF CL3-4           09/12/74

00001  001010 IDENTIFICATION DIVISION.                                                   CDTPDISK
00002  001020 PROGRAM-ID.     CDTDISK.                                                    CDTPDISK
00003  001030 AUTHOR.         SHELLY.                                                     CDTPDISK
00004  001040 INSTALLATION.   LONG BEACH.                                                 CDTPDISK
00005  001050 DATE-WRITTEN.   07/08/74.                                                   CDTPDISK
00006  001060 DATE-COMPILED.  09/12/74                                                    CDTPDISK
00007  001070 SECURITY.       UNCLASSIFIED.                                               CDTPDISK
00008  001080 REMARKS.        THIS PROGRAM READS A CARD AND A TAPE FILE                   CDTPDISK
00009  001090                 AND CREATES A SEQUENTIAL DISK FILE WHICH WILL              CDTPDISK
00010  001100                 BE USED TO LOAD AN INDEXED SEQUENTIAL MASTER               CDTPDISK
00011  001110                 FILE OR TO UPDATE AN INDEXED SEQUENTIAL MASTER             CDTPDISK
00012  001120                 FILE.                                                       CDTPDISK
00013  001130                                                                             CDTPDISK
00014  001140                                                                             CDTPDISK
00015  001150 ENVIRONMENT DIVISION.                                                       CDTPDISK
00016  001160 CONFIGURATION SECTION.                                                      CDTPDISK
00017  001170 SOURCE-COMPUTER.    IBM-360-F30.                                            CDTPDISK
00018  001180 OBJECT-COMPUTER.    IBM-360-F30.                                            CDTPDISK
00019  001190 SPECIAL-NAMES.                                                              CDTPDISK
00020  001200     C01 IS TO-TOP-OF-PAGE.                                                  CDTPDISK
00021  002010                                                                             CDTPDISK
00022  002020 INPUT-OUTPUT SECTION.                                                       CDTPDISK
00023  002030 FILE-CONTROL.                                                               CDTPDISK
00024  002040     SELECT CARDSIN                                                          CDTPDISK
00025  002050         ASSIGN TO SYS004-UR-2540R-S.                                        CDTPDISK
00026  002060     SELECT TAPEIN                                                           CDTPDISK
00027  002070         ASSIGN TO SYS005-UT-2400-S-TAPEIN.                                  CDTPDISK
00028  002080     SELECT DISKOUT                                                          CDTPDISK
00029  002090         ASSIGN TO SYS006-UT-2314-S-DISKOUT.                                 CDTPDISK
00030  002100     SELECT PRTFLE                                                           CDTPDISK
00031  002110         ASSIGN TO SYS007-UR-1403-S.                                         CDTPDISK
00032  002120                                                                             CDTPDISK
00033  002130                                                                             CDTPDISK
00034  002140                                                                             CDTPDISK
00035  002150 DATA DIVISION.                                                              CDTPDISK
00036  002160                                                                             CDTPDISK
00037  002170 FILE SECTION.                                                               CDTPDISK
00038  002180                                                                             CDTPDISK
00039  002190 FD CARDSIN                                                                  CDTPDISK
00040  002200     RECORD CONTAINS 80 CHARACTERS                                           CDTPDISK
00041  003010     LABEL RECORDS ARE OMITTED                                               CDTPDISK
00042  003020     DATA RECORD IS CARD-IO.                                                 CDTPDISK
00043  003030 01  CARD-IO.                                                                CDTPDISK
00044  003040     03  PART-NUMB-CD.                                                       CDTPDISK
00045  003050         05  DIV-CD          PICTURE XX.                                     CDTPDISK
00046  003060         05  PRIME-CD        PICTURE X(6).                                   CDTPDISK
00047  003070         05  DASH-CD         PICTURE X(5).                                   CDTPDISK
00048  003080     03  NAME-CD             PICTURE X(25).                                  CDTPDISK
00049  003090     03  QTY-ON-HAND-CD      PICTURE X(7).                                   CDTPDISK
00050  003100     03  QTY-ON-ORDER-CD     PICTURE X(7).                                   CDTPDISK
00051  003110     03  QTY-RESERVED-CD     PICTURE X(7).                                   CDTPDISK
00052  003120     03  NEXT-ASSEMBLY-CD.                                                   CDTPDISK
00053  003130         05  DIV-NA-CD       PICTURE XX.                                     CDTPDISK
00054  003140         05  PRIME-NA-CD     PICTURE X(6).                                   CDTPDISK
00055  003150         05  DASH-NA-CD      PICTURE X(5).                                   CDTPDISK
00056  003160     03  TYPE-CD             PICTURE X.                                      CDTPDISK
00057  003170     03  SOURCE-CD           PICTURE X.                                      CDTPDISK
00058  003180     03  UNIT-PRICE-CD       PICTURE X(6).                                   CDTPDISK
00059  003190                                                                             CDTPDISK
00060  003200                                                                             CDTPDISK
00061  004010 FD TAPEIN                                                                   CDTPDISK
00062  004020     BLOCK CONTAINS 4 RECORDS                                                CDTPDISK
00063  004030     RECORD CONTAINS 80 CHARACTERS                                           CDTPDISK
00064  004040     LABEL RECORDS ARE STANDARD                                              CDTPDISK
00065  004050     DATA RECORD IS TAPE-IO.                                                 CDTPDISK
00066  004060 01  TAPE-IO.                                                                CDTPDISK
00067  004070     03  PART-NUMB-TP.                                                       CDTPDISK
00068  004080         05  DIV-TP          PICTURE XX.                                     CDTPDISK
00069  004090         05  PRIME-TP        PICTURE X(6).                                   CDTPDISK
00070  004100         05  DASH-TP         PICTURE X(5).                                   CDTPDISK
00071  004110     03  NAME-TP             PICTURE X(25).                                  CDTPDISK
00072  004120     03  QTY-ON-HAND-TP      PICTURE X(7).                                   CDTPDISK
00073  004130     03  QTY-ON-ORDER-TP     PICTURE X(7).                                   CDTPDISK
00074  004140     03  QTY-RESERVED-TP     PICTURE X(7).                                   CDTPDISK
00075  004150     03  NEXT-ASSEMBLY-TP.                                                   CDTPDISK
00076  004160         05  DIV-NA-TP       PICTURE XX.                                     CDTPDISK
00077  004170         05  PRIME-NA-TP     PICTURE X(6).                                   CDTPDISK
00078  004180         05  DASH-NA-TP      PICTURE X(5).                                   CDTPDISK
00079  004190     03  TYPE-TP             PICTURE X.                                      CDTPDISK
00080  004200     03  SOURCE-TP           PICTURE X.                                      CDTPDISK
00081  005010     03  UNIT-PRICE-TP       PICTURE X(6).                                   CDTPDISK
00082  005020                                                                             CDTPDISK
00083  005030                                                                             CDTPDISK
00084  005040 FD  DISKOUT                                                                 CDTPDISK
00085  005050     BLOCK CONTAINS 44 RECORDS                                               CDTPDISK
00086  005060     RECORD CONTAINS 80 CHARACTERS                                           CDTPDISK
00087  005070     LABEL RECORDS ARE STANDARD                                              CDTPDISK
```

```
    2

00088   005080      DATA RECORD IS DISK-IO.                              CDTPDISK
00089   005090  01  DISK-IO                    PICTURE X(80).            CDTPDISK
00090   005100                                                          CDTPDISK
00091   005110                                                          CDTPDISK
00092   005120  FD  PRTFLE                                              CDTPDISK
00093   005130      RECORD CONTAINS 121 CHARACTERS                      CDTPDISK
00094   005140      LABEL RECORDS ARE OMITTED                           CDTPDISK
00095   005150      DATA RECORD IS PRINT-IOA.                           CDTPDISK
00096   005160  01  PRINT-IOA.                                          CDTPDISK
00097   005170      03  FILLER                 PICTURE X.                CDTPDISK
00098   005180      03  PRINT-IO.                                       CDTPDISK
00099   005190          05  CARD-PRT           PICTURE X(80).            CDTPDISK
00100   005200          05  FILLER             PICTURE XXX.              CDTPDISK
00101   006010          05  ERROR-PRT          PICTURE X(37).            CDTPDISK
00102   006020                                                          CDTPDISK
00103   006030                                                          CDTPDISK
00104   006040                                                          CDTPDISK
00105   006050  WORKING-STORAGE SECTION.                                CDTPDISK
00106   006060                                                          CDTPDISK
00107   006070  77  BAD-SWITCH                 PICTURE X      VALUE '0'. CDTPDISK
00108   006080  77  CARD-COUNT                 PICTURE S9(5)  VALUE ZERO CDTPDISK
00109   006090                                 USAGE  COMPUTATIONAL-3.   CDTPDISK
00110   006100  77  TAPE-COUNT                 PICTURE S9(5)  VALUE ZERO CDTPDISK
00111   006110                                 USAGE  COMPUTATIONAL-3.   CDTPDISK
00112   006120  77  PG-CNT                     PICTURE S999   VALUE ZERO CDTPDISK
00113   006130                                 USAGE  COMPUTATIONAL-3.   CDTPDISK
00114   006140  77  VARIABLE                   PICTURE 9.                CDTPDISK
00115   006150  77  SINGLE-SPACING             PICTURE 9      VALUE 1.   CDTPDISK
00116   006160                                                          CDTPDISK
00117   006170  77  DOUBLE-SPACING             PICTURE 9      VALUE 2.   CDTPDISK
00118   006180  77  LINE-COUNT                 PICTURE S999              CDTPDISK
00119   006190                                 USAGE COMPUTATIONAL-3.    CDTPDISK
00120   006200                                                          CDTPDISK
00121   007010  01  HEADER1.                                            CDTPDISK
00122   007020      03  FILLER                 PICTURE X(19)  VALUE SPACES. CDTPDISK
00123   007030      03  FILLER                 PICTURE X(72)  VALUE      CDTPDISK
00124   007040      'CARD IN ERROR'.                                    CDTPDISK
00125   007050      03  FILLER                 PICTURE X(5)   VALUE 'PAGE'. CDTPDISK
00126   007060      03  PG-H1                  PICTURE ZZ9.              CDTPDISK
00127   007070      03  FILLER                 PICTURE X(21)  VALUE SPACES. CDTPDISK
00128   007080                                                          CDTPDISK
00129   007090  01  WORK-AREA.                                          CDTPDISK
00130   007100      03  PART-NUMB-WK           PICTURE X(13).            CDTPDISK
00131   007110      03  NAME-WK                PICTURE X(25).            CDTPDISK
00132   007120      03  QTY-ON-HAND-WK         PICTURE X(7).             CDTPDISK
00133   007130      03  QTY-ON-HAND-WK9 REDEFINES QTY-ON-HAND-WK        CDTPDISK
00134   007140                                 PICTURE S9(7).            CDTPDISK
00135   007150      03  QTY-ON-ORDER-WK        PICTURE X(7).             CDTPDISK
00136   007160      03  QTY-ON-ORDER-WK9 REDEFINES QTY-ON-ORDER-WK      CDTPDISK
00137   007170                                 PICTURE S9(7).            CDTPDISK
00138   007180      03  QTY-RESERVED-WK        PICTURE X(7).             CDTPDISK
00139   007190      03  QTY-RESERVED-WK9 REDEFINES QTY-RESERVED-WK      CDTPDISK
00140   007200                                 PICTURE S9(7).            CDTPDISK
00141   008010      03  PART-NUMB-NA-WK        PICTURE X(13).            CDTPDISK
00142   008020      03  TYPE-WK                PICTURE X.                CDTPDISK
00143   008030      03  SOURCE-WK              PICTURE X.                CDTPDISK
00144   008040      03  UNIT-PRICE-WK          PICTURE X(6).             CDTPDISK
00145   008050                                                          CDTPDISK
00146   008060  01  LAST-MSG.                                           CDTPDISK
00147   008070      03  FILLER                 PICTURE X(18)  VALUE      CDTPDISK
00148   008080      'TOTAL VALID CARDS'.                                CDTPDISK
00149   008090      03  CARDS-RD               PICTURE ZZZZ9.            CDTPDISK
00150   008100      03  FILLER                 PICTURE X(27)  VALUE      CDTPDISK
00151   008110      ' TOTAL VALID TAPE RECORDS '.                       CDTPDISK
00152   008120      03  TAPE-RD                PICTURE ZZZZ9.            CDTPDISK
00153   008130                                                          CDTPDISK
00154   008140  01  BAD-WRITE-ERROR.                                    CDTPDISK
00155   008150      03  FILLER                 PICTURE X(49)  VALUE      CDTPDISK
00156   008160      '***DISKOUT EXTENT LIMIT EXCEEDED---RUN STOPPED***'. CDTPDISK
00157   008170                                                          CDTPDISK
00158   008180                                                          CDTPDISK
00159   008190  PROCEDURE DIVISION.                                     CDTPDISK
00160   008200                                                          CDTPDISK
00161   009010                                                          CDTPDISK
00162   009020  NOTE-001.                                               CDTPDISK
00163   009030      NOTE ***************************************************CDTPDISK
00164   009040      *  THIS PROGRAM CREATES A SEQUENTIAL DISK FILE FROM *CDTPDISK
00165   009050      *  CARD AND TAPE INPUT.                             *CDTPDISK
00166   009060      *                                                   *CDTPDISK
00167   009070      *  THE FIRST ROUTINE OPENS THE FILES AND READS A CARD. *CDTPDISK
00168   009080      *  IT THEN PERFORMS A CHECK ROUTINE TO VALIDATE NUMERIC *CDTPDISK
00169   009090      *  DATA.                                           *CDTPDISK
00170   009100      *************************************************************.CDTPDISK
00171   009110                                                          CDTPDISK
00172   009120  001-START.                                              CDTPDISK
00173   009130      OPEN INPUT  CARDSIN,                                CDTPDISK
00174   009140                  TAPEIN,                                 CDTPDISK
```

```
      3
00175  009150          OUTPUT DISKOUT,                                        CDTPDISK
00176  009160                 PRTFLE.                                         CDTPDISK
00177  009170     PERFORM 300-HEADER THRU 300-EXIT.                           CDTPDISK
00178  009180     MOVE SPACES TO PRINT-IO.                                    CDTPDISK
00179  009190                                                                 CDTPDISK
00180  009200 010-READ-CARDS.                                                 CDTPDISK
00181  010010     READ CARDSIN INTO WORK-AREA AT END GO TO 030-READ-TAPE.     CDTPDISK
00182  010020     PERFORM 200-CHECK-NUMB THRU 200-EXIT.                       CDTPDISK
00183  010030     IF BAD-SWITCH IS = '1',                                     CDTPDISK
00184  010040         MOVE '0' TO BAD-SWITCH,                                 CDTPDISK
00185  010050         GO TO 010-READ-CARDS.                                   CDTPDISK
00186  010060     ADD 1 TO CARD-COUNT.                                        CDTPDISK
00187  010070     PERFORM 100-WRITE-DISK THRU 100-EXIT.                       CDTPDISK
00188  010080     IF BAD-SWITCH IS = '1'                                      CDTPDISK
00189  010090         GO TO 400-END-TAPE.                                     CDTPDISK
00190  010100     GO TO 010-READ-CARDS.                                       CDTPDISK
00191  010110                                                                 CDTPDISK
00192  010120                                                                 CDTPDISK
00193  010130 NOTE-030.                                                       CDTPDISK
00194  010140     NOTE ***************************************************CDTPDISK
00195  010150     *   THIS ROUTINE IS ENTERED TO READ THE TAPE INPUT     *CDTPDISK
00196  010160     *   FILE AFTER THE CARD FILE HAS BEEN READ. IT READS    *CDTPDISK
00197  010170     *   THE TAPE AND THEN PERFORMS A ROUTINE TO CHECK       *CDTPDISK
00198  010180     *   THE NUMERIC FIELDS. IF ALL IS OK, THE RECORD IS     *CDTPDISK
00199  010190     *   WRITTEN ON THE DISK.                                *CDTPDISK
00200  010200     ***************************************************.CDTPDISK
00201  011010                                                                 CDTPDISK
00202  011020 030-READ-TAPE.                                                  CDTPDISK
00203  011030     READ TAPEIN INTO WORK-AREA AT END GO TO 400-END-TAPE.       CDTPDISK
00204  011040     PERFORM 200-CHECK-NUMB THRU 200-EXIT.                       CDTPDISK
00205  011050     IF BAD-SWITCH IS = '1'                                      CDTPDISK
00206  011060         MOVE '0' TO BAD-SWITCH                                  CDTPDISK
00207  011070         GO TO 030-READ-TAPE.                                    CDTPDISK
00208  011080     ADD 1 TO TAPE-COUNT.                                        CDTPDISK
00209  011090     PERFORM 100-WRITE-DISK THRU 100-EXIT.                       CDTPDISK
00210  011100     IF BAD-SWITCH IS = '1'                                      CDTPDISK
00211  011110         GO TO 400-END-TAPE.                                     CDTPDISK
00212  011120     GO TO 030-READ-TAPE.                                        CDTPDISK
00213  011130                                                                 CDTPDISK
00214  011140                                                                 CDTPDISK
00215  011150 NOTE-100.                                                       CDTPDISK
00216  011160     NOTE ***************************************************CDTPDISK
00217  011170     *   THIS ROUTINE IS ENTERED TO WRITE THE INPUT RECORD   *CDTPDISK
00218  011180     *   FROM CARDS OR TAPE ONTO THE SEQUENTIAL DISK FILE.    *CDTPDISK
00219  011190     ***************************************************.CDTPDISK
00220  011200                                                                 CDTPDISK
00221  012010 100-WRITE-DISK.                                                 CDTPDISK
00222  012020     WRITE DISK-IO FROM WORK-AREA                                CDTPDISK
00223  012030             INVALID KEY                                         CDTPDISK
00224  012040                 MOVE BAD-WRITE-ERROR TO PRINT-IO                CDTPDISK
00225  012050                 PERFORM 250-WRITE-ERR THRU 250-EXIT.            CDTPDISK
00226  012060 100-EXIT. EXIT.                                                 CDTPDISK
00227  012070                                                                 CDTPDISK
00228  012080                                                                 CDTPDISK
00229  012090 NOTE-200.                                                       CDTPDISK
00230  012100     NOTE ***************************************************CDTPDISK
00231  012110     *   THIS ROUTINE IS ENTERED TO VERIFY THAT ALL NUMERIC  *CDTPDISK
00232  012120     *   FIELDS IN THE INPUT RECORDS CONTAIN VALID DATA.      *CDTPDISK
00233  012130     *   THE NUMERIC FIELDS CAN CONTAIN EITHER ALL BLANKS,    *CDTPDISK
00234  012140     *   IN WHICH CASE ZEROS ARE MOVED TO THE FIELD OR THEY   *CDTPDISK
00235  012150     *   CAN CONTAIN NUMERIC VALUES. ANY OTHER VALUES ARE     *CDTPDISK
00236  012160     *   INVALID.                                             *CDTPDISK
00237  012170     ***************************************************.CDTPDISK
00238  012180                                                                 CDTPDISK
00239  012190 200-CHECK-NUMB.                                                 CDTPDISK
00240  012200     MOVE WORK-AREA TO CARD-PRT.                                 CDTPDISK
00241  013010     IF TYPE-WK IS < '1' OR TYPE-WK IS > '9'                     CDTPDISK
00242  013020         MOVE 'INVALID TYPE' TO ERROR-PRT,                       CDTPDISK
00243  013030         PERFORM 250-WRITE-ERR THRU 250-EXIT.                    CDTPDISK
00244  013040     IF SOURCE-WK IS = ' '                                       CDTPDISK
00245  013050         NEXT SENTENCE                                           CDTPDISK
00246  013060     ELSE                                                        CDTPDISK
00247  013070         IF SOURCE-WK IS < '1' OR SOURCE-WK IS > '2'             CDTPDISK
00248  013080             MOVE 'INVALID SOURCE' TO ERROR-PRT                  CDTPDISK
00249  013090             PERFORM 250-WRITE-ERR THRU 250-EXIT.                CDTPDISK
00250  013100     IF PART-NUMB-WK IS NOT NUMERIC                              CDTPDISK
00251  013110         MOVE 'PART NUMBER-NOT NUMERIC' TO ERROR-PRT             CDTPDISK
00252  013120         PERFORM 250-WRITE-ERR THRU 250-EXIT.                    CDTPDISK
00253  013130     IF UNIT-PRICE-WK = SPACES                                   CDTPDISK
00254  013140         MOVE '000000' TO UNIT-PRICE-WK,                         CDTPDISK
00255  013150     ELSE                                                        CDTPDISK
00256  013160         IF UNIT-PRICE-WK IS NOT NUMERIC                         CDTPDISK
00257  013170             MOVE 'UNIT PRICE-NOT NUMERIC' TO ERROR-PRT          CDTPDISK
00258  013180             PERFORM 250-WRITE-ERR THRU 250-EXIT.                CDTPDISK
00259  013190     IF QTY-ON-HAND-WK IS = SPACES,                             CDTPDISK
00260  013200         MOVE '0000000' TO QTY-ON-HAND-WK,                       CDTPDISK
00261  014010     ELSE                                                        CDTPDISK
```

```
    4

00262  014020          IF QTY-ON-HAND-WK9 IS NOT NUMERIC                    CDTPDISK
00263  014030              MOVE 'QUANTITY ON HAND-NOT NUMERIC' TO ERROR-PRT CDTPDISK
00264  014040              PERFORM 250-WRITE-ERR THRU 250-EXIT.             CDTPDISK
00265  014050          IF QTY-ON-ORDER-WK IS = SPACES,                      CDTPDISK
00266  014060              MOVE '0000000' TO QTY-ON-ORDER-WK,               CDTPDISK
00267  014070          ELSE                                                 CDTPDISK
00268  014080              IF QTY-ON-ORDER-WK9 IS NOT NUMERIC               CDTPDISK
00269  014090                  MOVE 'QUANTITY ON ORDER-NOT NUMERIC' TO ERROR-PRT CDTPDISK
00270  014100                  PERFORM 250-WRITE-ERR THRU 250-EXIT.         CDTPDISK
00271  014110          IF QTY-RESERVED-WK IS = SPACES,                      CDTPDISK
00272  014120              MOVE '0000000' TO QTY-RESERVED-WK,               CDTPDISK
00273  014130          ELSE                                                 CDTPDISK
00274  014140              IF QTY-RESERVED-WK9 IS NOT NUMERIC               CDTPDISK
00275  014150                  MOVE 'QUANTITY RESERVED-NOT NUMERIC' TO ERROR-PRT CDTPDISK
00276  014160                  PERFORM 250-WRITE-ERR THRU 250-EXIT.         CDTPDISK
00277  014170          IF PART-NUMB-NA-WK IS = SPACES                       CDTPDISK
00278  014180              MOVE '0000000000000' TO PART-NUMB-NA-WK          CDTPDISK
00279  014190          ELSE                                                 CDTPDISK
00280  014200              IF PART-NUMB-NA-WK NOT NUMERIC                   CDTPDISK
00281  015010                  MOVE 'NEXT ASSEMBLY-NOT NUMERIC' TO ERROR-PRT CDTPDISK
00282  015020                  PERFORM 250-WRITE-ERR THRU 250-EXIT.         CDTPDISK
00283  015030 200-EXIT.    EXIT.                                            CDTPDISK
00284  015040                                                               CDTPDISK
00285  015050                                                               CDTPDISK
00286  015060 NOTE-250.                                                     CDTPDISK
00287  015070          NOTE *********************************************************CDTPDISK
00288  015080          *    THIS ROUTINE IS ENTERED TO WRITE ERROR MESSAGES TO    *CDTPDISK
00289  015090          *    THE PRINTER. ON THE FIRST ERROR FOR EACH RECORD, THE  *CDTPDISK
00290  015100          *    ENTIRE RECORD AND THE ERROR MESSAGE IS WRITTEN. AFTER *CDTPDISK
00291  015110          *    THE FIRST LINE, ONLY THE ERROR MESSAGE IS WRITTEN.    *CDTPDISK
00292  015120          *********************************************************.CDTPDISK
00293  015130                                                               CDTPDISK
00294  015140 250-WRITE-ERR.                                                CDTPDISK
00295  015150          IF LINE-COUNT > 50                                   CDTPDISK
00296  015160              PERFORM 300-HEADER THRU 300-EXIT.                CDTPDISK
00297  015170          WRITE PRINT-IOA AFTER ADVANCING VARIABLE LINES.      CDTPDISK
00298  015180          ADD 1 TO LINE-COUNT.                                 CDTPDISK
00299  015190          MOVE SPACES TO PRINT-IO.                             CDTPDISK
00300  015200          MOVE '1' TO BAD-SWITCH.                              CDTPDISK
00301  016010          MOVE SINGLE-SPACING TO VARIABLE.                     CDTPDISK
00302  016020 250-EXIT.    EXIT.                                            CDTPDISK
00303  016030                                                               CDTPDISK
00304  016040                                                               CDTPDISK
00305  016050 NOTE-300.                                                     CDTPDISK
00306  016060          NOTE *********************************************************CDTPDISK
00307  016070          *    THIS ROUTINE IS ENTERED TO PRINT THE HEADER FOR THE   *CDTPDISK
00308  016080          *    ERROR EXCEPTION REPORT.                               *CDTPDISK
00309  016090          *********************************************************.CDTPDISK
00310  016100                                                               CDTPDISK
00311  016110 300-HEADER.                                                   CDTPDISK
00312  016120          ADD 1 TO PG-CNT.                                     CDTPDISK
00313  016130          MOVE PG-CNT TO PG-H1.                                CDTPDISK
00314  016140          MOVE HEADER1 TO PRINT-IO.                            CDTPDISK
00315  016150          WRITE PRINT-IOA AFTER ADVANCING TO-TOP-OF-PAGE.      CDTPDISK
00316  016160          MOVE DOUBLE-SPACING TO VARIABLE.                     CDTPDISK
00317  016170          MOVE ZERO TO LINE-COUNT.                             CDTPDISK
00318  016180 300-EXIT. EXIT.                                               CDTPDISK
00319  016190                                                               CDTPDISK
00320  016200                                                               CDTPDISK
00321  017010 NOTE-400.                                                     CDTPDISK
00322  017020          NOTE *********************************************************CDTPDISK
00323  017030          *    THIS ROUTINE IS ENTERED WHEN END-OF-FILE IS REACHED   *CDTPDISK
00324  017040          *    ON THE TAPE INPUT FILE. IT WRITES AN END MESSAGE ON   *CDTPDISK
00325  017050          *    THE PRINTER AND CLOSES THE FILES.                     *CDTPDISK
00326  017060          *********************************************************.CDTPDISK
00327  017070                                                               CDTPDISK
00328  017080 400-END-TAPE.                                                 CDTPDISK
00329  017090          MOVE CARD-COUNT TO CARDS-RD.                         CDTPDISK
00330  017100          MOVE TAPE-COUNT TO TAPE-RD.                          CDTPDISK
00331  017110          MOVE LAST-MSG TO PRINT-IO.                           CDTPDISK
00332  017120          MOVE DOUBLE-SPACING TO VARIABLE.                     CDTPDISK
00333  017130          PERFORM 250-WRITE-ERR THRU 250-EXIT.                 CDTPDISK
00334  017140          CLOSE CARDSIN,                                       CDTPDISK
00335  017150              TAPEIN,                                          CDTPDISK
00336  017160              DISKOUT,                                         CDTPDISK
00337  017170              PRTFLE.                                          CDTPDISK
00338  017180          STOP RUN.                                            CDTPDISK
```

CHAPTER 2

PROGRAMMING ASSIGNMENT

INTRODUCTION

The programming assignments in the next five chapters consist of a series of programs to be used in a Sales Commission System. The first program to be written is to create a sequential disk file from input data cards. This sequential disk file will be used as the input file to create an indexed sequential master file (Chapter 3).

The program will also be used to create a transaction file that will be used as the input file to update the indexed sequential file (Chapter 5). Thus, the program in this assignment is similar in function to the program used in Step 1 and Step 5 of the Inventory System explained in the text.

INSTRUCTIONS

From the cards illustrated below, a sequential disk file is to be created. The format of the input file is illustrated below.

The sequential disk output file should consist of records containing the same fields as the input cards. The record layout is to be determined by the programmer. The output file should be blocked. The blocking factor should be determined by the programmer.

The program should incorporate checking features to ensure that the Department Field and the Salesman Field contain absolute numeric values. The Current Sales Field, the Commission Rate field and the Current Sales Return field may contain either absolute numeric values or spaces. If they contain spaces, move zeros to the fields.

The type field must contain the values 1-7 to indicate the following.

1 - **LOAD**
2 - **NAME CHANGE**
3 - **Y-T-D Sales UPDATE**
4 - **COMMISSION RATE CHANGE**
5 - **Y-T-D Sales Return UPDATE**
6 - **ADDITION**
7 - **DELETION**

Note that any of the codes are valid as this program will be used to load records which will be used to create the master file and also to load records which comprise the transaction file used to update the master file.

An error report should be generated indicating any errors in punching in the numeric fields, and any invalid codes. The format of the report is to be designed by the programmer.

It should be noted the sequential output file created in this program must be sorted on department number and salesman number. This may be accomplished by sorting the cards prior to loading the file on the disk, or by using the **SORT** verb in the COBOL program itself, or by using an Utility Sort Program after the file has been loaded on the disk.

Valid test data cards are contained in Appendix G. Invalid test cards are also found in Appendix G. Both valid and invalid test data should be used when testing the program. It is suggested that the sequential disk file created be dumped to assure that the file was stored properly on the disk. This may be accomplished using a utility program.

INDEXED SEQUENTIAL ACCESS METHOD

CHAPTER 3

INDEXED
SEQUENTIAL
ACCESS METHOD

3

INTRODUCTION

Sequential processing, as has been shown, involves processing records one after another. Due to the addressing scheme used on direct access devices, another type of processing called **RANDOM PROCESSING** is possible. Random processing is a means by which non-sequential records may be read, written, and processed. Devices such as card readers and tape drives cannot process records randomly because there is no way, for example, to read the fourth record in an input stream and then read the first record because the first record must be read first, followed by the second, third, fourth, etc.

Direct access devices, however, offer the opportunity to read the fourth record in a file and then the first record in a file because the only thing governing which record is read is the record address which is presented to the channel.

The Indexed Sequential Access Method, which is explained in this chapter, allows **BOTH** sequential and random access to a file.

FILE STRUCTURE

The records of an indexed sequential file are organized on the basis of a collating sequence determined by a specific control field or "key" within the record. An indexed sequential file exists in space allocated on the disk called **PRIME** data areas, **OVERFLOW** areas, and **INDEX** areas.

When an index sequential file is initially established on the disk, or "loaded", all data records are loaded into an area called the **PRIME DATA AREA**. The data in this area is available to be processed by both sequential and random access methods. Figure 3-1 illustrates this concept.

91

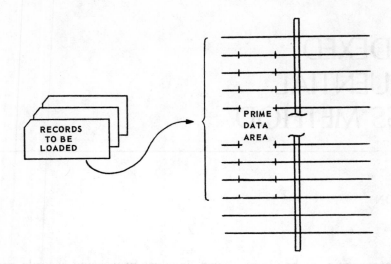

Figure 3-1 Prime Data Area

After the file is established, the user can **ADD** records without reorganizing the entire file as in sequential file organization. A new record added to an indexed sequential file is placed into a location on a track determined by the value of a ''key'' or control field in each record. To handle additions an **OVERFLOW AREA** exists.

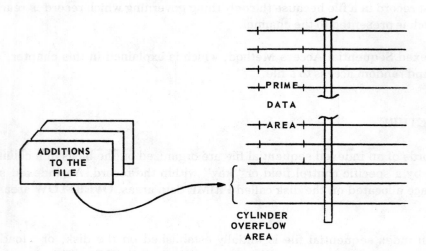

Figure 3-2 Cylinder Overflow Area

Two types of overflow areas may be used either separately or together--the cylinder overflow area and the independent overflow area. A **CYLINDER OVERFLOW AREA** is a track or tracks located on each cylinder within the prime data area extents. COBOL will allocate 4 tracks on a device using a **2316 DISK PACK**, but this default value can be changed by the programmer. The **INDEPENDENT OVERFLOW AREA** is a separate area outside the extents for the prime area and is used strictly as an overflow area.

The following diagram illustrates the concept of the prime data area, the cylinder overflow area, and the independent overflow area as they appear on the disk.

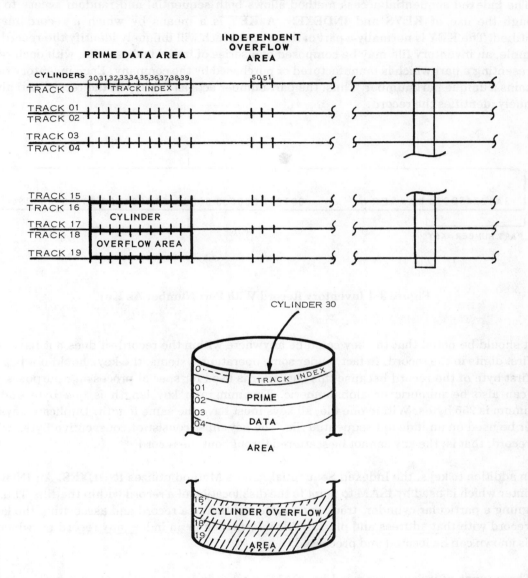

Figure 3-3 Prime Data Area And Overflow Area

In Figure 3-3, Cylinders 30-39 are assigned to be used for the prime data area and the cylinder overflow area. Track 0 is used for the Track Index and tracks 0 thru 15 can be used to store data when the file is loaded. Tracks 16 thru 19 are assigned to the Cylinder Overflow area. Thus, on each cylinder, tracks 16 thru 19 will be used for overflow. Cylinders 50-51 are used as the Independent Overflow area. All twenty tracks (0-19) will be used for the Independent Overflow Area.

KEYS AND INDEXES

The indexed sequential access method allows both sequential and random access to data through the use of **KEYS** and **INDEXES**. A **KEY** is a means by which a record may be identified. The **KEY** is normally a part of the record which will uniquely identify the record. For example, an inventory file may be composed of a series of individual records, with each record representing a part which is manufactured or purchased by the company. Each inventory record contains a unique part number. Thus, the part number acts as the key to the record and always uniquely identifies the record.

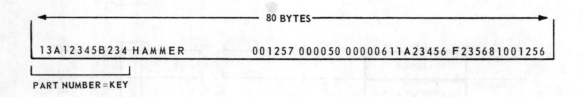

Figure 3-4 Inventory Record With Part Number As Key

It should be noted that the key could be anywhere within the record--it does not have to be the first digits in the record. In fact, under some operating systems, the key should not begin in the first byte of the record because this character is used for special processing purposes. The key can also be numeric or alphanumeric. The minimum key length is one byte and the maximum is 255 bytes. Within one file, all keys must have the same length. Duplicate keys can never be used on an indexed sequential file. The key must consist of consecutive bytes within the record, that is, the key cannot be scattered throughout the record.

In addition to keys, the Indexed Sequential Access Method utilizes **INDEXES**. An **INDEX** is a pointer which is used by **ISAM** to point to the disk location of a record within the file. Thus, by assigning a particular cylinder, track and record location to a record and associating the key of the record with that address and placing this information in an index, any record for which the key is known can be located and processed.

Three types of indexes are used by **ISAM**, a track index, a cylinder index, and a master index. The first two indexes are required and the master index is optional.

TRACK INDEX

The lowest level index used is the **TRACK INDEX**. A track index is built on every **CYLINDER** which is used in the indexed sequential file. Thus, if there were 10 cylinders used for the file, there would be 10 track indexes. The track index is built on the first track of each cylinder used in the file. Therefore, if the extents for the prime data area of the file were Cylinder 30 Track 0, through Cylinder 39 Track 19, each cylinder (30, 31, 32, etc.) would have a track index on its track 0. The track index is always contained on the cylinder for which it is the index and it contains index entries for only the cylinder on which it resides. See Figure 3-1.

The format of the track index and a schematic of the data records as they are stored on disk is illustrated in Figure 3-5. Note that the track index consists of a series of entries for the prime data area and the overflow area for each track, with each of these entries containing a **KEY** entry and a **DATA** entry.

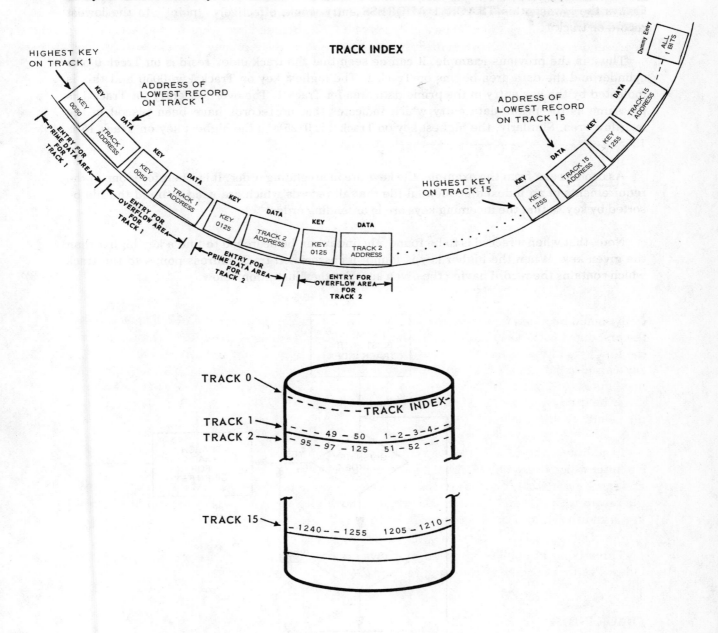

Figure 3-5 Track Index

The track index consists of two parts: (1) For the prime data area, the **KEY** entry in the track index specifies the **HIGHEST KEY** of a record on that track and the **DATA** entry specifies the **ADDRESS** of the **LOWEST RECORD** on that track; (2) For the overflow area, the **KEY** entry specifies the **HIGHEST KEY** associated with that track and the **DATA** entry specifies the **ADDRESS** of the **LOWEST RECORD** in the overflow area. If no overflow entry has been made, the second entry is the same as the first entry.

The **DATA** entry labelled **TRACK 1 ADDRESS** uses a cylinder number and a track number to specify the address of the lowest record on a track. For example, in Figure 3-3, the basic entries in the **TRACK 1 ADDRESS** would include "cylinder 30" (where cylinder 30 is the cylinder for which the track index is used) and "track 1". Since the first record on the track is always the lowest, this **TRACK 1 ADDRESS** entry would effectively "point" to the lowest record on track 1.

Thus, in the previous example, it can be seen that the track index resides on Track 0 of a cylinder and the data area begins on Track 1. The highest key on Track 1 is 0050 and this is indicated by the key entry in the prime data area for Track 1. The overflow entry for Track 1 is the same as the prime data entry which indicates that no records have been placed in the overflow area. Similarly, the highest key on Track 2 is 0125 and the highest key on Track 15 is 1255.

As can be seen from the example, the keys are in ascending order. It is, therefore, one of the requirements of an indexed sequential file that all records which are used to build the file be sorted by key so that the incoming keys are in ascending order.

Note, that when a record is to be found, the index can be searched to find a key higher than the given key. When the higher key is found, its associated track address points to the track which contains the record having the given key. See the illustration below.

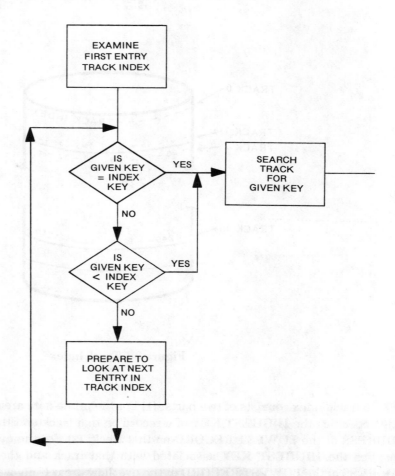

Figure 3-6 Logic For Finding Key In Track Index

In the example below, the logic illustrated in Figure 3-6 is used to find a record. The record to be found has a key of 0095. Since the highest key on track 1 is 0050, the next entry in the index is checked. It shows that the highest key on track 2 is 0125. Therefore, the desired record resides on track 2. The track is then read for the proper key and the record can then be retrieved.

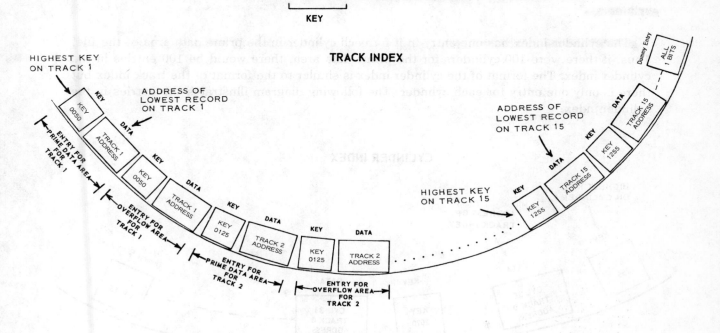

Figure 3-7 Record and Track Index

Note in the example that the last record in the track index is a dummy record which indicates the end of the track index--it is a record of all 1 bits. Therefore, to avoid any problems, a key should never be all 1 bits.

Note also that track 15 is the last entry in the index when the file is organized--this is because of the cylinder overflow feature.

CYLINDER INDEX

The **CYLINDER INDEX** is the intermediate index used by the Indexed Sequential Access Method. It has a function similar to that of the track index, except that it points to the cylinders in the file rather than the tracks within the cylinder. The cylinder index is built on a separate area of the disk from the prime data and overflow areas. Job control statements are used to specify the cylinder(s) to be used for the cylinder index. The cylinder index cannot be on the same cylinder as the prime data record area and it must be located on one or more consecutive cylinders.

The cylinder index has one entry in it for each cylinder in the prime data area of the file. Thus, if there were 100 cylinders for the prime data area, there would be 100 entries in the cylinder index. The format of the cylinder index is similar to the format of the track index but there is only one entry for each cylinder. The following diagram illustrates the entries in the cylinder index.

CYLINDER INDEX

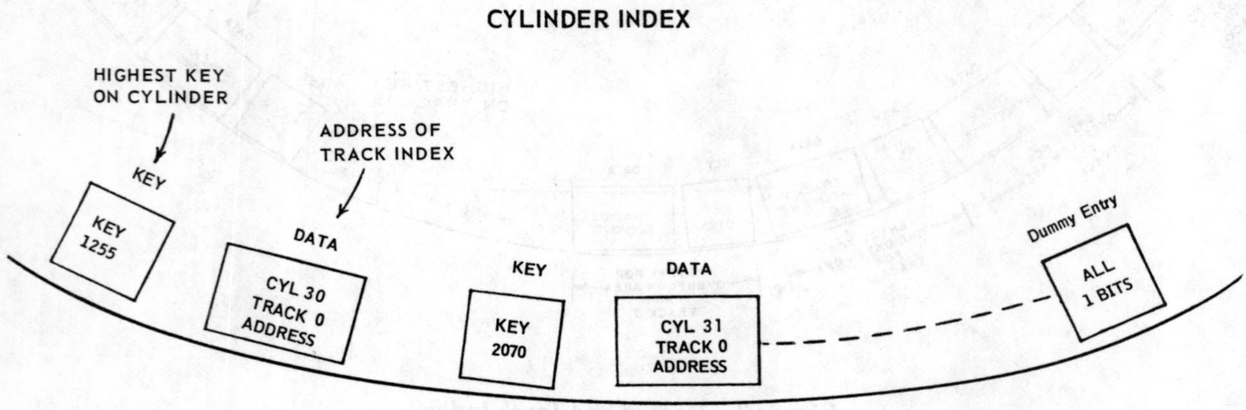

Figure 3-8 Cylinder Index

The entries in the cylinder index consist of the **HIGHEST KEY OF A RECORD** on the entire cylinder and the **ADDRESS OF THE TRACK INDEX** for that cylinder. The key area contains the highest key associated with the given cylinder. The data area contains the address of the associated track index. Thus, in the example, the highest key on cylinder 30 is 1255 and the address of the track index is cylinder 30, track 0. The track index for cylinder 30 is contained in Figure 3-5. The highest key on cylinder 31 is 2070 and the address of the track index is cylinder 31, track 0. This example assumes the prime data area begins on cylinder 30.

To retrieve record 95 the cylinder index is searched using the same logic as illustrated in Figure 3-6 and 3-7. In the example, record 95 would be compared to the first **KEY** entry in the cylinder index. Since record 95 is less than 1255, the associated track index whose address is specified in the **DATA** portion of the first entry is searched in the manner shown previously. In this example, the track index would be found on cylinder 30, track 0.

MASTER INDEX

The master index is an optional index which can be used if desired by the programmer. It contains the track address of each track in the cylinder index and the highest key referenced by the corresponding track. Its use is not recommended unless the cylinder index is more than four tracks. This is because it is more efficient, time-wise, to search a 4 track cylinder index than it is to search a master index and then the 4 track cylinder index.

The master index is built on the device specified in a special **APPLY** statement in the COBOL program. The master index must immediately precede the cylinder index on the disk volume. It may be more than one cylinder long.

MASTER INDEX

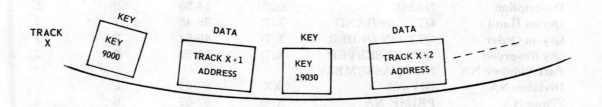

Figure 3-9 Master Index

The key portion of the master index specifies the highest key contained on a given track of the cylinder index and the data portion of the master index contains the address of the track in the cylinder index. In the example above, the master index is located on track X. Further, since the master index in the example is one track in length, and the cylinder index must immediately follow the master index, the first track of the cylinder index would be track (X + 1). Thus, track (X + 1) is specified in the data portion of the first entry in the master index.

By using these indexes, the indexed sequential access method can randomly retrieve any record for which the key is known. It can also process the records sequentially by beginning anywhere in the file (determined by key) and sequentially process the records by just reading the prime data and overflow areas. This flexibility of indexed sequential files makes it an extremely useful tool in many applications requiring diversified usage of the data on the file.

SAMPLE PROGRAM

The sample program presented in this chapter illustrates an application in which an inventory master file is being created. The input to the program is the sorted output of the disk file created in the sample program in Chapter 2. The input fields are the same as the output fields of the file created in Chapter 2. The file has been sorted on the key (positions 1-13) of the record. The figure below again illustrates the records as they are stored on the sequential disk file.

FIELD	FIELD NAME	PICTURE	POSITION	NO OF DIGITS	LENGTH
Part Number	PART-NUMB				
Division Number	DIV	XX	1-2	2	2
Prime Number	PRIME	X(6)	3-8	6	6
Dash Number	DASH	X(5)	9-13	5	5
Description	NAME	X(25)	14-38	25	25
Qty on Hand	QTY-ON-HAND	X(7)	39-45	7	7
Qty on Order	QTY-ON-ORDER	X(7)	46-52	7	7
Qty Reserved	QTY-RESERVED	X(7)	53-59	7	7
Part Number-NA	NEXT-ASSEMBLY				
Division-NA	DIV-NA	XX	60-61	2	2
Prime-NA	PRIME-NA	X(6)	62-67	6	6
Dash-NA	DASH-NA	X(5)	68-72	5	5
Type	TYPE	X	73	1	1
Source	SOURCE	X	74	1	1
Unit Price	UNIT-PRICE	X(6)	75-80	6	6

Figure 3-10 Sequential Disk Input File

A master file and an exception report are created in the sample program. The exception report lists errors in the input records such as invalid type codes, etc. The report format is illustrated in Figure 3-11.

PRINTER SPACING CHART

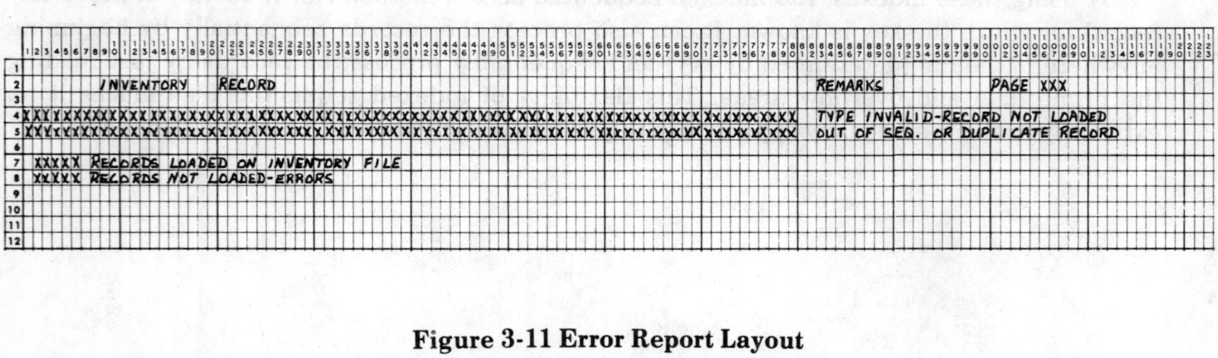

Figure 3-11 Error Report Layout

The output file is the master inventory file. It is an indexed sequential file. Its record layout is illustrated below.

FIELD	FIELD NAME	PICTURE	POSITION	NO OF DIGITS	LENGTH
Part Number	PART-NUMB-MSTR	Picture 9(13) Comp-3	1-7	13	7
Description	NAME-MSTR	Picture X(25)	8-32	25	25
Quantity on Hand	QTY-ON-HAND-MSTR	Picture S9(7) Comp-3	33-36	7	4
Quantity on Order	QTY-ON-ORDER-MSTR	Picture S9(7) Comp-3	37-40	7	4
Quantity Reserved	QTY-RESERVED-MSTR	Picture S9(7) Comp-3	41-44	7	4
Next Assembly Number	NEXT-ASSEMBLY-MSTR	Picture S9(13) Comp-3	45-51	13	7
Type	TYPE-MSTR	Picture X	52	1	1
Source	SOURCE-MSTR	Picture X	53	1	1
Unit Price	UNIT-PRICE-MSTR	Picture S9(7) Comp-3	54-57	6	4
Filler	FILLER	Picture X(7)	58-64	7	7

Figure 3-12 Inventory Master Record Layout

The record length of the master record is to be 64 bytes. The blocking factor is to be 54; therefore, there are to be 3456 bytes per block. Notice that 7 bytes of filler have been reserved in the master record. This is done in case another field must be added to the master record and is normally a good practice.

LOADING AN INDEXED SEQUENTIAL FILE

In order to "load" an indexed sequential file, that is, create the file, the **System Name**, **ACCESS IS SEQUENTIAL**, and **RECORD KEY IS** entries must be made in the File-Control paragraph of the Input-Output Section in the Environment Division. The required entries are illustrated below.

```
003090        SELECT INVMSTR
003100        ASSIGN TO SYS006-DA-2314-I-INVMSTR
003110        ACCESS IS SEQUENTIAL
003120        RECORD KEY IS PART-NUMB-MSTR.
```

Figure 3-13 SELECT Statement To Load Indexed Sequential File

The filename **INVMSTR** immediately follows the **SELECT** Statement in the same manner as has been used with previous file definitions. The **ASSIGN** clause indicates the type of device and the organization of the file through the use of the System-Name. **SYS006** is the symbolic name of the device to be used. It should be noted that this entry may not be necessary when using some compilers and operating systems. The class entry when defining an indexed sequential file which is to be loaded must be specified as **DA**, which indicates that file must be contained on a direct access device. An indexed sequential file cannot be contained on any device other than a direct access device.

The device entry is specified 2314 because this is the type of device which is to be used in the sample program. This entry would vary depending upon the type of device which is to be used for the file. The organization entry, I, indicates that the file is an indexed sequential file. This entry is required for all indexed sequential files, whether they are being initially loaded or whether the data in an indexed sequential file is being sequentially or randomly processed.

The last entry in the Select Statement is the **NAME** entry. This entry specifies the name which will be used on job control statements to relate the file defined in the COBOL program with the file defined on the job control statements. This entry, under the Disk Operating System, is optional and if it is not specified, the symbolic name should be used in the job control statements. Under other operating systems, however, it is required and it is recommended that it always be used to ensure as much compatibility as possible between different operating systems and computers.

The **ACCESS IS SEQUENTIAL** clause is always used as shown when an indexed sequential file is being created. As noted previously, the Indexed sequential Access Method utilizes keys and indexes as a means of locating records within the file. The **RECORD KEY IS** clause is used to identify the data field within the record on the indexed sequential file which is to be used as the key of the record. Thus, in the sample program, the data-name **PART-NUMB-MSTR** is to be used as the key of each record in the indexed sequential inventory master file. The field to be used as the key can be in any data format desired by the user. Thus, it can be alphabetic, alphanumeric, or numeric. In the sample program, **PART-NUMB-MSTR** is defined as a numeric, Computational-3 field, as illustrated in Figure 3-12.

APPLY CLAUSE

The **APPLY** Clause is specified in the **I-O CONTROL** paragraph of the Input-Output Section within the Environment Division and can be used to specify three options which are used with the loading of an indexed sequential file.

The three options which can be specified are **WRITE-VERIFY**, which indicates that records to be written on a mass storage device are to be checked after they are written to ensure that each record has been written correctly; **CYL-OVERFLOW**, which is used to specify the number of tracks per cylinder in the prime data area which are to be used for the cylinder overflow area, if the default value is not to be used; and **MASTER-INDEX**, which is used to indicate that a master index is to be created for the indexed sequential file being loaded.

If these three options were to be used in the sample program, the coding would be specified as illustrated in Figure 3-14.

```
003020  INPUT-OUTPUT SECTION.
003030  FILE-CONTROL.
003040      SELECT INVMSTR
003050          ASSIGN TO SYS001-DA-2314-I-INVMSTR
003060          ACCESS IS SEQUENTIAL
003070          RECORD KEY IS PART-NUMB-MSTR.
003080  I-O-CONTROL.
003090      APPLY WRITE-VERIFY ON INVMSTR.
003100      APPLY CYL-OVERFLOW OF 8 TRACKS ON INVMSTR.
003110      APPLY MASTER-INDEX TO 2314 ON INVMSTR.
003120  DATA DIVISION.
```

Figure 3-14 Example of APPLY Clauses

As can be seen from the example in Figure 3-14, the **I-O-CONTROL** paragraph must follow the **FILE-CONTROL** paragraph within the **INPUT-OUTPUT SECTION**. Each of the **APPLY** clauses has its own general format notation and this is illustrated in Figure 3-15.

Format Notation

APPLY WRITE-VERIFY ON file-name-1 [file-name-2]. . .

APPLY CYL-OVERFLOW OF integer **TRACKS ON** file-name-1 [file-name-2].... .

APPLY MASTER-INDEX TO device-number **ON** file-name-1 [file-name-2]. . .

Figure 3-15 General Formats of APPLY Clauses for Indexed Sequential Files

In the format for the **WRITE-VERIFY** clause, note that only the filename must be entered. The filename specified is the name of the file on which the verification is to take place. Thus, in Figure 3-14, the file **INVMSTR** will be verified when it is written.

The **CYL-OVERFLOW** entry specifies the number of tracks per cylinder which are to be used for the cylinder overflow area in an indexed sequential file. The "integer" value specifies the number of tracks to be used; for a 2314-type device, the maximum which can be specified is 18. As noted previously, the default value used for a 2314 if this clause is not specified is 4. Any number between 0 and 18 may be specified for integer. The filename entry again specifies the file on which this statement applies. In the example in Figure 3-14, the file **INVMSTR** is to have 8 tracks used for the cylinder overflow area.

The **MASTER-INDEX** entry specifies that a master index is to be used for the file defined with the filename. The device-number entry indicates the type of device to be used. Thus, in the example in Figure 3-14, the **INVMSTR** file is to have a master index on a 2314 device.

It should be noted that the **APPLY** clauses are optional and need not be specified. If the **WRITE-VERIFY** option is not specified, there is no write verification for an output file. If the **CYL-OVERFLOW** option is omitted, then four tracks per cylinder will be used for cylinder overflow on a 2314 device, and if the **MASTER-INDEX** is not used, there will be no master index for the file, only a cylinder and track index. Nor, it should be noted, are all of these clauses required if one of them is specified, that is, the **CYL-OVERFLOW** can be used without the other two clauses being used, and this is true of all the **APPLY** clauses.

DATA DIVISION

As with all other data files which are defined in COBOL, the indexed sequential file must be defined in the File Section of the Data Division as well as in the Environment Division. The definition of the file and a portion of the record to be stored in the file is illustrated in Figure 3-16.

```
005020   DATA DIVISION.
005030   FILE SECTION.
005040   FD  INVMSTR
005050       BLOCK CONTAINS 54 RECORDS
005060       RECORD CONTAINS 64 CHARACTERS
005070       LABEL RECORDS ARE STANDARD
005080       DATA RECORD IS MSTR-IO.
005090   01  MSTR-IO.
005100       03  PART-NUMB-MSTR        PICTURE 9(13)
005110                                 USAGE COMPUTATIONAL-3.
005120       03  NAME-MSTR             PICTURE X(25).
```

Figure 3-16 Data Division Entries For Indexed Sequential File

Note in Figure 3-16 that the File Section entries for an indexed sequential file do not differ from the definitions of other blocked files defined in Chapter 1 and Chapter 2. Each block will contain 54 records and each record will contain 64 characters. Thus, the block will contain 3456 bytes. It should also be noted that standard labels will be used for the file (**LABEL RECORDS ARE STANDARD**). All indexed sequential files must use standard labels.

The field which is used for the Record Key, **PART-NUMB-MSTR,**is also contained in Figure 3-16. It is a numeric field which is to be stored in the Computational-3 format. Each record in the file will be identifiable by the value contained in this field.

SEQUENTIAL DISK INPUT FILES

As noted previously, the input to the sample program is the sequential disk file created in the program in Chapter 2. This input file must be defined in both the Environment Division and the Data Division. The entries to define the file are shown in Figure 3-17.

```
003020        SELECT TRANSIN
003030          ASSIGN TO SYS004-UT-2314-S-TRANSIN.

004150   FD  TRANSIN
004160        BLOCK CONTAINS 44 RECORDS
004170        RECORD CONTAINS 80 CHARACTERS
004180        LABEL RECORDS ARE STANDARD
004190        DATA RECORD IS TRANS-IO.
```

Figure 3-17 Environment Division and Data Division Entries for Sequential Disk Input File

Note that the entries in the Environment and Data Divisions are identical to the entries for the sequential disk output file in Chapter 2. The only difference is the name of the disk I/O area. The determination of the use of the file, that is, whether the file is to be an input file or an output file, is made by the **OPEN** statement.

OPEN STATEMENT

The **OPEN** statement must be issued for both the sequential disk input file and the indexed sequential output file before any other processing is done with the files. The **OPEN** statement used in the sample program is illustrated in Figure 3-18.

EXAMPLE

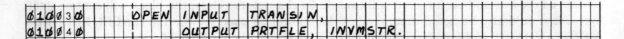

Figure 3-18 OPEN Statement for Disk Input File and Indexed Sequential Output File

Note in the example above that the sequential disk input file is opened as an input file and the indexed sequential file which is to be loaded is opened as an output file. The filename **PRTFLE** is for the exception report file. The **OPEN** statement checks the standard labels for the indexed sequential file and ensures that the indexes are readied to allow the file to be loaded.

In order to read the sequential disk input file, the **READ** statement is used in the same manner as card and tape files. The **AT END** processing is entered when the end-of-file marker on the disk is found. After the **READ** statement, the fields in the input record are moved to the fields in the output record, that is, the record which will be written on the Indexed Sequential Master file (see Figure 3-21).

WRITE STATEMENT

In order to write the records on the new indexed sequential file, the **WRITE** statement is used. The **WRITE** statement used in the sample program is illustrated in Figure 3-19.

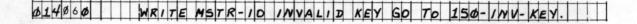

Figure 3-19 WRITE Statement To Load An Indexed Sequential File

The record-name following the **WRITE** statement is the name of the disk output I/O area defined in the File Section of the Data Division. This is the same as the **WRITE** statements used for other types of files. The **INVALID KEY** clause is a clause which is used with Indexed Sequential files to indicate the action to be taken when an abnormal situation occurs when the file is being loaded or retrieved. When the file is being loaded, the **INVALID KEY** routine (as specified by the statement **GO TO 150-INV-KEY**) is executed when a duplicate record is attempted to be loaded or when the key in the record to be loaded is out of sequence.

Previously it was mentioned that the records being loaded must be in an ascending sequence by key, that is, the key of each record being loaded must be higher than the key of the previous record loaded. This requirement is made because the indexes are based on the fact that each key is higher than the previous key. Thus, when a key in a record is out of sequence, it cannot be loaded on the file and the **INVALID KEY** routine will be executed.

In the sample program, as shown in Figure 3-19, when an invalid key status is found, the **150-INV-KEY** routine will be entered. This routine is shown below.

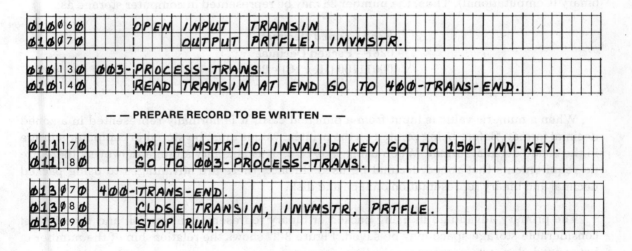

```
Ø14Ø8Ø    150-INV-KEY.
Ø14Ø9Ø        MOVE TRANS-IO TO RECORD-PRINT.
Ø141ØØ        MOVE 'OUT OF SEQ. OR DUPLICATE RECORD' TO MSG-PRINT.
Ø1411Ø        PERFORM 2ØØ-WRITE-PRT THRU 2ØØ-EXIT.
Ø1412Ø        ADD 1 TO BAD-RECS.
Ø1413Ø        GO TO ØØ3-PROCESS-TRANS.
```

Figure 3-20 Invalid Key Routine

The Invalid Key routine shown above moves the input record and an error message to the printer I/O area and then performs the **200-WRITE-PRT** routine to write the error message on the printer. It then adds 1 to the invalid records counter which is printed at the end of the program, and branches back to read the next input record. Note that the invalid record will not be written on the new indexed sequential file because when the invalid key routine is entered, no data transfer to the disk has taken place.

The following example illustrates the basic steps to be used when loading an indexed sequential file from sorted sequential input.

```
Ø1ØØ6Ø        OPEN INPUT TRANSIN
Ø1ØØ7Ø             OUTPUT PRTFLE, INVMSTR.

Ø1Ø13Ø    ØØ3-PROCESS-TRANS.
Ø1Ø14Ø        READ TRANSIN AT END GO TO 4ØØ-TRANS-END.

          — — PREPARE RECORD TO BE WRITTEN — —

Ø1117Ø        WRITE MSTR-IO INVALID KEY GO TO 15Ø-INV-KEY.
Ø1118Ø        GO TO ØØ3-PROCESS-TRANS.

Ø13Ø7Ø    4ØØ-TRANS-END.
Ø13Ø8Ø        CLOSE TRANSIN, INVMSTR, PRTFLE.
Ø13Ø9Ø        STOP RUN.
```

Figure 3-21 Routine To Load An Indexed Sequential File

Note in the routine shown above that the file to be loaded (**INVMSTR**) must be opened before any other processing is performed on it. The sorted sequential file must then be read and the fields in the input record moved to the fields in the output record. The new record is then written on the indexed sequential file. After all processing has been completed, the files must be closed as shown.

SUMMARY
LOAD INDEXED SEQUENTIAL FILE

The following entries are required in the Environment Division for loading an indexed sequential file:

- **ORGANIZATION SPECIFIED AS "I"** (indexed)
- **ACCESS IS SEQUENTIAL**
- **DEVICE SPECIFIED AS "DA"** (Direct-Access)
- **RECORD KEY IS** data-name

The following statements must be included in the Procedure Division.

- **OPEN OUTPUT** file-name
- **WRITE** record-name **[INVALID KEY]**
- **CLOSE** file-name

NUMERIC REPRESENTATION

As has been previously shown, numeric values on most computers can be represented in three different formats: zoned decimal (Display), packed decimal (Computational-3), and binary (Computational). Thus, the number 28 may be represented in computer storage as:

> **F2F8 - Zoned Decimal**
> **028F - Packed Decimal**
> **00011100 (Hex 1C) - Binary**

When a numeric value is input from a punched card, it is normally represented in a zoned decimal format. Before being printed on the printer, values must be stored in computer storage in the zoned decimal format. When using tape or disk as auxiliary storage, however, there are no requirements that zoned decimal be used. In fact, there are advantages to using packed decimal and binary representation on tape and disk.

The primary advantage in using packed or binary representation on disk and tape is that considerable storage space may be saved. Figure 3-22 shows the relationship of the number of bytes needed to store numbers in the three formats.

Numerical Value	ZONED DEC		PACKED DEC		BINARY		
	Rep	Bytes	Rep	Bytes	Rep	Hex	Bytes
9	F9	1	9F	1	0000 1001	09	1
99	F9 | F9	2	09 | 9F	2	0110 0011	63	1
999	F9 | F9 | F9	3	99 | 9F	2	0000 0011 | 1110 0111	03 | E7	2
9999	F9 | F9 | F9 | F9	4	09 | 99 | 9F	3	0010 0111 | 0000 1111	27 | 0F	2
99999	F9 | F9 | F9 | F9 | F9	5	99 | 99 | 9F	3	0000 0001 | 1000 0110 | 1001 1111	01 | 86 | 9F	3
999999	F9 | F9 | F9 | F9 | F9 | F9	6	09 | 99 | 99 | 9F	4	0000 1111 | 0100 0010 | 0011 1111	0F | 42 | 3F	3
9999999	F9 | F9 | F9 | F9 | F9 | F9 | F9	7	99 | 99 | 99 | 9F	4	1001 1000 | 1001 0110 | 0111 1111	98 | 96 | 7F	3

Figure 3-22 Required Storage For Zoned-Decimal, Packed and Binary Formats

Note from the chart in Figure 3-22 that a 7 digit number (9999999) requires 7 bytes when stored in the zoned-decimal format, 4 bytes when stored in the packed-decimal format, and only 3 bytes when stored in a binary format.

As can be seen from the table, binary representation takes less space to store data than either packed decimal or zoned decimal and packed decimal takes less than zoned decimal. The COBOL programmer must decide which data formats to use on disk and tape files. To do this requires an understanding of the binary data format and the use of the Computational format in COBOL programs.

COMPUTATIONAL FORMAT

Binary data is normally represented in a fixed-length format consisting of a one bit sign followed by a series of bits to represent the numeric values. The three commonly used lengths on the IBM System/360 and System/370 are a **HALFWORD**, a **FULLWORD**, and a **DOUBLEWORD**. A halfword consists of 2 bytes (16 bits), a fullword is 4 bytes long (32 bits), and a doubleword contains 8 bytes (64 bits). In some machines, however, binary data is usually stored in the same size field, usually a ''word'', or 32 bits.

COBOL determines which of the formats will be used to contain a binary value by the size of the number to be represented. It should be noted that the largest positive value which can be contained in a halfword is 32767. When determining which format to use, however, the COBOL compiler has no way of knowing the actual value which will be contained in a field. Thus, it must allow for the maximum value in any field and the maximum value in a five digit field is 99,999, which cannot be contained in a halfword. Thus, the most digits which can be contained in a halfword is 4 digits, with a maximum value of 9,999. Therefore, when a field has a **USAGE IS COMPUTATIONAL** clause, a halfword will be reserved by the COBOL compiler if the picture is specified as **PICTURES9, PICTURES99, PICTURES999, or PICTURES9999.**

Similarly, a fullword can contain the positive value 2,147,483,647, which consists of 10 digits. Since the highest value in the 10 digit field is 9,999,999,999, only a 9 digit field can be contained in a fullword. Thus, the COBOL compiler reserves a fullword when the picture is **PICTURE S9(5)** to **PICTURE S9(9).** A doubleword area is reserved for a **PICTURE S9(10)** to **PICTURE S9(18)** field. This is summarized below.

PICTURE	STORAGE RESERVED
S9 to S9(4)	Halfword
S9(5) to S9(9)	Fullword
S9(10) to S9(18)	Doubleword

Figure 3-23 Computer Storage for Computational Fields

ALIGNMENT

The internal structure of the IBM System/360 and System/370, as well as some other machines, dictates that halfwords, fullwords, and doublewords which are to be used for binary values must be on **BOUNDARIES** if the values in the fields are to be used in any computation operation. A boundary is an address which satisfies a necessary condition. For example, a halfword boundary is any address which has, as its low-order hexadecimal value a 0, 2, 4, 6, 8, A, C, or E, that is, a hexadecimal address which is divisible by 2. Any address which has one of these digits as the low-order value is considered to be on a halfword boundary. Note that the increment for halfword boundaries is 2, which is the size of a halfword field. A fullword boundary is any address in main storage which has as its low-order hexadecimal value a 0, 4, 8, or C, that is, a hexadecimal address which is divisible by 4. Note also that for a fullword, the increment is 4, which is the size of a fullword. A doubleword boundary is any address which ends in the digit 0 or 8.

When the COBOL compiler finds numeric fields defined by a **USAGE IS COMPUTATIONAL** clause, it reserves the amount of storage as shown in Figure 3-23. It does not, however, automatically align the fields upon the proper boundary. In order to have a Computational field properly aligned on a boundary, the **SYNCHRONIZED** clause must be used in the data field definition. An example of the **SYNCHRONIZED** clause is illustrated in Figure 3-24.

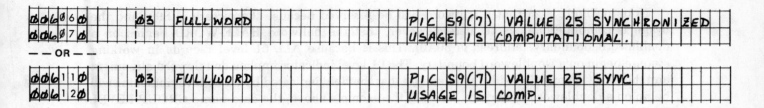

| 0 0 0 0 6 0 | | | 0 3 | FULLWORD | | | | | | | | PIC S9(7) VALUE 25 SYNCHRONIZED |
| 0 0 0 0 7 0 | | | | | | | | | | | | USAGE IS COMPUTATIONAL. |

— — OR — —

| 0 0 0 1 1 0 | | | 0 3 | FULLWORD | | | | | | | | PIC S9(7) VALUE 25 SYNC |
| 0 0 0 1 2 0 | | | | | | | | | | | | USAGE IS COMP. |

Figure 3-24 Example of Synchronized Clause

In the example above, the field **FULLWORD** is defined as a numeric field containing seven digits and is given an initial value of 25. It is specified as a Computational field and the **SYNCHRONIZED** clause is specified, which will cause the field to be four bytes in length (see Figure 3-23) and be on a full-word boundary. Note that the **SYNCHRONIZED** clause can be abbreviated **SYNC** and the Computational designation can be abbreviated **COMP**. In most cases, these abbreviations can be used with no loss of clarity in the program source listing.

As noted, when the **SYNCHRONIZED** clause is used, the field will be aligned on a halfword, fullword, or doubleword boundary, depending upon the size of the field. When alignment takes place, the compiler will take certain action depending upon the size of the field being defined and the status of the fields defined before the aligned field in the program. The actions of the compiler when dealing with aligned **COMP** fields is illustrated in the following examples.

Example 1: A halfword is to be defined in working storage. It is to be an elementary field. The field is defined as below.

0 0 0 0 3 0	0 1	GROUP-LEVEL.										
0 0 0 0 4 0			0 3	HALF-WORD								PIC S99 VALUE 25 SYNC
0 0 0 0 5 0												USAGE IS COMP.

Main Storage

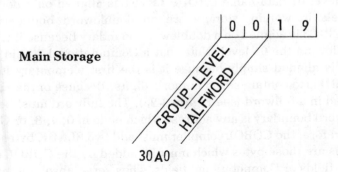

Figure 3-25 Halfword Defined in Working Storage

Note in Figure 3-25 that a halfword will be reserved because the picture is S99, and the usage is computational. Note also, however, that the halfword **HALF-WORD** begins on a doubleword boundary (address is 30A0). This is because **ALL** 01 level records in working storage begin on a Doubleword boundary. The 01 level indicator implies doubleword alignment and the COBOL compiler will always ensure that the field indicated by an 01 level indicator will begin on a doubleword boundary. Thus, in the example above, the data-name **GROUP-LEVEL** is aligned on a doubleword boundary. Since a doubleword boundary is also a halfword boundary, the halfword **HALF-WORD** is properly aligned and would appear as illustrated in Figure 3-25.

Example 2: A Computational-3 field is to be defined within an 01 group indicator and a fullword is to be defined following the Computational-3 field. The fields are defined as shown below.

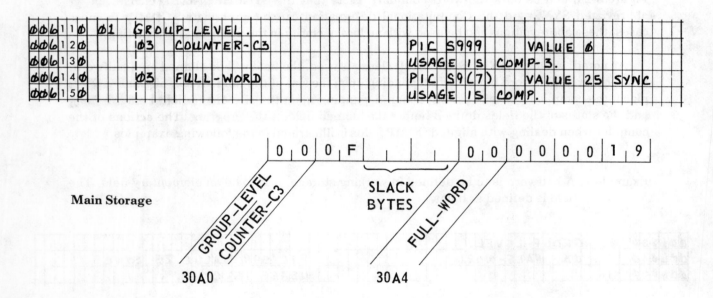

Figure 3-26 Computational-3 Field and Computational Field

In the example above, the level 01 data-name **GROUP-LEVEL** is aligned on a doubleword boundary because all 01 levels in working-storage are on doubleword boundaries. The Computational-3 field **COUNTER-C3** is aligned on a doubleword boundary because it is the first elementary level data-name following the 01 level. Note that a Computational-3 field requires no boundary alignment and it is aligned simply because it is the first elementary item. The Computational field **FULL-WORD** is to contain seven numeric digits. Because of the size of the field, the data must be contained in a fullword (see Figure 3-23). The fullword must be aligned on a fullword boundary. A fullword boundary is any address which ends in 0, 4, 8, or C, that is, any address divisible by 4. Therefore, the COBOL compiler must add two **SLACK** bytes in order to align the fullword. Slack bytes are those bytes which must be added by the COBOL compiler in order to align either 01 level fields or Computational fields. They serve absolutely no useful purpose other than to align fields. They cannot be referenced by the COBOL program and data cannot be stored in them by the COBOL program. Therefore, it is very desirable that slack bytes be kept to a minimum in a program because they waste storage within the program.

A better way to define the two fields in Example 2 is shown in the following example.

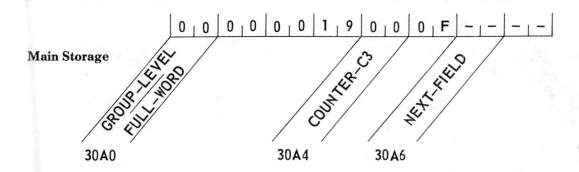

```
006050  01   GROUP-LEVEL.
006060       03   FULL-WORD                    PIC S9(7)      VALUE 25 SYNC
006070                                         USAGE IS COMP.
006080       03   COUNTER-C3                   PIC S999       VALUE 0
006090                                         USAGE IS COMP-3.
```

Main Storage

0 0 0 0 0 0 1 9 0 0 0 F – – – –

GROUP-LEVEL
FULL-WORD

COUNTER-C3

NEXT-FIELD

30A0   30A4   30A6

Figure 3-27 Computational Field and Computational-3 Field

Note in the example in Figure 3-27 that the Computational field **FULL-WORD** is defined immediately after the level 01 group field. Thus, since the level 01 field is on a doubleword boundary, the fullword reserved for the data in **FULL-WORD** will be on a fullword boundary. The Computational-3 field **COUNTER-C3** is defined after the Computational field and since it requires no boundary alignment, no slack bytes are inserted by the COBOL compiler. Thus, by defining the Computational field before the Computational-3 field, two bytes were saved in the Data Division.

Example 3: A fullword and a doubleword are to be defined within an 01 group indicator. The fields are defined as shown below.

007030	01	GROUP-LEVEL.							
007040		03	FULL-WORD			PIC S9(5)	VALUE 30 SYNC	
007050						USAGE IS Comp.		
007060		03	DOUBLE-WORD			PIC S9(12)	VALUE 100 SYNC	
007070						USAGE IS Comp.		

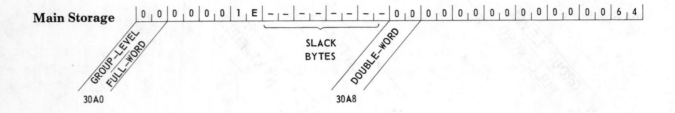

Main Storage

Figure 3-28 Fullword and Doubleword Areas

Note in Figure 3-28 that the fullword area **FULL-WORD** is located in the same positions as the group level field **GROUP-LEVEL** because the 01 level indicator is on a doubleword boundary and a doubleword boundary is always a fullword boundary. The doubleword **DOUBLE-WORD**, however, must also be on a doubleword boundary. Thus, four slack bytes must be inserted following the fullword in order to align **DOUBLE-WORD** on a doubleword boundary. These four slack bytes serve no useful purpose and, if possible, should be eliminated.

The following example illustrates another way to define the two fields which eliminates any slack bytes.

0	0	7	0	3	0		0	1			G	R	O	U	P	-	L	E	V	E	L	.																													
0	0	7	0	4	0						0	3			D	O	U	B	L	E	-	W	O	R	D										P	I	C		S	9	(|1|2|)			V	A	L	U	E		1	0	0		S	Y	N	C
0	0	7	0	5	0																												U	S	A	G	E		I	S		C	O	M	P	.											
0	0	7	0	6	0						0	3			F	U	L	L	-	W	O	R	D												P	I	C		S	9	(|5|)			V	A	L	U	E		3	0		S	Y	N	C
0	0	7	0	7	0																												U	S	A	G	E		I	S		C	O	M	P	.											

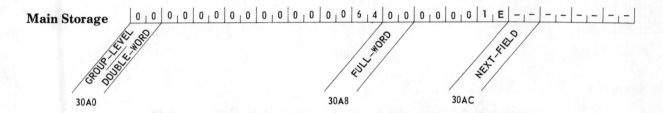

Main Storage 0 0 0 0 0 0 0 0 0 0 0 0 0 0 6 4 0 0 0 0 0 0 0 1 E - - - - - - - -

GROUP-LEVEL / DOUBLE-WORD   FULL-WORD   NEXT-FIELD

30A0   30A8   30AC

Figure 3-29 Doubleword and Fullword Areas

In the example in Figure 3-29, the slack bytes are eliminated because the doubleword area **DOUBLE-WORD** is defined before the fullword area **FULL-WORD**. This definition takes advantage of the fact that all 01 level indicators are aligned on a doubleword boundary in Working-Storage. Thus, the boundary determined for **GROUP-LEVEL** will also work for the doubleword **DOUBLEWORD** and no additional computer storage is required. After the doubleword, which requires eight bytes of computer storage, the fullword will follow properly aligned on a fullword boundary as shown.

As can be seen from the previous examples, binary fields must be given special consideration because of the alignment requirements. When designing a record which will be stored on auxiliary storage (i.e. tape or direct-access devices), slack bytes in binary fields should be eliminated if at all possible because the COBOL compiler will always insert them if necessary. Thus, records could be written on the disk or on tape with slack bytes included in the record. This, obviously, is a waste of auxiliary storage space.

If records cannot be designed in such a way as to eliminate slack bytes, it may be preferable to define the Computational fields within the record without the Synchronization clause. In this manner, the proper number of digits for the fields are reserved, but no boundary alignment takes place. When one of the fields in the record is to be used in computations, it can be moved to a computational field which is defined in Working-Storage with the Synchronization clause. In this manner, the computational fields within the record to be stored on auxiliary storage will not generate slack bytes, and the compiler will not have to manipulate the data prior to performing the computations, as it would if the data was not moved to the synchronized, or aligned, field in Working-Storage.

SIGN CONTROL

Binary numbers are always considered signed numbers. A positive number is represented by its true binary value and a negative number is represented in its two's complement form. A **COMPLEMENT NUMBER** is defined as that quantity which, when added to a number, would result in a zero answer and a "carry out" of the high-order position. For example, when the quantity 367 is added to 633, the answer is 000 with a carry out in the high-order position. This is illustrated in Figure 3-30.

$$
\begin{array}{r}
633 \\
+\ \ 367 \\
\hline
\text{"1" } 000
\end{array}
$$

Figure 3-30 Addition with a Carry Out in the High-Order Position

Thus, 367 is said to be the **COMPLEMENT** of 633. Notice that the example given is in the decimal number system. Thus, the complement number is called the "tens" complement because the decimal number system has a base 10. Every number in the decimal number system except zero has a "tens" complement. For example, the "tens" complement of 99 is 1.

Regardless of the numbering system, Complement Numbers can be found. Thus, in the binary numbering system, "twos" complement numbers can be found. The following example illustrates the technique for determining the "twos" complement of the binary number 10010010.

EXAMPLE

STEP 1: Subtract the number from all 1's (the highest digit value in the numbering system).

$$
\begin{array}{r}
11111111 \\
-\ 10010010 \\
\hline
01101101
\end{array}
$$

Figure 3-31 Subtraction of Number From Highest Value in Number Base

STEP 2: Add 1 to the low-order position of the result of the subtraction.

$$
\begin{array}{r}
01101101 \\
+\ \quad\quad\quad 1 \\
\hline
01101110 = \text{"Two's" complement of 10010010}
\end{array}
$$

Figure 3-32 Addition of 1 To Get Two's Complement

In order to check the result, the number (10010010) and its "two's" complement (01101110) can be added to verify that the definition of a complement number is satisfied.

$$
\begin{array}{r}
10010010 \\
+\ \underline{01101110} \\
\text{``1''}\ 00000000
\end{array}
$$

Figure 3-33 Verification of "Two's" Complement

As can be seen the answer is zero with a carry out in the high-order position.

The method shown above of subtracting the number from the highest digit in the numbering system and then adding one to obtain the complement number can be used for a number in any number base. Another method exists, however, to obtain the complement number of a number in the binary numbering system. This involves the "inverting" of the values in the binary number and then adding one and is illustrated in the example in Figure 3-34 and Figure 3-35.

EXAMPLE

STEP 1: "Invert" or switch binary digit.

10010010
↓↓↓↓↓↓↓↓ **Invert numbers**
01101101 - Note that each binary digit has been switched from 0 to 1 or from 1 to 0.

Figure 3-34 Inverting Binary Number

STEP 2: Add 1 to the result.

$$
\begin{array}{r}
01101101 \\
+\ \underline{\hspace{1.5em}1} \\
01101110 = \text{``Two's'' complement of } 10010010
\end{array}
$$

Figure 3-35 Addition of 1 To Get Two's Complement

Note that the answer obtained is the same as in the previous example.

As was mentioned, a positive binary number is represented in its true form while a negative number is represented in its complement form, and binary numbers are stored in halfwords, fullwords, or doublewords. Thus, the number + 100 represented in a halfword appears as follows:

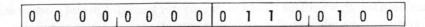

Figure 3-36 Decimal + 100 in Binary Form in a Halfword

Whenever halfwords, fullwords or doublewords contain data to be used in arithmetic operations, the high-order bit (bit 0) contains the "sign" of the number. Positive numbers contain a 0 in the sign bit position and negative numbers contain a 1 in the sign bit position.

POSITIVE binary numbers are represented in their TRUE form while NEGATIVE numbers are represented in their COMPLEMENT form. Thus, the number - 100 would be represented by its complement form as shown in Figure 3-37.

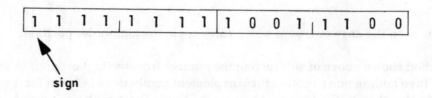

Figure 3-37 Decimal - 100 in Binary Form in a Halfword

Note that the high-order bit (bit 0) is a 1. This indicates that the number is negative, that is, it is represented in its complement form. Thus, the high-order bit is not truly a sign but rather an indication that the number is in true form (bit 0 = 0) or in complement form (bit 0 = 1).

It should be noted that the sign and the proper representation of the number in a binary format will take place whether the Synchronization clause is used or not, that is, it does not matter that the Computational field is not on a boundary in order for the data to be properly represented. It is necessary, however, that the high-order byte in the field remain with the field so that the field is properly signed whenever any computations are to be performed. Thus, one must be careful when manipulating binary fields to be sure that this high-order byte is not lost through the use of the Redefines clause or through some other error.

RECORD FORMATS

When determining the format of numeric fields to be used in a master record to be stored on auxiliary storage, the space required for the master record to be stored is only one consideration. The programmer must also consider the time that it takes to process the fields in the master when it is created, updated, or otherwise processed. He must also consider the computer storage required in the program being written to process the fields. As was noted previously, most arithmetic statements generated by the COBOL compiler expect the data to be operated upon to be in Computational-3 format. If it is not, the compiler ensures that it is by packing it before performing the arithmetic. The only exception to this is when both fields are in a binary format, which occurs only after both fields have been converted to binary.

In addition to the conversion instructions necessary for arithmetic operations, instructions must also be generated to transform the zoned-decimal numeric data, which is read from cards, into the binary data which would be stored in the master record. Special work areas may also be necessary. Because of the additional storage and execution time which is required to operate on numeric data stored in binary format, it was decided that the numeric fields in the inventory master record which is being developed in the sample program in the inventory system will be in packed-decimal format (Computational-3).

SAMPLE PROGRAM

The sample program in this chapter loads the indexed sequential master file from sorted sequential transactions.

The input file record layout is illustrated below.

FIELD	FIELD NAME	PICTURE	POSITION	NO OF DIGITS	LENGTH
Part Number	PART-NUMB				
Division Number	DIV	XX	1-2	2	2
Prime Number	PRIME	X(6)	3-8	6	6
Dash Number	DASH	X(5)	9-13	5	5
Description	NAME	X(25)	14-38	25	25
Qty on Hand	QTY-ON-HAND	X(7)	39-45	7	7
Qty on Order	QTY-ON-ORDER	X(7)	46-52	7	7
Qty Reserved	QTY-RESERVED	X(7)	53-59	7	7
Part Number-NA	NEXT-ASSEMBLY				
Division-NA	DIV-NA	XX	60-61	2	2
Prime-NA	PRIME-NA	X(6)	62-67	6	6
Dash-NA	DASH-NA	X(5)	68-72	5	5
Type	TYPE	X	73	1	1
Source	SOURCE	X	74	1	1
Unit Price	UNIT-PRICE	X(6)	75-80	6	6

The output record format is illustrated below.

FIELD	FIELD NAME	PICTURE	POSITION	NO OF DIGITS	LENGTH
Part Number	PART-NUMB-MSTR	Picture 9(13) Comp-3	1-7	13	7
Description	NAME-MSTR	Picture X(25)	8-32	25	25
Quantity on Hand	QTY-ON-HAND-MSTR	Picture S9(7) Comp-3	33-36	7	4
Quantity on Order	QTY-ON-ORDER-MSTR	Picture S9(7) Comp-3	37-40	7	4
Quantity Reserved	QTY-RESERVED-MSTR	Picture S9(7) Comp-3	41-44	7	4
Next Assembly Number	NEXT-ASSEMBLY-MSTR	Picture S9(13) Comp-3	45-51	13	7
Type	TYPE-MSTR	Picture X	52	1	1
Source	SOURCE-MSTR	Picture X	53	1	1
Unit Price	UNIT-PRICE-MSTR	Picture S9(7) Comp-3	54-57	6	4
Filler	FILLER	Picture X(7)	58-64	7	7

In the master record, the type field is used to indicate whether a record is an active record (type = 1) or a deleted record (type = 2).

A report is created in the program which lists all transactions which are in error. The format of the report is shown below.

PRINTER SPACING CHART

PROGRAM

The following is the listing of the program used to load the indexed sequential inventory master file. Important points to note include the following:

1. It is specified that the inventory master record contains 64 characters (line 55). Note that although the **PICTURE** entries (lines 59-74) total 80 digits, the numeric fields in the record are in Computational-3 format. Thus, the Record Contains Clause does not equal the total characters specified in the Picture clause. For example, on line 59 the 03 level entry specifies that the field **PART-NUMB-MSTR** has 13 digits, Picture 9(13), and is stored in the Computational-3 format. Thus, this entry reserves only seven bytes of storage because the 13 digits can be stored in 7 bytes when they are in a packed-decimal format.

2. Line 101 contains the 01 **WORKING-AREA**, and following it, the entries for the heading on the report and the total count at the end of the report. These fields are defined as level 03 entries, not level 01 entries. If the fields were defined as level 01 entries, each of them would require slack bytes to be aligned on a doubleword boundary and this is unnecessary.

3. All records used to load the indexed sequential file from the sequential input file should contain a code 8 in the **TYPE** field which represents a **LOAD**-type record. On the newly created master record, a "1" is moved to the **TYPE** field to indicate an active record (see line 162).

```
00001    001010 IDENTIFICATION DIVISION.                                       LOADISEQ
00002    001020 PROGRAM-ID.      LOADIS.                                       LOADISEQ
00003    001030 AUTHOR.          SHELLY.                                       LOADISEQ
00004    001040 INSTALLATION.    LONG BEACH.                                   LOADISEQ
00005    001050 DATE-WRITTEN.    07/11/74.                                     LOADISEQ
00006    001060 DATE-COMPILED.   09/12/74                                      LOADISEQ
00007    001070 SECURITY.        UNCLASSIFIED.                                 LOADISEQ
00008    001080 REMARKS.         THIS PROGRAM CREATES AN INDEXED SEQUENTIAL    LOADISEQ
00009    001090                  MASTER FILE FROM SORTED SEQUENTIAL LOAD       LOADISEQ
00010    001100                  RECORDS.                                      LOADISEQ
00011    001110                                                                LOADISEQ
00012    001120                                                                LOADISEQ
00013    001130 ENVIRONMENT DIVISION.                                          LOADISEQ
00014    001140 CONFIGURATION SECTION.                                         LOADISEQ
00015    001150 SOURCE-COMPUTER.    IBM-360-F30.                               LOADISEQ
00016    001160 OBJECT-COMPUTER.    IBM-360-F30.                               LOADISEQ
00017    001170 SPECIAL-NAMES.                                                 LOADISEQ
00018    001180     C01 IS TO-TOP-OF-PAGE.                                     LOADISEQ
00019    001190                                                                LOADISEQ
00020    001200 INPUT-OUTPUT SECTION.                                          LOADISEQ
00021    002010 FILE-CONTROL.                                                  LOADISEQ
00022    002020     SELECT TRANSIN                                             LOADISEQ
00023    002030         ASSIGN TO SYS004-UT-2314-S-TRANSIN.                    LOADISEQ
00024    002040     SELECT PRTFLE                                              LOADISEQ
00025    002050         ASSIGN TO SYS005-UR-1403-S.                            LOADISEQ
00026    002060     SELECT INVMSTR                                             LOADISEQ
00027    002070         ASSIGN TO SYS006-DA-2314-I-INVMSTR                     LOADISEQ
00028    002080         ACCESS IS SEQUENTIAL                                   LOADISEQ
00029    002090         RECORD KEY IS PART-NUMB-MSTR.                          LOADISEQ
00030    002100                                                                LOADISEQ
00031    002110                                                                LOADISEQ
00032    002120                                                                LOADISEQ
00033    002130 DATA DIVISION.                                                 LOADISEQ
00034    002140                                                                LOADISEQ
00035    002150 FILE SECTION.                                                  LOADISEQ
00036    002160                                                                LOADISEQ
00037    002170 FD  TRANSIN                                                    LOADISEQ
00038    002180     BLOCK CONTAINS 44 RECORDS                                  LOADISEQ
00039    002190     RECORD CONTAINS 80 CHARACTERS                             LOADISEQ
00040    002200     LABEL RECORDS ARE STANDARD                                 LOADISEQ
00041    003010     DATA RECORD IS TRANS-IO.                                   LOADISEQ
00042    003020 01  TRANS-IO.                                                  LOADISEQ
00043    003030     03  PART-NUMB-TRANS      PICTURE 9(13).                    LOADISEQ
00044    003040     03  NAME-TRANS           PICTURE X(25).                    LOADISEQ
00045    003050     03  QTY-UN-HAND-TRANS    PICTURE S9(7).                    LOADISEQ
00046    003060     03  QTY-ON-ORDER-TRANS   PICTURE S9(7).                    LOADISEQ
00047    003070     03  QTY-RESERVED-TRANS   PICTURE S9(7).                    LOADISEQ
00048    003080     03  NEXT-ASSEMBLY-TRANS  PICTURE S9(13).                   LOADISEQ
00049    003090     03  TYPE-TRANS           PICTURE X.                        LOADISEQ
00050    003100     03  SOURCE-TRANS         PICTURE X.                        LOADISEQ
00051    003110     03  UNIT-PRICE-TRANS     PICTURE S9(6).                    LOADISEQ
00052    003120                                                                LOADISEQ
00053    003130 FD  INVMSTR                                                    LOADISEQ
00054    003140     BLOCK CONTAINS 54 RECORDS                                  LOADISEQ
00055    003150     RECORD CONTAINS 64 CHARACTERS                             LOADISEQ
00056    003160     LABEL RECORDS ARE STANDARD                                 LOADISEQ
00057    003170     DATA RECORD IS MSTR-IO.                                    LOADISEQ
00058    003180 01  MSTR-IO.                                                   LOADISEQ
00059    003190     03  PART-NUMB-MSTR       PICTURE 9(13)                     LOADISEQ
00060    003200                              USAGE COMPUTATIONAL-3.            LOADISEQ
00061    004010     03  NAME-MSTR            PICTURE X(25).                    LOADISEQ
00062    004020     03  QTY-ON-HAND-MSTR     PICTURE S9(7)                     LOADISEQ
00063    004030                              USAGE COMPUTATIONAL-3.            LOADISEQ
00064    004040     03  QTY-ON-ORDER-MSTR    PICTURE S9(7)                     LOADISEQ
00065    004050                              USAGE COMPUTATIONAL-3.            LOADISEQ
00066    004060     03  QTY-RESERVED-MSTR    PICTURE S9(7)                     LOADISEQ
00067    004070                              USAGE COMPUTATIONAL-3.            LOADISEQ
00068    004080     03  NEXT-ASSEMBLY-MSTR   PICTURE S9(13)                    LOADISEQ
00069    004090                              USAGE COMPUTATIONAL-3.            LOADISEQ
00070    004100     03  TYPE-MSTR            PICTURE X.                        LOADISEQ
00071    004110     03  SOURCE-MSTR          PICTURE X.                        LOADISEQ
00072    004120     03  UNIT-PRICE-MSTR      PICTURE S9(7)                     LOADISEQ
00073    004130                              USAGE COMPUTATIONAL-3.            LOADISEQ
00074    004140     03  FILLER               PICTURE X(7).                     LOADISEQ
00075    004150                                                                LOADISEQ
00076    004160 FD  PRTFLE                                                     LOADISEQ
00077    004170     RECORD CONTAINS 121 CHARACTERS                            LOADISEQ
00078    004180     LABEL RECORDS ARE OMITTED                                  LOADISEQ
00079    004190     DATA RECORD IS PRINT-IOA.                                  LOADISEQ
00080    004200 01  PRINT-IOA.                                                 LOADISEQ
00081    005010     03  FILLER               PICTURE X.                        LOADISEQ
00082    005020     03  PRINT-IO.                                              LOADISEQ
00083    005030         05  RECORD-PRINT     PICTURE X(80).                    LOADISEQ
00084    005040         05  FILLER           PICTURE XX.                       LOADISEQ
00085    005050         05  MSG-PRINT        PICTURE X(38).                    LOADISEQ
00086    005060                                                                LOADISEQ
00087    005070                                                                LOADISEQ
```

```
       2
00088    005080 WORKING-STORAGE SECTION.                                               LOADISEQ
00089    005090 77  PG-CNT                 PICTURE S9(3)       VALUE ZERO              LOADISEQ
00090    005100                            USAGE COMPUTATIONAL-3.                      LOADISEQ
00091    005110 77  GOOD-RECS              PICTURE S9(5)       VALUE ZERO              LOADISEQ
00092    005120                            USAGE COMPUTATIONAL-3.                      LOADISEQ
00093    005130 77  BAD-RECS               PICTURE S9(5)       VALUE ZERO              LOADISEQ
00094    005140                            USAGE COMPUTATIONAL-3.                      LOADISEQ
00095    005150 77  VARIABLE               PICTURE 9.                                  LOADISEQ
00096    005160 77  SINGLE-SPACING         PICTURE 9           VALUE 1.                LOADISEQ
00097    005170 77  DOUBLE-SPACING         PICTURE 9           VALUE 2.                LOADISEQ
00098    005180 77  LINE-COUNT             PICTURE S999                                LOADISEQ
00099    005190                            USAGE COMPUTATIONAL-3.                      LOADISEQ
00100    005200                                                                        LOADISEQ
00101    006010 01  WORKING-AREA.                                                      LOADISEQ
00102    006020     03  HEADER1.                                                       LOADISEQ
00103    006030         05  FILLER         PICTURE X(80)       VALUE                   LOADISEQ
00104    006040         '    INVENTORY   RECORD'.                                      LOADISEQ
00105    006050         05  FILLER         PICTURE X(25)       VALUE                   LOADISEQ
00106    006060         '  REMARKS         PAGE'.                                      LOADISEQ
00107    006070         05  PG-H1          PICTURE ZZ9.                                LOADISEQ
00108    006080         05  FILLER         PICTURE X(12)       VALUE SPACES.           LOADISEQ
00109    006090     03  BAD-REC-PRT.                                                   LOADISEQ
00110    006100         05  FILLER         PICTURE X           VALUE ' '.              LOADISEQ
00111    006110         05  NUMB-BAD-PRT   PICTURE Z(4)9.                              LOADISEQ
00112    006120         05  FILLER         PICTURE X(26)       VALUE                   LOADISEQ
00113    006130         ' RECORDS NOT LOADED-ERRORS'.                                  LOADISEQ
00114    006140     03  GOOD-REC-PRT.                                                  LOADISEQ
00115    006150         05  FILLER         PICTURE X       VALUE ' '.                  LOADISEQ
00116    006160         05  NUMB-GOOD-PRT  PICTURE Z(4)9.                              LOADISEQ
00117    006170         05  FILLER         PICTURE X(33)    VALUE                      LOADISEQ
00118    006180         ' RECORDS LOADED ON INVENTORY FILE'.                           LOADISEQ
00119    006190                                                                        LOADISEQ
00120    006200                                                                        LOADISEQ
00121    007010                                                                        LOADISEQ
00122    007020 PROCEDURE DIVISION.                                                    LOADISEQ
00123    007030                                                                        LOADISEQ
00124    007040                                                                        LOADISEQ
00125    007050 NOTE-001.                                                              LOADISEQ
00126    007060     NOTE *******************************************************INVENTORY MASTER FILE.*LOADISEQ
00127    007070     *    THIS PROGRAM IS USED TO LOAD THE INVENTORY MASTER FILE. *LOADISEQ
00128    007080     *    THIS MASTER IS TO BE AN INDEXED SEQUENTIAL FILE.         *LOADISEQ
00129    007090     *                                                            *LOADISEQ
00130    007100     *    THE INPUT TO THE PROGRAM IS A SORTED SEQUENTIAL DISK     *LOADISEQ
00131    007110     *    FILE CREATED IN THE PREVIOUS CARD/TAPE TO DISK           *LOADISEQ
00132    007120     *    PROGRAM.                                                 *LOADISEQ
00133    007130     *    THIS FIRST ROUTINE OPENS THE FILES, AND PRINTS THE       *LOADISEQ
00134    007140     *    HEADING ON THE REPORT.                                   *LOADISEQ
00135    007150     ***********************************************************.LOADISEQ
00136    007160                                                                        LOADISEQ
00137    007170 001-MAIN.                                                              LOADISEQ
00138    007180     OPEN INPUT  TRANSIN,                                               LOADISEQ
00139    007190         OUTPUT PRTFLE, INVMSTR.                                        LOADISEQ
00140    007200     PERFORM 300-HEADER THRU 300-EXIT.                                  LOADISEQ
00141    008010     MOVE SPACES TO PRINT-IO.                                           LOADISEQ
00142    008020                                                                        LOADISEQ
00143    008030                                                                        LOADISEQ
00144    008040 NOTE-003.                                                              LOADISEQ
00145    008050     NOTE *********************************************************LOADISEQ
00146    008060     *    THIS ROUTINE READS THE TRANSACTION RECORD AND INSURES   *LOADISEQ
00147    008070     *    THAT THE TYPE CODE IS A LOAD (CODE = 8). IF IT IS,       *LOADISEQ
00148    008080     *    THE RECORD WILL BE LOADED ONTO THE FILE. IF IT IS NOT,   *LOADISEQ
00149    008090     *    AN ERROR MESSAGE IS PRINTED ON THE EXCEPTION REPORT.     *LOADISEQ
00150    008100     ***********************************************************.LOADISEQ
00151    008110                                                                        LOADISEQ
00152    008120 003-PROCESS-TRANS.                                                     LOADISEQ
00153    008130     READ TRANSIN AT END GO TO 400-TRANS-END.                           LOADISEQ
00154    008140     IF TYPE-TRANS IS NOT = '8'                                         LOADISEQ
00155    008150         GO TO 100-INV-TYPE.                                            LOADISEQ
00156    008160     MOVE PART-NUMB-TRANS TO PART-NUMB-MSTR.                            LOADISEQ
00157    008170     MOVE NAME-TRANS TO NAME-MSTR.                                      LOADISEQ
00158    008180     MOVE QTY-ON-HAND-TRANS TO QTY-ON-HAND-MSTR.                        LOADISEQ
00159    008190     MOVE QTY-ON-ORDER-TRANS TO QTY-ON-ORDER-MSTR.                      LOADISEQ
00160    008200     MOVE QTY-RESERVED-TRANS TO QTY-RESERVED-MSTR.                      LOADISEQ
00161    009010     MOVE NEXT-ASSEMBLY-TRANS TO NEXT-ASSEMBLY-MSTR.                    LOADISEQ
00162    009020     MOVE '1' TO TYPE-MSTR.                                             LOADISEQ
00163    009030     MOVE SOURCE-TRANS TO SOURCE-MSTR.                                  LOADISEQ
00164    009040     MOVE UNIT-PRICE-TRANS TO UNIT-PRICE-MSTR.                          LOADISEQ
00165    009050     WRITE MSTR-IO INVALID KEY GO TO 150-INV-KEY.                       LOADISEQ
00166    009060     ADD 1 TO GOOD-RECS.                                                LOADISEQ
00167    009070     GO TO 003-PROCESS-TRANS.                                           LOADISEQ
00168    009080                                                                        LOADISEQ
00169    009090                                                                        LOADISEQ
00170    009100 NOTE-100.                                                              LOADISEQ
00171    009110     NOTE ********************************************************* LOADISEQ
00172    009120     *    THIS ROUTINE IS ENTERED WHEN A TRANSACTION RECORD        *LOADISEQ
00173    009130     *    WITH AN INVALID TYPE CODE (THAT IS, A TYPE CODE OTHER     *LOADISEQ
00174    009140     *    THAN 8) IS READ. THIS ROUTINE MOVES AN ERROR MESSAGE     *LOADISEQ
```

```
      3

00175   009150      *   TO THE PRINT AREA AND WRITES THE ERROR MESSAGE.       *LOADISEQ
00176   009160      *****************************************************************.LOADISEQ
00177   009170                                                                  LOADISEQ
00178   009180  100-INV-TYPE.                                                   LOADISEQ
00179   009190      MOVE TRANS-IO TO RECORD-PRINT.                             LOADISEQ
00180   009200      MOVE 'TYPE INVALID-RECORD NOT LOADED' TO MSG-PRINT.        LOADISEQ
00181   010010      PERFORM 200-WRITE-PRT THRU 200-EXIT.                       LOADISEQ
00182   010020      ADD 1 TO BAD-RECS.                                         LOADISEQ
00183   010030      GO TO 003-PROCESS-TRANS.                                   LOADISEQ
00184   010040                                                                  LOADISEQ
00185   010050                                                                  LOADISEQ
00186   010060  NOTE-150.                                                       LOADISEQ
00187   010070      NOTE *****************************************************************.LOADISEQ
00188   010080      *   THIS ROUTINE IS ENTERED WHEN AN 'INVALID KEY' OCCURS   *LOADISEQ
00189   010090      *   WHEN LOADING THE FILE. THIS HAPPENS WHEN THE RECORD    *LOADISEQ
00190   010100      *   BEING LOADED IS OUT OF SEQUENCE OR WHEN A DUPLICATE    *LOADISEQ
00191   010110      *   RECORD IS READ. THE ROUTINE WRITES AN ERROR MESSAGE   *LOADISEQ
00192   010120      *   AND INCREMENTS THE BAD RECORD COUNT BY 1.             *LOADISEQ
00193   010130      *****************************************************************.LOADISEQ
00194   010140                                                                  LOADISEQ
00195   010150  150-INV-KEY.                                                    LOADISEQ
00196   010160      MOVE TRANS-IO TO RECORD-PRINT.                             LOADISEQ
00197   010170      MOVE 'OUT OF SEQ. OR DUPLICATE RECORD' TO MSG-PRINT.       LOADISEQ
00198   010180      PERFORM 200-WRITE-PRT THRU 200-EXIT.                       LOADISEQ
00199   010190      ADD 1 TO BAD-RECS.                                         LOADISEQ
00200   010200      GO TO 003-PROCESS-TRANS.                                   LOADISEQ
00201   011010                                                                  LOADISEQ
00202   011020                                                                  LOADISEQ
00203   011030  NOTE-200.                                                       LOADISEQ
00204   011040      NOTE *****************************************************************.LOADISEQ
00205   011050      *   THIS ROUTINE IS ENTERED TO WRITE TO THE PRINTER.       *LOADISEQ
00206   011060      *   ALL WRITES PERFORMED ON THE PRINTER ARE DONE IN THIS   *LOADISEQ
00207   011070      *   ROUTINE.                                               *LOADISEQ
00208   011080      *****************************************************************.LOADISEQ
00209   011090                                                                  LOADISEQ
00210   011100  200-WRITE-PRT.                                                  LOADISEQ
00211   011110      WRITE PRINT-IOA AFTER ADVANCING VARIABLE LINES.           LOADISEQ
00212   011120      ADD 1 TO LINE-COUNT.                                       LOADISEQ
00213   011130      MOVE SINGLE-SPACING TO VARIABLE.                           LOADISEQ
00214   011140      IF LINE-COUNT > 50                                        LOADISEQ
00215   011150          PERFORM 300-HEADER THRU 300-EXIT.                     LOADISEQ
00216   011160      MOVE SPACES TO PRINT-IO.                                   LOADISEQ
00217   011170  200-EXIT.    EXIT.                                             LOADISEQ
00218   011180                                                                  LOADISEQ
00219   011190                                                                  LOADISEQ
00220   011200  NOTE-300.                                                       LOADISEQ
00221   012010      NOTE *****************************************************************.LOADISEQ
00222   012020      *   THIS ROUTINE IS ENTERED TO PRINT THE HEADING FOR       *LOADISEQ
00223   012030      *   THE EXCEPTION REPORT.                                  *LOADISEQ
00224   012040      *****************************************************************.LOADISEQ
00225   012050                                                                  LOADISEQ
00226   012060  300-HEADER.                                                     LOADISEQ
00227   012070      ADD 1 TO PG-CNT.                                           LOADISEQ
00228   012080      MOVE PG-CNT TO PG-H1.                                      LOADISEQ
00229   012090      MOVE HEADER1 TO PRINT-IO.                                  LOADISEQ
00230   012100      WRITE PRINT-IOA AFTER ADVANCING TO-TOP-OF-PAGE.           LOADISEQ
00231   012110      MOVE ZERO TO LINE-COUNT.                                   LOADISEQ
00232   012120      MOVE DOUBLE-SPACING TO VARIABLE.                           LOADISEQ
00233   012130  300-EXIT.    EXIT.                                             LOADISEQ
00234   012140                                                                  LOADISEQ
00235   012150                                                                  LOADISEQ
00236   012160  NOTE-400.                                                       LOADISEQ
00237   012170      NOTE *****************************************************************.LOADISEQ
00238   012180      *   THIS ROUTINE IS ENTERED WHEN END-OF-FILE IS REACHED    *LOADISEQ
00239   012190      *   ON THE INPUT TRANSACTION FILE. IT PRINTS THE TOTAL     *LOADISEQ
00240   012200      *   RECORDS LOADED ON THE FILE AND THE TOTAL RECORDS IN    *LOADISEQ
00241   013010      *   ERROR THAT WERE NOT LOADED ON THE FILE. IT THEN        *LOADISEQ
00242   013020      *   CLOSES THE FILES AND ENDS THE JOB.                     *LOADISEQ
00243   013030      *****************************************************************.LOADISEQ
00244   013040                                                                  LOADISEQ
00245   013050  400-TRANS-END.                                                  LOADISEQ
00246   013060      MOVE DOUBLE-SPACING TO VARIABLE.                           LOADISEQ
00247   013070      MOVE GOOD-RECS TO NUMB-GOOD-PRT.                           LOADISEQ
00248   013080      MOVE GOOD-REC-PRT TO PRINT-IO.                             LOADISEQ
00249   013090      PERFORM 200-WRITE-PRT THRU 200-EXIT.                       LOADISEQ
00250   013100      MOVE SINGLE-SPACING TO VARIABLE.                           LOADISEQ
00251   013110      MOVE BAD-RECS TO NUMB-BAD-PRT.                             LOADISEQ
00252   013120      MOVE BAD-REC-PRT TO PRINT-IO.                              LOADISEQ
00253   013130      PERFORM 200-WRITE-PRT THRU 200-EXIT.                       LOADISEQ
00254   013140      CLOSE TRANSIN,                                             LOADISEQ
00255   013150            INVMSTR,                                             LOADISEQ
00256   013160            PRTFLE.                                              LOADISEQ
00257   013170      STOP RUN.                                                  LOADISEQ
```

CHAPTER 3

PROGRAMMING ASSIGNMENT

INSTRUCTIONS

This program uses the sorted sequential disk file as input (Chapter 2) to create an indexed sequential sales master file. The input record format was to be determined by the programmer in Chapter 2. The record format for the master file is also to be determined by the programmer. It should contain the following fields:

> 1 - Department Number
> 2 - Salesman Number
> 3 - Salesman Name
> 4 - Y-T-D Sales
> 5 - Y-T-D Sales Returns
> 6 - Commission Rate
> 7 - Type Field (active or deleted record)
> > NOTE: an active record will contain a "1" code. A deleted record a "2".

The Department Number and Salesman Number are to be used as the "Key" for the records on the indexed sequential file.

When the file is loaded, the Current Sales in the transaction record is to become the Y-T-D Sales in the master record and the Current Sales Returns in the transaction record is to become the Y-T-D Sales Returns in the master records. (See Chapter 2 Programming Assignment).

The value in the type field in the records to load the indexed sequential file must contain a "1" (new load). In addition, all active records in the master record will contain a "1" in the type code field. When a record is deleted, the type field will be changed to a "2".

All numeric fields are to be packed-decimal in format.

An Exception Report is to be prepared which will list records containing invalid codes in the Type field. A code "1" should be present to indicate a **LOAD**. In addition, duplicate records should be detected through the **INVALID KEY** routine used in the Write Statement.

Sample job control cards are illustrated in Appendix F. It is suggested that the prime data area be dumped and analyzed to assure that the file was properly created.

INDEXED SEQUENTIAL ACCESS METHOD - SEQUENTIAL RETRIEVAL

CHAPTER 4

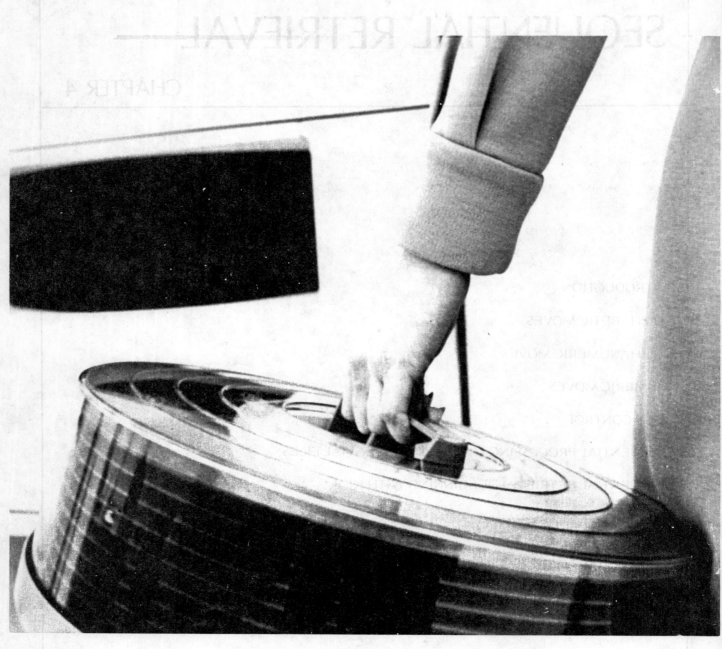

INDEXED SEQUENTIAL ACCESS METHOD – SEQUENTIAL RETRIEVAL   4

INTRODUCTION

After a master file, such as the inventory master file explained in Chapter 3, has been created, it is normally desirable to have a report listing its contents. The sample program presented in this chapter reads an indexed sequential master file and prints a list containing all the master records. The format of the report is illustrated in Figure 4-1.

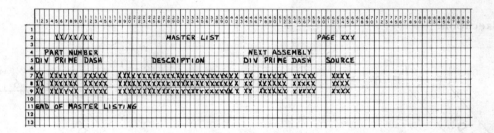

Figure 4-1 Format of Master List Report

In order to create the report, the master file must be retrieved sequentially.

In addition to illustrating the sequential retrieval of an indexed sequential file, this chapter illustrates some considerations when using the **MOVE** verb in a COBOL program.

ALPHABETIC MOVES

A field defined as an alphabetic field (Picture A) may contain only the letters of the alphabet or blanks. An alphabetic field can be moved to another alphabetic field or to an alphanumeric field (Picture X). It cannot be moved to a numeric field. This is because the data in an alphabetic field is not supposed to be numeric in content. An attempt to execute an invalid move will cause a compilation error. Also, a numeric field cannot be moved to an alphabetic field. Thus, the alphabetic field has a limited use as it can only be used for alphabetic characters. In general, it is best to define fields as alphanumeric instead of an alphabetic because an alphanumeric field allows much more flexibility than an alphabetic field.

ALPHANUMERIC MOVES

A field defined as an alphanumeric field (Picture X) may contain any valid character and is the most flexible of the three fields which can be defined using COBOL. A field defined as alphanumeric can be moved to an alphabetic field or an alphabetic field can be moved to an alphanumeric field. In addition, a numeric field in any of the numeric formats except floating-point can be moved to an alphanumeric field. It must be noted, however, that any numeric field which is moved to an alphanumeric field is moved in its exact format. Thus, a field which is Computational-3 in the numeric field will NOT be unpacked when it is moved to the alphanumeric field. This is illustrated in the following example.

EXAMPLE

```
006020 77  FIELDX                  PIC XXX.
006030 77  FIELD9                  PIC S999
006040                             USAGE COMP-3.

013070     MOVE FIELD9 TO FIELDX.
```

Before Execution:

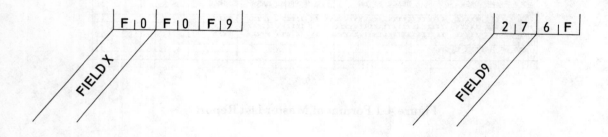

After Execution:

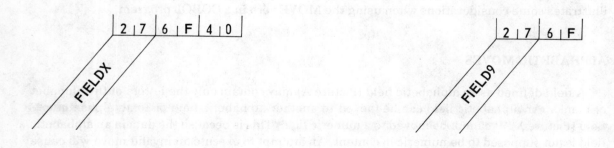

Figure 4-2 Example of Moving Computational-3 Field to Alphanumeric Field

Note in the example that the result in the alphanumeric field is NOT unpacked. It is stored in the same format as it was in **FIELD9**. In addition, the low-order byte in **FIELDX** contains a blank. Whenever the receiving field in an alphanumeric move is longer than the sending field, the receiving field is filled with blanks in its low-order positions. It should be noted that the only method to unpack a numeric field is to move a numeric field defined as Computational-3 to a numeric field defined as Display.

It should also be noted that all Group items are considered to be alphanumeric. Even if a Usage clause is included on the group level, any move to a group item would be handled as an alphanumeric move. Thus, if a group of counters were defined as Computational-3, a move of **ZEROS** to the group level will not properly zero the counters. This is illustrated in the following example.

EXAMPLE

Step 1: Define counters with a value of zero.

004020		03	COUNTERS		USAGE IS COMP-3.
004030		05	COUNTER1		PIC S9(3)	VALUE 0.
004040		05	COUNTER2		PIC S9(5)	VALUE 0.
004050		05	COUNTER3		PIC S9(5)	VALUE 0.

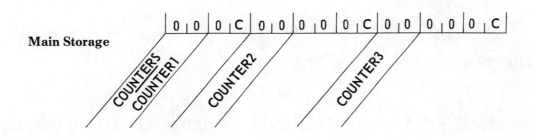

Main Storage

Figure 4-3 Counters Defined as Computational-3 Fields

Note that the fields labelled **COUNTER1, COUNTER2, and COUNTER3** are each packed-decimal fields with the value of zero.

Step 2: Add values to the counters.

003070		03	MONTH-IN		PIC S9(3)
003080					USAGE IS COMP-3.
003090		03	AMOUNT-IN		PIC S9(5)
003100					USAGE IS COMP-3.
003110		03	RETURN-IN		PIC S9(5)
003120					USAGE IS COMP-3.

012150		ADD MONTH-IN TO COUNTER1.
012160		ADD AMOUNT-IN TO COUNTER2.
012170		ADD RETURN-IN TO COUNTER3.

Before Execution:

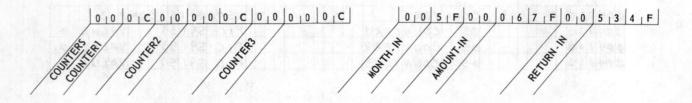

After Execution:

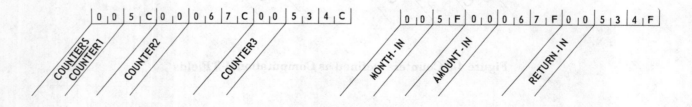

Figure 4-4 Example of Adding to Counters

Note that the values from the input fields are added to the counters and that the values in the counters are in packed-decimal format.

Step 3: Clear the counters with a group move.

014060		MOVE ZEROS TO COUNTERS.

Before Execution:

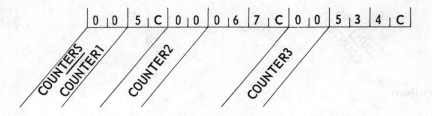

After Execution:

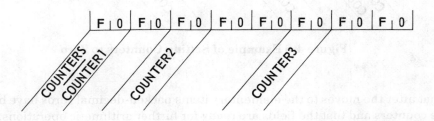

Figure 4-5 Example of Group Move to Computational-3 Fields

Note that after the figurative constant **ZEROS** is moved to the group level field **COUNTERS** the zeros are in zoned-decimal format, not packed-decimal format as desired. Thus, if the counters were used for further arithmetic operations, an abnormal program termination would occur because the fields are not properly signed. In order to zero the counters, a move must be executed to each of the elementary counters. The following instructions could be used.

EXAMPLE

```
014 100    MOVE ZEROS TO COUNTER1.
014 110    MOVE ZEROS TO COUNTER2.
014 120    MOVE ZEROS TO COUNTER3.
```

Before Execution:

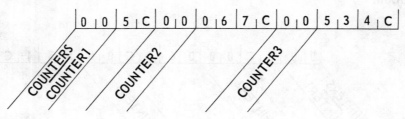

After Execution:

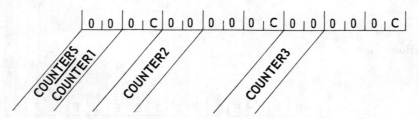

Figure 4-6 Example of Setting Counters to Zero

Note that after the moves to the elementary items packed-decimal zeros have been moved to each of the counters and that the fields are ready for further arithmetic operations.

As was noted previously, whenever the receiving field is alphanumeric and is longer than the sending field, the receiving field is filled with low-order blanks. In order to place these blanks in the receiving field, instructions must be generated within the Procedure Division. These instructions take main storage space and if possible, it is preferable that they not be needed. In order to get rid of these instructions, the sending and receiving fields must be the same length. Therefore, if the sending field is normally shorter than the receiving field, consideration should be given to extending the sending field to the same length as the receiving field. For example, the following illustration shows a sixteen byte receiving field and a 12 byte sending field.

EXAMPLE

```
003140      03  RECEIVING-FIELD              PIC X(16).
004160      03  SENDING-FIELD                PIC X(12)     VALUE
004170          'INVALID TYPE'.

016190      MOVE SENDING-FIELD TO RECEIVING-FIELD.
```

Figure 4-7 Example of Alphanumeric Move with Different Length Fields

In the example above, the value "**INVALID TYPE**" would be moved to **RECEIVING-FIELD** in the 12 high-order bytes of the field and the remaining four low-order bytes would be filled with blanks. The instructions to fill the low-order bytes with blanks would be generated in the Procedure Division. A better way to accomplish the same thing is illustrated in Figure 4-8.

EXAMPLE

```
ø ø 3 ø 2 ø       ø 3    R E C E I V I N G - F I E L D              P I C  X ( 1 6 ) .
ø ø 3 ø 4 ø       ø 3    S E N D I N G - F I E L D                 P I C  X ( 1 6 )
ø ø 3 ø 5 ø              ' I N V A L I D   T Y P E ' .
ø 1 6 ø 7 ø       M O V E  S E N D I N G - F I E L D  T O  R E C E I V I N G - F I E L D .
```

Figure 4-8 Example of Alphanumeric Move With Fields of Same Length

Note in the example above that the results of the move would be the same as the move shown in Figure 4-7. However, since the length of **SENDING-FIELD** is the same as the length of **RECEIVING-FIELD**, no instructions would be generated to fill **RECEIVING-FIELD** with low-order blanks. The blanks would be set in **SENDING-FIELD** by the Value clause. Thus, even though the length of **SENDING-FIELD** is four bytes longer than shown in Figure 4-7, there is a net savings because the bytes in the Procedure Division used for the instructions to move the low-order blanks are not needed. It should be noted also that this idea applies to alphabetic fields as well as alphanumeric fields.

When an alphanumeric move is generated by some COBOL compilers, a maximum of 256 bytes can be moved by the single machine-language instruction. If more than 256 bytes are to be moved, a special subroutine must be used by COBOL. Therefore, to avoid the use of a subroutine, alphanumeric moves should be kept to a maximum of 256 bytes.

NUMERIC MOVES

As noted previously, numeric fields can be represented in the zoned-decimal format, the packed-decimal format, or the binary format. Thus, in instances when a numeric field is being moved from one format to another, the move instruction also includes a conversion process from one format to the other. It is best, therefore, if possible, to have both fields in the same data mode. If this is not possible, additional coding may be generated for the conversions. The following list explains the conversions necessary between different modes of numeric data.

1. Move Display to Computational-3: The data in the Display field is packed to the Computational-3 field.

2. Move Display to Computational: Before the move is executed, the Display data is packed and converted to a binary format. The data is then stored in the Computational field.

3. Move Computational-3 to Computational: The data is moved to a work area, converted to binary, and then stored in the Computational field.

4. Move Computational to Computational-3: The Computational data is converted to a packed decimal format and then moved to the Computational-3 field.

5. Move Computational to Display: The data in the Computational field is converted to a packed decimal format in a work area and then is unpacked and moved to the Display field.

6. Move Computational-3 to Display: The Computational-3 field is unpacked to the Display field.

As can be seen from the list above, a single **MOVE** instruction in a COBOL program can cause a number of operations to occur, in addition to just moving the data from one location in main storage to another, dependent upon the mode in which the numeric data is stored. When the data is in the same mode, however, the only function which must be performed is the movement of the data-no conversion from one mode to another is required. Therefore, as noted previously, if at all possible, when numeric data is to be moved from location to location, it is best that it be in the same mode.

The conversions presented in the lists all assumed that the same number of digits were contained in the numeric field and that the fields were decimally aligned, that is, each field contained the same number of digits to the right of the decimal point. Whenever a numeric field contains a different number of digits, additional instructions may be generated by the COBOL compiler to move the data. For example, the following illustrates a move of a Display field containing three digits to a four digit decimal field.

EXAMPLE

```
002020  77  DISP1                          PIC S999.
002030  77  DISP2                          PIC S9999.

013050      MOVE DISP1 TO DISP2.
```

Figure 4-9 Example of Moving Different Size Display Fields

Whenever the receiving field in a numeric move is larger than the sending field, high-order zeros are inserted in the receiving field. Therefore, in the example above, in addition to generating the instructions to move the data in the field **DISP1** to the field **DISP2**, there must be instructions generated by the compiler to move the zero to the high-order byte in **DISP2**. If the fields were the same length, then the compiler would not generate any instructions to move zeros to **DISP2** and the main storage used for these instructions would be saved.

When a longer field is moved to a shorter field, as illustrated in Figure 4-10, no extra instructions must be generated by the compiler.

EXAMPLE

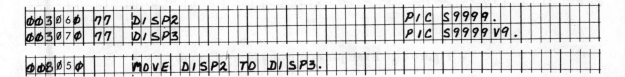

```
ΦΦ2Φ9Φ  77  DISP1                          PIC S999.
ΦΦ21ΦΦ  77  DISP2                          PIC S9999.

Φ16 12Φ        MOVE DISP2 TO DISP1.
```

Figure 4-10 Example of Moving Longer Field to Shorter Field

Although only the instruction needed to move the data from **DISP2** to **DISP1** will be generated by the compiler, all the data in the longer field (**DISP2**) will not be moved to the shorter field (**DISP1**) because the "to" field governs how many digits will be moved. Thus, only the three low-order digits of **DISP2** will be moved to **DISP1**. Whenever a longer field is moved to a shorter field, a **LEVEL-W** diagnostic will be generated by the compiler. The programmer should check all **LEVEL-W** diagnostics to ensure that the instruction will produce the desired result.

Note that when numeric fields of different lengths are used, the high-order bytes of the longer receiving fields are filled with zeros and when the shorter field is the receiving field, the low-order digits in the sending field are moved. This is directly opposite to alphanumeric fields, where longer receiving fields are filled with low-order blanks and, when the shorter field is the receiving field, the high-order bytes of the sending field are moved.

As noted, decimal alignment is assumed in the previous discussion of storage requirements for moves. When numeric fields are not decimally aligned, that is, when one numeric field contains more positions to the right of the decimal point that the other, the COBOL compiler must generate instructions to align the fields before any movement of the data can take place. Generally, these alignment instructions are very costly in terms of computer storage usage in the Procedure Division.

The following example illustrates a move instruction to move two non-aligned decimal fields.

```
ΦΦ3Φ6Φ  77  DISP2                          PIC S9999.
ΦΦ3Φ7Φ  77  DISP3                          PIC S9999V9.

ΦΦ8Φ5Φ        MOVE DISP2 TO DISP3.
```

Figure 4-11 Example of Moving Non-Aligned Display Fields

The **MOVE** Instruction illustrated in Figure 4-11 requires instructions not only to move the data from **DISP2** to **DISP3**, such as in previous examples, but also requires instructions in the procedure division to decimally align the data in the fields. This alignment must take place prior to the moving of the data to **DISP3**. If the field **DISP2** contained the Picture S9999V9, the only instruction required would be to move the data to **DISP3**. There would be no alignment instructions. Thus, by aligning decimal points in numeric fields, a great deal of storage can be saved in the instructions generated in the Procedure Division.

The following Move Statement requires instructions to both pack the display data and to align the decimal points.

```
004080  77  DISP2                              PIC S9999.
004090  77  COMP3                              PIC S999V9
004100                                         USAGE IS COMP-3.

011120      MOVE DISP2 TO COMP3.
```

Figure 4-12 Example of Moving Non-Aligned Display Field to Computational-3 Field

In the example above, more than twice the amount of main storage is used to cause the data to be moved than is required when moving a Display field to a Computational-3 field and the decimal points are aligned.

Even further conversions together with decimal alignment requirements will cause more inefficient usage of main storage. The following is an example of moving a Computational field to a Display field when the decimals are not aligned.

```
004140  77  BIN1                               PIC S999        SYNC
004150                                         USAGE IS COMP.
004160  77  DISP3                              PIC S999V9.

016180      MOVE BIN1 TO DISP3.
```

Figure 4-13 Example of Moving Non-Aligned

The Move instruction in Figure 4-13 will again generate over twice the number of bytes for instructions in the Procedure Division as would be generated if decimal alignment was not required. This is because both conversion and decimal alignment must take place when the data is moved.

It can be seen from the previous examples that consideration should always be given to the definitions of numeric fields. The indiscriminate use of mixed-modes can lead to excessive computer storage being used by the program and longer execution times than are necessary.

SIGN CONTROL

In the examples given previously in this chapter and in Chapters 2 and 3, most of the fields defined as numeric were given a picture with an "S", which indicated a signed field. For example, the Computational-3 field shown in Figure 4-12 contains the clause **PICTURE S999V9 Comp-3.** The "S" contained in the Picture clause indicates that the field can be signed, that is, it may contain a positive sign or a negative sign. On most machines which use the **EBCDIC** coding system, a positive sign is a hexadecimal "C" and a negative sign is a hexadecimal "D". Whenever any Move instructions or arithmetic instructions are performed on a field that is designated as signed, the result of the move or arithmetic operation may be positive or negative, and the field will be left as positive or negative by the coding developed by the COBOL compiler.

If the "S" is not included in the numeric picture, however, the COBOL compiler will generate instructions to ensure that the field will always contain the absolute value sign (usually a hexadecimal "F") after a move or after an arithmetic operation. The instruction to ensure the absolute sign in a field will, in most cases, require four bytes in the Procedure Division. Thus, whenever a numeric field which does not include the "S" in its picture is referenced in a move or arithmetic operation, four extra bytes of coding will be generated by the COBOL compiler.

The only time a numeric field should not contain an "S" in its picture clause is when it is mandatory that the field contain an absolute numeric value. In the sample program, the part number in the inventory record is the key of the record. Whenever the key on an indexed sequential file is referenced (as when sequentially or randomly retrieving a record from the file), the reference to the key must be identical to the key contained on the file. A numeric field with a sign of hexadecimal "C", although equivalent to a sign of hexadeciaml "F" when performing arithmetic operations, is not considered equivalent when being compared as a key on an indexed sequential file. Therefore, it is necessary to ensure that any reference to the key on an indexed sequential file is the same as the key in the record on the file. Thus, by not specifying an "S" in the Picture clause for the part number on the master file, it is ensured that the sign in the part number will always be a hexadecimal "F" and that any reference to the key in the record will be the same as the key which is stored in the record.

It should also be noted that any numeric fields which are defined as **USAGE IS COMPUTATIONAL** must be signed because all binary fields are considered signed numeric values.

SEQUENTIAL PROCESSING - INDEXED SEQUENTIAL FILES

As noted previously, indexed sequential files can be processed either randomly or in a sequential manner. Sequential processing can be used either to retrieve records from an indexed sequential file for use, for example, in a printed report, or to update (change) records currently in the file. In the sample program presented in this chapter, the indexed sequential inventory master file is to be retrieved sequentially to produce a report listing the part numbers in the inventory master file.

As with all files using Logical IOCS in COBOL, the indexed sequential file which is to be retrieved sequentially must be defined in the Environment Division and the Data Division. The clauses **ACCESS IS SEQUENTIAL** and **RECORD KEY IS** are used together with the indexed sequential entries required in the System Name. The following is the definition of the inventory master file to be retrieved sequentially which is used in the sample program.

EXAMPLE

```
002020  FILE-CONTROL.
002030      SELECT  INVMSTR
002040          ASSIGN TO SYS006-DA-2314-I-INVMSTR
002050          ACCESS IS SEQUENTIAL
002060          RECORD KEY IS PART-NUMB-MSTR.

003080  DATA DIVISION.
003090  FILE SECTION.
003100
003110  FD  INVMSTR
003120      BLOCK CONTAINS 54 RECORDS
003130      RECORD CONTAINS 64 CHARACTERS
003140      LABEL RECORDS ARE STANDARD
003150      DATA RECORD IS MSTR-IO.
003160  01  MSTR-IO.
003170      03  PART-NUMB-MSTR          PIC 9(13).
003180                                  USAGE COMP-3.
003190      03  NAME-MSTR               PIC X(25).
```

Figure 4-14 Environment and Data Division Entries for Sequential Retrieval

As can be seen from the example above, the **SELECT** statement is the same as shown for creating the indexed sequential file. The name of the file is **INVMSTR**, it will be held on the disk drive assigned to "SYS006" at the time of execution, and it will be on a 2314 direct access device. The "I" in the organization entry identifies the file as an indexed sequential file and the **ACCESS IS SEQUENTIAL** clause indicates that the file will be retrieved sequentially.

The **RECORD KEY IS** clause is used to identify the field within the record on the indexed sequential file which is used as the key for the file. In the sample program, the part number is used as the key to the file and the identifier for the part number is **PART-NUMB-MSTR**.

Unlike sequential processing when using sequential files, sequential processing when using indexed sequential files can begin at any point in the file. This is because, using the indexes, **ISAM** is able to locate any record in the file. Thus, when programming in COBOL, the user has the option of beginning sequential retrieval at the beginning of the file or with a record within the file which has a particular key.

The optional **NOMINAL KEY IS** clause is used to determine where sequential processing is to begin. If the **NOMINAL KEY IS** clause is not included in the **SELECT** statement, sequential retrieval will begin with the first record on the indexed sequential file. Thus, from the coding in the sample program illustrated in Figure 4-14, it can be seen that sequential retrieval will begin with the first record in the file because the **NOMINAL KEY IS** clause is not present.

The indexed sequential file which is to be sequentially retrieved must first be opened as an input file. The Open statement used in the sample program is illustrated below.

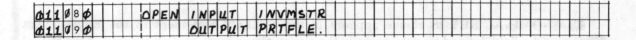

Figure 4-15 Example of OPEN Instruction

Whenever an indexed sequential file is to be used for sequential retrieval and is not to be updated in the same program, the file is opened as an input file. The report file **PRTFLE** is, of course, opened as an output file.

After the Open statement is issued, the file is ready to be processed. When processing is to begin with the first record in the file, the records on the file are read through the use of the **READ** Statement. The statement used in the sample program is shown in Figure 4-16.

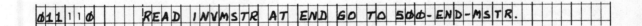

Figure 4-16 Example of READ Statement

The **READ** Statement will make the first record on the indexed sequential file ready for processing in the input area defined in the File Section of the Data Division. The optional "INTO" word could be used to cause the input record to be moved to an area defined in Working-Storage. When the last record on the file has been read, the end-of-file routine **500-END-MSTR** will be entered for end-of-file processing.

SEQUENTIAL RETRIEVAL - BEGINNING WITH KEY

As was noted previously, sequential retrieval of an indexed sequential file can begin with a record that is not the first record on the file. This is because each record on the indexed sequential file is uniquely identifiable because of the key associated with each record. Thus, by specifying a particular key of a record on the file, processing can begin with the record whose key is specified.

The **NOMINAL KEY IS** clause is used to specify the name of the field which will contain the key where sequential retrieval is to begin. The format of the Clause is illustrated below.

NOMINAL KEY IS data name

Figure 4-17 Format Notation for NOMINAL KEY IS Clause

The **NOMINAL KEY IS** clause appears in the **SELECT** Statement in the Environment Division. The field defined by data-name in the clause above must contain the key of the record which is to begin the sequential processing and should be defined in the Working-Storage Section of the Data Division. The key must be in the exact format as the key in the record. Thus, if retrieval were to begin with a record in the inventory master file, the key must be moved to the Nominal Key field in the Computational-3 format, because this is the format of the key on the file.

After the key which indicates where the sequential retrieval is to begin has been moved to the field defined in the Nominal Key clause, the **START** Statement must be issued after the file has been opened, but before a **READ** Statement is issued. The format of the **START** Statement is illustrated below.

START file-name **INVALID** KEY imperative-statement

Figure 4-18 Format Notation of START Statement

Note from Figure 4-18 that the word **START** is required. The file-name entry is the name of the indexed sequential file as defined in the Environment and Data Divisions. The **INVALID KEY** entry must specify a statement which directs the processing which is to occur if the key which is contained in the Nominal Key area and which is used for the search by the **START** Statement is not found in the file indicated by file-name.

A sample routine which could be used to begin sequential retrieval of an indexed sequential file at a given record within the file is illustrated below.

EXAMPLE

```
002020  FILE-CONTROL.
002030      SELECT INVMSTR
002040          ASSIGN TO SYS006-DA-2314-I-INVMSTR
002050          ACCESS IS SEQUENTIAL
002060          RECORD KEY IS PART-NUMB-MSTR
002070          NOMINAL KEY IS MSTR-KEY.

003020  DATA DIVISION.
003030  FILE SECTION.
003040
003050  FD  INVMSTR
003060      BLOCK CONTAINS 54 RECORDS
003070      RECORD CONTAINS 64 CHARACTERS
003080      LABEL RECORDS ARE STANDARD
003090      DATA RECORD IS MSTR-IO.
003100  01  MSTR-IO.
003110      03  PART-NUMB-MSTR              PIC 9(13)
003120                                      USAGE COMP-3.
003130      03  NAME-MSTR                   PIC X(25).

004090  WORKING-STORAGE SECTION.
004100  77  MSTR-KEY                        PIC 9(13)
004110                                      USAGE COMP-3.
004120  01  CARD-IN.
004130      03  CARD-KEY                    PIC 9(13).
004140      03  FILLER                      PIC X(67).

011020  PROCEDURE DIVISION.
011030  001-BEGIN.
011040      OPEN INPUT INVMSTR
011050           OUTPUT PRTFLE.
011060      ACCEPT CARD-IN.
011070      MOVE CARD-KEY TO MSTR-KEY.
011080      START INVMSTR INVALID KEY GO TO 200-BAD-KEY.
011090  010-READ-MSTR.
011100      READ INVMSTR AT END GO TO 500-END-MSTR.
```

Figure 4-19 Example of Routine to begin Sequential Retrieval At A Record With a Given Key

In the routine illustrated in Figure 4-19, the data-name specified in the **NOMINAL KEY IS** clause is **MSTR-KEY**, and it is defined as **Picture 9(13) Usage Computational-3**. Note that the picture of this field is identical to the data field which is used as the key in the record on the inventory master file (**RECORD KEY IS PART-NUMB-MSTR**). This is required because the key specified in the Nominal Key field must be the same as the key in the record.

The data card containing the desired beginning key is read by means of the **ACCEPT** statement. The Accept statement, as shown in the example, is used to read a card from the device assigned as the system card reader. The Accept statement will read the card and cause the contents of the card to be placed in the **CARD-IN** field. The first 13 characters of the card contain the key where sequential retrieval is to begin. This number is moved to the nominal key area (note that the zoned decimal data read in the card will be packed when it is moved to the nominal key area **MSTR-KEY**).

After the beginning key is moved to **MSTR-KEY**, the **START** Statement is issued. It causes the indexed sequential master file to be searched for the record whose key is contained in the field **MSTR-KEY** (the Nominal Key area). When this record is found in the indexes of the file, pointers are set so that when a Read statement is given, the first record read is the record with the given key. If a record with the key which is found in the Nominal Key area is not located in the indexes, then the **200-BAD-KEY** routine is entered. In most cases, an error message would be printed and the program terminated because the sequential retrieval cannot begin with the record indicated.

SEQUENTIAL RETRIEVAL - GENERIC KEY

In some applications, it is desirable to begin sequential retrieval of an indexed sequential file by specifying only a portion of the key of the file. For example, if it was desired to begin processing of the **INVMSTR** file with the first record in Division 6, then all of the records in divisions 1-5 would be bypassed. In most instances, it is not possible to know what the entire key of the first record in division 6 is and this record may change as records are added to the file. Therefore, some COBOL compilers allow retrieval to begin with a ''generic key'', that is, by specifying some portion of the key which is less than the entire key.

The following example illustrates the use of the generic key to retrieve the first record in Division 6 of the **INVMSTR** file.

EXAMPLE

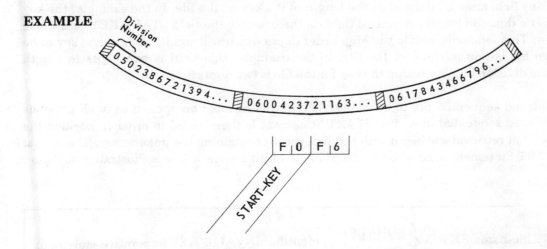

Figure 4-20 Example of Generic Key

Note in the example in Figure 4-20 that the records stored on the indexed sequential file contain, as the first two digits of the record, the division number. In the example, sequential retrieval is to begin with the first record in division six. The field, **START-KEY**, contains the value "06". This field, which must be defined in addition to the Nominal Key Field, must contain the portion of the key which is to be used to determine where sequential retrieval is to begin. The coding in the program to cause the pointers to be set to begin reading at division 6 is illustrated below.

EXAMPLE

```
002020        SELECT INVMSTR
002030            ASSIGN TO SYS006-DA-2314-I-INVMSTR
002040            ACCESS IS SEQUENTIAL
002050            RECORD KEY IS PART-NUMB-MSTR
002060            NOMINAL KEY IS MSTR-KEY.

005020    WORKING-STORAGE SECTION.
005030    77  MSTR-KEY                        PIC 9(13)
005040                                        USAGE COMP-3.
005050    77  START-KEY                       PIC 99.

011110    PROCEDURE DIVISION.
011120        OPEN INPUT INVMSTR
011130            OUTPUT PRTFLE.

012070        START INVMSTR KEY IS = START-KEY
012080            INVALID KEY GO TO 400-INV-KEY.
```

Figure 4-21 Example of GENERIC KEY Routine

Note from the example in Figure 4-21 that the file **INVMSTR** is defined in the same manner as when retrieval is to begin with a given key on the file, instead of a given generic key. The Nominal Key field must be defined as the length of the key on the file. In the example, the key is 13 numeric digits in length. A second field, in the example the field **START-KEY**, must also be defined. This field will contain the high-order digits which will signify the generic key to be used when beginning retrieval of the file. In the example, this field is two digits in length because the division number within the key for the file is two digits in length.

The indexed sequential file to be sequentially retrieved must be opened as in all previous uses of indexed sequential files. The **START** Statement is then issued in order to position the pointers so that retrieval will begin with the first record containing the generic key. The format of the **START** Statement used when retrieval begins with a generic key is illustrated in Figure 4-22.

$$\underline{START}\ \text{file-name}\ \underline{KEY}\ \text{IS}\ \left\{ \begin{array}{c} \underline{EQUAL}\ TO \\ = \end{array} \right\}\ \text{identifier}\ \underline{INVALID}\ \text{KEY imperative-statement}$$

Figure 4-22 Format Notation - START Statement

Note from Figure 4-22 that the Start Statement when used with a generic key retrieval has a slightly different format than that used when retrieval is to begin with the key of a record on a file (see Figure 4-18). The difference is due to the fact that an extra field, as specified by ''identifier'' in the format notation above (**START-KEY** in Figure 4-21) must be used to specify the portion of the key which is to be used to find the beginning record.

An Invalid Key occurs when the generic class it contains is not found in any of the keys in the indexed sequential file. Thus, in Figure 4-20, if there were no records on the file with a division number 06, the invalid key routine would be entered. As with sequential retrieval beginning with a key in the file, the ''imperative-statement'' is usually a **GO TO** or **PERFORM** statement which will direct control to an error routine to note that the desired generic key was not found in the file. In the example in Figure 4-21, the routine **400-INV-KEY** will be entered if the generic key is not found in the **INVMSTR** file.

SEQUENTIAL UPDATING - INDEXED SEQUENTIAL ACCESS METHOD

As has been noted previously, an indexed sequential file can be updated sequentially. Sequential updating of an indexed sequential file involves the changing of the records on the file. Additions cannot be made using the sequential update technique (see Chapter 5). Although sequential updating of an indexed sequential file is not illustrated in the sample program presented in this chapter, the following is a brief explanation of the process involved in sequential updating.

The process of sequentially updating an indexed sequential master file is essentially the same as when sequential files are updated. The master record and the transaction record are compared and when a match is found, the master record is updated. The Primary difference is that when an indexed sequential master file is updated sequentially, a new master file is NOT created. The master record to be updated is retrieved, updated, and rewritten back into the same place on the master file.

In order to sequentially update an indexed sequential file, both the **OPEN** statement and the **REWRITE** statement must be used. The following is an example of the Open statement to be used when an indexed sequential file is to be sequentially updated.

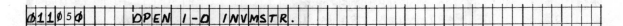

Figure 4-23 OPEN I-O Statement for Sequential Updating

The **OPEN I-O** statement is used when an indexed sequential file is going to be both retrieved (using the **READ** statement) and written (using the **REWRITE** statement). When sequential updating is to be performed on an indexed sequential file, the file must be opened as an I-O file.

The **REWRITE** command is used to rewrite a record which has been previously retrieved using a **READ** command. The format of the **REWRITE** statement is illustrated in Figure 4-24.

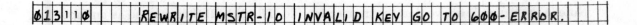

Figure 4-24 REWRITE Statement

The only operand used with the **REWRITE** statement when rewriting a sequentially retrieved record is the name of the master I/O area as described in the File Section of the Data Division. When the Rewrite statement is executed, the record which has been retrieved and updated is rewritten back onto the indexed sequential file in the same place it was when retrieved. The Invalid Key routine must be specified to indicate the processing which is to occur if a **REWRITE** statement has not been preceeded by a valid Read operation. In the example, the **600-ERROR** routine will be entered.

A typical routine to sequentially update an indexed sequential file is illustrated below.

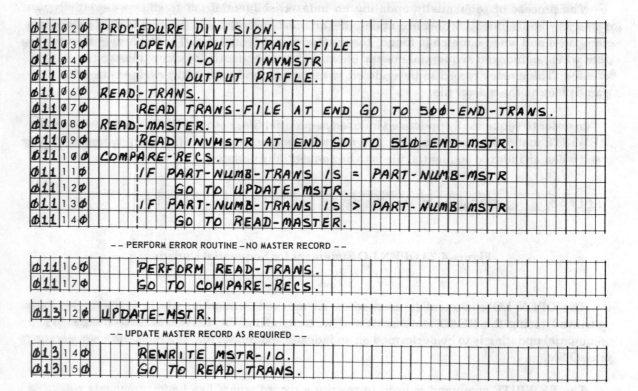

```
011020  PROCEDURE DIVISION.
011030      OPEN INPUT   TRANS-FILE
011040           I-O     INVMSTR
011050           OUTPUT  PRTFLE.
011060  READ-TRANS.
011070      READ TRANS-FILE AT END GO TO 500-END-TRANS.
011080  READ-MASTER.
011090      READ INVMSTR AT END GO TO 510-END-MSTR.
011100  COMPARE-RECS.
011110      IF PART-NUMB-TRANS IS = PART-NUMB-MSTR
011120          GO TO UPDATE-MSTR.
011130      IF PART-NUMB-TRANS IS > PART-NUMB-MSTR
011140          GO TO READ-MASTER.
         -- PERFORM ERROR ROUTINE -NO MASTER RECORD --
011160      PERFORM READ-TRANS.
011170      GO TO COMPARE-RECS.

013120  UPDATE-MSTR.
         -- UPDATE MASTER RECORD AS REQUIRED --
013140      REWRITE MSTR-IO.
013150      GO TO READ-TRANS.
```

Figure 4-25 Typical Sequential Update Routine

Note in the example above that the transaction file (**TRANS-FILE**) is opened as an input file, the indexed sequential master file which is to be updated (**INVMSTR**) is opened as an I-O file, and the exception report file (**PRTFLE**) is opened as an output file. The part number fields on the transaction file (**PART-NUMB-TRANS**) and the master file (**PART-NUMB-MSTR**) are compared and when an equal condition occurs, the master record is updated with the transaction data. It must be noted that any field in the master record EXCEPT the key of the record (in the example, the part number field **PART-NUMB-MSTR**) can be updated. If the key of a record is changed after it has been read into main storage, the indexes of the indexed sequential file will not reflect the correct key because the indexes are not altered when a record is updated sequentially. Therefore, the key of a record being updated must NEVER be changed during a sequential updating operation.

After the record has been updated with the transaction data, the master record is rewritten using the **REWRITE** command. The Rewrite command rewrites a record which has been previously retrieved using the Read command. The Rewrite command must never be issued unless a Read command has been issued prior to it. Note in the example, however, that a Read command can be issued with no Rewrite command following it. This is because a record which is not changed does not have to be rewritten as it is already on the file with the proper data. Therefore, the only time a Rewrite command must be issued is after a record on the master file has been updated. It should be noted also that when an indexed sequential file is opened as an I-O file it is perfectly legitimate to specify a Nominal Key field and begin the sequential processing at a record with a specific key rather than with the first record on the file. The Nominal Key field operates in the same manner as when the file is opened as an input file.

SAMPLE PROGRAM

INPUT

The input to the sample program is the inventory master file built in Chapter 3. The format of the file is shown below.

FIELD	FIELD NAME	PICTURE	POSITION	NO OF DIGITS	LENGTH
Part Number	PART-NUMB-MSTR	Picture 9(13) Comp-3	1-7	13	7
Description	NAME-MSTR	Picture X(25)	8-32	25	25
Quantity on Hand	QTY-ON-HAND-MSTR	Picture S9(7) Comp-3	33-36	7	4
Quantity on Order	QTY-ON-ORDER-MSTR	Picture S9(7) Comp-3	37-40	7	4
Quantity Reserved	QTY-RESERVED-MSTR	Picture S9(7) Comp-3	41-44	7	4
Next Assembly Number	NEXT-ASSEMBLY-MSTR	Picture S9(13) Comp-3	45-51	13	7
Type	TYPE-MSTR	PictureX	52	1	1
Source	SOURCE-MSTR	Picture X	53	1	1
Unit Price	UNIT-PRICE-MSTR	Picture S9(7) Comp-3	54-57	6	4
Filler	FILLER	Picture X(7)	58-64	7	7

OUTPUT

The output of the sample program is a printed report listing the parts on the master file. The format of the report is illustrated below.

PRINTER SPACING CHART

SOURCE LISTING

The source listing of the sample program to sequentially retrieve an indexed sequential file is contained on the following pages.

```
  1                                IBM DOS AMERICAN NATIONAL STANDARD COBOL          CBF CL3-4        09/12/74

00001    001010 IDENTIFICATION DIVISION.                                            PRTMASTR
00002    001020 PROGRAM-ID.    PRTMASTR.                                            PRTMASTR
00003    001030 AUTHOR.        SHELLY.                                              PRTMASTR
00004    001040 INSTALLATION.  LONG BEACH.                                          PRTMASTR
00005    001050 DATE-WRITTEN.  07/11/74.                                            PRTMASTR
00006    001060 DATE-COMPILED. 09/12/74.                                            PRTMASTR
00007    001070 SECURITY.      UNCLASSIFIED.                                        PRTMASTR
00008    001080 REMARKS.       THIS PROGRAM SEQUENTIALLY RETRIEVES THE             PRTMASTR
00009    001090                INVENTORY MASTER FILE AND CREATES A PRINTED         PRTMASTR
00010    001100                REPORT LISTING ALL OF THE PARTS ON THE FILE.        PRTMASTR
00011    001110                                                                    PRTMASTR
00012    001120                                                                    PRTMASTR
00013    001130 ENVIRONMENT DIVISION.                                              PRTMASTR
00014    001140 CONFIGURATION SECTION.                                             PRTMASTR
00015    001150 SOURCE-COMPUTER.    IBM-360-F30.                                   PRTMASTR
00016    001160 OBJECT-COMPUTER.    IBM-360-F30.                                   PRTMASTR
00017    001170 SPECIAL-NAMES.                                                     PRTMASTR
00018    001180     C01 IS TO-TOP-OF-PAGE.                                         PRTMASTR
00019    001190                                                                    PRTMASTR
00020    001200 INPUT-OUTPUT SECTION.                                              PRTMASTR
00021    002010                                                                    PRTMASTR
00022    002020 FILE-CONTROL.                                                      PRTMASTR
00023    002030     SELECT INVMSTR                                                 PRTMASTR
00024    002040         ASSIGN TO SYS006-DA-2314-I-INVMSTR                         PRTMASTR
00025    002050         ACCESS IS SEQUENTIAL                                       PRTMASTR
00026    002060         RECORD KEY IS PART-NUMB-MSTR.                              PRTMASTR
00027    002070     SELECT PRTFLE                                                  PRTMASTR
00028    002080         ASSIGN TO SYS005-UR-1403-S.                                PRTMASTR
00029    002090                                                                    PRTMASTR
00030    002100                                                                    PRTMASTR
00031    002110                                                                    PRTMASTR
00032    002120 DATA DIVISION.                                                     PRTMASTR
00033    002130                                                                    PRTMASTR
00034    002140 FILE SECTION.                                                      PRTMASTR
00035    002150                                                                    PRTMASTR
00036    002160 FD  INVMSTR                                                        PRTMASTR
00037    002170     BLOCK CONTAINS 54 RECORDS                                      PRTMASTR
00038    002180     RECORD CONTAINS 64 CHARACTERS                                  PRTMASTR
00039    002190     LABEL RECORDS ARE STANDARD                                     PRTMASTR
00040    002200     DATA RECORD IS MSTR-IO.                                        PRTMASTR
00041    003010 01  MSTR-IO.                                                       PRTMASTR
00042    003020     03  PART-NUMB-MSTR      PICTURE 9(13)                          PRTMASTR
00043    003030                             USAGE COMPUTATIONAL-3.                 PRTMASTR
00044    003040     03  NAME-MSTR           PICTURE X(25).                         PRTMASTR
00045    003050     03  QTY-ON-HAND-MSTR    PICTURE S9(7)                          PRTMASTR
00046    003060                             USAGE COMPUTATIONAL-3.                 PRTMASTR
00047    003070     03  QTY-ON-ORDER-MSTR   PICTURE S9(7)                          PRTMASTR
00048    003080                             USAGE COMPUTATIONAL-3.                 PRTMASTR
00049    003090     03  QTY-RESERVED-MSTR   PICTURE S9(7)                          PRTMASTR
00050    003100                             USAGE COMPUTATIONAL-3.                 PRTMASTR
00051    003110     03  NEXT-ASSEMBLY-MSTR  PICTURE S9(13)                         PRTMASTR
00052    003120                             USAGE COMPUTATIONAL-3.                 PRTMASTR
00053    003130     03  TYPE-MSTR           PICTURE X.                             PRTMASTR
00054    003140     03  SOURCE-MSTR         PICTURE X.                             PRTMASTR
00055    003150     03  UNIT-PRICE-MSTR     PICTURE S9(7)                          PRTMASTR
00056    003160                             USAGE COMPUTATIONAL-3.                 PRTMASTR
00057    003170     03  FILLER              PICTURE X(7).                          PRTMASTR
00058    003180                                                                    PRTMASTR
00059    003190 FD  PRTFLE                                                         PRTMASTR
00060    003200     RECORD CONTAINS 121 CHARACTERS                                 PRTMASTR
00061    004010     LABEL RECORDS ARE OMITTED                                      PRTMASTR
00062    004020     DATA RECORD IS PRINT-IOA.                                      PRTMASTR
00063    004030 01  PRINT-IOA.                                                     PRTMASTR
00064    004040     03  FILLER              PICTURE X.                             PRTMASTR
00065    004050     03  PRINT-IO.                                                  PRTMASTR
00066    004060         05  PART-NUMB-PRT   PICTURE ZZBZZZZZZZBZZZZZ.              PRTMASTR
00067    004070         05  FILLER          PICTURE XX.                            PRTMASTR
00068    004080         05  NAME-PRT        PICTURE X(25).                         PRTMASTR
00069    004090         05  FILLER          PICTURE X.                             PRTMASTR
00070    004100         05  NEXT-ASSEM-PRT  PICTURE ZZBZZZZZZZBZZZZZ.              PRTMASTR
00071    004110         05  FILLER          PICTURE XXX.                           PRTMASTR
00072    004120         05  SOURCE-PRT      PICTURE X(4).                          PRTMASTR
00073    004130         05  FILLER          PICTURE X(55).                         PRTMASTR
00074    004140                                                                    PRTMASTR
00075    004150                                                                    PRTMASTR
00076    004160 WORKING-STORAGE SECTION.                                           PRTMASTR
00077    004170 77  PG-COUNT                PICTURE S9(3)       VALUE ZERO         PRTMASTR
00078    004180                             USAGE COMPUTATIONAL-3.                 PRTMASTR
00079    004190 77  VARIABLE                PICTURE 9.                             PRTMASTR
00080    004200 77  SINGLE-SPACING          PICTURE 9           VALUE 1.           PRTMASTR
00081    005010 77  DOUBLE-SPACING          PICTURE 9           VALUE 2.           PRTMASTR
00082    005020 77  LINE-COUNT              PICTURE S999        VALUE ZERO         PRTMASTR
00083    005030                             USAGE COMPUTATIONAL-3.                 PRTMASTR
00084    005040 01  WORKING-AREA.                                                  PRTMASTR
00085    005050     03  HEADER1.                                                   PRTMASTR
00086    005060         05  FILLER          PICTURE X(4)        VALUE SPACES.      PRTMASTR
00087    005070         05  DATE-H1         PICTURE X(8).                          PRTMASTR
```

```
   2

00088   005080       05  FILLER          PICTURE X(25)      VALUE         PRTMASTR
00089   005090       '               MASTER LIS'.                        PRTMASTR
00090   005100       05  FILLER          PICTURE X(26)      VALUE         PRTMASTR
00091   005110       'T              PAGE '.                             PRTMASTR
00092   005120       05  PAGE-H1         PICTURE ZZ9.                     PRTMASTR
00093   005130       05  FILLER          PICTURE X(54)      VALUE SPACES. PRTMASTR
00094   005140   03  HEADER2.                                            PRTMASTR
00095   005150       05  FILLER          PICTURE X(44)      VALUE         PRTMASTR
00096   005160       '   PART NUMBER'.                                   PRTMASTR
00097   005170       05  FILLER          PICTURE X(76)      VALUE         PRTMASTR
00098   005180       'NEXT ASSEMBLY'.                                    PRTMASTR
00099   005190   03  HEADER3.                                            PRTMASTR
00100   005200       05  FILLER          PICTURE X(30)      VALUE         PRTMASTR
00101   006010       'DIV PRIME DASH         DESCRI'.                    PRTMASTR
00102   006020       05  FILLER          PICTURE X(30)      VALUE         PRTMASTR
00103   006030       'PTION        DIV PRIME DASH  '.                    PRTMASTR
00104   006040       05  FILLER          PICTURE X(60)      VALUE         PRTMASTR
00105   006050       'SOURCE'.                                           PRTMASTR
00106   006060                                                           PRTMASTR
00107   006070                                                           PRTMASTR
00108   006080                                                           PRTMASTR
00109   006090 PROCEDURE DIVISION.                                       PRTMASTR
00110   006100                                                           PRTMASTR
00111   006110                                                           PRTMASTR
00112   006120 NOTE-001.                                                 PRTMASTR
00113   006130       NOTE *************************************************PRTMASTR
00114   006140       *   THIS PROGRAM IS USED TO PRINT THE MASTER FILE AFTER  *PRTMASTR
00115   006150       *   IT HAS BEEN CREATED. THE INDEXED SEQUENTIAL MASTER IS *PRTMASTR
00116   006160       *   RETRIEVED SEQUENTIALLY AND A PRINTED REPORT IS   *PRTMASTR
00117   006170       *   CREATED.                                        *PRTMASTR
00118   006180       *************************************************** .PRTMASTR
00119   006190                                                           PRTMASTR
00120   006200 NOTE-002.                                                 PRTMASTR
00121   007010       NOTE *************************************************PRTMASTR
00122   007020       *   THIS ROUTINE IS ENTERED TO OPEN THE FILES AND PRINT *PRTMASTR
00123   007030       *   THE HEADER FOR THE FIRST PAGE.                  *PRTMASTR
00124   007040       *************************************************** .PRTMASTR
00125   007050                                                           PRTMASTR
00126   007060 002-START.                                                PRTMASTR
00127   007070       OPEN INPUT  INVMSTR,                                PRTMASTR
00128   007080            OUTPUT PRTFLE.                                 PRTMASTR
00129   007090       MOVE CURRENT-DATE TO DATE-H1.                       PRTMASTR
00130   007100       PERFORM 400-HEADER THRU 400-EXIT.                   PRTMASTR
00131   007110                                                           PRTMASTR
00132   007120                                                           PRTMASTR
00133   007130 NOTE-010.                                                 PRTMASTR
00134   007140       NOTE *************************************************PRTMASTR
00135   007150       *   THIS ROUTINE IS ENTERED TO SEQUENTIALLY RETRIEVE THE *PRTMASTR
00136   007160       *   INVENTORY MASTER FILE AND PRINT IT.             *PRTMASTR
00137   007170       *************************************************** .PRTMASTR
00138   007180                                                           PRTMASTR
00139   007190 010-READ-MSTR.                                            PRTMASTR
00140   007200       READ INVMSTR AT END GO TO 500-END-MSTR.             PRTMASTR
00141   008010       MOVE PART-NUMB-MSTR TO PART-NUMB-PRT.               PRTMASTR
00142   008020       MOVE NAME-MSTR TO NAME-PRT.                         PRTMASTR
00143   008030       MOVE NEXT-ASSEMBLY-MSTR TO NEXT-ASSEM-PRT.          PRTMASTR
00144   008040       IF SOURCE-MSTR = '1'                                PRTMASTR
00145   008050           MOVE 'MANU' TO SOURCE-PRT                       PRTMASTR
00146   008060       ELSE                                                PRTMASTR
00147   008070           MOVE 'VEND' TO SOURCE-PRT.                      PRTMASTR
00148   008080       PERFORM 200-WRITE-PRT THRU 200-EXIT.                PRTMASTR
00149   008090       GO TO 010-READ-MSTR.                                PRTMASTR
00150   008100                                                           PRTMASTR
00151   008110                                                           PRTMASTR
00152   008120 NOTE-200.                                                 PRTMASTR
00153   008130       NOTE *************************************************PRTMASTR
00154   008140       *   THIS ROUTINE IS ENTERED TO WRITE PRINTER RECORDS. *PRTMASTR
00155   008150       *   IT ISSUES THE WRITE FOR BOTH THE REPORT HEADINGS *PRTMASTR
00156   008160       *   AND THE BODY OF THE REPORT.                     *PRTMASTR
00157   008170       *************************************************** .PRTMASTR
00158   008180                                                           PRTMASTR
00159   008190 200-WRITE-PRT.                                            PRTMASTR
00160   008200       WRITE PRINT-IOA AFTER ADVANCING VARIABLE LINES.     PRTMASTR
00161   009010       ADD 1 TO LINE-COUNT.                                PRTMASTR
00162   009020       MOVE SINGLE-SPACING TO VARIABLE.                    PRTMASTR
00163   009030       IF LINE-COUNT > 50                                  PRTMASTR
00164   009040           PERFORM 400-HEADER THRU 400-EXIT.               PRTMASTR
00165   009050       MOVE SPACES TO PRINT-IO.                            PRTMASTR
00166   009060 200-EXIT.  EXIT.                                          PRTMASTR
00167   009070                                                           PRTMASTR
00168   009080                                                           PRTMASTR
00169   009090 NOTE-400.                                                 PRTMASTR
00170   009100       NOTE *************************************************PRTMASTR
00171   009110       *   THIS ROUTINE IS ENTERED WHENEVER THE END OF THE PAGE *PRTMASTR
00172   009120       *   IS REACHED ON THE PRINTER. IT PRINTS THE HEADER LINES *PRTMASTR
00173   009130       *   AND SETS THE SPACING FOR THE FIRST LINE ON THE REPORT. *PRTMASTR
00174   009140       *************************************************** .PRTMASTR
```

```
    3

00175   009150                                                                    PRTMASTR
00176   009160 400-HEADER.                                                        PRTMASTR
00177   009170     ADD 1 TO PG-COUNT.                                             PRTMASTR
00178   009180     MOVE PG-COUNT TO PAGE-H1.                                      PRTMASTR
00179   009190     MOVE HEADER1 TO PRINT-IO.                                      PRTMASTR
00180   009200     WRITE PRINT-IOA AFTER ADVANCING TO-TOP-OF-PAGE.                PRTMASTR
00181   010010     MOVE HEADER2 TO PRINT-IO.                                      PRTMASTR
00182   010020     MOVE DOUBLE-SPACING TO VARIABLE.                              PRTMASTR
00183   010030     PERFORM 200-WRITE-PRT THRU 200-EXIT.                          PRTMASTR
00184   010040     MOVE SINGLE-SPACING TO VARIABLE.                              PRTMASTR
00185   010050     MOVE HEADER3 TO PRINT-IO.                                      PRTMASTR
00186   010060     PERFORM 200-WRITE-PRT THRU 200-EXIT.                          PRTMASTR
00187   010070     MOVE DOUBLE-SPACING TO VARIABLE.                              PRTMASTR
00188   010080     MOVE 3 TO LINE-COUNT.                                          PRTMASTR
00189   010090 400-EXIT.   EXIT.                                                  PRTMASTR
00190   010100                                                                    PRTMASTR
00191   010110                                                                    PRTMASTR
00192   010120 NOTE-500.                                                          PRTMASTR
00193   010130     NOTE ******************************************************PRTMASTR
00194   010140     *   THIS ROUTINE IS ENTERED WHEN THE INVENTORY MASTER     *PRTMASTR
00195   010150     *   FILE REACHES END-OF-FILE. IT PRINTS AN ENDING MESSAGE *PRTMASTR
00196   010160     *   ON THE PRINTER AND CLOSES THE FILES, AND STOPS THE JOB. *PRTMASTR
00197   010170     ******************************************************.PRTMASTR
00198   010180                                                                    PRTMASTR
00199   010190 500-END-MSTR.                                                      PRTMASTR
00200   010200     MOVE 'END OF MASTER LISTING' TO PRINT-IO.                      PRTMASTR
00201   011010     MOVE DOUBLE-SPACING TO VARIABLE.                              PRTMASTR
00202   011020     PERFORM 200-WRITE-PRT THRU 200-EXIT.                          PRTMASTR
00203   011030     CLOSE INVMSTR,                                                 PRTMASTR
00204   011040           PRTFLE.                                                  PRTMASTR
00205   011050     STOP RUN.                                                      PRTMASTR
```

CHAPTER 4

PROGRAMMING ASSIGNMENT

INSTRUCTIONS

The master file created in the student programming assignment in Chapter 3 is to be used as input to create a Salesman Commission Rate Report. The report should contain:

      1. Department Number
      2. Salesman Number
      3. Salesman Name
      4. Commission Rate

The format of the report is to be designed by the programmer. The Report is a sequential listing of all salesmen contained on the master file.

INDEXED SEQUENTIAL ACCESS METHOD - RANDOM UPDATING

CHAPTER 5

INDEXED SEQUENTIAL ACCESS METHOD - RANDOM UPDATING $\qquad$ 5

INTRODUCTION

As was mentioned in Chapter 1, when a master file is created, it is normally necessary to update the file so that the master contains accurate, up-to-date information. The Indexed Sequential Access Method allows both sequential and random access to a file. Therefore, when using an indexed sequential master file, updating can take place both sequentially and randomly.

RANDOM FILE UPDATE

A **RANDOM** update takes place when a transaction is read and the corresponding master record for that transaction is randomly retrieved from the master file. When a random update is used, it must be possible to randomly retrieve any record on the master file. Random updating can only be performed on a direct access storage device.

A new master file is not created when random updating is used. Thus, a deletion does not eliminate the record from the file as with a sequential update. Instead, in random updating, the deleted record is "flagged" to indicate that the record is to be considered deleted upon subsequent processing runs. A deletion is flagged by recording some type of code on the master record. For example, in the sample program at the end of the chapter, a master record that is effectively deleted from the file is identified by a "2" in the type field of the master record. This code thus indicates that the record is considered deleted even though it is still physically part of the master file.

It must also be possible to add records to the file so that new information can be added to the file. The basic logic of the random update is shown in the flowchart illustrated below.

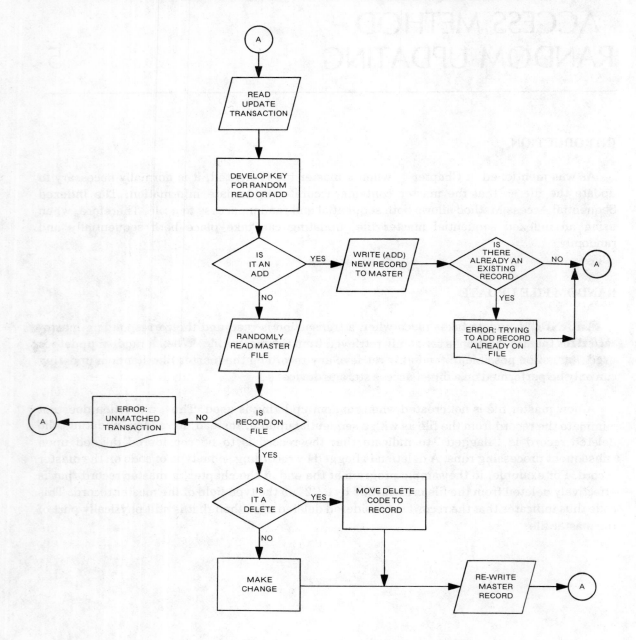

Figure 5-1 Basic Logic of a Random Update

Note that, although the results of the random update are the same as those of the sequential update, the techniques are quite different.

The choice of a sequential or random update is normally made by determining the type of file in use (sequential, indexed sequential, or direct access) and the amount of update activity which will be done against the master file. A sequential file cannot be conveniently updated by any method except the sequential method. A direct access file is normally updated randomly.

An indexed sequential file, however, can be easily updated using a sequential or random technique because records can be processed either sequentially or randomly. Therefore, when using an indexed sequential file, the decision to update randomly or sequentially is normally determined by how much update activity there will be against the master file. Although sequential updating is, when compared on a record to record basis, faster than random updating, it takes a high volume of update activity to make the sequential method faster on an overall run basis. This is because when the sequential method is used, all of the records on the master file must be read and compared to the update transactions. Thus, if the master file consisted of 10,000 records, 10,000 READ's must be issued to read the master records. If only 100 update transactions are being processed against a master file containing 10,000 records, random processing would be faster because, even though random retrieval is slower than sequential retrieval, only 100 master records would have to be retrieved as opposed to 10,000 with sequential updating. It should be noted that when using a sequential update with an indexed sequential file, a new master is NOT created. Instead, the record to be updated is re-written on the file after being changed.

ADDITION OF RECORDS TO INDEXED SEQUENTIAL FILES

As stated previously, one of the functions to be performed by an update program is the addition of records to the master file. Records to be added to the master file have keys which normally place them somewhere between the first and last record on the master file; however, the additions may fall behind the last record on the master file (that is, the key of the record to be added is greater than any key on the master file).

If ALL the records to be added to the master file have keys greater than the highest key on the file, the update records can be LOADED onto the file by making the proper entries in the job control statements and processing the records the same as when the file is being loaded initially (as illustrated in Chapter 3). This situation would normally occur when the file is being extended because a new group of part numbers, etc., were being added to the file. This is not the normal situation when performing an ordinary addition, deletion, and change update to a file.

When making additions to the file where the key of the new record is unknown before processing, the ADD function of ISAM is utilized. This allows records to be added anywhere in the file.

The method of adding records to an existing indexed sequential file is illustrated in the following examples. These examples illustrate the contents of the cylinder index, the track index, the prime data area and the overflow area, when the file is initially loaded and after records have been added to the file.

STEP 1: The file is loaded as shown in the program in Chapter 3. Cylinder 1 Track 1 contains records 6-20, Cylinder 1 Track 2 contains records 24-45. The highest record on Cylinder 1 is record 150, which is stored on Track 15.

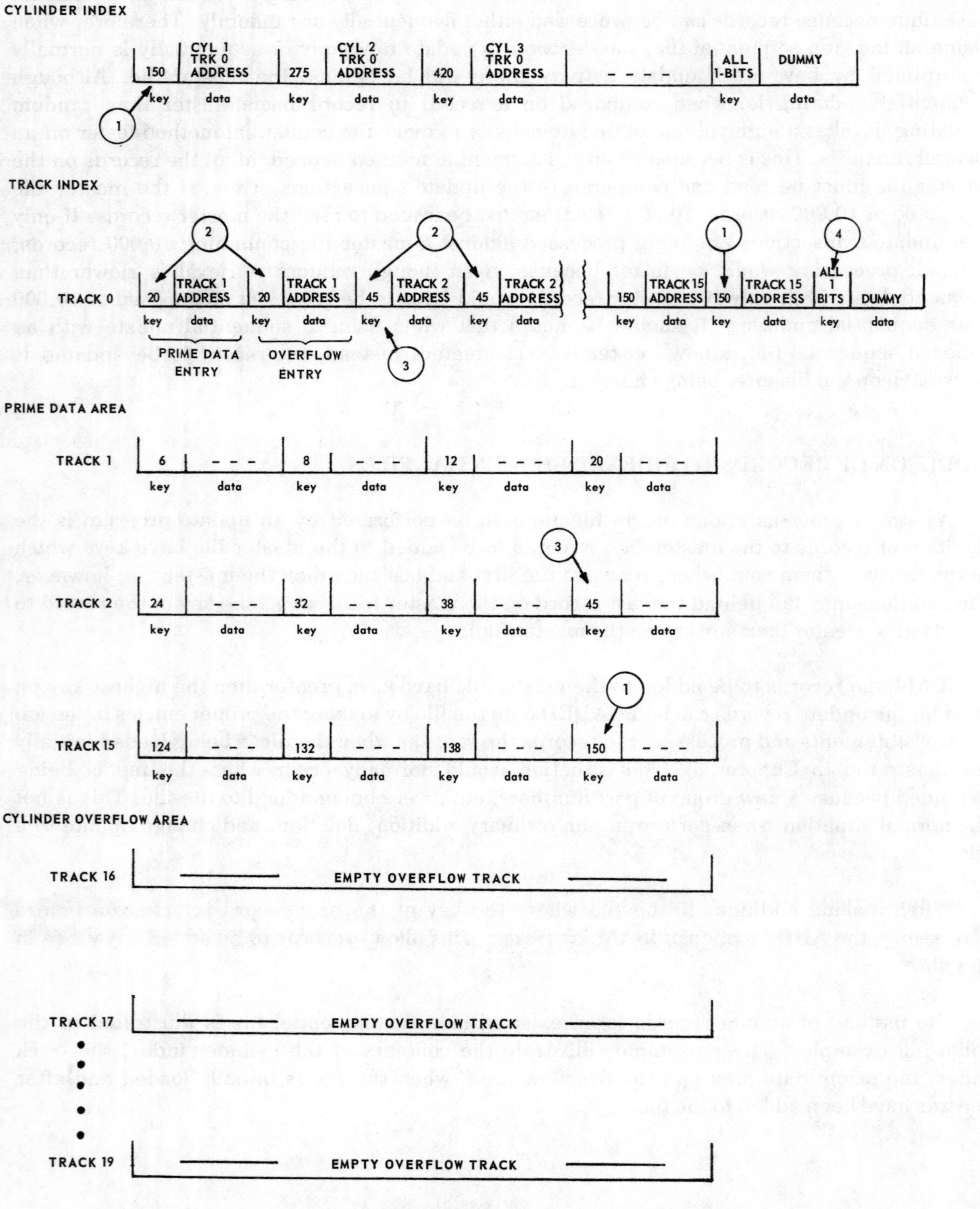

Figure 5-2 Indexes and Data Area - File is Loaded

Note in the example that tracks 16, 17, 18 and 19 are the overflow tracks for each cylinder in the prime data area. This is because COBOL automatically assigns four tracks to be used as cylinder overflow tracks when a 2314 device is used. Note also that only the first two tracks of the prime data area and the cylinder overflow area are shown. This is for illustration purposes and the complete file would be processed in the same manner as shown for these two tracks.

Important features of the file as it is organized are:

1. The highest key contained in the cylinder index for cylinder 1 corresponds to the highest key in the track index for track 15, the last track used for prime data. It is always true that the cylinder index contains the highest key which is on the corresponding cylinder. In the example the highest key on cylinder 1 is 150. Note the entries in the cylinder index and the track index.

2. There are always two entries in the track index for each track on the cylinder. The first entry is used for the prime data area, and the second entry is used for the overflow area when records are added to the file, as will be shown. When no records are contained in the overflow area, such as in the example in Figure 5-2, the entries both contain the same value indicating the highest key on the track. In the example, the highest key on track 1 is 20, the highest key on track 2 is 45, etc.

3. The key specified in the track index is always the highest key which is on the associated track.

4. The end of the track index is specified by a key of all 1-bits. It is possible to have data following the track index on track 0 if there is room on the track to write a block of data. When this is done, track 0 is called a **SHARED TRACK**. In the example, there was not enough room on track 0 to write a record, so the data begins on track 1.

It should also be noted that if the records being used for the file are blocked, the key used for the block and in the indexes is the highest key in the block. Thus, if the block of records appeared as illustrated below, the key for the block would be 125.

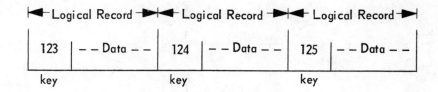

Figure 5-3 Block of Records With Keys

STEP 2: A record with a key of 18 is added to the file.

CYLINDER INDEX

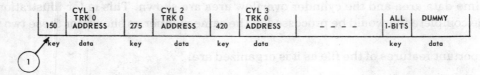

TRACK INDEX

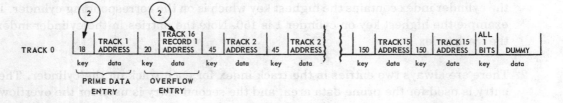

PRIME DATA AREA

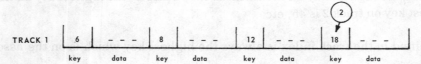

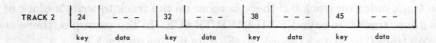

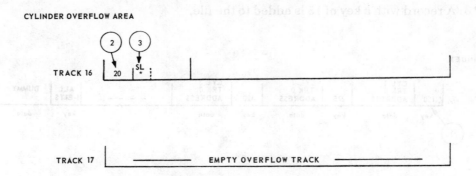

Figure 5-4 Indexes and Data Area - Record With Key of 18 is Added

After a record with a key = 18 has been added to the file, note the following:

1. The entries in the cylinder index have not been altered because the highest key on the cylinder has not been altered.

2. Record 18* was inserted between record 12 and record 20. **ISAM** always inserts a new record where it belongs on the prime data area to keep the keys in an ascending sequence. When record 18 was inserted, no room remained on the track for record 20, so it was moved to the overflow area. The track index reflects this move by altering its entries as shown. The first entry in the track index for track 1 contains the highest key physically stored on the track. This is key 18 because it became the highest key on the track. The second entry contains the highest key from track 1 which is in the overflow area. In the example, the key is 20. The data portion of the second entry for track 1 contains the track and record address of the record which would immediately follow the highest key physically stored on the track. In the example, this is record 20.

3. The sequence link field (S.L.) is established by **ISAM** for every record which goes into the overflow area. The sequence link field is used to link the records in the overflow area. The * indicates that there are no other records in the overflow area from track 1.

* When referencing the records in this example, a record with a key = 18 will be called record 18, etc.

STEP 3: A record with a key of 15 is added to the file.

CYLINDER INDEX

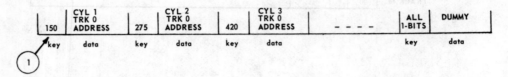

TRACK INDEX

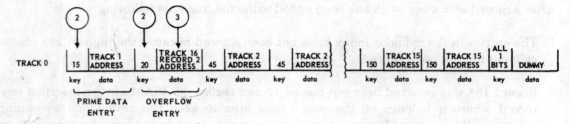

PRIME DATA AREA

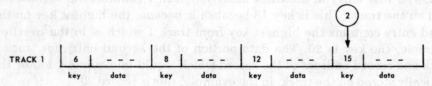

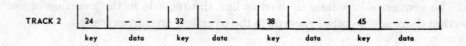

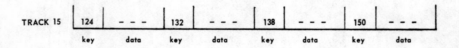

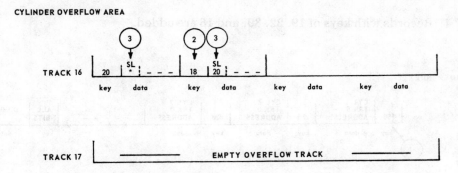

Figure 5-5 Indexes and Data Area - Record With Key of 15 is Added

After a record with a key of 15 has been added, note the following:

1. The cylinder index has not changed because the highest key on the cylinder has not been altered.

2. The first entry in the track index reflects the highest key stored on the track. Therefore, 15 is the key specified because **ISAM** inserted the record in its proper place on the track to keep the records in an ascending sequence by key. Therefore, record 18 was moved to the overflow area. Note, however, that the key value in the second entry of the track index still shows 20. This is because 20 is still the highest key value from track 1 in the overflow area.

3. The sequence link field is now used because there are two records from track 1 in the overflow area. The data in the second entry for track 1 in the track index now points to track 16, record 2. This is because record 18 is the next sequentially ascending record after the last record on track 1 (key = 15). The sequence link field in record 18 points to record 20 because it is the next sequentially ascending record from track 1. The sequence link field in record 20 indicates no more records are in the overflow area from track 1.

STEP 4: Records with keys of 19, 22, 39, and 16 are added.

CYLINDER INDEX

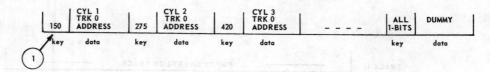

TRACK INDEX

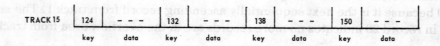

PRIME DATA AREA

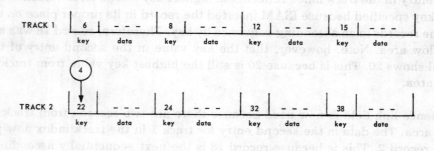

CYLINDER OVERFLOW AREA

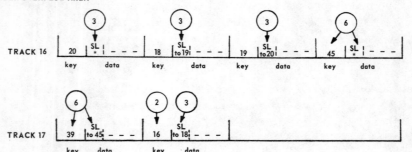

Figure 5-6 Indexes and Data Area - Records with Key of 19, 22, 39 and 16 are Added

When record 19 was added to the file, it was placed in the overflow area on track 16. Record 22 was placed as the first record on track 2 and record 45, which was originally on track 2 (see Figure 5-5), was placed in the overflow area on track 16. Record 39 was placed directly in the overflow area on track 17, as there was no room on track 16 in the overflow area. When record 16 was added, it was placed in the overflow area on track 17.

After the above records have been added, note the following:

1. The cylinder index has not been altered.

2. The key entries for track 1 in the track index are still the same. The highest key stored on the track is 15 and the highest key in the overflow area from track 1 is 20. Note, however, that the address in the second data entry for track 1 in the track index has changed. It now points to record 16. Record 16 was added directly to the overflow area because its key was higher than the highest key located on track 1 (15).

3. The sequence link fields in the overflow records for track 1 all point to the next sequentially ascending record from track 1. Thus, 16 points to 18, 18 points to 19 and 19 points to 20. Note that the sequence link field in record 18 was altered to point to record 19 when record 19 was added. Record 20 indicates no more linkages. Even though there are higher keys in the overflow area (39 and 45), they are not from track 1 in the prime data area and thus are not linked with record 20.

4. Record 22 was added to track 2. It was added to track 2 even though its key was lower than the previous low key (24) because it was higher than the highest key on track 1. Records are always added in this manner. The highest key on a track when a file is loaded remains the highest key when other processing is done against the file.

5. The entries in the track index have been modified to reflect the addition of records to track 2. The first entry for track 2 indicates that the highest key stored on track 2 is 38. This is because record 22 was added. The second key entry for track 2 indicates that 45 is the highest key associated with the track. The data for the second entry points to record 39 which is the next sequentially ascending record in the overflow area after the last record on track 2 (38).

6. Record 45 was moved to the overflow area when record 22 was added. Record 39 was added directly to the overflow area because its key was greater than the highest key in the prime data area. Its sequence link field points to record 45 because record 45 is the next sequentially ascending record from track 2.

More additions could be made to the file and processing would continue until the overflow areas were full. At that point, it would be necessary to reorganize the file to eliminate records in the overflow areas. It should be noted that after the cylinder overflow areas are full, an independent overflow area can be used to hold additional records.

All records in both the cylinder and independent overflow areas are unblocked even though the file may be blocked in the prime data areas.

RANDOM RETRIEVAL

Random retrieval and updating normally involves the retrieving of a master record from a file (based on a given key from the corresponding transaction record), updating the master record and re-writing the updated master record on the master file. When an indexed sequential file is randomly retrieved, a search of the indexes precedes the actual retrieval of the desired record. The search of the indexes locates the exact disk location of the record and the record is then read into computer storage. If it was desired to retrieve the record with a key of 19 from the previous example, the following routine would be followed (this assumes no master index):

1. The cylinder index is read and it is determined record 19 resides on cylinder 1. This is because the highest key on cylinder 1 is 150.

2. The track index is read and searched to find what track record 19 is on. It is found that the highest key associated with track 1 is 20, but that the highest key on track 1 in the prime data area is 15. Therefore, record 19, if it is on the file, must be in the overflow area.

3. The address of the first sequentially ascending record in the overflow area is obtained from the second data entry in the track index for track 1. This address is track 17, record 2.

4. The record at track 17, record 2 is read and the key is 16. However, the sequence link field points to another record, so that record is read. The key for the record is 18, but the sequence link field points to the next record from track 1. This record is record 19, so it is returned to computer storage in the I/O area or work area for random retrieval. The program can then process the record.

It should be noted that, had record 19 not been on the file, the next record would have been record 20. Since 20 is greater than 19 and the records are in ascending order, the **INVALID KEY** routine would have been entered, indicating that the record was not on the file.

SAMPLE PROGRAM

In the sample problem developed in this chapter, the indexed sequential inventory master file is to be updated with additions, deletions, and changes. It has been determined that random updating would be the most efficient method. The transaction file which contains the update transactions is a sequential disk file created using the program developed in Chapter 2, and illustrated in Step 5 of the systems flowchart in Figure 2-2. The format of the update transaction records (stored on the disk file) and the format of the records in the indexed sequential inventory master file are illustrated below.

Transaction Records

FIELD	FIELD NAME	PICTURE	POSITION	NO OF DIGITS	LENGTH
Part Number	PART-NUMB				
Division Number	DIV	XX	1-2	2	2
Prime Number	PRIME	X(6)	3-8	6	6
Dash Number	DASH	X(5)	9-13	5	5
Description	NAME	X(25)	14-38	25	25
Qty on Hand	QTY-ON-HAND	X(7)	39-45	7	7
Qty on Order	QTY-ON-ORDER	X(7)	46-52	7	7
Qty Reserved	QTY-RESERVED	X(7)	53-59	7	7
Part Number-NA	NEXT-ASSEMBLY				
Division-NA	DIV-NA	XX	60-61	2	2
Prime-NA	PRIME-NA	X(6)	62-67	6	6
Dash-NA	DASH-NA	X(5)	68-72	5	5
Type	TYPE	X	73	1	1
Source	SOURCE	X	74	1	1
Unit Price	UNIT-PRICE	X(6)	75-80	6	6

Master Records

FIELD	FIELD NAME	PICTURE	POSITION	NO OF DIGITS	LENGTH
Part Number	PART-NUMB-MSTR	Picture 9(13) Comp-3	1-7	13	7
Description	NAME-MSTR	Picture X(25)	8-32	25	25
Quantity on Hand	QTY-ON-HAND-MSTR	Picture S9(7) Comp-3	33-36	7	4
Quantity on Order	QTY-ON-ORDER-MSTR	Picture S9(7) Comp-3	37-40	7	4
Quantity Reserved	QTY-RESERVED-MSTR	Picture S9(7) Comp-3	41-44	7	4
Next Assembly Number	NEXT-ASSEMBLY-MSTR	Picture S9(13) Comp-3	45-51	13	7
Type	TYPE-MSTR	Picture X	52	1	1
Source	SOURCE-MSTR	Picture X	53	1	1
Unit Price	UNIT-PRICE-MSTR	Picture S9(7) Comp-3	54-57	6	4
Filler	FILLER	Picture X(7)	58-64	7	7

Figure 5-7 Transaction and Master Record Formats

Records that are to be deleted from the master file will be flagged by placing a '2' in the type-code field (**TYPE-MSTR**) of the master record. Duplicate records, or records with invalid keys which are read from the transaction file will be printed on the exception report.

ADDITIONS AND RANDOM RETRIEVAL - INDEXED SEQUENTIAL FILES

As with all indexed sequential files, the file definition to allow additions and random retrieval require entries in both the Environment Division and the Data Division. When making additions or performing random retrieval, the clauses **ACCESS IS RANDOM**, **RECORD KEY IS**, and **NOMINAL KEY IS** are used together with the proper entries in the **System Name**. The entries used in the sample program to define both the indexed sequential master file and the sequential transaction file are illustrated in Figure 5-8.

```
003020 FILE-CONTROL.
003030       SELECT INVMSTR
003040          ASSIGN TO SYS006-DA-2314-I-INVMSTR
003050          ACCESS IS RANDOM
003060          RECORD KEY IS PART-NUMB-MSTR
003070          NOMINAL KEY IS MSTR-KEY.
003080       SELECT TRANSIN
003090          ASSIGN TO SYS007-UT-2314-S-TRANSIN.

004020 DATA DIVISION.
004030 FILE SECTION.
004040 FD INVMSTR
004050    BLOCK CONTAINS 54 RECORDS
004060    RECORD CONTAINS 64 CHARACTERS
004070    LABEL RECORDS ARE STANDARD
004080    DATA RECORD IS MSTR-IO.
004090 01 MSTR-IO.
004100    03 PART-NUMB-MSTR         PICTURE 9(13)
004110                              USAGE COMPUTATIONAL-3.
004120    03 NAME-MSTR              PICTURE X(25).

005020 FD TRANSIN
005030    BLOCK CONTAINS 44 RECORDS
005040    RECORD CONTAINS 80 CHARACTERS
005050    LABEL RECORDS ARE STANDARD
005060    DATA RECORD IS TRANS-IO.
005070 01 TRANS-IO.
005080    03 PART-NUMB-TRANS        PICTURE 9(13).
005090    03 NAME-TRANS             PICTURE X(25).

007130 WORKING-STORAGE SECTION.
007140 77 MSTR-KEY                  PICTURE 9(13)
007150                              USAGE COMPUTATIONAL-3.
```

**Figure 5-8 Entries in Environment Division and Data Division
For Random Indexed Sequential File**

In the example above, note that the **SELECT** statement indicates that the name of the master file will be **INVMSTR** and that it will be on a 2314 direct access device, which will be assigned to "SYS006" at execution time. The "I" indicates that the file is an indexed sequential file.

The **ACCESS IS RANDOM** clause states that the file will be accessed randomly, that is, whenever a **READ** command is issued to the file, the record to be read will be retrieved randomly, not sequentially. The Access Is Random clause also implies that any **REWRITE** command issued will be a rewrite of a record previously retrieved randomly, and that any **WRITE** command issued will be a command to **ADD** a record to the already organized indexed sequential file.

The **RECORD KEY IS** clause identifies the field within the record that is the key for the record. In the sample program, this field is the part number field and is given the data-name **PART-NUMB-MSTR**. The **NOMINAL KEY IS** clause states the data-name of a field defined in Working-Storage which will contain the key of the record which is to be retrieved randomly. In the sample program, this field is named **MSTR-KEY**.

The transaction input file (**TRANSIN**) is defined in the same manner as when it was input to the program in Chapter 3 to load the indexed sequential file.

RANDOM UPDATING

As noted previously, when an indexed sequential file is to be updated randomly, it must be possible to both randomly retrieve and update a record on the file and to add new records to the file. In order to accomplish this, certain steps must be taken in the program to determine what update action should be accomplished and then perform the desired function. The following example illustrates the steps which should be taken to randomly update a record in an indexed sequential file.

Step 1: **OPEN** the transaction file as an input file and the indexed sequential file as an "I-O" file.

```
Ø11Ø2Ø        OPEN INPUT  TRANSIN
Ø11Ø3Ø             I-O    INVMSTR
Ø11Ø4Ø             OUTPUT PRTFLE.
```

Figure 5-9 OPENing of the Transaction File, Master File, and Report File

In the coding shown above, the transaction file is opened as an input file because it is a sequential disk file which contains the update transactions which will update the master file. The master file is opened as an "I-O" file so that both random retrieval and updating can take place and records can be added to the file. The output file **PRTFLE** is the error report file.

Step 2: **READ** the transaction input file.

```
Ø11Ø8Ø    Ø1Ø-READ-TRANS.
Ø11Ø9Ø        READ TRANSIN AT END GO TO 6ØØ-END-TRANS.
```

Figure 5-10 READing of the Transaction Input File

The transaction record to update the indexed sequential inventory master file is read from the sequential disk file. In addition to the data in the record to update the master record, a type code is contained in the record.

The type code field in the transaction records can contain the following codes:

1 = Add Record
2 = Delete Record
3 = Change Quantity on Hand
4 = Change Quantity on Order
5 = Change Quantity Reserved
6 = Change Next Assembly Part Number
7 = Change Source
8 = New Load
9 = Change Unit Price

When the transaction record is read, different routines must be entered depending upon the value in the type code field. Thus, the next step is to determine which of the processing routines in the update program should be entered.

Step 3: Determine which routine to enter in the update program through the use of the **GO TO. . . DEPENDING ON** statement.

```
012050        GO TO    200-ADD-REC
012060                 210-DEL-REC
012070                 220-CHNG-QOH
012080                 230-CHNG-QOO
012090                 240-CHNG-QRSV
012100                 250-CHNG-NA
012110                 260-CHNG-SRCE
012120                 270-BAD-TYPE
012130                 280-CHNG-UNIT
012140         DEPENDING ON TYPE-TRANS.
```

Figure 5-11 Example of GO TO . . . DEPENDING ON Statement To Determine Update Processing

The **GO TO** statement shown in Figure 5-11 will branch to the proper update routine based upon the numeric value contained in the **TYPE-TRANS** field in the transaction record. It should be recalled that the program which creates the transaction file (the sample program presented in Chapter 2) verifies that the type field contains the numeric values 1 through 9. Thus, one of the routines stated in the **GO TO** statement will always be entered. It should also be recalled that a type code of 8 is used to signify a ''load'' transaction and is invalid in the update program. Thus, if a value of 8 is contained in the type field, the routine **270-BAD-TYPE** will be entered to issue an error message on the exception report.

After the **GO TO** statement, a record on the master file will be updated or a new record will be added to the file. Step 4 assumes the transaction type code is equal to 2, which indicates the corresponding master record is to be deleted.

Step 4: Process the ''delete'' transaction.

```
013020  210-DELREC.
013030       PERFORM 320-READ-MSTR THRU 320-EXIT.
013040       IF INV-READ = '1'
013050            MOVE '0' TO INV-READ
013060            GO TO 010-READ-TRANS.
013070       MOVE '2' TO TYPE-MSTR.
013080       GO TO 225-RETURN.

014020  225-RETURN.
014030       REWRITE MSTR-IO INVALID KEY
014040            MOVE BAD-READ-MSG TO ERROR-PRT
014050            MOVE TRANS-IO TO RECORD-PRT
014060            PERFORM 430-WRITE-PRT THRU 430-EXIT.
014070       GO TO 010-READ-TRANS.

015020  320-READ-MSTR.
015030       MOVE PART-NUMB-TRANS TO MSTR-KEY.
015040       READ INVMSTR INVALID KEY
015050            MOVE '1' TO INV-READ
015060            MOVE NO-RECORD-MSG TO ERROR-PRT
015070            MOVE TRANS-IO TO RECORD-PRT
015080            PERFORM 430-WRITE-PRT THRU 430-EXIT
015090            GO TO 320-EXIT.
015100  320A-EXIT. EXIT.
015110  320A-CHK-TYPE.
015120       IF TYPE-MSTR IS = '2'
015130            MOVE '1' TO INV-READ
015140       MOVE NO-RECORD-MSG TO ERROR-PRT
015150       MOVE TRANS-IO TO RECORD-PRT
015160            PERFORM 430-WRITE-PRT THRU 430-EXIT.
015170  320-EXIT. EXIT.
```

Figure 5-12 Delete Routine in Random Update

The routine **210-DELREC** is entered when the type code in the transaction record is equal to 2, which indicates that the master record is to be deleted from the master file. The first task for the delete routine is to read the inventory master record randomly from the indexed sequential master file. This is accomplished by **PERFORM**ing the **320-READ-MSTR** routine.

The first **MOVE** statement in the **320-READ-MSTR** routine moves the part number from the transaction record to the **NOMINAL KEY** field as defined in the **SELECT** statement for the file (see Figure 5-8). The **NOMINAL KEY** field is **MSTR-KEY**. Before any random read is performed on an indexed sequential file, the key of the record to be retrieved MUST be stored in the **NOMINAL KEY** area in the exact same format and containing the exact same information that is in the key for the record in the indexes of the file. Thus, the field **MSTR-KEY** is an unsigned Computational-3 field, the same as the field for the key in the record (**PART-NUMB-MSTR**). When the field **PART-NUMB-TRANS** is moved to **MSTR-KEY**, the numeric data will be packed and signed with an absolute sign (hexadecimal "F"). This move ensures that the data in **MSTR-KEY** will be the same as the data in the indexes of the indexed sequential file. The contents of computer storage before and after the move are illustrated in the example in Figure 5-13.

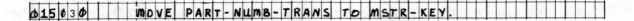

Before Execution:

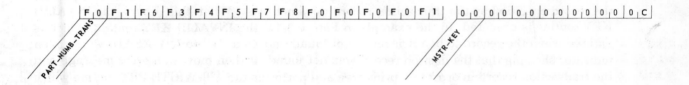

After Execution:

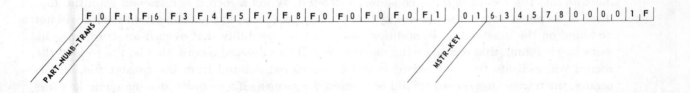

Figure 5-13 Example of Move Statement to Move the Key to the Nominal Key Area

Note in the example that, as described previously, the numeric data in **PART-NUMB-TRANS** is packed into the Nominal Key field **MSTR-KEY**. The Nominal Key field, after the move, contains the key for the record to be retrieved in the same format as the key is contained in the indexes of the indexed sequential file.

The **READ** statement is then issued to retrieve the record on the indexed sequential file whose key is stored in the Nominal Key area. The **READ** statement is again illustrated in Figure 5-14.

```
Ø15Ø4Ø          READ INVMSTR INVALID KEY
Ø15Ø5Ø                        MOVE '1' TO INV-READ
Ø15Ø6Ø                        MOVE NO-RECORD-MSG TO ERROR-PRT
Ø15Ø7Ø                        MOVE TRANS-IO TO RECORD-PRT
Ø15Ø8Ø                        PERFORM 43Ø-WRITE-PRT THRU 43Ø-EXIT
Ø15Ø9Ø                        GO TO 32Ø-EXIT.
Ø151ØØ  32ØA-EXIT. EXIT.
```

Figure 5-14 READ Statement to Randomly Retrieve a Record

The Read Statement in Figure 5-14 will read the record from the indexed sequential file whose key is stored in the Nominal Key area. When the execution of the **READ** is complete, the record will be available for processing in the I/O area defined for the file in the File Section of the Data Division.

Whenever a record is to be retrieved randomly by key, the possibility exists that the key presented in the transaction record does not correspond to any key on the master file, that is, the record specified by the transaction record does not exist. When this occurs, the **INVALID KEY** routine is executed. In the example in Figure 5-14, the **INVALID KEY** routine, which is entered when the record to be retrieved is not found, moves a ''1'' to **INV-READ**, which is an indicator showing that the desired record was not found. It then moves an error message and the transaction record in error to a print area and performs the **430-WRITE-PRT** routine which prints the error message on the exception report.

As was noted previously, when a record is deleted from an indexed sequential file, it is not physically removed from the file. Instead, some type of indicator must be placed in the record to indicate that the record is to be considered deleted. When a record is retrieved from the file, there is, as noted above, the possibility that the key presented in the transaction record will not be found on the master file. In addition, there is the possibility that even if a record with the same key is found, that record on the master file will be a deleted record, that is, the code in the record will indicate that the record is to be considered deleted from the master file. If this occurs, the transaction record should be treated the same as if a record with a matching key was not found on the file. Therefore, as illustrated in Figure 5-15, after the record is read, it is checked to see if it is a logically deleted record. If so, then an error message is printed on the exception report.

```
Ø151ØØ  32ØA-CHK-TYPE.
Ø1511Ø          IF TYPE-MSTR IS = '2'
Ø1512Ø                        MOVE '1' TO INV-READ
Ø1513Ø                        MOVE NO-RECORD-MSG TO ERROR-PRT
Ø1514Ø                        MOVE TRANS-IO TO RECORD-PRT
Ø1515Ø                        PERFORM 43Ø-WRITE-PRT THRU 43Ø-EXIT.
Ø1516Ø  32Ø-EXIT. EXIT.
```

Figure 5-15 Routine to Check for Deleted Record

As can be seen in Figure 5-15, if the record contains a type-code of ''2'', it is considered a deleted record on the file. An error message will be written on the Exception Report and the **INV-READ** switch will be set to ''1'', indicating that the record has not been found on the master file.

After the **320-READ-MSTR** routine is performed, the delete routine tests the **INV-READ** indicator to see if it contains a ''1'' (see Figure 5-12). If so, it indicates that the Invalid Key routine was entered when the read of the record was attempted and that the record specified in the transaction record was not retrieved. Therefore, no more processing can be performed on the delete transaction. Thus, the indicator is reset to zero and a branch is made back to the routine to read the next transaction record. It should be noted that this indicator is set in the **320-READ-MSTR** routine and checked in the delete routine. The reason that a branch to the routine to read the next transaction record (**010-READ-TRANS**) is not made in the **320-READ-MSTR** routine is that it would be a branch out of a ''Performed'' subroutine and this is NOT a good programming technique. As mentioned in Chapter 2 a ''Performed'' subroutine should always return to the statement following the Perform statement which called it and let the calling routine make any branch decisions.

If the record indicated in the transaction record was retrieved, the delete routine moves a ''2'' to the type field in the master record. It should be recalled that when randomly updating an indexed sequential file, a new file is NOT created. Thus, all records which were a part of the file when the update began will be a part of the file when the update is complete. Any record which is to be effectively deleted from the file must be ''flagged'' to indicate that in future processing the record is to be considered deleted even though it is still physically part of the file. In the sample program, a value ''2'' in the type field of the master record indicates that the record is to be considered deleted from the file.

After the master has been processed, that is, after the type field has been changed to a ''2'', the record must be rewritten on the master file. The delete routine branches to the **225-RETURN** routine to rewrite the updated record. The **225-RETURN** routine is again illustrated in Figure 5-16.

```
Ø14Ø2Ø 225-RETURN.
Ø14Ø3Ø     REWRITE MSTR-IO INVALID KEY
Ø14Ø4Ø                     MOVE BAD-READ-MSG TO ERROR-PRT
Ø14Ø5Ø                     MOVE TRANS-IO TO RECORD-PRT
Ø14Ø6Ø                     PERFORM 43Ø-WRITE-PRT THRU 43Ø-EXIT.
Ø14Ø7Ø     GO TO Ø1Ø-READ-TRANS.
```

Figure 5-16 Example of REWRITE Command

In the example in Figure 5-16, the record previously retrieved by the **READ** command and updated in the delete routine is rewritten on the indexed sequential master file by the **REWRITE** command. The data-name following the **REWRITE** verb is the name of the I/O area defined in the File Section of the Data Division for the indexed sequential file.

It should be noted that when randomly updating, the **REWRITE** command must not be issued if a **READ** command has not preceded it. Also, it is important to note that both the **RECORD KEY** and the **NOMINAL KEY** must not be altered in any way between the time the random **READ** is executed and the time the **REWRITE** is executed. The Record Key may be referenced through comparisons, etc., during update processing, but it must not be altered. This is a requirement because the indexes of the indexed sequential file are not altered during random updating and if the record key is changed, the indexes will not correspond to the key of the record on the file.

The Invalid Key clause must be included to indicate the processing which will take place if a valid Read operation has not preceded the **REWRITE** Statement. In the example, an error message will be written on the exception report and then the next transaction will be read.

The other update routines in the sample program, such as the changes to the quantity on hand routine, the changes to the unit price, etc., are processed in the same basic way as the delete processing. The records are randomly retrieved, updated, and rewritten back onto the indexed sequential master file.

ADDITIONS

The routine presented in Figure 5-11 determines what processing will occur depending upon the value in the **TYPE-TRANS** field in the transaction record. Step 4 as illustrated in Figure 5-12, assumed that the type code indicated that a master record was to be deleted. If the type code in the transaction record is equal to "1", it indicates that a record is to be added to the indexed sequential inventory master file. Thus, Step 5 in Figure 5-17, illustrates the routine which is entered when a new record is to be added to the master file.

Step 5: ADD a new record to the master file.

```
012020  200-ADDREC.
012030      MOVE PART-NUMB-TRANS TO PART-NUMB-MSTR.
012040      MOVE NAME-TRANS TO NAME-MSTR.
012050      MOVE QTY-ON-HAND-TRANS TO QTY-ON-HAND-MSTR.
012060      MOVE QTY-ON-ORDER-TRANS TO QTY-ON-ORDER-MSTR.
012070      MOVE QTY-RESERVED-TRANS TO QTY-RESERVED-MSTR.
012080      MOVE NEXT-ASSEMBLY-TRANS TO NEXT-ASSEMBLY-MSTR.
012090      MOVE '1' TO TYPE-MSTR.
012100      MOVE SOURCE-TRANS TO SOURCE-MSTR.
012110      MOVE UNIT-PRICE-TRANS TO UNIT-PRICE-MSTR.
012120      MOVE PART-NUMB-TRANS TO MSTR-KEY.
012130      MOVE MSTR-IO TO SAVE-MSTR.
012140      WRITE MSTR-IO INVALID KEY GO TO 340-INV-ADD.
012150      GO TO 010-READ-TRANS.

014020  225-RETURN.
014030      REWRITE MSTR-IO INVALID KEY
014040                  MOVE BAD-READ-MSG TO ERROR-PRT
014050                  MOVE TRANS-IO TO RECORD-PRT
014060                  PERFORM 430-WRITE-PRT THRU 430-EXIT.
014070      GO TO 010-READ-TRANS.

018020  340-INV-ADD.
018030      PERFORM 320-READ-MSTR THRU 320A-EXIT.
018040      IF TYPE-MSTR IS = '2'
018050          MOVE SAVE-MSTR TO MSTR-IO
018060          GO TO 225-RETURN
018070      ELSE
018080          MOVE DUPLICATE-MSG TO ERROR-PRT
018090          MOVE TRANS-IO TO RECORD-PRT
018100          PERFORM 430-WRITE-PRT THRU 430-EXIT
018110          GO TO 010-READ-TRANS.
```

Figure 5-17 Example of ADD Routine

The first portion of the **200-ADDREC** routine "builds" the output record by moving all the fields in the transaction input record to the output fields defined for the inventory master file. Note at pg/line 012130 that the entire record is saved in an area defined in Working-Storage. This is done in case there is a duplicate record on the master file. If a duplicate record is found, it will be read into the master I/O area and if the record to be added was not saved, it would be destroyed by the Read.

After the record has been built in the master I/O area, the **WRITE** command is used to add the record to the indexed sequential inventory master file. The data-name following the **WRITE** verb is the name of the Input/Output field defined in the File Section of the Data Division for the indexed sequential file. This is the same format used for all previous Write commands to the card punch, printer, etc.

As noted previously, two records with the same key cannot be contained in the same indexed sequential file. When adding records to an already established file, the possibility exists that a record which is to be added has the same key as a record already on the file. If this occurs, the **INVALID KEY** routine is entered.

In the example in Figure 5-17, when a record with a duplicate key is attempted to be added to the file, the **340-INV-ADD** routine is entered. This routine will first retrieve the record which is on the file by performing the **320-READ-MSTR** routine up to the exit point **320A-EXIT** (see Figure 5-12). Thus, the record will be retrieved, but the type will not be checked in the Read routine. This is because special processing must be performed for adding a record depending upon the content of the type field.

The reason that the record is read is because there is a possibility that the record on the master file is a record which has been previously deleted, that is, although still physically part of the master file, it is to be considered deleted in all processing. If this is the case, the new record can be added because it will be considered a new record. Thus, the next step in the **340-INV-ADD** routine is to check the value in the type field (**TYPE-MSTR**) in the master record. If it is equal to ''2'', it is a deleted record. When this occurs, the record to be added, which has been saved in the Working-Storage area **SAVE-MSTR**, is moved to the file I/O area (**MSTR-IO**) and a branch is taken to the **225-RETURN** routine to rewrite the new record in place of the old master record, which was a deleted record. Thus, in effect, the new record is added in place of the old, deleted master record.

If the record on the master file is not a deleted record, the new record to be added to the file is in error. Therefore, an error message and the record in error are moved to the printer area and they are written on the exception report by performing the **430-WRITE-PRT** routine. The **INVALID KEY** routine then returns to the **010-READ-TRANS** routine to read the next transaction record.

As shown in the previous steps, with the proper file definitions and use of the correct verbs, the indexed sequential file can be randomly updated and records can be added to the file. The following page summarizes the entries for random updating and additions.

SUMMARY
INDEXED SEQUENTIAL ACCESS METHOD
RANDOM UPDATING AND ADDITIONS

In order to randomly update an indexed sequential file and add records to the file, the following entries are required in the **SELECT** statement in the Environment Division.

- **DEVICE SPECIFIED AS "DA"** (Direct-Access)
- **ORGANIZATION SPECIFIED AS "I"** (Indexed)
- **ACCESS IS RANDOM**
- **RECORD KEY IS** data-name
- **NOMINAL KEY IS** data-name

In order to process the indexed sequential file, the following entries are made in the Procedure Division.

- **OPEN I-O** file-name (for indexed sequential file)
- **READ** file-name **INVALID KEY** any imperative statement(s) - used for random retrieval
- **REWRITE** record-name - used to rewrite a previously retrieved master record
- **WRITE** record-name **INVALID KEY** any imperative statement(s) - used to add records to the indexed sequential file
- **CLOSE** file-name

ARITHMETIC PROGRAMMING CONSIDERATIONS

Arithmetic operations, such as add, subtract, multiply, divide, compute, etc., can only be performed on data fields which are defined as numeric (Picture 9). These numeric fields can be defined using any **USAGE** clause desired, that is, the field may be Display, Computational, Computational-3, etc. Although all of the Usages are valid in arithmetic operations, the indiscriminate use of fields defined as different formats in arithmetic operations can lead to excessive usage of main storage and longer execution times than are desirable.

The following examples of Add instructions are given to illustrate the steps taken when adding fields of the same and different modes.

1. Add Display to Display: Both Display fields must be packed to work areas and they are then added. The answer is unpacked back to the Display answer field.

2. Add Computational-3 to Computational-3: A single add instruction adds the two fields.

3. Add Computational to Computational: The two fields are added in the binary mode.

4. Add Computational to Computational-3: The Computational field is converted to a Computational-3 field, or the Computational-3 field is converted to Computational, depending on the size of the field, and the two fields are added.

5. Add Computational-3 to Computational: The Computational-3 field is converted to Computational, or vice versa, depending on the sizes of the fields, the fields are added and then the answer is stored into the Computational field.

6. Add Computational to Display: Both the Computational and Display fields are converted to Computational-3, or the Display data is converted to Computational. They are then added and the answer is converted back to the Display mode.

7. Add Display to Computational: The Display field is converted to Computational or Computational-3, the fields are added, and the answer is stored in the Computational field.

8. Add Display to Computational-3: The Display field is packed and then the two fields are added.

9. Add Computational-3 to Display: The Display field is packed, the numbers are added, and the answer is unpacked to the Display field.

The most efficient arithmetic operations, in terms of main storage usage, occur when two Computational-3 fields are used. The most inefficient arithmetic statements occur when a Computational field is the receiving field for the answer of the arithmetic operation. Thus, when using Computational fields, the programmer must be aware of the additional instructions which will be generated.

It should be noted that the above examples are based on coding developed when all fields are the same length, are decimally aligned, and are on the proper boundaries. As with the **IF** Statements and the **MOVE** Statements discussed earlier, additional coding is developed when the fields are of different lengths, when decimal points are not aligned, and when boundary alignment must be handled in the Procedure Division. Thus, it is advantageous for the programmer to be aware of the steps which are taken by the compiler with which he is working so that the most efficient Procedure Division coding is generated when the program is compiled.

It is not intended that the programmer should analyze every statement that is written in the program in order to write in the most economical way in terms of main storage usage and execution time. It is necessary, however, that the programmer realize that there are various ways of accomplishing the same thing in COBOL programs and that some ways are better than others. This is especially true when performing comparisons, moving data, and performing arithmetic. Therefore, when coding COBOL programs, the programmer should think in terms of the best ways to accomplish these tasks in the program.

SAMPLE PROGRAM

The sample program presented in this chapter randomly updates the indexed sequential inventory master file.

INPUT

The input to the update program is the inventory master file and the update transaction records. The format of the update transaction records is illustrated below.

FIELD	FIELD NAME	PICTURE	POSITION	NO OF DIGITS	LENGTH
Part Number	PART-NUMB				
Division Number	DIV	XX	1-2	2	2
Prime Number	PRIME	X(6)	3-8	6	2
Dash Number	DASH	X(5)	9-13	5	5
Description	NAME	X(25)	14-38	25	25
Qty on Hand	QTY-ON-HAND	X(7)	39-45	7	7
Qty on Order	QTY-ON-ORDER	X(7)	46-52	7	7
Qty Reserved	QTY-RESERVED	X(7)	53-59	7	7
Part Number-NA	NEXT-ASSEMBLY				
Division-NA	DIV-NA	XX	60-61	2	2
Prime-NA	PRIME-NA	X(6)	62-67	6	6
Dash-NA	DASH-NA	X(5)	68-72	5	5
Type	TYPE	X	73	1	1
Source	SOURCE	X	74	1	1
Unit Price	UNIT-PRICE	X(6)	75-80	6	6

The format of the inventory master file records is shown below.

FIELD	FIELD NAME	PICTURE	POSITION	NO OF DIGITS	LENGTH
Part Number	PART-NUMB-MSTR	Picture 9(13) Comp-3	1-7	13	7
Description	NAME-MSTR	Picture X(25)	8-32	25	25
Quantity on Hand	QTY-ON-HAND-MSTR	Picture S9(7) Comp-3	33-36	7	4
Quantity on Order	QTY-ON-ORDER-MSTR	Picture S9(7) Comp-3	37-40	7	4
Quantity Reserved	QTY-RESERVED-MSTR	Picture S9(7) Comp-3	41-44	7	4
Next Assembly Number	NEXT-ASSEMBLY-MSTR	Picture S9(13) Comp-3	45-51	13	7
Type	TYPE-MSTR	Picture X	52	1	1
Source	SOURCE-MSTR	Picture X	53	1	1
Unit Price	UNIT-PRICE-MSTR	Picture S9(7) Comp-3	54-57	6	4
Filler	FILLER	Picture X(7)	58-64	7	7

OUTPUT

The output of the sample program is an updated inventory master and an error exception report. The format of the report is illustrated below.

PRINTER SPACING CHART

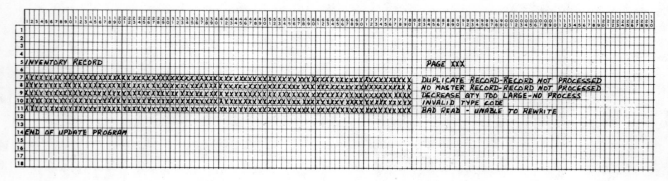

Figure 5-18 Printer Spacing Chart - Exception Report

PROGRAM

The program listing for the update program is presented on the following pages. Note that the **220-CHNG-QOH** routine changes the quantity on hand field (**QTY-ON-HAND-MSTR**) and also changes either the quantity on order field (**QTY-ON-ORDER-MSTR**) or the quantity reserved field (**QTY-RESERVED-MSTR**). This is because when the quantity on hand value is increased, the increases are assumed to be from orders which would be reflected in the quantity on order field. Thus, if the quantity on hand field is increased, the quantity on order field will be decreased by the same amount. If the decrease to the quantity on order field causes the value in the field to become negative, it is set to zero. This would occur when more parts were received than were on order. If the quantity on hand field is decreased, it is assumed these parts filled a reserve order, so the quantity reserved field is decreased by the same amount the quantity on hand is decreased. Again, if the value in the quantity reserved field becomes negative, it is set to zero because more parts were taken out of stock than were reserved. If the quantity on hand field in the transaction record causes the quantity on hand field in the master record to be less than zero, the transaction is considered an error transaction because there can never be less than zero parts on hand. If this occurs, an entry is made on the error exception report.

```
    1                         IBM DOS AMERICAN NATIONAL STANDARD COBOL              CBF CL3-4         09/12/74

    00001   001010 IDENTIFICATION DIVISION.                                                          UPDTMSTR
    00002   001020 PROGRAM-ID.      MSTUDAT.                                                          UPDTMSTR
    00003   001030 AUTHOR.          SHELLY.                                                           UPDTMSTR
    00004   001040 INSTALLATION.    LONG BEACH.                                                       UPDTMSTR
    00005   001050 DATE-WRITTEN. 07/11/74.                                                            UPDTMSTR
    00006   001060 DATE-COMPILED. 09/12/74                                                            UPDTMSTR
    00007   001070 SECURITY.        UNCLASSIFIED.                                                     UPDTMSTR
    00008   001080 REMARKS.        THIS PROGRAM RANDOMLY UPDATES THE INVENTORY                        UPDTMSTR
    00009   001090                 MASTER FILE WITH ADDITIONS, DELETIONS AND                          UPDTMSTR
    00010   001100                 CHANGES TO THE FIELDS IN THE MASTER RECORD.                        UPDTMSTR
    00011   001110                                                                                    UPDTMSTR
    00012   001120                                                                                    UPDTMSTR
    00013   001130 ENVIRONMENT DIVISION.                                                              UPDTMSTR
    00014   001140                                                                                    UPDTMSTR
    00015   001150 CONFIGURATION SECTION.                                                             UPDTMSTR
    00016   001160                                                                                    UPDTMSTR
    00017   001170 SOURCE-COMPUTER.        IBM-360-F30.                                               UPDTMSTR
    00018   001190 OBJECT-COMPUTER.        IBM-360-F30.                                               UPDTMSTR
    00019   001190 SPECIAL-NAMES.                                                                     UPDTMSTR
    00020   001200      C01 IS TO-TOP-OF-PAGE.                                                        UPDTMSTR
    00021   002010                                                                                    UPDTMSTR
    00022   002020 INPUT-OUTPUT SECTION.                                                              UPDTMSTR
    00023   002030 FILE-CONTROL.                                                                      UPDTMSTR
    00024   002040                                                                                    UPDTMSTR
    00025   002050      SELECT INVMSTR                                                                UPDTMSTR
    00026   002060         ASSIGN TO SYS006-DA-2314-I-INVMSTR                                         UPDTMSTR
    00027   002070         ACCESS IS RANDOM                                                           UPDTMSTR
    00028   002080         RECORD KEY IS PART-NUMB-MSTR                                               UPDTMSTR
    00029   002090         NOMINAL KEY IS MSTR-KEY.                                                   UPDTMSTR
    00030   002100      SELECT TRANSIN                                                                UPDTMSTR
    00031   002110         ASSIGN TO SYS007-UT-2314-S-TRANSIN.                                        UPDTMSTR
    00032   002120      SELECT PRTFLE                                                                 UPDTMSTR
    00033   002130         ASSIGN TO SYS005-UR-1403-S.                                                UPDTMSTR
    00034   002140                                                                                    UPDTMSTR
    00035   002150                                                                                    UPDTMSTR
    00036   002160                                                                                    UPDTMSTR
    00037   002170 DATA DIVISION.                                                                     UPDTMSTR
    00038   002180                                                                                    UPDTMSTR
    00039   002190 FILE SECTION.                                                                      UPDTMSTR
    00040   002200                                                                                    UPDTMSTR
    00041   003010 FD  INVMSTR                                                                        UPDTMSTR
    00042   003020      BLOCK CONTAINS 54 RECORDS                                                     UPDTMSTR
    00043   003030      RECORD CONTAINS 64 CHARACTERS                                                 UPDTMSTR
    00044   003040      LABEL RECORDS ARE STANDARD                                                    UPDTMSTR
    00045   003050      DATA RECORD IS MSTR-IO.                                                       UPDTMSTR
    00046   003060 01  MSTR-IO.                                                                       UPDTMSTR
    00047   003070      03   PART-NUMB-MSTR          PICTURE 9(13)                                    UPDTMSTR
    00048   003080                                   USAGE COMPUTATIONAL-3.                           UPDTMSTR
    00049   003090      03   NAME-MSTR               PICTURE X(25).                                   UPDTMSTR
    00050   003100      03   QTY-ON-HAND-MSTR        PICTURE S9(7)                                    UPDTMSTR
    00051   003110                                   USAGE COMPUTATIONAL-3.                           UPDTMSTR
    00052   003120      03   QTY-ON-ORDER-MSTR       PICTURE S9(7)                                    UPDTMSTR
    00053   003130                                   USAGE COMPUTATIONAL-3.                           UPDTMSTR
    00054   003140      03   QTY-RESERVED-MSTR       PICTURE S9(7)                                    UPDTMSTR
    00055   003150                                   USAGE COMPUTATIONAL-3.                           UPDTMSTR
    00056   003160      03   NEXT-ASSEMBLY-MSTR      PICTURE S9(13)                                   UPDTMSTR
    00057   003170                                   USAGE COMPUTATIONAL-3.                           UPDTMSTR
    00058   003180      03   TYPE-MSTR               PICTURE X.                                       UPDTMSTR
    00059   003190      03   SOURCE-MSTR             PICTURE X.                                       UPDTMSTR
    00060   003200      03   UNIT-PRICE-MSTR         PICTURE S9(7)                                    UPDTMSTR
    00061   004010                                   USAGE COMPUTATIONAL-3.                           UPDTMSTR
    00062   004020      03   FILLER                  PICTURE X(7).                                     UPDTMSTR
    00063   004030                                                                                    UPDTMSTR
    00064   004040 FD  PRTFLE                                                                         UPDTMSTR
    00065   004050      RECORD CONTAINS 121 CHARACTERS                                                UPDTMSTR
    00066   004060      LABEL RECORDS ARE OMITTED                                                     UPDTMSTR
    00067   004070      DATA RECORD IS PRINT-IOA.                                                     UPDTMSTR
    00068   004080 01  PRINT-IOA.                                                                     UPDTMSTR
    00069   004090      03   FILLER                  PICTURE X.                                       UPDTMSTR
    00070   004100      03   PRINT-IO.                                                                UPDTMSTR
    00071   004110          05   RECORD-PRT          PICTURE X(80).                                   UPDTMSTR
    00072   004120          05   FILLER              PICTURE XX.                                      UPDTMSTR
    00073   004130          05   ERROR-PRT           PICTURE X(38).                                   UPDTMSTR
    00074   004140                                                                                    UPDTMSTR
    00075   004150 FD  TRANSIN                                                                        UPDTMSTR
    00076   004160      BLOCK CONTAINS 44 RECORDS                                                     UPDTMSTR
    00077   004170      RECORD CONTAINS 80 CHARACTERS                                                 UPDTMSTR
    00078   004180      LABEL RECORDS ARE STANDARD                                                    UPDTMSTR
    00079   004190      DATA RECORD IS TRANS-IO.                                                      UPDTMSTR
    00080   004200 01  TRANS-IO.                                                                      UPDTMSTR
    00081   005010      03   PART-NUMB-TRANS         PICTURE 9(13).                                   UPDTMSTR
    00082   005020      03   NAME-TRANS              PICTURE X(25).                                   UPDTMSTR
    00083   005030      03   QTY-ON-HAND-TRANS       PICTURE S9(7).                                   UPDTMSTR
    00084   005040      03   QTY-ON-ORDER-TRANS      PICTURE S9(7).                                   UPDTMSTR
    00085   005050      03   QTY-RESERVED-TRANS      PICTURE S9(7).                                   UPDTMSTR
    00086   005060      03   NEXT-ASSEMBLY-TRANS     PICTURE S9(13).                                  UPDTMSTR
    00087   005070      03   TYPE-TRANS              PICTURE 9.                                        UPDTMSTR
```

```
      2

00088   005080    03  SOURCE-TRANS           PICTURE X.                    UPDTMSTR
00089   005090    03  UNIT-PRICE-TRANS       PICTURE S9(6).                UPDTMSTR
00090   005100                                                             UPDTMSTR
00091   005110                                                             UPDTMSTR
00092   005120 WORKING-STORAGE SECTION.                                    UPDTMSTR
00093   005130                                                             UPDTMSTR
00094   005140 77 PG-COUNT                    PICTURE S999    VALUE ZERO    UPDTMSTR
00095   005150                                USAGE COMPUTATIONAL-3.        UPDTMSTR
00096   005160 77 DUPLICATE-MSG               PICTURE X(38)    VALUE        UPDTMSTR
00097   005170    'DUPLICATE RECORD-RECORD NOT PROCESSED'.                 UPDTMSTR
00098   005180 77 NO-RECORD-MSG               PICTURE X(38)    VALUE        UPDTMSTR
00099   005190    'NO MASTER RECORD-RECORD NOT PROCESSED'.                 UPDTMSTR
00100   005200 77 END-MSG                     PICTURE X(21)    VALUE        UPDTMSTR
00101   006010    'END OF UPDATE PROGRAM'.                                 UPDTMSTR
00102   006020 77 QTY-MSG                     PICTURE X(38)    VALUE        UPDTMSTR
00103   006030    'DECREASE QTY TOO LARGE-NO PROCESS'.                     UPDTMSTR
00104   006040 77 TYPE-MSG                    PICTURE X(38)    VALUE        UPDTMSTR
00105   006050    'INVALID TYPE CODE'.                                     UPDTMSTR
00106   006060 77 BAD-READ-MSG                PICTURE X(38)    VALUE        UPDTMSTR
00107   006070    'BAD READ - UNABLE TO REWRITE'.                          UPDTMSTR
00108   006080 77 SAVE-MSTR                   PICTURE X(64).                UPDTMSTR
00109   006090 77 MSTR-KEY                    PICTURE 9(13)    VALUE 0      UPDTMSTR
00110   006100                                USAGE COMPUTATIONAL-3.        UPDTMSTR
00111   006110 77 INV-READ                    PICTURE X        VALUE '0'.   UPDTMSTR
00112   006120 77 ARITH-WORK                  PICTURE S9(7)                 UPDTMSTR
00113   006130                                USAGE COMPUTATIONAL-3.        UPDTMSTR
00114   006140 77 SIGN-SWITCH                 PICTURE X        VALUE '0'.   UPDTMSTR
00115   006150 77 ARITH-ANS                   PICTURE S9(7)                 UPDTMSTR
00116   006160                                USAGE COMPUTATIONAL-3.        UPDTMSTR
00117   006170 77 VARIABLE                    PICTURE 9.                    UPDTMSTR
00118   006180 77 SINGLE-SPACING              PICTURE 9        VALUE 1.     UPDTMSTR
00119   006190 77 DOUBLE-SPACING              PICTURE 9        VALUE 2.     UPDTMSTR
00120   006200 77 TRIPLE-SPACING              PICTURE 9        VALUE 3.     UPDTMSTR
00121   007010 77 LINE-COUNT                  PICTURE S999                  UPDTMSTR
00122   007020                                USAGE COMPUTATIONAL-3.        UPDTMSTR
00123   007030 01 HEADER1.                                                 UPDTMSTR
00124   007040    03  FILLER                  PICTURE X(83)    VALUE        UPDTMSTR
00125   007050    'INVENTORY RECORD'.                                      UPDTMSTR
00126   007060    03  FILLER                  PICTURE X(5)     VALUE 'PAGE'.UPDTMSTR
00127   007070    03  PG-H1              PICTURE ZZZ.                       UPDTMSTR
00128   007080    03  FILLER                  PICTURE X(29)    VALUE SPACES.UPDTMSTR
00129   007090                                                             UPDTMSTR
00130   007100                                                             UPDTMSTR
00131   007110                                                             UPDTMSTR
00132   007120 PROCEDURE DIVISION.                                         UPDTMSTR
00133   007130                                                             UPDTMSTR
00134   007140 NOTE-001.                                                   UPDTMSTR
00135   007150    NOTE ***********************************************************UPDTMSTR
00136   007160    *    THIS PROGRAM RANDOMLY UPDATES THE INVENTORY MASTER FILE,*UPDTMSTR
00137   007170    *    WHICH IS AN INDEXED SEQUENTIAL FILE, IN THREE WAYS -  *UPDTMSTR
00138   007180    *                                                         *UPDTMSTR
00139   007190    *         1-ADDITIONS - IT ADDS PART NUMBERS TO THE FILE. THE *UPDTMSTR
00140   007200    *                       ADDITION UPDATE TRANSACTIONS ARE  *UPDTMSTR
00141   008010    *                       EDITED IN THE CARD TO DISK PROGRAM.*UPDTMSTR
00142   008020    *                       THE ONLY ADDITION ERROR REPORTED OUT*UPDTMSTR
00143   008030    *                       OF THIS UPDATE IS WHEN A DUPLICATE *UPDTMSTR
00144   008040    *                       RECORD IS ATTEMPTED TO BE ADDED. IF*UPDTMSTR
00145   008050    *                       A DUPLICATE IS FOUND, THE DUPLICATE*UPDTMSTR
00146   008060    *                       RECORD IS READ. IF THE TYPE CODE IN*UPDTMSTR
00147   008070    *                       THE DUPLICATE RECORD INDICATES THE *UPDTMSTR
00148   008080    *                       RECORD IS DELETED, THE NEW RECORD IS*UPDTMSTR
00149   008090    *                       RE-WRITTEN IN ITS PLACE. OTHERWISE,*UPDTMSTR
00150   008100    *                       A MESSAGE IS PRINTED ON THE       *UPDTMSTR
00151   008110    *                       EXCEPTION REPORT.                 *UPDTMSTR
00152   008120    *         2-DELETIONS - ANY PART NUMBER ON THE INVENTORY FILE*UPDTMSTR
00153   008130    *                       MAY BE DELETED AT ANY TIME. THIS IS*UPDTMSTR
00154   008140    *                       ACCOMPLISHED BY MOVING A '2' TO THE*UPDTMSTR
00155   008150    *                       TYPE CODE IN THE RECORD. ONE ERROR*UPDTMSTR
00156   008160    *                       CAN OCCUR WITH DELETIONS - THE PART*UPDTMSTR
00157   008170    *                       NUMBER MAY NOT BE PRESENT ON THE FILE*UPDTMSTR
00158   008180    *         3-CHANGES   - CHANGES CAN BE MADE TO ANY RECORD *UPDTMSTR
00159   008190    *                       WHICH IS NOT A DELETED RECORD. CHANGES*UPDTMSTR
00160   008200    *                       CAN BE MADE TO THE FOLLOWING FIELDS -*UPDTMSTR
00161   009010    *                       QUANTITY ON HAND, QUANTITY ON ORDER,*UPDTMSTR
00162   009020    *                       QUANTITY RESERVED, NEXT ASSEMBLY  *UPDTMSTR
00163   009030    *                       PART NUMBER, OR SOURCE. WHENEVER A *UPDTMSTR
00164   009040    *                       CHANGE IS MADE TO THE QUANTITY ON HAND*UPDTMSTR
00165   009050    *                       A CHANGE IS MADE TO THE QUANTITY ON*UPDTMSTR
00166   009060    *                       ORDER (IT IS DECREASED IF THE QOH *UPDTMSTR
00167   009070    *                       IS INCREASED) OR THE QUANTITY     *UPDTMSTR
00168   009080    *                       RESERVED (IT IS DECREASED IF THE  *UPDTMSTR
00169   009090    *                       QUANTITY ON HAND IS DECREASED).   *UPDTMSTR
00170   009100    *                                                         *UPDTMSTR
00171   009110    *    THE CARD CODES IN THE TYPE FIELD TO UPDATE THE FILE ARE-*UPDTMSTR
00172   009120    *                                                         *UPDTMSTR
00173   009130    *         1 - ADD A RECORD                                *UPDTMSTR
00174   009140    *         2 - DELETE A RECORD                             *UPDTMSTR
```

```
     3

00175  009150  *          3 - CHANGE QUANTITY ON HAND                      *UPDTMSTR
00176  009160  *          4 - CHANGE QUANTITY ON ORDER                     *UPDTMSTR
00177  009170  *          5 - CHANGE QUANTITY RESERVED                     *UPDTMSTR
00178  009180  *          6 - CHANGE NEXT ASSEMBLY NUMBER                  *UPDTMSTR
00179  009190  *          7 - CHANGE SOURCE                                 UPDTMSTR
00180  009200  *          9 - CHANGE UNIT PRICE                             UPDTMSTR
00181  010010  *       ANY OTHER ENTRIES IN THE TYPE FIELD ARE INVALID IN THE  *UPDTMSTR
00182  010020  *       UPDATE TRANSACTIONS.                                *UPDTMSTR
00183  010030  *********************************************************************UPDTMSTR
00184  010040                                                             UPDTMSTR
00185  010050 NOTE-003.                                                   UPDTMSTR
00186  010060      NOTE **************************************************************UPDTMSTR
00187  010070  *       THIS ROUTINE OPENS THE FILES AND PRINTS THE HEADINGS  *UPDTMSTR
00188  010080  *       ON THE EXCEPTION REPORT.                            *UPDTMSTR
00189  010090  *********************************************************************UPDTMSTR
00190  010100                                                             UPDTMSTR
00191  010110 003-START.                                                  UPDTMSTR
00192  010120      OPEN INPUT  TRANSIN,                                   UPDTMSTR
00193  010130           OUTPUT PRTFLE,                                    UPDTMSTR
00194  010140           I-O    INVMSTR.                                   UPDTMSTR
00195  010150      PERFORM 500-HEADER THRU 500-EXIT.                      UPDTMSTR
00196  010160      MOVE SPACES TO PRINT-IO.                               UPDTMSTR
00197  010170                                                             UPDTMSTR
00198  010180 NOTE-010.                                                   UPDTMSTR
00199  010190      NOTE **************************************************************UPDTMSTR
00200  010200  *       THIS ROUTINE IS ENTERED TO READ THE TRANSACTION FILE. *UPDTMSTR
00201  011010  *       AFTER READING THE FILE, IT GOES TO THE PROPER PROCESSING*UPDTMSTR
00202  011020  *       ROUTINE DEPENDING UPON THE TRANSACTION CODE.       *UPDTMSTR
00203  011030  *********************************************************************UPDTMSTR
00204  011040                                                             UPDTMSTR
00205  011050 010-READ-TRANS.                                             UPDTMSTR
00206  011060      READ TRANSIN AT END GO TO 600-END-TRANS.              UPDTMSTR
00207  011070      GO TO   200-ADDREC,                                    UPDTMSTR
00208  011080              210-DELREC,                                    UPDTMSTR
00209  011090              220-CHNG-QOH,                                  UPDTMSTR
00210  011100              230-CHNG-QOO,                                  UPDTMSTR
00211  011110              240-CHNG-QRSV,                                 UPDTMSTR
00212  011120              250-CHNG-NA,                                   UPDTMSTR
00213  011130              260-CHNG-SRCE,                                 UPDTMSTR
00214  011140              270-BAD-TYPE,                                  UPDTMSTR
00215  011150              280-CHNG-UNIT                                  UPDTMSTR
00216  011160      DEPENDING ON TYPE-TRANS.                               UPDTMSTR
00217  011170                                                             UPDTMSTR
00218  011180 NOTE-200.                                                   UPDTMSTR
00219  011190      NOTE **************************************************************UPDTMSTR
00220  011200  *       THIS ROUTINE IS ENTERED WHEN THE TYPE CODE INDICATES AN*UPDTMSTR
00221  012010  *       ADD FUNCTION. IF THE PART NUMBER FOR THE TRANSACTION*UPDTMSTR
00222  012020  *       RECORD IS NOT ON THE MASTER FILE, THE RECORD IS ADDED.*UPDTMSTR
00223  012030  *       IF IT IS ON THE MASTER FILE, THE CODE IN THE MASTER*UPDTMSTR
00224  012040  *       IS CHECKED-IF IT IS A DELETED RECORD, THE NEW RECORD IS*UPDTMSTR
00225  012050  *       RE-WRITTEN. IF NOT, AN ERROR MESSAGE IS WRITTEN ON THE*UPDTMSTR
00226  012060  *       EXCEPTION REPORT.                                   *UPDTMSTR
00227  012070  *********************************************************************UPDTMSTR
00228  012080                                                             UPDTMSTR
00229  012090 200-ADDREC.                                                 UPDTMSTR
00230  012100      MOVE PART-NUMB-TRANS TO PART-NUMB-MSTR.                UPDTMSTR
00231  012110      MOVE NAME-TRANS TO NAME-MSTR.                          UPDTMSTR
00232  012120      MOVE QTY-ON-HAND-TRANS TO QTY-ON-HAND-MSTR.            UPDTMSTR
00233  012130      MOVE QTY-ON-ORDER-TRANS TO QTY-ON-ORDER-MSTR.          UPDTMSTR
00234  012140      MOVE QTY-RESERVED-TRANS TO QTY-RESERVED-MSTR.          UPDTMSTR
00235  012150      MOVE NEXT-ASSEMBLY-TRANS TO NEXT-ASSEMBLY-MSTR.        UPDTMSTR
00236  012160      MOVE '1' TO TYPE-MSTR.                                 UPDTMSTR
00237  012170      MOVE SOURCE-TRANS TO SOURCE-MSTR.                      UPDTMSTR
00238  012180      MOVE UNIT-PRICE-TRANS TO UNIT-PRICE-MSTR.              UPDTMSTR
00239  012190      MOVE PART-NUMB-TRANS TO MSTR-KEY.                      UPDTMSTR
00240  012200      MOVE MSTR-IO TO SAVE-MSTR.                             UPDTMSTR
00241  013010      WRITE MSTR-IO   INVALID KEY GO TO 340-INV-ADD.         UPDTMSTR
00242  013020      GO TO 010-READ-TRANS.                                  UPDTMSTR
00243  013030                                                             UPDTMSTR
00244  013040 NOTE-210.                                                   UPDTMSTR
00245  013050      NOTE **************************************************************UPDTMSTR
00246  013060  *       THIS ROUTINE IS ENTERED TO DELETE A RECORD FROM THE *UPDTMSTR
00247  013070  *       INVENTORY MASTER FILE. IT READS THE RECORD, MOVES A '2'*UPDTMSTR
00248  013080  *       TO THE TYPE FIELD AND RE-WRITES THE RECORD.        *UPDTMSTR
00249  013090  *********************************************************************UPDTMSTR
00250  013100                                                             UPDTMSTR
00251  013110 210-DELREC.                                                 UPDTMSTR
00252  013120      PERFORM 320-READ-MSTR THRU 320-EXIT.                   UPDTMSTR
00253  013130      IF INV-READ = '1'                                      UPDTMSTR
00254  013140          MOVE '0' TO INV-READ,                              UPDTMSTR
00255  013150          GO TO 010-READ-TRANS.                              UPDTMSTR
00256  013160      MOVE '2' TO TYPE-MSTR.                                 UPDTMSTR
00257  013170      GO TO 225-RETURN.                                      UPDTMSTR
00258  013180                                                             UPDTMSTR
00259  013190                                                             UPDTMSTR
00260  013200 NOTE-220.                                                   UPDTMSTR
00261  014010      NOTE **************************************************************UPDTMSTR
```

```
  4

00262  014020     *     THIS ROUTINE IS ENTERED TO CHANGE THE QUANTITY ON HAND   *UPDTMSTR
00263  014030     *     IN THE MASTER RECORD. WHENEVER THE QUANTITY ON HAND IS    *UPDTMSTR
00264  014040     *     CHANGED, THE QUANTITY ON ORDER OR THE QUANTITY            *UPDTMSTR
00265  014050     *     RESERVED IS ALSO CHANGED. IF THE QUANTITY ON HAND IS      *UPDTMSTR
00266  014060     *     INCREASED, THE QUANTITY ON ORDER IS DECREASED. IF         *UPDTMSTR
00267  014070     *     THE QUANTITY ON HAND IS DECREASED, THE QUANTITY           *UPDTMSTR
00268  014080     *     RESERVED IS DECREASED. IF THE QUANTITY ON HAND  IS        *UPDTMSTR
00269  014090     *     DECREASED BELOW ZERO, THE INPUT IS CONSIDERED TO BE       *UPDTMSTR
00270  014100     *     INVALID. IF, BECAUSE OF CHANGES TO THE QUANTITY ON        *UPDTMSTR
00271  014110     *     HAND, THE QTY ON ORDER OR QTY RESERVED GOES BELOW         *UPDTMSTR
00272  014120     *     ZERO, IT IS RESET TO ZERO.                               *UPDTMSTR
00273  014130     **************************************************************.UPDTMSTR
00274  014140                                                                    UPDTMSTR
00275  014150 220-CHNG-QOH.                                                      UPDTMSTR
00276  014160     PERFORM 320-READ-MSTR THRU 320-EXIT.                           UPDTMSTR
00277  014170     IF INV-READ NOT = '0'                                          UPDTMSTR
00278  014180         MOVE '0' TO INV-READ                                       UPDTMSTR
00279  014190         GO TO 010-READ-TRANS.                                      UPDTMSTR
00280  014200     MOVE QTY-ON-HAND-TRANS TO ARITH-WORK.                          UPDTMSTR
00281  015010     ADD QTY-ON-HAND-MSTR, ARITH-WORK GIVING ARITH-ANS.            UPDTMSTR
00282  015020     IF ARITH-ANS NEGATIVE                                          UPDTMSTR
00283  015030         MOVE QTY-MSG TO ERROR-PRT                                  UPDTMSTR
00284  015040         MOVE TRANS-IO TO RECORD-PRT                                UPDTMSTR
00285  015050         PERFORM 430-WRITE-PRT THRU 430-EXIT                        UPDTMSTR
00286  015060         GO TO 010-READ-TRANS.                                      UPDTMSTR
00287  015070     MOVE ARITH-ANS TO QTY-ON-HAND-MSTR.                            UPDTMSTR
00288  015080     IF ARITH-WORK IS NEGATIVE                                      UPDTMSTR
00289  015090         ADD QTY-RESERVED-MSTR, ARITH-WORK GIVING ARITH-ANS         UPDTMSTR
00290  015100         IF ARITH-ANS NEGATIVE,                                     UPDTMSTR
00291  015110             MOVE 0000000 TO QTY-RESERVED-MSTR                      UPDTMSTR
00292  015120         ELSE                                                       UPDTMSTR
00293  015130             MOVE ARITH-ANS TO QTY-RESERVED-MSTR                    UPDTMSTR
00294  015140     ELSE                                                           UPDTMSTR
00295  015150     SUBTRACT ARITH-WORK FROM QTY-ON-ORDER-MSTR GIVING ARITH-ANSUPDTMSTR
00296  015160         IF ARITH-ANS NEGATIVE                                      UPDTMSTR
00297  015170             MOVE 0000000 TO QTY-ON-ORDER-MSTR                      UPDTMSTR
00298  015180         ELSE                                                       UPDTMSTR
00299  015190             MOVE ARITH-ANS TO QTY-ON-ORDER-MSTR.                   UPDTMSTR
00300  015200                                                                    UPDTMSTR
00301  016010 225-RETURN.                                                        UPDTMSTR
00302  016020     REWRITE MSTR-IO INVALID KEY                                    UPDTMSTR
00303  016030         MOVE BAD-READ-MSG TO ERROR-PRT                             UPDTMSTR
00304  016040         MOVE TRANS-IO TO RECORD-PRT                                UPDTMSTR
00305  016050         PERFORM 430-WRITE-PRT THRU 430-EXIT.                       UPDTMSTR
00306  016060     GO TO 010-READ-TRANS.                                          UPDTMSTR
00307  016070                                                                    UPDTMSTR
00308  016080                                                                    UPDTMSTR
00309  016090 NOTE-230.                                                          UPDTMSTR
00310  016100     NOTE ***********************************************************UPDTMSTR
00311  016110     *     THIS ROUTINE IS ENTERED TO CHANGE THE QUANTITY           *UPDTMSTR
00312  016120     *     ON ORDER. IF THE CHANGE MAKES THE QTY ON ORDER IN        *UPDTMSTR
00313  016130     *     THE MASTER NEGATIVE, IT IS CONSIDERED AN ERROR.          *UPDTMSTR
00314  016140     **************************************************************.UPDTMSTR
00315  016150                                                                    UPDTMSTR
00316  016160 230-CHNG-QOO.                                                      UPDTMSTR
00317  016170     PERFORM 320-READ-MSTR THRU 320-EXIT.                           UPDTMSTR
00318  016180     IF INV-READ = '1'                                             UPDTMSTR
00319  016190         MOVE '0' TO INV-READ                                       UPDTMSTR
00320  016200         GO TO 010-READ-TRANS.                                      UPDTMSTR
00321  017010     MOVE QTY-ON-ORDER-TRANS TO ARITH-WORK.                         UPDTMSTR
00322  017020     ADD QTY-ON-ORDER-MSTR TO ARITH-WORK.                           UPDTMSTR
00323  017030     IF ARITH-WORK IS NEGATIVE,                                     UPDTMSTR
00324  017040         MOVE QTY-MSG TO ERROR-PRT                                  UPDTMSTR
00325  017050         MOVE TRANS-IO TO RECORD-PRT                                UPDTMSTR
00326  017060         PERFORM 430-WRITE-PRT THRU 430-EXIT                        UPDTMSTR
00327  017070         GO TO 010-READ-TRANS.                                      UPDTMSTR
00328  017080     MOVE ARITH-WORK TO QTY-ON-ORDER-MSTR.                          UPDTMSTR
00329  017090     GO TO 225-RETURN.                                              UPDTMSTR
00330  017100                                                                    UPDTMSTR
00331  017110                                                                    UPDTMSTR
00332  017120 NOTE-240.                                                          UPDTMSTR
00333  017130     NOTE ***********************************************************UPDTMSTR
00334  017140     *     THIS ROUTINE IS ENTERED TO CHANGE THE QUANTITY           *UPDTMSTR
00335  017150     *     RESERVED ON THE MASTER FILE. IF THE CHANGE CAUSES THE    *UPDTMSTR
00336  017160     *     QUANTITY RESERVED TO BE NEGATIVE, IT IS CONSIDERED       *UPDTMSTR
00337  017170     *     AN ERROR.                                                *UPDTMSTR
00338  017180     **************************************************************.UPDTMSTR
00339  017190                                                                    UPDTMSTR
00340  017200 240-CHNG-QRSV.                                                     UPDTMSTR
00341  018010     PERFORM 320-READ-MSTR THRU 320-EXIT.                           UPDTMSTR
00342  018020     IF INV-READ NOT = '0'                                          UPDTMSTR
00343  018030         MOVE '0' TO INV-READ                                       UPDTMSTR
00344  018040         GO TO 010-READ-TRANS.                                      UPDTMSTR
00345  018050     MOVE QTY-RESERVED-TRANS TO ARITH-WORK.                         UPDTMSTR
00346  018060     ADD QTY-RESERVED-MSTR TO ARITH-WORK.                           UPDTMSTR
00347  018070     IF ARITH-WORK IS NEGATIVE,                                     UPDTMSTR
00348  018080         MOVE QTY-MSG TO ERROR-PRT                                  UPDTMSTR
```

```
  5

00349  019090        MOVE TRANS-IO TO RECORD-PRT                          UPDTMSTR
00350  018100        PERFORM 430-WRITE-PRT THRU 430-EXIT                  UPDTMSTR
00351  018110        GO TO 010-READ-TRANS.                                UPDTMSTR
00352  018120    MOVE ARITH-WORK TO QTY-RESERVED-MSTR.                    UPDTMSTR
00353  018130    GO TO 225-RETURN.                                        UPDTMSTR
00354  018140                                                             UPDTMSTR
00355  018150 NOTE-250.                                                   UPDTMSTR
00356  018160    NOTE *****************************************************UPDTMSTR
00357  018170    *    THIS ROUTINE IS ENTERED TO CHANGE THE NEXT ASSEMBLY *UPDTMSTR
00358  018180    *    PART NUMBER. IT MOVES THE NEW PART NUMBER TO THE    *UPDTMSTR
00359  018190    *    MASTER RECORD.                                      *UPDTMSTR
00360  018200    ****************************************************.UPDTMSTR
00361  019010                                                             UPDTMSTR
00362  019020 250-CHNG-NA.                                                UPDTMSTR
00363  019030    PERFORM 320-READ-MSTR THRU 320-EXIT.                     UPDTMSTR
00364  019040    IF INV-READ IS = '1'                                     UPDTMSTR
00365  019050        MOVE '0' TO INV-READ,                                UPDTMSTR
00366  019060        GO TO 010-READ-TRANS.                                UPDTMSTR
00367  019070    MOVE NEXT-ASSEMBLY-TRANS TO NEXT-ASSEMBLY-MSTR.          UPDTMSTR
00368  019080    GO TO 225-RETURN.                                        UPDTMSTR
00369  019090                                                             UPDTMSTR
00370  019100                                                             UPDTMSTR
00371  019110 NOTE-260.                                                   UPDTMSTR
00372  019120    NOTE *****************************************************UPDTMSTR
00373  019130    *    THIS ROUTINE IS ENTERED TO CHANGE THE SOURCE ON     *UPDTMSTR
00374  019140    *    THE MASTER RECORD.                                  *UPDTMSTR
00375  019150    ****************************************************.UPDTMSTR
00376  019160                                                             UPDTMSTR
00377  019170 260-CHNG-SRCE.                                              UPDTMSTR
00378  019180    PERFORM 320-READ-MSTR THRU 320-EXIT.                     UPDTMSTR
00379  019190    IF INV-READ IS = '1'                                     UPDTMSTR
00380  019200        MOVE '0' TO INV-READ                                 UPDTMSTR
00381  020010        GO TO 010-READ-TRANS.                                UPDTMSTR
00382  020020    MOVE SOURCE-TRANS TO SOURCE-MSTR.                        UPDTMSTR
00383  020030    GO TO 225-RETURN.                                        UPDTMSTR
00384  020040                                                             UPDTMSTR
00385  020050                                                             UPDTMSTR
00386  020060 NOTE-270.                                                   UPDTMSTR
00387  020070    NOTE *****************************************************UPDTMSTR
00388  020080    *    THIS ROUTINE IS ENTERED WHEN AN INVALID TYPE CODE   *UPDTMSTR
00389  020090    *    IS FOUND IN THE TRANSACTION RECORD. IT MOVES THE    *UPDTMSTR
00390  020100    *    RECORD AND AN ERROR MESSAGE TO THE PRINTER I/O      *UPDTMSTR
00391  020110    *    AREA AND PRINTS THE ERROR MESSAGE. IT THEN GOES TO  *UPDTMSTR
00392  020120    *    READ THE NEXT TRANSACTION RECORD.                   *UPDTMSTR
00393  020130    ****************************************************.UPDTMSTR
00394  020140                                                             UPDTMSTR
00395  020150 270-BAD-TYPE.                                               UPDTMSTR
00396  020160    MOVE TYPE-MSG TO ERROR-PRT.                              UPDTMSTR
00397  020170    MOVE TRANS-IO TO RECORD-PRT.                             UPDTMSTR
00398  020180    PERFORM 430-WRITE-PRT THRU 430-EXIT.                     UPDTMSTR
00399  020190    GO TO 010-READ-TRANS.                                    UPDTMSTR
00400  020200                                                             UPDTMSTR
00401  021010                                                             UPDTMSTR
00402  021020 NOTE-280.                                                   UPDTMSTR
00403  021030    NOTE *****************************************************UPDTMSTR
00404  021040    *    THIS ROUTINE IS ENTERED TO CHANGE THE UNIT PRICE    *UPDTMSTR
00405  021050    *    ON THE MASTER RECORD. IT MOVES THE NEW UNIT PRICE   *UPDTMSTR
00406  021060    *    TO THE MASTER AND GOES TO WRITE THE UPDATED         *UPDTMSTR
00407  021070    *    RECORD.                                            *UPDTMSTR
00408  021080    ****************************************************.UPDTMSTR
00409  021090                                                             UPDTMSTR
00410  021100 280-CHNG-UNIT.                                              UPDTMSTR
00411  021110    PERFORM 320-READ-MSTR THRU 320-EXIT.                     UPDTMSTR
00412  021120    IF INV-READ IS = '1'                                     UPDTMSTR
00413  021130 .      MOVE '0' TO INV-READ                                 UPDTMSTR
00414  021140        GO TO 010-READ-TRANS.                                UPDTMSTR
00415  021150    MOVE UNIT-PRICE-TRANS TO UNIT-PRICE-MSTR.                UPDTMSTR
00416  021160    GO TO 225-RETURN.                                        UPDTMSTR
00417  021170                                                             UPDTMSTR
00418  021180                                                             UPDTMSTR
00419  021190 NOTE-320.                                                   UPDTMSTR
00420  021200    NOTE *****************************************************UPDTMSTR
00421  022010    *    THIS ROUTINE IS ENTERED TO RANDOMLY READ THE        *UPDTMSTR
00422  022020    *    INVENTORY MASTER. IT MOVES THE PART NUMBER FROM THE *UPDTMSTR
00423  022030    *    TRANSACTION RECORD TO THE NOMINAL KEY AREA AND ISSUES*UPDTMSTR
00424  022040    *    THE WRITE. ON AN INVALID KEY, IT PERFORMS THE READ  *UPDTMSTR
00425  022050    *    INVALID KEY ROUTINE.                                *UPDTMSTR
00426  022060    ****************************************************.UPDTMSTR
00427  022070                                                             UPDTMSTR
00428  022080 320-READ-MSTR.                                              UPDTMSTR
00429  022090    MOVE PART-NUMB-TRANS TO MSTR-KEY.                        UPDTMSTR
00430  022100    READ INVMSTR INVALID KEY                                 UPDTMSTR
00431  022110            MOVE '1' TO INV-READ                             UPDTMSTR
00432  022120            MOVE NO-RECORD-MSG TO ERROR-PRT                  UPDTMSTR
00433  022130            MOVE TRANS-IO TO RECORD-PRT                      UPDTMSTR
00434  022140            PERFORM 430-WRITE-PRT THRU 430-EXIT              UPDTMSTR
00435  022150            GO TO 320-EXIT.                                  UPDTMSTR
```

```
   6

00436    022160 320A-EXIT.  EXIT.                                         UPDTMSTR
00437    022170 320A-CHK-TYPE.                                            UPDTMSTR
00438    022180     IF TYPE-MSTR IS = '2'                                 UPDTMSTR
00439    022190         MOVE '1' TO INV-READ                              UPDTMSTR
00440    022200         MOVE NO-RECORD-MSG TO ERROR-PRT                   UPDTMSTR
00441    023010         MOVE TRANS-IO TO RECORD-PRT                       UPDTMSTR
00442    023020         PERFORM 430-WRITE-PRT THRU 430-EXIT.              UPDTMSTR
00443    023030 320-EXIT.  EXIT.                                          UPDTMSTR
00444    023040                                                           UPDTMSTR
00445    023050                                                           UPDTMSTR
00446    023060 NOTE-340.                                                 UPDTMSTR
00447    023070     NOTE ****************************************************UPDTMSTR
00448    023080     *    THIS ROUTINE IS ENTERED WHEN AN ADD IS ATTEMPTED OF *UPDTMSTR
00449    023090     *    A RECORD ALREADY ON THE FILE. IT DOES A RANDOM READ *UPDTMSTR
00450    023100     *    OF THE RECORD ON THE FILE AND CHECKS THE TYPE CODE. *UPDTMSTR
00451    023110     *    IF THE TYPE INDICATES AN ACTIVE RECORD, AN ERROR  *UPDTMSTR
00452    023120     *    MESSAGE IS WRITTEN ON THE PRINTER. IF IT IS A     *UPDTMSTR
00453    023130     *    DELETED RECORD, THE NEW RECORD IS RE-WRITTEN ONTO *UPDTMSTR
00454    023140     *    THE FILE.                                        *UPDTMSTR
00455    023150     ****************************************************.UPDTMSTR
00456    023160                                                           UPDTMSTR
00457    023170 340-INV-ADD.                                              UPDTMSTR
00458    023180     PERFORM 320-READ-MSTR THRU 320A-EXIT.                 UPDTMSTR
00459    023190     IF TYPE-MSTR IS = '2'                                 UPDTMSTR
00460    023200         MOVE SAVE-MSTR TO MSTR-IO                         UPDTMSTR
00461    024010         GO TO 225-RETURN,                                 UPDTMSTR
00462    024020     ELSE                                                  UPDTMSTR
00463    024030         MOVE DUPLICATE-MSG TO ERROR-PRT                   UPDTMSTR
00464    024040         MOVE TRANS-IO TO RECORD-PRT                       UPDTMSTR
00465    024050         PERFORM 430-WRITE-PRT THRU 430-EXIT              UPDTMSTR
00466    024060         GO TO 010-READ-TRANS.                             UPDTMSTR
00467    024070                                                           UPDTMSTR
00468    024080                                                           UPDTMSTR
00469    024090 NOTE-430.                                                 UPDTMSTR
00470    024100     NOTE ****************************************************UPDTMSTR
00471    024110     *    THIS ROUTINE IS ENTERED FOR ALL WRITES TO THE PRINTER. *UPDTMSTR
00472    024120     ****************************************************.UPDTMSTR
00473    024130                                                           UPDTMSTR
00474    024140 430-WRITE-PRT.                                            UPDTMSTR
00475    024150     WRITE PRINT-IOA AFTER ADVANCING VARIABLE LINES.       UPDTMSTR
00476    024160     ADD 1 TO LINE-COUNT.                                  UPDTMSTR
00477    024170     MOVE SINGLE-SPACING TO VARIABLE.                      UPDTMSTR
00478    024180     IF LINE-COUNT > 50                                    UPDTMSTR
00479    024190         PERFORM 500-HEADER THRU 500-EXIT.                 UPDTMSTR
00480    024200     MOVE SPACES TO PRINT-IO.                              UPDTMSTR
00481    025010 430-EXIT.  EXIT.                                          UPDTMSTR
00482    025020                                                           UPDTMSTR
00483    025030                                                           UPDTMSTR
00484    025040 NOTE-500.                                                 UPDTMSTR
00485    025050     NOTE ****************************************************UPDTMSTR
00486    025060     *    THIS ROUTINE IS ENTERED TO PRINT THE HEADING ON THE *UPDTMSTR
00487    025070     *    EXCEPTION REPORT.                                *UPDTMSTR
00488    025080     ****************************************************.UPDTMSTR
00489    025090                                                           UPDTMSTR
00490    025100 500-HEADER.                                               UPDTMSTR
00491    025110     ADD 1 TO PG-COUNT.                                    UPDTMSTR
00492    025120     MOVE PG-COUNT TO PG-H1.                               UPDTMSTR
00493    025130     MOVE HEADER1 TO PRINT-IO.                             UPDTMSTR
00494    025140     WRITE PRINT-IOA AFTER ADVANCING TO-TOP-OF-PAGE.       UPDTMSTR
00495    025150     MOVE ZERO TO LINE-COUNT.                              UPDTMSTR
00496    025160     MOVE DOUBLE-SPACING TO VARIABLE.                      UPDTMSTR
00497    025170 500-EXIT.  EXIT.                                          UPDTMSTR
00498    025180                                                           UPDTMSTR
00499    025190                                                           UPDTMSTR
00500    025200 NOTE-600.                                                 UPDTMSTR
00501    026010     NOTE ****************************************************UPDTMSTR
00502    026020     *    THIS ROUTINE IS ENTERED WHEN THE TRANSACTION FILE HAS *UPDTMSTR
00503    026030     *    REACHED EOF. IT PRINTS AS ENDING MESSAGE, CLOSES THE *UPDTMSTR
00504    026040     *    FILES, AND STOPS THE RUN.                        *UPDTMSTR
00505    026050     ****************************************************.UPDTMSTR
00506    026060                                                           UPDTMSTR
00507    026070 600-END-TRANS.                                            UPDTMSTR
00508    026080     MOVE TRIPLE-SPACING TO VARIABLE.                      UPDTMSTR
00509    026090     MOVE END-MSG TO PRINT-IO.                             UPDTMSTR
00510    026100     PERFORM 430-WRITE-PRT THRU 430-EXIT.                  UPDTMSTR
00511    026110     CLOSE TRANSIN,                                        UPDTMSTR
00512    026120           PRTFLE,                                         UPDTMSTR
00513    026130           INVMSTR.                                        UPDTMSTR
00514    026140     STOP RUN.                                             UPDTMSTR
```

CHAPTER 5

PROGRAMMING ASSIGNMENT

INSTRUCTIONS

The Sales Master File is to be updated by transactions. Suggested data for these transaction records are contained in the appendices. Using the program from the programming assignment in Chapter 2, create the sequential disk transaction file that is to be used as input to update the Sales Master File.

The Master File should be randomly updated. The following codes indicate the type of update to be performed.

> 2 - NAME CHANGE
> 3 - Y-T-D SALES UPDATE
> 4 - COMMISSION RATE CHANGE
> 5 - Y-T-D SALES RETURN UPDATE
> 6 - ADDITION
> 7 - DELETION

The Y-T-D Sales update is performed by adding Current Sales from the transaction records to the Y-T-D Sales from the master record. A similar procedure is followed in updating the Y-T-D Sales Return Field.

When a Name Change or Commission Rate Change occurs, the fields on the master record should be replaced by the contents of the transaction record.

When a record is to be deleted (code 7), a ''2'' should be moved to the Type Field in the Master Record indicating that the record is to be considered deleted from the master file. It should be noted that a type of ''1'' is invalid in the transaction record.

COBOL SUBROUTINES - SEGMENTATION

CHAPTER 6

COBOL SUBROUTINES - SEGMENTATION

6

INTRODUCTION

Although the inventory master file established in Chapter 3 and stored on the disk as an indexed sequential file contains the most up-to-date information, it is relatively useless unless this information can be presented in a usable form. Normally this information is presented as a printed report. Printed reports from the master file can be in many forms and present different information, dependent upon the needs of the users. In the sample program developed in this chapter, an Inventory Master Report, which will contain all the data in each data record, is prepared. The report layout for this report is shown in Figure 6-1.

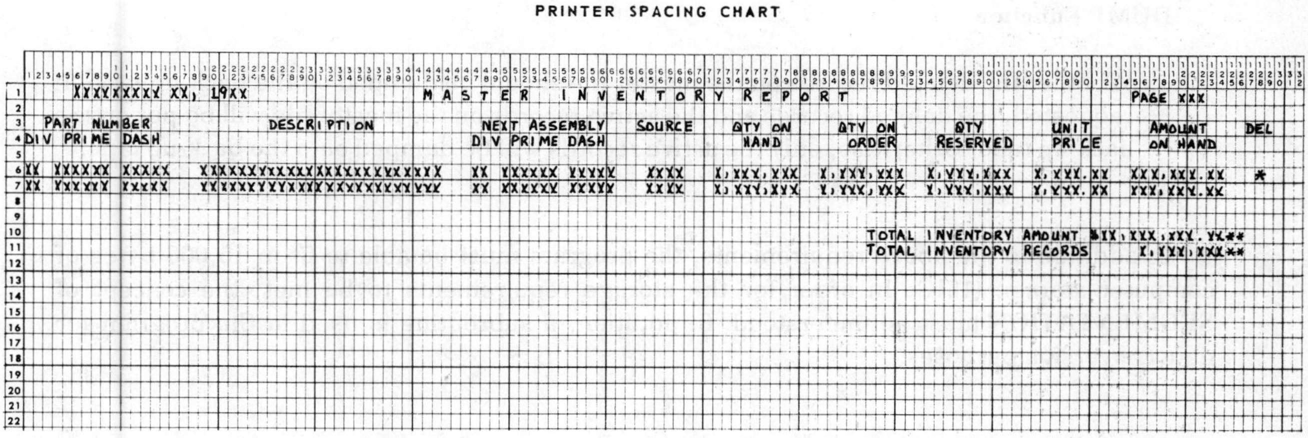

PRINTER SPACING CHART

Figure 6-1 Report Layout

In addition to this report, a back-up file is necessary for the indexed sequential master file stored on the disk. This back-up file is to be produced on magnetic tape and will be used to restore the inventory master file in case it becomes unusable.

It was decided that both the print function (to prepare the report) and the "dump" function (to create the back-up file) could be performed within the same program. To perform both functions within a single program, the program will read a control card and determine which function should be performed. In addition, certain control features will be introduced to the program through the use of the control card. The functions to be controlled by the control card include the following:

PRINT Function

1. Which part numbers will be printed. Either all the part numbers will be printed or a "from-to-range" can be requested and only the parts in the "from-to-range" will be printed.

2. Whether the deleted parts on the file should be printed. If requested, only the deleted parts will be printed. Otherwise, only the active parts will be printed.

DUMP Function

1. Whether the deleted records on the master file should be dumped on the back-up tape. If requested, the deleted records and the active records on the master file will be put on the back-up tape. Otherwise, only the active records will be dumped onto the back-up tape.

In addition to the above requirements, the program must be able to fit in 15,000 bytes of computer storage (15K). In order for the storage requirements to be met, the concept of **SEGMENTATION** must be understood. In addition, a subroutine is used in the program for data conversion purposes.

COBOL SUBPROGRAMS

It is possible to have subroutines written in a language other than COBOL, such as Assembler Language, to perform certain tasks which either could not be performed by using the COBOL language or which could be performed better using another language. Another use for separately written subroutines is when they are used to perform a function which has to be accomplished in more than one program. An example of this is the routine which is used by COBOL and Logical IOCS to read a card or write on the printer. These routines are necessary in many COBOL programs, so they are written once and included in many different programs.

Subroutines which are common to many programs do not have to be written in a language other than COBOL. Many occasions arise when the common task to be accomplished can be programmed in COBOL. Thus, the use of subroutines written in COBOL can save a great deal of time because they can be used many times in different programs. Subroutines which are compiled separately are referred to as **SUBPROGRAMS**.

As when using subprograms which are written in a programming language other than COBOL, the COBOL program which passes control to another program is called the "calling program", and the COBOL program which receives control (the **SUBPROGRAM**) is referred to as the "called program". Both programs are compiled as separate programs, but the resulting object modules, that is, the machine language output of a COBOL compilation, are linked together to form a single program. This is illustrated in the following example.

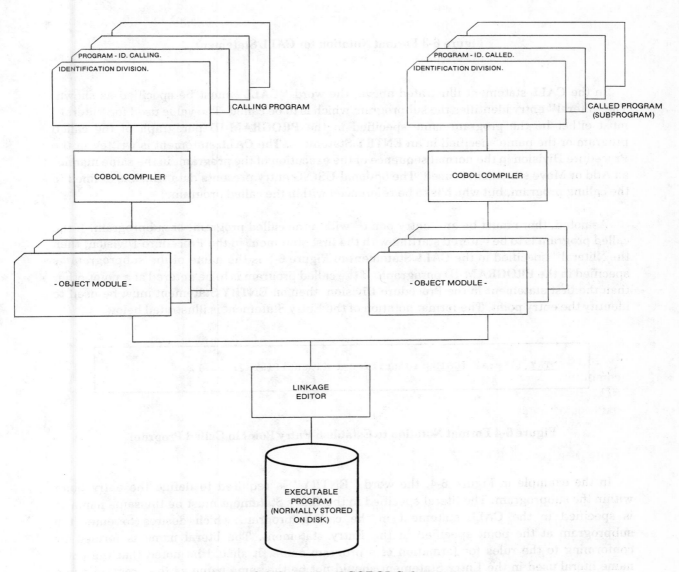

Figure 6-2 Example of COBOL Subprogram

Note in Figure 6-2 that the calling program (**CALLING**) and the called subprogram (**CALLED**) are each compiled as separate programs. Separate object modules are produced as a result of the separate compilations, and then these separate object modules are linked together by the Linkage Editor to form a single program which can then be executed. This executable program, which consists of the two user-written programs as well as other modules like the IOCS modules which are automatically included, is normally stored on a direct-access device from which it can be retrieved for execution.

To call a COBOL subprogram, the **CALL** statement is used in the calling program. The format notation of the **CALL** statement is illustrated in Figure 6-3.

```
CALL literal [USING identifier-1 [identifier-2] ...]
```

Figure 6-3 Format Notation for CALL Statement

In the **CALL** statement illustrated above, the word "CALL" must be specified as shown. The "literal" entry identifies the subprogram which is to be called. The value used for "literal" must either be the program-name specified in the **PROGRAM-ID** paragraph of the called program or the name specified in an **ENTRY** Statement. The **CALL** statement is written in the Procedure Division in the normal sequence of the execution of the program, in the same manner an Add or Move statement is used. The optional **USING** entry presents data which is defined in the calling program, but which is to be referenced within the called program.

As noted, there must be an "entry point" within the called program, or subprogram. If the called program is to be entered starting with the first statement in the Procedure Division, then the "literal" specified in the **CALL** Statement in Figure 6-3 is the name of the subprogram as specified in the **PROGRAM-ID** paragraph. If the called program is to be entered at a point other than the first statement in the Procedure Division, then an **ENTRY** Statement must be used to identify the entry point. The format notation of the Entry Statement is illustrated below.

```
ENTRY literal [USING identifier-1 [identifier-2] ...]
```

Figure 6-4 Format Notation to Establish Entry Point in Called Program

In the example in Figure 6-4, the word "ENTRY" is required to define the entry point within the subprogram. The literal specified in the Entry Statement must be the same name as is specified in the **CALL** statement in the calling program which desires to enter the subprogram at the point specified in the Entry statement. The literal name is formed by conforming to the rules for formation of a program-name. It should be noted that the entry name literal used in the Entry Statement should not be the same name as the program name specified in the Program-ID paragraph.

The optional **USING** clause is specified when data is being passed from the calling program to the called program. It gives the names in the called program which will be used to reference this data.

As noted, the COBOL subprogram can be entered at the first instruction in the Procedure Division, or at any Entry point within the Procedure Division. In either case, the calling program must issue the Call Statement specifying the desired entry point. This is illustrated in the following example.

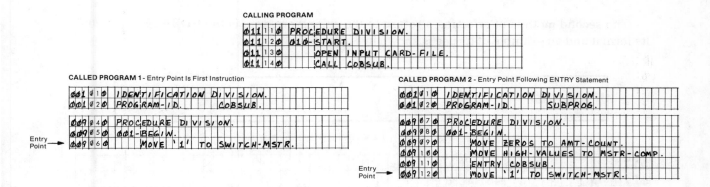

Figure 6-5 Example of Subprograms

In the example above, the **CALL COBSUB** statement will result in a branch to the entry point **COBSUB** in the called program. As noted previously, this entry point can be either the first instruction in the subprogram, such as with Called Program 1, or the instruction following the Entry Statement, such as in Called Program 2. Thus, as a result of the instructions generated by the Call Statement, the subprogram will be entered at the entry point and it will be executed in the normal manner, that is, as if it were part of the main calling program.

After the task of the subprogram has been completed, it is normally desirable to return to the calling program. A return to the statement following the Call Statement can be accomplished by two means in the called subprogram: The **EXIT PROGRAM** Statement and the **GOBACK** Statement.

The **EXIT PROGRAM** Statement format and an example are illustrated in Figure 6-6.

```
        paragraph-name.   EXIT PROGRAM.
```

```
0060 80       SUBTRACT GROSS-CALC FROM SALE-PRICE GIVING NET-AMT.
0060 90  EXIT-POINT. EXIT PROGRAM.
```

Figure 6-6 Example of EXIT PROGRAM Statement

The **EXIT PROGRAM** Statement must be immediately preceeded by a paragraph-name and must be the only statement in the paragraph. Thus, the only statement in the **EXIT-POINT** paragraph is the Exit Program Statement. When this statement is encountered in the subprogram, control is returned to the calling program at the statement immediately following the **CALL** Statement which called the subprogram.

The second method of effecting a return to the calling program is the **GOBACK** statement. Its format and an example of its use is shown in Figure 6-7.

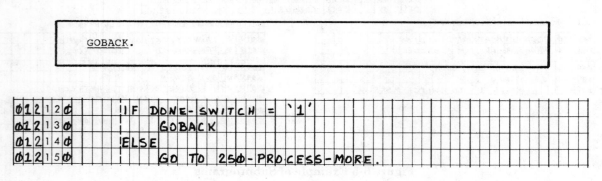

Figure 6-7 Example of GOBACK Statement

Note from the format notation illustrated above that the only statement necessary to cause a return to the calling program is the verb **GOBACK**. There are no special rules regarding the use of a paragraph-name such as with the Exit Program statement. Thus, the **GOBACK** statement can appear in any sentence within the program such as any other verb within the COBOL language can. In the coding example above, if the field **DONE-SWITCH** contains the value '1', the **GOBACK** statement will be executed which will cause control to return to the calling program at the statement following the **CALL** statement which invoked the subprogram.

The following example illustrates the use of the **CALL** statement, the **ENTRY** statement and the **GOBACK** statement. Note that the subprogram will be entered at the statement immediately following the **ENTRY** statement on pg/line 009110, and that control will be returned to the calling program at pg/line 011060 as a result of the **GOBACK** statement at pg/line 012130.

EXAMPLE

CALLING PROGRAM

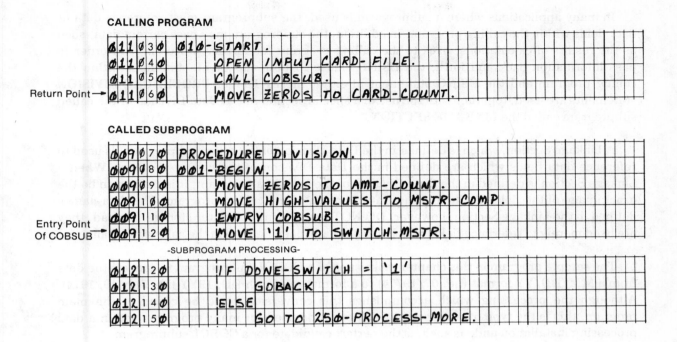

Figure 6-8 Example of Returning to Calling Program

As can be seen from the example in Figure 6-8, the subprogram which is entered using the **CALL** statement is used in a manner similar to a subroutine which is performed. The subprogram is entered at the entry point and continues processing until it returns to the calling program using either the **EXIT PROGRAM** or the **GOBACK** statements. The primary difference, in addition to the fact that Perform rules do not apply to called subprograms, is that the called subprogram is compiled separately from the calling program and is included in the program when the program is link-edited prior to execution.

It should also be noted that a subprogram is not restricted to one entry point. If the subprogram is written to perform several different tasks, it can be entered at more than one point by merely specifying more than one **ENTRY** statement within the Procedure Division. With each Entry statement, however, a different Entry Point name must be used. It is not allowable to have two different entry points with the same Entry Point name.

LINKAGE SECTION

In many applications where a subprogram is used, the subprogram must reference data or data fields within the calling program. In addition, the subprogram may pass certain data, such as the results of calculations, back to the calling program for further processing. In order to pass information back and forth, the USING clause in both the CALL statement within the calling program and the USING statement in either the ENTRY or PROCEDURE DIVISION statements are used, together with the use of a special section in the Data Division of the called subprogram called the LINKAGE SECTION.

A Linkage Section, which is defined in the Data Division of the called subprogram, is used to reference data fields which are defined in the Data Division of the calling program. When a Linkage Section is defined in the Data Division of the called subprogram, it is defined to be the exact image of the fields defined in the Data Division of the calling program. The data-names defined in the Linkage Section, however, DO NOT reserve any computer storage. Instead, they are used merely to reference fields which have already been defined in the calling program.

The sample program in this chapter makes use of a COBOL Subprogram to convert the date from a MM/DD/YY format (i.e. 07/19/74) to a format of Month DD, 19YY (i.e. July 19, 1974). Although the processing which accomplishes this conversion could be coded in the main program, this is the type of processing which could be used for many programs within a data processing installation and, as such, is the perfect candidate for a COBOL subprogram.

In order to successfully execute the subprogram, the current date or a date which is to be converted must be passed to the called subprogram from the calling program. In addition, there must be a field in the calling program where the subprogram can place the converted date. The coding used in the sample program and the subprogram is illustrated in Figure 6-9.

CALLING PROGRAM

```
004140 DATA DIVISION.

005160 WORKING-STORAGE SECTION.
005170 01  DATE-PASSED                    PICTURE X(8).
005180 01  DATE-RECEIVED                  PICTURE X(18).
```

CALLED SUBPROGRAM

```
002020 DATA DIVISION.

003040 WORKING-STORAGE SECTION.

004020 LINKAGE SECTION.
004030 01  DATE-GIVEN.
004040     03  MONTH-GIVEN               PIC 99.
004050     03  FILLER                    PIC X.
004060     03  DAY-GIVEN1                PIC X.
004070     03  DAY-GIVEN2                PIC X.
004080     03  FILLER                    PIC X.
004090     03  YEAR-GIVEN1               PIC X.
004100     03  YEAR-GIVEN2               PIC X.
004110 01  DATE-RETURNED.
004120     03  DATE-ALL-RETURNED         PIC X(18).
004130     03  DATE-PIECES-RETURNED REDEFINES DATE-ALL-RETURNED
004140         OCCURS 18 TIMES           PIC X.
004150     03  MONTH-RETURNED REDEFINES DATE-ALL-RETURNED.
004160         05  MONTH-NAME-RETURNED PIC X(9).
004170         05  FILLER                PIC X(9).
```

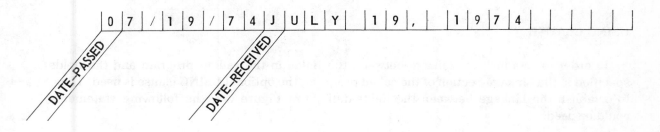

Figure 6-9 Example of the Use of the LINKAGE SECTION

The entries in the Working-Storage Section of the calling program define two fields which are to be referenced in the subprogram - the field in which the date in the format **MM/DD/YY** is to be passed (**DATE-PASSED**) and the field in which the converted date is to be received (**DATE-RECEIVED**). It should be noted that the field is 18 digits in length because this is the longest date which can be returned (September 21, 1974). These entries in the Working-Storage Section of the calling program reserve computer storage and the calling program will place the date into the **DATE-PASSED** field.

In the called subprogram, the **LINKAGE SECTION** is used. It does not reserve computer storage. It merely references storage already reserved by the entries in Working-Storage of the calling program. Thus, when the name **DATE-GIVEN** is referenced in the Procedure Division of the called subprogram, it would be referencing the same storage location as the data-name **DATE-PASSED** in the calling program.

As can be seen from the example, there is no need that the references in the Linkage Section be defined in exactly the same manner as those in the calling program although they must be the same length as those in the calling program. The fields in the Calling Program are defined as eight and eighteen character alphanumeric fields. In the called program, the fields total eight and eighteen digits, respectively, but they are defined in different formats. This is because the called program is to perform certain functions which require the fields to be in these different formats.

Also, it should be noted that the fields **DATE-PASSED** and **DATE-RECEIVED** are defined with the level number 01, and the fields in the called program are also defined as level 01. Whenever a Linkage Section is used, the fields must be defined either as level 01 or level 77 fields. In addition, they must be defined with the same level number in both the calling and the called programs. Thus, if a field is defined as a level 01 field in the calling program, it must also be defined as a level 01 field in the called program. This is because the compiler will automatically align an 01 field on a doubleword boundary and if the field in the calling program is on a doubleword boundary, the field in the called program should be also. The same holds true for a level 77 field, that is a 77 level field in the calling program should not be defined as a level 01 entry in the called program, but should be defined as a level 77 field.

USING CLAUSE

In order to establish the linkage between the fields in the calling program and the fields specified in the Linkage Section of the called program, the optional **USING** clause is used. Thus, to establish the Linkage between the fields defined in Figure 6-9, the following statements could be used.

CALLING PROGRAM

```
011090      CALL DTECONV USING DATE-PASSED, DATE-RECEIVED.
```

CALLED PROGRAM - Entry Point Is First Instruction

```
006110  PROCEDURE DIVISION USING DATE-GIVEN, DATE-RETURNED.
```

CALLED PROGRAM - Entry Point Follows ENTRY Statement

```
006170      ENTRY DTECONV USING DATE-GIVEN, DATE-RETURNED.
```

Figure 6-10 Example of the Use of the USING Clause

Note in Figure 6-10, that the entry point in the subprogram is established either by the Program-ID in the case where the first statement in the subprogram is to be the entry point or by the **ENTRY** Statement. The linkage to the subroutine is established by the **CALL** statement in the calling program. The **USING** clause in the **CALL** statement indicates that the address of the fields **DATE-PASSED** and **DATE-RECEIVED** are to be passed to the called subprogram so that it may reference the data in the calling program. The **USING** clause in the subprogram, as specified with either the Procedure Division statement of the Entry statement, identifies the Linkage Section entries in the called subprogram which will be used to reference the data in the calling program.

When the Call Statement takes place, the called subprogram will reference those fields which are indicated in the call statement in the calling program. Therefore, the entries in the Linkage Section, as illustrated in Figure 6-9, must be specified in the same sequence as those in the calling program when using the **USING** clause. As noted previously, all entries in the Linkage Section of the called subprogram must be identical to those in the Working-Storage Section of the calling program and these fields must be defined with either a level 01 or a level 77 indication.

OVERLAYS AND SEGMENTATION

In some applications, such as the sample program presented in this chapter, there are storage requirements placed on a program, that is, the program can be no larger than a given number of bytes. In some instances this presents no problem because the entire program can fit into the required number of bytes. In other instances, however, the entire program may be too large to fit into the storage area alloted for the program. When this occurs, it may be necessary to break the program up into a number of independent segments which can then be executed as a single program to produce the required results. All of these independent segments cannot be in computer storage at one time because together they are too large for the allocated storage. Therefore, these segments must **OVERLAY** one another. Overlaying is the technique of replacing one segment of a program in computer storage with another segment of the same program. The segment which is brought into storage can then be executed until it has completed its task at which time it can be overlayed by another segment. Thus, a number of different segments of a program can each be executed in the same area of computer storage. These separate segments are referred to as **OVERLAYS**.

In the sample program, the storage requirements state that the program must be less than 15K in length. It is not possible, however, for the entire program to be included in 15K or less; therefore, overlays are used.

The sample program has three distinct functions: Interpret the control card, dump the inventory master file onto tape, and print the desired report from the master file. Thus, the program could logically be broken into three overlay segments. By making one overlay segment to interpret the card, one to dump the inventory master and one to print the report, the program could satisfy the computer storage requirements. Therefore, the program is designed to use three overlay segments.

The storage allocation for the three overlay segments is illustrated in the following diagram. Note that there is a root segment, a segment to read the control card, a segment to dump the master file, and a segment to print the report.

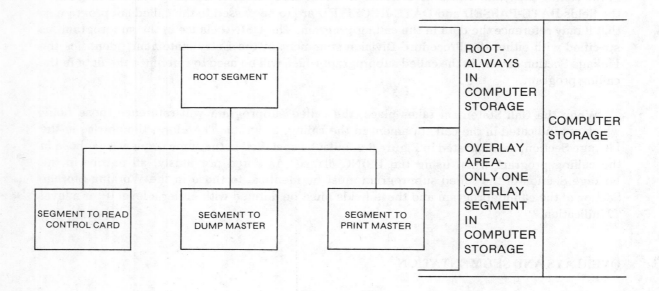

Figure 6-11 Computer Storage Allocation With Overlay Phases

Note in Figure 6-11 that the overlay segment to read the control card, the overlay segment to dump the master file onto tape, and the overlay segment to print the master file will all be in the same portion of computer storage. In addition, there is a "root segment" which contains the File Definitions which are used in the program as well as the Data Division of the program. The overlay segments can all reference this data which is stored in the Root Segment. The root segment is in computer storage at all times during the execution of the program. In addition, in the sample program at the end of the chapter, the root segment determines which other segments will be executing at any given time. It does this by Performing the proper segment depending upon the function to be performed by the program.

SECTION DESIGNATIONS

Since each overlay segment is not in computer storage at the same time, they must be available to be brought into storage when it is determined that it is time for them to be executed. The Operating Systems which control the processing on a computer also provide some type of library in which these segments can be stored and retrieved when necessary. For example, when using the IBM System/360/370 Disk Operating System, the segments are stored in the Core Image Library.

Segments of a program which are to be used as overlays are written just as if they were a part of a COBOL program which was not going to contain overlays. The only difference is that the program is divided into sections which constitute the overlayable segments. The coding necessary to divide a program is illustrated below.

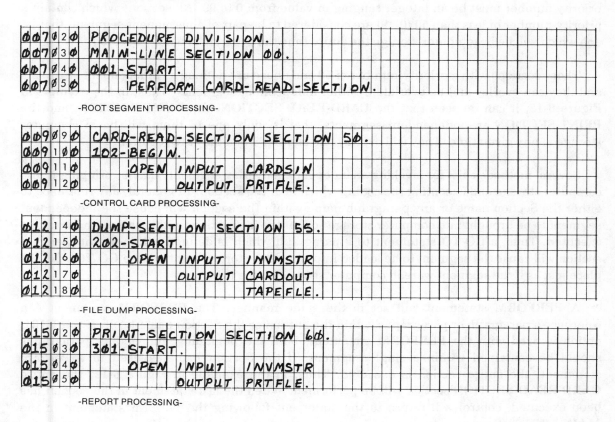

```
007020  PROCEDURE DIVISION.
007030  MAIN-LINE SECTION 00.
007040  001-START.
007050      PERFORM CARD-READ-SECTION.
```
-ROOT SEGMENT PROCESSING-

```
009090  CARD-READ-SECTION SECTION 50.
009100  102-BEGIN.
009110      OPEN INPUT  CARDSIN
009120           OUTPUT PRTFLE.
```
-CONTROL CARD PROCESSING-

```
012140  DUMP-SECTION SECTION 55.
012150  202-START.
012160      OPEN INPUT  INVMSTR
012170           OUTPUT CARDOUT
012180           TAPEFLE.
```
-FILE DUMP PROCESSING-

```
015020  PRINT-SECTION SECTION 60.
015030  301-START.
015040      OPEN INPUT  INVMSTR
015050           OUTPUT PRTFLE.
```
-REPORT PROCESSING-

Figure 6-12 Example of Segmentation

Note from the example in Figure 6-12 that the root section is defined immediately following the Procedure Division heading. The format notation of the Section Statement is illustrated below.

```
section-name SECTION [priority-number].
```

Figure 6-13 Format Notation for Section Statement

Note from the format notation in Figure 6-13 that the section-name must be specified. It is a name which is formed by the same rules as data-names. The word **SECTION** must be specified as indicated. The priority-number in the Section statement is the indicator which specifies if the section is to be an ''independent segment'', that is, one which can overlay and be overlaid. The priority number must be an integer ranging in value from 0 to 99. All sections which contain a priority-number of less than 50 (0-49) are considered to be part of a permanent segment, that is, one which will be in computer storage the entire time the program is being executed.

Those sections with a priority-number of 50 and above are defined as independent segments and they can overlay and be overlaid by other independent segments. Thus, in the example in Figure 6-12, it can be seen that the **CARD-READ-SECTION**, the **DUMP-SECTION**, and the **PRINT-SECTION** are independent segments, that is, only one of them will be in computer storage at any given time. They will overlay one another when they are required.

Several methods exist for invoking an independent overlay segment, that is, bringing it into computer storage and executing the coding which is in the section. In general, any reference to either the Section name or any paragraph name within the section will cause the independent segment to be brought into computer storage so that the instructions within the segment can be executed. Thus, a **GO TO** statement to a paragraph which is defined within an independent section will cause the segment to be loaded into computer storage and then the **GO TO** will take place just as if the segment were in computer storage all the time.

A **PERFORM** statement will act in the same manner. The **PERFORM** statement can reference a paragraph or paragraphs within the section or the Section name itself. If the **THRU** option is used with the **PERFORM** statement, both the beginning and ending paragraphs should be contained within a single segment. If the Section name is used in a Perform statement, the entire section is executed. Thus, in the example in Figure 6-12, the entire **CARD-READ-SECTION** section will be performed. When the last statement in the section has been executed, control will return to the statement following the Perform statement in the **MAIN-LINE** Section.

In the sample program, the Root Segment is used to determine which other segments are brought into computer storage and executed. The root section is illustrated below.

```
0 0 7 0 2 0  PROCEDURE DIVISION.
0 0 7 0 3 0  MAIN-LINE SECTION 00.
0 0 7 0 4 0  001-START.
0 0 7 0 5 0      PERFORM CARD-READ-SECTION.
0 0 7 0 6 0      IF PRINT-DUMP = '1' GO TO 010-PRINT-PGM.
0 0 7 0 7 0      PERFORM DUMP-SECTION.
0 0 7 0 8 0      GO TO 050-STOP-IT.
0 0 7 0 9 0  010-PRINT-PGM.
0 0 7 1 0 0      PERFORM PRINT-SECTION.
0 0 7 1 1 0  050-STOP-IT.
0 0 7 1 2 0      STOP RUN.
```

Figure 6-14 Example of ROOT Segment

In the example in Figure 6-14, it can be seen that the **CARD-READ-SECTION** is performed as the first step in the root segment. This section reads the control card which is input to the program and determines the type of processing which is to take place. If the switch **PRINT-DUMP** is equal to '1', then the print program is to be executed; otherwise, the dump program will be executed. Note that both the print and the dump segments are invoked through the use of the Perform verb. In both cases, when the Perform verb is executed, the given segment will be loaded into computer storage and the entire section will then be performed in the same manner as paragraphs have been performed in previous programs.

VIRTUAL STORAGE

As was noted previously, one problem which programmers have frequently encountered has been keeping a program to a size which will fit into the computer storage. If this was not possible, then the overlay techniques described can be used so that a program which is actually larger than the storage allocated for its execution can still be executed.

With the advent of the IBM System/370 and other new computers, the concept of **VIRTUAL STORAGE** has been introduced. As a result of virtual storage on the System/370 and some other computers, the programmer need not worry about the size of his program. It can be written to be any size and, without resorting to the techniques of overlaying segments, will fit into the computer's storage because the computer hardware and operating system will automatically take care of the storage allocations. In order to see how this virtual storage takes place, it is necessary to understand the concepts of segmentation and paging.

SEGMENTATION AND PAGING

In the previous example of overlays, it was noted that the program was segmented through the use of priority-numbers used with the **SECTION** statement. When programming for a virtual storage environment, the programmer need not segment his program in this manner because the operating system will perform this task automatically. The program is divided into segments because this is the manner in which the program will be executed. Figure 6-15 illustrates this concept.

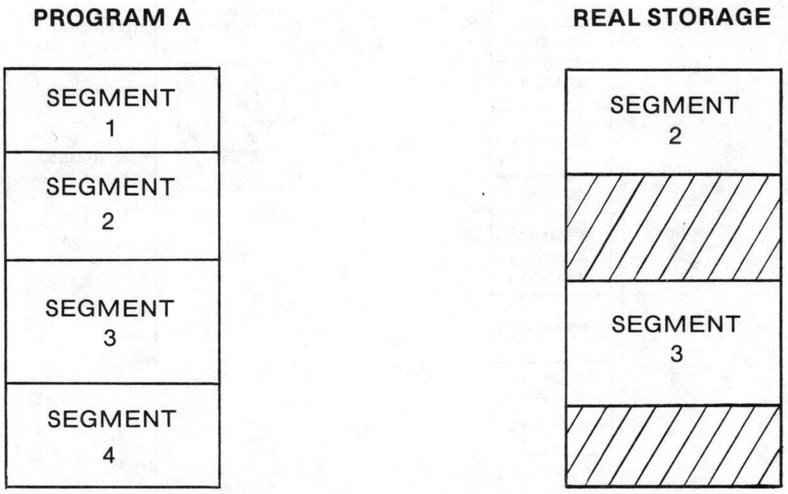

PROGRAM A   REAL STORAGE

Figure 6-15 Example of Segmented Program

In Figure 6-15, it can be seen that the program is divided into four segments. In real storage, that is, the actual computer storage, only segment 2 and segment 3 are resident. This is because at the given time above, these are the only segments of the program which are necessary to carry out the execution of the program. If, as the program is executing, the coding in segment 4 is required, then the operating system would automatically load segment 4 into real storage so that its instructions could be executed.

It should be noted that this concept is not altogether different from that of overlaying discussed previously, but there are several important distinctions. First, the programmer need not be concerned with the segmentation, as this is done by the operating system when the program is link-edited and prepared for execution. Secondly, and this is very important, when using a virtual storage system, any segment of any program can be loaded into any portion of real storage at any time. This is because of both hardware and software features which allow a segment of a program to be placed anywhere in real storage at any time for execution.

In the example in Figure 6-15, it does not appear that there is a significant advantage using a system such as this because it appears that the program can in fact fit into real storage and if it cannot, then overlaying would be a simple matter. When one program is being executed, this may be true, but the real value of a virtual storage system is when many programs are being executed at the same time. This situation is illustrated in Figure 6-16.

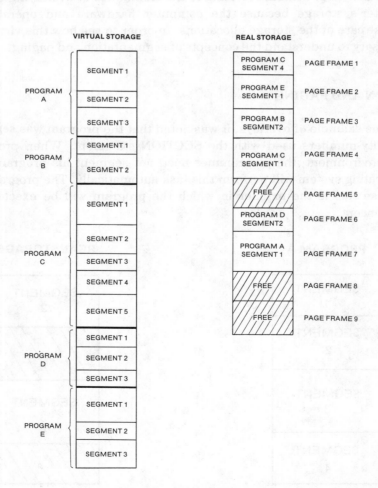

Figure 6-16 Example of Virtual Storage

In the example in Figure 6-16, it can be seen that there are five programs which are stored in virtual storage. Each of these programs have been segmented by the operating system. In real storage, that is, the actual computer storage, various segments of these programs have been placed for execution.

Real storage is divided into "page frames" by the operating system and it is into these page frames that the segments of the programs stored in virtual storage are loaded for execution. Within these "page frames" in real storage, the segments of the programs need not be stored in a contiguous manner. For example, segment 4 of Program C is in page frame 1 and segment 1 of Program C is in page frame 4. These are the only segments of Program C which are required for the execution of Program C at the given time illustrated in Figure 6-16. At another time in the execution of the program, other segments of the program will be required and these segments will be loaded into real storage at whatever locations may be available when they are needed.

Note also in Figure 6-16, that there are three allocated page frames (5, 8, and 9) which are currently not in use. If one of the programs executing in real storage required another segment stored in virtual storage, the operating system would "page" the proper segment and place it in one of the free page frames. If all of the page frames contain a segment from a program, the operating system will determine, through the use of an algorithm, which program has priority and will bring a segment of the program with priority into a page frame currently occupied by a segment of a program without priority. When it is time for the lower priority program to have time for execution, the operating system will load the segment required back into real storage, in the same or different page frame than that which it occupied previously.

The programs which are stored in virtual storage are actually stored, totally, on a direct-access device on which space has been reserved to act as virtual storage. The entire program is stored on the direct-access device, but only the segments actually required for execution at any given time are loaded into the page frames of real computer storage. As they are needed, other segments of the program stored in virtual storage, on a direct-access device, are "paged" into real storage.

On the System/370, the maximum size of virtual storage is over 16 million bytes. It would be prohibitively expensive to have this much real storage on a computer. Therefore, through the use of virtual storage, large programs which would not otherwise fit into real storage can be executed, and many programs can take advantage of "multiprogramming" to increase the throughput of a computer manyfold.

SAMPLE PROGRAM

The sample program, as was noted, reads a control card and determines the functions to be performed by the program as a result of the contents of the control card. The format of the card is illustrated in Figure 6-17.

PRINT CARD

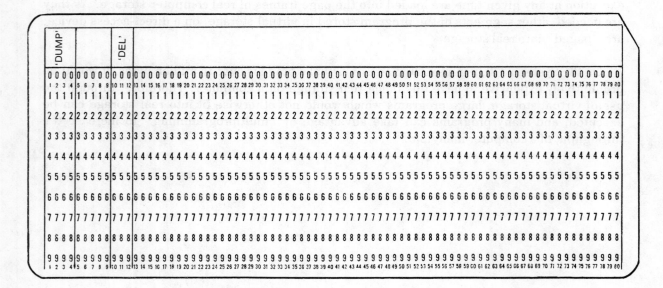

DUMP CARD

Figure 6-17 Control Card Formats

The control card is read by the **CARD-READ-SECTION** segment. The entries in the cards have the following meanings:

Print Card

Col 1-5:   '**PRINT**' - This entry indicates that the print function is to be performed by the program.

Col 10-22: Beginning part number or blank - This entry, if used, gives the 13 digit beginning part number. If the number is stated, the report to be printed will begin with the part number given. If the report is to begin at the beginning of the file, this entry must be left blank.

Col 25-37: Ending part number or blank - This entry, if used, gives the ending part number for the report. If this entry is specified, the report will end with the part number given. If an ending part number is not given, this field must be left blank.

Col 40-42: '**DEL**' - If this entry is specified, the report will contain only the deleted parts on the master file. If it is left blank, the active parts will be printed.

Dump Card

Col 1-4:   '**DUMP**' - This entry indicates that the dump function is to be performed by the program.

Col 10-12: '**DEL**' - This entry is included if the deleted parts as well as the active parts are to be dumped onto the back-up tape. If this entry is included, a card will be punched for each deleted record so that, if the file is restored to the disk after it is dumped, the records can be deleted by using the update program presented in Chapter 5. It should be noted that the type code in each of the records which are written on tape is changed to '8' so that the tape to disk program (Chapter 2) and the load program (Chapter 3) can be used to restore the master file.

The control card is read and indicators are set so that either the print or dump segments will be executed.

In addition to the control card, the inventory master file is input to the program. The format of the file is illustrated in Figure 6-18.

MASTER FILE

FIELD	FIELD NAME	PICTURE	POSITION	NO OF DIGITS	LENGTH
Part Number	PART-NUMB-MSTR	Picture 9(13) Comp-3	1-7	13	7
Description	NAME-MSTR	Picture X(25)	8-32	25	25
Quantity on Hand	QTY-ON-HAND-MSTR	Picture S9(7) Comp-3	33-36	7	4
Quantity on Order	QTY-ON-ORDER-MSTR	Picture S9(7) Comp-3	37-40	7	4
Quantity Reserved	QTY-RESERVED-MSTR	Picture S9(7) Comp-3	41-44	7	4
Next Assembly Number	NEXT-ASSEMBLY-MSTR	Picture S9(13) Comp-3	45-51	13	7
Type	TYPE-MSTR	Picture X	52	1	1
Source	SOURCE-MSTR	Picture X	53	1	1
Unit Price	UNIT-PRICE-MSTR	Picture S9(7) Comp-3	54-57	6	4
Filler	FILLER	Picture X(7)	58-64	7	7

Figure 6-18 Master File Format

COPY STATEMENT

Throughout the programs developed in the inventory system, it will be noted that the definition of the inventory master file in the File Section of the Data Division has been the same. Whenever a file definition is to be used in a number of different programs, it is normally desirable to write the file definition once, and then be able to include it in the source statements of each program. This can be accomplished through the use of the **COPY** statement.

The Copy statement can be used in the Environment or Data Division in a COBOL source program. It copies source statements which have been catalogued in an Operating System Library into the COBOL program at the point it is encountered in the program. The format notations of the Copy statement are illustrated in Figure 6-19.

FORMAT NOTATIONS

Option 1
(Within the Input-Output Section)

FILE-CONTROL.   COPY library-name.
I-O-CONTROL.

Option 2
(Within the File-Control Paragraph)
SELECT file-name COPY library-name.

Option 3
(Within a file area description entry or within the Working-Storage or Linkage Section)
01 data-name COPY library-name.

Option 4
(Within the Working-Storage or Linkage Section)
77 data-name COPY library-name.

Option 5
(Within the File Section)
FD file-name COPY library-name.

Option 6 (Within the Procedure Division):

section-name SECTION [priority-number]. COPY statement.
paragraph-name. COPY statement.

Figure 6-19 Format Notation of COPY Statement

In the examples shown in Figure 6-19, the "library-name" entry is the name which is used when the entry to be copied is catalogued in the user's library. It is an external name and must follow the rules for external name formation. When Options 1, 2, and 5 are used as shown in Figure 6-19, the data contained in the library replaces the **COPY** library-name statement. Thus, the data in the library is contained in the source program when the compilation is completed. When Options 3 and 4 are used, the data-name specified in the statement which includes the **COPY** clause is used as the data-name for the entry, even though a corresponding data-name is contained in the information copied from the library. Any reference to the 01 or 77 level data-names retrieved from the library as a result of using Options 3 or 4 should reference the name defined in the data-name portion of the statement, not the corresponding data-name which is retrieved from the library.

As noted, in the inventory system developed in the sample programs, the inventory master file is defined in each of the programs. The Copy statement which could be used to copy the definition of the master file into the source program is shown in Figure 6-20.

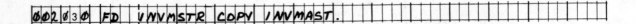

Figure 6-20 Example of Copy Statement in Sample Program

Note in the example shown above that the "FD" statement is included as when the file is defined if not using the Copy statement. The file-name **INVMSTR** is also included as without the Copy statement and it is the name which must be referenced whenever the file-name is referenced in the Procedure Division. The **COPY** verb is then stated with the library-name of **INVMAST**. This library-name is the name given to the source coding which is catalogued on the user's library.

As a result of the coding shown in Figure 6-20, the following coding would be included in the source program when it is compiled.

```
00050   003100 DATA DIVISION.                                           PRTMSTR
00051   003110 FILE SECTION.                                            PRTMSTR
00052   003120 FD  INVMSTR COPY INVMAST.                                PRTMSTR
00053 C 001010    BLOCK CONTAINS 54 RECORDS                             INVMAST
00054 C 001020    RECORD CONTAINS 64 CHARACTERS                         INVMAST
00055 C 001030    LABEL RECORDS ARE STANDARD                            INVMAST
00056 C 001040    DATA RECORD IS MSTR-IO.                               INVMAST
00057 C 001050 01 MSTR-IO.                                              INVMAST
00058 C 001060    03  PART-NUMB-MSTR          PIC 9(13)                 INVMAST
00059 C 001070                                USAGE COMP-3.             INVMAST
00060 C 001080    03  PART-NUMB-MSTR-X        REDEFINES PART-NUMB-MSTR  INVMAST
00061 C 001090                                PIC X(7).                 INVMAST
00062 C 001100    03  NAME-MSTR               PIC X(25).                INVMAST
00063 C 001110    03  QTY-ON-HAND-MSTR        PIC S9(7)                 INVMAST
00064 C 001120                                USAGE COMP-3.             INVMAST
00065 C 001130    03  QTY-ON-ORDER-MSTR       PIC S9(7)                 INVMAST
00066 C 001140                                USAGE COMP-3.             INVMAST
00067 C 001150    03  QTY-RESERVED-MSTR       PIC S9(7)                 INVMAST
00068 C 001160                                USAGE COMP-3.             INVMAST
00069 C 001170    03  NEXT-ASSEMBLY-MSTR      PIC S9(13)                INVMAST
00070 C 001180                                USAGE COMP-3.             INVMAST
00071 C 001190    03  TYPE-MSTR               PIC X.                    INVMAST
00072 C 001200    03  SOURCE-MSTR             PIC X.                    INVMAST
00073 C 002010    03  UNIT-PRICE-MSTR         PIC S9(7)                 INVMAST
00074 C 002020                                USAGE COMP-3.             INVMAST
00075 C 002030    03  FILLER                  PIC X(7).                 INVMAST
```

Figure 6-21 Source Listing Using Copy Statement

Note that the file definition and the I/O area for the master file are included as a result of the Copy statement. The coding which is received from the library is prefixed with the letter of the alphabet "C", which indicates that it was included because of the Copy statement.

PROGRAM

The following is the source listing of the sample program to create the master back-up file and the printed reports.

```
     1                          IBM DOS AMERICAN NATIONAL STANDARD COBOL        CBF CL3-4        10/25/74

  00001    001010 IDENTIFICATION DIVISION.                                      PRTMSTR
  00002    001020 PROGRAM-ID.     DUMPLIST.                                      PRTMSTR
  00003    001030 AUTHOR.         GBS.                                          PRTMSTR
  00004    001040 INSTALLATION.   LONG BEACH.                                   PRTMSTR
  00005    001050 DATE-WRITTEN.   09/11/74.                                     PRTMSTR
  00006    001060 DATE-COMPILED.  10/25/74                                      PRTMSTR
  00007    001070 SECURITY.       UNCLASSIFIED.                                 PRTMSTR
  00008    001080 REMARKS.        THIS PROGRAM PREPARES A PRINTED REPORT, AND   PRTMSTR
  00009    001090                 CREATES A BACK-UP TAPE OF THE INVENTORY MASTER PRTMSTR
  00010    001100                 FILE, IT DOES THESE TASKS IN 15K OF MAIN      PRTMSTR
  00011    001110                 STORAGE.  IN ORDER TO FIT IN THE REQUIRED STORAGE PRTMSTR
  00012    001120                 THE PROGRAM USES INDEPENDENT OVERLAYABLE      PRTMSTR
  00013    001130                 SEGMENTS.  IT USES FOUR DIFFERENT SEGMENTS.   PRTMSTR
  00014    001140                 1) A ROOT SEGMENT WHICH PERMANENTLY RESIDES   PRTMSTR
  00015    001150                 IN MAIN STORAGE AND CONROLS  WHICH OVERLAYABLE PRTMSTR
  00016    001160                 ARE BEING USED.  THE ROOT SEGMENT ALSO CONTAINS PRTMSTR
  00017    001170                 ALL OF THE INPUT/OUTPUT AREAS, WORKING STORAGE PRTMSTR
  00018    001180                 AND FILE DEFINITIONS USED IN THE PROGRAM;     PRTMSTR
  00019    001190                 2) A SEGMENT TO READ AND INTERPRET THE CONTROL PRTMSTR
  00020    001200                 CARD WHICH INDICATES THE PROCESSING WHICH IS TO PRTMSTR
  00021    002010                 OCCUR WITHIN THE PROGRAMS; 3) A SEGMENT TO CREATE PRTMSTR
  00022    002020                 THE PRINTED REPORTS; 4) A SEGMENT            PRTMSTR
  00023    002030                 TO CREATE THE BACK-UP TAPE OF THE INVENTORY   PRTMSTR
  00024    002040                 MASTER FILE.                                  PRTMSTR
  00025    002050                                                               PRTMSTR
  00026    002060 ENVIRONMENT DIVISION.                                         PRTMSTR
  00027    002070 CONFIGURATION SECTION.                                        PRTMSTR
  00028    002080 SOURCE-COMPUTER.  IBM-360-F30.                                PRTMSTR
  00029    02090 OBJECT-COMPUTER.  IBM-360-F30.                                 PRTMSTR
  00030    002100 SPECIAL-NAMES.                                                PRTMSTR
  00031    002110     C01 IS TO-TOP-OF-PAGE.                                    PRTMSTR
  00032    002120                                                               PRTMSTR
  00033    002130 INPUT-OUTPUT SECTION.                                         PRTMSTR
  00034    002140 FILE-CONTROL.                                                 PRTMSTR
  00035    002150     SELECT INVMSTR                                            PRTMSTR
  00036    002160        ASSIGN TO SYS006-DA-2314-I-INVMSTR                     PRTMSTR
  00037    002170        ACCESS IS SEQUENTIAL                                   PRTMSTR
  00038    002180        RECORD KEY IS PART-NUMB-MSTR                           PRTMSTR
  00039    002190        NOMINAL KEY IS MSTR-KEY.                               PRTMSTR
  00040    002200     SELECT PRTFLE                                             PRTMSTR
  00041    003010        ASSIGN TO SYS005-UR-1403-S.                            PRTMSTR
  00042    003020     SELECT TAPEFLE                                            PRTMSTR
  00043    003030        ASSIGN TO SYS007-UT-2400-S-TAPEFLE.                    PRTMSTR
  00044    003040     SELECT CARDOUT                                            PRTMSTR
  00045    003050        ASSIGN TO SYS008-UR-2540P-S.                           PRTMSTR
  00046    003060     SELECT CARDSIN                                            PRTMSTR
  00047    003070        ASSIGN TO SYS004-UR-2540R-S.                           PRTMSTR
  00048    003080                                                               PRTMSTR
  00049    003090                                                               PRTMSTR
  00050    003100 DATA DIVISION.                                                PRTMSTR
  00051    003110 FILE SECTION.                                                 PRTMSTR
  00052    003120 FD  INVMSTR COPY INVMAST.                                     PRTMSTR
  00053  C 001010     BLOCK CONTAINS 54 RECORDS                                 INVMAST
  00054  C 001020     RECORD CONTAINS 64 CHARACTERS                             INVMAST
  00055  C 001030     LABEL RECORDS ARE STANDARD                                INVMAST
  00056  C 001040     DATA RECORD IS MSTR-IO.                                   INVMAST
  00057  C 001050 01  MSTR-IO.                                                  INVMAST
  00058  C 001060     03  PART-NUMB-MSTR          PIC 9(13)                     INVMAST
  00059  C 001070                                 USAGE COMP-3.                 INVMAST
  00060  C 001080     03  PART-NUMB-MSTR-X        REDEFINES PART-NUMB-MSTR      INVMAST
  00061  C 001090                                 PIC X(7).                     INVMAST
  00062  C 001100     03  NAME-MSTR               PIC X(25).                    INVMAST
  00063  C 001110     03  QTY-ON-HAND-MSTR        PIC S9(7)                     INVMAST
  00064  C 001120                                 USAGE COMP-3.                 INVMAST
  00065  C 001130     03  QTY-ON-ORDER-MSTR       PIC S9(7)                     INVMAST
  00066  C 001140                                 USAGE COMP-3.                 INVMAST
  00067  C 001150     03  QTY-RESERVED-MSTR       PIC S9(7)                     INVMAST
  00068  C 001160                                 USAGE COMP-3.                 INVMAST
  00069  C 001170     03  NEXT-ASSEMBLY-MSTR      PIC S9(13)                    INVMAST
  00070  C 001180                                 USAGE COMP-3.                 INVMAST
  00071  C 001190     03  TYPE-MSTR               PIC X.                        INVMAST
  00072  C 001200     03  SOURCE-MSTR             PIC X.                        INVMAST
  00073  C 002010     03  UNIT-PRICE-MSTR         PIC S9(7)                     INVMAST
  00074  C 002020                                 USAGE COMP-3.                 INVMAST
  00075  C 002030     03  FILLER                  PIC X(7).                     INVMAST
  00076    003130                                                               PRTMSTR
  00077    003140 FD  TAPEFLE                                                   PRTMSTR
  00078    003150     BLOCK CONTAINS 4 RECORDS                                  PRTMSTR
  00079    003160     RECORD CONTAINS 80 CHARACTERS                             PRTMSTR
  00080    003170     LABEL RECORDS ARE STANDARD                                PRTMSTR
  00081    003180     DATA RECORD IS TAPE-IO.                                   PRTMSTR
  00082    003190 01  TAPE-IO.                                                  PRTMSTR
  00083    003200     03  PART-NUMB-TP      PICTURE 9(13).                      PRTMSTR
  00084    004010     03  NAME-TP           PICTURE X(25).                      PRTMSTR
  00085    004020     03  QTY-ON-HAND-TP    PICTURE 9(7).                       PRTMSTR
  00086    004030     03  QTY-ON-ORDER-TP   PICTURE 9(7).                       PRTMSTR
  00087    004040     03  QTY-RESERVED-TP   PICTURE 9(7).                       PRTMSTR
```

```
                 2
00088  004050    03  NEXT-ASSEMBLY-TP   PICTURE 9(13).                      PRTMSTR
00089  004060    03  TYPE-TP            PICTURE X.                          PRTMSTR
00090  004070    03  SOURCE-TP          PICTURE X.                          PRTMSTR
00091  004080    03  UNIT-PRICE-TP      PICTURE 9(6).                       PRTMSTR
00092  004090                                                               PRTMSTR
00093  004100 FD CARDOUT                                                    PRTMSTR
00094  004110    RECORD CONTAINS 80 CHARACTERS                              PRTMSTR
00095  004120    LABEL RECORDS ARE OMITTED                                  PRTMSTR
00096  004130    DATA RECORD IS CARD-IO.                                    PRTMSTR
00097  004140 01 CARD-IO.                                                   PRTMSTR
00098  004150    03  PART-NUMB-CARD     PICTURE 9(13).                      PRTMSTR
00099  004160    03  NAME-CARD          PICTURE X(25).                      PRTMSTR
00100  004170    03  QTY-ON-HAND-CARD   PICTURE 9(7).                       PRTMSTR
00101  004180    03  QTY-ON-ORDER-CARD  PICTURE 9(7).                       PRTMSTR
00102  004190    03  QTY-RESERVED-CARD  PICTURE 9(7).                       PRTMSTR
00103  004200    03  NEXT-ASSEMBLY-CARD PICTURE 9(13).                      PRTMSTR
00104  005010    03  TYPE-CARD          PICTURE X.                          PRTMSTR
00105  005020    03  SOURCE-CARD        PICTURE X.                          PRTMSTR
00106  005030    03  UNIT-PRICE-CARD    PICTURE 9(6).                       PRTMSTR
00107  005040                                                               PRTMSTR
00108  005050 FD CARDSIN                                                    PRTMSTR
00109  005060    RECORD  CONTAINS 80 CHARACTERS                             PRTMSTR
00110  005070    LABEL RECORDS ARE OMITTED                                  PRTMSTR
00111  005080    DATA RECORDS ARE CARD-IOD, CARD-IOP.                       PRTMSTR
00112  005090 01 CARD-IOD.                                                  PRTMSTR
00113  005100    03  DUMP-CARD          PICTURE X(4).                       PRTMSTR
00114  005110    03  FILLER             PICTURE X(5).                       PRTMSTR
00115  005120    03  DELETE-CARD        PICTURE XXX.                        PRTMSTR
00116  005130    03  FILLER             PICTURE X(68).                      PRTMSTR
00117  005140 01 CARD-IOP.                                                  PRTMSTR
00118  005150    03  PRINT-CARD         PICTURE X(5).                       PRTMSTR
00119  005160    03  FILLER             PICTURE X(4).                       PRTMSTR
00120  005170    03  PART-START-CARD    PICTURE 9(13).                      PRTMSTR
00121  005180    03  PART-START-CARD-X  REDEFINES PART-START-CARD           PRTMSTR
00122  005190                           PICTURE X(13).                      PRTMSTR
00123  005200    03  FILLER             PICTURE XX.                         PRTMSTR
00124  006010    03  PART-END-CARD      PICTURE 9(13).                      PRTMSTR
00125  006020    03  PART-END-CARD-X    REDEFINES PART-END-CARD             PRTMSTR
00126  006030                           PICTURE X(13).                      PRTMSTR
00127  006040    03  FILLER             PICTURE XX.                         PRTMSTR
00128  006050    03  DEL-CARD           PICTURE XXX.                        PRTMSTR
00129  006060    03  FILLER             PICTURE X(38).                      PRTMSTR
00130  006070                                                               PRTMSTR
00131  006080 FD PRTFLE                                                     PRTMSTR
00132  006090    RECORD CONTAINS 133 CHARACTERS                             PRTMSTR
00133  006100    LABEL RECORDS ARE OMITTED                                  PRTMSTR
00134  006110    DATA RECORD IS PRINT-IOA.                                  PRTMSTR
00135  006120 01 PRINT-IOA.                                                 PRTMSTR
00136  006130    03  FILLER             PICTURE X.                          PRTMSTR
00137  006140    03  PRINT-IO.                                              PRTMSTR
00138  006150        05 FIRST-PART.                                         PRTMSTR
00139  006160           07 PART-NUMB-PT PICTURE 99B9(6)B9(5).               PRTMSTR
00140  006170           07 FILLER       PICTURE XXX.                        PRTMSTR
00141  006180           07 NAME-PT      PICTURE X(25).                      PRTMSTR
00142  006190           07 FILLER       PICTURE XXX.                        PRTMSTR
00143  006200           07 NA-PT-NO-PT  PICTURE 99B9(6)B9(5).               PRTMSTR
00144  007010           07 FILLER       PICTURE XXX.                        PRTMSTR
00145  007020           07 SOURCE-PT    PICTURE X(4).                       PRTMSTR
00146  007030           07 FILLER       PICTURE X.                          PRTMSTR
00147  007040        05 MASTER-PRT.                                         PRTMSTR
00148  007050           07 FILLER       PICTURE XX.                         PRTMSTR
00149  007060           07 QOH-MPT      PICTURE Z,ZZZ,ZZZ.                  PRTMSTR
00150  007070           07 FILLER       PICTURE XX.                         PRTMSTR
00151  007080           07 QOO-MPT      PICTURE Z,ZZZ,ZZZ.                  PRTMSTR
00152  007090           07 FILLER       PICTURE XX.                         PRTMSTR
00153  007100           07 QRSV-MPT     PICTURE Z,ZZZ,ZZZ.                  PRTMSTR
00154  007110           07 UNIT-PRC-MPT PICTURE ZZZ,ZZZ.ZZ.                 PRTMSTR
00155  007120           07 FILLER       PICTURE X.                          PRTMSTR
00156  007130           07 AMOUNT-MPT   PICTURE ZZZZ,ZZZ.ZZ.               PRTMSTR
00157  007140           07 FILLER       PICTURE XXX.                        PRTMSTR
00158  007150           07 DEL-MPT      PICTURE X.                          PRTMSTR
00159  007160           07 FILLER       PICTURE X(4).                       PRTMSTR
00160  007170        05 TOT-MPT         REDEFINES MASTER-PRT.               PRTMSTR
00161  007180           07 FILLER       PICTURE X(18).                      PRTMSTR
00162  007190           07 MSG-TOT-MPT  PICTURE X(22).                      PRTMSTR
00163  007200           07 AMT-TOT-MPT  PICTURE $$$$,$$$,$$$.99.            PRTMSTR
00164  008010           07 TOT-AST-MPT  PICTURE XX.                         PRTMSTR
00165  008020           07 FILLER       PICTURE X(6).                       PRTMSTR
00166  008030        05 TOT-REC-MPT     REDEFINES MASTER-PRT.               PRTMSTR
00167  008040           07 FILLER       PICTURE X(18).                      PRTMSTR
00168  008050           07 MSG-REC-MPT  PICTURE X(23).                      PRTMSTR
00169  008060           07 FILLER       PICTURE X(5).                       PRTMSTR
00170  008070           07 RECS-MPT     PICTURE Z,ZZZ,ZZZ.                  PRTMSTR
00171  008080           07 RECS-AST-MPT PICTURE XX.                         PRTMSTR
00172  008090           07 FILLER       PICTURE X(6).                       PRTMSTR
00173  008100                                                               PRTMSTR
00174  008110                                                               PRTMSTR
```

```
        3

00175   008120 WORKING-STORAGE SECTION.                                      PRTMSTR
00176   008130 77  ASTERISKS              PICTURE XX          VALUE '**'.     PRTMSTR
00177   008140 77  CARD-ERROR             PICTURE X(49)       VALUE          PRTMSTR
00178   008150      'CONTROL CARD IN ERROR - CORRECT AND RE-SUBMIT'.         PRTMSTR
00179   008160 77  VARIABLE               PICTURE 9.                         PRTMSTR
00180   008170 77  SINGLE-SPACING         PICTURE 9           VALUE 1.       PRTMSTR
00181   008180 77  DOUBLE-SPACING         PICTURE 9           VALUE 2.       PRTMSTR
00182   008190 77  TRIPLE-SPACING         PICTURE 9           VALUE 3.       PRTMSTR
00183   008200 77  AMOUNT-MSG-MSTR        PICTURE X(22)       VALUE          PRTMSTR
00184   009010      'TOTAL INVENTORY AMOUNT'.                                PRTMSTR
00185   009020 77  REC-MSG-MSTR           PICTURE X(23)       VALUE          PRTMSTR
00186   009030      'TOTAL INVENTORY RECORDS'.                               PRTMSTR
00187   009040 77  RECORD-COUNT           PICTURE S9(7)       VALUE ZERO     PRTMSTR
00188   009050                            USAGE COMPUTATIONAL-3.             PRTMSTR
00189   009060 77  AMOUNT-COUNT1          PICTURE S9(9)V99    VALUE ZERO     PRTMSTR
00190   009070                            USAGE COMPUTATIONAL-3.             PRTMSTR
00191   009080 77  PG-COUNT               PICTURE S9(3)       VALUE ZERO     PRTMSTR
00192   009090                            USAGE COMPUTATIONAL-3.             PRTMSTR
00193   009100 77  LINE-COUNT             PICTURE S9(3)       VALUE ZERO     PRTMSTR
00194   009110                            USAGE COMPUTATIONAL-3.             PRTMSTR
00195   009120 77  AMT-HOLD               PICTURE S9(9)V99                   PRTMSTR
00196   009130                            USAGE COMPUTATIONAL-3.             PRTMSTR
00197   009140 77  NO-DIV-MSG             PICTURE X(47)       VALUE          PRTMSTR
00198   009150      'REQUESTED PART NUMBER NOT ON FILE-JOB CANCELLED'.       PRTMSTR
00199   009160 77  INV-HEAD               PICTURE X(51)       VALUE          PRTMSTR
00200   009170      '   M A S T E R   I N V E N T O R Y   R E P O R T'.      PRTMSTR
00201   009180 77  COMM-LINE1             PICTURE X(69)       VALUE          PRTMSTR
00202   009190      '  PART NUMBER         DESCRIPTION         NEXT ASSEMBLYPRTMSTR
00203   009200-     '  SOURCE'.                                              PRTMSTR
00204   010010 77  LINE1-MSTR             PICTURE X(63)       VALUE          PRTMSTR
00205   010020      '  QTY ON     QTY ON     QTY     UNIT     AMOUNT    DELPRTMSTR
00206   010030-     ' '.                                                     PRTMSTR
00207   010040 77  LINE2-MSTR             PICTURE X(63)       VALUE          PRTMSTR
00208   010050      '   HAND      ORDER    RESERVED    PRICE    ON HAND'.    PRTMSTR
00209   010060 77  COMM-LINE2             PICTURE X(69)       VALUE          PRTMSTR
00210   010070      'DIV PRIME DASH                          DIV PRIME DASHPRTMSTR
00211   010080-     ' '.                                                     PRTMSTR
00212   010090 77  MSTR-KEY               PICTURE 9(13)                      PRTMSTR
00213   010100                            USAGE COMPUTATIONAL-3.             PRTMSTR
00214   010110 77  MSTR-KEY-X             REDEFINES MSTR-KEY                 PRTMSTR
00215   010120                            PICTURE X(7).                      PRTMSTR
00216   010130 01  DATE-PASSED            PICTURE X(8).                      PRTMSTR
00217   010140 01  DATE-RECEIVED          PICTURE X(18).                     PRTMSTR
00218   010150 01  HEADING-1.                                                PRTMSTR
00219   010160     03  FILLER             PICTURE X(5)        VALUE SPACES.  PRTMSTR
00220   010170     03  DATE-H1            PICTURE X(18).                     PRTMSTR
00221   010180     03  FILLER             PICTURE X(14)       VALUE SPACES.  PRTMSTR
00222   010190     03  MAINHEAD           PICTURE X(51)       VALUE SPACES.  PRTMSTR
00223   010200     03  FILLER             PICTURE X(27)       VALUE SPACES.  PRTMSTR
00224   011010     03  FILLER             PICTURE X(5)        VALUE 'PAGE'.  PRTMSTR
00225   011020     03  PG-H1              PICTURE ZZ9.                       PRTMSTR
00226   011030     03  FILLER             PICTURE X(9)        VALUE ' '.     PRTMSTR
00227   011040                                                               PRTMSTR
00228   011050 01  CONTROL-SWITCHES.                                         PRTMSTR
00229   011060     03  PRINT-DUMP         PICTURE X.                         PRTMSTR
00230   011070     03  START-PT-NO        PICTURE 9(13)                      PRTMSTR
00231   011080                            USAGE COMPUTATIONAL-3.             PRTMSTR
00232   011090     03  START-PT-NO-X      REDEFINES START-PT-NO              PRTMSTR
00233   011100                            PICTURE X(7).                      PRTMSTR
00234   011110     03  END-PT-NO          PICTURE 9(13)                      PRTMSTR
00235   011120                            USAGE COMPUTATIONAL-3.             PRTMSTR
00236   011130     03  END-PT-NO-X        REDEFINES END-PT-NO                PRTMSTR
00237   011140                            PICTURE X(7).                      PRTMSTR
00238   011150     03  DEL-SWITCH         PICTURE X           VALUE '0'.     PRTMSTR
00239   011160                                                               PRTMSTR
00240   011170                                                               PRTMSTR
00241   011180                                                               PRTMSTR
00242   011190 PROCEDURE DIVISION.                                           PRTMSTR
00243   011200                                                               PRTMSTR
00244   012010 MAIN-LINE SECTION  00.                                        PRTMSTR
00245   012020                                                               PRTMSTR
00246   012030 NOTE-001.                                                     PRTMSTR
00247   012040     NOTE **********************************************PRTMSTR
00248   012050     *   THIS SECTION IS MERELY THE ROOT PHASE FOR THE    *PRTMSTR
00249   012060     *   OVERLAY SECTIONS WHICH WILL EITHER PRINT THE MASTER  *PRTMSTR
00250   012070     *   FILE OR CREATE A BACK-UP TAPE.                   *PRTMSTR
00251   012080     **********************************************.PRTMSTR
00252   012090                                                               PRTMSTR
00253   012100 001-START.                                                    PRTMSTR
00254   012110     PERFORM CARD-READ-SECTION.                                PRTMSTR
00255   012120     IF  PRINT-DUMP = '1' GO TO 010-PRINT-PGM.                 PRTMSTR
00256   012130     PERFORM DUMP-SECTION.                                     PRTMSTR
00257   012140     GO TO 050-STOPIT.                                         PRTMSTR
00258   012150                                                               PRTMSTR
00259   012160 010-PRINT-PGM.                                                PRTMSTR
00260   012170     PERFORM PRINT-SECTION.                                    PRTMSTR
00261   012180                                                               PRTMSTR
```

```
     4

00262  012190 050-STOPIT.                                                  PRTMSTR
00263  012200     STOP RUN.                                                PRTMSTR
00264  013010                                                             PRTMSTR
00265  013020                                                             PRTMSTR
00266  013030                                                             PRTMSTR
00267  013040 CARD-READ-SECTION  SECTION    50.                          PRTMSTR
00268  013050                                                             PRTMSTR
00269  013060                                                             PRTMSTR
00270  013070 NOTE-101.                                                   PRTMSTR
00271  013080     NOTE ************************************************** *PRTMSTR
00272  013090     *    THIS SECTION IS ENTERED TO READ AND INTERPRET     *PRTMSTR
00273  013100     *    THE CONTROL CARD AND PASS THE INFORMATION IN THE   *PRTMSTR
00274  013110     *    CONTROL CARD TO EITHER THE DUMP OR PRINT SECTIONS. *PRTMSTR
00275  013120     *    THE CONTROL CARD WHICH IS READ BY THIS PROGRAM HAS THE *PRTMSTR
00276  013130     *    FOLLOWING FORMAT-                                  *PRTMSTR
00277  013140     *    PRINT CARD - COL 1-5      'PRINT'                   PRTMSTR
00278  013150     *                 COL 10-22    13 DIGIT PART NUMBER     *PRTMSTR
00279  013160     *                              INDICATING THE FIRST PART *PRTMSTR
00280  013170     *                              NUMBER TO BE RETRIEVED- THIS*PRTMSTR
00281  013180     *                              OPERAND IS OPTIONAL.     *PRTMSTR
00282  013190     *                 COL 25-37    13 DIGIT PART NUMBER     *PRTMSTR
00283  013200     *                              INDICATING THE LAST PART *PRTMSTR
00284  014010     *                              NUMBER TO BE RETRIEVED.- *PRTMSTR
00285  014020     *                              THIS OPERAND IS OPTIONAL. *PRTMSTR
00286  014030     *                 COL 40-42    'DEL' - INCLUDED IF DELETED *PRTMSTR
00287  014040     *                              PARTS ARE TO BE PRINTED  *PRTMSTR
00288  014050     *                              INSTEAD OF ACTIVE PARTS. *PRTMSTR
00289  014060     *    DUMP CARD  - COL 1-4      'DUMP'                    *PRTMSTR
00290  014070     *                 COL 10-12    'DEL' - INCLUDED IF       *PRTMSTR
00291  014080     *                              DELETED PARTS AS WELL AS  *PRTMSTR
00292  014090     *                              ACTIVE PARTS ARE TO BE    *PRTMSTR
00293  014100     *                              DUMPED. IN THIS CASE, A CARD*PRTMSTR
00294  014110     *                              IS PUNCHED BY THE DUMP    *PRTMSTR
00295  014120     *                              PHASE FOR EACH DELETED    *PRTMSTR
00296  014130     *                              RECORD.                   *PRTMSTR
00297  014140     ************************************************** .PRTMSTR
00298  014150                                                             PRTMSTR
00299  014160 NOTE-102.                                                   PRTMSTR
00300  014170     NOTE ************************************************** *PRTMSTR
00301  014180     *    THIS ROUTINE OPENS THE CARD AND PRINTER FILES AND  *PRTMSTR
00302  014190     *    READS THE CARD.  IT THEN CHECKS EACH FIELD IN THE  *PRTMSTR
00303  014200     *    CARD AND SETS THE APPROPRIATE SWITCHES, ETC.       *PRTMSTR
00304  015010     ************************************************** .PRTMSTR
00305  015020                                                             PRTMSTR
00306  015030                                                             PRTMSTR
00307  015040 102-BEGIN.                                                  PRTMSTR
00308  015050     OPEN INPUT  CARDSIN,                                    PRTMSTR
00309  015060          OUTPUT PRTFLE.                                     PRTMSTR
00310  015070     READ CARDSIN AT END GO TO 110-NO-CARD.                  PRTMSTR
00311  015080     IF DUMP-CARD = 'DUMP'                                   PRTMSTR
00312  015090         GO TO 120-DO-DUMP.                                  PRTMSTR
00313  015100     IF PRINT-CARD = 'PRINT'                                 PRTMSTR
00314  015110         GO TO 130-DO-PRINT.                                 PRTMSTR
00315  015120                                                             PRTMSTR
00316  015130                                                             PRTMSTR
00317  015140 NOTE-110.                                                   PRTMSTR
00318  015150     NOTE ************************************************** *PRTMSTR
00319  015160     *    THIS ROUTINE IS ENTERED WHEN NO CONTROL CARD OR AN *PRTMSTR
00320  015170     *    INVALID CONTROL CARD IS FOUND. IT PRINTS AN ERROR  *PRTMSTR
00321  015180     *    MESSAGE ON THE PRINTER AND STOPS THE RUN.          *PRTMSTR
00322  015190     ************************************************** .PRTMSTR
00323  015200                                                             PRTMSTR
00324  016010 110-NO-CARD.                                                PRTMSTR
00325  016020     MOVE CARD-ERROR TO PRINT-IO.                            PRTMSTR
00326  016030     WRITE PRINT-IOA AFTER ADVANCING TO-TOP-OF-PAGE.         PRTMSTR
00327  016040     PERFORM 150-CLOSE-FILES THRU 150-EXIT.                  PRTMSTR
00328  016050     STOP RUN.                                               PRTMSTR
00329  016060                                                             PRTMSTR
00330  016070                                                             PRTMSTR
00331  016080 NOTE-120.                                                   PRTMSTR
00332  016090     NOTE ************************************************** *PRTMSTR
00333  016100     *    THIS ROUTINE IS ENTERED TO CHECK THE DUMP CARD. THE *PRTMSTR
00334  016110     *    ONLY VALID IS 'DEL' IN COLUMN 10.                  *PRTMSTR
00335  016120     ************************************************** .PRTMSTR
00336  016130                                                             PRTMSTR
00337  016140 120-DO-DUMP.                                                PRTMSTR
00338  016150     MOVE '0' TO PRINT-DUMP.                                 PRTMSTR
00339  016160     IF DELETE-CARD = 'DEL'                                  PRTMSTR
00340  016170         MOVE '1' TO DEL-SWITCH                              PRTMSTR
00341  016180     ELSE                                                    PRTMSTR
00342  016190         IF DELETE-CARD NOT = SPACES                         PRTMSTR
00343  016200             GO TO 110-NO-CARD                               PRTMSTR
00344  017010         ELSE                                                PRTMSTR
00345  017020             MOVE '0' TO DEL-SWITCH.                         PRTMSTR
00346  017030     GO TO 150-CLOSE-FILES.                                  PRTMSTR
00347  017040                                                             PRTMSTR
00348  017050 NOTE-130.                                                   PRTMSTR
```

```
    5
    00349   017060        NOTE **************************************************PRTMSTR
    00350   017070        *    THIS ROUTINE IS ENTERED TO CHECK THE VALID ENTRIES IN  *PRTMSTR
    00351   017080        *    THE PRINT CARD. THE VALID ENTRIES ARE EXPLAINED IN      *PRTMSTR
    00352   017090        *    NOTE-101.                                               *PRTMSTR
    00353   017100        **************************************************.PRTMSTR
    00354   017110                                                          PRTMSTR
    00355   017120 130-DO-PRINT.                                            PRTMSTR
    00356   017130        MOVE '1' TO PRINT-DUMP.                           PRTMSTR
    00357   017140        IF PART-START-CARD-X = SPACES                     PRTMSTR
    00358   017150            MOVE LOW-VALUE TO START-PT-NO-X               PRTMSTR
    00359   017160        ELSE                                             PRTMSTR
    00360   017170            MOVE PART-START-CARD TO START-PT-NO.          PRTMSTR
    00361   017180        IF PART-END-CARD-X = SPACES                       PRTMSTR
    00362   017190            MOVE HIGH-VALUE TO END-PT-NO-X                PRTMSTR
    00363   017200        ELSE                                             PRTMSTR
    00364   018010            MOVE PART-END-CARD TO END-PT-NO.              PRTMSTR
    00365   018020        IF DEL-CARD = 'DEL'                               PRTMSTR
    00366   018030            MOVE '1' TO DEL-SWITCH                        PRTMSTR
    00367   018040        ELSE                                             PRTMSTR
    00368   018050            IF DEL-CARD NOT = SPACES                      PRTMSTR
    00369   018060                GO TO 110-NO-CARD                         PRTMSTR
    00370   018070            ELSE                                         PRTMSTR
    00371   018080                MOVE '0' TO DEL-SWITCH.                   PRTMSTR
    00372   018090        GO TO 150-CLOSE-FILES.                            PRTMSTR
    00373   018100                                                          PRTMSTR
    00374   018110                                                          PRTMSTR
    00375   018120 NOTE-150.                                                PRTMSTR
    00376   018130        NOTE **************************************************PRTMSTR
    00377   018140        *    THIS ROUTINE IS ENTERED TO CLOSE THE FILES AND        *PRTMSTR
    00378   018150        *    RETURN TO THE ROOTPHASE.                              *PRTMSTR
    00379   018160        **************************************************.PRTMSTR
    00380   018170                                                          PRTMSTR
    00381   018180 150-CLOSE-FILES.                                         PRTMSTR
    00382   018190        CLOSE PRTFLE,                                     PRTMSTR
    00383   018200            CARDSIN.                                      PRTMSTR
    00384   019010                                                          PRTMSTR
    00385   019020 150-EXIT. EXIT.                                          PRTMSTR
    00386   019030                                                          PRTMSTR
    00387   019040                                                          PRTMSTR
    00388   019050 DUMP-SECTION  SECTION   55.                              PRTMSTR
    00389   019060                                                          PRTMSTR
    00390   019070                                                          PRTMSTR
    00391   019080 NOTE-201.                                                PRTMSTR
    00392   019090        NOTE **************************************************PRTMSTR
    00393   019100        *    THIS SECTION READS THE INVENTORY MASTER FILE AND       *PRTMSTR
    00394   019110        *    CREATES A BACK-UP FILE ON MAGNETIC TAPE. THE RECORD     *PRTMSTR
    00395   019120        *    FORMAT IS THE SAME AS THE TAPE USED AS INPUT IN THE     *PRTMSTR
    00396   019130        *    CHAPTER 2 PROGRAM. THIS ALLOWS THE FILE TO BE RE-LOADED *PRTMSTR
    00397   019140        *    FROM THE BACK-UP TAPE BY THE PROGRAMS IN CHAPTER 2 AND  *PRTMSTR
    00398   019150        *    CHAPTER 3. ALL THE RECORDS WHICH ARE WRITTEN ON THE     *PRTMSTR
    00399   019160        *    TAPE HAVE THE TYPE CODE CHANGED TO '8' SO THAT THEY     *PRTMSTR
    00400   019170        *    WILL APPEAR AS NEW-LOAD RECORDS. IF DELETED RECORDS     *PRTMSTR
    00401   019180        *    ARE WRITTEN ON THE BACK-UP FILE, DELETE CARDS ARE       *PRTMSTR
    00402   019190        *    PUNCHED SO THAT THE DELETED RECORDS ON THE FILE CAN BE  *PRTMSTR
    00403   019200        *    RE-DELETED USING THE UPDATE ROUTINE IN CHAPTER 5.       *PRTMSTR
    00404   020010        **************************************************.PRTMSTR
    00405   020020                                                          PRTMSTR
    00406   020030                                                          PRTMSTR
    00407   020040 NOTE-202.                                                PRTMSTR
    00408   020050        NOTE **************************************************PRTMSTR
    00409   020060        *    THIS ROUTINE OPENS THE THREE FILES AND READS THE        *PRTMSTR
    00410   020070        *    INVENTORY MASTER.  IT THEN DECIDES WHETHER OR NOT       *PRTMSTR
    00411   020080        *    THE RECORD SHOULD BE WRITTEN ON THE TAPE AND WHETHER    *PRTMSTR
    00412   020090        *    OR NOT A DELETE CARD SHOULD BE PUNCHED.                 *PRTMSTR
    00413   020100        **************************************************.PRTMSTR
    00414   020110                                                          PRTMSTR
    00415   020120 202-START.                                               PRTMSTR
    00416   020130        OPEN INPUT  INVMSTR,                              PRTMSTR
    00417   020140            OUTPUT CARDOUT,                               PRTMSTR
    00418   020150               TAPEFLE.                                   PRTMSTR
    00419   020160                                                          PRTMSTR
    00420   020170 210-READ-MSTR.                                           PRTMSTR
    00421   020180        READ INVMSTR AT END GO TO 220-END-MSTR.           PRTMSTR
    00422   020190        IF DEL-SWITCH = '0' AND TYPE-MSTR = '2'           PRTMSTR
    00423   020200            GO TO 210-READ-MSTR.                          PRTMSTR
    00424   021010        MOVE PART-NUMB-MSTR TO PART-NUMB-TP.              PRTMSTR
    00425   021020        MOVE NAME-MSTR TO NAME-TP.                        PRTMSTR
    00426   021030        MOVE QTY-ON-HAND-MSTR TO QTY-ON-HAND-TP.          PRTMSTR
    00427   021040        MOVE QTY-ON-ORDER-MSTR TO QTY-ON-ORDER-TP.        PRTMSTR
    00428   021050        MOVE QTY-RESERVED-MSTR TO QTY-RESERVED-TP.        PRTMSTR
    00429   021060        MOVE NEXT-ASSEMBLY-MSTR TO NEXT-ASSEMBLY-TP.      PRTMSTR
    00430   021070        MOVE '8' TO TYPE-TP.                              PRTMSTR
    00431   021080        MOVE SOURCE-MSTR TO SOURCE-TP.                    PRTMSTR
    00432   021090        MOVE UNIT-PRICE-MSTR TO UNIT-PRICE-TP.            PRTMSTR
    00433   021100        WRITE TAPE-IO.                                    PRTMSTR
    00434   021110        IF DEL-SWITCH = '1' AND TYPE-MSTR = '2'           PRTMSTR
    00435   021120            NEXT SENTENCE                                 PRTMSTR
```

```
       6

00436  021130     ELSE                                                      PRTMSTR
00437  021140         GO TO 210-READ-MSTR.                                  PRTMSTR
00438  021150     MOVE SPACES TO CARD-IO.                                   PRTMSTR
00439  021160     MOVE PART-NUMB-MSTR TO PART-NUMB-CARD.                    PRTMSTR
00440  021170     MOVE '2' TO TYPE-CARD.                                    PRTMSTR
00441  021180     WRITE CARD-IO.                                            PRTMSTR
00442  021190     GO TO 210-READ-MSTR.                                      PRTMSTR
00443  021200                                                               PRTMSTR
00444  022010                                                               PRTMSTR
00445  022020 NOTE-220.                                                     PRTMSTR
00446  022030     NOTE ***************************************************PRTMSTR
00447  022040     *    THIS ROUTINE IS ENTERED WHEN THE MASTER FILE REACHES *PRTMSTR
00448  022050     *    END OF FILE. IT CLOSES THE FILES AND RETURNS TO THE  *PRTMSTR
00449  022060     *    ROOT PHASE.                                          *PRTMSTR
00450  022070     ***************************************************.PRTMSTR
00451  022080                                                               PRTMSTR
00452  022090 220-END-MSTR.                                                 PRTMSTR
00453  022100     CLOSE INVMSTR,                                            PRTMSTR
00454  022110           TAPEFLE,                                            PRTMSTR
00455  022120           CARDOUT.                                            PRTMSTR
00456  022130                                                               PRTMSTR
00457  022140                                                               PRTMSTR
00458  022150                                                               PRTMSTR
00459  022160 PRINT-SECTION  SECTION  60.                                   PRTMSTR
00460  022170                                                               PRTMSTR
00461  022180                                                               PRTMSTR
00462  022190 NOTE-301.                                                     PRTMSTR
00463  022200     NOTE ***************************************************PRTMSTR
00464  023010     *    THIS SECTION IS USED TO PRINT THE MASTER FILE.  IT   *PRTMSTR
00465  023020     *    GENERATES A COMPLETE LISTING OF THE  MASTER FILE     *PRTMSTR
00466  023030     *    SHOWING ALL RECORDS ON THE MASTER FILE.              *PRTMSTR
00467  023040     *    THIS PROGRAM IS ENTERED FROM THE ROOT SECTION AFTER  *PRTMSTR
00468  023050     *    ANOTHER OVERLAY SEGMENT HAS INTERPRETED THE CONTROL CARD*PRTMSTR
00469  023060     *    AND SET THE APPROPRIATE SWITCHES, ETC. IF A PART     *PRTMSTR
00470  023070     *    NUMBER RANGE (PRIME AND DASH) IS ENTERED ON THE      *PRTMSTR
00471  023080     *    CONTROL CARD, ONLY PART NUMBERS FALLING IN THE RANGE *PRTMSTR
00472  023090     *    ARE PRINTED. IF A DELETED PARTS LIST IS REQUESTED,   *PRTMSTR
00473  023100     *    ONLY THOSE PART NUMBERS WHICH ARE DELETED ARE PRINTED. *PRTMSTR
00474  023110     *    OTHERWISE, ONLY THE ACTIVE PART NUMBERS ARE PRINTED. *PRTMSTR
00475  023120     ***************************************************PRTMSTR
00476  023130                                                               PRTMSTR
00477  023140     ***************************************************PRTMSTR
00478  023150     *    THIS ROUTINE IS ENTERED TO DETERMINE WHERE TO BEGIN  *PRTMSTR
00479  023160     *    RETRIEVAL (EITHER AT THE START OF THE FILE OR AT A    *PRTMSTR
00480  023170     *    PARTICULAR KEY) AND TO OPEN THE FILES.               *PRTMSTR
00481  023180     ***************************************************.PRTMSTR
00482  023190                                                               PRTMSTR
00483  023200 301-START.                                                    PRTMSTR
00484  024010     OPEN INPUT  INVMSTR,                                      PRTMSTR
00485  024020          OUTPUT PRTFLE.                                       PRTMSTR
00486  024030     IF START-PT-NO-X NOT = LOW-VALUES                         PRTMSTR
00487  024040         MOVE START-PT-NO-X TO MSTR-KEY-X                      PRTMSTR
00488  024050         START INVMSTR INVALID KEY                             PRTMSTR
00489  024060             GO TO 330-INV-KEY.                                PRTMSTR
00490  024070     MOVE CURRENT-DATE TO DATE-PASSED.                         PRTMSTR
00491  024080     CALL 'DTECONV' USING DATE-PASSED, DATE-RECEIVED.          PRTMSTR
00492  024090     MOVE  DATE-RECEIVED TO DATE-H1.                           PRTMSTR
00493  024100     PERFORM 350-HEADER THRU 350-EXIT.                         PRTMSTR
00494  024110                                                               PRTMSTR
00495  024120                                                               PRTMSTR
00496  024130 NOTE-310.                                                     PRTMSTR
00497  024140     NOTE ***************************************************PRTMSTR
00498  024150     *    THIS ROUTINE IS ENTERED TO READ THE INVENTORY MASTER *PRTMSTR
00499  024160     *    FILE. IT FIRST DETERMINES THAT THE RECORD IS WITHIN  *PRTMSTR
00500  024170     *    THE PART NUMBER RANGES AND THEN IF THE DELETED RECORDS *PRTMSTR
00501  024180     *    ARE DESIRED. AFTER THE DETERMINATIONS, THE RECORD IS *PRTMSTR
00502  024190     *    PRINTED, PROVIDED THE RECORD IS VALID               *PRTMSTR
00503  024200     ***************************************************.PRTMSTR
00504  025010                                                               PRTMSTR
00505  025020 310-READ-MSTR.                                                PRTMSTR
00506  025030     READ INVMSTR AT END GO TO 360-END-MSTR.                   PRTMSTR
00507  025040     IF PART-NUMB-MSTR-X IS > END-PT-NO-X                      PRTMSTR
00508  025050         GO TO 360-END-MSTR.                                   PRTMSTR
00509  025060     NOTE *** MASTER RECORD IS WITHIN DESIRED RANGE***.        PRTMSTR
00510  025070     IF DEL-SWITCH IS = '1'                                    PRTMSTR
00511  025080         IF TYPE-MSTR IS = '2'                                 PRTMSTR
00512  025090             GO TO 320-OK-TO-PRINT
00513  025100         ELSE
00514  025110             GO TO 310-READ-MSTR.                              PRTMSTR
00515  025120     IF TYPE-MSTR IS = '2'                                     PRTMSTR
00516  025130         GO TO 310-READ-MSTR.                                  PRTMSTR
00517  025140                                                               PRTMSTR
00518  025150 320-OK-TO-PRINT.                                              PRTMSTR
00519  025160     MOVE PART-NUMB-MSTR TO PART-NUMB-PT.                      PRTMSTR
00520  025170     MOVE NAME-MSTR TO NAME-PT.                                PRTMSTR
00521  025180     MOVE NEXT-ASSEMBLY-MSTR TO NA-PT-NO-PT.                   PRTMSTR
00522  025190     IF SOURCE-MSTR IS = '1'                                   PRTMSTR
```

```
       7

00523   025200          MOVE 'MANU' TO SOURCE-PT                              PRTMSTR
00524   026010      ELSE                                                      PRTMSTR
00525   026020          MOVE 'VEND' TO SOURCE-PT.                             PRTMSTR
00526   026030      MOVE QTY-ON-HAND-MSTR TO QOH-MPT.                         PRTMSTR
00527   026040      MOVE QTY-ON-ORDER-MSTR TO QOO-MPT.                        PRTMSTR
00528   026050      MOVE QTY-RESERVED-MSTR TO QRSV-MPT.                       PRTMSTR
00529   026060      MOVE UNIT-PRICE-MSTR TO UNIT-PRC-MPT.                     PRTMSTR
00530   026070      COMPUTE AMT-HOLD = UNIT-PRICE-MSTR * QTY-ON-HAND-MSTR.    PRTMSTR
00531   026080      MOVE AMT-HOLD TO AMOUNT-MPT.                              PRTMSTR
00532   026090      ADD AMT-HOLD TO AMOUNT-COUNT1.                            PRTMSTR
00533   026100      IF TYPE-MSTR IS = '2'                                     PRTMSTR
00534   026110          MOVE '*' TO DEL-MPT.                                  PRTMSTR
00535   026120      ADD 1 TO RECORD-COUNT.                                    PRTMSTR
00536   026130      PERFORM 340-WRITE-RPT THRU 340-EXIT.                      PRTMSTR
00537   026140      ADD 1 TO LINE-COUNT.                                      PRTMSTR
00538   026150      MOVE SINGLE-SPACING TO VARIABLE.                          PRTMSTR
00539   026160      IF LINE-COUNT > 55                                        PRTMSTR
00540   026170          PERFORM 350-HEADER THRU 350-EXIT                      PRTMSTR
00541   026180          MOVE 0 TO LINE-COUNT.                                 PRTMSTR
00542   026190      GO TO 310-READ-MSTR.                                      PRTMSTR
00543   026200                                                                PRTMSTR
00544   027010                                                                PRTMSTR
00545   027020  NOTE-330.                                                     PRTMSTR
00546   027030      NOTE ***********************************************   *   PRTMSTR
00547   027040      * THIS ROUTINE IS ENTERED WHEN SPECIFIED STARTING        *PRTMSTR
00548   027050      * RECORD IS NOT FOUND ON THE MASTER FILE. AN ERROR MESSAGE *PRTMSTR
00549   027060      * IS PRINTED ON THE REPORT AND THE PROGRAM IS THEN        *PRTMSTR
00550   027070      * TERMINATED.                                             *PRTMSTR
00551   027080      ***********************************************************.PRTMSTR
00552   027090                                                                PRTMSTR
00553   027100  330-INV-KEY.                                                  PRTMSTR
00554   027110      MOVE NO-DIV-MSG TO PRINT-IO.                              PRTMSTR
00555   027120      PERFORM 340-WRITE-RPT THRU 340-EXIT.                      PRTMSTR
00556   027130      PERFORM 370-CLOSE THRU 370-EXIT.                          PRTMSTR
00557   027140      GOBACK.                                                   PRTMSTR
00558   027150                                                                PRTMSTR
00559   027160                                                                PRTMSTR
00560   027170  NOTE-340.                                                     PRTMSTR
00561   027180      NOTE ***********************************************   *   PRTMSTR
00562   027190      *   THIS SUBROUTINE IS ENTERED TO WRITE TO THE PRINTER.  *PRTMSTR
00563   027200      *   THIS IS THE ONLY WRITE COMMAND TO THE PRINTER        *PRTMSTR
00564   028010      *   EXCEPT FOR THE FIRST LINE IN THE HEADING.            *PRTMSTR
00565   028020      ***********************************************************.PRTMSTR
00566   028030                                                                PRTMSTR
00567   028040  340-WRITE-RPT.                                                PRTMSTR
00568   028050      WRITE PRINT-IOA AFTER ADVANCING VARIABLE LINES.           PRTMSTR
00569   028060      MOVE SPACES TO PRINT-IO.                                  PRTMSTR
00570   028070  340-EXIT. EXIT.                                               PRTMSTR
00571   028080                                                                PRTMSTR
00572   028090                                                                PRTMSTR
00573   028100  NOTE-350.                                                     PRTMSTR
00574   028110      NOTE ***********************************************   *   PRTMSTR
00575   028120      *   THIS ROUTINE IS ENTERED TO WRITE THE HEADINGS FOR THE *PRTMSTR
00576   028130      *   REPORT.                                               *PRTMSTR
00577   028140      ***********************************************************.PRTMSTR
00578   028150                                                                PRTMSTR
00579   028160  350-HEADER.                                                   PRTMSTR
00580   028170      ADD 1 TO PG-COUNT.                                        PRTMSTR
00581   028180      MOVE PG-COUNT TO PG-H1.                                   PRTMSTR
00582   028190      MOVE INV-HEAD TO MAINHEAD.                                PRTMSTR
00583   028200      MOVE HEADING-1 TO PRINT-IO.                               PRTMSTR
00584   029010      WRITE PRINT-IOA AFTER ADVANCING TO-TOP-OF-PAGE.           PRTMSTR
00585   029020      MOVE DOUBLE-SPACING TO VARIABLE.                          PRTMSTR
00586   029030      MOVE LINE1-MSTR TO MASTER-PRT.                            PRTMSTR
00587   029040      MOVE COMM-LINE1 TO FIRST-PART.                            PRTMSTR
00588   029050      PERFORM 340-WRITE-RPT THRU 340-EXIT.                      PRTMSTR
00589   029060      MOVE SINGLE-SPACING TO VARIABLE.                          PRTMSTR
00590   029070      MOVE COMM-LINE2 TO FIRST-PART.                            PRTMSTR
00591   029080      MOVE LINE2-MSTR TO MASTER-PRT.                            PRTMSTR
00592   029090      PERFORM 340-WRITE-RPT THRU 340-EXIT.                      PRTMSTR
00593   029100      MOVE DOUBLE-SPACING TO VARIABLE.                          PRTMSTR
00594   029110  350-EXIT. EXIT.                                               PRTMSTR
00595   029120                                                                PRTMSTR
00596   029130                                                                PRTMSTR
00597   029140  NOTE-360.                                                     PRTMSTR
00598   029150      NOTE ***********************************************   ***PRTMSTR
00599   029160      *   THIS ROUTINE IS ENTERED WHEN END-OF-FILE IS REACHED   *PRTMSTR
00600   029170      *   ON THE INVENTORY FILE. IT PRINTS THE PROPER TOTAL     *PRTMSTR
00601   029180      *   LINES, CLOSES THE FILES AND STOPS THE RUN.            *PRTMSTR
00602   029190      ***********************************************************.PRTMSTR
00603   029200                                                                PRTMSTR
00604   030010  360-END-MSTR.                                                 PRTMSTR
00605   030020      MOVE AMOUNT-MSG-MSTR TO MSG-TOT-MPT.                      PRTMSTR
00606   030030      MOVE AMOUNT-COUNT1 TO AMT-TOT-MPT.                        PRTMSTR
00607   030040      MOVE ASTERISKS TO TOT-AST-MPT.                            PRTMSTR
00608   030050      MOVE TRIPLE-SPACING TO VARIABLE.                          PRTMSTR
00609   030060      PERFORM 340-WRITE-RPT THRU 340-EXIT.                      PRTMSTR
```

```
      8

   00610   030070        MOVE SINGLE-SPACING TO VARIABLE.                                      PRTMSTR
   00611   030080        MOVE REC-MSG-MSTR TO MSG-REC-MPT.                                      PRTMSTR
   00612   030090        MOVE RECORD-COUNT TO RECS-MPT.                                         PRTMSTR
   00613   030100        MOVE ASTERISKS TO RECS-AST-MPT.                                        PRTMSTR
   00614   030110        PERFORM 340-WRITE-RPT THRU 340-EXIT.                                   PRTMSTR
   00615   030120                                                                               PRTMSTR
   00616   030130 370-CLOSE.                                                                    PRTMSTR
   00617   030140        CLOSE INVMSTR,                                                         PRTMSTR
   00618   030150               PRTFLE.                                                         PRTMSTR
   00619   030160 370-EXIT.                                                                     PRTMSTR
```

```
     1                             IBM DOS AMERICAN NATIONAL STANDARD COBOL        CBF CL3-4          10/25/74

 00001   001010 IDENTIFICATION DIVISION.                                              DATESUB
 00002   001020 PROGRAM-ID.      DTECONV.                                             DATESUB
 00003   001030 AUTHOR.          TJC.                                                 DATESUB
 00004   001040 INSTALLATION.    LONG BEACH.                                          DATESUB
 00005   001050 DATE-WRITTEN.    07/05/74.                                            DATESUB
 00006   001060 DATE-COMPILED. 10/25/74                                               DATESUB
 00007   001070 SECURITY.        UNCLASSIFIED.                                        DATESUB
 00008   001080 REMARKS.         THIS SUBROUTINE CONVERTS THE DATE FROM               DATESUB
 00009   001090                  A FORMAT OF MM/DD/YY TO A FORMAT OF                  DATESUB
 00010   001100                  MONTH DD, 19YY.                                      DATESUB
 00011   001110 ENVIRONMENT DIVISION.                                                 DATESUB
 00012   001120 CONFIGURATION SECTION.                                                DATESUB
 00013   001130 SOURCE-COMPUTER. IBM-360-F30.                                         DATESUB
 00014   001140 OBJECT-COMPUTER. IBM-360-F30.                                         DATESUB
 00015   001150                                                                       DATESUB
 00016   001160                                                                       DATESUB
 00017   001170 DATA DIVISION.                                                        DATESUB
 00018   001180                                                                       DATESUB
 00019   001190 WORKING-STORAGE SECTION.                                              DATESUB
 00020   001200 77 SUB-SCRIPT                 PIC S99       SYNC                       DATESUB
 00021   002010                               USAGE COMP.                             DATESUB
 00022   002020 01  TABLE-MONTHS.                                                     DATESUB
 00023   002030     03  ALL-MONTHS.                                                   DATESUB
 00024   002040         05  FILLER            PIC X(11)     VALUE                      DATESUB
 00025   002050             'JANUARY  09'.                                            DATESUB
 00026   002060         05  FILLER            PIC X(11)     VALUE                      DATESUB
 00027   002070             'FEBRUARY 10'.                                            DATESUB
 00028   002080         05  FILLER            PIC X(11)     VALUE                      DATESUB
 00029   002090             'MARCH    07'.                                            DATESUB
 00030   002100         05  FILLER            PIC X(11)     VALUE                      DATESUB
 00031   002110             'APRIL    07'.                                            DATESUB
 00032   002120         05  FILLER            PIC X(11)     VALUE                      DATESUB
 00033   002130             'MAY      05'.                                            DATESUB
 00034   002140         05  FILLER            PIC X(11)     VALUE                      DATESUB
 00035   002150             'JUNE     06'.                                            DATESUB
 00036   002160         05  FILLER            PIC X(11)     VALUE                      DATESUB
 00037   002170             'JULY     06'.                                            DATESUB
 00038   002180         05  FILLER            PIC X(11)     VALUE                      DATESUB
 00039   002190             'AUGUST   08'.                                            DATESUB
 00040   002200         05  FILLER            PIC X(11)     VALUE                      DATESUB
 00041   003010             'SEPTEMBER11'.                                            DATESUB
 00042   003020         05  FILLER            PIC X(11)     VALUE                      DATESUB
 00043   003030             'OCTOBER  09'.                                            DATESUB
 00044   003040         05  FILLER            PIC X(11)     VALUE                      DATESUB
 00045   003050             'NOVEMBER 10'.                                            DATESUB
 00046   003060         05  FILLER            PIC X(11)     VALUE                      DATESUB
 00047   003070             'DECEMBER 10'.                                            DATESUB
 00048   003080                                                                       DATESUB
 00049   003090     03  TBLOKUP REDEFINES ALL-MONTHS     OCCURS 12 TIMES.             DATESUB
 00050   003100                                                                       DATESUB
 00051   003110         05  MONTH-NAME        PIC X(9).                               DATESUB
 00052   003120         05  MONTH-DISPL       PIC 99.                                 DATESUB
 00053   003130                                                                       DATESUB
 00054   003140 LINKAGE SECTION.                                                      DATESUB
 00055   003150 01  DATE-GIVEN.                                                       DATESUB
 00056   003160     03  MONTH-GIVEN           PIC 99.                                 DATESUB
 00057   003170     03  FILLER                PIC X.                                  DATESUB
 00058   003180     03  DAY-GIVEN1            PIC X.                                  DATESUB
 00059   003190     03  DAY-GIVEN2            PIC X.                                  DATESUB
 00060   003200     03  FILLER                PIC X.                                  DATESUB
 00061   004010     03  YEAR-GIVEN1           PIC X.                                  DATESUB
 00062   004020     03  YEAR-GIVEN2           PIC X.                                  DATESUB
 00063   004030 01  DATE-RETURNED.                                                    DATESUB
 00064   004040     03  DATE-ALL-RETURNED     PIC X(18).                              DATESUB
 00065   004050     03  DATE-PIECES-RETURNED REDEFINES DATE-ALL-RETURNED              DATESUB
 00066   004060         OCCURS 18 TIMES       PIC X.                                  DATESUB
 00067   004070     03  MONTH-RETURNED REDEFINES DATE-ALL-RETURNED.                   DATESUB
 00068   004080         05  MONTH-NAME-RETURNED PIC X(9)                              DATESUB
 00069   004090         05  FILLER            PIC X(9).                               DATESUB
 00070   004100 PROCEDURE DIVISION  USING DATE-GIVEN, DATE-RETURNED.                  DATESUB
 00071   004110                                                                       DATESUB
 00072   004120                                                                       DATESUB
 00073   004130 001-NOTE.                                                             DATESUB
 00074   004140     NOTE ***************************************************DATESUB
 00075   004150     *    THIS ROUTINE CONVERTS MM/DD/YY DATES TO          *DATESUB
 00076   004160     *    A MONTH-NAME, DAY, AND YEAR FORMAT (EX:          *DATESUB
 00077   004170     *    JUNE 28, 1947). IT DOES THIS BY FIRST            *DATESUB
 00078   004180     *    FINDING THE NAME OF THE MONTH IN A TABLE         *DATESUB
 00079   004190     *    WHICH IS ORGANIZED BY THE NUMBER OF THE          *DATESUB
 00080   004200     *    MONTH.                                           *DATESUB
 00081   005010     *         THE TABLE ENTRY CONTAINS THE               *DATESUB
 00082   005020     *    NAME OF THE MONTH AND ALSO THE NUMBER           *DATESUB
 00083   005030     *    OF CHARACTERS TO WHERE THE DAY SHOULD           *DATESUB
 00084   005040     *    BE MOVED. THIS IS DONE SO THERE ARE NOT         *DATESUB
 00085   005050     *    LARGE GAPS BETWEEN THE NAME OF THE MONTH        *DATESUB
 00086   005060     *    AND THE DAY IN THE MONTH.                       *DATESUB
 00087   005070     *                                                    *DATESUB
```

```
         2
00088    005080    *    THE METHOD USED IS TO TREAT EACH DIGIT IN           *DATESUB
00089    005090    *    THE OUTPUT FIELD AS SINGE SUBSCRIPTED               *DATESUB
00090    005100    *    VARIABLES. THEREFORE, THE VALUES, EXCEPT            *DATESUB
00091    005110    *    FOR THE MONTH NAME, ARE MOVED ONE                   *DATESUB
00092    005120    *    CHARACTER AT A TIME.                                *DATESUB
00093    005130    *****************************************************************.DATESUB
00094    005140                                                             DATESUB
00095    005150 010-PROCESS.                                                DATESUB
00096    005160     MOVE SPACES TO DATE-ALL-RETURNED.                       DATESUB
00097    005170     MOVE MONTH-NAME (MONTH-GIVEN) TO MONTH-NAME-RETURNED.   DATESUB
00098    005180     MOVE MONTH-DISPL (MONTH-GIVEN)  TO SUB-SCRIPT.          DATESUB
00099    005190     IF DAY-GIVEN1 NOT = 0                                   DATESUB
00100    005200        MOVE DAY-GIVEN1 TO DATE-PIECES-RETURNED (SUB-SCRIPT) DATESUB
00101    006010        ADD 1 TO SUB-SCRIPT.                                 DATESUB
00102    006020     MOVE DAY-GIVEN2 TO DATE-PIECES-RETURNED (SUB-SCRIPT).   DATESUB
00103    006030     ADD 1 TO SUB-SCRIPT.                                    DATESUB
00104    006040     MOVE ',' TO DATE-PIECES-RETURNED (SUB-SCRIPT).          DATESUB
00105    006050     ADD 2 TO SUB-SCRIPT.                                    DATESUB
00106    006060     MOVE '1' TO DATE-PIECES-RETURNED (SUB-SCRIPT).          DATESUB
00107    006070     ADD 1 TO SUB-SCRIPT.                                    DATESUB
00108    006080     MOVE '9' TO DATE-PIECES-RETURNED (SUB-SCRIPT).          DATESUB
00109    006090     ADD 1 TO SUB-SCRIPT.                                    DATESUB
00110    006100     MOVE YEAR-GIVEN1 TO DATE-PIECES-RETURNED (SUB-SCRIPT).  DATESUB
00111    006110     ADD 1 TO SUB-SCRIPT.                                    DATESUB
00112    006120     MOVE YEAR-GIVEN2 TO DATE-PIECES-RETURNED (SUB-SCRIPT).  DATESUB
00113    006130     GOBACK.                                                 DATESUB
```

CHAPTER 6

PROGRAMMING ASSIGNMENT

INSTRUCTIONS

From the Sales Master File created in Chapter 3, two reports are to be prepared, a Net Sales Report and a Commission Report. In addition, a back-up tape for the Sales Master file is to be created.

The Net Sales Report is to contain the Department Number, Salesman Number, Salesman Name, Y-T-D Sales, Y-T-D Sales Returns and the Net Sales (Y-T-D Sales - Sales Returns).

The Commission Report is to contain the Department Number, the Salesman Number, Salesman Name, Net Sales, Commission Rate, and Commission (Commission Rate x Net Sales).

The back-up tape should include all fields on the master record.

A control card is to be used to determine whether the reports or the back-up tape are to be produced.

Other functions to be determined by the control card include the following:

Print Function:

1. Which report will be produced. Either the Net Sales Report or the Commission Report.

2. Which Salesman Numbers will be printed. Either all salesman numbers will be printed or a ''From-To'' range will be printed.

The entries in the control card will be the following:

1. Col 1-4: ''**DUMP**'' - This entry indicates that a back-up file is to be created.

2. Col 1-5: ''**PRINT**'' - This indicates that one of the two printed reports is to be produced.

   A. Col 10-12: ''**NET**'' - This indicates that the Net Sales Report is to be produced.

   OR

   B. Col 10-19: ''**COMMISSION**'' - This indicates that the Commission Report is to be produced.

C. Col 25-29: "**XXXXX**" or omitted - If present, this entry specifies a beginning department number and salesman number for the report.

D. Col 30-34: "**XXXXX**" or omitted - If present, this entry specifies an ending department number and salesman number for the report.

In addition, the program should be segmented into a root phase and three independent segments - one to read and interpret the control card, one to create the back-up file, and one to create the printed reports.

REPORT WRITER

CUSTOMER	IND	ST	TERR	D	INV	SP	PRODUCT	SC	TR	QUANTITY	AMOUNT
357705-00	070	42	6111	1	35776	19	71642801	13	001	1.00	12.3
							TOTAL				82.6
357705-00	070	42	6111	1	36832	19	53351501	03	001	12.00	15.9
357705-00	070	42	6111	1	36832	19	51642501	06	001	1.00	6.1
357705-00	070	42	6111	1	36832	19	50232712	02	001	3.00	39.5
							TOTAL				61.6
357849-00	070	42	0801	8	36720	19	89952005	05	001	2.00	5.3

REPORT WRITER   7

INTRODUCTION

In previous programs, many reports have been prepared by defining the print file in the Environment and Data Divisions, specifying the format of the output record in the Data Division, and preparing the output record by moving data from input records and Working Storage into the specific areas of the output record. The Write verb was then used to cause the record to be written. Associated with this processing have been routines to update the page numbers, process the line counter, and perform heading routines to write headings on the report.

COBOL has another method which can be used to prepare printed reports. This is called the **REPORT WRITER** feature. The Report Writer feature allows the COBOL programmer to merely define the characteristics of the report which is to be produced by the program and then by issuing one imperative verb, the report is automatically produced.

In order to illustrate the use of the Report Writer feature, a sample program in this chapter will read a file of sales cards and produce a Sales Analysis Report. The card input is illustrated in Figure 7-1.

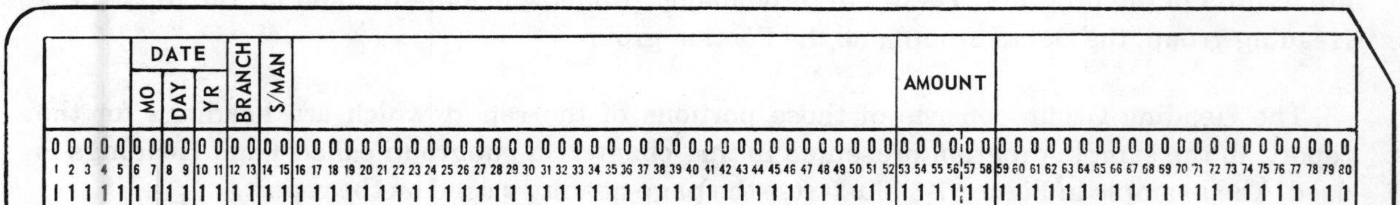

Figure 7-1 Input Card Format

The format of the Sales Analysis Report to be produced is illustrated below.

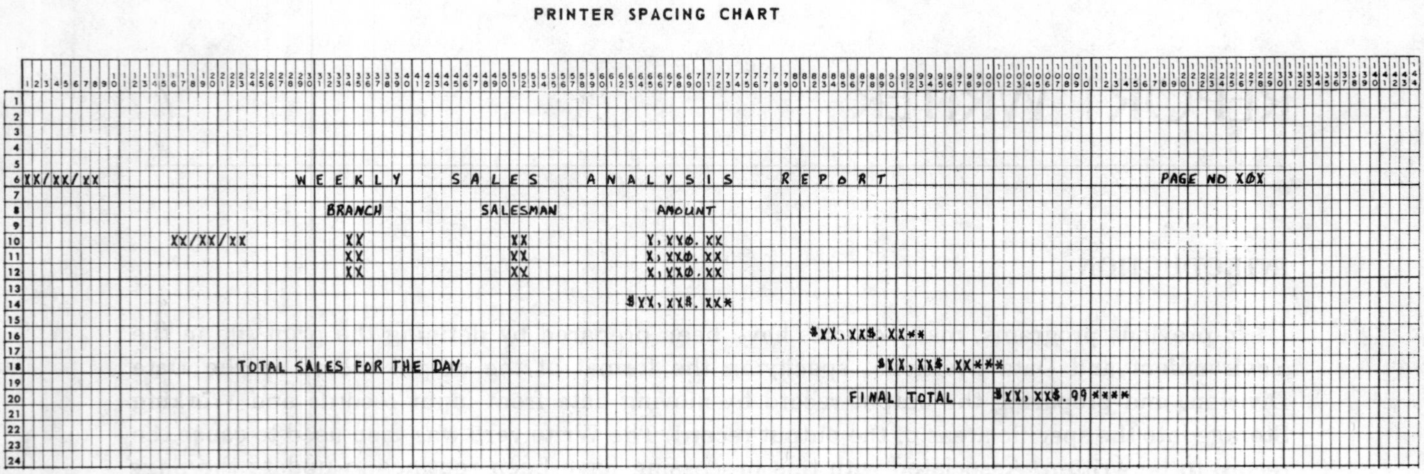

PRINTER SPACING CHART

Figure 7-2 Printer Spacing Chart for Output Report

As can be seen from the printer spacing chart in Figure 7-2, the report consists of detail data for each card which is read, a total amount whenever there is a change in salesman number, a total for each change in branch, a total for each change in date, and a final total. In addition, the date is group indicated on the report.

When utilizing the Report Writer feature of the ANSI COBOL compiler, each portion of the report is given a name so that it can be identified when the detail specifications for the report are written in the program. There are three major groups which are defined for the report: the Heading group, the Detail group, and the Footing group.

The Heading Group consists of those portions of the report which are headings for the report. In the sample program presented in this chapter, a subgroup called Page Headings is used. The example in Figure 7-3 illustrates the page headings used on the report.

EXAMPLE

```
10/08/74              W E E K L Y   S A L E S   A N A L Y S I S   R E P O R T                PAGE NO.  1
                           BRANCH        SALESMAN         AMOUNT                   PAGE HEADINGS
              06/05/74       15            21             40.00
                             15            21             43.50
                             15            21             24.50
                             15            21            390.00
                             15            21            610.00

                                                       $1,108.00*

              06/05/74       15            79             49.60
                             15            79             56.00
                             15            79            576.00
                             15            79            390.00

                                                       $1,071.60*

                                                                    $2,179.60**

              06/05/74       39            12             72.16
                             39            12             72.90
                             39            12            105.00
                             39            12             14.10
                             39            12             21.25
                             39            12            336.00
                             39            12            316.00
                             39            12             77.90
                             39            12             37.80
                             39            12             15.64

                                                       $1,068.75*

              06/05/74       39            54              8.37
                             39            54             25.60
                             39            54             42.30
                             39            54             29.60
                             39            54             48.00

                                                        $153.87*

                                                                    $1,222.62**
                           TOTAL SALES FOR THE DAY                  $3,402.22***
```

Figure 7-3 Example of Page Headings

Note in Figure 7-3 that the Page Headings consist of two printed lines. These lines are called page headings because they will be printed on each page of the report, that is, each time a new page is begun the page headings will be printed before any other information on the report.

In addition to page headings, which are quite common on printed reports, the Report Writer allows two other types of headings: Report Headings and Control Headings. Report headings are printed at the start of a report and they are printed only once. For example, if an accounts receivable ledger was to be prepared, the first page of the report may contain only the report heading, ACCOUNTS RECEIVABLE LEDGER, and perhaps the date. In this manner, the entire report can be identified by a Report Heading.

A Control Heading is printed whenever a control break occurs in a given field. For example, if it was required, whenever a change in the salesman field in the input card took place, a heading of some type could be printed. In the sample program, a control heading is not required.

The second major group is the Detail Group. Detail lines are printed on the report as each detail input record is processed. The detail lines on the report generated by the sample program are illustrated below.

EXAMPLE

```
10/08/74              W E E K L Y    S A L E S    A N A L Y S I S    R E P O R T              PAGE NO.  1

                         BRANCH        SALESMAN         AMOUNT

                06/05/74    15            21             40.00 ◄
                            15            21             43.50 ◄──────  DETAIL LINES
                            15            21             24.50 ◄
                            15            21            390.00
                            15            21            610.00
GROUP-INDICATED
  DETAIL LINE                                          $1,108.00*


                06/05/74    15            79             49.60
                            15            79             56.00
                            15            79            576.00
                            15            79            390.00

                                                      $1,071.60*

                                                                      $2,179.60**


                06/05/74    39            12             72.16
                            39            12             72.90
                            39            12            105.00
                            39            12             14.10
                            39            12             21.25
                            39            12            336.00
                            39            12            316.00
                            39            12             77.90
                            39            12             37.80
                            39            12             15.64

                                                      $1,068.75*


                06/05/74    39            54              8.37
                            39            54             25.60
                            39            54             42.30
                            39            54             29.60
                            39            54             48.00

                                                       $153.87*
                                                                      $1,222.62**

                      TOTAL SALES FOR THE DAY                        $3,402.22***
```

Figure 7-4 Example of Detail Lines

As can be seen from the example above, the detail lines are printed as each single input record is read and processed by the program. Detail lines can contain any information which is desired by the programmer, but they are normally printed each time an input record is read. It should also be noted that detail lines, as illustrated in Figure 7-4, can be group-indicated. Thus, the date is group-indicated, that is, it is printed as identification only once for the entire group of related detail records.

The third major group which is defined for the report is the Footing Group. The footing group consists of three types: Control Footings, Page Footings, and Report Footings. In the sample program, Control footings are utilized and are illustrated in Figure 7-5.

EXAMPLE

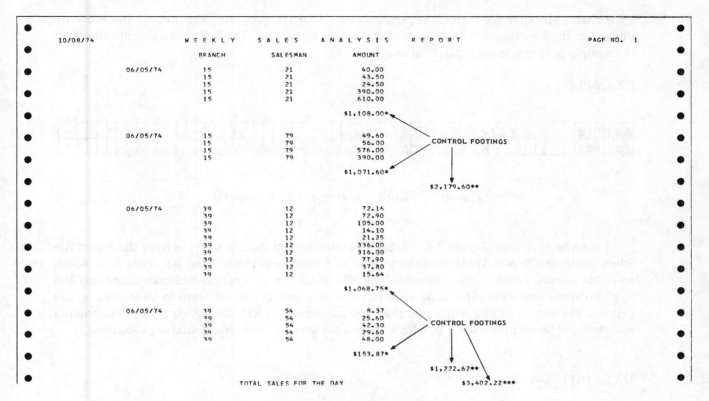

Figure 7-5 Example of Control Footings

Note in the example above that the entries on the report which are designated control footings are printed whenever a control break occurs, that is, when there is a change in salesman number, a salesman total is printed, when there is a change in branch number, a branch total is printed, and when there is a change in date, a date total is printed. In addition, a final total is printed and is also considered a control footing.

Page footings are printed as the last lines on each page, if this is desired on the report. This type of footing is normally printed whenever figures are contained on the page and it would be convenient for the reader to have a total for these figures at the end of each page. They may also be used in other applications such as invoices where invoice totals must be printed at the end of each invoice.

Report totals are totals which are to be printed only once at the conclusion of the report. These figures are normally summary totals or analysis figures of the data contained within the body of the report.

In order to create a report using the Report Writer feature, the file must be defined and the specifications must be given showing not only what lines are to be considered headings, detail, or footing lines, but also the physical layout of the report, such as which fields are to be contained in which columns, and what the vertical spacing of the report will be. The entries to perform these functions are contained in the Environment and Data Divisions of the COBOL program.

ENVIRONMENT DIVISION ENTRIES

As with all other files which are utilized in a COBOL program, the Report file must be defined in the Environment Division with the Select Statement. The Select Statement utilized in the sample program is illustrated below.

EXAMPLE

```
002110        SELECT REPORT-FILE
002120          !   ASSIGN TO SYS008-UR-1403-S.
```

Figure 7-6 SELECT Statement for Report File

As can be seen from Figure 7-6, the Select Statement for the file which is to be the report file when using the Report Writer is the same as has been previously used for other files which were for printed reports. The filename **REPORT-FILE** is a programmer-chosen name and the System-Name entries are the same as have been used for files which were to be written on the printer. The report will be written on the device assigned to SYS008 by job control statements and the 1403 printer to be used is a Unit Record device which has sequential organization.

DATA DIVISION

The majority of the file definition for a printer file using the Report Writer is made in the Data Division. As with previous files, the file must be defined in the File Section of the Data Division using the "FD" statement. The coding used in the sample program is illustrated in Figure 7-7.

EXAMPLE

```
003110  FD  REPORT-FILE
003120      RECORD CONTAINS 133 CHARACTERS
003130      LABEL RECORDS ARE OMITTED
003140      REPORT IS SALES-REPORT.
```

Figure 7-7 File Definition for Report File

The FD Statement used to define the Report File used with the Report Writer is quite similar to the statements used for previous report files. The filename must be the same name which is used in the Select Statement. The Record Contains Clause specifies that 133 characters will be used for the print line in the same manner as for previous file definitions. It should be noted that if this clause is not specified, the compiler will assume that 133 characters are to be used but for good program documentation, this clause should be included. As before, there is no label processing when using printer files.

A new entry which is used for the Report Writer is the **REPORT IS** clause. The format notation for this entry is illustrated below.

```
{REPORT IS   }
{            }   report-name-1 [report-name-2]...
{REPORTS ARE}
```

Figure 7-8 Format Notation for REPORT IS Clause

Note from the format notation in Figure 7-8 that the **REPORT** or **REPORTS** word is required. In addition, one or more "report-name" must be specified. The "report-name" is a programmer-chosen name which must follow the same rules as file names and is used to link the FD Statement with the RD Statement which is specified in the Report Section of the Data Division (see next section). The report-name is used to identify each report which is to be generated by the Report Writer. As can be seen, more than one report can be generated from a single report file. In the sample program, only one report is to be generated and the name specified in Figure 7-7, **SALES-REPORT**, is to be the name of the report.

REPORT SECTION

When utilizing the Report Writer, it is necessary to define both the format of the page on the report and each line within the page. As will be noted from Figure 7-7, this is not done with an I/O area, such as has been done previously, that is, the **DATA RECORD IS** clause is not used in the FD Statement. Rather, when using the Report Writer, a separate section called the Report Section is utilized. Within this section, both the page format and the line formats are defined. For each report which is to be created from the Report File defined with the FD Statement, there must be a corresponding RD entry in the Report Section of the Data Division. The RD Statement used in the sample program is illustrated in Figure 7-9.

```
003020 DATA DIVISION.
004060 REPORT SECTION.
004080 RD  SALES-REPORT
004090     CONTROLS ARE FINAL, DATE-CD, BRANCH-CD, SALESMAN-CD
004100     PAGE LIMIT IS 52 LINES
004110     HEADING 1
004120     FIRST DETAIL 5
004130     LAST DETAIL 46
004140     FOOTING 52.
```

Figure 7-9 Example of File Section and RD Statement

From Figure 7-9 it can be seen that the Report Section header **REPORT SECTION** is specified in the same manner as the File Section header and the Working-Storage Section header. The Report Section should follow both the File Section and the Working-Storage Section in the Data Division.

The RD Statement in the Report Section is used to define the physical characteristics of the page which will be produced by the Report Writer. The first entry in the Report Description entry (RD) is the report-name **SALES-REPORT**, which is the same name which is specified in the FD entry in the File Section of the Data Division (see Figure 7-7). These two names must be identical and must be specified as shown.

The next entry in the Report Description statement is the **CONTROL** Clause. The Control Clause is used to indicate those fields which are to be used as control fields within the report, that is, those fields which are to cause control breaks on the report. The general format of the Control Clause is illustrated in Figure 7-10.

```
{CONTROL IS  }   {FINAL                           }
{            }   {identifier-1 [identifier-2]...  }
{CONTROLS ARE}   {FINAL  identifier-1 [identifier-2]...}
```

Figure 7-10 Format Notation for CONTROL Clause

Note from the format notation illustrated above that the word **CONTROL** or **CONTROLS** is required. If a final total is to be printed, such as in the sample program, the word **FINAL** must next be specified (see Figure 7-9). This indicates that at the conclusion of all of the input cards a final total should be printed on the report.

The identifiers specified after **FINAL** are fields which are defined elsewhere in the program and which are the control fields for the report, that is, they are the fields on which control break processing is to take place. In the example in Figure 7-9, the fields specified are **DATE-CD**, **BRANCH-CD**, and **SALESMAN-CD**. These fields are defined for the input card as shown in Figure 7-11.

EXAMPLE

```
ØØ2Ø2Ø FD  SALESMAN-FILE
ØØ2Ø3Ø     RECORD CONTAINS 80 CHARACTERS
ØØ2Ø4Ø     LABEL RECORDS ARE OMITTED
ØØ2Ø5Ø     DATA RECORD IS SALES-CARD.
ØØ2Ø6Ø 01  SALES-CARD.
ØØ2Ø7Ø     Ø3  FILLER                        PIC X(5).
ØØ2Ø8Ø     Ø3  DATE-CD.
ØØ2Ø9Ø         Ø5  MONTH-CD                  PIC XX.
ØØ21ØØ         Ø5  DAY-CD                    PIC XX.
ØØ211Ø         Ø5  YEAR-CD                   PIC XX.
ØØ212Ø     Ø3  BRANCH-CD                     PIC XX.
ØØ213Ø     Ø3  SALESMAN-CD                   PIC XX.
ØØ214Ø     Ø3  FILLER                        PIC X(37).
ØØ215Ø     Ø3  AMOUNT-CD                     PIC 9999V99.
ØØ216Ø     Ø3  FILLER                        PIC X(22).
```

Figure 7-11 Example of Control Fields Definition

Note from the example in Figure 7-11 that the fields defined as control fields in the Control Clause are defined in the input record for the card input file. The sequence in which the control fields are specified in the Control Clause is critical (see Figure 7-9). They must be specified from the most major to the minor control field, that is, the **DATE-CD** field is the highest level control field and it is specified immediately following the **FINAL** entry. The next highest is the **BRANCH-CD** field and it is next in the list. The lowest level of control break is the **SALESMAN-CD** field. It should be noted again that in the Control Clause, the control fields must be specified in the order of major to minor.

The next entry in the RD Statement is the **PAGE** Clause. The general format of the Page Clause is illustrated in Figure 7-12.

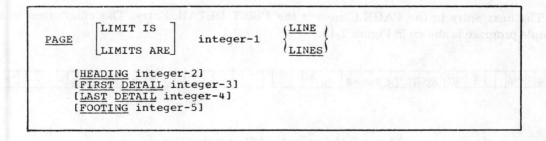

Figure 7-12 General Format of PAGE Clause

The Page Clause is used to specify the vertical spacing which is to take place on the page of the report in terms of the first and last lines to be used for various portions of the report. The first entry is the **PAGE** entry and the entry used for the sample program is illustrated in Figure 7-13.

EXAMPLE

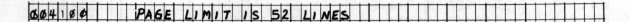

Figure 7-13 Example of PAGE Clause

The Page Limit entry is used to specify the maximum number of lines which can be printed on each page of the report. In the example above, the maximum is 52 lines. This maximum includes all heading lines, detail lines, and footing lines on a given page. Thus, its function is similar to the line count which has been used in previous programs to determine when page overflow has occurred and a new page should be started.

The next entry in the **PAGE** Clause is the Heading Entry. It is again illustrated in Figure 7-14.

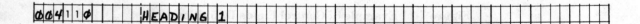

Figure 7-14 Example of Heading Entry

Note from the format notation illustrated in Figure 7-12, and the example above, that the word **HEADING** is required and the only entry required is an integer value. This integer value specifies the absolute line on which the Headings on the report are to begin. It should be noted that all absolute lines specified in the **PAGE** clause are relative to the first line of printing on a page. The location of the first line on a page is indicated by controls on the printer itself. For example, on the IBM 1403 printer, a punch in Channel 1 of the carriage control tape indicates the first line of the page. In the example, it can be seen that the headings of the report in the sample program are to begin on the first line of the page, that is, the integer value specified is 1.

The next entry in the **PAGE** Clause is the **FIRST DETAIL** Entry. The entry used in the sample program is shown in Figure 7-15.

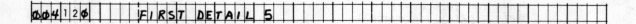

Figure 7-15 Example of First Detail Entry

The First Detail Entry is used to specify the absolute line on the report where the first detail record can be printed. In the example in Figure 7-15, the entry "5" states that the first detail line of the report is to be printed on line 5 of the report. In addition, if control headings are to be used with the report, they will not be printed above the value specified for integer-2, which, in the sample program is the value "5".

Thus far, it can be seen that the first four lines of the page will be used for page headings and that the detail lines will begin on the fifth line of the report. It remains, then, to specify where the detail lines will terminate on the report and where the last line of the report can be printed on the page. This is accomplished with the **LAST DETAIL** and **FOOTING** entries as illustrated in Figure 7-16.

Figure 7-16 Example of Last Detail and Footing Entries

The **LAST DETAIL** entry specifies the last line on the report where a detail line can be printed. In the example, this line is specified as line 46 of the report. No detail line, nor control heading will be printed past this line on the report. The **FOOTING** entry indicates the last line on which control footings will be printed, and is indicated as line 52 for the sample program. It should be noted that page footings will be printed after the line specified for the Footing entry. In the sample program, there are no page footings, so the value specified for the Footing entry is the same as the value specified for the Page Limit (both are equal to 52).

REPORT GROUPS

After the Report Definition (RD) statement, the format of the report and the fields which may be used for control breaks have been defined. It remains, however, to define each line which is to be printed on the report. A report generated by the Report Writer consists of one or more **REPORT GROUPS**. A Report Group is a grouping of related entries similar to the description of a data record which is used in COBOL programs. Report Groups consist of three main categories: Heading Groups, Detail Groups, and Footing Groups.

In order to define a report group, a report group description is made for each report group which is to be printed on the report. In the sample program, there are six report groups: the page headings, the detail lines, the control footing group for the salesman number, the control footing group for the branch, the control footing group for the date, and the control footing group for the final total. Each of these report groups must be defined in order to be properly printed on the report.

In addition, the report groups must appear in the program in the same sequence as they are to be printed on the report. Thus, the first report group which must be defined is the page-heading group. The entries to define this group are shown below.

EXAMPLE

```
004020 01  HEADINGS               TYPE IS PAGE HEADING.
004030     03  LINE 1.
004040         05  COLUMN 1            PIC X(8)
004050                                 SOURCE CURRENT-DATE.
004060         05  COLUMN 29           PIC X(61)         VALUE
004070             'WEEKLY        SALES        ANALYSIS        R
004080-            'EPORT'.
004090         05  COLUMN 118          PIC X(8)          VALUE
004100             'PAGE NO.'.
004110         05  COLUMN 126          PIC ZZ9
004120                                 SOURCE PAGE-COUNTER.
004130     03  LINE 3.
004140         05  COLUMN 32           PIC X(43)         VALUE
004150             'BRANCH        SALESMAN        AMOUNT'.
```

Figure 7-17 Example of Heading Report Group

Note from Figure 7-17 the similarity between the definition of the Report Group and the data definition for files which have been seen in previous programs. Each of the items within the report group are defined in a hierarchial manner.

The level-01 entry is used to define a report group. The report group description must contain a report group entry (level-01) and it must be the first entry within the report group. The format notation for the report group description is illustrated below.

```
01     [data-name-1]
       [LINE Clause]
       [NEXT GROUP Clause]
       TYPE Clause
       [USAGE Clause].
```

Figure 7-18 Format Notation for Report Group Description

Note from the format notation in Figure 7-18, and the example in Figure 7-17, that the report group description entry must begin with level-01. The next entry in Figure 7-17 is the data-name-1 entry. In the example, it is the data-name **HEADINGS**. This name may be any programmer-chosen name which conforms to the rules regarding formation of data-names. As can be seen from Figure 7-18, the only required entry is the **TYPE** entry. This value specifies the type of report group which is being defined. The format of the type entry is illustrated below.

```
              ┌ REPORT HEADING ┐
              │ RH             │
              │ PAGE HEADING   │
              │ PH             │
              │ CONTROL HEADING│   ┌ identifier-n ┐
              │ CH             │   │ FINAL        │
  TYPE IS     │ DETAIL         │
              │ DE             │
              │ CONTROL FOOTING│   ┌ identifier-n ┐
              │ CF             │   │ FINAL        │
              │ PAGE FOOTING   │
              │ PF             │
              │ REPORT FOOTING │
              └ RF             ┘
```

Figure 7-19 Format Notation for TYPE Clause

In Figure 7-19, it can be seen that the **TYPE** Clause is used to define all of the various types of report groups which are found on a report when utilizing the Report Writer. In the example in Figure 7-17, the report group being defined is the Page Heading group, so the entry **PAGE HEADING** is used. It should be noted that, if desired, the abbreviation PH could also have been used.

In order to define the report group to be used for the Page Headings, only the data-name and Type entries must be used. It remains, however, to define the lines and data to be printed for the page headings. There are two requirements: the line on the page must be identified and the data must be specified. In order to show the line on which the headings are to be printed, the group item description can be used. A group item description can be used when more than one printed line is to appear within a report group. In the sample program, two lines are to be printed within the heading report group, so the group item description entry is used. The general format and the coding used in the sample program are illustrated in Figure 7-20.

EXAMPLE

Format Notation - Group Item Description

```
level number [data-name-1]
     [LINE clause]
     [USAGE clause].
```

```
LINE NUMBER IS     {integer-1        }
                   {PLUS integer-2   }
                   {NEXT PAGE        }
```

Coding

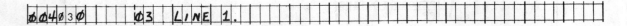

Figure 7-20 Format Notation and Coding for Line Clause

Note from the format notation for the group item that a level number must be specified. Since the Report Group is defined using a level-01 indicator, the level number used for the group item definition can be any number 02-48. In the example above, the level-03 indicator is used. Since it is not required that a data-name be used with the group item definition, one is not used in the example in Figure 7-20. The optional **LINE** clause, however, is used. This clause is used to specify the line on which the item is to be printed. As can be seen from the format notation for the **LINE** Clause, the word **LINE** is required. The line number can be specified in any one of three different formats. In the example in Figure 7-20, it is specified as "integer-1", that is, the value "1" is given. Whenever the integer value is used, it specifies the absolute line on the report. Thus, the data which is to follow the group item will be printed on the first line of the report. It will be recalled that the page heading data is to be printed in the first four lines of the report.

After the group item description has been used to indicate the line on which the data is to be printed, the format of the line must be specified. This is accomplished through the use of the Elementary Item entry. The formats of the statements used and the actual statements from the sample program are illustrated in Figure 7-21.

EXAMPLE

Format Notation

```
level number [data-name-1]
      [BLANK WHEN ZERO Clause]
      [COLUMN Clause]
      [GROUP Clause]
      [JUSTIFIED Clause]
      [LINE Clause]
      [PICTURE Clause]
      [RESET Clause]
           SOURCE
      [    SUM       Clause   ]
           VALUE
      [USAGE Clause].
```

```
COLUMN NUMBER IS integer
```

```
SOURCE IS      identifier-1
```

Coding

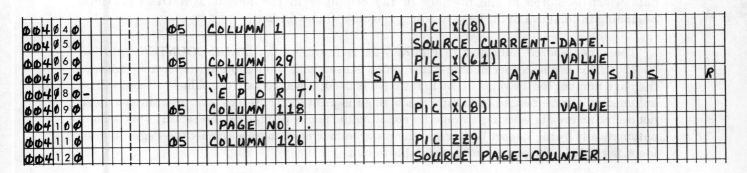

Figure 7-21 Format Notation and Coding for Elementary Item

In the format notation for the definition of the Elementary Item, it can be seen that there are a number of entries, all of which are optional. Thus, only those required for the creation of the headings will be discussed at this time. Later, other entries will be explained.

Note first that the level number used with the elementary items in the page headings is 05. This is subordinate to the group item definition of level-03 (see Figure 7-20). Therefore, all of the elementary items shown in Figure 7-21 with the level number 05 will be contained on the first line of the report because this is the line specified by the level-03 group item definition.

The first element for each of the elementary items is the Column Clause, whose format notation is also illustrated. Note that the word **COLUMN** is required. The value specified for "integer" must be a number from 1 to 132 which specifies the column in which the field defined will begin on the report. Thus, from the example in Figure 7-21, it can be seen that the Current Date will begin in column 1, the heading for the Weekly Sales Analysis Report will begin in column 29, and so on.

The **PICTURE** (PIC) clause is used with the Report Writer in the same manner as it is used with other elementary item definitions in COBOL programs. In the example the date will be stored in an alphanumeric field which is eight digits in length. Note that editing can be performed in the same manner also, as the page number is to be zero suppressed. It should also be noted that there are no filler clauses required when defining the line for the Report Writer. The Report Writer will automatically assure that there are spaces where data is not to be printed. Only the Column clauses are required to define where data is to be printed.

The **VALUE** Clause is also used with the Report Writer in the same manner as with the other elementary items in previous COBOL programs. Thus, the Value Clause is used to specify the values which are to appear in the Page Heading.

A clause which is particular to the Report Writer is the **SOURCE** Clause. This clause indicates the source of the data which is to be placed in the field for the report. The "identifier-1" value can be any data name which is identified in the File Section, the Working-Storage Section, or the Linkage Section. In the example, the source for the data to be printed on the report beginning in column 1 is the identifier **CURRENT-DATE**. It will be recalled that this is a special data name which is defined in COBOL and represents the current date which is stored in the memory of the computer in the format MM/DD/YY. Thus, beginning in column 1 of the page heading, the date will be printed.

The other source indicated in Figure 7-21 is the identifier **PAGE-COUNTER** (pg/line 004120). This is also a special data-name which is used with the Report Writer to keep track of the page number for the report. The first time it is used, it will contain the value "1" and will be automatically incremented each time a new page is printed. Therefore, the programmer need not define an area in working-storage for counting the pages printed on the report. This is done automatically by the Report Writer and the programmer need merely specify the Page-Counter identifier to have the page number available to him.

The next line of the page heading is defined in a similar manner to that used for the first line, that is, with a group item definition and the elementary item definitions. The coding used for the second line of the report is illustrated in Figure 7-22.

Figure 7-22 Coding for Next Line of Page Headings

As can be seen from Figure 7-22, the next line of the page heading will begin on line 3 of the report. Thus, the heading will be double spaced. It will also be recalled that the first line of detail printing is to begin on line 5 of the report (see Figure 7-9). Therefore, there will be double spacing between the last line in the page heading and the first line of the detail printing.

DETAIL LINES

As was noted previously, the report which is generated by the Report Writer consists of report groups. In the previous examples, the Page Heading report group was defined. Since the report groups are printed in the sequence in which they are found in the program, the next report group which must be defined is the Detail Report Group. The definition and specifications for the detail report group are illustrated in Figure 7-23.

EXAMPLE

```
005020  01  DETAIL-LINE        LINE PLUS 1
005030                         TYPE IS DETAIL.
005040      03  COLUMN 16 GROUP INDICATE PIC XX
005050                              SOURCE MONTH-CD.
005060      03  COLUMN 18 GROUP INDICATE PIC X          VALUE '/'.
005070      03  COLUMN 19 GROUP INDICATE PIC XX
005080                              SOURCE DAY-CD.
005090      03  COLUMN 21 GROUP INDICATE PIC X          VALUE '/'.
005100      03  COLUMN 22 GROUP INDICATE PIC XX
005110                              SOURCE YEAR-CD.
005120      03  COLUMN 33           PIC XX
005130                              SOURCE BRANCH-CD.
005140      03  COLUMN 51           PIC XX
005150                              SOURCE SALESMAN-CD.
005160      03  COLUMN 65           PIC Z,ZZZ.99
005170                              SOURCE AMOUNT-CD.
```

Figure 7-23 Definition of DETAIL Line

As with the Page Headings, the report group for the Detail line is defined using a level-01 indicator. The data-name **DETAIL-LINE** is given to the line to be printed at detail time. The detail line consists only of one line, that is, one line will be printed on the report each time a detail record is read. Therefore, the group item definition, such as with the page headings, is not necessary for the detail line, and only the Report Group Description and the Elementary Item Descriptions are used to define the detail line.

The spacing for the single line which is defined for the detail line is indicated as **LINE PLUS 1** on the report group description level. This entry specifies that the detail line will be printed after single spacing the printer following the last line which was printed. Therefore, the detail lines will be single-spaced on the report. In addition, the counter which keeps track of the number of lines printed on the page is incremented by the value specified. When the ''Line Plus'' statement is used, it specifies that the spacing is to take place before the line defined is printed.

The **TYPE IS DETAIL** clause identifies the report group as a detail group. It should be noted that the word Detail could be abbreviated DE (see Figure 7-19). The Detail specification for the line indicates that it will be printed for each detail record which is read and processed in the Procedure Division. There are no other specifications which must be made for the report group so the next entries are made to define the elementary items which are to make up the detail line.

As was noted previously, the report is to be group-indicated with the date which is contained within the input card. Therefore, the fields which are to be group-indicated must be specified on the elementary item level. In the example, it can be seen that the fields beginning in columns 16, 18, 19, 21, and 22 are to be group-indicated because the **GROUP INDICATE** Clause is specified for these fields. The format of the Group Indicate clause is illustrated below.

```
GROUP INDICATE
```

Figure 7-24 Format Notation for GROUP INDICATE Clause

Whenever the Group Indicate Clause is specified for a field to be printed on a detail line, the fields will be printed whenever there is a control break on any of the fields specified in the RD statement as control fields. Thus, in the sample program, whenever there is a control break on the **SALESMAN-CD** field, the **BRANCH-CD** field, or the **DATE-CD** field, the fields specified as Group Indicate fields will be printed on the detail lines (see Figure 7-3).

The remaining entries in the Detail Line contain the same types of clauses as in the Page Heading report group. Note that the source fields for the values to be contained on the detail line are the fields which are read from the input card (see Figure 7-11). It was noted previously that the sources for the data to be printed on the report can come from fields defined in the File Section, the Working-Storage Section, or the Linkage Section of the Data Division.

It will also be noted that the field beginning in column 65 of the detail line, with the source **AMOUNT-CD**, will be edited and zero-suppressed. Any editing which can be performed when creating reports without the Report Writer can be used with it. The rules which apply to editing, however, such as the fields to be edited must be numeric in content, must be adhered to the same as when the report writer is not being used.

CONTROL FOOTING - REPORT GROUPS

After the Page Heading report group and the Detail report group have been defined, any control footing report groups which are required for the report must be defined. In the sample program, there are three control footing report groups - one for the control break on the salesman number (SALESMAN-CD), one for the break on the branch (BRANCH-CD), and one for the date (DATE-CD). In addition, the **FINAL** total, which is considered a control footing, must also be specified. The coding used in the sample program to define these control footing report groups is illustrated below.

EXAMPLE

```
006010  01  SALESMAN-TOTAL      LINE PLUS 2
006020                          TYPE IS CONTROL FOOTING SALESMAN-CD
006030                          NEXT GROUP PLUS 2.
006040      03  COLUMN 63                   PIC $$$,$$$.99
006050                                      SUM AMOUNT-CD.
006060      03  COLUMN 73                   PIC X           VALUE '*'.
006070
006080  01  BRANCH-TOTAL        LINE PLUS 2
006090                          TYPE IS CONTROL FOOTING BRANCH-CD
006100                          NEXT GROUP PLUS 2.
006110      03  COLUMN 82                   PIC $$$,$$$.99
006120                                      SUM AMOUNT-CD.
006130      03  COLUMN 92                   PIC XX          VALUE '**'.
006140
006150  01  DATE-TOTAL          LINE PLUS 2
006160                          TYPE IS CONTROL FOOTING DATE-CD
006170                          NEXT GROUP PLUS 2.
006180      03  COLUMN 41                   PIC X(23)       VALUE
006190      'TOTAL SALES FOR THE DAY'.
007010      03  COLUMN 89                   PIC $$$,$$$.99
007020                                      SUM AMOUNT-CD.
007030      03  COLUMN 99                   PIC XXX         VALUE '***'.
007040
007050  01  FINAL-TOTAL         LINE PLUS 1
007060                          TYPE IS CONTROL FOOTING FINAL.
007070      03  COLUMN 86                   PIC X(15)       VALUE
007080      'FINAL TOTAL'.
007090      03  COLUMN 101                  PIC $$$,$$$.99
007100                                      SUM AMOUNT-CD.
007110      03  COLUMN 111                  PIC X(4)        VALUE '****'.
```

Figure 7-25 Description of Control Footing Report Groups

As can be seen from the example in Figure 7-25, each of the report groups for the control footing lines (Salesman, Branch, Date, and Total) are defined in the same manner as the Detail lines, that is, the report group definition is given by the level-01 entry and each field which is to be printed on the line is defined by an elementary item entry on the 03-level.

As was noted previously, the report groups should be defined in the same sequence within the Report Section of the COBOL program as they will be printed on the report. Thus, the report group for the salesman is first, for the branch is second, for the date is third, and for the final total is last. It should be noted that this is directly opposite to the sequence in which the control fields are defined in the Control Clause of the RD Statement where the highest control level is defined first, followed by the next highest, and so on down to the lowest level.

As illustrated in Figure 7-25, each of the report groups is given a data-name. In addition, the type is specified and the spacing of the line relative to the rest of the lines on the report is indicated. As noted, the ''Line Plus'' Clause specifies that prior to printing the line defined in the report group, the printer should be spaced the number of times indicated. Thus, the report groups for the salesman total, the branch total, and the date total will all be spaced twice before printing.

The **TYPE** Clause must be used to indicate the type of report group which is being defined, and when the report group is to be printed. In the case of all four report groups defined in Figure 7-25, they are specified as Control Footing report groups. Whenever a Control Heading or Control Footing report group is defined, it is also necessary to define the control field associated with the control report group. Therefore, following the ''Type Is Control Footing'' entry, the identifier of the field which is the control field must be specified. Thus, for the salesman report group, the field **SALESMAN-CD** is entered. This indicates that when the value in the field **SALESMAN-CD** changes, that is, when there is a control break for that field, the Control Footing Report group will be printed.

The same type of entries are made for the control fields **BRANCH-CD**, **DATE-CD**, and the special name **FINAL**. The report groups associated with these identifiers will be printed only when a control break occurs for these fields.

In addition to specifying the control field identifier, it will be noted from Figure 7-25, that another entry has been used - the **NEXT GROUP** Clause. The Next Group Clause is used to cause spacing of the printer after a line has been printed. The format notation for the **NEXT GROUP** Clause is shown below.

```
                          (integer-1           )
NEXT GROUP IS             {PLUS integer-2      }
                          (NEXT PAGE            )
```

Figure 7-26 Format Notation for NEXT GROUP Clause

The Next Group Clause is used to cause spacing of the printer after a line is printed. It will be recalled that the "Line Plus" clause is used to cause spacing before the line is printed. Therefore, through the use of the "Line Plus" clause and the "Next Group" clause, any spacing desired can be effected on the report. One important element of the Next Group clause must be recognized, however, and that is that only when a control break occurs for the field which is the control field for the given report group will the clause cause any skipping. Thus, only when there is a control break for the field **SALESMAN-CD** will the Next Group clause on the pg/line 006030 in Figure 7-25, have any effect. If the control break is caused by a change in date or a change in branch number, the Next Group clause will not cause any spacing after the line is printed. The report created and the results of the spacing commands used are illustrated below.

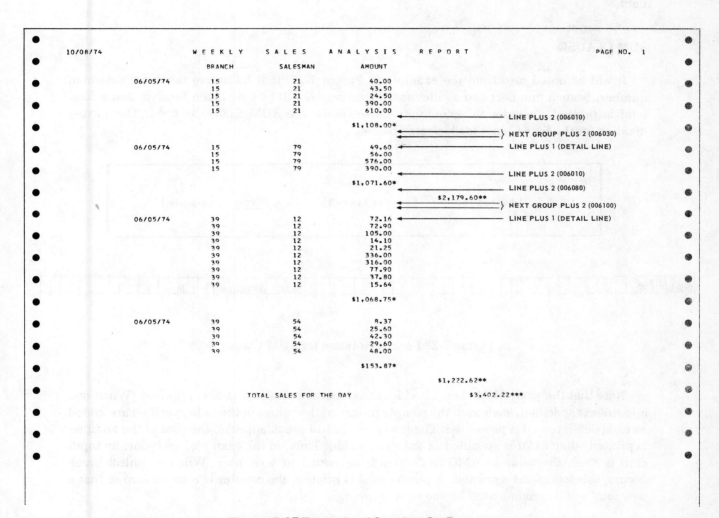

Figure 7-27 Example of Spacing On Report

In the example in Figure 7-27, the spacing which takes place on the report together with the pg/line from the coding in Figure 7-25 causing the spacing is shown. It will be noted that when a control break takes place on the salesman number (from 21 to 79 within branch 15) the "Line Plus 2" entry (pg/line 006010) causes double spacing to occur before the total ($1,108.00) is printed. Note, also, that following the total, the Next Group clause specified for the Salesman Total (pg/line 006030) caused the spacing requested because a change in Salesman Number had taken place. Following the total for salesman number 79, however, no spacing took place as a result of the Next Group entry because the change which caused the total to be printed was a change in branch number (from 15 to 39) and not salesman number. Thus, as noted, when the Next Group clause is used with Control Footing Report Groups, it only has an effect when the control field with which it is associated changes without any change in a higher level control field.

SUM CLAUSE

It will be noted also from the example in Figure 7-27, that totals are taken for salesman number, branch number, and as illustrated previously, will also be taken for date and a final total is printed. In order to accumulate these totals, the **SUM** Clause is used. The format notation for the Sum Clause is illustrated below.

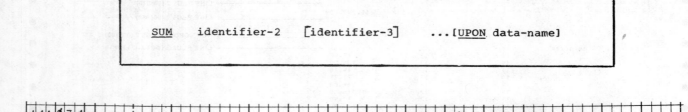

Figure 7-28 Format Notation for SUM Clause

Note that the word **SUM** is required for the clause. Identifier-2 is also required. When one identifier is specified, such as in the sample program, the values in the field specified are added as each detail record is processed. Then, when a control break appears, the sum of the addition is printed when **SUM** is specified as the source field. Thus, in the example, each time an input card is read, the value in **AMOUNT-CD** will be added to a counter. When a control break occurs, this total will be printed. After the total is printed, the counter is reset to zero so that a new total will be accumulated for the next grouping.

In Figure 7-25, it can be seen that the Sum clause is used for all of the Control Footing Report Groups. It should be noted that when there is a control break in salesman number, the counter for the salesman will be printed and then reset automatically to zero, but this does not reset the counters for the other control fields. Thus, even though the **SUM** Clause specifies the same field for all four control levels, different counters are established by the Report Writer for each control level.

PROCEDURE DIVISION ENTRIES

As can be seen from the previous discussion, the entire format of the report, the fields to be used as data fields and also as counters are defined in the Report Section of the Data Division. Thus, in the Procedure Division, it is not necessary to perform the detail calculations and the movement of data which has been necessary in previous programs. All that is necessary is that a command is given to instruct that the report is to be created. The coding developed by the compiler will construct the report.

There are five statements that are required in order to create a report using the Report Writer: The **OPEN** Statement, the **INITIATE** Statement, the **GENERATE** Statement, the **TERMINATE** Statement, and the **CLOSE** Statement. The Procedure Division for the sample program using these statements is illustrated below.

EXAMPLE

```
008020 001-START.
008030        OPEN INPUT SALESMAN-FILE
008040             OUTPUT REPORT-FILE.
008050        INITIATE SALES-REPORT.
008060
008070 005-READ-PRINT.
008080        READ SALESMAN-FILE AT END GO TO 010-END-CARDS.
008090        GENERATE DETAIL-LINE.
008100        GO TO 005-READ-PRINT.
008110
008120 010-END-CARDS.
008130        TERMINATE SALES-REPORT.
008140        CLOSE SALESMAN-FILE
008150              REPORT-FILE.
008160        STOP RUN.
```

Figure 7-29 Procedure Division

Note from the example above that the first step in the Procedure Division is to Open the report file. The Open Verb is used in exactly the same manner as has been used in all previous programs, that is, the file-name as defined in the Select Statement and the FD statement is used with the Open verb.

Next, the **INITIATE** statement must be issued for the Report file. The format notation for the Initiate Statement is illustrated below.

```
INITIATE report-name-1 [report-name-2] ...
```

Figure 7-30 Format Notation for INITIATE Statement

As can be seen, the word **INITIATE** must be stated together with the report-name. The report-name is the name used in the RD Statement when defining the characteristics of the report to be generated. Thus, in the example, the name **SALES-REPORT** is used because this is the report-name used in the RD Statement (see Figure 7-9). The Initiate statement is issued only once for each report which is to be generated. Thus it, like the Open Statement, must be issued prior to entering the processing loop.

Within the **005-READ-PRINT** routine it can be seen from Figure 7-29, that an input card is read and then the **GENERATE** Statement is issued. The Generate statement causes the heading, detail, and footing lines to be printed. In addition, it updates any counters which are specified by the **SUM** Clause, updates any counters which are specified by the Page-Counter when a new page is printed, and generally takes care of printing the report. The format notation for the Generate Statement is illustrated below.

```
GENERATE identifier
```

Figure 7-31 Format Notation for GENERATE Statement

The identifier which is used with the Generate Statement must be the name of the detail report group within the report to be printed. In the example, the name used is **DETAIL-LINE** because this is the data-name associated with the detail report group (see Figure 7-22). No other entries are specified with the Generate Statement.

After all the detail records have been read and the report printed, the **010-END-CARDS** routine is entered. Prior to closing the report file, the **TERMINATE** Statement must be issued. The format of the Terminate statement is illustrated below.

```
TERMINATE report-name-1 [report-name-2] ...
```

Figure 7-32 Format Notation for TERMINATE Statement

Note from the format illustrated in Figure 7-32 that the only entry used with the word **TERMINATE** is the report-name. As with the Initiate statement, this report name in the sample program is **SALES-REPORT** which is defined in the RD Statement.

Following the Terminate Statement, the file must be closed the same as any other file which is to be written on the printer. Thus, in Figure 7-29, the **REPORT-FILE** is closed and then the program is terminated.

SAMPLE PROGRAM

The sample program in this chapter reads a file of Sales Cards and creates the printed report using the Report Writer feature of the COBOL compiler. The input and the output for the program are shown below.

INPUT

OUTPUT

PRINTER SPACING CHART

SOURCE LISTING

The source listing for the program is contained on this and the following pages.

```
   1                              IBM DOS AMERICAN NATIONAL STANDARD COBOL        360N CB482 PTF0009      10/08/74

    CBL ZWB,SUPMAP,CLIST
    00001    001010 IDENTIFICATION DIVISION.                                          RPTWRTR
    00002    001020 PROGRAM-ID.  RPTGEN.                                              RPTWRTR
    00003    001030 AUTHOR.      TJC.                                                 RPTWRTR
    00004    001040 INSTALLATION.  LONG BEACH.                                        RPTWRTR
    00005    001050 DATE-WRITTEN.  07/25/74.                                          RPTWRTR
    00006    001060 DATE-COMPILED. 10/08/74.                                          RPTWRTR
    00007    001070 SECURITY.      UNCLASSIFIED.                                      RPTWRTR
    00008    001080 REMARKS.       THIS PROGRAM PREPARES A SALES REPORT              RPTWRTR
    00009    001090                UTILIZING THE REPORT GENERATOR FEATURE            RPTWRTR
    00010    001100                OF ANSI COBOL. THE PROGRAM REPORTS EACH           RPTWRTR
    00011    001110                DETAIL SALES RECORD. IT ALSO TAKES A              RPTWRTR
    00012    001120                MINOR TOTAL UPON A CHANGE OF SALESMAN             RPTWRTR
    00013    001130                NUMBER, AN INTERMEDIATE TOTAL ON CHANGE           RPTWRTR
    00014    001140                OF BRANCH, AND A MAJOR TOTAL ON A CHANGE          RPTWRTR
    00015    001150                OF DATE. A FINAL TOTAL IS ALSO TAKEN.             RPTWRTR
    00016    001160                                                                  RPTWRTR
    00017    001170                                                                  RPTWRTR
    00018    001180 ENVIRONMENT DIVISION.                                            RPTWRTR
    00019    001190                                                                  RPTWRTR
    00020    001200 CONFIGURATION SECTION.                                           RPTWRTR
    00021    002010 SOURCE-COMPUTER.  IBM-360-F30.                                   RPTWRTR
    00022    002020 OBJECT-COMPUTER.  IBM-360-F30.                                   RPTWRTR
    00023    002030                                                                  RPTWRTR
    00024    002040 INPUT-OUTPUT SECTION.                                            RPTWRTR
    00025    002050 FILE-CONTROL.                                                    RPTWRTR
    00026    002060     SELECT SALESMAN-FILE                                         RPTWRTR
    00027    002070         ASSIGN TO SYS007-UR-2540R-S.                             RPTWRTR
    00028    002080     SELECT REPORT-FILE                                           RPTWRTR
    00029    002090         ASSIGN TO SYS008-UR-1403-S.                              RPTWRTR
    00030    002100                                                                  RPTWRTR
    00031    002110                                                                  RPTWRTR
    00032    002120 DATA DIVISION.                                                   RPTWRTR
    00033    002130 FILE SECTION.                                                    RPTWRTR
    00034    002140 FD  SALESMAN-FILE                                                RPTWRTR
    00035    002150     RECORD CONTAINS 80 CHARACTERS                                RPTWRTR
    00036    002160     LABEL RECORDS ARE OMITTED                                    RPTWRTR
    00037    002170     DATA RECORD IS SALES-CARD.                                   RPTWRTR
    00038    002180 01  SALES-CARD.                                                  RPTWRTR
    00039    002190     03  FILLER                    PIC X(5).                      RPTWRTR
    00040    002200     03  DATE-CD.                                                 RPTWRTR
    00041    003010         05  MONTH-CD              PIC XX.                        RPTWRTR
    00042    003020         05  DAY-CD                PIC XX.                        RPTWRTR
    00043    003030         05  YEAR-CD               PIC XX.                        RPTWRTR
    00044    003040     03  BRANCH-CD                 PIC XX.                        RPTWRTR
    00045    003050     03  SALESMAN-CD               PIC XX.                        RPTWRTR
    00046    003060     03  FILLER                    PIC X(37).                     RPTWRTR
    00047    003070     03  AMOUNT-CD                 PIC 9999V99.                   RPTWRTR
    00048    003080     03  FILLER                    PIC X(22).                     RPTWRTR
    00049    003090                                                                  RPTWRTR
    00050    003100 FD  REPORT-FILE                                                  RPTWRTR
    00051    003110     RECORD CONTAINS 133 CHARACTERS                               RPTWRTR
    00052    003120     LABEL RECORDS ARE OMITTED                                    RPTWRTR
    00053    003130     REPORT IS SALES-REPORT.                                      RPTWRTR
    00054    003140                                                                  RPTWRTR
    00055    003150                                                                  RPTWRTR
    00056    003160 REPORT SECTION.                                                  RPTWRTR
    00057    003170                                                                  RPTWRTR
    00058    003180 RD  SALES-REPORT                                                 RPTWRTR
    00059    003190     CONTROLS ARE FINAL, DATE-CD, BRANCH-CD, SALESMAN-CD          RPTWRTR
    00060    003200     PAGE LIMIT IS 52 LINES                                       RPTWRTR
    00061    004010     HEADING 1                                                    RPTWRTR
    00062    004020     FIRST DETAIL 5                                               RPTWRTR
    00063    004030     LAST DETAIL 46                                               RPTWRTR
    00064    004040     FOOTING 52.                                                  RPTWRTR
    00065    004050                                                                  RPTWRTR
    00066    004060 01  HEADINGS              TYPE IS PAGE HEADING.                  RPTWRTR
    00067    004070     03  LINE 1.                                                  RPTWRTR
    00068    004080         05  COLUMN 1.         PIC X(8)                           RPTWRTR
    00069    004090                 SOURCE CURRENT-DATE.                             RPTWRTR
    00070    004100         05  COLUMN 29         PIC X(61)     VALUE                RPTWRTR
    00071    004110             'W E E K L Y     S A L E S     A N A L Y S I S    R· RPTWRTR
    00072    004120-            'E P O R T'.                                         RPTWRTR
    00073    004130         05  COLUMN 118        PIC X(8)      VALUE                RPTWRTR
    00074    004140             'PAGE NO.'.                                          RPTWRTR
    00075    004150         05  COLUMN 126        PIC ZZ9                            RPTWRTR
    00076    004160                 SOURCE PAGE-COUNTER.                             RPTWRTR
    00077    004170     03  LINE 3.                                                  RPTWRTR
    00078    004180         05  COLUMN 32         PIC X(43)     VALUE                RPTWRTR
    00079    004190             'BRANCH     SALESMAN        AMOUNT'.                 RPTWRTR
```

```
     2

00080  004200                                                                      RPTWRTR
00081  005010 01  DETAIL-LINE        LINE PLUS 1                                    RPTWRTR
00082  005020                        TYPE IS DETAIL.                                RPTWRTR
00083  005030      03  COLUMN 16 GROUP INDICATE PIC XX                             RPTWRTR
00084  005040                                   SOURCE MONTH-CD.                    RPTWRTR
00085  005050      03  COLUMN 18 GROUP INDICATE PIC X          VALUE '/'.          RPTWRTR
00086  005060      03  COLUMN 19 GROUP INDICATE PIC XX                             RPTWRTR
00087  005070                                   SOURCE DAY-CD.                      RPTWRTR
00088  005080      03  COLUMN 21 GROUP INDICATE PIC X          VALUE '/'.          RPTWRTR
00089  005090      03  COLUMN 22 GROUP INDICATE PIC XX                             RPTWRTR
00090  005100                                   SOURCE YEAR-CD.                     RPTWRTR
00091  005110      03  COLUMN 33                PIC XX                              RPTWRTR
00092  005120                                   SOURCE BRANCH-CD.                   RPTWRTR
00093  005130      03  COLUMN 51                PIC XX                              RPTWRTR
00094  005140                                   SOURCE SALESMAN-CD.                 RPTWRTR
00095  005150      03  COLUMN 65                PIC Z,ZZZ.99                        RPTWRTR
00096  005160                                   SOURCE AMOUNT-CD.                   RPTWRTR
00097  005170                                                                      RPTWRTR
00098  005180 01  SALESMAN-TOTAL     LINE PLUS 2                                    RPTWRTR
00099  005190                        TYPE IS CONTROL FOOTING SALESMAN-CD            RPTWRTR
00100  005200                        NEXT GROUP PLUS 2.                             RPTWRTR
00101  006010      03  COLUMN 63                PIC $$$,$$$.99                      RPTWRTR
00102  006020                                   SUM AMOUNT-CD.                      RPTWRTR
00103  006030      03  COLUMN 73                PIC X          VALUE '*'.           RPTWRTR
00104  006040                                                                      RPTWRTR
00105  006050 01  BRANCH-TOTAL       LINE PLUS 2                                    RPTWRTR
00106  006060                        TYPE IS CONTROL FOOTING BRANCH-CD              RPTWRTR
00107  006070                        NEXT GROUP PLUS 2.                             RPTWRTR
00108  006080      03  COLUMN 82                PIC $$$,$$$.99                      RPTWRTR
00109  006090                                   SUM AMOUNT-CD.                      RPTWRTR
00110  006100      03  COLUMN 92                PIC XX         VALUE '**'.          RPTWRTR
00111  006110                                                                      RPTWRTR
00112  006120 01  DATE-TOTAL         LINE PLUS 2                                    RPTWRTR
00113  006130                        TYPE IS CONTROL FOOTING DATE-CD                RPTWRTR
00114  006140                        NEXT GROUP PLUS 2.                             RPTWRTR
00115  006150      03  COLUMN 41                PIC X(23)      VALUE                RPTWRTR
00116  006160          'TOTAL SALES FOR THE DAY'.                                   RPTWRTR
00117  006170      03  COLUMN 89                PIC $$$,$$$.99                      RPTWRTR
00118  006180                                   SUM AMOUNT-CD.                      RPTWRTR
00119  006190      03  COLUMN 99                PIC XXX        VALUE '***'.         RPTWRTR
00120  006200                                                                      RPTWRTR
00121  007010 01  FINAL-TOTAL        LINE PLUS 1                                    RPTWRTR
00122  007020                        TYPE IS CONTROL FOOTING FINAL.                 RPTWRTR
00123  007030      03  COLUMN 86                PIC X(15)      VALUE                RPTWRTR
00124  007040          'FINAL TOTAL'.                                               RPTWRTR
00125  007050      03  COLUMN 101               PIC $$$,$$$.99                      RPTWRTR
00126  007060                                   SUM AMOUNT-CD.                      RPTWRTR
00127  007070      03  COLUMN 111               PIC X(4)       VALUE '****'.        RPTWRTR
00128  007080                                                                      RPTWRTR
00129  007090                                                                      RPTWRTR
00130  007100                                                                      RPTWRTR
00131  007110 PROCEDURE DIVISION.                                                   RPTWRTR
00132  007120                                                                      RPTWRTR
00133  007130 001-NOTE.                                                            *RPTWRTR
00134  007140      NOTE ***********************************************************RPTWRTR
00135  007150      *    THIS PROGRAM PRODUCES A SALES ANALYSIS REPORT USING        *RPTWRTR
00136  007160      *    THE REPORT WRITER FEATURE OF ANSI COBOL. THE FIRST         *RPTWRTR
00137  007170      *    STEP IS TO OPEN BOTH THE CARD INPUT AND THE PRINTER        *RPTWRTR
00138  007180      *    OUTPUT FILE, AND TO INITIATE THE REPORT FILE. THE          *RPTWRTR
00139  007190      *    CARD FILE IS THEN READ AND THE REPORT IS                   *RPTWRTR
00140  007200      *    GENERATED. AT THE END OF THE CARD INPUT, THE REPORT        *RPTWRTR
00141  008010      *    IS TERMINATED AND FILES ARE CLOSED.                        *RPTWRTR
00142  008020      ************************************************************.RPTWRTR
00143  008030                                                                      RPTWRTR
00144  008040 001-START.                                                            RPTWRTR
00145  008050      OPEN INPUT  SALESMAN-FILE                                        RPTWRTR
00146  008060           OUTPUT REPORT-FILE.                                         RPTWRTR
00147  008070      INITIATE SALES-REPORT.                                           RPTWRTR
00148  008080                                                                      RPTWRTR
00149  008090 005-READ-PRINT.                                                       RPTWRTR
00150  008100      READ SALESMAN-FILE AT END GO TO 010-END-CARDS.                   RPTWRTR
00151  008110      GENERATE DETAIL-LINE.                                            RPTWRTR
00152  008120      GO TO 005-READ-PRINT.                                            RPTWRTR
00153  008130                                                                      RPTWRTR
00154  008140 010-END-CARDS.                                                        RPTWRTR
00155  008150      TERMINATE SALES-REPORT.                                          RPTWRTR
00156  008160      CLOSE SALESMAN-FILE                                              RPTWRTR
00157  008170            REPORT-FILE.                                               RPTWRTR
00158  008180      STOP RUN.                                                        RPTWRTR
```

CHAPTER 7

PROGRAMMING ASSIGNMENT

INSTRUCTIONS

The following report is prepared monthly by hand by the merchandising department.

NOVASKEIN FASHIONS, INC.
MERCHANDISE CONTROL

DATE 7-1-6-

DEPT NO.	DEPARTMENT AND CLASSIFICATION	MONTH'S SALES		ON HAND		ON ORDER	
		UNITS	RETAIL AMOUNT	UNITS	RETAIL AMOUNT	UNITS	RETAIL AMOUNT
18	COLLEGE WEAR						
	BLOUSES	435	$ 2,070.50	355	$ 1,566.02	95	$ 308.58
	SKIRTS	150	1,075.28	155	1,275.70	84	748.56
	SWEATERS	204	1,059.65	229	1,102.99	108	496.32
	JACKETS	117	1,839.64	125	2,010.40	36	609.36
	DRESSES	427	12,703.25	296	8,806.00	365	10,858.75
	COATS	285	17,784.00	148	9,235.20	207	12,916.80
	BELTS LEATHER	134	502.50	102	382.50	96	360.00
		1752	$37,034.82	1410	$24,378.81	991	$26,298.37
24	SPORTSWEAR						
	BLOUSES	216	$ 1,028.16	134	637.84	225	1,071.00
	SKIRTS	473	4,337.41	246	2,255.82	450	4,126.50

It has been decided to convert the report to a computer program. The card input to the program is illustrated below.

There will be one input card for each classification, that is, one card for blouses in department 18, one card for skirts in department 18, etc. In addition to the totals shown on the report above, a final total of all units and retail amounts is to be printed at the conclusion of the report. The format of the report is to be determined by the programmer. In addition, the programmer should develop test data to adequately test the program.

PROGRAM DESIGN, IMPLEMENTATION AND DOCUMENTATION

CHAPTER 8

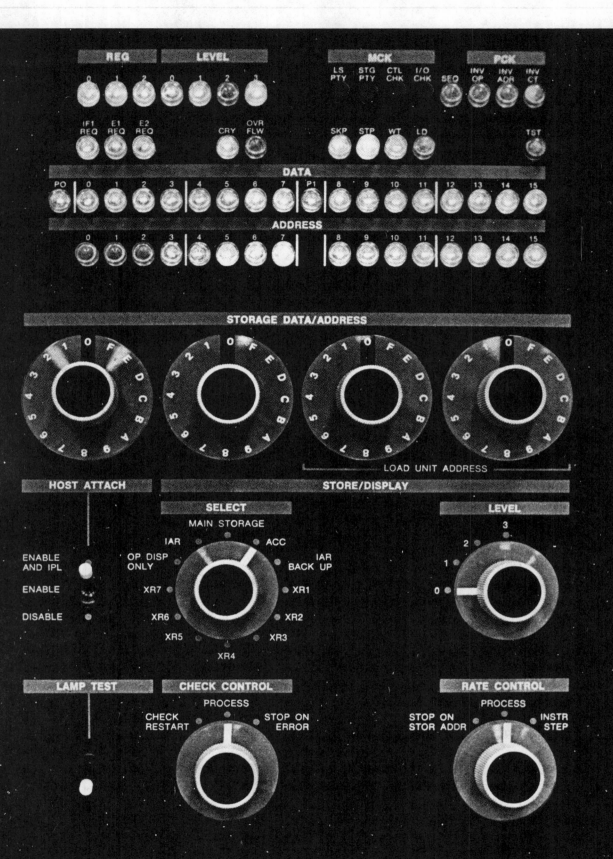

PROGRAM DESIGN, IMPLEMENTATION AND DOCUMENTATION   8

INTRODUCTION

In Chapter 2, it was mentioned that the programmer should have four major goals in mind when performing a programming assignment: 1) Completing the program in as little time as possible with as much accuracy and completeness as possible; 2) Having the program consume as little computer storage as possible; 3) Having the program execute as fast as possible; 4) Design the program so that future debugging and maintenance performed by a programmer other than the original programmer will be as easy a task as possible. Throughout this text, numerous examples have been given for good coding techniques which will lead to accomplishing the goals set forth above. An often overlooked phase of programming, however, is the manner in which the programmer approaches the problem which is to be solved by his program. The coding in the program is certainly one of the most important aspects of solving a problem on a computer, but merely coding a program in an efficient manner does not ensure a properly completed project. Many other areas are equally important when a programmer is given a programming assignment. The following is a list of some areas to which a programmer should pay close attention and some suggested steps and techniques to be used in the solving of a programming problem.

1 - UNDERSTAND THE PROBLEM: Although this sounds as if it is unnecessary, many of the problems encountered by the programmers and users of programs are as a result of the programmer not understanding the problem or misunderstanding the problem. It is vitally necessary that the programmer fully understand what is to be accomplished by his program and how it is to be accomplished. This includes an understanding of the input to the program, the output required, and the steps which are to be taken to produce the output. The programmer and the analyst or other person requesting the program must completely agree on all areas of processing within the program before any work is performed on the program itself.

2 - PREPARE A PRELIMINARY PROGRAM FLOWCHART: This is an absolutely vital step in writing a program and no further steps should be performed on a program until the preliminary flowchart has been prepared. It is at this point that the programmer determines all of the logic which is to be incorporated into his program. In addition, all programming techniques which are to be used in the program, such as subroutines, table look-ups, etc., are specifically defined and logically included into the program. Decisions such as manipulation of data for the most efficient usage must be made at this point. This flowchart must be very detailed so that the programmer can code directly from the flowchart, literally translating the flowchart from decision and processing statements into COBOL source statements.

3 - **DESK CHECK PRELIMINARY FLOWCHART**: After the preliminary flowchart has been prepared, it must be checked carefully for any errors which may have been inadvertently included in it. The programmer should ensure that the logic of the program includes all the processing which is to be accomplished by the program. This means that the input and output are being handled properly, all decisions are being made properly, and all error possibilities have been properly checked for and will be handled in the correct manner. It is at this point that the major errors in the program logic and processing should be caught. Coding of the program should not begin until the programmer is satisfied that every aspect of the program is correct and that the source coding produced will be correct.

4 - **CODE THE PROGRAM AND SUBMIT FOR KEYPUNCHING**: After the detailed flowchart has been prepared and checked, the program can be coded. The program should be coded directly from the preliminary flowchart. The Procedure Division should be an almost one-for-one translation of the flowchart. Careful attention to detail when coding the program can save a great deal of time and trouble when the program is being debugged. Such things as invalid punctuation, and misspelled data-names, procedure-names and reserved words should be carefully avoided. Numerous Note statements should be used in the coding for clarification and explanation. Every routine and each unique processing technique should be explained by a Note statement. In addition to easing the maintenance task at a later date, the use of Note statements many times eases the debugging chore for the original programmer. Keypunching instructions should also be included on the coding sheets. There is nothing more frustrating to a programmer than to have all the zeros in his program punched as the letter of the alphabet O and vice versa. A simple statement as to which is which can sometimes save several days of correction time.

5 - **CHECK KEYPUNCHING**: When the punched program is returned, the programmer should check the punched deck against the coding forms to ensure that the punching is correct. Although an initial compilation will flag any punctuation or spelling errors, it will not indicate errors such as omitted cards, punctuation in the wrong place, or misplaced cards. It may take much more time to correct these errors after a compilation than before the initial compilation. Therefore, the programmer should always check the punched deck against the coding sheets. It is almost always more economical in terms of cost, and many times in terms of time for the programmer to do as much checking as possible at his desk rather than relying on the computer to do the checking.

6 - **SUBMIT THE PROGRAM FOR INITIAL COMPILATION**: After the punched deck has been checked for errors and corrected, the program should be submitted for compilation. The programmer must prepare the necessary job control cards for the compilation. Care must be taken by the programmer to ensure that the job control cards are correct and complete. Errors in job control can be very costly in terms of time because a run on the computer is essentially negated by invalid job control.

7 - **CORRECT ERRORS IN THE COMPILATION**: When the initial compilation is returned from the computer, the programmer must correct any compilation errors. If possible, all diagnostic errors should be eliminated in the program. Normally, if errors are to be left uncorrected, they should only be Level-W diagnostics which deal either with alignment problems or with situations where the receiving field on a Move or arithmetic statement is not large enough to accept the complete sending field. However, all diagnostics must be analyzed. It should NEVER be assumed that a Level-W diagnostic is acceptable. Only after an analysis should this be concluded.

Normally, a second compilation should be all that is necessary to have a correct compilation. All errors in the initial compilation should be corrected on the second compilation. In some instances, a third compilation may be necessary, but in the majority of cases, two compilations should be enough.

8 - DESK CHECK THE CORRECT COMPILATION: "Desk checking" a program refers to the process of "playing computer" with a program source listing. The programmer analyses EVERY statement in the program to ensure that each statement, technique and routine will perform exactly as it is intended. This checking should include the file definitions, the data definitions, and the processing statements in the Procedure Division. Each path which the program can take should be followed in order to check each part of the program.

This desk checking procedure should include a close correlation between the program source listing and the preliminary flowchart to ensure that all processing steps taken in the program will accomplish the desired goal. Too much emphasis cannot be placed on the importance of desk checking a program before it is tested. Many errors which would occur during test runs will be eliminated before the program is ever tested. The combination of carefully checking the preliminary flowchart before coding the program and then carefully going through the program, following all logical paths and correcting any errors, will, in most cases, eliminate most of the logic and processing errors which have occurred in the writing of the program.

9 - PREPARE JOB CONTROL CARDS FOR TESTING: The preparation of the job control cards which will be used for testing a program should be done in as careful a manner as the preparation of the program itself. An error in a job control card can result in lost time on the computer because the run will be aborted before any testing is accomplished. In addition, an incorrect value in a job control card may lead to test results which are difficult to interpret because the error is not immediately apparent in the program itself. Whenever a program is being tested, a list of the job control cards must always be part of the test results received by the programmer because an error in job control can cause invalid results the same as an error in the program.

10 - PREPARE TEST DATA: It is the experience of many programmers that the preparation of adequate test data to test a program is more difficult than writing the program itself. In many cases it is extremely difficult to develop adequate test data, but it is an absolute necessity if the program is to be debugged properly. Unique test data must be prepared to test a program and should include data to test all decisions made in the program, all techniques and routines used in the program, and all error possibilities which can occur in a program. The data used to test a program should never be "live data", that is, data which will be or has been used in the same or a related program. The theory that if an error or other situation can occur, it will occur in the "live data" simply is not true. The programmer must design test data which adequately tests ALL possible situations which can occur in his program. Most failures of programs after they have been put into production, that is, after they are being used in the system for which they were written, occur because the programmer did not design adequate test data and therefore did not test for all situations. Particular attention should be paid to routines which are executed only for the first record on a file and end-of-file and other routines which are executed at the end of a program. Different combinations of beginning and ending data can produce different results and all possible combinations should be tested.

11 - **TEST PROGRAM USING "VALID" TEST DATA:** The first several tests of a program should use "perfect" test data, that is, data which contains no errors and which should produce the desired results. The first tests should test all the major logic in the program and each major routine. The concept of using all combinations of test data on the first tests under the theory that all portions of the program will be tested is not valid. The tests should be designed to test specific portions of the program. For example, in a random update of an indexed sequential file, the first tests may test only the "addition routine" to ensure that records are being added properly. Then the random access routines could be tested to ensure that they are working properly. A step-by-step approach to testing a program is normally much more effective than a "shotgun" approach where everything is tested all at the same time.

After each test run, the test results should be analyzed very carefully and ALL errors in the results should be corrected. For example, if the program were designed to take a minor total the totals may not be correct on the printed report. Obviously, this error must be corrected. However, the report may also show that the page number is not being incremented properly and there may be garbage characters in the heading line. All of these errors should be corrected before resubmitting the program for another test run.

12 - **TEST THE PROGRAM USING ALL TEST DATA:** After all the routines have been checked using valid test data, the program must be tested using invalid data and combinations of valid data which will produce errors. This phase of testing is very critical because it is the errors which can occur which will make the program fail after it is in production. Normally, writing a program which will work with valid data is relatively easy. The difficulty in programming is making a program work with invalid data. Thus, the programmer must take great care in preparing the test data and using it in the correct manner to ensure that the program will work properly regardless of the data which is input to the program.

13 - **VERIFY TEST RESULTS WITH ANALYST:** After the program has been completely tested, the test results should be reviewed by the analyst in charge to ensure that all functions of the program are being performed properly and that nothing has been omitted from the program. This verification should include an analysis of the test data and the results of the test runs.

14 - **PREPARE FINAL DOCUMENTATION:** After the program has been verified as complete, the programmer should prepare the final documentation of the program so that any future maintenance or corrections can be made to the program with a minimum of effort. Although documentation standards within industry vary to a great extent, the following information should be the minimum contained in a properly documented program:

   A) Title Page: The Title Page should contain the program name, a program number or some unique identification, the name of the original programmer, and the date.

B) Revision Page: The revision page should be a form to document the history of the program. Contents should include the name of the original programmer or programmers, the date the program became operational, and the time required to program the project. In a chart form, provision should be made to document subsequent revisions to the program, a brief description of the revisions, the name of the programmer making the revision, the time required to make the revision, and the date the revised program was operational.

C) Abstract or General Description: The program abstract should contain a general description of the program, its basic purpose and features, frequency of use, and the input, output, and processing performed. The abstract provides an overview of the function of the program.

D) Records Layouts: Record layouts include multiple card layout forms, printer spacing charts, and/or disk and tape record layouts. These forms should specifically define the format of the input and output, the blocking factors and record sizes, an estimated number of records to be processed by the program, and the requirements for disk and tape storage space.

E) Systems Flowchart: The systems flowchart documents the flow of data through the system, provides a visual means of identifying the input and output files being used, and illustrates required steps in the total processing cycle.

F) Detailed Description: This part of the documentation manual should provide a detailed description of the program including special editing, such as checks for valid numeric fields, sequence checking, checking for maximum field size, and reasonableness checks, any table used within the program, special forms used, special carriage control tapes required, special operating instructions, and the size of computer storage required for the program.

G) Program Logic: The detailed program logic must be illustrated through the use of program flowcharts and/or decision tables.

H) Program Listing: The program listing should list all source code, storage maps, and job control statements required to execute the program.

I) Test Data: A listing of the test data used to test the program, as well as the output of the program, should be provided in the program documentation manual. This test data should include sufficient data to test all routines within the program.

J) Operation Instructions: Instructions must be prepared to direct the operator in the execution of the program. Such elements as job control statements required, specification of the devices to be used, report forms and carriage control tapes to be used, timing estimates, special switch settings, any error messages to which the operator must respond, the source of the input to the program and the distribution of the output of the program must be explicitly stated so that the operator can properly run the program.

When a programmer follows these steps, he can be assured that the program he is writing will be a complete and correct program. If any of the steps described are omitted, he runs the risk that the final program will not be a reliable, accurate program. If this occurs, all of the effort put into the program will have been of little use because the user of the program is not receiving the product to which he is entitled.

PROGRAMMING ASSIGNMENT

CASE STUDY

The final programming assignment incorporates many of the concepts studied in the previous chapters. Upon solution of the problem, the student should be able to solve a variety of business type programming problems using the COBOL programming language.

INSTRUCTIONS

A survey sheet has been sent to colleges and universities throughout the United States to determine what data processing courses are offered at their school. The format of the survey sheet is illustrated below.

DATA PROCESSING COURSE SURVEY

SCHOOL NAME_____

SCHOOL ADDRESS_____

CITY_____

STATE_____

CONTACT_____

CHECK FOLLOWING COURSES OFFERED:

_____ Introduction to Data Processing

_____ Introduction to Computer Programming

_____ IBM System/360 Assembler Language Programming

_____ IBM System/360 Advanced Assembler Language Programming

_____ IBM System/360 COBOL Programming

_____ IBM System/360 RPG Programming

_____ IBM System/360 Advanced RPG Programming

_____ IBM System/360 PL/I Programming

_____ IBM System/360 Advanced PL/I Programming

_____ IBM System/360 Fortran IV Programming

_____ Data Processing Systems

_____ IBM System/360 Job Control Language

_____ Systems Programming

(OTHERS)

_____   _____

_____   _____

_____   _____

_____   _____

From the information received upon return of the survey sheets, a printed report is to be prepared containing all of the schools which respond to the survey, the address of the school, the person to contact at the school, and the courses which they offer. The report is to be in alphabetic sequence by state and by school within state.

A master file to be stored on a direct-access device is to be created which will contain the following information: School Name, School Address, person to contact, and all courses offered by the school. It is estimated that the maximum number of responses to the survey will be 5000. All of the fields in the master record except school and the state should be able to be updated. Allowance must be made for adding courses for a school and deleting courses for a school. In addition, it must be possible to add and delete schools from the master file. The update activity for the file is estimated to be relatively small, perhaps 50 to 100 update transactions when the file is updated monthly.

The state will be the two digit zip-code name for a state (for example, California is CA). The maximum number of characters which will be allowed in the School Name is 40. It is estimated that the maximum number of courses offered at any one school will be 30.

The input formats, the report formats, master file format, and all processing for this system is to be designed and the programs written to produce the reports and the master file. This system should include all necessary error checking and other necessary controls to ensure that all the processing is accomplished properly. The necessary test data for the system is to be prepared.

APPENDICES

DISK AND TAPE CONCEPTS

INTRODUCTION TO MAGNETIC TAPE

Magnetic tape used with computer systems is similar to the tape used in audio tape recorders. Physically, the tape is composed of a plastic material normally one-half inch wide and coated on one side with a metallic oxide on which data may be recorded in the form of magnetic spots. The data recorded on magnetic tape may include numbers, letters of the alphabet, or special characters. Data is recorded in a series of parallel channels or tracks along the length of the tape. It is the presence or absence of magnetic spots on the tape that forms the representation of meaningful characters.

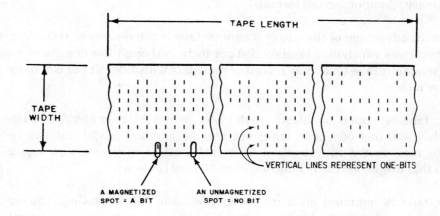

Figure A-1 Data Recorded on a Section of Magnetic Tape

Computers using the Extended Binary Coded Decimal Interchange Code normally use 9 channel magnetic tape. The tape consists of 9 horizontal channels with one of the channels reserved for parity checking. The following diagram illustrates the coding structure and bit configurations for 9 channel tape.

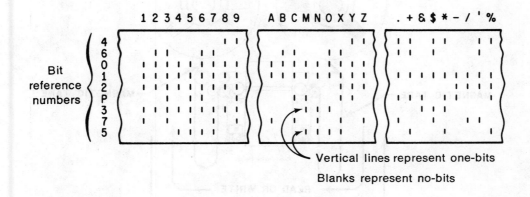

Figure A-2 Nine Channel Tape

The bit assignments indicated are based upon the coding structure of EBCDIC using the zoned decimal format. It should be noted that the bit assignments were selected for maximum reliability and performance. Those bits utilized most frequently in representing data are recorded near the center of the tape. The bit positions used less frequently are recorded on the outer edges of the tape where reading or writing errors are more likely to occur. The numbers to the left of the tape segment reference positions 0-7 of the byte. Note that position 7 of the byte is the second channel from the bottom on 9 channel tape. Bit position 6 is the second channel from the top, etc. For example, the bit configuration for the number "one" in EBCDIC is 1111 0001. This same bit configuration is contained on 9 channel magnetic tape by referencing the bit positions as indicated.

When using 9 channel tape, data may also be recorded in packed decimal (Computational-3) format or a binary (Computational) format.

An important advantage of the use of magnetic tape is the density of recording, that is, the number of characters which may be recorded per inch. Although the density of magnetic tape varies, most magnetic tape units may record or read data with a density of 800 bytes per inch or 1600 bytes per inch.

Magnetic tape is wound on plastic reels 10½ inches in diameter. A full reel contains approximately 2,400 feet of usable tape, but lengths as short as 50 feet can be used. It is interesting to note that a fully utilized 10½ inch reel of magnetic tape can contain data equivalent to that in 480,000 cards punched in all 80 card columns.

Magnetic tape is mounted on a magnetic tape unit for processing. During reading or writing, tape is moved from the file reel through a vacuum column, across a read-write head, through another vacuum column and to the machine take-up reel. Reading or writing takes place as the tape is moved across a read-write head. The tape-transport speed of the magnetic tape units varies from approximately 18.75 inches per second to 200 inches per second.

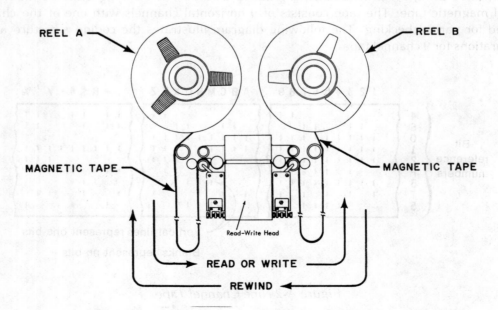

Figure A-3 Schematic of a Magnetic Tape Drive

Because of the density of magnetic tape and the speed at which the tape is transported past the read-write head, extremely fast input/output speeds are possible. To obtain the "effective" data transfer rate, that is, the speed at which data may be transferred to the Central Processing Unit from magnetic tape, the tape transport speed is multiplied by the tape density. For example, a magnetic tape unit with a tape transport speed of 112.5 inches per second, processing magnetic tape with a density of 800 bytes per inch has an "effective" data transfer rate of 90,000 characters per second.

SEQUENTIAL FILE PROCESSING

Although tape drives operate in different modes, they all process data in a sequential access method. Sequential processing means that records are read or written one after another. Card readers and card punches operate in a sequential manner because cards are read or punched one after another. Thus, when using magnetic tape, records are read and written sequentially. In addition, the records stored on magnetic tape are normally arranged sequentially on the basis of some central field or "key" such as the item number of individual records, the salesman number, etc.

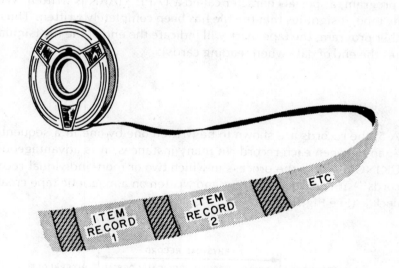

Figure A-4 Illustration of Records Arranged Sequentially on Magnetic Tape

After each record is written sequentially on a magnetic tape, there is an inter-block-gap (IBG) created (also called an IRG or inter-record-gap). This inter-block or inter-record-gap is a blank space on the tape approximately .6 inch long and indicates to the magnetic tape drive that the end of the record has been reached. This inter-block-gap is necessary to allow for the starting and stopping, acceleration and deceleration, of the magnetic tape unit, and is required for correct reading and writing of records. Data to be read begins with the first character after an inter-block-gap and continues to the next inter-block-gap.

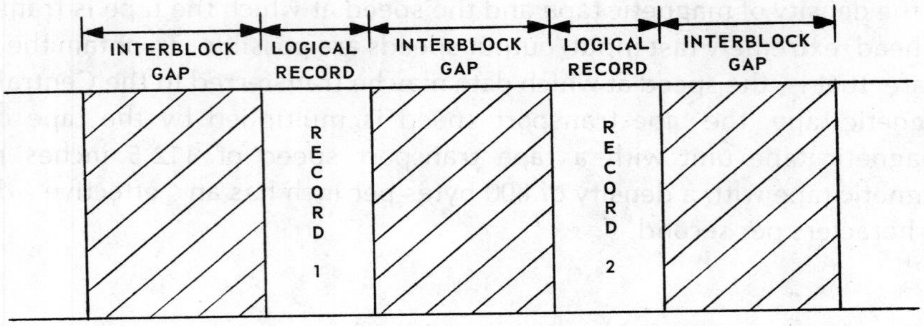

INTERBLOCK GAP | LOGICAL RECORD | INTERBLOCK GAP | LOGICAL RECORD | INTERBLOCK GAP

RECORD 1   RECORD 2

Figure A-5 Illustration of Records Stored on Magnetic Tape

When writing on tape, the records are written sequentially with inter-block-gaps between each record. During writing, the gap is automatically produced at the end of each record or block of records.

When all the records of the FILE (that is, the group of related records on the tape) have been written by the program, a special character called a TAPE MARK is written. When a tape mark is written on the tape, it signifies that the file has been completely written. Thus, when the tape is read by another program, the tape mark will indicate the end of the file (similar to the way the /* card indicates the end of data when reading cards).

BLOCKING

In Figure A-5, the records are shown to be written one by one in a sequential manner with an inter-block-gap between each record. In many instances, it is advantageous to BLOCK the records. BLOCKING refers to the process in which two or more individual records (referred to as ''logical records'') are grouped together and written on a magnetic tape creating a ''physical record'' or ''block''. (See Figure A-6).

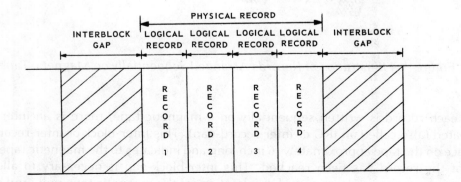

PHYSICAL RECORD

INTERBLOCK GAP | LOGICAL RECORD | LOGICAL RECORD | LOGICAL RECORD | LOGICAL RECORD | INTERBLOCK GAP

RECORD 1 | RECORD 2 | RECORD 3 | RECORD 4

Figure A-6 Illustration of Blocked Records

Blocking has two major advantages: (1) More records can be written on the tape because a number of records are recorded between each inter-block-gap, thus reducing the number of gaps on the tape; (2) The records can be read faster because two or more records can be read before the read operation is stopped by the inter-block-gap. The limiting factor in blocking records is the amount of computer storage available for input/output operations, as there must be enough room in storage to store the complete block of data to be processed. Thus, the larger the block of records, the more computer storage that must be allocated for storing the block. For example, if fifty 80 byte records comprise a physical record, then 4,000 bytes of computer storage are required when the physical record is transferred from magnetic tape to computer storage or from computer storage to magnetic tape. The programmer or analyst must make the determination as to what size block can be used so that there is enough storage available and the blocking is as efficient as possible.

The number of logical records comprising the "physical record" is called the BLOCKING FACTOR.

TAPE MARKERS

Magnetic tape must have some blank space at the beginning and end of the tape to allow threading through the feed mechanism of the tape unit. Special markers called "reflective strips" are placed on the tape to enable the tape unit to sense the beginning and end of the usable portion of the tape. The tape unit senses these markers as either the LOAD POINT marker which indicates where reading or writing is to begin or as the END-OF-TAPE marker which indicates approximately where writing is to stop.

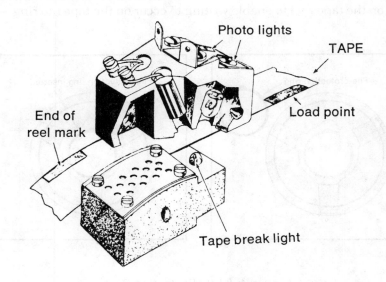

Figure A-7 Load Point and End-Of-Tape Markers

The markers are small pieces of transparent plastic with a thin film of aluminum on one side. At least 10 feet of tape must be allowed from the beginning of the tape to the LOAD POINT marker and approximately 14 feet are normally allowed between the END-OF-TAPE marker and the end of the tape.

TAPE UNIT POSITIONING

When a magnetic tape is loaded onto a magnetic tape drive, the tape is positioned at the LOAD POINT. As the tape is read or written, it progresses by being taken up on the take-up reel. Thus, when the reading or writing of the tape file is complete and the tape mark has been written or read, there will be tape on the take-up reel. Two commands are available to return the tape to the ''user reel'' -- the rewind command and the rewind and unload command. When the rewind command is executed, all the tape on the take-up reel is wound back on the ''user reel'' until the load point is reached. At that time the tape drive is readied and the tape is ready to be read or written again. When the rewind and unload command is used, the tape is wound back on the ''user reel'' and then the tape is unloaded, that is, it is taken out of a ''ready'' status and it is possible for the operator to dismount the tape.

There are times when one file is larger than one VOLUME (that is, one reel of tape). When this happens, a tape mark is written at the end of the first volume and a second volume must be mounted by the operator so that the file may be continued. When this situation occurs, the file is called a MULTI-VOLUME file. It is also possible to have more than one file on a tape volume. This is called a MULTI-FILE volume.

FILE PROTECTION DEVICE

Because the writing operation automatically erases any previous information on the tape, a file protection device is provided to prevent accidental erasure. A plastic ring must be fitted into a circular groove on the tape reel to enable writing to occur on the tape (no ring — no write).

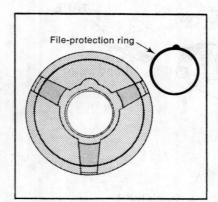 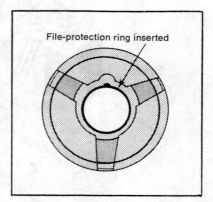

Figure A-8 File Protection Ring

When this ring is removed only reading can take place. This technique tends to prevent accidental writing on a reel of tape as the operator must insert the ring in the reel for writing to occur.

MAGNETIC TAPE LABELING

Installations utilizing magnetic tape as a form of input and output normally maintain a tape "library". This library may consist of hundreds and even thousands of reels of tape containing the data to be processed. It is essential, therefore, that an effective means of identifying the individual reels of tape be developed. In actual practice, two types of labels are normally used to identify tape volumes or reels: an External Label and an Internal Label.

An External Label is written on some type of gummed label and is attached to the reel of tape. It normally contains information such as the volume number, that is, the unique number which identifies the volume or reel of tape, the "owner's name", that is, the programmer, department, etc., who is currently using the reel of tape, the date on which the tape may be "scratched" or used again, and a description of the contents of the data on the tape. Additional information may be included depending on the needs of the installation. This external label is used for identification purposes by the computer operator and the tape librarian.

An Internal Label is written directly on the tape by the computer. It is recorded in the same manner as data is recorded on the tape. It contains such information as the volume serial number, the data set name or identifer, the creation and expiration dates, etc. This internal label may be placed on the tape through the use of Standard Labels. These labels allow the user to uniquely identify each file or data set which is created on tape.

The format of an internal label or labels which are found on magnetic tape will normally be determined by the type of computer and the operating system which is used with the computer. Typically, however, the internal labels consist of at least three different types — a Volume Label, a Header Label, and a Trailer Label. An example of a labeled tape is shown in Figure A-9.

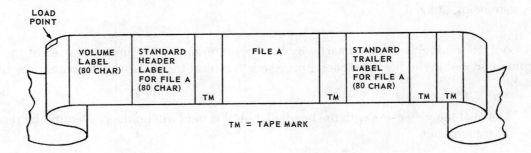

Figure A-9 Standard Tape Labels

The Volume Label is normally the first record on the magnetic tape volume and serves to identify the entire reel of tape. In most instances, the volume serial number which identifies the tape is written in this label and there may be additional information dependent upon the needs of the operating system.

The Header Label which is written on the magnetic tape is normally used to identify each of the files which may be contained upon the tape. It will be noted that it is possible for more than one file to be stored on a single volume of tape and if this occurs, then there will usually be a header label for each file which is on the tape. A header label will normally include at least the following information:

1. Label Identifier - This field contains a special value which identifies the record as a header record.

2. Tape Serial Number - This number normally corresponds to the serial number which is found in the Volume Label.

3. File Serial Number - This may be some unique number identifying the file, or it may be the same number as the tape serial number.

4. Sequence Number - This is a value which indicates the sequence of the file contained on the tape if the file consists of more than one tape volume (a Multi-Volume File).

5. File Identification - This is normally a unique name which is selected by the analyst or programmer to identify the file by name.

6. Creation Date - This field will identify the date on which the file was created.

7. Retention Cycle - This field will normally indicate the number of days a file is to be retained after it has been created or will give a date beyond which the tape may be used for another file.

These fields are basic to most header labels which are utilized in labeling tape files. Additional fields and, hence, additional control, may be present depending upon the operating system being utilized.

A Trailer Label is used primarily by the operating system to ensure that all of the records contained within the file have been processed. A typical trailer label will contain the following data:

1. Label Identifier - As with the header label, this field will uniquely identify the record as a trailer label.

2. Block Count - This field will contain the total number of physical records or blocks which have been written on the file. When the file is read as input, the number of records read will be counted, and after all of the records have been read, the number read will be compared to the value in this block count. If the values are not equal, it indicates that there has been a read error on the tape drive and corrective action must be taken.

3. Tape Record Count - This may be a similar count to that of the block count only it is a count of the number of logical records on the file rather than the number of physical records.

Trailer labels may also contain any additional control information which may be applicable to either the operating system or the particular program or application.

NON-LABELLED AND USER-LABELLED TAPES

There is normally not a requirement, unless by installation standards, that magnetic tape files be labelled, although it is normally the best operating procedure to have labelled tapes. If labels are not used on a tape file or a tape volume, then the first record on the tape will be a data record in the file. The use or non-use of labels can be specified in the File Definition within the COBOL program.

There also may be provisions within the operating system being used which allow for user-written labels, that is, labels which contain any information which the user wishes to write in them. Special user label routines must be called in the COBOL program through the use of entries in the Declarative Section of the COBOL program.

RECORD FORMATS

Records on a magnetic tape can be of several formats. These formats are chosen by the programmer or analyst depending upon the use of the record and what type of data will be contained in the record.

The two types of records are FIXED and VARIABLE. In addition, the fixed and variable length records may be BLOCKED or UNBLOCKED.

A FIXED-LENGTH record is one which always contains the same number of bytes. Thus, when a file is defined as having fixed-length records and the record length is 120, all records on the file contain 120 bytes. Normally, the fields in the record are defined in the File Section of the Data Division in the same manner used for the card reader and printer.

Fixed-length records can be blocked or unblocked. When they are unblocked, each physical record will be 120 bytes long. When the fixed-length records are blocked, the physical record contains more than one logical record. Thus, if a blocking factor of five is used, that is, there are five logical records for each block or physical record, then the BLOCKSIZE or block length would be 600 bytes (120 bytes/rec times 5 recs/block).

A VARIABLE-LENGTH record is one which may contain a variable number of bytes in each record, that is, each record may contain the same or a different number of bytes. Variable-length records are used when different amounts of data may be available for each record. Variable-length records may be either blocked or unblocked, depending upon the application.

TAPE DISADVANTAGES

Although magnetic tape is an effective input/output media because of its high density and fast data transfer rate, the use of magnetic tape has several significant disadvantages. These disadvantages include the following:

1. Because records are stored on magnetic tape sequentially, transactions against master files stored on tape must be batched and sorted into sequence before processing.

2. Additions or deletions from a master file require that a new file must be created no matter how few the number of additions or deletions.

3. To extract a single record from a magnetic tape file (for example, the last record stored on a tape reel) requires that each record on the file be examined until the proper "key" identifying the record is found, at which time the record is processed as required.

4. In file updating procedures where there is little activity against the file the use of magnetic tape is normally inefficient. For example, if a master file containing 10,000 records is to be updated but only 100 records are to be processed against the entire master file, the sequential file organization characteristic of magnetic tape requires that the entire master file of 10,000 records be processed.

DIRECT ACCESS STORAGE DEVICES

Another type of input/output device which is an effective storage media for many applications is a DIRECT ACCESS STORAGE DEVICE (DASD). Direct access storage devices may process files organized sequentially as with magnetic tape, but also offer the advantage of "random" retrieval of individual records from a file. Although a number of direct access devices are currently available, the IBM 2311 disk drive is representative of all direct-access devices and will serve as a general example for similar units. The 2311 disk storage drive is illustrated in Figure A-10.

Figure A-10 2311 Disk Drive

The 2311 disk drive is a single unit which allows the mounting of removable disk "packs" (2316 disk packs). The packs when removed from the drive are enclosed in protective covers. Each pack consists of six disks mounted on a vertical shaft. The disks are 14 inches in diameter and are made of metal with a magnetic oxide coating on both sides of the disk. There are ten recording surfaces on each pack. The top surface of the upper disk and the bottom surface of the lower disk are not used for recording data. A disk pack is illustrated in Figure A-11.

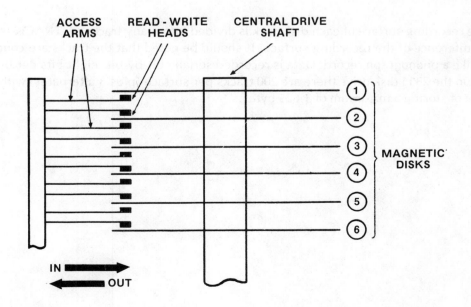

Figure A-11 Schematic of Disk Unit

The disks rotate at 2400 revolutions per minute. To transfer data to or from the recording surface requires some type of "access" mechanism. On the 2311 disk drive the access mechanism consists of a group of access arms consisting of read/write heads that move together as a unit in and out between the recording surfaces of the disk pack. These comb-type access arms can move to 203 different positions on the surface of the disk as there are 203 discrete recording positions within a disk surface. It should be noted that only 200 positions are normally used for recording data. Three alternate areas are supplied if any of the first 200 positions are defective.

RECORDING OF DATA

Data is recorded on the surface of the disks in the form of magnetic spots along a series of concentric circular recording positions on each disk recording surface.

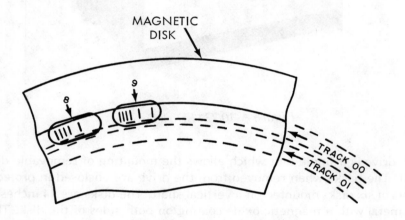

Figure A-12 Segment of Disk Recording Surface

The recording surface of each disk pack is divided into many tracks. A TRACK is defined as a circumference of the recording surface. It should be noted that the tracks are concentric, not spiral like a phonograph record. Data is recorded serially bit-by-bit, eight bits per byte, along a track. On the 2311 disk drive there are 200 tracks per surface (plus 3 alternates) with each track capable of storing a maximum of 3,625 bytes.

The following is a schematic drawing illustrating the 200 tracks on a recording surface.

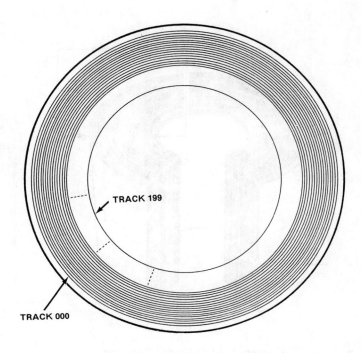

TRACK 199

TRACK 000

Figure A-13 Schematic of Disk Recording Track Position

CYLINDER CONCEPT

Each concentric circle as one looks "three dimensionally" from the top of the disk pack is called a CYLINDER. A "cylinder of data" is defined as the amount of data that is accessible with one positioning of the access mechanism. This is an important concept since movement of the access mechanism represents a significant portion of the time required to access and transfer data.

CYLINDER CONCEPT

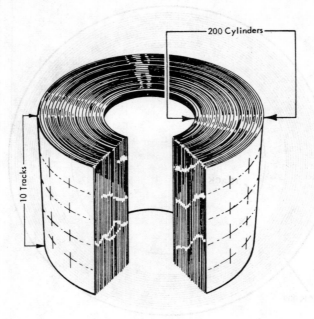

Figure A-14 Cylinder Concept

Each 2316 disk pack has 200 cylinders which is equal to the number of positions to which the access mechanism can move. Each cylinder has ten tracks, which is equal to the number of recording surfaces. Thus, a cylinder has a maximum capacity of 36,250 bytes (3,625 bytes per track, 10 tracks per cylinder). A pack has a maximum capacity of 7.25 million bytes (36,250 bytes per cylinder, 200 cylinders per pack).

RECORDS

Each track can hold a maximum of 3,625 characters. Of course, every record which is recorded on the disk is not 3,625 characters long. Therefore, more than one record can be recorded on a track. These records are separated by a gap similar in function to the inter-block-gap on tape. One method of referencing a particular record on a track is by a "record number". This record number specifies the relative location of the record on the track and uniquely identifies its position on the track.

In order to develop an address for a record on a disk pack, the program specifies the cylinder number, the track number and the record number.

The track number refers to the number of the disk surface. The first recording surface is called track 0, the second recording surface track 1, etc. See the illustration below.

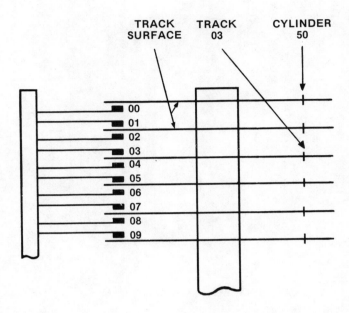

Figure A-15 Data Record Recorded on Disk

In the example above, if data is recorded beginning on cylinder 50, track 3, one could specify the address of "RECORD2" by indicating that it resides on cylinder 50, track 3, record 2.

DISK LABELS

Labels are normally used for disk files. The labels provide the pertinent information about the disk file. They give the file a name, a creation and expiration date, the location of the file on the disk pack, and other necessary data.

SUMMARY - FORMAT NOTATION

Throughout this publication, basic formats are prescribed for various elements of COBOL. These generalized descriptions are intended to guide the programmer in writing his own statements. They are presented in a uniform system of notation, explained in the following paragraphs. Although it is not part of COBOL, this notation is useful in describing COBOL.

1. All words printed entirely in capital letters are <u>reserved words</u>. These are words that have preassigned meanings in COBOL. In all formats, words in capital letters represent an actual occurrence of those words. If any such word is incorrectly spelled, it will not be recognized as a reserved word and may cause an error in the program.

2. All underlined reserved words are required unless the portion of the format containing them is itself optional. These are <u>key words</u>. If any such word is missing or is incorrectly spelled, it is considered an error in the program. Reserved words <u>not</u> underlined may be included or omitted at the option of the programmer. These words are used only for the sake of readability; they are called <u>optional words</u> and, when used, must be correctly spelled.

3. The characters +, -, <, >, =, when appearing in formats, although not underlined, are required when such formats are used.

4. All punctuation and other special characters (except those symbols cited in the following paragraphs) represent the actual occurrence of those characters. Punctuation is essential where it is shown. Additional punctuation can be inserted, according to the rules for punctuation specified in this publication.

5. Words that are printed in lower-case letters represent information to be supplied by the programmer. All such words are defined in the accompanying text.

6. In order to facilitate references to them in text, some lower-case words are followed by a hyphen and a digit or letter. This modification does not change the syntactical definition of the word.

7. Certain entries in the formats consist of a capitalized word(s) followed by the word "Clause" or "Statement." These designate clauses or statements that are described in other formats, in appropriate sections of the text.

8. Square brackets ([ ]) are used to indicate that the enclosed item may be used or omitted, depending on the requirements of the particular program. When two or more items are stacked within brackets, one or none of them may occur.

9. Braces ({ }) enclosing vertically stacked items indicate that one of the enclosed items is obligatory.

10. The ellipsis (...) indicates that the immediately preceding unit may occur once, or any number of times in succession. A <u>unit</u> means either a single lower-case word, or a group of lower-case words and one or more reserved words enclosed in brackets or braces. If a term is enclosed in brackets or braces, the entire unit of which it is a part must be repeated when repetition is specified.

```
IDENTIFICATION DIVISION — BASIC FORMATS

{IDENTIFICATION DIVISION.}
{ID DIVISION.            }

PROGRAM-ID. program-name.

AUTHOR. [comment-entry] . . .

INSTALLATION. [comment-entry] . . .

DATE-WRITTEN. [comment-entry] . . .

DATE-COMPILED. [comment-entry] . . .

SECURITY. [comment-entry] . . .

REMARKS. [comment-entry] . . .
```

It will be noted in the formats shown above and in subsequent format notations that some of the entries are shaded. These shaded portions of the formats depict additions which IBM has made to the basic ANSI COBOL Compiler and for those compilers executed on an IBM machine, these entries will be applicable. On other compilers, they may or may not be applicable.

ENVIRONMENT DIVISION — BASIC FORMATS

ENVIRONMENT DIVISION.

CONFIGURATION SECTION.

SOURCE-COMPUTER. *computer-name.*

OBJECT-COMPUTER. *computer-name* [MEMORY SIZE *integer* $\left\{ \begin{matrix} \text{WORDS} \\ \text{CHARACTERS} \\ \text{MODULES} \end{matrix} \right\}$].

SPECIAL-NAMES. [*function-name-1* IS *mnemonic-name*] . . .

   [*function-name-2* [IS *mnemonic-name*]

          $\left\{ \begin{matrix} \underline{\text{ON}} \text{ STATUS } \underline{\text{IS}} \text{ condition-name-1 } [\underline{\text{OFF}} \text{ STATUS } \underline{\text{IS}} \text{ condition-name-2}] \\ \underline{\text{OFF}} \text{ STATUS } \underline{\text{IS}} \text{ condition-name-2 } [\underline{\text{ON}} \text{ STATUS } \underline{\text{IS}} \text{ condition-name-1}] \end{matrix} \right\}$] . . .

   [CURRENCY SIGN IS *literal*]

   [DECIMAL-POINT IS COMMA].

INPUT-OUTPUT SECTION.

FILE-CONTROL.

   {SELECT [OPTIONAL] *file-name*

   ASSIGN TO [*integer*] *system-name-1* [*system-name-2*] . . .

        [FOR MULTIPLE $\left\{ \begin{matrix} \text{REEL} \\ \text{UNIT} \end{matrix} \right\}$]

   RESERVE $\left\{ \begin{matrix} \text{NO} \\ \text{integer} \end{matrix} \right\}$ ALTERNATE $\left[\begin{matrix} \text{AREA} \\ \text{AREAS} \end{matrix} \right]$

   $\left\{ \begin{matrix} \text{FILE-LIMIT IS} \\ \text{FILE-LIMITS ARE} \end{matrix} \right\}$ $\left\{ \begin{matrix} \text{data-name-1} \\ \text{literal-1} \end{matrix} \right\}$ THRU $\left\{ \begin{matrix} \text{data-name-2} \\ \text{literal-2} \end{matrix} \right\}$

     [$\left\{ \begin{matrix} \text{data-name-3} \\ \text{literal-3} \end{matrix} \right\}$ THRU $\left\{ \begin{matrix} \text{data-name-4} \\ \text{literal-4} \end{matrix} \right\}$] . . .

   ACCESS MODE IS $\left\{ \begin{matrix} \text{SEQUENTIAL} \\ \text{RANDOM} \end{matrix} \right\}$

   PROCESSING MODE IS SEQUENTIAL

   ACTUAL KEY IS *data-name*

   NOMINAL KEY IS *data-name*

   RECORD KEY IS *data-name*

   TRACK-AREA IS *integer* CHARACTERS.} . . .

I-O-CONTROL.

   RERUN ON *system-name* EVERY *integer* RECORDS OF *file-name*

   SAME [RECORD] AREA FOR *file-name-1* {*file-name-2*} . . .

   MULTIPLE FILE TAPE CONTAINS *file-name-1* [POSITION *integer-1*]

        [*file-name-2* [POSITION *integer-2*]] . . .

   APPLY WRITE-ONLY ON *file-name-1* [*file-name-2*] . . .

   APPLY EXTENDED-SEARCH ON *file-name-1* [*file-name-2*] . . .

   APPLY WRITE-VERIFY ON *file-name-1* [*file-name-2*] . . .

   APPLY CYL-OVERFLOW OF *integer* TRACKS ON *file-name-1* [*file-name-2*] . . .

   APPLY $\left\{ \begin{matrix} \text{MASTER-INDEX} \\ \text{CYL-INDEX} \end{matrix} \right\}$ TO *device-number* ON *file-name-1* [*file-name-2*] . . .

   APPLY CORE-INDEX TO *data-name* ON *file-name-1* [*file-name-2*] . . . .

DATA DIVISION — BASIC FORMATS

DATA DIVISION.

FILE SECTION.

FD *file-name*

BLOCK CONTAINS [*integer-1* TO] *integer-2* $\begin{Bmatrix} \text{CHARACTERS} \\ \text{RECORDS} \end{Bmatrix}$

RECORD CONTAINS [*integer-1* TO] *integer-2* CHARACTERS

RECORDING MODE IS *mode*

LABEL $\begin{Bmatrix} \text{RECORD IS} \\ \text{RECORDS ARE} \end{Bmatrix}$ $\begin{Bmatrix} \text{OMITTED} \\ \text{STANDARD} \\ \text{\textit{data-name-1} [\textit{data-name-2}] ...} \end{Bmatrix}$

VALUE OF *data-name-1* IS $\begin{Bmatrix} \textit{data-name-2} \\ \textit{literal-1} \end{Bmatrix}$ [*data-name-3* IS $\begin{Bmatrix} \textit{data-name-4} \\ \textit{literal-2} \end{Bmatrix}$] ...

DATA $\begin{Bmatrix} \text{RECORD IS} \\ \text{RECORDS ARE} \end{Bmatrix}$ *data-name-1* [*data-name-2*] ... .

01-49 $\begin{Bmatrix} \textit{data-name-1} \\ \text{FILLER} \end{Bmatrix}$

REDEFINES *data-name-2*

BLANK WHEN ZERO

$\begin{Bmatrix} \text{JUSTIFIED} \\ \text{JUST} \end{Bmatrix}$ RIGHT

$\begin{Bmatrix} \text{PICTURE} \\ \text{PIC} \end{Bmatrix}$ IS *character string*

$\begin{Bmatrix} \text{SYNCHRONIZED} \\ \text{SYNC} \end{Bmatrix}$ $\begin{bmatrix} \text{LEFT} \\ \text{RIGHT} \end{bmatrix}$

[USAGE IS] $\begin{Bmatrix} \text{INDEX} \\ \text{DISPLAY} \\ \begin{Bmatrix} \text{COMPUTATIONAL} \\ \text{COMP} \end{Bmatrix} \\ \begin{Bmatrix} \text{COMPUTATIONAL-1} \\ \text{COMP-1} \end{Bmatrix} \\ \begin{Bmatrix} \text{COMPUTATIONAL-2} \\ \text{COMP-2} \end{Bmatrix} \\ \begin{Bmatrix} \text{COMPUTATIONAL-3} \\ \text{COMP-3} \end{Bmatrix} \\ \text{DISPLAY-ST} \end{Bmatrix}$

88 *condition-name* $\begin{Bmatrix} \text{VALUE IS} \\ \text{VALUES ARE} \end{Bmatrix}$ *literal-1* [THRU *literal-2*]

[*literal-3*] [THRU *literal-4*]] ... .

66 *data-name-1* RENAMES *data-name-2* [THRU *data-name-3*] .

NOTE: Formats of the OCCURS Clause are included with **TABLE HANDLING** formats.

WORKING-STORAGE SECTION.

77   *data-name-1*

01-49   {*data-name-1*}
        {FILLER   }

REDEFINES *data-name-2*

BLANK WHEN ZERO

{JUSTIFIED} RIGHT
{JUST   }

{PICTURE} IS *character string*
{PIC   }

{SYNCHRONIZED} [LEFT]
{SYNC   }   [RIGHT]

[USAGE IS] ⎰ INDEX
            ⎱ DISPLAY
              {COMPUTATIONAL}
              {COMP   }
              {COMPUTATIONAL-1}
              {COMP-1   }
              {COMPUTATIONAL-2}
              {COMP-2   }
              {COMPUTATIONAL-3}
              {COMP-3   }
              DISPLAY-ST

VALUE IS *literal*.

88   *condition-name* {VALUE IS } *literal-1* [THRU *literal-2*]
                       {VALUES ARE}

        [*literal-3*] [THRU *literal-4*]] . . . .

66   *data-name-1* RENAMES *data-name-2* [THRU *data-name-3*] .

NOTE: Formats of the OCCURS Clause are included with TABLE HANDLING formats.

LINKAGE SECTION.

77 *data-name-1*

01-49 $\begin{Bmatrix} data\text{-}name\text{-}1 \\ \text{FILLER} \end{Bmatrix}$

REDEFINES *data-name-2*

BLANK WHEN ZERO

$\begin{Bmatrix} \text{JUSTIFIED} \\ \text{JUST} \end{Bmatrix}$ RIGHT

$\begin{Bmatrix} \text{PICTURE} \\ \text{PIC} \end{Bmatrix}$ IS *character string*

$\begin{Bmatrix} \text{SYNCHRONIZED} \\ \text{SYNC} \end{Bmatrix}$ $\begin{bmatrix} \text{LEFT} \\ \text{RIGHT} \end{bmatrix}$

[USAGE IS] $\begin{Bmatrix} \text{INDEX} \\ \text{DISPLAY} \\ \begin{Bmatrix} \text{COMPUTATIONAL} \\ \text{COMP} \end{Bmatrix} \\ \begin{Bmatrix} \text{COMPUTATIONAL-1} \\ \text{COMP-1} \end{Bmatrix} \\ \begin{Bmatrix} \text{COMPUTATIONAL-2} \\ \text{COMP-2} \end{Bmatrix} \\ \begin{Bmatrix} \text{COMPUTATIONAL-3} \\ \text{COMP-3} \end{Bmatrix} \\ \text{DISPLAY-ST} \end{Bmatrix}$

88 *condition-name* $\begin{Bmatrix} \text{VALUE IS} \\ \text{VALUES ARE} \end{Bmatrix}$ *literal-1* [THRU *literal-2*]

        [*literal-3*] [THRU *literal-4*]] . . . .

66 *data-name-1* RENAMES *data-name-2* [THRU *data-name-3*] .

NOTE: Formats of the OCCURS Clause are included with TABLE HANDLING formats.

PROCEDURE DIVISION — BASIC FORMATS

$$\left\{ \begin{array}{l} \underline{\text{PROCEDURE}} \ \underline{\text{DIVISION}}. \\ \underline{\text{PROCEDURE}} \ \underline{\text{DIVISION}} \ \underline{\text{USING}} \ identifier\text{-}1 \ [identifier\text{-}2] \ \ldots \ . \end{array} \right\}$$

ACCEPT Statement

$$\underline{\text{ACCEPT}} \ identifier \ [\underline{\text{FROM}} \ \left\{ \begin{array}{l} \underline{\text{CONSOLE}} \\ mnemonic\text{-}name \end{array} \right\} \ ]$$

ADD Statement

FORMAT 1

$$\underline{\text{ADD}} \ \left\{ \begin{array}{l} identifier\text{-}1 \\ literal\text{-}1 \end{array} \right\} \left[\begin{array}{l} identifier\text{-}2 \\ literal\text{-}2 \end{array} \right] \ldots \underline{\text{TO}} \ identifier\text{-}m \ [\underline{\text{ROUNDED}}]$$

$$[identifier\text{-}n \ [\underline{\text{ROUNDED}}]] \ldots [\text{ON} \ \underline{\text{SIZE}} \ \underline{\text{ERROR}} \ imperative\text{-}statement]$$

FORMAT 2

$$\underline{\text{ADD}} \ \left\{ \begin{array}{l} identifier\text{-}1 \\ literal\text{-}1 \end{array} \right\} \left\{ \begin{array}{l} identifier\text{-}2 \\ literal\text{-}2 \end{array} \right\} \left[\begin{array}{l} identifier\text{-}3 \\ literal\text{-}3 \end{array} \right] \ldots$$

$$\underline{\text{GIVING}} \ identifier\text{-}m \ [\underline{\text{ROUNDED}}] \ [\text{ON} \ \underline{\text{SIZE}} \ \underline{\text{ERROR}} \ imperative\text{-}statement]$$

FORMAT 3

$$\underline{\text{ADD}} \ \left\{ \begin{array}{l} \underline{\text{CORRESPONDING}} \\ \underline{\text{CORR}} \end{array} \right\} \ identifier\text{-}1 \ \underline{\text{TO}} \ identifier\text{-}2 \ [\underline{\text{ROUNDED}}]$$

$$[\text{ON} \ \underline{\text{SIZE}} \ \underline{\text{ERROR}} \ imperative\text{-}statement]$$

ALTER Statement

$$\underline{\text{ALTER}} \ procedure\text{-}name\text{-}1 \ \underline{\text{TO}} \ [\underline{\text{PROCEED}} \ \underline{\text{TO}}] \ procedure\text{-}name\text{-}2$$

$$[procedure\text{-}name\text{-}3 \ \underline{\text{TO}} \ [\underline{\text{PROCEED}} \ \underline{\text{TO}}] \ procedure\text{-}name\text{-}4] \ldots$$

CALL Statement

$$\underline{\text{CALL}} \ literal\text{-}1 \ [\underline{\text{USING}} \ identifier\text{-}1 \ [identifier\text{-}2] \ldots]$$

CLOSE Statement

$$\underline{\text{CLOSE}} \ file\text{-}name\text{-}1 \left[\begin{array}{l} \underline{\text{REEL}} \\ \underline{\text{UNIT}} \end{array} \right] [\text{WITH} \ \left\{ \begin{array}{l} \underline{\text{NO}} \ \underline{\text{REWIND}} \\ \underline{\text{LOCK}} \end{array} \right\} \ ]$$

$$[file\text{-}name\text{-}2 \left[\begin{array}{l} \underline{\text{REEL}} \\ \underline{\text{UNIT}} \end{array} \right] [\text{WITH} \ \left\{ \begin{array}{l} \underline{\text{NO}} \ \underline{\text{REWIND}} \\ \underline{\text{LOCK}} \end{array} \right\} \ ]] \ldots$$

COMPUTE Statement

$$\underline{\text{COMPUTE}} \ identifier\text{-}1 \ [\underline{\text{ROUNDED}}] = \left\{ \begin{array}{l} arithmetic\text{-}expression \\ identifier\text{-}2 \\ literal\text{-}1 \end{array} \right\}$$

$$[\text{ON} \ \underline{\text{SIZE}} \ \underline{\text{ERROR}} \ imperative\text{-}statement]$$

DECLARATIVE Section

PROCEDURE DIVISION.

DECLARATIVES.

{section-name SECTION. USE sentence.

{paragraph-name. {sentence} ...} ...} ...

END DECLARATIVES.

DISPLAY Statement

$$\text{DISPLAY} \begin{Bmatrix} identifier\text{-}1 \\ literal\text{-}1 \end{Bmatrix} \begin{bmatrix} identifier\text{-}2 \\ literal\text{-}2 \end{bmatrix} ... [\underline{\text{UPON}} \begin{Bmatrix} \underline{\text{CONSOLE}} \\ \underline{\text{SYSPCH}} \\ \underline{\text{SYSPUNCH}} \\ mnemonic\text{-}name \end{Bmatrix}]$$

DIVIDE Statement

FORMAT 1

$$\underline{\text{DIVIDE}} \begin{Bmatrix} identifier\text{-}1 \\ literal\text{-}1 \end{Bmatrix} \underline{\text{INTO}} \; identifier\text{-}2 \; [\underline{\text{ROUNDED}}]$$

$$[\text{ON} \; \underline{\text{SIZE}} \; \underline{\text{ERROR}} \; imperative\text{-}statement]$$

FORMAT 2

$$\underline{\text{DIVIDE}} \begin{Bmatrix} identifier\text{-}1 \\ literal\text{-}1 \end{Bmatrix} \begin{Bmatrix} \underline{\text{INTO}} \\ \underline{\text{BY}} \end{Bmatrix} \begin{Bmatrix} identifier\text{-}2 \\ literal\text{-}2 \end{Bmatrix} \underline{\text{GIVING}} \; identifier\text{-}3 \; [\underline{\text{ROUNDED}}]$$

$$[\underline{\text{REMAINDER}} \; identifier\text{-}4] \; [\text{ON} \; \underline{\text{SIZE}} \; \underline{\text{ERROR}} \; imperative\text{-}statement]$$

ENTER Statement

$$\underline{\text{ENTER}} \; language\text{-}name \; [routine\text{-}name].$$

ENTRY Statement

$$\underline{\text{ENTRY}} \; literal \; [\underline{\text{USING}} \; identifier\text{-}1 \; [identifier\text{-}2] \; .. \;]$$

EXAMINE Statement

FORMAT 1

$$\underline{\text{EXAMINE}} \; identifier \; \underline{\text{TALLYING}} \begin{Bmatrix} \underline{\text{UNTIL}} \; \underline{\text{FIRST}} \\ \underline{\text{ALL}} \\ \underline{\text{LEADING}} \end{Bmatrix} literal\text{-}1$$

$$[\underline{\text{REPLACING}} \; \underline{\text{BY}} \; literal\text{-}2]$$

FORMAT 2

$$\underline{\text{EXAMINE}} \; identifier \; \underline{\text{REPLACING}} \begin{Bmatrix} \underline{\text{ALL}} \\ \underline{\text{LEADING}} \\ \underline{\text{FIRST}} \\ \underline{\text{UNTIL}} \; \underline{\text{FIRST}} \end{Bmatrix} literal\text{-}1 \; \underline{\text{BY}} \; literal\text{-}2$$

EXIT Statement

paragraph-name. EXIT [PROGRAM].

GOBACK Statement

GOBACK.

GO TO Statement

FORMAT 1

<u>GO</u> <u>TO</u> *procedure-name-1*

FORMAT 2

<u>GO</u> <u>TO</u> *procedure-name-1* [*procedure-name-2*] . . . <u>DEPENDING</u> ON *identifier*

FORMAT 3

<u>GO</u> <u>TO</u>.

IF Statement

<u>IF</u> *condition* THEN $\begin{Bmatrix} \underline{NEXT}\ \underline{SENTENCE} \\ statement\text{-}1 \end{Bmatrix}$ $\begin{Bmatrix} \underline{OTHERWISE} \\ \underline{ELSE} \end{Bmatrix}$ $\begin{Bmatrix} \underline{NEXT}\ \underline{SENTENCE} \\ statement\text{-}2 \end{Bmatrix}$

MOVE Statement

FORMAT 1

<u>MOVE</u> $\begin{Bmatrix} identifier\text{-}1 \\ literal \end{Bmatrix}$ <u>TO</u> *identifier-2* [*identifier-3*] . . .

FORMAT 2

<u>MOVE</u> $\begin{Bmatrix} \underline{CORRESPONDING} \\ \underline{CORR} \end{Bmatrix}$ *identifier-1* <u>TO</u> *identifier-2*

MULTIPLY Statement

FORMAT 1

<u>MULTIPLY</u> $\begin{Bmatrix} identifier\text{-}1 \\ literal\text{-}1 \end{Bmatrix}$ <u>BY</u> *identifier-2* [<u>ROUNDED</u>]

[ON <u>SIZE</u> <u>ERROR</u> *imperative-statement*]

FORMAT 2

<u>MULTIPLY</u> $\begin{Bmatrix} identifier\text{-}1 \\ literal\text{-}1 \end{Bmatrix}$ <u>BY</u> $\begin{Bmatrix} identifier\text{-}2 \\ literal\text{-}2 \end{Bmatrix}$ <u>GIVING</u> *identifier-3*

[<u>ROUNDED</u>] [ON <u>SIZE</u> <u>ERROR</u> *imperative-statement*]

NOTE Statement

<u>NOTE</u> *character string*

OPEN Statement

<u>OPEN</u> [<u>INPUT</u> {*file-name* $\begin{bmatrix} \underline{REVERSED} \\ WITH\ \underline{NO}\ \underline{REWIND} \end{bmatrix}$ } . . .]

[<u>OUTPUT</u> {*file-name* [WITH <u>NO</u> <u>REWIND</u>]} . . .]

[<u>I-O</u> {*file-name*} . . .]

PERFORM Statement

FORMAT 1

PERFORM procedure-name-1 [THRU procedure-name-2]

FORMAT 2

PERFORM procedure-name-1 [THRU procedure-name-2] $\left\{\begin{array}{l} identifier\text{-}1 \\ integer\text{-}1 \end{array}\right\}$ TIMES

FORMAT 3

PERFORM procedure-name-1 [THRU procedure-name-2] UNTIL condition-1

FORMAT 4

PERFORM procedure-name-1 [THRU procedure-name-2]

VARYING $\left\{\begin{array}{l} index\text{-}name\text{-}1 \\ identifier\text{-}1 \end{array}\right\}$ FROM $\left\{\begin{array}{l} index\text{-}name\text{-}2 \\ literal\text{-}2 \\ identifier\text{-}2 \end{array}\right\}$ BY

$\left\{\begin{array}{l} literal\text{-}3 \\ identifier\text{-}3 \end{array}\right\}$ UNTIL condition-1

[AFTER $\left\{\begin{array}{l} index\text{-}name\text{-}4 \\ identifier\text{-}4 \end{array}\right\}$ FROM $\left\{\begin{array}{l} index\text{-}name\text{-}5 \\ literal\text{-}5 \\ identifier\text{-}5 \end{array}\right\}$ BY

$\left\{\begin{array}{l} literal\text{-}6 \\ identifier\text{-}6 \end{array}\right\}$ UNTIL condition-2

[AFTER $\left\{\begin{array}{l} index\text{-}name\text{-}7 \\ identifier\text{-}7 \end{array}\right\}$ FROM $\left\{\begin{array}{l} index\text{-}name\text{-}8 \\ literal\text{-}8 \\ identifier\text{-}8 \end{array}\right\}$ BY -

$\left\{\begin{array}{l} literal\text{-}9 \\ identifier\text{-}9 \end{array}\right\}$ UNTIL condition-3]]

READ Statement

READ file-name RECORD [INTO identifier] $\left\{\begin{array}{l} \text{AT END} \\ \text{INVALID KEY} \end{array}\right\}$ imperative-statement

REWRITE Statement

REWRITE record-name [FROM identifier] INVALID KEY imperative-statement

SEEK Statement

SEEK file-name RECORD

START Statement

    <u>START</u> *file-name* <u>INVALID</u> KEY *imperative-statement*

STOP Statement

    <u>STOP</u> $\left\{ \begin{array}{l} \underline{RUN} \\ literal \end{array} \right\}$

SUBTRACT Statement

FORMAT 1

    <u>SUBTRACT</u> $\left\{ \begin{array}{l} identifier\text{-}1 \\ literal\text{-}1 \end{array} \right\}$ $\left[\begin{array}{l} identifier\text{-}2 \\ literal\text{-}2 \end{array} \right]$ . . . <u>FROM</u> *identifier-m* [<u>ROUNDED</u>]

        [*identifier-n* [<u>ROUNDED</u>]] . . . [ON <u>SIZE</u> <u>ERROR</u> *imperative-statement*]

FORMAT 2

    <u>SUBTRACT</u> $\left\{ \begin{array}{l} identifier\text{-}1 \\ literal\text{-}1 \end{array} \right\}$ $\left[\begin{array}{l} identifier\text{-}2 \\ literal\text{-}2 \end{array} \right]$ . . . <u>FROM</u> $\left\{ \begin{array}{l} identifier\text{-}m \\ literal\text{-}m \end{array} \right\}$ <u>GIVING</u>

        identifier-n [<u>ROUNDED</u>] [ON <u>SIZE</u> <u>ERROR</u> *imperative-statement*]

FORMAT 3

    <u>SUBTRACT</u> $\left\{ \begin{array}{l} \underline{CORRESPONDING} \\ \underline{CORR} \end{array} \right\}$ *identifier-1* <u>FROM</u> *identifier-2* [<u>ROUNDED</u>]

        [ON <u>SIZE</u> <u>ERROR</u> *imperative-statement*]

TRANSFORM Statement

    <u>TRANSFORM</u> *identifier-3* CHARACTERS <u>FROM</u> $\left\{ \begin{array}{l} figurative\text{-}constant\text{-}1 \\ nonnumeric\text{-}literal\text{-}1 \\ identifier\text{-}1 \end{array} \right\}$

        <u>TO</u> $\left\{ \begin{array}{l} figurative\text{-}constant\text{-}2 \\ nonnumeric\text{-}literal\text{-}2 \\ identifier\text{-}2 \end{array} \right\}$

USE Sentence

FORMAT 1

Option 1:

USE $\begin{Bmatrix} \underline{BEFORE} \\ \underline{AFTER} \end{Bmatrix}$ STANDARD [BEGINNING] $\begin{bmatrix} REEL \\ FILE \\ UNIT \end{bmatrix}$

$\qquad$ LABEL PROCEDURE ON $\begin{Bmatrix} \{file\text{-}name\} \ldots \\ \underline{OUTPUT} \\ \underline{INPUT} \\ \underline{I\text{-}O} \end{Bmatrix}$

Option 2:

USE $\begin{Bmatrix} \underline{BEFORE} \\ \underline{AFTER} \end{Bmatrix}$ STANDARD [ENDING] $\begin{bmatrix} REEL \\ FILE \\ UNIT \end{bmatrix}$

$\qquad$ LABEL PROCEDURE ON $\begin{Bmatrix} \{file\text{-}name\} \ldots \\ \underline{OUTPUT} \\ \underline{INPUT} \\ \underline{I\text{-}O} \end{Bmatrix}$.

FORMAT 2

USE AFTER STANDARD ERROR PROCEDURE

$\qquad$ ON $\begin{Bmatrix} \{file\text{-}name\text{-}1\} \\ file\text{-}name\text{-}2 \ \underline{GIVING} \ data\text{-}name\text{-}1 \ [data\text{-}name\text{-}2] \\ \underline{INPUT} \\ \underline{OUTPUT} \\ \underline{I\text{-}O} \end{Bmatrix}$.

WRITE Statement

FORMAT 1

WRITE record-name [FROM identifier-1]

$\qquad \left[\begin{Bmatrix} \underline{BEFORE} \\ \underline{AFTER} \end{Bmatrix} \text{ADVANCING} \begin{Bmatrix} identifier\text{-}2 \text{ LINES} \\ integer \text{ LINES} \\ mnemonic\text{-}name \end{Bmatrix} \right]$

$\qquad \left[\text{AT } \begin{Bmatrix} \underline{END\text{-}OF\text{-}PAGE} \\ \underline{EOP} \end{Bmatrix} imperative\text{-}statement \right]$

FORMAT 2

WRITE record-name [FROM identifier-1]

$\qquad$ AFTER POSITIONING $\begin{Bmatrix} identifier\text{-}2 \\ integer \end{Bmatrix}$ LINES

$\qquad \left[\text{AT } \begin{Bmatrix} \underline{END\text{-}OF\text{-}PAGE} \\ \underline{EOP} \end{Bmatrix} imperative\text{-}statement \right]$

FORMAT 3

WRITE record-name [FROM identifier-1] INVALID KEY imperative-statement

TABLE HANDLING — BASIC FORMATS

Data Division Table Handling Formats

OCCURS Clause

FORMAT 1

OCCURS *integer* TIMES

[INDEXED BY *index-name-1* [*index-name-2*] . . .]

FORMAT 2

OCCURS *integer* TIMES [DEPENDING ON *data-name*]

[INDEXED BY *index-name-1* [*index-name-2*] . . .]

USAGE IS INDEX Clause

[USAGE IS] INDEX

Procedure Division Table Handling Formats

SET Statement

FORMAT 1

$$\text{SET} \left\{ \begin{array}{ll} \textit{index-name-1} & [\textit{index-name-2}] \ldots \\ \textit{identifier-1} & [\textit{identifier-2}\ ] \ldots \end{array} \right\} \text{TO} \left\{ \begin{array}{l} \textit{index-name-3} \\ \textit{identifier-3} \\ \textit{literal-1} \end{array} \right\}$$

FORMAT 2

$$\text{SET } \textit{index-name-4} \ [\textit{index-name-5}] \ldots \left\{ \begin{array}{l} \underline{\text{UP BY}} \\ \underline{\text{DOWN}} \ \underline{\text{BY}} \end{array} \right\} \left\{ \begin{array}{l} \textit{identifier-4} \\ \textit{literal-2} \end{array} \right\}$$

SEGMENTATION — BASIC FORMATS

Priority Numbers in Procedure Division

section-name SECTION [*priority-number*].

SOURCE PROGRAM LIBRARY FACILITY

COPY Statement

COPY *library name* [SUPPRESS].

DEBUGGING LANGUAGE — BASIC FORMATS

Procedure Division Debugging Formats

EXHIBIT Statement

$$\underline{\text{EXHIBIT}} \left\{ \begin{array}{l} \underline{\text{NAMED}} \\ \underline{\text{CHANGED}} \ \underline{\text{NAMED}} \\ \underline{\text{CHANGED}} \end{array} \right\} \left\{ \begin{array}{l} \textit{identifier-1} \\ \textit{nonnumeric-literal-1} \end{array} \right\} \left[\begin{array}{l} \textit{identifier-2} \\ \textit{nonnumeric-literal-2} \end{array} \right] \cdots$$

ON (Count-conditional) Statement

$$\underline{\text{ON}} \ \textit{integer-1} \ [\underline{\text{AND}} \ \underline{\text{EVERY}} \ \textit{integer-2}] \ [\underline{\text{UNTIL}} \ \textit{integer-3}]$$

$$\left\{ \begin{array}{l} \textit{imperative-statement} \ldots \\ \underline{\text{NEXT}} \ \underline{\text{SENTENCE}} \end{array} \right\} \left\{ \begin{array}{l} \underline{\text{ELSE}} \\ \underline{\text{OTHERWISE}} \end{array} \right\} \left\{ \begin{array}{l} \textit{statement} \ldots \\ \underline{\text{NEXT}} \ \underline{\text{SENTENCE}} \end{array} \right\}$$

READY/RESET TRACE Statement

$$\left\{ \begin{array}{l} \underline{\text{READY}} \\ \underline{\text{RESET}} \end{array} \right\} \ \underline{\text{TRACE}}$$

Compile-Time Debugging Packet

DEBUG Card

$$\underline{\text{DEBUG}} \qquad \textit{location}$$

FORMAT CONTROL — BASIC FORMATS

EJECT Statement

1	Area B
	EJECT

SKIP1, SKIP2, SKIP3 Statements

1	Area B
	$\left\{ \begin{array}{l} \underline{\text{SKIP1}} \\ \underline{\text{SKIP2}} \\ \underline{\text{SKIP3}} \end{array} \right\}$

COBOL REFERENCE SUMMARY

CHARACTER SET

The complete COBOL character set consists of the following 51 characters:

Digits 0 through 9
Letters A through Z
Special characters:
  Blank or space
  + Plus sign
  - Minus sign or hyphen
  * Check protection symbol, asterisk
  / Slash
  = Equal sign
  > Inequality sign (greater than)
  < Inequality sign (less than)
  $ Dollar sign
  , Comma
  . Period or decimal point
  ' Quotation mark
  (Left parenthesis
) Right parenthesis
  ; Semicolon

Of the previous set, the following characters are used for words:

0 through 9
A through Z
- (hyphen)

The following characters are used for punctuation:

  ' Quotation mark
  (Left parenthesis
) Right parenthesis
  , Comma
  . Period
  ; Semicolon

The following characters are used in arithmetic expressions:

  + Addition
  - Subtraction
  * Multiplication
  / Division
  ** Exponentiation

The following characters are used in relation tests:

  > Greater than
  < Less than
  = Equal to

All of the preceding characters are contained in the COBOL character set. In addition, the programmer can use, as characters in non-numeric literals, any characters (except the quotation mark) included in the IBM Extended Binary-Coded-Decimal Interchange Code; however, such characters may be unacceptable to COBOL for other computers.

WORD FORMATION

A word is composed of a combination of not more than 30 characters, chosen from the following set of 37 characters:

0 through 9 (digits)
A through Z (letters)
- (hyphen)

A word must not begin or end with a hyphen. A word is ended by a space, or by proper punctuation. Embedded hyphens are permitted. All words in COBOL are either reserved words, which have preassigned meanings in COBOL, or programmer-supplied names. Each type of name is discussed in the section of this publication in which it is first mentioned.

TYPES OF NAMES

There are three types of <u>names</u> used in a COBOL program:

1. A <u>data-name</u> is a word that contains at least one alphabetic character and identifies a data item in the Data Division. The following are formed according to the rules for data-names:

   > file-names
   > sort-file-description-names
   > record-names
   > report-names

2. A <u>condition-name</u> is a name given to a specific value, set of values, or range of values, within the complete set of values that a particular data item may assume. The data item itself is called a conditional variable. The condition-name must contain at least one alphabetic character (see "Data Division" and the discussion of "Special-Names" in "Environment Division").

3. A <u>procedure-name</u> is either a paragraph-name or a section-name. A procedure-name may be composed solely of numeric characters. Two numeric procedure-names are equivalent if, and only if, they are composed of the same number of digits and have the same value (see "Procedure Division"). The following are formed according to the rules for procedure-names:

   > library-names
   > program-names

QUALIFICATION OF NAMES

Every name used in a COBOL source program must be unique within the source program, either because no other name has the identical spelling, or because the name exists within a hierarchy of names (so that the name can be made unique by mentioning one or more of the higher levels of the hierarchy). The higher levels are called qualifiers when used in this way, and the process is called qualification.

The following rules apply to the qualification of names:

1. The word OF or IN must precede each qualifying name, and the names must appear in ascending order of hierarchy.
2. A qualifier must be of a higher level and within the same hierarchy as the name it is qualifying.
3. The same name must not appear at two levels in a hierarchy in such a manner that it would appear to qualify itself.
4. The highest level qualifier must be unique. Each qualifying name must be unique at its own level within the hierarchy of the immediately higher qualifier.
5. Qualification when not needed is permitted.
6. Qualifiers must not be subscripted, although the entire qualified name may be subscripted.
7. The total number of characters x cannot exceed 300 where:
   $x = T + 4N$
   T is the number of characters in all names, and
   N is the number of data names, including their qualifiers.
8. Regardless of qualification, procedure names and data names must not be the same.

COBOL RESERVED WORDS

The following is a list of reserved words. It should be noted that all of the words in the list are not reserved words for all COBOL compilers. It is the best policy, however, to not use any of the words in the list as data-names or procedure-names. This will eliminate any possibility of using reserved words on any COBOL compiler.

ACCEPT
ACCESS
ACTUAL
ADD
ADDRESS
ADVANCING
AFTER
ALL
ALPHABETIC
ALTER
ALTERNATE
AND
APPLY
ARE
AREA
AREAS
ASCENDING
ASSIGN
AT
AUTHOR

BASIS
BEFORE
BEGINNING
BLANK
BLOCK
BY

CALL
CANCEL
CF
CH
CHANGED
CHARACTERS
CLOCK-UNITS
CLOSE
COBOL
CODE
COLUMN
COM-REG
COMMA
COMP
COMP-1
COMP-2
COMP-3
COMPUTATIONAL
COMPUTATIONAL-1
COMPUTATIONAL-2
COMPUTATIONAL-3
COMPUTE
CONFIGURATION
CONSOLE
CONSTANT
CONTAINS
CONTROL
CONTROLS
COPY
CORE-INDEX
CORR
CORRESPONDING
CSP
CURRENCY
CURRENT-DATE
CYL-INDEX
CYL-OVERFLOW
C01
C02
C03
C04

C05
C06
C07
C08
C09
C10
C11
C12

DATA
DATE-COMPILED
DATE-WRITTEN
DE
DEBUG
DECIMAL-POINT
DECLARATIVES
DELETE
DEPENDING
DESCENDING
DETAIL
DISP
DISPLAY
DISPLAY-ST
DISPLAY-n
DIVIDE
DIVISION
DOWN

EJECT
ELSE
END
END-OF-PAGE
ENDING
ENTER
ENTRY
ENVIRONMENT
EOP
EQUAL
EQUALS
ERROR
EVERY
EXAMINE
EXCEEDS
EXHIBIT
EXIT
EXTENDED-SEARCH

FD
FILE
FILE-CONTROL
FILE-LIMIT
FILE-LIMITS
FILLER
FINAL
FIRST
FOOTING
FOR
FROM

GENERATE
GIVING
GO
GOBACK
GREATER
GROUP

HEADING
HIGH-VALUE
HIGH-VALUES
HOLD

I-O
I-O-CONTROL
ID
IDENTIFICATION
IF
IN
INDEX
INDEX-n
INDEXED
INDICATE
INITIATE
INPUT
INPUT-OUTPUT
INSERT
INSTALLATION
INTO
INVALID
IS

JUST
JUSTIFIED

KEY
KEYS

LABEL
LABEL-RETURN
LAST
LEADING
LEAVE
LEFT
LESS
LIBRARY
LIMIT
LIMITS
LINAGE
LINAGE-COUNTER
LINE
LINE-COUNTER
LINES
LINKAGE
LOCK
LOW-VALUE
LOW-VALUES
LOWER-BOUND
LOWER-BOUNDS

MASTER-INDEX
MEMORY
MODE
MODULES
MORE-LABELS
MOVE
MULTIPLE
MULTIPLY

NAMED
NEGATIVE
NEXT
NO
NOMINAL
NOT
NOTE
NSTD-REELS
NUMBER
NUMERIC
OBJECT-COMPUTER
OBJECT-PROGRAM
OCCURS
OF

OFF
OH
OMITTED
ON
OPEN
OPTIONAL
OR
OTHERWISE
OUTPUT
OV
OVERFLOW

PAGE
PAGE-COUNTER
PERFORM
PF
PH
PIC
PICTURE
PLUS
POSITION
POSITIONING
POSITIVE
PREPARED
PRINT-SWITCH
PRIORITY
PROCEDURE
PROCEED
PROCESS
PROCESSING
PROGRAM
PROGRAM-ID

QUOTE
QUOTES

RANDOM
RANCE
RD
READ
READY
RECORD
RECORD-OVERFLOW
RECORDING
RECORDS
REDEFINES
REEL
RELEASE
REMAINDER
REMARKS
RENAMES
REORG-CRITERIA
REPLACING
REPORT
REPORTING
REPORTS
REREAD
RERUN
RESERVE
RESET
RETURN
RETURN-CODE
REVERSED
REWIND
REWRITE
RF
RH
RIGHT
ROUNDED
RUN

SA
SAME
SD
SEARCH
SECTION
SECURITY
SEEK
SEGMENT-LIMIT
SELECT
SELECTED
SENTENCE
SEQUENTIAL
SET
SIGN
SIZE
SKIP1
SKIP2
SKIP3
SORT
SORT-CORE-SIZE
SORT-FILE-SIZE
SORT-MODE-SIZE
SORT-RETURN
SOURCE
SOURCE-COMPUTER
SPACE
SPACES
SPECIAL-NAMES
STANDARD
START
STATUS
STOP
SUBTRACT
SUM
SUPERVISOR
SUPPRESS
SUSPEND
SYNC
SYNCHRONIZED
SYSIN
SYSIPT
SYSLST
SYSOUT
SYSPCH
SYSPUNCH
S01
S02

TALLY
TALLYING
TAPE
TERMINATE
THAN
THEN
THROUGH
THRU
TIME-OF-DAY
TIMES
TO
TOTALED
TOTALING
TRACE
TRACK
TRACK-AREA
TRACK-LIMIT
TRACKS
TRANSFORM
TYPE

UNEQUAL
UNIT
UNTIL
UP
UPON
UPPER-BOUND
UPPER-BOUNDS
UPSI-0
UPSI-1
UPSI-2
UPSI-3
UPSI-4
UPSI-5
UPSI-6
UPSI-7
USAGE
USE
USING

VALUE
VALUES
VARYING

WHEN
WITH
WORDS
WORKING-STORAGE
WRITE
WRITE-ONLY
WRITE-VERIFY

ZERO
ZEROES
ZEROS

LITERALS

A literal is a constant that is not identified by a data-name in a program, but is completely defined by its own identity. A literal is either non-numeric (alphabetic or alphanumeric), numeric, or floating-point.

Non-Numeric Literals

A non-numeric literal must be bounded by quotation marks and may consist of any combination of characters in the IBM EBCDIC set, except quotation marks. All spaces enclosed by the quotation marks are included as part of the literal. A non-numeric literal may not exceed 120 characters in length.

The following are examples of non-numeric literals:

'EXAMINE CLOCK NUMBER'
'12565'
'PAGE 144 MISSING'

Numeric Literals

A numeric literal must contain at least one and not more than 18 digits. A numeric literal may consist of the characters 0 through 9, the plus sign or the minus sign, and the decimal point. It may contain only one sign character and only one decimal point. The sign, if present, must appear as the leftmost character in the numeric literal. If a numeric literal is unsigned, it is assumed to be positive.

A decimal point may appear anywhere within the numeric literal, except as the rightmost character. If a numeric literal does not contain a decimal point, it is considered to be a whole number.

The following are examples of numeric literals:

            1506798
            +12572.6
            -256.75
            .16

FIGURATIVE CONSTANTS

Figurative constants are a special type of literal. They are values that have been assigned fixed data-names. Figurative constants must not be bounded by quotation marks.

ZERO may be used in many places in a program as a numeric literal. It may not, however, be used in an arithmetic statement. The use of ZERO as a non-numeric literal is permitted. All other figurative constants are considered non-numeric. The singular and plural forms of figurative constants are equivalent and may be used interchangeably.

ZERO ZEROS ZEROES	Represents one or more zeros.
SPACE SPACES	Represents one or more blanks or spaces.
HIGH-VALUE HIGH-VALUES	Represents one or more appearances of the highest value in the computer's collating sequence. (Hexadecimal 'FF')
LOW-VALUE LOW-VALUES	Represents one or more appearances of the lowest value in the computer's collating sequence. (Hexadecimal '00')
ALL 'character'	Represents one or more occurrences of the single character bounded by quotation marks. Character may not be a quotation mark.
QUOTE QUOTES	Represents the character '. Note that the use of the word QUOTE to represent the character ' at object time is not equivalent to the use of the symbol ' to bound a non-numeric literal.

When a figurative constant is used in such a way that the exact number of characters required cannot be determined, only one character is generated. For example, the statement DISPLAY ZEROES would produce one zero character since, in this case, the length of the sequence of zeros to be displayed cannot be determined.

COBOL PROGRAM SHEET

The purpose of the program sheet is to provide a standard way of writing COBOL source programs.

The Identification, Environment, Data, and Procedure Divisions which constitute a COBOL source program are written in the stated order. This program sheet, despite its necessary restrictions, is of a relatively free form. The programmer should note, however, that the rules for using it are precise and must be followed exactly. These rules take precedence over any other rules, with respect to spacing.

COBOL Program Sheet

System			Punching Instructions									Sheet of
Program			Graphic							Card	*	Identification
Programmer		Date	Punch							Form #		73 80

Sequence (PAGE) (SERIAL)	CONT.	A	B	COBOL Statement

SEQUENCE NUMBER: (COLUMNS 1-6)

The sequence number must consist only of digits; letters and special characters should not be used. The sequence number has no effect on the source program and need not be written. If the programmer supplies sequence numbers in each program card, the compiler will check the source program cards and will indicate any errors in their sequence. If these columns are blank, no sequence error will be indicated.

CONTINUATION INDICATOR: (COLUMN 7)

When a non-numeric literal is of a length such that it cannot be contained on one line of a coding sheet, the following rules apply:

1. On every line containing a portion of a literal to be continued, the portion of the literal that is to be continued must not be terminated with a quotation mark.
2. On every line containing a portion of a literal being continued, the portion of the literal being continued must be immediately preceded by a quotation mark. This quotation mark may appear anywhere in Margin B, and may not be preceded by anything but spaces.
3. A hyphen must be punched in column 7 of each line in which the literal is being continued.

SOURCE PROGRAM STATEMENTS: (COLUMNS 8-72)

These columns are used for writing the COBOL source program.

PROGRAM IDENTIFICATION CODE: (COLUMNS 73-80)

These columns can be used to identify the program. Any character from the COBOL character set may be used, including the blank. The program identification code has no effect on the object program or the compiler.

MARGIN RESTRICTIONS

AREA A AND AREA B

Area A, columns 8 through 11, is reserved for the beginning of
division headers, section-names, paragraph-names, level indicators, and
certain level numbers. Area B occupies columns 12 through 72.

The division header must be the first line in a division. The
division header starts in Area A with the division-name, followed by a
space and the word DIVISION, and a period.

The name of a section starts in Area A of any line following the
division header. The section-name is followed by a space, the word
SECTION, and a period. If program segmentation is desired, a space and
a priority number may follow the word SECTION. No other text may appear
on the same line as the section-header, except USE and COPY sentences.

The name of a paragraph starts in Area A of any line following the
division header. It is followed by a period followed by a space.

A paragraph consists of one or more successive sentences. The first
sentence in a paragraph begins anywhere in Area B of either the same
line as paragraph-name or the immediately following line. Each
successive line in the paragraph starts anywhere in Area B.

PUNCTUATION

The following general rules of punctuation apply in writing COBOL
source programs:

1. When any punctuation mark is indicated in a format in this
    publication, it is required.
2. A period, semicolon or comma, when used, must not be preceded by a
    space, but must be followed by a space.
3. A left parenthesis must not be followed immediately by a space; a
    right parenthesis must not be preceded immediately by a space.
4. At least one space must appear between two successive words and/or
    parenthetical expressions and/or literals. Two or more successive
    spaces are treated as a single space, except in non-numeric
    literals.
5. When an arithmetic operator or an equal sign is used, it must be
    preceded by a space and followed by another space.
6. When the period or comma, or arithmetic operator characters are
    used in the PICTURE clause as editing characters, they are governed
    by rules for report items only.
7. A comma may be used as a separator between successive operands of a
    statement. A comma or semicolon may be used to separate a series
    of clauses , and a semicolon or the word THEN may be used to
    separate a series of statements.

TYPES OF DATA ITEMS

Several types of data items can be described in a COBOL source program. These data items are described in the following text. The format
of the Record Description entry used to describe each of these items
appears under the discussion of Record Description entries.

Alphabetic Item

An alphabetic item may contain any combination of the characters A
through Z and space. Each alphabetic character is stored in a separate
byte.

Alphanumeric Item

An alphanumeric item consists of any combination of characters in the
IBM EBCDIC set. Each alphanumeric character is stored in a separate
byte.

Report Item

A report item is an alphanumeric item containing only digits and/or
special editing characters. It must not exceed 127 characters in
length. A report item can be used only as a receiving field for numeric
data. Each report character is stored in a separate byte (see PICTURE
and BLANK WHEN ZERO clauses), except P and V which occupy no storage,
and CR and DB which occupy two bytes each.

Elementary Items

An elementary item is a data item containing no subordinate items.
For example, an 03 level data item followed immediately by another 03
item is an elementary item. Elementary items always have the picture
clause specified.

Group Items

A group item is defined as a field having further subdivisions, so
that it contains one or more elementary items. In addition, a group
item may contain other groups. An item is a group item if, and only if,
its level number is less than the level number of the immediately succeeding item, unless the succeeding level is 88. If an item is not a
group item, then it is an elementary item, or, in the case of level 88,
it is a condition-name.

The maximum length for any elementary or group item in a tape system
is 4092 bytes. For a disk file, maximum length depends upon the particular disk model; 3625, 4096, and 2000 bytes for the IBM 2311, 2314,
and 2321 direct-access devices respectively. An exception to these
stated lengths is the use of a fixed-length Working-Storage group item,
which may be as long as 32,767 bytes. If an IBM 2314 direct-access
device is available, it should be used since it offers the advantage of
longer track records.

Group items never have a picture associated with them.

Fixed-Point Items

Fixed-point items may be defined as external decimal, internal decimal, or binary. External decimal corresponds to the form in which information is represented initially for card input, or finally for printed or punched output. Such items may be converted (by moving) to the internal machine formats described as internal decimal or binary. Except when an item is a single digit in length, these formats require less storage than the external decimal format and can be used to save space on volumes. The binary mode of representation is particularly efficient for data-names used as subscripts. Computational results are the same, regardless of the particular format selected provided the intermediate computational results do not require more than 18 digit positions.

EXTERNAL DECIMAL ITEM: Decimal numbers in the System/360 zoned format are external decimal items.Each digit of a number is represented by a single byte, with the four low-order bits of each eight-bit byte containing the value of a digit. The four high-order bits of each byte are zone bits; the zone bits of the low-order byte represent the sign of the item. The maximum length of an external decimal item is 18 digits. For items whose PICTURE does not contain an S, the sign position is occupied by a bit configuration interpreted as positive but which does not represent an overpunch.

INTERNAL DECIMAL ITEM: An internal decimal item consists of numeric characters 0 through 9 plus a sign, and represents a value not exceeding 18 digits in length. It appears in storage as "packed" decimal. One byte contains two digits with the low-order byte containing the low-order digit followed by the sign of the item. For items whose PICTURE does not contain an S, the sign position is occupied by a bit configuration interpreted as positive but which does not represent an overpunch.

BINARY ITEM: A binary item may be considered decimally as consisting of numeric characters 0 through 9 plus a sign. It occupies two bytes (a half-word), four bytes (a full-word), or eight bytes (two words), corresponding to specified decimal lengths of 1 to 4 digits, 5 to 9 digits, and 10 to 18 digits, respectively. The leftmost bit of the reserved area is the operational sign.

If the item is used as a resultant data name in an arithmetic statement, and no ON SIZE ERROR option is specified, the area may be set to a number greater than that specified in the PICTURE clause.

If the item is used as an operand, it is assumed that the area contains a number less than or equal to that specified in the PICTURE clause.

An Example of binary represented decimal:

If the number is +1234 and,

Picture and Usage Are:	Machine Representation Is:
PICTURE S9999 COMPUTATIONAL.	|0 000|0100|1101|0010| S BYTE

S=Sign   a "1" in position S means number is negative.

                a "0" in position S means number is positive.

PROCEDURE DIVISION

The Procedure Division of a source program specifies those procedures needed to solve a given problem. These steps (computations, logical decisions, input/output, etc.) are expressed in meaningful statements, similar to English, which employ the concept of verbs to denote actions, statements and sentences to describe procedures. The Procedure Division must begin in Area A with the header PROCEDURE DIVISION followed by a period.

The discussion that follows describes the units of expression that constitute the Procedure Division and the way in which they may be combined.

Its constituent parts, in order of hierarchy, are:

- Section

- Paragraph

- Sentence

- Expression

- Statement

SECTIONS

> A section is composed of one or more successive paragraphs and must begin with a section-header beginning in Margin A. A section-header consists of a unique section-name conforming to the rules for procedure-name formation, followed by the word SECTION and a period. A section header must appear on a line by itself, except in the Declaratives portion of the Procedure Division, where it may only be followed immediately by a USE sentence or an INCLUDE statement. The INCLUDE statement is discussed in Section 7. A section-name need not immediately follow the words PROCEDURE DIVISION or END DECLARATIVES. A section ends at the next section-name or at the end of the Procedure Division, or, in the case of Declaratives, at the next section-name or at END DECLARATIVES.

PARAGRAPHS

> A paragraph is a logical entity consisting of one or more sentences. Each paragraph must begin with a paragraph-name starting in Margin A.
>
> A paragraph-name must not be duplicated within the same section. When used as operands in Procedure Division statements, non-unique paragraph-names may be uniquely qualified by writing IN or OF after the paragraph-name, followed by the name of the section in which the paragraph is contained. A paragraph ends at the next paragraph-name or section-name, or at the end of the Procedure Division. In the case of Declaratives, a paragraph ends at the next paragraph-name, section-name, or at END DECLARATIVES.

SENTENCES

A sentence is a single statement or a series of statements terminated by a period and followed by a space. A single comma or semicolon or the word THEN may be used as a separator between statements. A sentence must be contained within Margin B.

EXPRESSIONS

An expression may be defined as a meaningful combination of names, literals, COBOL words, and/or operators which may be reduced to a single value. This definition will become clear after the reader has studied the two types of expressions employed in COBOL, the "arithmetic" expression and the "conditional" expression.

STATEMENTS

A statement consists of a COBOL verb or the word IF or ON, followed by any appropriate operands (data-names, file-names, or literals) and other COBOL words that are necessary for the completion of the statement. The three types of statements are: compiler-directing, imperative, and conditional.

Types of Statements

COMPILER-DIRECTING STATEMENT: A compiler-directing statement directs the compiler to take certain actions at compilation time. A compiler-statement contains one of the compiler-directing verbs and its operands. Compiler-directing statements (except for NOTE, COPY, and INCLUDE) must appear as separate single sentences.

IMPERATIVE STATEMENT: An imperative statement specifies an unconditional action to be taken by the object program. An imperative statement consists of a COBOL verb and its operands, excluding the Compiler-Directing verbs and the conditional statements. An imperative statement may also consist of a series of imperative statements.

CONDITIONAL STATEMENT: A conditional statement is a statement containing a condition that is tested to determine which of alternate paths of program flow to take.

ARITHMETIC STATEMENTS AND OPTIONS

The following rules apply to the arithmetic statements:

1. All data-names used in arithmetic statements must represent elementary numeric data items that are defined in the Data Division of the program, except when they are the operands of the GIVING option.
    Operands of the GIVING option can be either elementary numeric or report.
2. The maximum size of any data-name or literal is 18 decimal digits.
3. Intermediate result fields generated for the evaluation of fixed-point arithmetic expressions assure the accuracy of the result field, except where high order truncation is necessary.
4. Decimal point alignment is supplied automatically throughout computations.

The ROUNDED and SIZE ERROR options apply to all the arithmetic statements. The GIVING option applies to all arithmetic statements but COMPUTE.

GIVING Option: If the GIVING option is written, the value of the data-name that follows the word GIVING will be made equal to the calculated result of the arithmetic operation. The data-name that follows GIVING is not used in the computation and may contain editing symbols.

If the GIVING option is not written, the operand following the words TO, FROM, BY, and INTO in the ADD, SUBTRACT, MULTIPLY, and DIVIDE statements, respectively, must be a data-name. This data-name is used in the computation and is made equal to the result.

ROUNDED Option: If, after decimal-point alignment, the number of places in the calculated result are greater than the number of places associated with the data-name whose value is to be set equal to the calculated result, truncation occurs unless the ROUNDED option has been specified.

When the ROUNDED option is specified, the least significant digit of the resultant data-name has its value increased by 1 whenever the most significant digit of the excess is greater than or equal to 5.

Rounding of a computed negative result is performed by rounding the absolute value of the computed result and then making the final result negative (unless the final result is zero).

SIZE ERROR Option: Whenever the number of integral places in the calculated result exceeds the number of integral places specified for the resultant data-name, a size error condition arises.

If the SIZE ERROR option has been specified and a size error condition arises, the value of the resultant data-name is not altered and the series of imperative statements specified for the condition is executed.

If the SIZE ERROR option has not been specified and a size error condition arises, no assumption should be made about the final result; but the program flow is not interrupted.

It should be noted that the SIZE ERROR option applies only to final calculated results. When a size error occurs in the handling of intermediate results, no assumption should be made about the final result.

An arithmetic statement, if written with a SIZE ERROR option, is not an imperative statement. Rather, it is a conditional statement and is prohibited in contexts where only imperative statements are allowed.

PERMISSIBLE MOVES

Source Field \ Receiving Field	GR	AL	AN	ED	BI	NE	ANE	ID	EF	IF	SN	SR
Group (GR)	Y	Y	Y	Y¹	Y¹	Y¹	Y¹	Y¹	Y¹	Y¹	Y¹	Y¹
Alphabetic (AL)	Y	Y	Y	N	N	N	Y	N	N	N	N	N
Alphanumeric (AN)	Y	Y	Y	Y⁴	Y⁴	Y⁴	Y	Y⁴	Y⁴	Y⁴	Y⁴	Y⁴
External Decimal (ED)	Y¹	N	Y²	Y	Y	Y	Y²	Y	Y	Y	Y	Y
Binary (BI)	Y¹	N	Y²	Y	Y	Y	Y²	Y	Y	Y	Y	Y
Numeric Edited (NE)	Y	N	Y	N	N	N	Y	N	N	N	N	N
Alphanumeric Edited (ANE)	Y	Y	Y	N	N	N	Y	N	N	N	N	N
ZEROS (numeric or alphanumeric)	Y	N	Y	Y³	Y³	Y³	Y	Y³	Y³	Y³	Y³	Y³
SPACES (AL)	Y	Y	Y	N	N	N	Y	N	N	N	N	N
HIGH-VALUE, LOW-VALUE, QUOTES	Y	N	Y	N	N	N	Y	N	N	N	N	N
ALL literal	Y	Y	Y	Y⁵	Y⁵	Y⁵	Y	Y⁵	N	N	N	N
Numeric Literal	Y¹	N	Y²	Y	Y	Y	Y²	Y	Y	Y	Y	Y
Nonnumeric Literal	Y	Y	Y	Y⁵	Y⁵	Y⁵	Y	Y⁵	N	N	N	N
Internal Decimal (ID)	Y¹	N	Y²	Y	Y	Y	Y²	Y	Y	Y	Y	Y
External Floating-point (EF)	Y¹	N	N	Y	Y	Y	N	Y	Y	Y	Y	Y
Internal Floating-point (IF)	Y¹	N	N	Y	Y	Y	N	Y	Y	Y	Y	Y
Sterling Nonreport (SN)	Y¹	N	Y	Y	Y	Y	N	Y	Y	Y	Y	Y
Sterling Report (SR)	Y	N	Y	N	N	N	Y	N	N	N	N	N
Floating-point Literal	Y¹	N	N	Y	Y	Y	N	Y	Y	Y	Y	Y

¹Move without conversion (like AN to AN)
²Only if the decimal point is at the right of the least significant digit
³Numeric move
⁴The alphanumeric field is treated as an ED (integer) field
⁵The literal must consist only of numeric characters and is treated as an ED integer field

PERMISSIBLE COMPARISONS

First Operand \ Second Operand	GR	AL	AN	ANE	NE	FC* NNL	ZR NL	ED	BI	ID	EF	IF	SR	SN	IN	IDI
Group (GR)	NN	NN	NN	NN	NN	NN	NN	NN	NN	NN	NN	NN	NN	NN		
Alphabetic (AL)	NN	NN	NN	NN	NN	NN	NN	NN			NN		NN	NN		
Alphanumeric (AN)	NN	NN	NN	NN	NN	NN	NN	NN			NN		NN	NN		
Alphanumeric Edited (ANE)	NN	NN	NN	NN	NN	NN	NN	NN			NN		NN	NN		
Numeric Edited (NE)	NN	NN	NN	NN	NN	NN	NN	NN			NN		NN	NN		
Figurative Constant (FC)* & Nonnumeric Literal (NNL)	NN	NN	NN	NN	NN			NN			NN		NN	NN		
Fig. Constant ZERO (ZR) & Numeric Literal (NL)	NN	NN	NN	NN	NN			NU	NU	NU	NU	NU	NN	NU	IO[1]	
External Decimal (ED)	NN	NN	NN	NN	NN	NN	NU	NU	NU	NU	NU	NU	NN	NU	IO[1]	
Binary (BI)	NN						NU	NU	NU	NU	NU	NU		NU	IO[1]	
Internal Decimal (ID)	NN						NU	NU	NU	NU	NU	NU		NU	IO[1]	
External Floating Point (EF)	NN	NN	NN	NN	NN	NN	NU	NU	NU	NU	NU	NU	NN	NU		
Internal Floating Point (IF)	NN						NU	NU	NU	NU	NU	NU		NU		
Sterling Report (SR)	NN	NN	NN	NN	NN	NN	NN	NN			NN		NN	NN		
Sterling Nonreport (SN)	NN	NN	NN	NN	NN	NN	NU	NU	NU	NU	NU	NU	NN	NU		
Index Name (IN)							IO[1]	IO[1]	IO[1]	IO[1]					IO	IV
Index Data Item (IDI)															IV	IV

*FC includes all Figurative Constants except ZERO.
[1]Valid only if the numeric item is an integer.

    NN = comparison as described for nonnumeric operands
    NU = comparison as described for numeric operands
    IO = comparison as described for two index-names
    IV = comparison as described for index data items

COMPUTER STORAGE REQUIREMENTS FOR COBOL STATEMENTS

The program listing on the following pages has been compiled to illustrate the computer storage requirements for various statements in the COBOL language. These include the MOVE, IF, ADD, WRITE, READ, OPEN, CLOSE, and PERFORM Statements. This program was compiled on a System/360, Model 30, using the Disk Operating System ANSI COBOL compiler. The following examples illustrate how this information can be used in order to find the typical storage requirements for these statements.

Example 1: A PERFORM Statement is given in Statement 47 on page 318. The machine language instructions which are generated as a result of this statement are shown on page 323. Note that eight machine language instructions have been generated as a result of the PERFORM statement and a total of 30 bytes of storage are used by these instructions (the machine language instructions are shown in their hexadecimal format). Thus, each Perform Statement which is issued in a COBOL program using the DOS ANSI COBOL compiler will require 30 bytes of computer storage.

Example 2: At statement 133 on page 319, an ADD Statement is written which will add the contents of a three byte display field (Statement 27 on page 318) to the contents of a four byte binary field with one byte to the right of the decimal place (Statement 29 on page 318). The machine language instructions which are generated in order to accomplish the addition operation are illustrated on page 330. Note that eleven instructions are generated in order to perform the add operation and that these instructions require 52 bytes of computer storage. Thus, it can be seen that by mixing the modes and not having decimal alignment, a large amount of computer storage is required for the single addition operation.

Example 3: In statement 259 on page 320, an ADD Statement adds two fields (Statement 35 and statement 38 on page 318) which are the same length, decimally aligned, and both are Computational-3 fields. The single machine language Add instruction which is generated is contained on page 337. Note that only one add instruction is required when the fields are both Computational-3, are the same length, and are decimally aligned, in contrast to the instructions which are generated for the Add Statement in Example 2.

The other statements which are contained within the listing can be similarly compared in order to illustrate the difference in the instructions which are generated for differently defined fields and also the listing can be used to see the computer storage requirements for other COBOL statements.

```
   1                              IBM DOS AMERICAN NATIONAL STANDARD COBOL          CBF CL3-4         09/17/74

 00001              IDENTIFICATION DIVISION.
 00002              PROGRAM-ID. TESTS.
 00003              ENVIRONMENT DIVISION.
 00004              CONFIGURATION SECTION.
 00005              SOURCE-COMPUTER. IBM-360-F30.
 00006              INPUT-OUTPUT SECTION.
 00007              FILE-CONTROL.
 00008                  SELECT CARDSIN
 00009      001170          ASSIGN TO SYS007-UR-2540R-S.
 00010                  SELECT PRTFLE
 00011      001190          ASSIGN TO SYS013-UR-1403-S.
 00012              DATA DIVISION.
 00013              FILE SECTION.
 00014              FD  CARDSIN
 00015                  RECORDING MODE IS F
 00016                  RECORD CONTAINS 80 CHARACTERS
 00017                  LABEL RECORDS ARE OMITTED
 00018                  DATA RECORD IS CARDS-IO.
 00019              01  CARDS-IO                 PICTURE X(80).
 00020              FD  PRTFLE
 00021                  RECORD CONTAINS 133 CHARACTERS
 00022                  LABEL RECORDS ARE OMITTED
 00023                  RECORDING MODE IS F
 00024                  DATA RECORD IS PRINT-IO.
 00025              01  PRINT-IO                 PICTURE X(133).
 00026              WORKING-STORAGE SECTION.
 00027              77 DISP1 PICTURE S999.
 00028              77 BIN1 PICTURE S9(3) COMPUTATIONAL.
 00029              77 BIN2 PICTURE S999V9 COMPUTATIONAL.
 00030              77 BIN3 PICTURE S999 COMPUTATIONAL.
 00031              77 DISP2 PICTURE S9999.
 00032              77 DISP3 PICTURE S999V9.
 00033              77 DISP4 PICTURE S999.
 00034              77 DISP5 PICTURE 999.
 00035              77 COMP1 PICTURE S999 COMPUTATIONAL-3.
 00036              77 COMP2 PICTURE S9999 COMPUTATIONAL-3.
 00037              77 COMP3 PICTURE S999V9 COMPUTATIONAL-3.
 00038              77 COMP4 PICTURE S999 COMPUTATIONAL-3.
 00039              77 COMP5 PICTURE 9999 COMPUTATIONAL-3.
 00040              PROCEDURE DIVISION.
 00041              START-IT.
 00042                  OPEN INPUT CARDSIN.
 00043                  OPEN OUTPUT PRTFLE.
 00044                  READ CARDSIN AT END GO TO END-CARD.
 00045              END-CARD.
 00046                  WRITE PRINT-IO AFTER ADVANCING DISP1 LINES.
 00047                  PERFORM PARA THRU PARB.
 00048                  CLOSE PRTFLE.
 00049                  CLOSE CARDSIN.
 00050                  IF BIN1 = BIN3     GO TO A-1.
 00051                  IF BIN1 = BIN2     GO TO A-1.
 00052              A-1.
 00053                  IF BIN1 = DISP1  GO TO A-1.
 00054                  IF BIN1 = DISP2  GO TO A-1.
 00055                  IF BIN1 = DISP3  GO TO A-1.
 00056                  IF BIN1 = DISP5  GO TO A-1.
 00057                  IF BIN2 = DISP1  GO TO A-1.
 00058              PARA.
 00059                  IF BIN2 = DISP2  GO TO A-1.
 00060                  IF BIN2 = DISP3  GO TO A-1.
 00061                  IF BIN2 = DISP5  GO TO A-1.
 00062                  IF DISP1 = DISP4  GO TO A-1.
 00063                  IF DISP1 = DISP2  GO TO A-1.
 00064                  IF DISP1 = DISP3  GO TO A-1.
 00065                  IF DISP1 = DISP5  GO TO A-1.
 00066                  IF BIN1 = COMP1  GO TO A-1.
 00067                  IF BIN1 = COMP2  GO TO A-1.
 00068              PARB.
 00069                  IF BIN1 = COMP3  GO TO A-1.
 00070                  IF BIN1 = COMP5  GO TO A-1.
 00071                  IF BIN2 = COMP1  GO TO A-1.
 00072                  IF BIN2 = COMP2  GO TO A-1.
 00073                  IF BIN2 = COMP3  GO TO A-1.
 00074                  IF BIN2 = COMP5  GO TO A-1.
 00075                  IF COMP5 = BIN2  GO TO A-1.
 00076                  IF DISP1 = COMP1  GO TO A-1.
 00077                  IF DISP1 = COMP2  GO TO A-1.
 00078                  IF DISP1 = COMP3  GO TO A-1.
 00079                  IF DISP1 = COMP5  GO TO A-1.
 00080                  IF DISP2 = COMP1  GO TO A-1.
 00081                  IF DISP2 = COMP2  GO TO A-1.
 00082                  IF DISP2 = COMP3  GO TO A-1.
 00083                  IF DISP2 = COMP5  GO TO A-1.
 00084                  IF DISP3 = COMP1  GO TO A-1.
 00085                  IF DISP3 = COMP2  GO TO A-1.
 00086                  IF DISP3 = COMP3  GO TO A-1.
 00087              PARC.
```

```
 2

00088          IF DISP3 = COMP5  GO TO A-1.
00089          IF DISP5 = COMP1  GO TO A-1.
00090          IF DISP5 = COMP2  GO TO A-1.
00091          IF DISP5 = COMP3  GO TO A-1.
00092          IF COMP1 = COMP4 GO TO A-1.
00093          IF DISP5 = COMP5  GO TO A-1.
00094          IF COMP1 = COMP2 GO TO A-1.
00095          IF COMP1 = COMP3  GO TO A-1.
00096          IF COMP1 = COMP5  GO TO A-1.
00097          IF DISP2 = DISP3 GO TO A-1.
00098          IF DISP2 = DISP5 GO TO A-1.
00099          IF DISP3 = DISP5  GO TO A-1.
00100          IF COMP2 = COMP3 GO TO A-1.
00101          IF COMP2 = COMP5 GO TO A-1.
00102          IF COMP3 = COMP5  GO TO A-1.
00103
00104
00105
00106          MOVE     BIN1 TO BIN3.
00107          ADD      BIN1 TO BIN3.
00108          MOVE     BIN3 TO BIN1.
00109          ADD      BIN3 TO BIN1.
00110          MOVE BIN1 TO BIN2.
00111          ADD BIN1 TO BIN2.
00112          MOVE     BIN2 TO BIN1.
00113          ADD      BIN2 TO BIN1.
00114          MOVE BIN1 TO DISP1.
00115          ADD BIN1 TO DISP1.
00116          MOVE DISP1 TO BIN1.
00117          ADD      DISP1 TO BIN1.
00118          MOVE BIN1 TO DISP2.
00119          ADD      BIN1 TO DISP2.
00120          MOVE     DISP2 TO BIN1.
00121          ADD      DISP2 TO BIN1.
00122          MOVE     BIN1 TO DISP3.
00123          ADD      BIN1 TO DISP3.
00124          MOVE     DISP3 TO BIN1.
00125          ADD      DISP3 TO BIN1.
00126          MOVE     BIN1 TO DISP5.
00127          ADD      BIN1 TO DISP5.
00128          MOVE     DISP5 TO BIN1.
00129          ADD      DISP5 TO BIN1.
00130          MOVE     BIN2 TO DISP1.
00131          ADD      BIN2 TO DISP1.
00132          MOVE DISP1 TO BIN2.
00133          ADD DISP1 TO BIN2. ──────② 
00134          MOVE     BIN2 TO DISP2.
00135          ADD      BIN2 TO DISP2.
00136          MOVE     DISP2 TO BIN2.
00137          ADD      DISP2 TO BIN2.
00138          MOVE     BIN2 TO DISP3.
00139          ADD      BIN2 TO DISP3.
00140          MOVE     DISP3 TO BIN2.
00141          ADD      DISP3 TO BIN2.
00142          MOVE     BIN2 TO DISP5.
00143          ADD      BIN2 TO DISP5.
00144          MOVE     DISP5 TO BIN2.
00145          ADD      DISP5 TO BIN2.
00146          MOVE     DISP1 TO DISP4.
00147          ADD      DISP1 TO DISP4.
00148          MOVE     DISP4 TO DISP1.
00149          ADD      DISP4 TO DISP1.
00150          MOVE DISP1 TO DISP2.
00151          ADD      DISP1 TO DISP2.
00152          MOVE     DISP2 TO DISP1.
00153          ADD      DISP2 TO DISP1.
00154          MOVE     DISP1 TO DISP3.
00155          ADD      DISP1 TO DISP3.
00156          MOVE DISP3 TO DISP1.
00157          ADD      DISP3 TO DISP1.
00158          MOVE     DISP1 TO DISP5.
00159          ADD      DISP1 TO DISP5.
00160          MOVE     DISP5 TO DISP1.
00161          ADD      DISP5 TO DISP1.
00162          MOVE     BIN1 TO COMP1.
00163          ADD      BIN1 TO COMP1.
00164          MOVE     COMP1 TO BIN1.
00165          ADD      COMP1 TO BIN1.
00166          MOVE     BIN1 TO COMP2.
00167          ADD      BIN1 TO COMP2.
00168          MOVE     COMP2 TO BIN1.
00169          ADD      COMP2 TO BIN1.
00170          MOVE     BIN1 TO COMP3.
00171          ADD      BIN1 TO COMP3.
00172          MOVE     COMP3 TO BIN1.
00173          ADD      COMP3 TO BIN1.
00174          MOVE     BIN1 TO COMP5.
```

```
  3

00175              ADD     BIN1 TO COMP5.
00176              MOVE    COMP5 TO BIN1.
00177              ADD     COMP5 TO BIN1.
00178              MOVE    BIN2 TO COMP1.
00179              ADD     BIN2 TO COMP1.
00180              MOVE    COMP1 TO BIN2.
00181              ADD     COMP1 TO BIN2.
00182              MOVE    BIN2 TO COMP2.
00183              ADD     BIN2 TO COMP2.
00184              MOVE    COMP2 TO BIN2.
00185              ADD     COMP2 TO BIN2.
00186              MOVE    BIN2 TO COMP3.
00187              ADD     BIN2 TO COMP3.
00188              MOVE    COMP3 TO BIN2.
00189              ADD     COMP3 TO BIN2.
00190              MOVE    BIN2 TO COMP5.
00191              ADD     BIN2 TO COMP5.
00192              MOVE    COMP5 TO BIN2.
00193              ADD     COMP5 TO BIN2.
00194              MOVE    DISP1 TO COMP1.
00195              ADD     DISP1 TO COMP1.
00196              MOVE    COMP1 TO DISP1.
00197              ADD     COMP1 TO DISP1.
00198              MOVE    DISP1 TO COMP2.
00199              ADD     DISP1 TO COMP2.
00200       MOVE COMP2 TO DISP1.
00201       ADD  COMP2 TO DISP1.
00202       MOVE DISP1 TO COMP3.
00203       ADD DISP1 TO COMP3.
00204              MOVE    COMP3 TO DISP1.
00205              ADD     COMP3 TO DISP1.
00206              MOVE    DISP1 TO COMP5.
00207              ADD     DISP1 TO COMP5.
00208              MOVE    COMP5 TO DISP1.
00209              ADD     COMP5 TO DISP1.
00210              MOVE    DISP2 TO COMP1.
00211              ADD     DISP2 TO COMP1.
00212              MOVE    COMP1 TO DISP2.
00213              ADD     COMP1 TO DISP2.
00214              MOVE    DISP2 TO COMP2.
00215              ADD     DISP2 TO COMP2.
00216              MOVE    COMP2 TO DISP2.
00217              ADD     COMP2 TO DISP2.
00218              MOVE    DISP2 TO COMP3.
00219              ADD     DISP2 TO COMP3.
00220              MOVE    COMP3 TO DISP2.
00221              ADD     COMP3 TO DISP2.
00222              MOVE    DISP2 TO COMP5.
00223              ADD     DISP2 TO COMP5.
00224              MOVE    COMP5 TO DISP2.
00225              ADD     COMP5 TO DISP2.
00226              MOVE    DISP3 TO COMP1.
00227              ADD     DISP3 TO COMP1.
00228              MOVE    COMP1 TO DISP3.
00229              ADD     COMP1 TO DISP3.
00230              MOVE    DISP3 TO COMP2.
00231              ADD     DISP3 TO COMP2.
00232              MOVE    COMP2 TO DISP3.
00233              ADD     COMP2 TO DISP3.
00234              MOVE    DISP3 TO COMP3.
00235              ADD     DISP3 TO COMP3.
00236              MOVE    COMP3 TO DISP3.
00237              ADD     COMP3 TO DISP3.
00238              MOVE    DISP3 TO COMP5.
00239              ADD     DISP3 TO COMP5.
00240              MOVE    COMP5 TO DISP3.
00241              ADD     COMP5 TO DISP3.
00242              MOVE    DISP5 TO COMP1.
00243              ADD     DISP5 TO COMP1.
00244              MOVE    COMP1 TO DISP5.
00245              ADD     COMP1 TO DISP5.
00246              MOVE    DISP5 TO COMP2.
00247              ADD     DISP5 TO COMP2.
00248              MOVE    COMP2 TO DISP5.
00249              ADD     COMP2 TO DISP5.
00250              MOVE    DISP5 TO COMP3.
00251              ADD     DISP5 TO COMP3.
00252              MOVE    COMP3 TO DISP5.
00253              ADD     COMP3 TO DISP5.
00254              MOVE    DISP5 TO COMP5.
00255              ADD     DISP5 TO COMP5.
00256              MOVE    COMP5 TO DISP5.
00257              ADD     COMP5 TO DISP5.
00258              MOVE    COMP1 TO COMP4.
00259              ADD     COMP1 TO COMP4.          ◀───── ③
00260              MOVE    COMP4 TO COMP1.
00261              ADD     COMP4 TO COMP1.
```

```
 4

 00262          MOVE    COMP1 TO COMP2.
 00263          ADD     COMP1 TO COMP2.
 00264          MOVE    COMP2 TO COMP1.
 00265          ADD     COMP2 TO COMP1.
 00266          MOVE    COMP1 TO COMP3.
 00267          ADD     COMP1 TO COMP3.
 00268          MOVE    COMP3 TO COMP1.
 00269          ADD     COMP3 TO COMP1.
 00270          MOVE    COMP1 TO COMP5.
 00271          ADD     COMP1 TO COMP5.
 00272          MOVE    COMP5 TO COMP1.
 00273          ADD     COMP5 TO COMP1.
 00274          MOVE    DISP2 TO DISP3.
 00275          ADD     DISP2 TO DISP3.
 00276          MOVE    DISP3 TO DISP2.
 00277          ADD     DISP3 TO DISP2.
 00278          MOVE    DISP2 TO DISP5.
 00279          ADD     DISP2 TO DISP5.
 00280          MOVE    DISP5 TO DISP2.
 00281          ADD     DISP5 TO DISP2.
 00282          MOVE    DISP3 TO DISP5.
 00283          ADD     DISP3 TO DISP5.
 00284          MOVE    DISP5 TO DISP3.
 00285          ADD     DISP5 TO DISP3.
 00286          MOVE    COMP2 TO COMP3.
 00287          ADD     COMP2 TO COMP3.
 00288          MOVE    COMP3 TO COMP2.
 00289          ADD     COMP3 TO COMP2.
 00290          MOVE    COMP2 TO COMP5..
 00291          ADD     COMP2 TO COMP5.
 00292          MOVE    COMP5 TO COMP2.
 00293          ADD     COMP5 TO COMP2.
 00294          MOVE    COMP3 TO COMP5.
 00295          ADD     COMP3 TO COMP5.
 00296          MOVE    COMP5 TO COMP3.
 00297          ADD     COMP5 TO COMP3.
 00298          STOP RUN.
```

```
            6


                    MEMORY MAP

                        TGT                 00360

                  SAVE AREA                 00360
                  SWITCH                    003A8
                  TALLY                     003AC
                  SORT SAVE                 003B0
                  ENTRY-SAVE                003B4
                  SORT CORE SIZE            003B8
                  NSTD-REELS                003BC
                  SORT RET                  003BE
                  WORKING CELLS             003C0
                  SORT FILE SIZE            004F0
                  SORT MODE SIZE            004F4
                  PGT-VN TBL                004F8
                  TGT-VN TBL                004FC
                  SORTAB ADDRESS            00500
                  LENGTH OF VN TBL          00504
                  LNGTH OF SORTAB           00506
                  PGM ID                    00508
                  A(INIT1)                  00510
                  UPSI SWITCHES             00514
                  OVERFLOW CELLS            0051C
                  BL CELLS                  0051C
                  DTFADR CELLS              00528
                  TEMP STORAGE              00530
                  TEMP STORAGE-2            00540
                  TEMP STORAGE-3            00540
                  TEMP STORAGE-4            00548
                  BLL CELLS                 00548
                  VLC CELLS                 0054C
                  SBL CELLS                 0054C
                  INDEX CELLS               0054C
                  SUBADR CELLS              0054C
                  ONCTL CELLS               0054C
                  PFMCTL CELLS              0054C
                  PFMSAV CELLS              0054C
                  VN CELLS                  00550
                  SAVE AREA =2              00554
                  XSASW CELLS               00554
                  XSA CELLS                 00554
                  PARAM CELLS               00554
                  RPTSAV AREA               00554
                  CHECKPT CTR               00554
                  IOPTR CELLS               00554

    LITERAL POOL (HEX)

    00648 (LIT+0)      000A010C  0000000A  585BC2D6  D7C5D540  00855B5B  C2C3D3D6
    00660 (LIT+24)     E2C5


                        PGT                 00560

                  OVERFLOW CELLS            00560
                  VIRTUAL CELLS             00560
                  PROCEDURE NAME CELLS      00568
                  GENERATED NAME CELLS      0057C
                  SUBDTF ADDRESS CELLS      00640
                  VNI CELLS                 00640
                  LITERALS                  00648
                  DISPLAY LITERALS          00662


    REGISTER ASSIGNMENT

      REG 6    BL =3
      REG 7    BL =1
      REG 8    BL =2

      42                   000662                     START   EQU   *
                           000662  41 10 C 0F0                LA    1,0F0(0,12)        LIT+8
                           000666  58 00 D 1C8                L     0,1C8(0,13)        DTF=1
                           00066A  18 40                      LR    4,0
                           00066C  07 00                      BCR   0,0
                           00066E  05 F0                      BALR  15,0
                           000670  50 00 F 008                ST    0,008(0,15)
                           000674  45 00 F 00C                BAL   0,00C(0,15)
                           000678  00000000                   DC    X'00000000'
                           00067C  0A 02                      SVC   2
      43                   00067E  41 10 C 0F0                LA    1,0F0(0,12)        LIT+8
                           000682  58 00 D 1CC                L     0,1CC(0,13)        DTF=2
                           000686  18 40                      LR    4,0
                           000688  07 00                      BCR   0,0
```

```
     7
                 00068A   05 F0                          BALR  15,0
                 00068C   50 00 F 008                    ST    0,008(0,15)
                 000690   45 00 F 00C                    BAL   0,00C(0,15)
                 000694   00000000                       DC    X'00000000'
                 000698   0A 02                          SVC   2
                 00069A   50 20 D 1C0                    ST    2,1C0(0,13)      BL =2
                 00069E   58 80 D 1C0                    L     8,1C0(0,13)      BL =2
     44          0006A2   58 10 D 1C8                    L     1,1C8(0,13)      DTF=1
                 0006A6   58 F0 C 01C                    L     15,01C(0,12)     GN=01
                 0006AA   91 20 1 010                    TM    010(1),X'20'
                 0006AE   07 1F                          BCR   1,15
                 0006B0   41 F0 C 01C                    LA    15,01C(0,12)     GN=01
                 0006B4   D2 02 1 01D F 001              MVC   01D(3,1),001(15)
                 0006B8   58 F0 1 010                    L     15,010(0,1)
                 0006BE   45 E0 F 008                    BAL   14,008(0,15)
                 0006C2   50 20 D 1BC                    ST    2,1BC(0,13)      BL =1
                 0006C6   58 70 D 1BC                    L     7,1BC(0,13)      BL =1
                 0006CA   58 F0 C 008                    L     15,008(0,12)     PN=01
                 0006CE   07 FF                          BCR   15,15
     44          0006D0                       GN=01      EQU   *
                 0006D0   58 10 C 008                    L     1,008(0,12)      PN=01
                 0006D4   07 F1                          BCR   15,1
     45          0006D6                       PN=01      EQU   *
     46          0006D6   58 10 D 1CC                    L     1,1CC(0,13)      DTF=2
                 0006DA   41 40 6 000                    LA    4,000(0,6)       DNM=1-202
                 0006DE   58 20 D 1C0                    L     2,1C0(0,13)      BL =2
                 0006E2   48 30 C 0F8                    LH    3,0F8(0,12)      LIT+16
                 0006E6   58 F0 C 004                    L     15,004(0,12)     V(ILBDSPAO)
                 0006EA   05 EF                          BALR  14,15
                 0006EC   84                             DC    X'84'
                 0006ED   03                             DC    X'03'
                 0006EE   00                             DC    X'00'
                 0006EF   00                             DC    X'00'
                 0006F0   50 20 D 1C0                    ST    2,1C0(0,13)      BL =2
                 0006F4   58 80 D 1C0                    L     8,1C0(0,13)      BL =2
     47 ←        0006F8                       GN=02      EQU   *
          ①      0006F8   58 00 D 1F0    -4             L     0,1F0(0,13)      VN=01
                 0006FC   50 00 D 1EC    -4             ST    0,1EC(0,13)      PSV=1
                 000700   58 00 C 024    -4             L     0,024(0,12)      GN=03
                 000704   50 00 D 1F0    -4             ST    0,1F0(0,13)      VN=01
                 000708   58 10 C 010    -4             L     1,010(0,12)      PN=03
                 00070C   07 F1          -2             BCR   15,1
                 00070E                       GN=03      EQU   *
                 00070E   58 00 D 1EC    -4             L     0,1EC(0,13)      PSV=1
                 000712   50 00 D 1F0    -4             ST    0,1F0(0,13)      VN=01
     48          000716   58 00 D 1CC                    L     0,1CC(0,13)      DTF=2
                 00071A   18 40                          LR    4,0
                 00071C   41 10 C 0FA                    LA    1,0FA(0,12)      LIT+18
                 000720   07 00                          BCR   0,0
                 000722   05 F0                          BALR  15,0
                 000724   50 00 F 008                    ST    0,008(0,15)
                 000728   45 00 F 00C                    BAL   0,00C(0,15)
                 00072C   00000000                       DC    X'00000000'
                 000730   0A 02                          SVC   2
     49          000732   58 00 D 1C8                    L     0,1C8(0,13)      DTF=1
                 000736   18 40                          LR    4,0
                 000738   41 10 C 0FA                    LA    1,0FA(0,12)      LIT+18
                 00073C   07 00                          BCR   0,0
                 00073E   05 F0                          BALR  15,0
                 000740   50 00 F 008                    ST    0,008(0,15)
                 000744   45 00 F 00C                    BAL   0,00C(0,15)
                 000748   00000000                       DC    X'00000000'
                 00074C   0A 02                          SVC   2
     50          00074E   D2 03 D 1E0 6 003              MVC   1E0(4,13),003(6)  TS3=1     DNM=1-217
                 000754   48 30 D 1E0                    LH    3,1E0(0,13)       TS3=1
                 000758   D2 03 D 1E0 6 007              MVC   1E0(4,13),007(6)  TS3=1     DNM=1-245
                 00075E   49 30 D 1E0                    CH    3,1E0(0,13)       TS3=1
                 000762   58 F0 C 028                    L     15,028(0,12)      GN=04
                 000766   07 7F                          BCR   7,15
     50          000768   58 10 C 00C                    L     1,00C(0,12)       PN=02
                 00076C   07 F1                          BCR   15,1
     51          00076E                       GN=04      EQU   *
                 00076E   D2 03 D 1E0 6 003              MVC   1E0(4,13),003(6)  TS3=1     DNM=1-217
                 000774   48 30 D 1E0                    LH    3,1E0(0,13)       TS3=1
                 000778   4C 30 C 0E8                    MH    3,0E8(0,12)       LIT+0
                 00077C   D2 03 D 1E0 6 005              MVC   1E0(4,13),005(6)  TS3=1     DNM=1-231
                 000782   48 50 D 1E0                    LH    5,1E0(0,13)       TS3=1
                 000786   1B 53                          SR    5,3
                 000788   58 F0 C 00C                    L     15,00C(0,12)      PN=02
                 00078C   07 7F                          BCR   7,15
     51          00078E   58 10 C 00C                    L     1,00C(0,12)       PN=02
                 000792   07 F1                          BCR   15,1
     52          000794                       PN=02      EQU   *
     53          000794   F2 72 D 1D0 6 000              PACK  1D0(8,13),000(3,6)  TS=01   DNM=1-202
                 00079A   4F 30 D 1D0                    CVB   3,1D0(0,13)       TS=01
                 00079E   D2 03 D 1E0 6 003              MVC   1E0(4,13),003(6)  TS3=1     DNM=1-217
                 0007A4   48 50 D 1E0                    LH    5,1E0(0,13)       TS3=1
```

```
       8

                  0007A8  19 53                          CR    5,3
                  0007AA  58 F0 C 02C                    L     15,02C(0,12)          GN=05
                  0007AE  07 7F                          BCR   7,15
         53       0007B0  58 10 C 00C                    L     1,00C(0,12)           PN=02
                  0007B4  07 F1                          BCR   15,1
         54       0007B6                    GN=05         EQU   *
                  0007B6  F2 73 D 1D0 6 009              PACK  1D0(8,13),009(4,6)    TS=01      DNM=1-259
                  0007BC  4F 30 D 1D0                    CVB   3,1D0(0,13)           TS=01
                  0007C0  D2 03 D 1E0 6 003              MVC   1E0(4,13),003(6)      TS3=1      DNM=1-217
                  0007C6  48 50 D 1E0                    LH    5,1E0(0,13)           TS3=1
                  0007CA  19 53                          CR    5,3
                  0007CC  58 F0 C 030                    L     15,030(0,12)          GN=06
                  0007D0  07 7F                          BCR   7,15
         54       0007D2  58 10 C 00C                    L     1,00C(0,12)           PN=02
                  0007D6  07 F1                          BCR   15,1
         55       0007D8                    GN=06         EQU   *
                  0007D8  F2 73 D 1D0 6 00D              PACK  1D0(8,13),00D(4,6)    TS=01      DNM=1-274
                  0007DE  D2 03 D 1E0 6 003              MVC   1E0(4,13),003(6)      TS3=1      DNM=1-217
                  0007E4  48 30 D 1E0                    LH    3,1E0(0,13)           TS3=1
                  0007E8  4C 30 C 0E8                    MH    3,0E8(0,12)           LIT+0
                  0007EC  4F 50 D 1D0                    CVB   5,1D0(0,13)           TS=01
                  0007F0  1B 53                          SR    5,3
                  0007F2  58 F0 C 034                    L     15,034(0,12)          GN=07
                  0007F6  07 7F                          BCR   7,15
         55       0007F8  58 10 C 00C                    L     1,00C(0,12)           PN=02
                  0007FC  07 F1                          BCR   15,1
         56       0007FE                    GN=07         EQU   *
                  0007FE  F2 72 D 1D0 6 014              PACK  1D0(8,13),014(3,6)    TS=01      DNM=1-304
                  000804  4F 30 D 1D0                    CVB   3,1D0(0,13)           TS=01
                  000808  D2 03 D 1E0 6 003              MVC   1E0(4,13),003(6)      TS3=1      DNM=1-217
                  00080E  48 50 D 1E0                    LH    5,1E0(0,13)           TS3=1
                  000812  19 53                          CR    5,3
                  000814  58 F0 C 038                    L     15,038(0,12)          GN=08
                  000818  07 7F                          BCR   7,15
         56       00081A  58 10 C 00C                    L     1,00C(0,12)           PN=02
                  00081E  07 F1                          BCR   15,1
         57       000820                    GN=08         EQU   *
                  000820  F2 72 D 1D0 6 000              PACK  1D0(8,13),000(3,6)    TS=01      DNM=1-202
                  000826  4F 30 D 1D0                    CVB   3,1D0(0,13)           TS=01
                  00082A  4C 30 C 0E8                    MH    3,0E8(0,12)           LIT+0
                  00082E  D2 03 D 1E0 6 005              MVC   1E0(4,13),005(6)      TS3=1      DNM=1-231
                  000834  4B 30 D 1E0                    SH    3,1E0(0,13)           TS3=1
                  000838  58 F0 C 010                    L     15,010(0,12)          PN=03
                  00083C  07 7F                          BCR   7,15
         57       00083E  58 10 C 00C                    L     1,00C(0,12)           PN=02
                  000842  07 F1                          BCR   15,1
         58       000844                    PN=03         EQU   *
         59       000844  F2 73 D 1D0 6 009              PACK  1D0(8,13),009(4,6)    TS=01      DNM=1-259
                  00084A  4F 30 D 1D0                    CVB   3,1D0(0,13)           TS=01
                  00084E  4C 30 C 0E8                    MH    3,0E8(0,12)           LIT+0
                  000852  D2 03 D 1E0 6 005              MVC   1E0(4,13),005(6)      TS3=1      DNM=1-231
                  000858  4B 30 D 1E0                    SH    3,1E0(0,13)           TS3=1
                  00085C  58 F0 C 03C                    L     15,03C(0,12)          GN=09
                  000860  07 7F                          BCR   7,15
         59       000862  58 10 C 00C                    L     1,00C(0,12)           PN=02
                  000866  07 F1                          BCR   15,1
         60       000868                    GN=09         EQU   *
                  000868  F2 73 D 1D0 6 00D              PACK  1D0(8,13),00D(4,6)    TS=01      DNM=1-274
                  00086E  4F 30 D 1D0                    CVB   3,1D0(0,13)           TS=01
                  000872  D2 03 D 1E0 6 005              MVC   1E0(4,13),005(6)      TS3=1      DNM=1-231
                  000878  48 50 D 1E0                    LH    5,1E0(0,13)           TS3=1
                  00087C  19 53                          CR    5,3
                  00087E  58 F0 C 040                    L     15,040(0,12)          GN=010
                  000882  07 7F                          BCR   7,15
         60       000884  58 10 C 00C                    L     1,00C(0,12)           PN=02
                  000888  07 F1                          BCR   15,1
         61       00088A                    GN=010        EQU   *
                  00088A  F2 72 D 1D0 6 014              PACK  1D0(8,13),014(3,6)    TS=01      DNM=1-304
                  000890  4F 30 D 1D0                    CVB   3,1D0(0,13)           TS=01
                  000894  4C 30 C 0E8                    MH    3,0E8(0,12)           LIT+0
                  000898  D2 03 D 1E0 6 005              MVC   1E0(4,13),005(6)      TS3=1      DNM=1-231
                  00089E  4B 30 D 1E0                    SH    3,1E0(0,13)           TS3=1
                  0008A2  58 F0 C 044                    L     15,044(0,12)          GN=011
                  0008A6  07 7F                          BCR   7,15
         61       0008A8  58 10 C 00C                    L     1,00C(0,12)           PN=02
                  0008AC  07 F1                          BCR   15,1
         62       0008AE                    GN=011        EQU   *
                  0008AE  F2 72 D 1D0 6 000              PACK  1D0(8,13),000(3,6)    TS=01      DNM=1-202
                  0008B4  F2 72 D 1D8 6 011              PACK  1D8(8,13),011(3,6)    TS=09      DNM=1-289
                  0008BA  F9 11 D 1D6 D 1DE              CP    1D6(2,13),1DE(2,13)   TS=07      TS=015
                  0008C0  58 F0 C 048                    L     15,048(0,12)          GN=012
                  0008C4  07 7F                          BCR   7,15
         62       0008C6  58 10 C 00C                    L     1,00C(0,12)           PN=02
                  0008CA  07 F1                          BCR   15,1
         63       0008CC                    GN=012        EQU   *
                  0008CC  F2 72 D 1D8 6 000              PACK  1D8(8,13),000(3,6)    TS=09      DNM=1-202
                  0008D2  F2 73 D 1D0 6 009              PACK  1D0(8,13),009(4,6)    TS=01      DNM=1-259
```

```
          9

          0008D8  F9 12 D 1DE D 1D5          CP    1DE(2,13),1D5(3,13)    TS=015      TS=06
          0008DE  58 F0 C 04C                L     15,04C(0,12)           GN=013
          0008E2  07 7F                      BCR   7,15
     63   0008E4  58 10 C 00C                L     1,00C(0,12)            PN=02
          0008E8  07 F1                      BCR   15,1
     64   0008EA                      GN=013 EQU   *
          0008EA  F2 72 D 1D8 6 000          PACK  1D8(8,13),000(3,6)     TS=09       DNM=1-202
          0008F0  F2 73 D 1D0 6 00D          PACK  1D0(8,13),00D(4,6)     TS=01       DNM=1-274
          0008F6  FC 31 D 1DC C 0EA          MP    1DC(4,13),0EA(2,12)    TS=013      LIT+2
          0008FC  FB 22 D 1D5 D 1DD          SP    1D5(3,13),1DD(3,13)    TS=06       TS=014
          000902  58 F0 C 050                L     15,050(0,12)           GN=014
          000906  07 7F                      BCR   7,15
     64   000908  58 10 C 00C                L     1,00C(0,12)            PN=02
          00090C  07 F1                      BCR   15,1
     65   00090E                      GN=014 EQU   *
          00090E  F2 72 D 1D8 6 000          PACK  1D8(8,13),000(3,6)     TS=09       DNM=1-202
          000914  F2 72 D 1D0 6 014          PACK  1D0(8,13),014(3,6)     TS=01       DNM=1-304
          00091A  F9 11 D 1DE D 1D6          CP    1DE(2,13),1D6(2,13)    TS=015      TS=07
          000920  58 F0 C 054                L     15,054(0,12)           GN=015
          000924  07 7F                      BCR   7,15
     65   000926  58 10 C 00C                L     1,00C(0,12)            PN=02
          00092A  07 F1                      BCR   15,1
     66   00092C                      GN=015 EQU   *
          00092C  F8 71 D 1D8 6 017          ZAP   1D8(8,13),017(2,6)     TS=09       DNM=1-319
          000932  4F 30 D 1D8                CVB   3,1D8(0,13)            TS=09
          000936  D2 03 D 1E0 6 003          MVC   1E0(4,13),003(6)       TS3=1       DNM=1-217
          00093C  48 50 D 1E0                LH    5,1E0(0,13)            TS3=1
          000940  19 53                      CR    5,3
          000942  58 F0 C 058                L     15,058(0,12)           GN=016
          000946  07 7F                      BCR   7,15
     66   000948  58 10 C 00C                L     1,00C(0,12)            PN=02
          00094C  07 F1                      BCR   15,1
     67   00094E                      GN=016 EQU   *
          00094E  F8 72 D 1D8 6 019          ZAP   1D8(8,13),019(3,6)     TS=09       DNM=1-334
          000954  4F 30 D 1D8                CVB   3,1D8(0,13)            TS=09
          000958  D2 03 D 1E0 6 003          MVC   1E0(4,13),003(6)       TS3=1       DNM=1-217
          00095E  48 50 D 1E0                LH    5,1E0(0,13)            TS3=1
          000962  19 53                      CR    5,3
          000964  58 F0 C 014                L     15,014(0,12)           PN=04
          000968  07 7F                      BCR   7,15
     67   00096A  58 10 C 00C                L     1,00C(0,12)            PN=02
          00096E  07 F1                      BCR   15,1
     68   000970                      PN=04  EQU   *
     69   000970  D2 03 D 1E0 6 003          MVC   1E0(4,13),003(6)       TS3=1       DNM=1-217
          000976  48 30 D 1E0                LH    3,1E0(0,13)            TS3=1
          00097A  4C 30 C 0E8                MH    3,0E8(0,12)            LIT+0
          00097E  F8 72 D 1D8 6 01C          ZAP   1D8(8,13),01C(3,6)     TS=09       DNM=1-352
          000984  4F 50 D 1D8                CVB   5,1D8(0,13)            TS=09
          000988  1B 53                      SR    5,3
          00098A  58 F0 C 05C                L     15,05C(0,12)           GN=017
          00098E  07 7F                      BCR   7,15
     69   000990  58 10 C 00C                L     1,00C(0,12)            PN=02
          000994  07 F1                      BCR   15,1
     70   000996                      GN=017 EQU   *
          000996  F8 72 D 1D8 6 021          ZAP   1D8(8,13),021(3,6)     TS=09       DNM=1-382
          00099C  4F 30 D 1D8                CVB   3,1D8(0,13)            TS=09
          0009A0  D2 03 D 1E0 6 003          MVC   1E0(4,13),003(6)       TS3=1       DNM=1-217
          0009A6  48 50 D 1E0                LH    5,1E0(0,13)            TS3=1
          0009AA  19 53                      CR    5,3
          0009AC  58 F0 C 060                L     15,060(0,12)           GN=018
          0009B0  07 7F                      BCR   7,15
     70   0009B2  58 10 C 00C                L     1,00C(0,12)            PN=02
          0009B6  07 F1                      BCR   15,1
     71   0009B8                      GN=018 EQU   *
          0009B8  F8 71 D 1D8 6 017          ZAP   1D8(8,13),017(2,6)     TS=09       DNM=1-319
          0009BE  4F 30 D 1D8                CVB   3,1D8(0,13)            TS=09
          0009C2  4C 30 C 0E8                MH    3,0E8(0,12)            LIT+0
          0009C6  D2 03 D 1E0 6 005          MVC   1E0(4,13),005(6)       TS3=1       DNM=1-231
          0009CC  4B 30 D 1E0                SH    3,1E0(0,13)            TS3=1
          0009D0  58 F0 C 064                L     15,064(0,12)           GN=019
          0009D4  07 7F                      BCR   7,15
     71   0009D6  58 10 C 00C                L     1,00C(0,12)            PN=02
          0009DA  07 F1                      BCR   15,1
     72   0009DC                      GN=019 EQU   *
          0009DC  F8 72 D 1D8 6 019          ZAP   1D8(8,13),019(3,6)     TS=09       DNM=1-334
          0009E2  4F 30 D 1D8                CVB   3,1D8(0,13)            TS=09
          0009E6  4C 30 C 0E8                MH    3,0E8(0,12)            LIT+0
          0009EA  D2 03 D 1E0 6 005          MVC   1E0(4,13),005(6)       TS3=1       DNM=1-231
          0009F0  4B 30 D 1E0                SH    3,1E0(0,13)            TS3=1
          0009F4  58 F0 C 068                L     15,068(0,12)           GN=020
          0009F8  07 7F                      BCR   7,15
     72   0009FA  58 10 C 00C                L     1,00C(0,12)            PN=02
          0009FE  07 F1                      BCR   15,1
     73   000A00                      GN=020 EQU   *
          000A00  F8 72 D 1D8 6 01C          ZAP   1D8(8,13),01C(3,6)     TS=09       DNM=1-352
          000A06  4F 30 D 1D8                CVB   3,1D8(0,13)            TS=09
          000A0A  D2 03 D 1E0 6 005          MVC   1E0(4,13),005(6)       TS3=1       DNM=1-231
```

```
10

          000A10   48 50 D 1E0              LH    5,1E0(0,13)          TS3=1
          000A14   19 53                    CR    5,3
          000A16   58 F0 C 06C              L     15,06C(0,12)         GN=021
          000A1A   07 7F                    BCR   7,15
   73     000A1C   58 10 C 00C              L     1,00C(0,12)          PN=02
          000A20   07 F1                    BCR   15,1
   74     000A22              GN=021        EQU   *
          000A22   F8 72 D 1D8 6 021        ZAP   1D8(8,13),021(3,6)   TS=09         DNM=1-382
          000A28   4F 30 D 1D8              CVB   3,1D8(0,13)          TS=09
          000A2C   4C 30 C 0E8              MH    3,0E8(0,12)          LIT+0
          000A30   D2 03 D 1E0 6 005        MVC   1E0(4,13),005(6)     TS3=1         DNM=1-231
          000A36   4B 30 D 1E0              SH    3,1E0(0,13)          TS3=1
          000A3A   58 F0 C 070              L     15,070(0,12)         GN=022
          000A3E   07 7F                    BCR   7,15
   74     000A40   58 10 C 00C              L     1,00C(0,12)          PN=02
          000A44   07 F1                    BCR   15,1
   75     000A46              GN=022        EQU   *
          000A46   F8 72 D 1D8 6 021        ZAP   1D8(8,13),021(3,6)   TS=09         DNM=1-382
          000A4C   4F 30 D 1D8              CVB   3,1D8(0,13)          TS=09
          000A50   4C 30 C 0E8              MH    3,0E8(0,12)          LIT+0
          000A54   D2 03 D 1E0 6 005        MVC   1E0(4,13),005(6)     TS3=1         DNM=1-231
          000A5A   48 50 D 1E0              LH    5,1E0(0,13)          TS3=1
          000A5E   1B 53                    SR    5,3
          000A60   58 F0 C 074              L     15,074(0,12)         GN=023
          000A64   07 7F                    BCR   7,15
   75     000A66   58 10 C 00C              L     1,00C(0,12)          PN=02
          000A6A   07 F1                    BCR   15,1
   76     0J0A6C              GN=023        EQU   *
          000A6C   F2 72 D 1D8 6 000        PACK  1D8(8,13),000(3,6)   TS=09         DNM=1-202
          000A72   F9 11 D 1DE 6 017        CP    1DE(2,13),017(2,6)   TS=015        DNM=1-319
          000A78   53 F0 C 078              L     15,078(0,12)         GN=024
          000A7C   07 7F                    BCR   7,15
   76     000A7E   58 10 C 00C              L     1,00C(0,12)          PN=02
          000A82   07 F1                    BCR   15,1
   77     000A84              GN=024        EQU   *
          000A84   F2 72 D 1D8 6 000        PACK  1D8(8,13),000(3,6)   TS=09         DNM=1-202
          000A8A   F9 12 D 1DE 6 019        CP    1DE(2,13),019(3,6)   TS=015        DNM=1-334
          000A90   58 F0 C 07C              L     15,07C(0,12)         GN=025
          000A94   07 7F                    BCR   7,15
   77     000A96   58 10 C 00C              L     1,00C(0,12)          PN=02
          000A9A   07 F1                    BCR   15,1
   78     000A9C              GN=025        EQU   *
          000A9C   F2 72 D 1D8 6 000        PACK  1D8(8,13),000(3,6)   TS=09         DNM=1-202
          000AA2   FC 31 D 1DC C 0EA        MP    1DC(4,13),0EA(2,12)  TS=013        LIT+2
          000AA8   F8 72 D 1D0 6 01C        ZAP   1D0(8,13),01C(3,6)   TS=01         DNM=1-352
          000AAE   FB 22 D 1D5 D 1DD        SP    1D5(3,13),1DD(3,13)  TS=06         TS=014
          000AB4   58 F0 C 080              L     15,080(0,12)         GN=026
          000AB8   07 7F                    BCR   7,15
   78     000ABA   58 10 C 00C              L     1,00C(0,12)          PN=02
          000ABE   07 F1                    BCR   15,1
   79     000AC0              GN=026        EQU   *
          000AC0   F2 72 D 1D8 6 000        PACK  1D8(8,13),000(3,6)   TS=09         DNM=1-202
          000AC6   F9 12 D 1DE 6 021        CP    1DE(2,13),021(3,6)   TS=015        DNM=1-382
          000ACC   58 F0 C 084              L     15,084(0,12)         GN=027
          000AD0   07 7F                    BCR   7,15
   79     000AD2   58 10 C 00C              L     1,00C(0,12)          PN=02
          000AD6   07 F1                    BCR   15,1
   80     000AD8              GN=027        EQU   *
          000AD8   F2 73 D 1D8 6 009        PACK  1D8(8,13),009(4,6)   TS=09         DNM=1-259
          000ADE   F9 21 D 1DD 6 017        CP    1DD(3,13),017(2,6)   TS=014        DNM=1-319
          000AE4   58 F0 C 088              L     15,088(0,12)         GN=028
          000AE8   07 7F                    BCR   7,15
   80     000AEA   58 10 C 00C              L     1,00C(0,12)          PN=02
          000AEE   07 F1                    BCR   15,1
   81     000AF0              GN=028        EQU   *
          000AF0   F2 73 D 1D8 6 009        PACK  1D8(8,13),009(4,6)   TS=09         DNM=1-259
          000AF6   F9 22 D 1DD 6 019        CP    1DD(3,13),019(3,6)   TS=014        DNM=1-334
          000AFC   58 F0 C 08C              L     15,08C(0,12)         GN=029
          000B00   07 7F                    BCR   7,15
   81     000B02   58 10 C 00C              L     1,00C(0,12)          PN=02
          000B06   07 F1                    BCR   15,1
   82     000B08              GN=029        EQU   *
          000B08   F2 73 D 1D8 6 009        PACK  1D8(8,13),009(4,6)   TS=09         DNM=1-259
          000B0E   FC 41 D 1DB C 0EA        MP    1DB(5,13),0EA(2,12)  TS=012        LIT+2
          000B14   F8 72 D 1D0 6 01C        ZAP   1D0(8,13),01C(3,6)   TS=01         DNM=1-352
          000B1A   FB 32 D 1D4 D 1DD        SP    1D4(4,13),1DD(3,13)  TS=05         TS=014
          000B20   58 F0 C 090              L     15,090(0,12)         GN=030
          000B24   07 7F                    BCR   7,15
   82     000B26   58 10 C 00C              L     1,00C(0,12)          PN=02
          000B2A   07 F1                    BCR   15,1
   83     000B2C              GN=030        EQU   *
          000B2C   F2 73 D 1D8 6 009        PACK  1D8(8,13),009(4,6)   TS=09         DNM=1-259
          000B32   F9 22 D 1DD 6 021        CP    1DD(3,13),021(3,6)   TS=014        DNM=1-382
          000B38   58 F0 C 094              L     15,094(0,12)         GN=031
          000B3C   07 7F                    BCR   7,15
   83     000B3E   58 10 C 00C              L     1,00C(0,12)          PN=02
          000B42   07 F1                    BCR   15,1
```

```
      11

84        000844                                  GN=031    EQU    *
          000844    F2 73 D 1D8 6 00D              PACK   1D8(8,13),00D(4,6)    TS=09     DNM=1-274
          00084A    F8 71 D 1D0 6 017              ZAP    1D0(8,13),017(2,6)    TS=01     DNM=1-319
          000850    FC 31 D 1D4 C OEA              MP     1D4(4,13),OEA(2,12)   TS=05     LIT+2
          000856    FB 22 D 1D5 D 1DD              SP     1D5(3,13),1DD(3,13)   TS=06     TS=014
          00085C    58 F0 C 098                    L      15,098(0,12)          GN=032
          000860    07 7F                          BCR    7,15
84        000862    58 10 C 00C                    L      1,00C(0,12)           PN=02
          000866    07 F1                          BCR    15,1
85        000868                                  GN=032    EQU    *
          000868    F2 73 D 1D8 6 00D              PACK   1D8(8,13),00D(4,6)    TS=09     DNM=1-274
          00086E    F8 72 D 1D0 6 019              ZAP    1D0(8,13),019(3,6)    TS=01     DNM=1-334
          000874    FC 41 D 1D3 C OEA              MP     1D3(5,13),OEA(2,12)   TS=04     LIT+2
          00087A    FB 32 D 1D4 D 1DD              SP     1D4(4,13),1DD(3,13)   TS=05     TS=014
          000880    58 F0 C 09C                    L      15,09C(0,12)          GN=033
          000884    07 7F                          BCR    7,15
85        000886    58 10 C 00C                    L      1,00C(0,12)           PN=02
          00088A    07 F1                          BCR    15,1
86        00088C                                  GN=033    EQU    *
          00088C    F2 73 D 1D8 6 00D              PACK   1D8(8,13),00D(4,6)    TS=09     DNM=1-274
          000892    F9 22 D 1DD 6 01C              CP     1DD(3,13),01C(3,6)    TS=014    DNM=1-352
          000898    58 F0 C 0A0                    L      15,0A0(0,12)          GN=034
          00089C    07 7F                          BCR    7,15
86        0008 9E   58 10 C 00C                    L      1,00C(0,12)           PN=02
          0008A2    07 F1                          BCR    15,1
          0008A4                                  GN=034    EQU    *
          0008A4    58 10 D 1F0                    L      1,1F0(0,13)           VN=01
          0008A8    07 F1                          BCR    15,1
87        0008AA                                  PN=05     EQU    *
88        0008AA    F2 73 D 1D8 6 00D              PACK   1D8(8,13),00D(4,6)    TS=09     DNM=1-274
          0008B0    F8 72 D 1D0 6 021              ZAP    1D0(8,13),021(3,6)    TS=01     DNM=1-382
          0008B6    FC 41 D 1D3 C OEA              MP     1D3(5,13),OEA(2,12)   TS=04     LIT+2
          0008BC    FB 32 D 1D4 D 1DD              SP     1D4(4,13),1DD(3,13)   TS=05     TS=014
          0008C2    58 F0 C 0A4                    L      15,0A4(0,12)          GN=035
          0008C6    07 7F                          BCR    7,15
88        0008C8    58 10 C 00C                    L      1,00C(0,12)           PN=02
          0008CC    07 F1                          BCR    15,1
89        0008CE                                  GN=035    EQU    *
          0008CE    F2 72 D 1D8 6 014              PACK   1D8(8,13),014(3,6)    TS=09     DNM=1-304
          0008D4    F9 11 D 1DE 6 017              CP     1DE(2,13),017(2,6)    TS=015    DNM=1-319
          0008DA    58 F0 C 0A8                    L      15,0A8(0,12)          GN=036
          0008DE    07 7F                          BCR    7,15
89        0008E0    58 10 C 00C                    L      1,00C(0,12)           PN=02
          0008E4    07 F1                          BCR    15,1
90        0008E6                                  GN=036    EQU    *
          0008E6    F2 72 D 1D8 6 014              PACK   1D8(8,13),014(3,6)    TS=09     DNM=1-304
          0008EC    F9 12 D 1DE 6 019              CP     1DE(2,13),019(3,6)    TS=015    DNM=1-334
          0008F2    58 F0 C 0AC                    L      15,0AC(0,12)          GN=037
          0008F6    07 7F                          BCR    7,15
90        0008F8    58 10 C 00C                    L      1,00C(0,12)           PN=02
          0008FC    07 F1                          BCR    15,1
91        0008FE                                  GN=037    EQU    *
          0008FE    F2 72 D 1D8 6 014              PACK   1D8(8,13),014(3,6)    TS=09     DNM=1-304
          000C04    FC 31 D 1DC C OEA              MP     1DC(4,13),OEA(2,12)   TS=013    LIT+2
          000C0A    F8 72 D 1D0 6 01C              ZAP    1D0(8,13),01C(3,6)    TS=01     DNM=1-352
          000C10    FB 22 D 1D5 D 1DD              SP     1D5(3,13),1DD(3,13)   TS=06     TS=014
          000C16    58 F0 C 0B0                    L      15,0B0(0,12)          GN=038
          000C1A    07 7F                          BCR    7,15
91        000C1C    58 10 C 00C                    L      1,00C(0,12)           PN=02
          000C20    07 F1                          BCR    15,1
92        000C22                                  GN=038    EQU    *
          000C22    F9 11 6 017 6 01F              CP     017(2,6),01F(2,6)     DNM=1-319  DNM=1-367
          000C28    58 F0 C 084                    L      15,084(0,12)          GN=039
          000C2C    07 7F                          BCR    7,15
92        000C2E    58 10 C 00C                    L      1,00C(0,12)           PN=02
          000C32    07 F1                          BCR    15,1
93        000C34                                  GN=039    EQU    *
          000C34    F2 72 D 1D8 6 014              PACK   1D8(8,13),014(3,6)    TS=09     DNM=1-304
          000C3A    F9 12 D 1DE 6 021              CP     1DE(2,13),021(3,6)    TS=015    DNM=1-382
          000C40    58 F0 C 088                    L      15,0B8(0,12)          GN=040
          000C44    07 7F                          BCR    7,15
93        000C46    58 10 C 00C                    L      1,00C(0,12)           PN=02
          000C4A    07 F1                          BCR    15,1
94        000C4C                                  GN=040    EQU    *
          000C4C    F9 12 6 017 6 019              CP     017(2,6),019(3,6)     DNM=1-319  DNM=1-334
          000C52    58 F0 C 08C                    L      15,08C(0,12)          GN=041
          000C56    07 7F                          BCR    7,15
94        000C58    58 10 C 00C                    L      1,00C(0,12)           PN=02
          000C5C    07 F1                          BCR    15,1
95        000C5E                                  GN=041    EQU    *
          000C5E    F8 71 D 1D8 6 017              ZAP    1D8(8,13),017(2,6)    TS=09     DNM=1-319
          000C64    FC 31 D 1DC C OEA              MP     1DC(4,13),OEA(2,12)   TS=013    LIT+2
          000C6A    F8 72 D 1D0 6 01C              ZAP    1D0(8,13),01C(3,6)    TS=01     DNM=1-352
          000C70    FB 22 D 1D5 D 1DD              SP     1D5(3,13),1DD(3,13)   TS=06     TS=014
          000C76    58 F0 C 0C0                    L      15,0C0(0,12)          GN=042
          000C7A    07 7F                          BCR    7,15
95        000C7C    58 10 C 00C                    L      1,00C(0,12)           PN=02
```

```
       12

              000C80   07 F1                          BCR   15,1
       96     000C82                     GN=042        EQU   *
              000C82   F9 12 6 017 6 021              CP    017(2,6),021(3,6)      DNM=1-319      DNM=1-382
              000C88   58 F0 C 0C4                    L     15,0C4(0,12)           GN=043
              000C8C   07 7F                          BCR   7,15
       96     000C8E   58 10 C 00C                    L     1,00C(0,12)            PN=02
              000C92   07 F1                          BCR   15,1
       97     000C94                     GN=043        EQU   *
              000C94   F2 73 D 1D8 6 009              PACK  1D8(8,13),009(4,6)     TS=09          DNM=1-259
              000C9A   F2 73 D 1D0 6 00D              PACK  1D0(8,13),00D(4,6)     TS=01          DNM=1-274
              000CA0   FC 41 D 1DB C 0EA              MP    1DB(5,13),0EA(2,12)    TS=012         LIT+2
              000CA6   FB 32 D 1D4 D 1DD              SP    1D4(4,13),1DD(3,13)    TS=05          TS=014
              000CAC   58 F0 C 0C8                    L     15,0C8(0,12)           GN=044
              000CB0   07 7F                          BCR   7,15
       97     000CB2   58 10 C 00C                    L     1,00C(0,12)            PN=02
              000CB6   07 F1                          BCR   15,1
       98     000CB8                     GN=044        EQU   *
              000CB8   F2 73 D 1D8 6 009              PACK  1D8(8,13),009(4,6)     TS=09          DNM=1-259
              000CBE   F2 72 D 1D0 6 014              PACK  1D0(8,13),014(3,6)     TS=01          DNM=1-304
              000CC4   F9 21 D 1DD D 1D6              CP    1DD(3,13),1D6(2,13)    TS=014         TS=07
              000CCA   58 F0 C 0CC                    L     15,0CC(0,12)           GN=045
              000CCE   07 7F                          BCR   7,15
       98     000CD0   58 10 C 00C                    L     1,00C(0,12)            PN=02
              000CD4   07 F1                          BCR   15,1
       99     000CD6                     GN=045        EQU   *
              000CD6   F2 73 D 1D8 6 00D              PACK  1D8(8,13),00D(4,6)     TS=09          DNM=1-274
              000CDC   F2 72 D 1D0 6 014              PACK  1D0(8,13),014(3,6)     TS=01          DNM=1-304
              000CE2   FC 31 D 1D4 C 0EA              MP    1D4(4,13),0EA(2,12)    TS=05          LIT+2
              000CE8   FB 22 D 1D5 D 1DD              SP    1D5(3,13),1DD(3,13)    TS=06          TS=014
              000CEE   58 F0 C 0D0                    L     15,0D0(0,12)           GN=046
              000CF2   07 7F                          BCR   7,15
       99     000CF4   58 10 C 00C                    L     1,00C(0,12)            PN=02
              000CF8   07 F1                          BCR   15,1
      100     000CFA                     GN=046        EQU   *
              000CFA   F8 72 D 1D8 6 019              ZAP   1D8(8,13),019(3,6)     TS=09          DNM=1-334
              000D00   FC 41 D 1DB C 0EA              MP    1DB(5,13),0EA(2,12)    TS=012         LIT+2
              000D06   F8 72 D 1D0 6 01C              ZAP   1D0(8,13),01C(3,6)     TS=01          DNM=1-352
              000D0C   FB 32 D 1D4 D 1DD              SP    1D4(4,13),1DD(3,13)    TS=05          TS=014
              000D12   58 F0 C 0D4                    L     15,0D4(0,12)           GN=047
              000D16   07 7F                          BCR   7,15
      100     000D18   58 10 C 00C                    L     1,00C(0,12)            PN=02
              000D1C   07 F1                          BCR   15,1
      101     000D1E                     GN=047        EQU   *
              000D1E   F9 22 6 019 6 021              CP    019(3,6),021(3,6)      DNM=1-334      DNM=1-382
              000D24   58 F0 C 0D8                    L     15,0D8(0,12)           GN=048
              000D28   07 7F                          BCR   7,15
      101     000D2A   58 10 C 00C                    L     1,00C(0,12)            PN=02
              000D2E   07 F1                          BCR   15,1
      102     000D30                     GN=048        EQU   *
              000D30   F8 72 D 1D8 6 021              ZAP   1D8(8,13),021(3,6)     TS=09          DNM=1-382
              000D36   FC 41 D 1DB C 0EA              MP    1DB(5,13),0EA(2,12)    TS=012         LIT+2
              000D3C   FB 32 D 1DC 6 01C              SP    1DC(4,13),01C(3,6)     TS=013         DNM=1-352
              000D42   58 F0 C 0DC                    L     15,0DC(0,12)           GN=049
              000D46   07 7F                          BCR   7,15
      102     000D48   58 10 C 00C                    L     1,00C(0,12)            PN=02
              000D4C   07 F1                          BCR   15,1
      106     000D4E                     GN=049        EQU   *
              000D4E   D2 01 6 007 6 003              MVC   007(2,6),003(6)        DNM=1-245      DNM=1-217
      107     000D54   D2 03 D 1E0 6 003              MVC   1E0(4,13),003(6)       TS3=1          DNM=1-217
              000D5A   48 30 D 1E0                    LH    3,1E0(0,13)            TS3=1
              000D5E   D2 03 D 1E0 6 007              MVC   1E0(4,13),007(6)       TS3=1          DNM=1-245
              000D64   4A 30 D 1E0                    AH    3,1E0(0,13)            TS3=1
              000D68   4E 30 D 1D8                    CVD   3,1D8(0,13)            TS=09
              000D6C   D7 05 D 1D8 D 1D8              XC    1D8(6,13),1D8(13)      TS=09          TS=09
              000D72   4F 30 D 1D8                    CVB   3,1D8(0,13)            TS=09
              000D76   40 30 D 1E0                    STH   3,1E0(0,13)            TS3=1
              000D7A   D2 01 6 007 D 1E0              MVC   007(2,6),1E0(13)       DNM=1-245      TS3=1
      108     000D80   D2 01 6 003 6 007              MVC   003(2,6),007(6)        DNM=1-217      DNM=1-245
      109     000D86   D2 03 D 1E0 6 007              MVC   1E0(4,13),007(6)       TS3=1          DNM=1-245
              000D8C   48 30 D 1E0                    LH    3,1E0(0,13)            TS3=1
              000D90   D2 03 D 1E0 6 003              MVC   1E0(4,13),003(6)       TS3=1          DNM=1-217
              000D96   4A 30 D 1E0                    AH    3,1E0(0,13)            TS3=1
              000D9A   4E 30 D 1D8                    CVD   3,1D8(0,13)            TS=09
              000D9E   D7 05 D 1D8 D 1D8              XC    1D8(6,13),1D8(13)      TS=09          TS=09
              000DA4   4F 30 D 1D8                    CVB   3,1D8(0,13)            TS=09
              000DA8   40 30 D 1E0                    STH   3,1E0(0,13)            TS3=1
              000DAC   D2 01 6 003 D 1E0              MVC   003(2,6),1E0(13)       DNM=1-217      TS3=1
      110     000DB2   D2 03 D 1E0 6 003              MVC   1E0(4,13),003(6)       TS3=1          DNM=1-217
              000DB8   48 30 D 1E0                    LH    3,1E0(0,13)            TS3=1
              000DBC   4C 30 C 0E8                    MH    3,0E8(0,12)            LIT+0
              000DC0   40 30 D 1E0                    STH   3,1E0(0,13)            TS3=1
      111     000DC4   D2 01 6 005 D 1E0              MVC   005(2,6),1E0(13)       DNM=1-231      TS3=1
              000DCA   D2 03 D 1E0 6 003              MVC   1E0(4,13),003(6)       TS3=1          DNM=1-217
              000DD0   48 30 D 1E0                    LH    3,1E0(0,13)            TS3=1
              000DD4   4C 30 C 0E8                    MH    3,0E8(0,12)            LIT+0
              000DD8   D2 03 D 1E0 6 005              MVC   1E0(4,13),005(6)       TS3=1          DNM=1-231
              000DDE   4A 30 D 1E0                    AH    3,1E0(0,13)            TS3=1
```

```
      13

            000DE2  4E 30 D 1D8            CVD   3,1D8(0,13)         TS=09
            000DE6  D7 04 D 1D8 D 1D8      XC    1D8(5,13),1D8(13)   TS=09        TS=09
            000DEC  94 0F D 1DD            NI    1DD(13),X'0F'       TS=09+5
            000DF0  4F 30 D 1D8            CVB   3,1D8(0,13)         TS=09
            000DF4  40 30 D 1E0            STH   3,1E0(0,13)         TS3=1
            000DF8  D2 01 6 005 D 1E0      MVC   005(2,6),1E0(13)    DNM=1-231    TS3=1
      112   000DFE  D2 03 D 1E0 6 005      MVC   1E0(4,13),005(6)    TS3=1        DNM=1-231
            000E04  48 20 D 1E0            LH    2,1E0(0,13)         TS3=1
            000E08  8E 20 0 020            SRDA  2,020(0)
            000E0C  5D 20 C 0EC            D     2,0EC(0,12)         LIT+4
            000E10  40 30 D 1E0            STH   3,1E0(0,13)         TS3=1
            000E14  D2 01 6 003 D 1E0      MVC   003(2,6),1E0(13)    DNM=1-217    TS3=1
      113   000E1A  D2 03 D 1E0 6 003      MVC   1E0(4,13),003(6)    TS3=1        DNM=1-217
            000E20  48 30 D 1E0            LH    3,1E0(0,13)         TS3=1
            000E24  4C 30 C 0E8            MH    3,0E8(0,12)         LIT+0
            000E28  D2 03 D 1E0 6 005      MVC   1E0(4,13),005(6)    TS3=1        DNM=1-231
            000E2E  4A 30 D 1E0            AH    3,1E0(0,13)         TS3=1
            000E32  4E 30 D 1D8            CVD   3,1D8(0,13)         TS=09
            000E36  D7 04 D 1D8 D 1D8      XC    1D8(5,13),1D8(13)   TS=09        TS=09
            000E3C  94 0F D 1DD            NI    1DD(13),X'0F'       TS=09+5
            000E40  F1 76 D 1D8 D 1D8      MVO   1D8(8,13),1D8(7,13) TS=09        TS=09
            000E46  4F 30 D 1D8            CVB   3,1D8(0,13)         TS=09
            000E4A  40 30 D 1E0            STH   3,1E0(0,13)         TS3=1
            000E4E  D2 01 6 003 D 1E0      MVC   003(2,6),1E0(13)    DNM=1-217    TS3=1
      114   000E54  D2 03 D 1E0 6 003      MVC   1E0(4,13),003(6)    TS3=1        DNM=1-217
            000E5A  48 30 D 1E0            LH    3,1E0(0,13)         TS3=1
            000E5E  4E 30 D 1D8            CVD   3,1D8(0,13)         TS=09
            000E62  F3 21 6 000 D 1DE      UNPK  000(3,6),1DE(2,13)  DNM=1-202    TS=015
      115   000E68  F2 72 D 1D8 6 000      PACK  1D8(8,13),000(3,6)  TS=09        DNM=1-202
            000E6E  D2 03 D 1E0 6 003      MVC   1E0(4,13),003(6)    TS3=1        DNM=1-217
            000E74  48 30 D 1E0            LH    3,1E0(0,13)         TS3=1
            000E78  4E 30 D 1D0            CVD   3,1D0(0,13)         TS=01
            000E7C  FA 21 D 1D5 D 1DE      AP    1D5(3,13),1DE(2,13) TS=06        TS=015
            000E82  F3 22 6 000 D 1D5      UNPK  000(3,6),1D5(3,13)  DNM=1-202    TS=06
      116   000E88  F2 72 D 1D8 6 000      PACK  1D8(8,13),000(3,6)  TS=09        DNM=1-202
            000E8E  4F 30 D 1D8            CVB   3,1D8(0,13)         TS=09
            000E92  40 30 D 1E0            STH   3,1E0(0,13)         TS3=1
            000E96  D2 01 6 003 D 1E0      MVC   003(2,6),1E0(13)    DNM=1-217    TS3=1
      117   000E9C  F2 72 D 1D8 6 000      PACK  1D8(8,13),000(3,6)  TS=09        DNM=1-202
            000EA2  4F 30 D 1D8            CVB   3,1D8(0,13)         TS=09
            000EA6  D2 03 D 1E0 6 003      MVC   1E0(4,13),003(6)    TS3=1        DNM=1-217
            000EAC  4A 30 D 1E0            AH    3,1E0(0,13)         TS3=1
            000EB0  4E 30 D 1D8            CVD   3,1D8(0,13)         TS=09
            000EB4  D7 05 D 1D8 D 1D8      XC    1D8(6,13),1D8(13)   TS=09        TS=09
            000EBA  4F 30 D 1D8            CVB   3,1D8(0,13)         TS=09
            000EBE  40 30 D 1E0            STH   3,1E0(0,13)         TS3=1
            000EC2  D2 01 6 003 D 1E0      MVC   003(2,6),1E0(13)    DNM=1-217    TS3=1
      118   000EC8  D2 03 D 1E0 6 003      MVC   1E0(4,13),003(6)    TS3=1        DNM=1-217
            000ECE  48 30 D 1E0            LH    3,1E0(0,13)         TS3=1
            000ED2  4E 30 D 1D8            CVD   3,1D8(0,13)         TS=09
            000ED6  F3 31 6 009 D 1DE      UNPK  009(4,6),1DE(2,13)  DNM=1-259    TS=015
      119   000EDC  F2 73 D 1D8 6 009      PACK  1D8(8,13),009(4,6)  TS=09        DNM=1-259
            000EE2  D2 03 D 1E0 6 003      MVC   1E0(4,13),003(6)    TS3=1        DNM=1-217
            000EE8  48 30 D 1E0            LH    3,1E0(0,13)         TS3=1
            000EEC  4E 30 D 1D0            CVD   3,1D0(0,13)         TS=01
            000EF0  FA 22 D 1D5 D 1DD      AP    1D5(3,13),1DD(3,13) TS=06        TS=014
            000EF6  F3 32 6 009 D 1D5      UNPK  009(4,6),1D5(3,13)  DNM=1-259    TS=06
      120   000EFC  F2 73 D 1D8 6 009      PACK  1D8(8,13),009(4,6)  TS=09        DNM=1-259
            000F02  D7 05 D 1D8 D 1D8      XC    1D8(6,13),1D8(13)   TS=09        TS=09
            000F08  4F 30 D 1D8            CVB   3,1D8(0,13)         TS=09
            000F0C  40 30 D 1E0            STH   3,1E0(0,13)         TS3=1
            000F10  D2 01 6 003 D 1E0      MVC   003(2,6),1E0(13)    DNM=1-217    TS3=1
      121   000F16  F2 73 D 1D8 6 009      PACK  1D8(8,13),009(4,6)  TS=09        DNM=1-259
            000F1C  4F 30 D 1D8            CVB   3,1D8(0,13)         TS=09
            000F20  D2 03 D 1E0 6 003      MVC   1E0(4,13),003(6)    TS3=1        DNM=1-217
            000F26  4A 30 D 1E0            AH    3,1E0(0,13)         TS3=1
            000F2A  4E 30 D 1D8            CVD   3,1D8(0,13)         TS=09
            000F2E  D7 05 D 1D8 D 1D8      XC    1D8(6,13),1D8(13)   TS=09        TS=09
            000F34  4F 30 D 1D8            CVB   3,1D8(0,13)         TS=09
            000F38  40 30 D 1E0            STH   3,1E0(0,13)         TS3=1
            000F3C  D2 01 6 003 D 1E0      MVC   003(2,6),1E0(13)    DNM=1-217    TS3=1
      122   000F42  D2 03 D 1E0 6 003      MVC   1E0(4,13),003(6)    TS3=1        DNM=1-217
            000F48  48 30 D 1E0            LH    3,1E0(0,13)         TS3=1
            000F4C  4C 30 C 0E8            MH    3,0E8(0,12)         LIT+0
            000F50  4E 30 D 1D8            CVD   3,1D8(0,13)         TS=09
            000F54  F3 32 6 00D D 1DD      UNPK  00D(4,6),1DD(3,13)  DNM=1-274    TS=014
      123   000F5A  F2 73 D 1D8 6 00D      PACK  1D8(8,13),00D(4,6)  TS=09        DNM=1-274
            000F60  D2 03 D 1E0 6 003      MVC   1E0(4,13),003(6)    TS3=1        DNM=1-217
            000F66  48 30 D 1E0            LH    3,1E0(0,13)         TS3=1
            000F6A  4C 30 C 0E8            MH    3,0E8(0,12)         LIT+0
            000F6E  4E 30 D 1D0            CVD   3,1D0(0,13)         TS=01
            000F72  FA 22 D 1D5 D 1DD      AP    1D5(3,13),1DD(3,13) TS=06        TS=014
            000F78  F3 32 6 00D D 1D5      UNPK  00D(4,6),1D5(3,13)  DNM=1-274    TS=06
      124   000F7E  F2 73 D 1D8 6 00D      PACK  1D8(8,13),00D(4,6)  TS=09        DNM=1-274
            000F84  4F 30 D 1D8            CVB   3,1D8(0,13)         TS=09
            000F88  18 23                  LR    2,3
            000F8A  8E 20 0 020            SRDA  2,020(0)
```

```
14

          000F8E  5D 20 C OEC         D     2,OEC(0,12)         LIT+4
          000F92  40 30 D 1EO         STH   3,1EO(0,13)         TS3=1
125       000F96  D2 01 6 003 D 1EO   MVC   003(2,6),1EO(13)    DNM=1-217     TS3=1
          000F9C  F2 73 D 1D8 6 00D   PACK  1D8(8,13),00D(4,6)  TS=09         DNM=1-274
          000FA2  4F 30 D 1D8         CVB   3,1D8(0,13)         TS=09
          000FA6  D2 03 D 1EO 6 003   MVC   1EO(4,13),003(6)    TS3=1         DNM=1-217
          000FAC  48 50 D 1EO         LH    5,1EO(0,13)         TS3=1
          000FB0  4C 50 C OE8         MH    5,OE8(0,12)         LIT+0
          000FB4  1A 35               AR    3,5
          000FB6  4E 30 D 1D8         CVD   3,1D8(0,13)         TS=09
          000FBA  D7 04 D 1D8 D 1D8   XC    1D8(5,13),1D8(13)   TS=09         TS=09
          000FC0  94 OF D 1DD         NI    1DD(13),X'OF'       TS=09+5
          000FC4  F1 76 D 1D8 D 1D8   MVO   1D8(8,13),1D8(7,13) TS=09         TS=09
          000FCA  4F 30 D 1D8         CVB   3,1D8(0,13)         TS=09
          000FCE  40 30 D 1EO         STH   3,1EO(0,13)         TS3=1
126       000FD2  D2 01 6 003 D 1EO   MVC   003(2,6),1EO(13)    DNM=1-217     TS3=1
          000FD8  D2 03 D 1EO 6 003   MVC   1EO(4,13),003(6)    TS3=1         DNM=1-217
          000FDE  48 30 D 1EO         LH    3,1EO(0,13)         TS3=1
          000FE2  4E 30 D 1D8         CVD   3,1D8(0,13)         TS=09
          000FE6  F3 21 6 014 D 1DE   UNPK  014(3,6),1DE(2,13)  DNM=1-304     TS=015
127       000FEC  96 FO 6 016         OI    016(6),X'FO'        DNM=1-304+2
          000FFO  F2 72 D 1D8 6 014   PACK  1D8(8,13),014(3,6)  TS=09         DNM=1-304
          000FF6  D2 03 D 1EO 6 003   MVC   1EO(4,13),003(6)    TS3=1         DNM=1-217
          000FFC  48 30 D 1EO         LH    3,1EO(0,13)         TS3=1
          001000  4E 30 D 1DO         CVD   3,1DO(0,13)         TS=01
          001004  FA 21 D 1D5 D 1DE   AP    1D5(3,13),1DE(2,13) TS=06         TS=015
          00100A  F3 22 6 014 D 1D5   UNPK  014(3,6),1D5(3,13)  TS=06
          001010  96 FO 6 016         OI    016(6),X'FO'        DNM=1-304+2
128       001014  F2 72 D 1D8 6 014   PACK  1D8(8,13),014(3,6)  TS=09         DNM=1-304
          00101A  4F 30 D 1D8         CVB   3,1D8(0,13)         TS=09
          00101E  40 30 D 1EO         STH   3,1EO(0,13)         TS3=1
          001022  D2 01 6 003 D 1EO   MVC   003(2,6),1EO(13)    DNM=1-217     TS3=1
129       001028  F2 72 D 1D8 6 014   PACK  1D8(8,13),014(3,6)  TS=09         DNM=1-304
          00102E  4F 30 D 1D8         CVB   3,1D8(0,13)         TS=09
          001032  D2 03 D 1EO 6 003   MVC   1EO(4,13),003(6)    TS3=1         DNM=1-217
          001038  4A 30 D 1EO         AH    3,1EO(0,13)         TS3=1
          00103C  4E 30 D 1D8         CVD   3,1D8(0,13)         TS=09
          001040  D7 05 D 1D8 D 1D8   XC    1D8(6,13),1D8(13)   TS=09         TS=09
          001046  4F 30 D 1D8         CVB   3,1D8(0,13)         TS=09
          00104A  40 30 D 1EO         STH   3,1EO(0,13)         TS3=1
130       00104E  D2 01 6 003 D 1EO   MVC   003(2,6),1EO(13)    DNM=1-217     TS3=1
          001054  D2 03 D 1EO 6 005   MVC   1EO(4,13),005(6)    TS3=1         DNM=1-231
          00105A  48 20 D 1EO         LH    2,1EO(0,13)         TS3=1
          00105E  8E 20 0 020         SRDA  2,020(0)
          001062  5D 20 C OEC         D     2,OEC(0,12)         LIT+4
          001066  4E 30 D 1D8         CVD   3,1D8(0,13)         TS=09
131       00106A  F3 21 6 000 D 1DE   UNPK  000(3,6),1DE(2,13)  DNM=1-202     TS=015
          001070  F2 72 D 1D8 6 000   PACK  1D8(8,13),000(3,6)  TS=09         DNM=1-202
          001076  D2 03 D 1EO 6 005   MVC   1EO(4,13),005(6)    TS3=1         DNM=1-231
          00107C  48 30 D 1EO         LH    3,1EO(0,13)         TS3=1
          001080  4E 30 D 1DO         CVD   3,1DO(0,13)         TS=01
          001084  FC 31 D 1DC C OEA   MP    1DC(4,13),OEA(2,12) TS=013        LIT+2
          00108A  FA 22 D 1D5 D 1DD   AP    1D5(3,13),1DD(3,13) TS=06         TS=014
          001090  F1 76 D 1DO D 1DO   MVO   1DO(8,13),1DO(7,13) TS=01         TS=01
          001096  F3 22 6 000 D 1D5   UNPK  000(3,6),1D5(3,13)  DNM=1-202     TS=06
132       00109C  F2 72 D 1D8 6 000   PACK  1D8(8,13),000(3,6)  TS=09         DNM=1-202
          0010A2  4F 30 D 1D8         CVB   3,1D8(0,13)         TS=09
          0010A6  4C 30 C OE8         MH    3,OE8(0,12)         LIT+0
          0010AA  40 30 D 1EO         STH   3,1EO(0,13)         TS3=1
          0010AE  D2 01 6 005 D 1EO   MVC   005(2,6),1EO(13)    DNM=1-231     TS3=1
133  ⌐    0010B4  F2 72 D 1D8 6 000   -6    PACK  1D8(8,13),000(3,6)  TS=09   DNM=1-202
     |    0010BA  4F 30 D 1D8         -4    CVB   3,1D8(0,13)          TS=09
     |    0010BE  4C 30 C OE8         -4    MH    3,OE8(0,12)          LIT+0
  (2)|    0010C2  D2 03 D 1EO 6 005   -4    MVC   1EO(4,13),005(6)     TS3=1  DNM=1-231
     |    0010C8  4A 30 D 1EO         -4    AH    3,1EO(0,13)          TS3=1
     |    0010CC  4E 30 D 1D8         -4    CVD   3,1D8(0,13)          TS=09
     |    0010D0  D7 04 D 1D8 D 1D8   -6    XC    1D8(5,13),1D8(13)    TS=09  TS=09
     |    0010D6  94 OF D 1DD         -4    NI    1DD(13),X'OF'        TS=09+5
     |    0010DA  4F 30 D 1D8         -4    CVB   3,1D8(0,13)          TS=09
     |    0010DE  40 30 D 1EO         -4    STH   3,1EO(0,13)          TS3=1
     └    0010E2  D2 01 6 005 D 1EO   -6    MVC   005(2,6),1EO(13)     DNM=1-231  TS3=1
134       0010E8  D2 03 D 1EO 6 005   MVC   1EO(4,13),005(6)    TS3=1         DNM=1-231
          0010EE  48 20 D 1EO         LH    2,1EO(0,13)         TS3=1
          0010F2  8E 20 0 020         SRDA  2,020(0)
          0010F6  5D 20 C OEC         D     2,OEC(0,12)         LIT+4
          0010FA  4E 30 D 1D8         CVD   3,1D8(0,13)         TS=09
135       0010FE  F3 31 6 009 D 1DE   UNPK  009(4,6),1DE(2,13)  DNM=1-259     TS=015
          001104  F2 73 D 1D8 6 009   PACK  1D8(8,13),009(4,6)  TS=09         DNM=1-259
          00110A  D2 03 D 1EO 6 005   MVC   1EO(4,13),005(6)    TS3=1         DNM=1-231
          001110  48 30 D 1EO         LH    3,1EO(0,13)         TS3=1
          001114  4E 30 D 1DO         CVD   3,1DO(0,13)         TS=01
          001118  FC 41 D 1D8 C OEA   MP    1D8(5,13),OEA(2,12) TS=012        LIT+2
          00111E  FA 32 D 1D4 D 1DD   AP    1D4(4,13),1DD(3,13) TS=05         TS=014
          001124  F1 76 D 1DO D 1DO   MVO   1DO(8,13),1DO(7,13) TS=01         TS=01
          00112A  F3 32 6 009 D 1D5   UNPK  009(4,6),1D5(3,13)  DNM=1-259     TS=06
136       001130  F2 73 D 1D8 6 009   PACK  1D8(8,13),009(4,6)  TS=09         DNM=1-259
          001136  D7 05 D 1D8 D 1D8   XC    1D8(6,13),1D8(13)   TS=09         TS=09
```

15

```
        00113C  FC 31 D 1DC C 0EA    MP     1DC(4,13),0EA(2,12)    TS=013       LIT+2
        001142  4F 30 D 1D8          CVB    3,1D8(0,13)            TS=09
        001146  40 30 D 1E0          STH    3,1E0(0,13)            TS3=1
        00114A  D2 01 6 005 D 1E0    MVC    005(2,6),1E0(13)       DNM=1-231    TS3=1
137     001150  F2 73 D 1D8 6 009    PACK   1D8(8,13),009(4,6)     TS=09        DNM=1-259
        001156  4F 30 D 1D8          CVB    3,1D8(0,13)            TS=09
        00115A  4C 30 C 0E8          MH     3,0E8(0,12)            LIT+0
        00115E  D2 03 D 1E0 6 005    MVC    1E0(4,13),005(6)       TS3=1        DNM=1-231
        001164  4A 30 D 1E0          AH     3,1E0(0,13)            TS3=1
        001168  4E 30 D 1D8          CVD    3,1D8(0,13)            TS=09
        00116C  D7 04 D 1D8 D 1D8    XC     1D8(5,13),1D8(13)      TS=09        TS=09
        001172  94 0F D 1DD          NI     1DD(13),X'0F'          TS=09+5
        001176  4F 30 D 1D8          CVB    3,1D8(0,13)            TS=09
        00117A  40 30 D 1E0          STH    3,1E0(0,13)            TS3=1
        00117E  D2 01 6 005 D 1E0    MVC    005(2,6),1E0(13)       DNM=1-231    TS3=1
138     001184  D2 03 D 1E0 6 005    MVC    1E0(4,13),005(6)       TS3=1        DNM=1-231
        00118A  48 30 D 1E0          LH     3,1E0(0,13)            TS3=1
        00118E  4E 30 D 1D8          CVD    3,1D8(0,13)            TS=09
        001192  F3 32 6 00D D 1DD    UNPK   00D(4,6),1DD(3,13)     DNM=1-274    TS=014
139     001198  F2 73 D 1D8 6 00D    PACK   1D8(8,13),00D(4,6)     TS=09        DNM=1-274
        00119E  D2 03 D 1E0 6 005    MVC    1E0(4,13),005(6)       TS3=1        DNM=1-231
        0011A4  48 30 D 1E0          LH     3,1E0(0,13)            TS3=1
        0011A8  4E 30 D 1D0          CVD    3,1D0(0,13)            TS=01
        0011AC  FA 22 D 1D5 D 1DD    AP     1D5(3,13),1DD(3,13)    TS=06        TS=014
        0011B2  F3 32 6 00D D 1D5    UNPK   00D(4,6),1D5(3,13)     DNM=1-274    TS=06
140     0011B8  F2 73 D 1D8 6 00D    PACK   1D8(8,13),00D(4,6)     TS=09        DNM=1-274
        0011BE  4F 30 D 1D8          CVB    3,1D8(0,13)            TS=09
        0011C2  40 30 D 1E0          STH    3,1E0(0,13)            TS3=1
        0011C6  D2 01 6 005 D 1E0    MVC    005(2,6),1E0(13)       DNM=1-231    TS3=1
141     0011CC  F2 73 D 1D8 6 00D    PACK   1D8(8,13),00D(4,6)     TS=09        DNM=1-274
        0011D2  4F 30 D 1D8          CVB    3,1D8(0,13)            TS=09
        0011D6  D2 03 D 1E0 6 005    MVC    1E0(4,13),005(6)       TS3=1        DNM=1-231
        0011DC  4A 30 D 1E0          AH     3,1E0(0,13)            TS3=1
        0011E0  4E 30 D 1D8          CVD    3,1D8(0,13)            TS=09
        0011E4  D7 04 D 1D8 D 1D8    XC     1D8(5,13),1D8(13)      TS=09        TS=09
        0011EA  94 0F D 1DD          NI     1DD(13),X'0F'          TS=09+5
        0011EE  4F 30 D 1D8          CVB    3,1D8(0,13)            TS=09
        0011F2  40 30 D 1E0          STH    3,1E0(0,13)            TS3=1
        0011F6  D2 01 6 005 D 1E0    MVC    005(2,6),1E0(13)       DNM=1-231    TS3=1
142     0011FC  D2 03 D 1E0 6 005    MVC    1E0(4,13),005(6)       TS3=1        DNM=1-231
        001202  48 20 D 1E0          LH     2,1E0(0,13)            TS3=1
        001206  8F 20 0 020          SRDA   2,020(0)
        00120A  5D 20 C 0EC          D      2,0EC(0,12)            LIT+4
        00120E  4E 30 D 1D8          CVD    3,1D8(0,13)            TS=09
        001212  F3 21 6 014 D 1DE    UNPK   014(3,6),1DE(2,13)     DNM=1-304    TS=015
        001218  96 F0 6 016          OI     016(6),X'F0'           DNM=1-304+2
143     00121C  F2 72 D 1D8 6 014    PACK   1D8(8,13),014(3,6)     TS=09        DNM=1-304
        001222  D2 03 D 1E0 6 005    MVC    1E0(4,13),005(6)       TS3=1        DNM=1-231
        001228  48 30 D 1E0          LH     3,1E0(0,13)            TS3=1
        00122C  4E 30 D 1D0          CVD    3,1D0(0,13)            TS=01
        001230  FC 31 D 1DC C 0EA    MP     1DC(4,13),0EA(2,12)    TS=013       LIT+2
        001236  FA 22 D 1D5 D 1DD    AP     1D5(3,13),1DD(3,13)    TS=06        TS=014
        00123C  F1 76 D 1D0 D 1DD    MVO    1D0(8,13),1DD(7,13)    TS=01        TS=06
        001242  F3 22 6 014 D 1D5    UNPK   014(3,6),1D5(3,13)     DNM=1-304    TS=06
        001248  96 F0 6 016          OI     016(6),X'F0'           DNM=1-304+2
144     00124C  F2 72 D 1D8 6 014    PACK   1D8(8,13),014(3,6)     TS=09        DNM=1-304
        001252  4F 30 D 1D8          CVB    3,1D8(0,13)            TS=09
        001256  4C 30 C 0E8          MH     3,0E8(0,12)            LIT+0
        00125A  40 30 D 1E0          STH    3,1E0(0,13)            TS3=1
        00125E  D2 01 6 005 D 1E0    MVC    005(2,6),1E0(13)       DNM=1-231    TS3=1
145     001264  F2 72 D 1D8 6 014    PACK   1D8(8,13),014(3,6)     TS=09        DNM=1-304
        00126A  4F 30 D 1D8          CVB    3,1D8(0,13)            TS=09
        00126E  4C 30 C 0E8          MH     3,0E8(0,12)            LIT+0
        001272  D2 03 D 1E0 6 005    MVC    1E0(4,13),005(6)       TS3=1        DNM=1-231
        001278  4A 30 D 1E0          AH     3,1E0(0,13)            TS3=1
        00127C  4E 30 D 1D8          CVD    3,1D8(0,13)            TS=09
        001280  D7 04 D 1D8 D 1D8    XC     1D8(5,13),1D8(13)      TS=09        TS=09
        001286  94 0F D 1DD          NI     1DD(13),X'0F'          TS=09+5
        00128A  4F 30 D 1D8          CVB    3,1D8(0,13)            TS=09
        00128E  40 30 D 1E0          STH    3,1E0(0,13)            TS3=1
        001292  D2 01 6 005 D 1E0    MVC    005(2,6),1E0(13)       DNM=1-231    TS3=1
146     001298  D2 02 6 011 6 000    MVC    011(3,6),000(6)        DNM=1-289    DNM=1-202
147     00129E  F2 72 D 1D8 6 000    PACK   1D8(8,13),000(3,6)     TS=09        DNM=1-202
        0012A4  F2 72 D 1D0 6 011    PACK   1D0(8,13),011(3,6)     TS=01        DNM=1-289
        0012AA  FA 21 D 1DD D 1D6    AP     1DD(3,13),1D6(2,13)    TS=014       TS=07
        0012B0  F3 22 6 011 D 1DD    UNPK   011(3,6),1DD(3,13)     DNM=1-289    TS=014
148     0012B6  D2 02 6 000 6 011    MVC    000(3,6),011(6)        DNM=1-202    DNM=1-289
149     0012BC  F2 72 D 1D8 6 011    PACK   1D8(8,13),011(3,6)     TS=09        DNM=1-289
        0012C2  F2 72 D 1D0 6 000    PACK   1D0(8,13),000(3,6)     TS=01        DNM=1-202
        0012C8  FA 21 D 1DD D 1D6    AP     1DD(3,13),1D6(2,13)    TS=014       TS=07
        0012CE  F3 22 6 000 D 1DD    UNPK   000(3,6),1DD(3,13)     DNM=1-202    TS=014
150     0012D4  D2 02 6 00A 6 000    MVC    00A(3,6),000(6)        DNM=1-259+1  DNM=1-202
        0012DA  92 F0 6 009          MVI    009(6),X'F0'           DNM=1-259
151     0012DE  F2 72 D 1D8 6 000    PACK   1D8(8,13),000(3,6)     TS=09        DNM=1-202
        0012E4  F2 73 D 1D0 6 009    PACK   1D0(8,13),009(4,6)     TS=01        DNM=1-259
        0012EA  FA 22 D 1DD D 1D5    AP     1DD(3,13),1D5(3,13)    TS=014       TS=06
        0012F0  F3 32 6 009 D 1DD    UNPK   009(4,6),1DD(3,13)     DNM=1-259    TS=014
```

```
    16

152    0012F6  D2 02 6 000 6 00A    MVC   000(3,6),00A(6)        DNM=1-202      DNM=1-259+1
153    0012FC  F2 73 D 1D8 6 009    PACK  1D8(8,13),009(4,6)     TS=09          DNM=1-259
       001302  F2 72 D 1D0 6 000    PACK  1D0(8,13),000(3,6)     TS=01          DNM=1-202
       001308  FA 21 D 1DD D 1D6    AP    1DD(3,13),1D6(2,13)    TS=014         TS=07
       00130E  F3 22 6 000 D 1DD    UNPK  000(3,6),1DD(3,13)     DNM=1-202      TS=014
154    001314  D2 02 6 00D 6 000    MVC   00D(3,6),000(6)        DNM=1-274      DNM=1-202
       00131A  92 F0 6 010          MVI   010(6),X'F0'           DNM=1-274+3
       00131E  D3 00 6 010 6 002    MVZ   010(1,6),002(6)        DNM=1-274+3    DNM=1-202+2
       001324  96 F0 6 00F          OI    00F(6),X'F0'           DNM=1-274+2
155    001328  F2 72 D 1D8 6 000    PACK  1D8(8,13),000(3,6)     TS=09          DNM=1-202
       00132E  F2 73 D 1D0 6 00D    PACK  1D0(8,13),00D(4,6)     TS=01          DNM=1-274
       001334  FC 31 D 1DC C 0EA    MP    1DC(4,13),0EA(2,12)    TS=013         LIT+2
       00133A  FA 22 D 1DD D 1D5    AP    1DD(3,13),1D5(3,13)    TS=014         TS=06
       001340  F3 32 6 00D D 1DD    UNPK  00D(4,6),1DD(3,13)     DNM=1-274      TS=014
156    001346  D2 02 6 000 6 00D    MVC   000(3,6),00D(6)        DNM=1-202      DNM=1-274
       00134C  D3 00 6 002 6 010    MVZ   002(1,6),010(6)        DNM=1-202+2    DNM=1-274+3
157    001352  F2 73 D 1D8 6 00D    PACK  1D8(8,13),00D(4,6)     TS=09          DNM=1-274
       001358  F2 72 D 1D0 6 000    PACK  1D0(8,13),000(3,6)     TS=01          DNM=1-202
       00135E  FC 31 D 1D4 C 0EA    MP    1D4(4,13),0EA(2,12)    TS=05          LIT+2
       001364  FA 22 D 1DD D 1D5    AP    1DD(3,13),1D5(3,13)    TS=014         TS=06
       00136A  F1 76 D 1D8 D 1D8    MVO   1D8(8,13),1D8(7,13)    TS=09          TS=09
       001370  F3 22 6 000 D 1DD    UNPK  000(3,6),1DD(3,13)     DNM=1-202      TS=014
158    001376  D2 02 6 014 6 000    MVC   014(3,6),000(6)        DNM=1-304      DNM=1-202
       00137C  96 F0 6 016          OI    016(6),X'F0'           DNM=1-304+2
159    001380  F2 72 D 1D8 6 000    PACK  1D8(8,13),000(3,6)     TS=09          DNM=1-202
       001386  F2 72 D 1D0 6 014    PACK  1D0(8,13),014(3,6)     TS=01          DNM=1-304
       00138C  FA 21 D 1DD D 1D6    AP    1DD(3,13),1D6(2,13)    TS=014         TS=07
       001392  F3 22 6 014 D 1DD    UNPK  014(3,6),1DD(3,13)     DNM=1-304      TS=014
       001398  96 F0 6 016          OI    016(6),X'F0'           DNM=1-304+2
160    00139C  D2 02 6 000 6 014    MVC   000(3,6),014(6)        DNM=1-202      DNM=1-304
       0013A2  94 0F 6 002          NI    002(6),X'0F'           DNM=1-202+2
       0013A6  96 C0 6 002          OI    002(6),X'C0'           DNM=1-202+2
161    0013AA  F2 72 D 1D8 6 014    PACK  1D8(8,13),014(3,6)     TS=09          DNM=1-304
       0013B0  F2 72 D 1D0 6 000    PACK  1D0(8,13),000(3,6)     TS=01          DNM=1-202
       0013B6  FA 21 D 1DD D 1D6    AP    1DD(3,13),1D6(2,13)    TS=014         TS=07
       0013BC  F3 22 6 000 D 1DD    UNPK  000(3,6),1DD(3,13)     DNM=1-202      TS=014
162    0013C2  D2 03 D 1E0 6 003    MVC   1E0(4,13),003(6)       TS3=1          DNM=1-217
       0013C8  48 30 D 1E0          LH    3,1E0(0,13)            TS3=1
       0013CC  4E 30 D 1D8          CVD   3,1D8(0,13)            TS=09
       0013D0  F8 11 6 017 D 1DE    ZAP   017(2,6),1DE(2,13)     DNM=1-319      TS=015
163    0013D6  D2 03 D 1E0 6 003    MVC   1E0(4,13),003(6)       TS3=1          DNM=1-217
       0013DC  48 30 D 1E0          LH    3,1E0(0,13)            TS3=1
       0013E0  4E 30 D 1D8          CVD   3,1D8(0,13)            TS=09
       0013E4  FA 11 6 017 D 1DE    AP    017(2,6),1DE(2,13)     DNM=1-319      TS=015
164    0013EA  F8 71 D 1D8 6 017    ZAP   1D8(8,13),017(2,6)     TS=09          DNM=1-319
       0013F0  4F 30 D 1D8          CVB   3,1D8(0,13)            TS=09
       0013F4  40 30 D 1E0          STH   3,1E0(0,13)            TS3=1
       0013F8  D2 01 6 003 D 1E0    MVC   003(2,6),1E0(13)       DNM=1-217      TS3=1
165    0013FE  F8 71 D 1D8 6 017    ZAP   1D8(8,13),017(2,6)     TS=09          DNM=1-319
       001404  4F 30 D 1D8          CVB   3,1D8(0,13)            TS=09
       001408  D2 03 D 1E0 6 003    MVC   1E0(4,13),003(6)       TS3=1          DNM=1-217
       00140E  4A 30 D 1E0          AH    3,1E0(0,13)            TS3=1
       001412  4E 30 D 1D8          CVD   3,1D8(0,13)            TS=09
       001416  D7 05 D 1D8 D 1D8    XC    1D8(6,13),1D8(13)      TS=09          TS=09
       00141C  4F 30 D 1D8          CVB   3,1D8(0,13)            TS=09
       001420  40 30 D 1E0          STH   3,1E0(0,13)            TS3=1
       001424  D2 01 6 003 D 1E0    MVC   003(2,6),1E0(13)       DNM=1-217      TS3=1
166    00142A  D2 03 D 1E0 6 003    MVC   1E0(4,13),003(6)       TS3=1          DNM=1-217
       001430  48 30 D 1E0          LH    3,1E0(0,13)            TS3=1
       001434  4E 30 D 1D8          CVD   3,1D8(0,13)            TS=09
       001438  F8 21 6 019 D 1DE    ZAP   019(3,6),1DE(2,13)     DNM=1-334      TS=015
167    00143E  D2 03 D 1E0 6 003    MVC   1E0(4,13),003(6)       TS3=1          DNM=1-217
       001444  48 30 D 1E0          LH    3,1E0(0,13)            TS3=1
       001448  4E 30 D 1D8          CVD   3,1D8(0,13)            TS=09
       00144C  FA 21 6 019 D 1DE    AP    019(3,6),1DE(2,13)     DNM=1-334      TS=015
       001452  94 0F 6 019          NI    019(6),X'0F'           DNM=1-334
168    001456  F8 72 D 1D8 6 019    ZAP   1D8(8,13),019(3,6)     TS=09          DNM=1-334
       00145C  D7 05 D 1D8 D 1D8    XC    1D8(6,13),1D8(13)      TS=09          TS=09
       001462  4F 30 D 1D8          CVB   3,1D8(0,13)            TS=09
       001466  40 30 D 1E0          STH   3,1E0(0,13)            TS3=1
       00146A  D2 01 6 003 D 1E0    MVC   003(2,6),1E0(13)       DNM=1-217      TS3=1
169    001470  F8 72 D 1D8 6 019    ZAP   1D8(8,13),019(3,6)     TS=09          DNM=1-334
       001476  4F 30 D 1D8          CVB   3,1D8(0,13)            TS=09
       00147A  D2 03 D 1E0 6 003    MVC   1E0(4,13),003(6)       TS3=1          DNM=1-217
       001480  4A 30 D 1E0          AH    3,1E0(0,13)            TS3=1
       001484  4E 30 D 1D8          CVD   3,1D8(0,13)            TS=09
       001488  D7 05 D 1D8 D 1D8    XC    1D8(6,13),1D8(13)      TS=09          TS=09
       00148E  4F 30 D 1D8          CVB   3,1D8(0,13)            TS=09
       001492  40 30 D 1E0          STH   3,1E0(0,13)            TS3=1
       001496  D2 01 6 003 D 1E0    MVC   003(2,6),1E0(13)       DNM=1-217      TS3=1
170    00149C  D2 03 D 1E0 6 003    MVC   1E0(4,13),003(6)       TS3=1          DNM=1-217
       0014A2  48 30 D 1E0          LH    3,1E0(0,13)            TS3=1
       0014A6  4C 30 C 0E8          MH    3,0E8(0,12)            LIT+0
       0014AA  4E 30 D 1D8          CVD   3,1D8(0,13)            TS=09
       0014AE  F8 22 6 01C D 1DD    ZAP   01C(3,6),1DD(3,13)     DNM=1-352      TS=014
171    0014B4  D2 03 D 1E0 6 003    MVC   1E0(4,13),003(6)       TS3=1          DNM=1-217
       0014BA  48 30 D 1E0          LH    3,1E0(0,13)            TS3=1
```

```
     17

 172
      0014BE  4C 30 C OE8           MH    3,0E8(0,12)           LIT+0
      0014C2  4E 30 D 1D8           CVD   3,1D8(0,13)           TS=09
      0014C6  FA 22 6 01C D 1DD     AP    01C(3,6),1DD(3,13)    DNM=1-352      TS=014
      0014CC  94 OF 6 01C           NI    01C(6),X'OF'          DNM=1-352
      0014D0  F8 72 D 1D8 6 01C     ZAP   1D8(8,13),01C(3,6)    TS=09          DNM=1-352
      0014D6  4F 30 D 1D8           CVB   3,1D8(0,13)           TS=09
      0014DA  18 23                 LR    2,3
      0014DC  8E 20 0 020           SRDA  2,020(0)
      0014E0  5D 20 C OEC           D     2,0EC(0,12)           LIT+4
      0014E4  40 30 D 1EO           STH   3,1EO(0,13)           TS3=1

 173  0014E8  D2 01 6 003 D 1EO     MVC   003(2,6),1EO(13)      DNM=1-217      TS3=1
      0014EE  F8 72 D 1D8 6 01C     ZAP   1D8(8,13),01C(3,6)    TS=09          DNM=1-352
      0014F4  4F 30 D 1D8           CVB   3,1D8(0,13)           TS=09
      0014F8  D2 03 D 1EO 6 003     MVC   1EO(4,13),003(6)      TS3=1          DNM=1-217
      0014FE  48 50 D 1EO           LH    5,1EO(0,13)           TS3=1
      001502  4C 50 C OE8           MH    5,0E8(0,12)           LIT+0
      001506  1A 35                 AR    3,5
      001508  4E 30 D 1D8           CVD   3,1D8(0,13)           TS=09

 174  00150C  D7 04 D 1D8 D 1D8     XC    1D8(5,13),1D8(13)     TS=09          TS=09
      001512  94 OF D 1DD           NI    1DD(13),X'OF'         TS=09+5
      001516  F1 76 D 1D8 D 1D8     MVO   1D8(8,13),1D8(7,13)   TS=09          TS=09
      00151C  4F 30 D 1D8           CVB   3,1D8(0,13)           TS=09
      001520  40 30 D 1EO           STH   3,1EO(0,13)           TS3=1
      001524  D2 01 6 003 D 1EO     MVC   003(2,6),1EO(13)      DNM=1-217      TS3=1
      00152A  D2 03 D 1EO 6 003     MVC   1EO(4,13),003(6)      TS3=1          DNM=1-217
      001530  48 30 D 1EO           LH    3,1EO(0,13)           TS3=1
      001534  4E 30 D 1D8           CVD   3,1D8(0,13)           TS=09

 175  001538  F8 21 6 021 D 1DE     ZAP   021(3,6),1DE(2,13)    DNM=1-382      TS=015
      00153E  96 OF 6 023           OI    023(6),X'OF'          DNM=1-382+2
      001542  D2 03 D 1EO 6 003     MVC   1EO(4,13),003(6)      TS3=1          DNM=1-217
      001548  48 30 D 1EO           LH    3,1EO(0,13)           TS3=1
      00154C  4E 30 D 1D8           CVD   3,1D8(0,13)           TS=09

 176  001550  FA 21 6 021 D 1DE     AP    021(3,6),1DE(2,13)    DNM=1-382      TS=015
      001556  94 OF 6 021           NI    021(6),X'OF'          DNM=1-382
      00155A  96 OF 6 023           OI    023(6),X'OF'          DNM=1-382+2
      00155E  F8 72 D 1D8 6 021     ZAP   1D8(8,13),021(3,6)    TS=09          DNM=1-382
      001564  D7 05 D 1D8 D 1D8     XC    1D8(6,13),1D8(13)     TS=09          TS=09
      00156A  4F 30 D 1D8           CVB   3,1D8(0,13)           TS=09
      00156E  40 30 D 1EO           STH   3,1EO(0,13)           TS3=1

 177  001572  D2 01 6 003 D 1EO     MVC   003(2,6),1EO(13)      DNM=1-217      TS3=1
      001578  F8 72 D 1D8 6 021     ZAP   1D8(8,13),021(3,6)    TS=09          DNM=1-382
      00157E  4F 30 D 1D8           CVB   3,1D8(0,13)           TS=09
      001582  D2 03 D 1EO 6 003     MVC   1EO(4,13),003(6)      TS3=1          DNM=1-217
      001588  4A 30 D 1EO           AH    3,1EO(0,13)           TS3=1
      00158C  4E 30 D 1D8           CVD   3,1D8(0,13)           TS=09
      001590  D7 05 D 1D8 D 1D8     XC    1D8(6,13),1D8(13)     TS=09          TS=09
      001596  4F 30 D 1D8           CVB   3,1D8(0,13)           TS=09
      00159A  40 30 D 1EO           STH   3,1EO(0,13)           TS3=1
      00159E  D2 01 6 003 D 1EO     MVC   003(2,6),1EO(13)      DNM=1-217      TS3=1

 178  0015A4  D2 03 D 1EO 6 005     MVC   1EO(4,13),005(6)      TS3=1          DNM=1-231
      0015AA  48 20 D 1EO           LH    2,1EO(0,13)           TS3=1
      0015AE  8E 20 0 020           SRDA  2,020(0)
      0015B2  5D 20 C OEC           D     2,0EC(0,12)           LIT+4
      0015B6  4E 30 D 1D8           CVD   3,1D8(0,13)           TS=09

 179  0015BA  F8 11 6 017 D 1DE     ZAP   017(2,6),1DE(2,13)    DNM=1-319      TS=015
      0015C0  D2 03 D 1EO 6 005     MVC   1EO(4,13),005(6)      TS3=1          DNM=1-231
      0015C6  48 30 D 1EO           LH    3,1EO(0,13)           TS3=1
      0015CA  4E 30 D 1D8           CVD   3,1D8(0,13)           TS=09
      0015CE  F8 71 D 1D0 6 017     ZAP   1D0(8,13),017(2,6)    TS=01          DNM=1-319
      0015D4  FC 31 D 1D4 C OEA     MP    1D4(4,13),0EA(2,12)   TS=05          LIT+2
      0015DA  FA 22 D 1DD D 1D5     AP    1DD(3,13),1D5(3,13)   TS=014         TS=06
      0015E0  F1 76 D 1D8 D 1D8     MVO   1D8(8,13),1D8(7,13)   TS=09          TS=09

 180  0015E6  F8 11 6 017 D 1DE     ZAP   017(2,6),1DE(2,13)    DNM=1-319      TS=014+1
      0015EC  F8 71 D 1D8 6 017     ZAP   1D8(8,13),017(2,6)    TS=09          DNM=1-319
      0015F2  4F 30 D 1D8           CVB   3,1D8(0,13)           TS=09
      0015F6  4C 30 C OE8           MH    3,0E8(0,12)           LIT+0
      0015FA  40 30 D 1EO           STH   3,1EO(0,13)           TS3=1

 181  0015FE  D2 01 6 005 D 1EO     MVC   005(2,6),1EO(13)      DNM=1-231      TS3=1
      001604  F8 71 D 1D8 6 017     ZAP   1D8(8,13),017(2,6)    TS=09          DNM=1-319
      00160A  4F 30 D 1D8           CVB   3,1D8(0,13)           TS=09
      00160E  4C 30 C OE8           MH    3,0E8(0,12)           LIT+0
      001612  D2 03 D 1EO 6 005     MVC   1EO(4,13),005(6)      TS3=1          DNM=1-231
      001618  4A 30 D 1EO           AH    3,1EO(0,13)           TS3=1
      00161C  4E 30 D 1D8           CVD   3,1D8(0,13)           TS=09
      001620  D7 04 D 1D8 D 1D8     XC    1D8(5,13),1D8(13)     TS=09          TS=09
      001626  94 OF D 1DD           NI    1DD(13),X'OF'         TS=09+5
      00162A  4F 30 D 1D8           CVB   3,1D8(0,13)           TS=09
      00162E  40 30 D 1EO           STH   3,1EO(0,13)           TS3=1

 182  001632  D2 01 6 005 D 1EO     MVC   005(2,6),1EO(13)      DNM=1-231      TS3=1
      001638  D2 03 D 1EO 6 005     MVC   1EO(4,13),005(6)      TS3=1          DNM=1-231
      00163E  48 20 D 1EO           LH    2,1EO(0,13)           TS3=1
      001642  8E 20 0 020           SRDA  2,020(0)
      001646  5D 20 C OEC           D     2,0EC(0,12)           LIT+4
      00164A  4E 30 D 1D8           CVD   3,1D8(0,13)           TS=09
      00164E  F8 21 6 019 D 1DE     ZAP   019(3,6),1DE(2,13)    DNM=1-334      TS=015

 183  001654  D2 03 D 1EO 6 005     MVC   1EO(4,13),005(6)      TS3=1          DNM=1-231
      00165A  48 30 D 1EO           LH    3,1EO(0,13)           TS3=1
```

```
18

          00165E  4E 30 D 1D8         CVD   3,1D8(0,13)              TS=09
          001662  F8 72 D 1DD 6 019   ZAP   1DD(8,13),019(3,6)       TS=01        DNM=1-334
          001668  FC 41 D 1D3 C OEA   MP    1D3(5,13),OEA(2,12)      TS=04        LIT+2
          00166E  FA 32 D 1DC D 1D5   AP    1DC(4,13),1D5(3,13)      TS=013       TS=06
          001674  F1 76 D 1D8 D 1D8   MVO   1D8(8,13),1D8(7,13)      TS=09        TS=09
          00167A  F8 22 6 019 D 1DD   ZAP   019(3,6),1DD(3,13)       DNM=1-334    TS=014
          001680  94 0F 6 019         NI    019(6),X'0F'             DNM=1-334
   184    001684  F8 72 D 1D8 6 019   ZAP   1D8(8,13),019(3,6)       TS=09        DNM=1-334
          00168A  D7 05 D 1D8 D 1D8   XC    1D8(6,13),1D8(13)        TS=09        TS=09
          001690  FC 31 D 1DC C OEA   MP    1DC(4,13),OEA(2,12)      TS=013       LIT+2
          001696  4F 30 D 1D8         CVB   3,1D8(0,13)              TS=09
          00169A  40 30 D 1E0         STH   3,1E0(0,13)              TS3=1
          00169E  D2 01 6 005 D 1E0   MVC   005(2,6),1E0(13)         DNM=1-231    TS3=1
   185    0016A4  F8 72 D 1D8 6 019   ZAP   1D8(8,13),019(3,6)       TS=09        DNM=1-334
          0016AA  4F 30 D 1D8         CVB   3,1D8(0,13)              TS=09
          0016AE  4C 30 C OE8         MH    3,0E8(0,12)              LIT+0
          0016B2  D2 03 D 1E0 6 005   MVC   1E0(4,13),005(6)         TS3=1        DNM=1-231
          0016B8  4A 30 D 1E0         AH    3,1E0(0,13)              TS3=1
          0016BC  4E 30 D 1D8         CVD   3,1D8(0,13)              TS=09
          0016C0  D7 04 D 1D8 D 1D8   XC    1D8(5,13),1D8(13)        TS=09        TS=09
          0016C6  94 0F D 1DD         NI    1DD(13),X'0F'            TS=09+5
          0016CA  4F 30 D 1D8         CVB   3,1D8(0,13)              TS=09
          0016CE  40 30 D 1E0         STH   3,1E0(0,13)              TS3=1
          0016D2  D2 01 6 005 D 1E0   MVC   005(2,6),1E0(13)         DNM=1-231    TS3=1
   186    0016D8  D2 03 D 1E0 6 005   MVC   1E0(4,13),005(6)         TS3=1        DNM=1-231
          0016DE  48 30 D 1E0         LH    3,1E0(0,13)              TS3=1
          0016E2  4E 30 D 1D8         CVD   3,1D8(0,13)              TS=09
          0016E6  F8 22 6 01C D 1DD   ZAP   01C(3,6),1DD(3,13)       DNM=1-352    TS=014
   187    0016EC  D2 03 D 1E0 6 005   MVC   1E0(4,13),005(6)         TS3=1        DNM=1-231
          0016F2  48 30 D 1E0         LH    3,1E0(0,13)              TS3=1
          0016F6  4E 30 D 1D8         CVD   3,1D8(0,13)              TS=09
          0016FA  FA 22 6 01C D 1DD   AP    01C(3,6),1DD(3,13)       DNM=1-352    TS=014
          001700  94 0F 6 01C         NI    01C(6),X'0F'             DNM=1-352
   188    001704  F8 72 D 1D8 6 01C   ZAP   1D8(8,13),01C(3,6)       TS=09        DNM=1-352
          00170A  4F 30 D 1D8         CVB   3,1D8(0,13)              TS=09
          00170F  40 30 D 1E0         STH   3,1E0(0,13)              TS3=1
          001712  D2 01 6 005 D 1E0   MVC   005(2,6),1E0(13)         DNM=1-231    TS3=1
   189    001718  F8 72 D 1D8 6 01C   ZAP   1D8(8,13),01C(3,6)       TS=09        DNM=1-352
          00171E  4F 30 D 1D8         CVB   3,1D8(0,13)              TS=09
          001722  D2 03 D 1E0 6 005   MVC   1E0(4,13),005(6)         TS3=1        DNM=1-231
          001728  4A 30 D 1E0         AH    3,1E0(0,13)              TS3=1
          00172C  4E 30 D 1D8         CVD   3,1D8(0,13)              TS=09
          001730  D7 04 D 1D8 D 1D8   XC    1D8(5,13),1D8(13)        TS=09        TS=09
          001736  94 0F D 1DD         NI    1DD(13),X'0F'            TS=09+5
          00173A  4F 30 D 1D8         CVB   3,1D8(0,13)              TS=09
          00173E  40 30 D 1E0         STH   3,1E0(0,13)              TS3=1
          001742  D2 01 6 005 D 1E0   MVC   005(2,6),1E0(13)         DNM=1-231    TS3=1
   190    001748  D2 03 D 1E0 6 005   MVC   1E0(4,13),005(6)         TS3=1        DNM=1-231
          00174E  48 20 D 1E0         LH    2,1E0(0,13)              TS3=1
          001752  8E 20 0 020         SRDA  2,020(0)
          001756  5D 20 C OEC         D     2,0EC(0,12)              LIT+4
          00175A  4E 30 D 1D8         CVD   3,1D8(0,13)              TS=09
          00175E  F8 21 6 021 D 1DE   ZAP   021(3,6),1DE(2,13)       DNM=1-382    TS=015
          001764  96 0F 6 023         OI    023(6),X'0F'             DNM=1-382+2
   191    001768  D2 03 D 1E0 6 005   MVC   1E0(4,13),005(6)         TS3=1        DNM=1-231
          00176E  48 30 D 1E0         LH    3,1E0(0,13)              TS3=1
          001772  4E 30 D 1D8         CVD   3,1D8(0,13)              TS=09
          001776  F8 72 D 1DD 6 021   ZAP   1DD(8,13),021(3,6)       TS=01        DNM=1-382
          00177C  FC 41 D 1D3 C OEA   MP    1D3(5,13),OEA(2,12)      TS=04        LIT+2
          001782  FA 32 D 1DC D 1D5   AP    1DC(4,13),1D5(3,13)      TS=013       TS=06
          001788  F1 76 D 1D8 D 1D8   MVO   1D8(8,13),1D8(7,13)      TS=09        TS=09
          00178E  F8 22 6 021 D 1DD   ZAP   021(3,6),1DD(3,13)       DNM=1-382    TS=014
          001794  94 0F 6 021         NI    021(6),X'0F'             DNM=1-382
          001798  96 0F 6 023         OI    023(6),X'0F'             DNM=1-382+2
   192    00179C  F8 72 D 1D8 6 021   ZAP   1D8(8,13),021(3,6)       TS=09        DNM=1-382
          0017A2  D7 05 D 1D8 D 1D8   XC    1D8(6,13),1D8(13)        TS=09        TS=09
          0017A8  FC 31 D 1DC C OEA   MP    1DC(4,13),OEA(2,12)      TS=013       LIT+2
          0017AE  4F 30 D 1D8         CVB   3,1D8(0,13)              TS=09
          0017B2  40 30 D 1E0         STH   3,1E0(0,13)              TS3=1
          0017B6  D2 01 6 005 D 1E0   MVC   005(2,6),1E0(13)         DNM=1-231    TS3=1
   193    0017BC  F8 72 D 1D8 6 021   ZAP   1D8(8,13),021(3,6)       TS=09        DNM=1-382
          0017C2  4F 30 D 1D8         CVB   3,1D8(0,13)              TS=09
          0017C6  4C 30 C OE8         MH    3,0E8(0,12)              LIT+0
          0017CA  D2 03 D 1E0 6 005   MVC   1E0(4,13),005(6)         TS3=1        DNM=1-231
          0017D0  4A 30 D 1E0         AH    3,1E0(0,13)              TS3=1
          0017D4  4E 30 D 1D8         CVD   3,1D8(0,13)              TS=09
          0017D8  D7 04 D 1D8 D 1D8   XC    1D8(5,13),1D8(13)        TS=09        TS=09
          0017DE  94 0F D 1DD         NI    1DD(13),X'0F'            TS=09+5
          0017E2  4F 30 D 1D8         CVB   3,1D8(0,13)              TS=09
          0017E6  40 30 D 1E0         STH   3,1E0(0,13)              TS3=1
          0017EA  D2 01 6 005 D 1E0   MVC   005(2,6),1E0(13)         DNM=1-231    TS3=1
   194    0017F0  F2 72 D 1D8 6 000   PACK  1D8(8,13),000(3,6)       TS=09        DNM=1-202
          0017F6  F8 11 6 017 D 1DE   ZAP   017(2,6),1DE(2,13)       DNM=1-319    TS=015
   195    0017FC  F2 72 D 1D8 6 000   PACK  1D8(8,13),000(3,6)       TS=09        DNM=1-202
          001802  FA 11 6 017 D 1DE   AP    017(2,6),1DE(2,13)       DNM=1-319    TS=015
   196    001808  F3 21 6 000 6 017   UNPK  000(3,6),017(2,6)        DNM=1-202    DNM=1-319
   197    00180E  F2 72 D 1D8 6 000   PACK  1D8(8,13),000(3,6)       TS=09        DNM=1-202
```

```
  19

        001814   FA 21 D 1DD 6 017      AP    1DD(3,13),017(2,6)     TS=014      DNM=1-319
        00181A   F3 22 6 000 D 1DD      UNPK  000(3,6),1DD(3,13)     DNM=1-202   TS=014
  198   001820   F2 72 D 1D8 6 000      PACK  1D8(8,13),000(3,6)     TS=09       DNM=1-202
        001826   F8 21 6 019 D 1DE      ZAP   019(3,6),1DE(2,13)     DNM=1-334   TS=015
  199   00182C   F2 72 D 1D8 6 000      PACK  1D8(8,13),000(3,6)     TS=09       DNM=1-202
        001832   FA 21 6 019 D 1DE      AP    019(3,6),1DE(2,13)     DNM=1-334   TS=015
        001838   94 0F 6 019            NI    019(6),X'0F'           DNM=1-334
  200   00183C   F3 22 6 000 6 019      UNPK  000(3,6),019(3,6)      DNM=1-202   DNM=1-334
  201   001842   F2 72 D 1D8 6 000      PACK  1D8(8,13),000(3,6)     TS=09       DNM=1-202
        001848   FA 22 D 1DD 6 019      AP    1DD(3,13),019(3,6)     TS=014      DNM=1-334
        00184E   F3 22 6 000 D 1DD      UNPK  000(3,6),1DD(3,13)     DNM=1-202   TS=014
  202   001854   F2 72 D 1D8 6 000      PACK  1D8(8,13),000(3,6)     TS=09       DNM=1-202
        00185A   FC 31 D 1DC C 0EA      MP    1DC(4,13),0EA(2,12)    TS=013      LIT+2
        001860   F8 22 6 01C D 1DD      ZAP   01C(3,6),1DD(3,13)     DNM=1-352   TS=014
  203   001866   F2 72 D 1D8 6 000      PACK  1D8(8,13),000(3,6)     TS=09       DNM=1-202
        00186C   FC 31 D 1DC C 0EA      MP    1DC(4,13),0EA(2,12)    TS=013      LIT+2
        001872   FA 22 6 01C D 1DD      AP    01C(3,6),1DD(3,13)     DNM=1-352   TS=014
        001878   94 0F 6 01C            NI    01C(6),X'0F'           DNM=1-352
  204   00187C   F8 72 D 1D8 6 01C      ZAP   1D8(8,13),01C(3,6)     TS=09       DNM=1-352
        001882   F1 76 D 1D8 D 1D8      MVO   1D8(8,13),1D8(7,13)    TS=09       TS=09
        001888   F3 21 6 000 D 1DE      UNPK  000(3,6),1DE(2,13)     DNM=1-202   TS=015
  205   00188E   F2 72 D 1D8 6 000      PACK  1D8(8,13),000(3,6)     TS=09       DNM=1-202
        001894   FC 31 D 1DC C 0EA      MP    1DC(4,13),0EA(2,12)    TS=013      LIT+2
        00189A   FA 22 D 1DD 6 01C      AP    1DD(3,13),01C(3,6)     TS=014      DNM=1-352
        0018A0   F1 76 D 1D8 D 1D8      MVO   1D8(8,13),1D8(7,13)    TS=09       TS=09
  206   0018A6   F3 22 6 000 D 1DD      UNPK  000(3,6),1DD(3,13)     DNM=1-202   TS=014
        0018AC   F2 72 D 1D8 6 000      PACK  1D8(8,13),000(3,6)     TS=09       DNM=1-202
        0018B2   F8 21 6 021 D 1DE      ZAP   021(3,6),1DE(2,13)     DNM=1-382   TS=015
        0018B8   96 0F 6 023            OI    023(6),X'0F'           DNM=1-382+2
  207   0018BC   F2 72 D 1D8 6 000      PACK  1D8(8,13),000(3,6)     TS=09       DNM=1-202
        0018C2   FA 21 6 021 D 1DE      AP    021(3,6),1DE(2,13)     DNM=1-382   TS=015
        0018C8   94 0F 6 021            NI    021(6),X'0F'           DNM=1-382
        0018CC   96 0F 6 023            OI    023(6),X'0F'           DNM=1-382+2
  208   0018D0   F3 22 6 000 6 021      UNPK  000(3,6),021(3,6)      DNM=1-202   DNM=1-382
        0018D6   94 0F 6 002            NI    002(6),X'0F'           DNM=1-202+2
        0018DA   96 C0 6 002            OI    002(6),X'C0'           DNM=1-202+2
  209   0018DE   F2 72 D 1D8 6 000      PACK  1D8(8,13),000(3,6)     TS=09       DNM=1-202
        0018E4   FA 22 D 1DD 6 021      AP    1DD(3,13),021(3,6)     TS=014      DNM=1-382
        0018EA   F3 22 6 000 D 1DD      UNPK  000(3,6),1DD(3,13)     DNM=1-202   TS=014
  210   0018F0   F2 73 D 1D8 6 009      PACK  1D8(8,13),009(4,6)     TS=09       DNM=1-259
        0018F6   F8 11 6 017 D 1DE      ZAP   017(2,6),1DE(2,13)     DNM=1-319   TS=014+1
  211   0018FC   F2 73 D 1D8 6 009      PACK  1D8(8,13),009(4,6)     TS=09       DNM=1-259
        001902   FA 12 6 017 D 1DD      AP    017(2,6),1DD(3,13)     DNM=1-319   TS=014
  212   001908   F3 31 6 009 6 017      UNPK  009(4,6),017(2,6)      DNM=1-259   DNM=1-319
  213   00190E   F2 73 D 1D8 6 009      PACK  1D8(8,13),009(4,6)     TS=09       DNM=1-259
        001914   FA 21 D 1DD 6 017      AP    1DD(3,13),017(2,6)     TS=014      DNM=1-319
        00191A   F3 32 6 009 D 1DD      UNPK  009(4,6),1DD(3,13)     DNM=1-259   TS=014
  214   001920   F2 73 D 1D8 6 009      PACK  1D8(8,13),009(4,6)     TS=09       DNM=1-259
        001926   F8 22 6 019 D 1DD      ZAP   019(3,6),1DD(3,13)     DNM=1-334   TS=014
  215   00192C   F2 73 D 1D8 6 009      PACK  1D8(8,13),009(4,6)     TS=09       DNM=1-259
        001932   FA 22 6 019 D 1DD      AP    019(3,6),1DD(3,13)     DNM=1-334   TS=014
        001938   94 0F 6 019            NI    019(6),X'0F'           DNM=1-334
  216   00193C   F3 32 6 009 6 019      UNPK  009(4,6),019(3,6)      DNM=1-259   DNM=1-334
  217   001942   F2 73 D 1D8 6 009      PACK  1D8(8,13),009(4,6)     TS=09       DNM=1-259
        001948   FA 22 D 1DD 6 019      AP    1DD(3,13),019(3,6)     TS=014      DNM=1-334
        00194E   F3 32 6 009 D 1DD      UNPK  009(4,6),1DD(3,13)     DNM=1-259   TS=014
  218   001954   F2 73 D 1D8 6 009      PACK  1D8(8,13),009(4,6)     TS=09       DNM=1-259
        00195A   FC 41 D 1DB C 0EA      MP    1DB(5,13),0EA(2,12)    TS=012      LIT+2
        001960   F8 22 6 01C D 1DD      ZAP   01C(3,6),1DD(3,13)     DNM=1-352   TS=014
        001966   94 0F 6 01C            NI    01C(6),X'0F'           DNM=1-352
  219   00196A   F2 73 D 1D8 6 009      PACK  1D8(8,13),009(4,6)     TS=09       DNM=1-259
        001970   FC 41 D 1DB C 0EA      MP    1DB(5,13),0EA(2,12)    TS=012      LIT+2
        001976   FA 22 6 01C D 1DD      AP    01C(3,6),1DD(3,13)     DNM=1-352   TS=014
        00197C   94 0F 6 01C            NI    01C(6),X'0F'           DNM=1-352
  220   001980   F8 72 D 1D8 6 01C      ZAP   1D8(8,13),01C(3,6)     TS=09       DNM=1-352
        001986   F1 76 D 1D8 D 1D8      MVO   1D8(8,13),1D8(7,13)    TS=09       TS=09
        00198C   F3 31 6 009 6 1DE      UNPK  009(4,6),1DE(2,13)     DNM=1-259   TS=015
  221   001992   F2 73 D 1D8 6 009      PACK  1D8(8,13),009(4,6)     TS=09       DNM=1-259
        001998   FC 41 D 1DB C 0EA      MP    1DB(5,13),0EA(2,12)    TS=012      LIT+2
        00199E   FA 32 D 1DC 6 01C      AP    1DC(4,13),01C(3,6)     TS=013      DNM=1-352
        0019A4   F1 76 D 1D8 D 1D8      MVO   1D8(8,13),1D8(7,13)    TS=09       TS=09
        0019AA   F3 32 6 009 D 1DD      UNPK  009(4,6),1DD(3,13)     DNM=1-259   TS=014
  222   0019B0   F2 73 D 1D8 6 009      PACK  1D8(8,13),009(4,6)     TS=09       DNM=1-259
        0019B6   F8 22 6 021 D 1DD      ZAP   021(3,6),1DD(3,13)     DNM=1-382   TS=014
        0019BC   96 0F 6 023            OI    023(6),X'0F'           DNM=1-382+2
  223   0019C0   F2 73 D 1D8 6 009      PACK  1D8(8,13),009(4,6)     TS=09       DNM=1-259
        0019C6   FA 22 6 021 D 1DD      AP    021(3,6),1DD(3,13)     DNM=1-382   TS=014
        0019CC   94 0F 6 021            NI    021(6),X'0F'           DNM=1-382
        0019D0   96 0F 6 023            OI    023(6),X'0F'           DNM=1-382+2
  224   0019D4   F3 32 6 009 6 021      UNPK  009(4,6),021(3,6)      DNM=1-259   DNM=1-382
        0019DA   94 0F 6 00C            NI    00C(6),X'0F'           DNM=1-259+3
        0019DE   96 C0 6 00C            OI    00C(6),X'C0'           DNM=1-259+3
  225   0019E2   F2 73 D 1D8 6 009      PACK  1D8(8,13),009(4,6)     TS=09       DNM=1-259
        0019E8   FA 22 D 1DD 6 021      AP    1DD(3,13),021(3,6)     TS=014      DNM=1-382
        0019EE   F3 32 6 009 D 1DD      UNPK  009(4,6),1DD(3,13)     DNM=1-259   TS=014
  226   0019F4   F2 73 D 1D8 6 000      PACK  1D8(8,13),000(4,6)     TS=09       DNM=1-274
        0019FA   F1 76 D 1D8 D 1D8      MVO   1D8(8,13),1D8(7,13)    TS=09       TS=09
```

```
     20

227      001A00  F8 11 6 017 D 1DE     ZAP   017(2,6),1DE(2,13)    DNM=1-319    TS=015
         001A06  F2 73 D 1D8 6 00D     PACK  1D8(8,13),00D(4,6)    TS=09        DNM=1-274
         001A0C  F8 71 D 1D0 6 017     ZAP   1D0(8,13),017(2,6)    TS=01        DNM=1-319
         001A12  FC 31 D 1D4 C 0EA     MP    1D4(4,13),0EA(2,12)   TS=05        LIT+2
         001A18  FA 22 D 1DD D 1D5     AP    1DD(3,13),1D5(3,13)   TS=014       TS=06
         001A1E  F1 76 D 1D8 D 1D8     MVO   1D8(8,13),1D8(7,13)   TS=09        TS=09
         001A24  F8 11 6 017 D 1DE     ZAP   017(2,6),1DE(2,13)    DNM=1-319    TS=014+1
228      001A2A  F8 71 D 1D8 6 017     ZAP   1D8(8,13),017(2,6)    TS=09        DNM=1-319
         001A30  FC 31 D 1DC C 0EA     MP    1DC(4,13),0EA(2,12)   TS=013       LIT+2
         001A36  F3 32 6 00D D 1DD     UNPK  00D(4,6),1DD(3,13)    DNM=1-274    TS=014
229      001A3C  F2 73 D 1D8 6 00D     PACK  1D8(8,13),00D(4,6)    TS=09        DNM=1-274
         001A42  F8 71 D 1D0 6 017     ZAP   1D0(8,13),017(2,6)    TS=01        DNM=1-319
         001A48  FC 31 D 1D4 C 0EA     MP    1D4(4,13),0EA(2,12)   TS=05        LIT+2
         001A4E  FA 22 D 1D5 D 1DD     AP    1D5(3,13),1DD(3,13)   TS=06        TS=014
         001A54  F3 32 6 00D D 1D5     UNPK  00D(4,6),1D5(3,13)    DNM=1-274    TS=06
230      001A5A  F2 73 D 1D8 6 00D     PACK  1D8(8,13),00D(4,6)    TS=09        DNM=1-274
         001A60  F1 76 D 1D8 D 1D8     MVO   1D8(8,13),1D8(7,13)   TS=09        TS=09
         001A66  F8 21 6 019 D 1DE     ZAP   019(3,6),1DE(2,13)    DNM=1-334    TS=015
231      001A6C  F2 73 D 1D8 6 00D     PACK  1D8(8,13),00D(4,6)    TS=09        DNM=1-274
         001A72  F8 72 D 1D0 6 019     ZAP   1D0(8,13),019(3,6)    TS=01        DNM=1-334
         001A78  FC 41 D 1D3 C 0EA     MP    1D3(5,13),0EA(2,12)   TS=04        LIT+2
         001A7E  FA 32 D 1DC D 1D5     AP    1DC(4,13),1D5(3,13)   TS=013       TS=06
         001A84  F1 76 D 1D8 D 1D8     MVO   1D8(8,13),1D8(7,13)   TS=09        TS=09
         001A8A  F8 22 6 019 D 1DD     ZAP   019(3,6),1DD(3,13)    DNM=1-334    TS=014
         001A90  94 0F 6 019           NI    019(6),X'0F'          DNM=1-334
232      001A94  F8 72 D 1D8 6 019     ZAP   1D8(8,13),019(3,6)    TS=09        DNM=1-334
         001A9A  FC 41 D 1DB C 0EA     MP    1DB(5,13),0EA(2,12)   TS=012       LIT+2
         001AA0  F3 32 6 00D D 1DD     UNPK  00D(4,6),1DD(3,13)    DNM=1-274    TS=014
233      001AA6  F2 73 D 1D8 6 00D     PACK  1D8(8,13),00D(4,6)    TS=09        DNM=1-274
         001AAC  F8 72 D 1D0 6 019     ZAP   1D0(8,13),019(3,6)    TS=01        DNM=1-334
         001AB2  FC 41 D 1D3 C 0EA     MP    1D3(5,13),0EA(2,12)   TS=04        LIT+2
         001AB8  FA 32 D 1D4 D 1DD     AP    1D4(4,13),1DD(3,13)   TS=05        TS=014
         001ABE  F3 33 6 00D D 1D4     UNPK  00D(4,6),1D4(4,13)    DNM=1-274    TS=05
234      001AC4  F2 73 D 1D8 6 00D     PACK  1D8(8,13),00D(4,6)    TS=09        DNM=1-274
         001ACA  F8 22 6 01C D 1DD     ZAP   01C(3,6),1DD(3,13)    DNM=1-352    TS=014
235      001AD0  F2 73 D 1D8 6 00D     PACK  1D8(8,13),00D(4,6)    TS=09        DNM=1-274
         001AD6  FA 22 6 01C D 1DD     AP    01C(3,6),1DD(3,13)    DNM=1-352    TS=014
         001ADC  94 0F 6 01C           NI    01C(6),X'0F'          DNM=1-352
236      001AE0  F3 32 6 00D 6 01C     UNPK  00D(4,6),01C(3,6)     DNM=1-274    DNM=1-352
237      001AE6  F2 73 D 1D8 6 00D     PACK  1D8(8,13),00D(4,6)    TS=09        DNM=1-274
         001AEC  FA 22 D 1DD 6 01C     AP    1DD(3,13),01C(3,6)    TS=014       DNM=1-352
         001AF2  F3 32 6 00D D 1DD     UNPK  00D(4,6),1DD(3,13)    DNM=1-274    TS=014
238      001AF8  F2 73 D 1D8 6 00D     PACK  1D8(8,13),00D(4,6)    TS=09        DNM=1-274
         001AFE  F1 76 D 1D8 D 1D8     MVO   1D8(8,13),1D8(7,13)   TS=09        TS=09
         001B04  F8 21 6 021 D 1DE     ZAP   021(3,6),1DE(2,13)    DNM=1-382    TS=015
         001B0A  96 0F 6 023           OI    023(6),X'0F'          DNM=1-382+2
239      001B0E  F2 73 D 1D8 6 00D     PACK  1D8(8,13),00D(4,6)    TS=09        DNM=1-274
         001B14  F8 72 D 1D0 6 021     ZAP   1D0(8,13),021(3,6)    TS=01        DNM=1-382
         001B1A  FC 41 D 1D3 C 0EA     MP    1D3(5,13),0EA(2,12)   TS=04        LIT+2
         001B20  FA 32 D 1DC D 1D5     AP    1DC(4,13),1D5(3,13)   TS=013       TS=06
         001B26  F1 76 D 1D8 D 1D8     MVO   1D8(8,13),1D8(7,13)   TS=09        TS=09
         001B2C  F8 22 6 021 D 1DD     ZAP   021(3,6),1DD(3,13)    DNM=1-382    TS=014
         001B32  94 0F 6 021           NI    021(6),X'0F'          DNM=1-382
         001B36  96 0F 6 023           OI    023(6),X'0F'          DNM=1-382+2
240      001B3A  F8 72 D 1D8 6 021     ZAP   1D8(8,13),021(3,6)    TS=09        DNM=1-382
         001B40  FC 41 D 1DB C 0EA     MP    1DB(5,13),0EA(2,12)   TS=012       LIT+2
         001B46  F3 32 6 00D D 1DD     UNPK  00D(4,6),1DD(3,13)    DNM=1-274    TS=014
         001B4C  94 0F 6 010           NI    010(6),X'0F'          DNM=1-274+3
         001B50  96 C0 6 010           OI    010(6),X'C0'          DNM=1-274+3
241      001B54  F2 73 D 1D8 6 00D     PACK  1D8(8,13),00D(4,6)    TS=09        DNM=1-274
         001B5A  F8 72 D 1D0 6 021     ZAP   1D0(8,13),021(3,6)    TS=01        DNM=1-382
         001B60  FC 41 D 1D3 C 0EA     MP    1D3(5,13),0EA(2,12)   TS=04        LIT+2
         001B66  FA 32 D 1D4 D 1DD     AP    1D4(4,13),1DD(3,13)   TS=05        TS=014
         001B6C  F3 33 6 00D D 1D4     UNPK  00D(4,6),1D4(4,13)    DNM=1-274    TS=05
242      001B72  F2 72 D 1D8 6 014     PACK  1D8(8,13),014(3,6)    TS=09        DNM=1-304
         001B78  F8 11 6 017 D 1DE     ZAP   017(2,6),1DE(2,13)    DNM=1-319    TS=015
         001B7E  94 F0 6 018           NI    018(6),X'F0'          DNM=1-319+1
         001B82  96 0C 6 018           OI    018(6),X'0C'          DNM=1-319+1
243      001B86  F2 72 D 1D8 6 014     PACK  1D8(8,13),014(3,6)    TS=09        DNM=1-304
         001B8C  FA 11 6 017 D 1DE     AP    017(2,6),1DE(2,13)    DNM=1-319    TS=015
244      001B92  F3 21 6 014 6 017     UNPK  014(3,6),017(2,6)     DNM=1-304    DNM=1-319
         001B98  96 F0 6 016           OI    016(6),X'F0'          DNM=1-304+2
245      001B9C  F2 72 D 1D8 6 014     PACK  1D8(8,13),014(3,6)    TS=09        DNM=1-304
         001BA2  FA 21 D 1DD 6 017     AP    1DD(3,13),017(2,6)    TS=014       DNM=1-319
         001BA8  F3 22 6 014 D 1DD     UNPK  014(3,6),1DD(3,13)    DNM=1-304    TS=014
         001BAE  96 F0 6 016           OI    016(6),X'F0'          DNM=1-304+2
246      001BB2  F2 72 D 1D8 6 014     PACK  1D8(8,13),014(3,6)    TS=09        DNM=1-304
         001BB8  F8 21 6 019 D 1DE     ZAP   019(3,6),1DE(2,13)    DNM=1-334    TS=015
         001BBE  94 F0 6 01B           NI    01B(6),X'F0'          DNM=1-334+2
         001BC2  96 0C 6 01B           OI    01B(6),X'0C'          DNM=1-334+2
247      001BC6  F2 72 D 1D8 6 014     PACK  1D8(8,13),014(3,6)    TS=09        DNM=1-304
         001BCC  FA 21 6 019 D 1DE     AP    019(3,6),1DE(2,13)    DNM=1-334    TS=015
         001BD2  94 0F 6 019           NI    019(6),X'0F'          DNM=1-334
248      001BD6  F3 22 6 014 6 019     UNPK  014(3,6),019(3,6)     DNM=1-304    DNM=1-334
         001BDC  96 F0 6 016           OI    016(6),X'F0'          DNM=1-304+2
249      001BE0  F2 72 D 1D8 6 014     PACK  1D8(8,13),014(3,6)    TS=09        DNM=1-304
         001BE6  FA 22 D 1DD 6 019     AP    1DD(3,13),019(3,6)    TS=014       DNM=1-334
```

```
21

         001BEC  F3 22 6 014 D 1DD    UNPK  014(3,6),1DD(3,13)     DNM=1-304      TS=014
         001BF2  96 F0 6 016          OI    016(6),X'F0'           DNM=1-304+2
250      001BF6  F2 72 D 1D8 6 014    PACK  1D8(8,13),014(3,6)     TS=09          DNM=1-304
         001BFC  FC 31 D 1DC C 0EA    MP    1DC(4,13),0EA(2,12)    TS=013         LIT+2
         001C02  F8 22 6 01C D 1DD    ZAP   01C(3,6),1DD(3,13)     DNM=1-352      TS=014
         001C08  94 F0 6 01E          NI    01E(6),X'F0'           DNM=1-352+2
         001C0C  96 0C 6 01E          OI    01E(6),X'0C'           DNM=1-352+2
251      001C10  F2 72 D 1D8 6 014    PACK  1D8(8,13),014(3,6)     TS=09          DNM=1-304
         001C16  FC 31 D 1DC C 0EA    MP    1DC(4,13),0EA(2,12)    TS=013         LIT+2
         001C1C  FA 22 6 01C D 1DD    AP    01C(3,6),1DD(3,13)     DNM=1-352      TS=014
         001C22  94 0F 6 01C          NI    01C(6),X'0F'           DNM=1-352
252      001C26  F8 72 D 1D8 6 01C    ZAP   1D8(8,13),01C(3,6)     TS=09          DNM=1-352
         001C2C  F1 76 D 1D8 D 1D8    MVO   1D8(8,13),1D8(7,13)    TS=09          TS=09
         001C32  F3 21 6 014 D 1DE    UNPK  014(3,6),1DE(2,13)     DNM=1-304      TS=015
         001C38  96 F0 6 016          OI    016(6),X'F0'           DNM=1-304+2
253      001C3C  F2 72 D 1D8 6 014    PACK  1D8(8,13),014(3,6)     TS=09          DNM=1-304
         001C42  FC 31 D 1DC C 0EA    MP    1DC(4,13),0EA(2,12)    TS=013         LIT+2
         001C48  FA 22 D 1DD 6 01C    AP    1DD(3,13),01C(3,6)     TS=014         DNM=1-352
         001C4E  F1 76 D 1D8 D 1D8    MVO   1D8(8,13),1D8(7,13)    TS=09          TS=09
         001C54  F3 22 6 014 D 1DD    UNPK  0143(3,6),1DD(3,13)    DNM=1-304      TS=014
         001C5A  96 F0 6 016          OI    016(6),X'F0'           DNM=1-304+2
254      001C5E  F2 72 D 1D8 6 014    PACK  1D8(8,13),014(3,6)     TS=09          DNM=1-304
         001C64  F8 21 6 021 D 1DE    ZAP   021(3,6),1DE(2,13)     DNM=1-382      TS=015
         001C6A  96 0F 6 023          OI    023(6),X'0F'           DNM=1-382+2
255      001C6E  F2 72 D 1D8 6 014    PACK  1D8(8,13),014(3,6)     TS=09          DNM=1-304
         001C74  FA 21 6 021 D 1DE    AP    021(3,6),1DE(2,13)     DNM=1-382      TS=015
         001C7A  94 0F 6 021          NI    021(6),X'0F'           DNM=1-382
         001C7E  96 0F 6 023          OI    023(6),X'0F'           DNM=1-382+2
256      001C82  F3 22 6 014 6 021    UNPK  014(3,6),021(3,6)      DNM=1-304      DNM=1-382
         001C88  96 F0 6 016          OI    016(6),X'F0'           DNM=1-304+2
257      001C8C  F2 72 D 1D8 6 014    PACK  1D8(8,13),014(3,6)     TS=09          DNM=1-304
         001C92  FA 22 D 1DD 6 021    AP    1DD(3,13),021(3,6)     TS=014         DNM=1-382
         001C98  F3 22 6 014 D 1DD    UNPK  014(3,6),1DD(3,13)     DNM=1-304      TS=014
         001C9E  96 F0 6 016          OI    016(6),X'F0'           DNM=1-304+2
258      001CA2  F8 11 6 01F 6 017    ZAP   01F(2,6),017(2,6)      DNM=1-367      DNM=1-319
259  ③   001CA8  FA 11 6 01F 6 017    AP    01F(2,6),017(2,6)      DNM=1-367      DNM=1-319
260      001CAE  F8 11 6 017 6 01F    ZAP   017(2,6),01F(2,6)      DNM=1-319      DNM=1-367
261      001CB4  FA 11 6 017 6 01F    AP    017(2,6),01F(2,6)      DNM=1-319      DNM=1-367
262      001CBA  F8 21 6 019 6 017    ZAP   019(3,6),017(2,6)      DNM=1-334      DNM=1-319
263      001CC0  FA 21 6 019 6 017    AP    019(3,6),017(2,6)      DNM=1-334      DNM=1-319
         001CC6  94 0F 6 019          NI    019(6),X'0F'           DNM=1-334
264      001CCA  F8 11 6 017 6 01A    ZAP   017(2,6),01A(2,6)      DNM=1-319      DNM=1-334+1
265      001CD0  FA 12 6 017 6 019    AP    017(2,6),019(3,6)      DNM=1-319      DNM=1-334
266      001CD6  F8 71 D 1D8 6 017    ZAP   1D8(8,13),017(2,6)     TS=09          DNM=1-319
         001CDC  FC 31 D 1DC C 0EA    MP    1DC(4,13),0EA(2,12)    TS=013         LIT+2
         001CE2  F8 22 6 01C D 1DD    ZAP   01C(3,6),1DD(3,13)     DNM=1-352      TS=014
267      001CE8  F8 71 D 1D8 6 017    ZAP   1D8(8,13),017(2,6)     TS=09          DNM=1-319
         001CEE  FC 31 D 1DC C 0EA    MP    1DC(4,13),0EA(2,12)    TS=013         LIT+2
         001CF4  FA 22 6 01C D 1DD    AP    01C(3,6),1DD(3,13)     DNM=1-352      TS=014
         001CFA  94 0F 6 01C          NI    01C(6),X'0F'           DNM=1-352
268      001CFE  F8 72 D 1D8 6 01C    ZAP   1D8(8,13),01C(3,6)     TS=09          DNM=1-352
         001D04  F1 76 D 1D8 D 1D8    MVO   1D8(8,13),1D8(7,13)    TS=09          TS=09
         001D0A  F8 11 6 017 D 1DE    ZAP   017(2,6),1DE(2,13)     DNM=1-319      TS=015
269      001D10  F8 71 D 1D8 6 017    ZAP   1D8(8,13),017(2,6)     TS=09          DNM=1-319
         001D16  FC 31 D 1DC C 0EA    MP    1DC(4,13),0EA(2,12)    TS=013         LIT+2
         001D1C  FA 22 D 1DD 6 01C    AP    1DD(3,13),01C(3,6)     TS=014         DNM=1-352
         001D22  F1 76 D 1D8 D 1D8    MVO   1D8(8,13),1D8(7,13)    TS=09          TS=09
         001D28  F8 11 6 017 D 1DE    ZAP   017(2,6),1DE(2,13)     DNM=1-319      TS=014+1
270      001D2E  F8 21 6 021 6 017    ZAP   021(3,6),017(2,6)      DNM=1-382      DNM=1-319
         001D34  96 0F 6 023          OI    023(6),X'0F'           DNM=1-382+2
271      001D38  FA 21 6 021 6 017    AP    021(3,6),017(2,6)      DNM=1-382      DNM=1-319
         001D3E  94 0F 6 021          NI    021(6),X'0F'           DNM=1-382
         001D42  96 0F 6 023          OI    023(6),X'0F'           DNM=1-382+2
272      001D46  F8 11 6 017 6 022    ZAP   017(2,6),022(2,6)      DNM=1-319      DNM=1-382+1
         001D4C  94 F0 6 018          NI    018(6),X'F0'           DNM=1-319+1
         001D50  96 0C 6 018          OI    018(6),X'0C'           DNM=1-319+1
273      001D54  FA 12 6 017 6 021    AP    017(2,6),021(3,6)      DNM=1-319      DNM=1-382
274      001D5A  D2 02 6 00D 6 00A    MVC   00D(3,6),00A(6)        DNM=1-274      DNM=1-259+1
         001D60  92 F0 6 010          MVI   010(6),X'F0'           DNM=1-274+3
         001D64  D3 00 6 010 6 00C    MVZ   010(1,6),00C(6)        DNM=1-274+3    DNM=1-259+3
         001D6A  96 F0 6 00F          OI    00F(6),X'F0'           DNM=1-274+2
275      001D6E  F2 73 D 1D8 6 009    PACK  1D8(8,13),009(4,6)     TS=09          DNM=1-259
         001D74  F2 73 D 1D0 6 00D    PACK  1D0(8,13),00D(4,6)     TS=01          DNM=1-274
         001D7A  FC 41 D 1DB C 0EA    MP    1DB(5,13),0EA(2,12)    TS=012         LIT+2
         001D80  FA 32 D 1DC D 1D5    AP    1DC(4,13),1D5(3,13)    TS=013         TS=06
         001D86  F3 33 6 00D D 1DC    UNPK  00D(4,6),1DC(4,13)     DNM=1-274      TS=013
276      001D8C  D2 02 6 00A 6 00D    MVC   00A(3,6),00D(6)        DNM=1-259+1    DNM=1-274
         001D92  92 F0 6 009          MVI   009(6),X'F0'           DNM=1-259
         001D96  D3 00 6 00C 6 010    MVZ   00C(1,6),010(6)        DNM=1-259+3    DNM=1-274+3
277      001D9C  F2 73 D 1D8 6 00D    PACK  1D8(8,13),00D(4,6)     TS=09          DNM=1-274
         001DA2  F2 73 D 1D0 6 009    PACK  1D0(8,13),009(4,6)     TS=01          DNM=1-259
         001DA8  FC 41 D 1D3 C 0EA    MP    1D3(5,13),0EA(2,12)    TS=04          LIT+2
         001DAE  FA 32 D 1DC D 1D5    AP    1DC(4,13),1D5(3,13)    TS=013         TS=06
         001DB4  F1 76 D 1D8 D 1D8    MVO   1D8(8,13),1D8(7,13)    TS=09          TS=09
         001DBA  F3 32 6 009 D 1DD    UNPK  009(4,6),1DD(3,13)     DNM=1-259      TS=014
278      001DC0  D2 02 6 014 6 00A    MVC   014(3,6),00A(6)        DNM=1-304      DNM=1-259+1
         001DC6  96 F0 6 016          OI    016(6),X'F0'           DNM=1-304+2
```

```
   22

 279    001DCA  F2 73 D 1D8 6 009      PACK    1D8(8,13),009(4,6)      TS=09          DNM=1-259
        001DD0  F2 72 D 1D0 6 014      PACK    1D0(8,13),014(3,6)      TS=01          DNM=1-304
        001DD6  FA 21 D 1DD D 1D6      AP      1DD(3,13),1D6(2,13)     TS=014         TS=07
        001DDC  F3 22 6 014 D 1DD      UNPK    014(3,6),1DD(3,13)      DNM=1-304      TS=014
        001DE2  96 F0 6 016            OI      016(6),X'F0'            DNM=1-304+2
 280    001DE6  D2 02 6 00A 6 014      MVC     00A(3,6),014(6)         DNM=1-259+1    DNM=1-304
        001DEC  92 F0 6 009            MVI     009(6),X'F0'            DNM=1-259
        001DF0  94 OF 6 00C            NI      00C(6),X'0F'            DNM=1-259+3
        001DF4  96 C0 6 00C            OI      00C(6),X'C0'            DNM=1-259+3
 281    001DF8  F2 72 D 1D8 6 014      PACK    1D8(8,13),014(3,6)      TS=09          DNM=1-304
        001DFE  F2 73 D 1D0 6 009      PACK    1D0(8,13),009(4,6)      TS=01          DNM=1-259
        001E04  FA 22 D 1DD D 1D5      AP      1DD(3,13),1D5(3,13)     TS=014         TS=06
        001E0A  F3 32 6 009 D 1DD      UNPK    009(4,6),1DD(3,13)      DNM=1-259      TS=014
 282    001E10  D2 02 6 014 6 00D      MVC     014(3,6),00D(6)         DNM=1-304      DNM=1-274
 283    001E16  F2 73 D 1D8 6 00D      PACK    1D8(8,13),00D(4,6)      TS=09          DNM=1-274
        001E1C  F2 72 D 1D0 6 014      PACK    1D0(8,13),014(3,6)      TS=01          DNM=1-304
        001E22  FC 31 D 104 C 0EA      MP      104(4,13),0EA(2,12)     TS=05          LIT+2
        001E28  FA 22 D 1DD D 1D5      AP      1DD(3,13),1D5(3,13)     TS=014         TS=06
        001E2E  F1 76 D 1D8 D 1D8      MVO     1D8(8,13),1D8(7,13)     TS=09          TS=09
        001E34  F3 22 6 014 D 1DD      UNPK    014(3,6),1DD(3,13)      DNM=1-304      TS=014
        001E3A  96 F0 6 016            OI      016(6),X'F0'            DNM=1-304+2
 284    001E3E  D2 02 6 00D 6 014      MVC     00D(3,6),014(6)         DNM=1-274      DNM=1-304
        001E44  92 F0 6 010            MVI     010(6),X'F0'            DNM=1-274+3
        001E48  D3 00 6 010 6 016      MVZ     010(1,6),016(6)         DNM=1-274+3    DNM=1-304+2
        001E4E  96 F0 6 00F            OI      00F(6),X'F0'            DNM=1-274+3
        001E52  94 OF 6 010            NI      010(6),X'0F'            DNM=1-274+3
        001E56  96 C0 6 010            OI      010(6),X'C0'            DNM=1-274+3
 285    001E5A  F2 72 D 1D8 6 014      PACK    1D8(8,13),014(3,6)      TS=09          DNM=1-304
        001E60  F2 73 D 1D0 6 00D      PACK    1D0(8,13),00D(4,6)      TS=01          DNM=1-274
        001E66  FC 31 D 1DC C 0EA      MP      1DC(4,13),0EA(2,12)     TS=013         LIT+2
        001E6C  FA 22 D 1DD D 1D5      AP      1DD(3,13),1D5(3,13)     TS=014         TS=06
        001E72  F3 32 6 00D D 1DD      UNPK    00D(4,6),1DD(3,13)      DNM=1-274      TS=014
 286    001E78  F8 72 D 1D8 6 014      ZAP     1D8(8,13),014(3,6)      TS=09          DNM=1-334
        001E7E  FC 41 D 1DB C 0EA      MP      1DB(5,13),0EA(2,12)     TS=012         LIT+2
        001E84  F8 22 6 01C D 1DD      ZAP     01C(3,6),1DD(3,13)      DNM=1-352      TS=014
        001E8A  94 OF 6 01C            NI      01C(6),X'0F'            DNM=1-352
 287    001E8E  F8 72 D 1D8 6 019      ZAP     1D8(8,13),019(3,6)      TS=09          DNM=1-334
        001E94  FC 41 D 1DB C 0EA      MP      1DB(5,13),0EA(2,12)     TS=012         LIT+2
        001E9A  FA 22 6 01C D 1DD      AP      01C(3,6),1DD(3,13)      DNM=1-352      TS=014
        001EA0  94 OF 6 01C            NI      01C(6),X'0F'            DNM=1-352
 288    001EA4  F8 72 D 1D8 6 01C      ZAP     1D8(8,13),01C(3,6)      TS=09          DNM=1-352
        001EAA  F1 76 D 1D8 D 1D8      MVO     1D8(8,13),1D8(7,13)     TS=09          TS=09
        001EB0  F8 21 6 019 D 1DE      ZAP     019(3,6),1DE(2,13)      DNM=1-334      TS=015
 289    001EB6  F8 72 D 1D8 6 019      ZAP     1D8(8,13),019(3,6)      TS=09          DNM=1-334
        001EBC  FC 41 D 1DB C 0EA      MP      1DB(5,13),0EA(2,12)     TS=012         LIT+2
        001EC2  FA 32 D 1DC 6 01C      AP      1DC(4,13),01C(3,6)      TS=013         DNM=1-352
        001EC8  F1 76 D 1D8 D 1D8      MVO     1D8(8,13),1D8(7,13)     TS=09          TS=09
        001ECE  F8 22 6 019 D 1DD      ZAP     019(3,6),1DD(3,13)      DNM=1-334      TS=014
        001ED4  94 OF 6 019            NI      019(6),X'0F'            DNM=1-334
 290    001ED8  F8 22 6 021 6 019      ZAP     021(3,6),019(3,6)       DNM=1-382      DNM=1-334
        001EDE  96 OF 6 023            OI      023(6),X'0F'            DNM=1-382+2
 291    001EE2  FA 22 6 021 6 019      AP      021(3,6),019(3,6)       DNM=1-382      DNM=1-334
        001EE8  94 OF 6 021            NI      021(6),X'0F'            DNM=1-382
        001EEC  96 OF 6 023            OI      023(6),X'0F'            DNM=1-382+2
 292    001EF0  F8 22 6 019 6 021      ZAP     019(3,6),021(3,6)       DNM=1-334      DNM=1-382
        001EF6  94 F0 6 01B            NI      01B(6),X'F0'            DNM=1-334+2
        001EFA  96 OC 6 01B            OI      01B(6),X'0C'            DNM=1-334+2
 293    001EFE  FA 22 6 019 6 021      AP      019(3,6),021(3,6)       DNM=1-334      DNM=1-382
        001F04  94 OF 6 019            NI      019(6),X'0F'            DNM=1-334
 294    001F08  F8 72 D 1D8 6 01C      ZAP     1D8(8,13),01C(3,6)      TS=09          DNM=1-352
        001F0E  F1 76 D 1D8 D 1D8      MVO     1D8(8,13),1D8(7,13)     TS=09          TS=09
        001F14  F8 21 6 021 D 1DE      ZAP     021(3,6),1DE(2,13)      DNM=1-382      TS=015
        001F1A  96 OF 6 023            OI      023(6),X'0F'            DNM=1-382+2
 295    001F1E  F8 72 D 1D8 6 021      ZAP     1D8(8,13),021(3,6)      TS=09          DNM=1-382
        001F24  FC 41 D 1DB C 0EA      MP      1DB(5,13),0EA(2,12)     TS=012         LIT+2
        001F2A  FA 32 D 1DC 6 01C      AP      1DC(4,13),01C(3,6)      TS=013         DNM=1-352
        001F30  F1 76 D 1D8 D 1D8      MVO     1D8(8,13),1D8(7,13)     TS=09          TS=09
        001F36  F8 22 6 021 D 1DD      ZAP     021(3,6),1DD(3,13)      DNM=1-382      TS=014
        001F3C  94 OF 6 021            NI      021(6),X'0F'            DNM=1-382
        001F40  96 OF 6 023            OI      023(6),X'0F'            DNM=1-382+2
 296    001F44  F8 72 D 1D8 6 021      ZAP     1D8(8,13),021(3,6)      TS=09          DNM=1-382
        001F4A  FC 41 D 1DB C 0EA      MP      1DB(5,13),0EA(2,12)     TS=012         LIT+2
        001F50  F8 22 6 01C D 1DD      ZAP     01C(3,6),1DD(3,13)      DNM=1-352      TS=014
        001F56  94 OF 6 01C            NI      01C(6),X'0F'            DNM=1-352
        001F5A  94 F0 6 01E            NI      01E(6),X'F0'            DNM=1-352+2
        001F5E  96 OC 6 01E            OI      01E(6),X'0C'            DNM=1-352+2
 297    001F62  F8 72 D 1D8 6 021      ZAP     1D8(8,13),021(3,6)      TS=09          DNM=1-382
        001F68  FC 41 D 1DB C 0EA      MP      1DB(5,13),0EA(2,12)     TS=012         LIT+2
        001F6E  FA 22 6 01C D 1DD      AP      01C(3,6),1DD(3,13)      DNM=1-352      TS=014
        001F74  94 OF 6 01C            NI      01C(6),X'0F'            DNM=1-352
 298    001F78  0A OE                  SVC     14
        001F7A  0A OE                  SVC     14
        001F7C  50 D0 5 008      INIT2 ST      13,008(0,5)
        001F80  50 50 D 004            ST      5,004(0,13)
        001F84  58 20 C 000            L       2,000(0,12)             VIR=1
        001F88  95 00 2 000            CLI     000(2),X'00'
        001F8C  07 79                  BCR     7,9
```

```
23

001F8E  92 FF 2 000          MVI   000(2),X'FF'
001F92  96 10 D 048          OI    048(13),X'10'        SWT+0
001F96  50 E0 D 054   INIT3  ST    14,054(0,13)
001F9A  05 F0                BALR  15,0
001F9C  91 20 D 048          TM    048(13),X'20'        SWT+0
001FA0  47 E0 F 016          BC    14,016(0,15)
001FA4  58 00 B 048          L     0,048(0,11)
001FA8  98 2D B 050          LM    2,13,050(11)
001FAC  58 E0 D 054          L     14,054(0,13)
001FB0  07 FE                BCR   15,14
001FB2  96 20 D 048          OI    048(13),X'20'        SWT+0
001FB6  41 60 0 004          LA    6,004(0,0)
001FBA  41 10 C 008          LA    1,008(0,12)          PN=01
001FBE  41 70 C 0E8          LA    7,0E8(0,12)          LIT+0
001FC2  06 70                BCTR  7,0
001FC4  05 50                BALR  5,0
001FC6  58 40 1 000          L     4,000(0,1)
001FCA  1E 4B                ALR   4,11
001FCC  50 40 1 000          ST    4,000(0,1)
001FD0  87 16 5 000          BXLE  1,6,000(5)
001FD4  41 80 D 1BC          LA    8,1BC(0,13)          OVF=1
001FD8  41 70 D 1CF          LA    7,1CF(0,13)          TS=01-1
001FDC  05 10                BALR  1,0
001FDE  58 00 8 000          L     0,000(0,8)
001FE2  1E 0B                ALR   0,11
001FE4  50 00 8 000          ST    0,000(0,8)
001FE8  87 86 1 000          BXLE  8,6,000(1)
001FEC  D2 03 D 1F0 C 0E0    MVC   1F0(4,13),0E0(12)    VN=01      VNI=1
001FF2  58 60 D 1C4          L     6,1C4(0,13)          BL =3
001FF6  58 70 D 1BC          L     7,1BC(0,13)          BL =1
001FFA  58 80 D 1C0          L     8,1C0(0,13)          BL =2
001FFE  58 E0 D 054          L     14,054(0,13)
002002  07 FE                BCR   15,14
000000  05 F0         INIT1  BALR  15,0
000002  07 00                BCR   0,0
000004  90 0E F 00A          STM   0,14,00A(15)
000008  47 F0 F 082          BC    15,082(0,15)
00000C                       DS    30F
000084  58 C0 F 0C6          L     12,0C6(0,15)
000088  58 E0 C 000          L     14,000(0,12)         VIR=1
00008C  58 D0 F 0CA          L     13,0CA(0,15)
000090  95 00 E 000          CLI   000(14),X'00'
000094  47 70 F 0A2          BC    7,0A2(0,15)
000098  96 10 D 048          OI    048(13),X'10'        SWT+0
00009C  92 FF E 000          MVI   000(14),X'FF'
0000A0  47 F0 F 0AC          BC    15,0AC(0,15)
0000A4  98 CE F 03A          LM    12,14,03A(15)
0000A8  90 EC D 00C          STM   14,12,00C(13)
0000AC  18 5D                LR    5,13
0000AE  98 9F F 0BA          LM    9,15,0BA(15)
0000B2  91 10 D 048          TM    048(13),X'10'        SWT+0
0000B6  07 19                BCR   1,9
0000B8  07 FF                BCR   15,15
0000BA  07 00                BCR   0,0
0000BC  00001F96             ADCON L4(INIT3)
0000C0  00000000             ADCON L4(INIT1)
0000C4  00000000             ADCON L4(INIT1)
0000C8  00000560             ADCON L4(PGT)
0000CC  00000360             ADCON L4(TGT)
0000D0  00000662             ADCON L4(START)
0000D4  00001F7C             ADCON L4(INIT2)
0000D8  C3D6C2C6F0F0F0F1     DC    X'C3D6C2C6F0F0F0F1'
0000E0  E3C5E2E3E2404040     DC    X'E3C5E2E3E2404040'
```

JOB CONTROL TO CATALOG IN SOURCE STATEMENT LIBRARY

The following listing contains the job control statements used to catalog the file definition and I/0 area definitions for the inventory master file which is used by the "COPY" statement in Chapter 6. Similar job control statements can be used for the program assignment at the end of Chapter 6 if the Disk Operating System is in use.

```
// JOB CASHMAN
// EXEC MAINT
 CATALS C.INVMAST
 BKEND
001010      BLOCK CONTAINS 54 RECORDS                              INVMAST
001020      RECORD CONTAINS 64 CHARACTERS                          INVMAST
001030      LABEL RECORDS ARE STANDARD                             INVMAST
001040      DATA RECORD IS MSTR-IO.                                INVMAST
001050 01   MSTR-IO.                                               INVMAST
001060      03   PART-NUMB-MSTR          PIC 9(13)                 INVMAST
001070                                   USAGE COMP-3.             INVMAST
001080      03   PART-NUMB-MSTR-X        REDEFINES PART-NUMB-MSTR  INVMAST
001090                                   PIC X(7).                 INVMAST
001100      03   NAME-MSTR               PIC X(25).                INVMAST
001110      03   QTY-ON-HAND-MSTR        PIC S9(7)                 INVMAST
001120                                   USAGE COMP-3.             INVMAST
001130      03   QTY-ON-ORDER-MSTR       PIC S9(7)                 INVMAST
001140                                   USAGE COMP-3.             INVMAST
001150      03   QTY-RESERVED-MSTR       PIC S9(7)                 INVMAST
001160                                   USAGE COMP-3.             INVMAST
001170      03   NEXT-ASSEMBLY-MSTR      PIC S9(13)                INVMAST
001180                                   USAGE COMP-3.             INVMAST
001190      03   TYPE-MSTR               PIC X.                    INVMAST
001200      03   SOURCE-MSTR             PIC X.                    INVMAST
002010      03   UNIT-PRICE-MSTR         PIC S9(7)                 INVMAST
002020                                   USAGE COMP-3.             INVMAST
002030      03   FILLER                  PIC X(7).                 INVMAST
 BKEND C.INVMAST
/*
```

SAMPLE JOB CONTROL

The following listings contain the job control statements which were used to execute the sample programs presented in the text.

```
// JOB CASHMAN                                          CHAPTER 1
// OPTION LINK,SYM
// EXEC FCOBOL

- Source Deck -

/*
// LBLTYP TAPE
// EXEC LNKEDT
// ASSGN SYS007,X'00C'
// ASSGN SYS013,X'00E'
// ASSGN SYS027,X'182'
// TLBL MSTROUT,'MASTER FILE',,111111
// UPSI 10000000
// EXEC

- Test Data to Load Master -

/*
// ASSGN SYS024,X'182'
// TLBL MSTRIN,'MASTER FILE',,111111
// ASSGN SYS027,X'183'
// TLBL MSTROUT,'MASTER UPDATED',,111111
// UPSI 00000000
// EXEC

- Test Data to Update Master -

/*
/&
```

CHAPTER 2

```
// JOB CASHMAN
// OPTION LINK
   INCLUDE
```

- Object Deck - Chapter 2 -

```
/*
// EXEC LNKEDT
// ASSGN SYS004,X'00C'
// TLBL TAPEIN,'CHAP3 INPUT'
// ASSGN SYS005,IGN
// DLBL DISKOUT,'CHAP3 OUTPUT AREA',66/001,SD
// EXTENT SYS006,111111,1,0,3880,20
// ASSGN SYS006,X'132'
// ASSGN SYS007,X'00E'
// EXEC
```

- Test Data to Load Indexed Sequential File -

```
/*
// OPTION LINK
   INCLUDE
```

CHAPTER 3

- Object Deck - Chapter 3 -

```
/*
// LBLTYP NSD(02)
// EXEC LNKEDT
// DLBL TRANSIN,'CHAP3 OUTPUT AREA',66/001,SD
// EXTENT SYS004,111111,1,0,3880,20
// ASSGN SYS004,X'132'
// ASSGN SYS005,X'00E'
// DLBL INVMSTR,'CHAP4 ISAM AREA',66/001,ISC
// EXTENT SYS006,111111,4,1,3900,20
// EXTENT SYS006,111111,1,2,3920,20
// ASSGN SYS006,X'132'
// EXEC
// OPTION LINK
   INCLUDE
```

CHAPTER 4

- Object Deck - Chapter 4 -

```
/*
// LBLTYP NSD(02)
// EXEC LNKEDT
// DLBL INVMSTR,'CHAP4 ISAM AREA',66/001,ISE
// EXTENT SYS006,111111,4,1,3900,20
// EXTENT SYS006,111111,1,2,3920,20
// ASSGN SYS006,X'132'
// ASSGN SYS005,X'00E'
// EXEC
```

```
// OPTION LINK
 INCLUDE
```

- Object Deck - Chapter 2 -

```
// EXEC LNKEDT
// ASSGN SYS004,X'00C'
// TLBL TAPEIN,'CHAP6 INPUT'
// ASSGN SYS005,IGN
// DLBL DISKOUT,'CHAP6 INPUT AREA',66/001,SD
// EXTENT SYS006,111111,1,0,3860,20
// ASSGN SYS006,X'132'
// ASSGN SYS007,X'00E'
// EXEC
```

- Test Data to Update Indexed Sequential File -

```
/*
// OPTION LINK
 INCLUDE
```

- Object Deck - Chapter 5 -

```
/*
// LBLTYP NSD(02)
// EXEC LNKEDT
// DLBL INVMSTR,'CHAP4 ISAM AREA',66/001,ISE
// EXTENT SYS006,111111,4,1,3900,20
// EXTENT SYS006,111111,1,2,3920,20
// ASSGN SYS006,X'132'
// DLBL TRANSIN,'CHAP6 INPUT AREA',66/001,SD
// EXTENT SYS007,111111,1,0,3860,20
// ASSGN SYS007,X'132'
// ASSGN SYS005,X'00E'
// EXEC
/*
```

Note:

The program in Chapter 6 utilizes the segmentation feature of the ANSI COBOL compiler as well as a subprogram which is called from the root segment. Whenever the segmentation feature is utilized, the COBOL compiler automatically generates the required job control statements to cause the program phases to be identified properly. When, however, a subprogram is to be used with one of the segments, it must be first compiled and an object module obtained. This object module must then be inserted in the object module produced by the compilation of the segmented program within the segment which calls it. Therefore, in order to illustrate this, some of the control statements which are generated by the COBOL compiler are shown below, together with the statements which are submitted by the programmer. The statements which are generated by the compiler are indicated.

```
// OPTION LINK,LISTX,DUMP                                    CHAPTER 6
// ASSGN SYS004,X'132'
 INCLUDE
 CATALR DUMPLIST            - COMPILER GENERATED
 PHASE DUMPLIST,ROOT        - COMPILER GENERATED
- Object Deck - Root Segment -

 CATALR DTECONV             - COMPILER GENERATED   Must be
                              (SUBPROGRAM)         inserted by
- Object Deck - DTECONV Subprogram                 programmer
                                                   after compilation

 CATALR DUMPLI50            - COMPILER GENERATED
 PHASE DUMPLI50,*           - COMPILER GENERATED
- Object Deck - Card-Read-Section -

 CATALR DUMPLI55            - COMPILER GENERATED
 PHASE DUMPLI55,DUMPLI50    - COMPILER GENERATED
- Object Deck - Dump-Section -

 CATALR DUMPLI60            - COMPILER GENERATED
 PHASE DUMPLI60,DUMPLI55    - COMPILER GENERATED

 Object Deck - Print-Section -
```

```
// EXEC LNKEDT
// ASSGN SYS006,X'132'
// ASSGN SYS005,X'00E'
// ASSGN SYS007,IGN
// ASSGN SYS008,IGN
// ASSGN SYS004,X'00C'
// DLBL INVMSTR,'CHAP4 ISAM AREA',66/001,ISE
// EXTENT SYS006,111111,4,1,3900,20
// EXTENT SYS006,111111,1,2,3920,20
// EXEC
PRINT     0112345600001   0112345900001   - PROGRAM CONTROL CARD
/*
/&
```

```
// JOB CASHMAN                                          CHAPTER 7
// OPTION LINK,SYM
// ASSGN SYS004,X'132'
// EXEC FCOBOL
```

- Source Deck - Chapter 7 -

```
/*
// EXEC LNKEDT
// ASSGN SYS007,X'00C'
// ASSGN SYS008,X'00E'
// EXEC
```

- Test Data - Chapter 7 -

```
/*
/&
```

APPENDIX G

TEST DATA FOR PROGRAMMING ASSIGNMENTS

This appendix contains suggested test data to be used in the programming assignments presented in Chapters 1, 2, and 5. The input to the programs in the other chapters are disk files created from this input.

Chapter 1 - Sequential Update

For this assignment, two sets of data are used. The first is to load the sequential master file and the second set is to update the master file. In addition to valid data for the program, invalid data is provided. It is suggested that the program first be tested using the valid data to ensure that all major functions of the program are being performed. The data with errors can then be included to check out the error routines.

Data To Create the Master File

Valid Data:

Dept. No. (1-2)	Salesman No. (3-5)	Name (8-25)	Current Sales (26-32)	Mo. Emp. (42-43)	Type (56)
60	100	James R. Gellded	0819066	04	1
60	179	Eric C. Damson	0352502	02	1
60	292	Joan I. French	0332000	02	1
60	409	Mick Ick	0410122	02	1
60	607	Al Catraz	0582507	03	1
60	825	Don M. Tillman	1230444	05	1
70	214	Sylvia Serene	0079067	03	1
70	310	Marie M. Gormally	0389002	06	1
70	332	Anna J. Held	0244000	09	1
70	689	Sophon DePeters	0437788	09	1
70	802	Michael Shea	0642033	08	1
80	102	Arthur A. Ballser	0883000	09	1
80	282	James Lewis	1984055	10	1
80	322	Jean H. Harleton	0780899	06	1
80	505	Jack Goup	0154001	04	1
80	921	Mary Vergen	1802000	09	1
90	105	Dick Hertz	0878044	06	1
90	215	Anne Chovey	0607050	07	1
90	315	Jim Nayseum	1274000	08	1
90	574	Chester Fester	0754366	10	1

Invalid Data:

Dept. No. (1-2)	Salesman No. (3-5)	Name (8-25)	Current Sales (26-32)	Mo. Emp. (42-43)	Type (56)
90	315	Jim Nayseum	0973642	03	2

Data To Update The Master File

Valid Data:

Dept. No. (1-2)	Salesman No. (3-5)	Name (8-25)	Current Sales (26-32)	Mo. Emp. (42-43)	Type (56)
60	179		0004067		3
60	409		0027643		3
60	607				2
60	825		0000100		3
60	927	Kate Hillary	0020105	01	1
80	505		0036743		3
90	215				2
90	574		0007243		3

Invalid Data:

Dept. No. (1-2)	Salesman No. (3-5)	Name (8-25)	Current Sales (26-32)	Mo. Emp. (42-43)	Type (56)
70	214	Sylvia Serene	0027385	06	1
80	914				2
85	213		0002167		3

Chapter 2 - Card to Disk

The program written for the programming assignment in Chapter 2 is used for two purposes: To build the sequential disk file which will be input to load the Sales Master file (Chapter 3) and to build a sequential disk file which will contain transactions to update the master file (Chapter 5). Thus, one set of data is presented for loading the master file and one set of data for updating the master. As in Chapter 1, both valid and invalid data is included.

Data To Load The Master File

Valid Data:

Dept. No. (1-2)	Salesman No. (3-5)	Name (6-25)	Current Sales (33-39)	Comm Rate (40-41)	Sales Returns (50-55)	Type (56)
10	004	William C. Ather	0067524	10	000000	1
10	185	Suzy Mae DeWitt	0090019	10	001020	1
10	300	Kim Kant	0030000	10	000000	1
10	325	C. Joanna Trye	0020539	10	000220	1
10	730	Betty Wyllknott	0105144	10	002310	1
10	960	Toulouse T. Estes	0035000	10	000000	1
20	111	Hu Flun Dun	0075006	12	001140	1
20	304	Steve V. Fromm	0120000	12	001832	1
20	590	Clarence N. Neil	0095023	12	002324	1
20	801	Harry T. Scheiber	0032508	12	000520	1
20	956	Thomas A. Wangley	0015000	12	000275	1
30	030	Ruth W. Alloren	0000000	15	000000	1
30	181	Edward D. Delbert	0130554	15	000000	1
30	318	Carol S. Haney	0145000	15	006019	1
30	487	Mildred J. King	0180429	15	005322	1
30	834	Harris T. Trawley	0055000	15	001329	1
40	027	Elaine Alhouer	0022066	12	000400	1
40	171	Nan S. Costa	0055000	12	000903	1
40	317	Pete R. Puller	0039500	12	001180	1
40	721	Betty Lou Sanderpantz	0100000	12	002346	1

Invalid Data:

Dept. No. (1-2)	Salesman No. (3-5)	Name (6-25)	Current Sales (33-39)	Comm Rate (40-41)	Sales Returns (50-55)	Type (56)
10	04B	Michael H. Shea	0082009	10	004680	1
10	050	Grace B. Groler	0205420	15	048369	6
7A	214	Rick T. Edmonson	0033057	10	000000	1
60	179	Eric C. Damson	0180888	2C	000000	1
90	574	Chester Fester	0059030	12	000000	A
40	721	Betty Lou Sanderpantz	0100000	12	002346	1

Data To Update The Master File

Valid Data:

Dept. No. (1-2)	Salesman No. (3-5)	Name (6-25)	Current Sales (33-39)	Comm Rate (40-41)	Sales Returns (50-55)	Type (56)
10	004	William I. Ather				2
10	004		006467			3
10	004				00500	5
10	730			12		4
20	111		0005000			3
20	304		0065000			3
20	590			15		4
20	590		0072024			3
20	590				000600	5
20	673	Stephen U. Teller	0177009	12	032222	6
20	956					7
30	030					7
30	318	Marie S. Haney				2
30	487			10		4
40	317	Nancy S. Costa				2
40	317		001700			3
40	317				003400	5
50	734	Reed M. Owney	0053066	10	001132	6

Invalid Data:

Dept. No. (1-2)	Salesman No. (3-5)	Name (6-25)	Current Sales (33-39)	Comm Rate (40-41)	Sales Returns (50-55)	Type (56)
10	185	Suzy Mae DeWitt	0090019	10	001020	6
10	304					7
20	300		0006437			3
40	171	Nan S. Costa	0056002	12	000903	6
40	721			15		1

It should be noted that the invalid test data used as input for the program is necessary only to test the error routines in the program and need not be corrected or used in subsequent programs.

DEBE AND DITTO UTILITIES

In order to properly test the programs written in the student assignments, the files created should be printed to ensure that the files have been created properly or updated properly. Two Utility programs are especially useful in displaying files - DEBE and DITTO.

DEBE

```
I.DEBE        V.M 0.0        88 BLOCKS .        SYSTEM SOURCE-STATEMENT LIBRARY

              BKEND   I.DEBE

       DEBE2                                                          0001
              TITLE 'DOS DEBE UTILITY PROGRAM'                        DEBE0002
       ***********************************************************     DEBE0003
       ***********************************************************     DEBE0004
       **                                                     **      DEBE0005
       **              DOS DEBE UTILITY PROGRAM               **      DEBE0006
       **                                                     **      DEBE0007
       ***********************************************************     DEBE0008
       ***********************************************************     DEBE0009
       *                                                       *      DEBE0010
       * INSTRUCTIONS,                                         *      DEBE0011
       * ------------                                          *      DEBE0012
       *                                                       *      DEBE0013
       * DOS DEBE CAN BE RUN FROM CONTROL CARD READER OR CONSOLE TYPEWRITER *  DEBE0014
       *                                                       *      DEBE0015
       * TO START A UTILITY RUN -                              *      DEBE0016
       * // EXEC DEBE   DEBE WILL INTERROGATE THE COMREG TO SEE IF THIS IS A *  DEBE0017
       *                CONSOLE EXEC OR SYSIN EXEC             *      DEBE0018
       *                IF SYSIN IS NOT ASSIGN CONSOLE EXEC IS ASSUME *  DEBE0019
       *     SYSXXX=001 TO 255 IS NECESSARY TO PROCESS /* OR /& AS DATA*  DEBE0020
       *     SYSIPT TREATS /* AS END OF CARD FILES, /& WILL FORCE EOJ.*  DEBE0021
       *                                                       *      DEBE0022
       * FROM READER, '// EXEC DEBE' MUST BE FOLLOWED BY -     *      DEBE0023
       *     '$$ DEBE XX,INPUT=SYSXXX,OUTPUT=SYSXXX,NUM=XXXX,SIZE=XXXX,*  DEBE0024
       *                LOXTNT=XXXXXXX,HIXTNT=XXXXXXX,VOLID=XXXXXX '  DEBE0025
       *     $$ DEBE XX MUST BE IN COLS 1-10 FOLLOWED BY THE KEYWORD *  DEBE0026
       *     PARAMETERS IN ANY ORDER SEPARATED BY COMMAS AND DELIMITED*  DEBE0027
       *     BY A BLANK.                                       *      DEBE0028
       *     IF THE READER IS NOT A 2540 OR TAPE AN INDICATION THAT IT*  DEBE0029
       *     HAS CONTROL CARDS IS REQUESTED FROM THE CONSOLE OTHERWISE*  DEBE0030
       *     CONTROL WILL BE FROM THE CONSOLE.                 *      DEBE0031
       *     IF THE READER IS ASSIGNED TO A LOGICAL UNIT (001-255) *   DEBE0032
       *     A /& CARD WILL BE TREATED AS DATA AND             *      DEBE0033
       *     A /* CARD WITH COL 3 NON-BLANK WILL BE TREATED AS DATA *  DEBE0034
       *     (BLANKING COL-3) OTHERWISE IT WILL DELIMIT CARD FILES. *  DEBE0035
       *                                                       *      DEBE0036
       * FROM CONSOLE, '// EXEC DEBE' WILL INTERROGATE THE CONSOLE WITH *  DEBE0037
       *     'PROG ID=XX' AND REQUIRED PAKAMETERS.             *      DEBE0038
       *                                                       *      DEBE0039
       * $$ DEBE XX/PROG ID=XX,   XX IS THE UTILITY PROGRAM IDENTIFICATION *  DEBE0040
       *                                                       *      DEBE0041
       * INPUT=SYSXXX IS SYMBOLIC LOGICAL UNIT ASSIGNED TO TAPE OR DASD INPUT*  DEBE0042
       *     XXX =000 TO 255.  (EOB ASSUMES SYS004)            *      DEBE0043
       *                                                       *      DEBE0044
       * OUTPUT=SYSXXX IS SYMBOLIC LOGICAL UNIT ASSIGNED TO TAPE/DASD OUTPUT.*  DEBE0045
       *     XXX =000 TO 255.  (EOB ASSUMES SYS005)            *      DEBE0046
       *                                                       *      DEBE0047
       * NUM=XXXX IS NUMBER OF FILES, TAPE RECORDS(BLOCKS), CARDS OR BLOCKING*  DEBE0048
       *          FACTOR(CARDS PER BLOCK).                     *      DEBE0049
       *     XXXX = 0001 IS DEFAULT OPTION.                    *      DEBE0050
       *                                                       *      DEBE0051
       * SIZE=XXXX IS RECORD SIZE(NUMBER OF CHARACTERS) PER PRINT LINE. *  DEBE0052
       *     XXXX = 0120 IS MAXIMUM VALUE AND DEFAULT OPTION.  *      DEBE0053
       *                                                       *      DEBE0054
       * LOXTNT,HIXTNT=XXXXXXX IS CCCHH00 (2311/2314) OR CSSXYTT (2321). *  DEBE0055
       *     CCC = CYLINDER         DEVICE TYPE IN PUB TABLE IS CHECKED FOR *  DEBE0056
       *     HH  = HEAD             2311  2314 OR 2321         *      DEBE0057
       *     00  = MUST BE ZEROS                               *      DEBE0058
       *     C   = CELL                                        *      DEBE0059
       *     SS  = SUBCELL                                     *      DEBE0060
       *     X   = STRIP                                       *      DEBE0061
       *     Y   =CYLINDER                                     *      DEBE0062
       *     TT  = TRACK.                                      *      DEBE0063
       *                                                       *      DEBE0064
       * VOLID=XXXXXX IS THE TAPE VOLUME SERIAL NUMBER.        *      DEBE0065
       *                                                       *      DEBE0066
       *                                                       *      DEBE0067
       *          ALL VALUES MUST BE IN DECIMAL.               *      DEBE0068
       *                                                       *      DEBE0069
       *                                                       *      DEBE0070
       * TO STOP A UTILITY RUN -                               *      DEBE0071
       * IN THE BACKGROUND THE EXTERNAL INTERRUPT KEY MUST BE PRESSED, *  DEBE0072
       * IN THE FOREGROUNDS THE CONSOLE REQUEST KEY MUST BE PRESSED AND THE *  DEBE0073
       *          REPLY 'MSG F1' OR 'MSG F2'-EOB ENTERED.      *      DEBE0074
       *                                                       *      DEBE0075
       *                                                       *      DEBE0076
       *  ID           OPERATION            ASSOCIATED PARAMETERS *   DEBE0077
       * /  /                               /IN /OUT/NUM/SIZ/LOX/HIX/VOL/* DEBE0078
       * /----/------------------------------/---/---/---/---/---/---/---/* DEBE0079
       * / CC / CARD TO CARD                / X /   /   /   /   /   /   /* DEBE0080
       * /----/------------------------------/---/---/---/---/---/---/---/* DEBE0081
       * / CP / CARD TO PRINT               / X /   /   /   /   /   /   /* DEBE0082
       * /----/------------------------------/---/---/---/---/---/---/---/* DEBE0083
       * / CT / CARD TO TAPE                / X /   /   /   /   /   /   /* DEBE0084
       * /----/------------------------------/---/---/---/---/---/---/---/* DEBE0085
       * / GP / GANG PUNCH                  /   /   / C /   /   /   /   /* DEBE0086
```

355

```
*  /----/------------------------------------/---/---/---/---/---/---/---/* DEBE0087
*  / DK / DISK TO PRINT (2311,2314 OR2321)/ X /   /   /   /   /   /   /* DEBE0088
*  /----/------------------------------------/---/---/---/---/---/---/---/* DEBE0089
*  / LC / SYSLOG TO CARD (MAX 80 CHARS)     /   /   /   /   /   /   /   /* DEBE0090
*  /----/------------------------------------/---/---/---/---/---/---/---/* DEBE0091
*  / IT / INITIALIZE TAPE                   /   / X /   /   /   /   / X /* DEBE0092
*  /----/------------------------------------/---/---/---/---/---/---/---/* DEBE0093
*  / TC / TAPE TO CARD                      / X /   / F /   /   /   /   /* DEBE0094
*  /----/------------------------------------/---/---/---/---/---/---/---/* DEBE0095
*  / TF / TAPE TO TAPE FILE                 / X / X / F /   /   /   /   /* DEBE0096
*  /----/------------------------------------/---/---/---/---/---/---/---/* DEBE0097
*  / TT / TAPE TO TAPE RECORD               / X / X / R /   /   /   /   /* DEBE0098
*  /----/------------------------------------/---/---/---/---/---/---/---/* DEBE0099
*  / TD / TAPE FILES TO HEX DISPLAY         / X /   / F / X /   /   /   /* DEBE0100
*  /----/------------------------------------/---/---/---/---/---/---/---/* DEBE0101
*  / TP / TAPE FILES TO CHARACTER PRINT     / X /   / F / X /   /   /   /* DEBE0102
*  /----/------------------------------------/---/---/---/---/---/---/---/* DEBE0103
*  / TH / TAPE RECORDS TO HEX DISPLAY       / X /   / R / X /   /   /   /* DEBE0104
*  /----/------------------------------------/---/---/---/---/---/---/---/* DEBE0105
*  / TR / TAPE RECORDS TO CHARACTER PRINT   / X /   / R / X /   /   /   /* DEBE0106
*  /----/------------------------------------/---/---/---/---/---/---/---/* DEBE0107
*  / TL / 'SYSOUT'TAPE TO LIST &/OR CARD    / X /   / F /   /   /   /   /* DEBE0108
*  /----/------------------------------------/---/---/---/---/---/---/---/* DEBE0109
*  / SF / FORWARD SPACE TAPE FILE           / X /   / F /   /   /   /   /* DEBE0110
*  /----/------------------------------------/---/---/---/---/---/---/---/* DEBE0111
*  / SR / FORWARD SPACE TAPE RECORD         / X /   / R /   /   /   /   /* DEBE0112
*  /----/------------------------------------/---/---/---/---/---/---/---/* DEBE0113
*  / BF / BACK SPACE TAPE FILE              / X /   / F /   /   /   /   /* DEBE0114
*  /----/------------------------------------/---/---/---/---/---/---/---/* DEBE0115
*  / BR / BACK SPACE TAPE RECORD            / X /   / R /   /   /   /   /* DEBE0116
*  /----/------------------------------------/---/---/---/---/---/---/---/* DEBE0117
*  / RW / REWIND TAPE                       / X /   /   /   /   /   /   /* DEBE0118
*  /----/------------------------------------/---/---/---/---/---/---/---/* DEBE0119
*  / RU / REWIND UNLOAD TAPE                / X /   /   /   /   /   /   /* DEBE0120
*  /----/------------------------------------/---/---/---/---/---/---/---/* DEBE0121
*  / WT / WRITE TAPEMARK                    /   / X /   /   /   /   /   /* DEBE0122
*  /----/------------------------------------/---/---/---/---/---/---/---/* DEBE0123
*  / CV / CHANGE DASD VOL SERIAL NUMBER     /   /   /   /   /   /   /   /* DEBE0124
*  /----/------------------------------------/---/---/---/---/---/---/---/* DEBE0125
*  / CD / DUMP TAPE MADE FROM CORE DUMP     / X /   /   /   /   /   /   /* DEBE0126
*  /----/------------------------------------/---/---/---/---/---/---/---/* DEBE0127
*  / CR / READ  CONTROL CARD                /   /   /   /   /   /   /   /* DEBE0128
*  /----/------------------------------------/---/---/---/---/---/---/---/* DEBE0129
*  / EJ / EOJ 'DEBE'                        /   /   /   /   /   /   /   /* DEBE0130
*  /----/------------------------------------/---/---/---/---/---/---/---/* DEBE0131
*                                               B=BLOCKING FACTOR  * DEBE0132
*                                               C=NUMBER OF CARDS  * DEBE0133
*                                               F=NUMBER OF FILES  * DEBE0134
*                                               R=NUMBER OF RECORDS* DEBE0135
*                                                                  * DEBE0136
*******************************************************************************  DEBE0137
*                                                                  * DEBE0138
*  GENERAL INFORMATION,                                            * DEBE0139
*  -------------------                                             * DEBE0140
*                                                                  * DEBE0141
*  DOS DEBE IS SELF RELOCATING.                                    * DEBE0142
*                                                                  * DEBE0143
*  OPERATOR COMMUNICATIONS (OC=YES) MUST BE SPECIFIED IN THE SUPERVISOR* DEBE0144
*  OR AN ILLEGAL SVC MESSAGE WILL OCCUR.                           * DEBE0145
*                                                                  * DEBE0146
*  THE FOLLOWING ASSIGNMENTS ARE REQUIRED FOR DEBE (BG OR F1 & F2),* DEBE0147
*        SYSLST FOR OUTPUT PRINTER;                                * DEBE0148
*        SYSPCH FOR OUTPUT PUNCH;                                  * DEBE0149
*        SYSLOG FOR CONSOLE INQUIRIES, REPLIES AND MESSAGES;       * DEBE0150
*        SYSXXX FOR CARD INPUT, XXX=IPT OR 001-255 (SEE INSTRUCTIONS)* DEBE0151
*        SYSXXX FOR TAPE AND DISK INPUT AND TAPE OUTPUT, XXX=001-255.* DEBE0152
*  THE DESIRED DEVICE ASSIGNMENTS MUST BE MADE BEFORE EXECUTING DEBE.* DEBE0153
*                                                                  * DEBE0154
*  A VALID SIGN WILL BE FORCED ON NUMERIC ENTRIES TO PREVENT PROGRAM* DEBE0155
*  CHECKS AND PROCESSING CONTINUES.                                * DEBE0156
*                                                                  * DEBE0157
*  IF READER RUNS OUT OF CONTROL CARDS BEFORE EJ IS FOUND, CONTROL IS* DEBE0158
*  GIVEN TO CONSOLE. ON OTHER THAN A 2540 OR TAPE ONE NON-CONTROL CARD* DEBE0159
*  WILL HAVE BEEN READ.                                            * DEBE0160
*                                                                  * DEBE0161
*        ANY VALID PUNCH IN COL-4 THOUGHT 71 WILL CAUSE A /* OR /& * DEBE0162
*        TO BE TREATED AS DATA CARDS IF THE INPUT DEVICE IS ASSGN  * DEBE0163
*        TO PROGRAMMER UNIT                                        * DEBE0164
*                                                                  * DEBE0165
*  '$$ NO' AS CARD FILE DELIMITER IN READER WILL PREVENT A TAPE MARK* DEBE0166
*  BEING WRITTEN ON OUTPUT TAPE AND CALLS NEXT PROG ID.            * DEBE0167
*                                                                  * DEBE0168
*  ANY OUTPUT TAPE IS MODE SET FROM THE PUB TABLE ON THE FIRST WRITE* DEBE0169
*  COMMAND (INCLUDING WTM) OF EACH NEW PROG ID.                    * DEBE0170
*                                                                  * DEBE0171
*  THE MAXIMUM SIZE OF INPUT TAPE RECORDS IS CALCULATED FROM THE   * DEBE0172
*  PARTITION'S AVAILABLE STORAGE. IF ANY RECORD EXCEEDS THIS MAXIMUM* DEBE0173
*  SIZE THE OPERATOR IS ALERTED AND MAY CANCEL OR CONTINUE (PROCESSING* DEBE0174
*  SHORT RECORDS).                                                 * DEBE0175
*                                                                  * DEBE0176
```

```
* DASD FILE PROTECT WHEN SPECIFIED IS CANCELLED FOR DEBE'S PARTITION  * DEBE0177
* BY $$BSYSWR TRANSIENT AND IS ACTIVATED AT EOJ BY JOB CONTROL.        * DEBE0178
*                                                                      * DEBE0179
*********************************************************************** DEBE0180
*********************************************************************** DEBE0181
**                                                                 ** DEBE0182
**        // JOB DEBE SAMPLE CONTROL CARDS                         ** DEBE0183
**        // ASSGN SYSLOG,X'01F'                                   ** DEBE0184
**        // ASSGN SYSLST,X'00E'                                   ** DEBE0185
**        // ASSGN SYSPCH,X'00D'                                   ** DEBE0186
**        // ASSGN SYS001,X'00C'                                   ** DEBE0187
**        // ASSGN SYS002,X'180'                                   ** DEBE0188
**        // ASSGN SYS003,X'181'                                   ** DEBE0189
**        // ASSGN SYS004,X'190'                                   ** DEBE0190
**        // ASSGN SYS005,X'198'                                   ** DEBE0191
**        // EXEC DEBE                                             ** DEBE0192
**        $$ DEBE CC                                               ** DEBE0193
**        *** DATA CARDS HERE. ***                                ** DEBE0194
**        /*    ANY PUNCH IN COL-4 THOUGHT COL-71                 ** DEBE0195
**        *** MORE DATA CARDS. ***                                ** DEBE0196
**        /*    END OF CARD DATA.                                 ** DEBE0197
**        $$ DEBE CP                                               ** DEBE0198
**        *** DATA CARDS HERE. ***                                ** DEBE0199
**        /*    END OF CARD DATA.                                 ** DEBE0200
**        $$ DEBE CT,OUTPUT=SYS002,NUM=0010                       ** DEBE0201
**        *** CARD DATA HERE ***                                  ** DEBE0202
**        /*X                                                     ** DEBE0203
**        *** MORE DATA CARDS. ***                                ** DEBE0204
**        /* END OF CARD DATA                                     ** DEBE0205
**        $$ DEBE GP,NUM=0010                                     ** DEBE0206
**        *** DATA CARDS HERE. ***                                ** DEBE0207
**        /*    END OF CARD DATA.                                 ** DEBE0208
**        $$ DEBE DC,INPUT=SYS005,LOXTNT=0188318,HIXTNT=0199419   ** DEBE0209
**        $$ DEBE DK,INPUT=SYS004,LOXTNT=1990000,HIXTNT=1990900   ** DEBE0210
**        $$ DEBE LC                                              ** DEBE0211
**        $$ DEBE IT,OUTPUT=SYS002,VOLID=000001                   ** DEBE0212
**        $$ DEBE TC,INPUT=SYS002,NUM=0001                        ** DEBE0213
**        $$ DEBE TT,INPUT=SYS002,OUTPUT=SYS003,NUM=0002          ** DEBE0214
**        $$ DEBE TF,INPUT=SYS002,OUTPUT=SYS003,NUM=0002          ** DEBE0215
**        $$ DEBE TD,INPUT=SYS002,SIZE=0080,NUM=0002              ** DEBE0216
**        $$ DEBE TP,INPUT=SYS002,NUM=0002,SIZE=0080              ** DEBE0217
**        $$ DEBE TH,INPUT=SYS002,NUM=0004,SIZE=0080              ** DEBE0218
**        $$ DEBE TR,INPUT=SYS002,NUM=0001,SIZE=0080              ** DEBE0219
**        $$ DEBE TL,INPUT=SYS002,NUM=0001                        ** DEBE0220
**        $$ DEBE SF,INPUT=SYS002,NUM=0002                        ** DEBE0221
**        $$ DEBE SR,INPUT=SYS002,NUM=0001                        ** DEBE0222
**        $$ DEBE HF,INPUT=SYS002,NUM=0002                        ** DEBE0223
**        $$ DEBE BP,INPUT=SYS002,NUM=0004                        ** DEBE0224
**        $$ DEBE RR,INPUT=SYS002                                 ** DEBE0225
**        $$ DEBE RU,INPUT=SYS002                                 ** DEBE0226
**        $$ DEBE WT,OUTPUT=SYS002                                ** DEBE0227
**        $$ DEBE EJ                                              ** DEBE0228
**        /& END OF JOB DEBE                                      ** DEBE0229
**                                                                 ** DEBE0230
**                                                                 ** DEBE0231
*********************************************************************** DEBE0232
*********************************************************************** DEBE0233
**                                                                 ** DEBE0234
**        TO LINK FOR OPERATION IN A BATCH- JOB SYSTEM            ** DEBE0235
**        // JOB  LINK DEBE FOR A BATCH-JOB ONLY SYSTEM           ** DEBE0236
**        // OPTION CATAL                                         ** DEBE0237
**           PHASE DEBE,S                                         ** DEBE0238
**           INCLUDE RELODEBE                                     ** DEBE0239
**        /*                                                      ** DEBE0240
**        // EXEC LNKEDT                                          ** DEBE0241
**        /*                                                      ** DEBE0242
**        /&                                                      ** DEBE0243
**                                                                 ** DEBE0244
*********************************************************************** DEBE0245
*********************************************************************** DEBE0246
**                                                                 ** DEBE0247
**                                                                 ** DEBE0248
**        TO LINK FOR OPERATION IN A MULTIPROGRAMMING SYSTEM      ** DEBE0249
**                                                                 ** DEBE0250
**        // JOB  LINK  DEBE FOR A MPS SYSTEM                     ** DEBE0251
**        // OPTION CATAL                                         ** DEBE0252
**           PHASE DEBE,+0                                        ** DEBE0253
**           INCLUDE RELODEBE                                     ** DEBE0254
**        /*                                                      ** DEBE0255
**        // EXEC LNKEDT                                          ** DEBE0256
**        /*                                                      ** DEBE0257
**        /&                                                      ** DEBE0258
**                                                                 ** DEBE0259
*********************************************************************** DEBE0260
*********************************************************************** DEBE0261

        BKEND
```

DITTO

```
  I.DITTO     V.M 0.0          50 BLOCKS        SYSTEM SOURCE-STATEMENT LIBRARY

               BKEND   I.DITTO

        *                                                                    * DITT0001
        * CODE   ALTERNATE    DESCRIPTION                                     * DITT0002
        * ----   ---------    -----------                                     * DITT0003
        * CCU      CC         CARD TO CARD                                    * DITT0004
        * CCS      --         CARD TO CARD WITH SEQ. NUMBERS AND DECK NAME    * DITT0005
        * CPU      CP         CARD TO PRINTER IN CHARACTER FORMAT             * DITT0006
        * CHU      CH         CARD TO PRINTER IN CHARACTER AND HEX FORMAT     * DITT0007
        * CTU      CT         CARD TO TAPE UNBLOCKED                          * DITT0008
        * CTR      --         CARD TO TAPE REBLOCKED                          * DITT0009
        * DDR      --         DISK TO PRINTER IN CHAR. AND HEX FORMAT REBLOCKED * DITT0010
        * DDU      DD         DISK TO PRINTER IN CHAR. AND HEX FORMAT UNBLOCKED * DITT0011
        * DIO +    --         DISK IDENTIFICATION CHANGE (CHANGE VOL. SER. NUM.)* DITT0012
        * DRL +    --         DISK RECORD LOAD. ALTER KEY AND/OR DATA PORTION * DITT0013
        *                     OF ANY DISK RECORD                              * DITT0014
        * DRS +    --         DISK RECORD SCAN. SCAN DISK FOR MATCHING KEY OR * DITT0015
        *                     END OF FILE RECORD.                               DITT0016
        * SDU      SD         DISK DUMP FOR SPLIT CYLINDER FILES              * DITT0017
        * SDP      --         DISK DUMP REBLOCKED FOR SPLIT CYLINDER FILES    * DITT0018
        * SKS +    --         DISK RECORD SCAN FOR SPLIT CYLINDER FILES       * DITT0019
        * EOF      --         WRITE DISK END-OF-FILE RECORD                   * DITT0020
        * BSF      --         BACK SPACE TAPE FILE                            * DITT0021
        * BSR      --         BACK SPACE TAPE RECORD                          * DITT0022
        * ERG      --         ERASE RECORD GAP                                * DITT0023
        * FSF      --         FORWARD SPACE TAPE FILE                         * DITT0024
        * FSR      --         FORWARD SPACE TAPE RECORD                       * DITT0025
        * INT +    --         INITIALIZE TAPE - DOS STANDARD FORMAT           * DITT0026
        * REW      --         REWIND TAPE                                     * DITT0027
        * RUN      --         REWIND AND UNLOAD TAPE                          * DITT0028
        * TCR      TC         TAPE TO CARD UNBLOCKED OR BLOCKED               * DITT0029
        * TFA      --         TAPE TO PRINTER USING TYPE A FORMS CONTROL      * DITT0030
        * TFD      --         TAPE TO PRINTER USING TYPE D FORMS CONTROL      * DITT0031
        * TPU      TP         TAPE TO PRINTER UNBLOCKED IN CHAR. FORMAT       * DITT0032
        * TPR      --         TAPE TO PRINTER REBLOCKED IN CHAR. FORMAT       * DITT0033
        * THU      TH         TAPE TO PRINTER UNBLOCKED IN CHAR. AND HEX FORMAT * DITT0034
        * THR      --         TAPE TO PRINTER REBLOCKED IN CHAR. AND HEX FORMAT * DITT0035
        * TRL +    --         TAPE RECORD LOAD. COPY TAPE TO TAPE WITH ALTERING * DITT0036
        *                     OF LENGTH AND/OR DATA OF SPECIFIC RECORDS       * DITT0037
        * TRS +    --         TAPE RECORD SCAN. SEARCH TAPE FOR LOGICAL RECORD * DITT0038
        *                     USING 1-35 POSITION SCAN ARGUMENT              * DITT0039
        * TTU      TT         TAPE TO TAPE  (01 TO 99 FILES FROM CONSOLE ONLY) * DITT0040
        * WTM      --         WRITE TAPE MARK                                 * DITT0041
        * CCL +    --         CANCEL CARD INPUT FUNCTION                      * DITT0042
        * EOJ      --         END OF JOB                                      * DITT0043
        *                                                                    * DITT0044
        * + DENOTES FUNCTIONS NOT AVAILABLE WITH CONTROL CARD OPERATION.      * DITT0045
        *                                                                    * DITT0046
        ******************************************************************* DITT0047
               EJECT                                                          DITT0048
        ******************************************************************* DITT0049
        *                                                                    * DITT0050
        * * * * *     CONTROL CARD OPERATION  * * * * * * * * * * * * *      * DITT0051
        *   CC 1-7      $$DITTO                                              * DITT0052
        *   CC 10-12    FUNCTION CODE                                        * DITT0053
        *   CC 16       PARAMETER 1,......, PARAMETER N                      * DITT0054
        *   PARAMETER               DESCRIPTION                              * DITT0055
        *   ---------               -----------                             * DITT0056
        *   INPUT=SYSNNN            LOGICAL INPUT DEVICE                     * DITT0057
        *   OUTPUT=SYSNNN           LOGICAL OUTPUT DEVICE                    * DITT0058
        *   BEGIN=CCCHH             LOWER DISK EXTENT                        * DITT0059
        *   END=CCCHH               UPPER DISK EXTENT                        * DITT0060
        *   NBLKS=NNNN              NUMBER OF TAPE BLOCKS                    * DITT0061
        *   RECSIZE=NNNNN           LOGICAL RECORD SIZE                      * DITT0062
        *   BLKFACTOR=NNN           OUTPUT BLOCKING FACTOR (CTR)             * DITT0063
        *   DECKTYPE=XXX            CCS DECKTYPE                             * DITT0064
        *                           CCS IS A CARD-TO-CARD COPY WITH SEQ      * DITT0065
        *                           NUMBERS AND DECK IDENTIFICATION NAME     * DITT0066
        *                           ADDED. THREE DECKTYPES ARE AVAILABLE.    * DITT0067
        *                                                                    * DITT0068
        *                           DECKTYPE=COB IS USED TO SEQUENCE AND     * DITT0069
        *                           NAME 'COBOL' SOURCE DECKS. SEQ  NUMBERS  * DITT0070
        *                           WILL BE PLACED IN CC 1-6 AND A 0-8       * DITT0071
        *                           POSITION DECKNAME PLACED IN CC 73-80.    * DITT0072
        *                                                                    * DITT0073
        *                           DECKTYPE=RPG  IS USED TO FOR 'RPG'       * DITT0074
        *                           SOURCE DECKS. SEQ NUMBERS WILL BE        * DITT0075
        *                           PLACED IN CC 1-5 AND A 0-6 POSITION      * DITT0076
        *                           DECKNAME PLACED IN CC 75-80.             * DITT0077
        *                           DECKTYPE=BAL  IS USED FOR 'ASSEMBLER'    * DITT0078
        *                           AND 'FORTRAN' SOURCE DECKS,'JOB CONTROL' * DITT0079
        *                           DECKS, ETC. SEQUENCE NUMBERS WILL BE     * DITT0080
        *                           PLACED IN CC 77-80 AND A 0-4 POSITION    * DITT0081
        *                           DECKNAME PLACED IN CC 73-76.             * DITT0082
        *                                                                    * DITT0083
        *   DECKNAME=X....X         CCS DECKNAME (0-8) CHARACTERS.           * DITT0084
        *                           DECKNAMES WHICH ARE LESS IN              * DITT0085
        *                           LENGTH THAN REQUIRED WILL BE LEFT        * DITT0086
```

```
*                         JUSTIFIED AND PADDED WITH BLANKS.              * DITT0087
*                                                                       * DITT0088
*                                                                       * DITT0089
*         TO READ JOB CONTROL WITHOUT STOPPING USE AMPERSAND INSTEAD    * DITT0090
*         OF FIRST CHARACTER OF CODE   USE BLANK CARD AS DELIMITER.     * DITT0091
*         EXAMPLE   INSTEAD OF CCU FOR CARD TO CARD USE &CU             * DITT0092
*********************************************************************** DITT0093
      EJECT                                                              DITT0094
*********************************************************************** DITT0095
*                                                                       * DITT0096
* * * * * * * *     PARAMETER REQUIREMENTS  * * * * * * * * * * * * *   * DITT0097
*                                                                       * DITT0098
*  CC  1-7 CC 10-12 C 16                                                * DITT0099
*  ------- -------- ----                                                * DITT0100
*  $$DITTO    CCS    DECKTYPE=XXX,DECKNAME=XX...X                       * DITT0101
*  $$DITTO    CCU                                                       * DITT0102
*  $$DITTO    CPU                                                       * DITT0103
*  $$DITTO    CHU                                                       * DITT0104
*  $$DITTO    CTR    OUTPUT=SYSNNN,BLKFACTOR=NNN                        * DITT0105
*  $$DITTO    CTU    OUTPUT=SYSNNN                                      * DITT0106
*  $$DITTO    DDU    INPUT=SYSNNN,BEGIN=CCCHH,END=CCCHH                 * DITT0107
*  $$DITTO    DDR    INPUT=SYSNNN,BEGIN=CCCHH,END=CCCHH,RECSIZE=NNNNN   * DITT0108
*  $$DITTO    SDR    INPUT=SYSNNN,BEGIN=CCCHH,END=CCCHH,RECSIZE=NNNNN   * DITT0109
*  $$DITTO    SDU    INPUT=SYSNNN,BEGIN=CCCHH,END=CCCHH                 * DITT0110
*  $$DITTO    TPU    INPUT=SYSNNN(,NBLKS=NNNN)                          * DITT0111
*  $$DITTO    THU    INPUT=SYSNNN(,NBLKS=NNNN)                          * DITT0112
*  $$DITTO    THR    INPUT=SYSNNN,RECSIZE=NNNNN(,NBLKS=NNNN)            * DITT0113
*  $$DITTO    TFA    INPUT=SYSNNN                                       * DITT0114
*  $$DITTO    TFD    INPUT=SYSNNN                                       * DITT0115
*  $$DITTO    TCR    INPUT=SYSNNN                                       * DITT0116
*  $$DITTO    TPR    INPUT=SYSNNN,RECSIZE=NNNNN(,NBLKS=NNNN)            * DITT0117
*  $$DITTO    TTU    INPUT=SYSNNN,OUTPUT=SYSNNN                         * DITT0118
*  $$DITTO    WTM    OUTPUT=SYSNNN                                      * DITT0119
*  $$DITTO    REW    OUTPUT=SYSNNN                                      * DITT0120
*  $$DITTO    RUN    OUTPUT=SYSNNN                                      * DITT0121
*  $$DITTO    FSF    OUTPUT=SYSNNN                                      * DITT0122
*  $$DITTO    BSF    OUTPUT=SYSNNN                                      * DITT0123
*  $$DITTO    FSR    OUTPUT=SYSNNN,NBLKS=NNNN                           * DITT0124
*  $$DITTO    BSR    OUTPUT=SYSNNN,NBLKS=NNNN                           * DITT0125
*  $$DITTO    EOJ                                                       * DITT0126
*                                                                       * DITT0127
*                                                                       * DITT0128
*********************************************************************** DITT0129
      EJECT                                                              DITT0130
*********************************************************************** DITT0131
*                                                                       * DITT0132
* * * * * * * * * * *  CONSOLE OPERATIONS  * * * * * * * * * * * * *    * DITT0133
*                                                                       * DITT0134
*                                                                       * DITT0135
*                                                                       * DITT0136
*         ALL CONSOLE COMMUNICATION IS IN TERMS OF PHYSICAL HARDWARD    * DITT0137
*         I/O ADDRESS, ELIMINATING THE NEED FOR KNOWLEDGE OF CURRENT    * DITT0138
*         LOGICAL ASSIGNMENT.                                           * DITT0139
*         TAPE DENSITY AND MODE SETTINGS MAY BE ENTERED VIA THE         * DITT0140
*         CONSOLE.                                                      * DITT0141
*         TAPE ADDRESS REPLIES ARE ENTERED IN THE FORM OF 'CCUMM'       * DITT0142
*         WHERE C=CHANNEL, UU=UNIT ADDRESS, AND MM=THE DENSITY AND      * DITT0143
*         MODE SETTING. FOR NINE-TRACK SINGLE DENSITY TAPES, BLANKS     * DITT0144
*         OR ZEROS MAY BE SUBSTITUTED FOR CO, OR THE MM PARAMETER       * DITT0145
*         MAY BE OMITTED.                                               * DITT0146
*                                                                       * DITT0147
*                                                                       * DITT0148
*  TO CATALOG DITTO                                                     * DITT0149
*                                                                       * DITT0150
*  // JOB CATALOG DITTO                                                 * DITT0151
*  // OPTION CATAL                                                      * DITT0152
*    PHASE DITTO,S      OR    PHASE DITTO,+0                            * DITT0153
*    INCLUDE RELDITTO                                                   * DITT0154
*  INCLUDE DITRANS1                                                     * DITT0155
*  INCLUDE DITRANS2                                                     * DITT0156
*  /*                                                                   * DITT0157
*  // EXEC LNKEDT                                                       * DITT0158
*  /&                                                                   * DITT0159
*                                                                       * DITT0160
*                                                                       * DITT0161
*         C. A. ALEXANDER    IBM    DETROIT, MICHIGAN                   * DITT0162
*********************************************************************** DITT0163

      BKEND
```

BLOCKING FACTOR TABLE

One of the decisions which must be made by an analyst or programmer when designing a file to be stored on a magnetic tape or direct-access device is the size of the block or physical record which is to be used for the file. One of the factors to be considered when deciding block size is the amount of computer storage which is available for input/output areas. There must be sufficient space in computer storage to store the entire physical record or block. In addition, when programming in COBOL, two I/O areas are normally used unless the Reserve No Alternate Area clause is specified, so there must be sufficient room for two blocks.

Another consideration when deciding the block size is the device on which the file is to be stored. When utilizing magnetic tape, the block size can be as large as desired. When utilizing direct-access devices, however, there is a maximum number of bytes which can be stored on a single track of a direct-access device and a block should normally be kept equal to or less than this size. In addition, if sufficient storage is not available to store the maximum size block on the track, then consideration must be given to the next best blocking size. The table in Figure I-1 can be used for determining the most efficient block sizes.

Maximum Bytes per Record Formatted without keys				Records per Track	Maximum Bytes per Record Formatted with keys			
2311	2314 2319	2321	3330		2311	2314 2319	2321	3330
3625	7294	2000	13030	1	3605	7249	1984	12974
1740	3520	935	6447	2	1720	3476	920	6391
1131	2298	592	4253	3	1111	2254	576	4197
830	1693	422	3156	4	811	1649	406	3100
651	1332	320	2498	5	632	1288	305	2442
532	1092	253	2059	6	512	1049	238	2003
447	921	205	1745	7	428	877	190	1689
384	793	169	1510	8	364	750	154	1454
334	694	142	1327	9	315	650	126	1271
295	615	119	1181	10	275	571	103	1125
263	550	101	1061	11	244	506	85	1005
236	496	86	962	12	217	452	70	906
213	450	73	877	13	194	407	58	821
193	411	62	805	14	174	368	47	749
177	377	53	742	15	158	333	38	686
162	347	44	687	16	143	304	29	631
149	321	37	639	17	130	277	21	583
138	298	30	596	18	119	254	15	540
127	276	24	557	19	108	233	9	501
118	258	20	523	20	99	215		467
109	241	15	491	21	90	198		435
102	226	10	463	22	82	183		407
95	211	6	437	23	76	168		381
88	199		413	24	69	156		357
82	187		391	25	63	144		335
77	176		371	26	58	133		315
72	166		352	27	53	123		296
67	157		335	28	48	114		279
63	148		318	29	44	105		262
59	139		303	30	40	96		247

Figure I-1 Record Capacities on DASD

In order to use the table in Figure I-1, first find the proper column for the device to be used to store the file. In the table, there are specifications for the 2311 disk drive, the 2314 and 2319 disk drives, the 2321 device, and the 3330 device. It must also be determined if the file is to contain keys. Normally, when a sequential file is utilized, there will not be keys associated with the file, but when indexed sequential files are used there are keys.

The records per track column indicates the number of physical records, or blocks, which can be stored with the maximum length as specified in each of the columns for each of the devices. For example, if the length of a physical record or block is 3520 bytes, then two of these records will be stored on a single track of a 2314 disk drive. If the physical record is 3600 bytes in length, only one record will be stored on the track because this is greater than the maximum for two records.

The following examples will illustrate the use of the table when determining the block lengths which should be used.

Example 1: Assume that the logical record length of records to be stored on a file is 100 bytes. The analyst or programmer must determine what the most efficient blocking factor is. If the programmer blocks the records 2 records per block, he will get a maximum of 23 physical records on the track (1) because each physical record or block will be 200 bytes in length (100 X 2), and 200 is greater than 199, but less than 211. Therefore, he will be able to store 46 logical records on the track (2 logical records/block X 23 blocks/track). If, however, he makes the blocking factor 72, that is, 72 logical records/block, he can store 72 logical records on a track because 7200 is greater than 3520, but less than 7294 and therefore, one physical record or block can be stored on the track (2).

Thus, it can be seen that by increasing the blocking factor, more logical records will be able to be stored on the track of the direct-access device.

Example 2: Assume that the logical record length of records to be stored on a file is 80 bytes, and assume further that the programmer has determined that he has enough computer storage to have a maximum block size of 3600 bytes. Therefore, a maximum block size of 3600 bytes would be the largest block length which could be used (80 X 45). Note, however, that 3600 is greater than 3520 and therefore, only one physical record or block of 3600 could be stored on a track (3), and the maximum number of logical records to be stored is 45.

If, however, the programmer reduced the number of records in the block (i.e. the blocking factor) to 44, he would be able to store 88 logical records on the track because 80 X 44 is equal to 3520 and this is the maximum size of a block which will allow two blocks to be stored on a single track (4). Thus, by reducing the blocking factor by 1 record per block, the programmer was able to store nearly twice the number of records on a single track.

By utilizing this table, the analyst or programmer should be able to determine the most efficient blocking factors dependent upon the size of the logical record and the type of device being used.

INDEX